DATE DUE

AP 26 '96	NO 25 04		
MY 17 '96	NO 10 05		
RENEW			
MY 30 '96			
OC 30 '96			
AP 16 '97			
NO 18 97			
FE 30 '98			
MR 9 '97			
MY 25 '99			
APR 0 3 2001			
APR 2 4 2001			
DE 18 05			

DEMCO 38-296

THE SOCIAL
ORGANIZATION OF
SEXUALITY

THE SOCIAL
ORGANIZATION OF
SEXUALITY

Sexual Practices
in the United States

Edward O. Laumann, John H. Gagnon,

Robert T. Michael, and Stuart Michaels

THE UNIVERSITY OF CHICAGO PRESS
CHICAGO AND LONDON

EDWARD O. LAUMANN is the George Herbert Mead Distinguished Service Professor in the Department of Sociology at the University of Chicago. He has served as dean of the Social Sciences Division and provost of the university. In 1990, Laumann was named a fellow of the American Association for the Advancement of Science. JOHN H. GAGNON is professor of sociology at the State University of New York, Stony Brook. He is a member of the National Academy of Sciences Committee on AIDS Research and past president of the International Academy of Sex Research. ROBERT T. MICHAEL is the Eliakim Hastings Moore Distinguished Service Professor and dean of the Harris Graduate School of Public Policy Studies at the University of Chicago. From 1984 to 1989 he served as director of the National Opinion Research Center (NORC). STUART MICHAELS, a researcher at the University of Chicago, was project manager of the National Health and Social Life Survey (NHSLS).

The University of Chicago Press, Chicago 60637
The University of Chicago Press, Ltd., London
© 1994 by Edward O. Laumann, Robert T. Michael,
CSG Enterprises, Inc., and Stuart Michaels
All rights reserved. Published 1994
Printed in the United States of America

03 02 01 00 99 98 97 96 95 94 1 2 3 4 5
ISBN: 0-226-46957-3 (cloth)

Library of Congress Cataloging-in-Publication Data

The Social organization of sexuality : sexual practices in the United States / Edward O. Laumann
    . . . [et al.].
        p.   cm.
    Includes bibliographical references and indexes.
    1. Sex customs—United States.   2. Sexual behavior surveys—United States.   I. Laumann, Edward O.
    HQ18.U5S59   1994
    306.7'0973—dc20   94–3736
                                                                                CIP

♾The paper used in this publication meets the minimum requirements of the American National Standard for Information Sciences—Permanence of Paper for Printed Library Materials, ANSI Z39.48-1984.

CONTENTS

ILLUSTRATIONS

TABLES

ACKNOWLEDGMENTS

A project of the scope and duration of ours accumulates many debts along the way, and we wish to express our thanks to the many people who have helped us in our undertaking. The private foundations that supported the National Health and Social Life Survey, on which this book is based, made the study possible. The Robert Wood Johnson Foundation awarded us funding in 1991 to conduct the survey and to analyze it; without their leadership, we could not have gone forward. The Henry J. Kaiser Family Foundation of Menlo Park, the Rockefeller Foundation, the Andrew Mellon Foundation, the John D. and Catherine T. MacArthur Foundation, the New York Community Trust, and the American Foundation for AIDS Research added critically needed resources as we were conducting the survey in the field, permitting us to better train our interviewers and substantially expand our sample size. With their support, the survey was completed and the analysis undertaken. Subsequently, the Ford Foundation provided crucial additional resources that supported a more extensive data analysis.

The design of our study was undertaken several years earlier under contract in 1988 to the U.S. Department of Health and Human Services' National Institute for Child Health and Human Development (NICHD). It was in response to that institute's request for proposals in mid-1987 that our team was formed and our efforts begun, and we wish to express our appreciation and admiration to the staff of NICHD's Demographic and Behavioral Sciences Branch of the Population Research Center, Jeff Evans, and especially our project officer on that early contract, Virginia Cain and the branch chief, Wendy Baldwin, for their guidance, support, and encouragement throughout the past several years' efforts. In both the political struggles of the Reagan and Bush era and the intellectual challenges of designing a study of adult sexual behavior, Virginia and Wendy were our colleagues, and we gratefully express our appreciation and our indebtedness to them. They were all one might hope that government scientists and advocates of the public health might be.

Our other major debt is to the remarkable institution that has collected the survey data and made the study happen in the literal sense. The top management, the survey operations team, and the survey field staff of the National Opinion Research Center (NORC) got behind this project from the outset, weathered the political and funding storms, and remained resolute in their support of the effort to obtain scientific evidence about adult sexual behavior. NORC itself funded from its own very limited resources the initial fielding of a few questions about adult sexual behavior in 1988 and 1989, added to its flagship survey, the General Social Survey (GSS), which is funded annually by the National Science Foundation. Had NORC not been willing to begin the now seven-year annual series of sexual behavior questions, or had the independent board of the GSS or its principal investigators, James Davis and Tom Smith, been unwilling to accommodate our two minutes of questions about sex, we would not have had the evidence that respondents are willing to answer these questions or the evidence that we use in this volume that respondents to a sex survey answer questions about sex just as they answer questions in a general household survey. That evidence has helped convince us of the veracity of our findings.

A final institutional acknowledgment is due to the University of Chicago. During the seven-year course of this project, one of us, Edward Laumann, served as dean of the Social Science Division and as the provost of the university, while another of us, Robert Michael, served as director of NORC and as founding dean of the Harris Graduate School of Public Policy Studies. The university willingly accommodated the research project's demands on our time and uniformly offered only support for a project that had considerable downside risks. We two are most grateful to the senior administration, especially Hanna H. Gray, Jonathan Kleinbard, and Arthur Sussman.

During the period of the project, John Gagnon has been professor of sociology at the State University of New York at Stony Brook. He would like to acknowledge the continuing support provided by his department and the university in the form of leaves of absence and research support, not only for this project, but for his prior research in human sexuality.

Numerous other individuals have helped us with this enterprise. We have been blessed with outstanding graduate students and staff employees who have helped us craft the survey questionnaire and write proposals and reports, manage others, and generally move the project forward; others have played a key role in helping check and analyze the data. These include Judy Birgen, Mary Blair-Loy, Christopher Browning, Aaron Buckley, Rita Butzer, Stephen Ellingson, James Farrer, Joel Feinleib, Ethan Ligon, Kara Joyner, Grace Kao, Fang Li, Nora Leibowitz, Lucy Mackey, Lisa Markovitz, Martina Morris, Kristen Olson, Yan Phoa, Michael Reynolds, William Schempp, Philip Schumm, Patricia Styer, Cynthia Veldman, and Ezra Zuckerman. We wish to make particular acknowledgment of the contributions of Martina Morris, our first senior research assistant, who played an especially critical role in the early stages of the project in helping us identify and direct the research team that prepared the successful response to the NICHD request for proposals and subsequently helped design and execute the pilot work on the interview instrument itself. Several of these students also participated in drafting specific chapters of the volume under our direction, and that fact is noted in the relevant chapters.

We were greatly assisted by the sure-footed guidance of a number of people through the complex pathways toward securing the private funding for the project. We especially want to acknowledge the helpful guidance of Jose Barzellato (the Ford Foundation), Joel Cantor (the Robert Wood Johnson Foundation), Robert Ebert (formerly at the Milbank Memorial Fund), Elizabeth McCormick (Rockefeller Family and Associates), Carolyn Makinson (the Andrew Mellon Foundation), Denis Prager (the John D. and Catherine T. MacArthur Foundation), Kenneth Prewitt (the Rockefeller Foundation), Steven Schroeder (the Robert Wood Johnson Foundation), Mark Smith (the Kaiser Family Foundation), and David Willis (formerly at the Milbank Memorial Fund).

NORC staff members made major contributions, and these include Julie Antelman, Norman Bradburn, Barbara Campbell, Susan Campbell, Woody Carter, Carol Ann Emmons, Martin R. Frankel, Jeff Hackett, Richard Kulka, Kay Malloy, Sally Murphy, Mary O'Brien, Patricia Phillips, Richard M. Rubin, Alicia Schoua-Glusberg, Kristine Talley, Roger Tourangeau, Ellen Williams, Rebecca Zahavi, and Pearl Zinner.

In addition to the three federal government scientists discussed above, others from other federal agencies also provided support, assistance, and constructive professional criticism at one point or another; these include Duane Alexander (director, NICHD), Arthur Campbell (deputy director, Center for Population Research, NICHD), William Darrow (chief, Behavioral and Prevention Research Branch, Division of STD/HIV Prevention, Centers for Disease Control and Prevention), Florence Haseltine (director of NICHD's Population Research Center), Geraldine McQuillan (senior infectious disease epidemiology adviser in the National Health and Nutrition Examination Survey), Jacqueline Wilson (National Survey of Family Growth), and Ronald Wilson (special assistant for HIV, National Center for Health Statistics).

Early on in the study, we had a national advisory group that met on two occasions in 1988 and provided suggestions and reactions to our plans. This opportunity to get advice at an early stage in the project was of great help to us. That group (and their affiliations at that time) included Joan Aron (assistant professor of biostatistics, Johns Hopkins University), Marshall H. Becker (associate dean, School of Public Health, University of Michigan), Larry Bumpass (professor of sociology [demography], University of Wisconsin—Madison), Don Des Jarlais (sociologist, Beth Israel Hospital and Narcotic and Drug Institute), Frank F. Furstenberg, Jr. (professor of sociology, University of Pennsylvania), Dr. Beatrix A. Hamburg (psychiatrist, Mt. Sinai Hospital, New York City), Dr. Edward W. Hook (chief, Sexually Transmitted Disease Clinical Services, Baltimore City Health Department), Dr. Philip L. Lee (professor of social medicine, University of California, San Francisco), Peter V. Marsden (professor of sociology, Harvard University), Jane Menken (professor of sociology, University of Pennsylvania), Anne Firth Murray (William and Flora Hewlett Foundation), Anne R. Pebley (assistant professor of demography, Princeton

University), Howard Schuman (director, Survey Research Center, University of Michigan), Burton Singer (Department of Epidemiology and Public Health, Yale University), Richard Udry (professor of sociology, University of North Carolina), and William J. Wilson (professor of sociology, University of Chicago).

Of course, our colleagues offered much informal advice as well throughout the period of planning and executing the project, by reading drafts and commenting on our workshop presentations. Unless otherwise noted, all the individuals mentioned are at the University of Chicago. We want to acknowledge, in particular, the help of Barry Adam (University of Windsor), Joan Aron (Johns Hopkins University), William Axinn, Stephen Berkowitz (University of Vermont), Wayne Baker, Allan Bloom, Norman Bradburn, Julie Brines (University of Washington), Richard Carroll (Northwestern University), George Chauncey, James Coleman, John Comaroff, Mihaly Csikszentmihalyi, Susan Fisher, Roger Gould, John P. Heinz (Northwestern University), Gilbert Herdt, Richard Herrell, Dennis Hogan (Pennsylvania State University), Joseph Hotz, James Koopman (University of Michigan), Nancy Lansdale (Pennsylvania State University), Martin Marty, Douglas Massey, Martha McClintock, David Ostrow, M.D. (University of Michigan), William Parish, Richard Posner, Ira Reiss (University of Minnesota), Robert Sampson, Pepper Schwartz (University of Washington), Mark Siegler, M.D., George Steinmetz, Stephen Stigler, Ross Stolzenberg, Fred Strodtbeck, Marta Tienda, Linda Waite, Robert Willis, and Kazuo Yamaguchi.

We also needed and obtained advice and support on the political front as we unsuccessfully attempted to obtain the required Office of Management and Budget approval for conducting our study with the federal moneys that we had previously been awarded through competitive contracting. Those on Capitol Hill who supported our efforts included Senators Daniel Patrick Moynihan (New York) and Paul Simon (Illinois) and Representative John Porter (Illinois). Our political adviser throughout this period was lobbyist William Bailey at the American Psychological Association, who guided us through an unfamiliar process. Additional lobbying efforts were made on our behalf by Stacey Beckhardt and Judy Auerbach at the Consortium of Social Science Associations (COSSA), and advice was offered and efforts made as well by Marjorie Benton, Carl Bitler, Mary Brandon, Theodore Cooper, M.D., Warwick Coppleson, M.D., Ronald Durnford, William Harms, Irving Harris, Anne Heinz, John Heinz, Vicki Otten, Paula Wolff, and Susanne Woolsey.

We owe a special debt to the 3,432 people whom we will never knowingly meet but who each gave us an hour and a half of their time and answered our questions about themselves and their sexual experiences. In so doing, they provided us with the raw material on which this volume is based. Managing a widely distributed project staff with co-principal investigators in two states and a national field staff and the myriad interdependent tasks of political interventions, scholarly agenda, and public and private funding initiatives would simply have been impossible without the heroic efforts of our wonderfully talented team of administrators, Alice Rollins, Cynthia Veldman, and Conray Weathers. They deserve special recognition for all that they accomplished.

This has been an exceptionally engrossing project, and our families and friends have put up with too many stories and suffered through our many setbacks as well as our several successes. We thank them for the support and encouragement they steadfastly gave us.

A Companion Volume

This book is one of two that report the findings from a national survey of adult sexual behavior. This book is written for professional social scientists, counselors, and health professionals. It is intended to be the book of record that systematically lays out the theory informing the study, the study design, and a detailed statistical report and analysis of the data. Written in tandem and published at the same time, the second book, *Sex in America,* by Robert T. Michael, John H. Gagnon, Edward O. Laumann, and Gina Kolata, published by Little, Brown, is intended to reach a more general audience. We have selected many highlights from the study and presented them with interpretation in a manner that we hope will help inform many about this important aspect of public and private social behavior.

PROLOGUE

For most of us, sexual behavior is private. With whom we make love, how and when we do so, and even why we do so are among our most intimate and private matters. But sexual behavior has many public consequences that make this most private of activities of public concern and a frequent target of public policy. This book is intended to help inform the private and the public choices that we make about issues regarding sexual behavior. It is both surprising and disturbing how empirically ill informed we as a nation are about important aspects of sexual behavior. Our primary motivation in writing this book is to provide useful information about sexual behavior in the United States today.

Social science research about sexual behavior has been intermittent and unsustained, typically focused empirically either on specific topics about sexuality, such as age at first intercourse, or on narrowly defined subpopulations, such as women of childbearing age, teenagers, college students, unmarried mothers, or homosexuals. Wide-ranging research on sexuality has not been a major concern among social scientists. The best-known contributors to research on sex over the past century were biologists, such as Alfred Kinsey, or medical clinicians, such as William Masters and Virginia Johnson. What has been contributed by social scientists has come primarily from the disciplines of psychology, anthropology, sociology, and social demography. There are exceptions to these generalizations, of course, and there have been important contributions to our understanding of normative orientations toward such sexual conduct as teenage, premarital, and extramarital sexuality or of fertility behavior, adolescent social relations, sexual deviance, and other phenomena related to sexuality.

There are important tools in the social sciences that have made considerable contributions to the understanding of other social behaviors and that can be applied to sexual behavior. These include the mathematical tools of theoretical models of social interaction as well as the statistical tools of well-crafted survey questionnaires asked of probability samples of respondents. Survey research, for example, is now widely used by politicians and by consumer product market researchers, and formal modeling and survey data are used extensively in many arenas of private enterprise and government decision making. But neither the formal modeling of the motivations and repercussions of

social behavior nor empirical data documenting behavior have yet been focused on the sexual behavior of the general population in the United States.
This book begins to do this, with a strong emphasis on the empirical evidence
obtained from a 1992 nationwide survey of adults.

The survey was designed by a multidisciplinary group of social scientists.
Laumann is a sociologist who specializes in analyzing the various relationships
that people have with each other as a set of overlapping "social networks."
Gagnon is also a sociologist and has studied sexual behavior extensively from
a more social psychological and cultural perspective. Michael is an economist
who specializes in economic behavior as it occurs within families. Michaels is
a sociologist with a special interest in developing techniques for studying
highly sensitive topics in general surveys of the population. Several members
of the research team bring experience in demographic research. Together, we
bring different sets of methods and interests to the study of sexual behavior,
each of which played an important role in framing the design of the national
survey.

Inquiry about sexual behavior is controversial for at least three reasons.
First, there are those on both sides of the political spectrum who oppose the
gathering and the publicizing of information about sex. Some of these people
strongly oppose one or another sexual practice and contend that reporting incidence may legitimate and even encourage certain behaviors. Others have strong
opinions about the right to engage in certain sexual practices and wish to increase public tolerance of those practices. They contend that, if only a small
percentage of people is reported to engage in those practices, such information
might encourage efforts to forbid those practices or to ostracize those people
involved in them. We contend that orchestrated ignorance about basic human
behavior has never been wise public policy. Anti-intellectualism and fear are
not convincing arguments against inquiry and knowledge.

Second, there are those who contend that sex is private and should not be
brought into the public light in general and particularly that there is no justification for the use of federal government support of such inquiry. While we
contend that public health, public education, and public well-being generally
are enhanced by knowledge about sexual behavior and that numerous public
repercussions of many sexual activities warrant governmental support of their
study, the survey on which this book is based was funded by nongovernment
sources. The study itself was greatly influenced, however, by the leadership of
the federal government's National Institute of Child Health and Human Development, which initially challenged us to bring the tools we knew to the task of
understanding sexual behavior.

Third, there are those who feel, as did sex researcher Alfred Kinsey fifty
years ago, that it is not possible to conduct an inquiry on the basis of accurate
and honest reporting of sexual behavior by a statistically random sample
of people. That nearly 3,500 respondents cooperated with us on the ninety-

minute, detailed personal survey that has become the data set on which this book is based offers unequivocal evidence that this is not so.

The case to be made in favor of inquiry into sexual behavior includes the following points. First, an informed citizenry is essential in a democratic society, and, while sex is essentially private, it has many public aspects as well. These require us as a democracy to make judgments and reach agreements about the rules by which we all will live—rules about the treatment of homosexuals, about the legality and availability of and methods of paying for abortions, about public nudity, about sexual harassment, rape, and gender discrimination, about contraceptives, about sexually transmitted infections, and on and on. Information is imperative if we are to make wise collective judgments.

Second, even in our private sexual lives we need guidance from counselors who offer medical advice, religious or ethical guidance, or psychological guidance as we confront the complexities and mysteries of our sexual being. Those counselors need information from somewhere. As we discussed our survey plans and the content of our inquiry with professional counselors from many walks of life, we have been impressed with how much these men and women wish to have and eagerly seek better information to inform their counsel. What is true for professional counselors is no less true of each of us as we counsel our children, our friends, our loved ones, and as we make our own decisions. Be it in the formal curricula in schools or in informal discussions among friends, the absence of information, not its availability, should be frightening to us all.

The devastating outbreak of the AIDS epidemic in the 1980s caught the public health community ill informed about sexual behavior. Better information might have improved the epidemiological models used to anticipate the spread of that disease. Better information might have enabled public health educators to identify more effectively the targeted population to whom to address a more effective message in their efforts to alter the behaviors associated with a high risk of disease and death. Ignorance is never an effective policy instrument for advancing well-being, and policy makers in the medical community urgently need to know more about sexual practices, their prevalences, and their distributions among the population. We should be better prepared for the next urgent need for this information.

Our primary goal in this book is to provide information about the sexual behavior of adults in the United States. There are many facts presented in the chapters that follow and many broad and fine-grained patterns reported in detail. We interpret these findings, speculate on the motives and social forces that underlie them, and suggest their meaning as we see it. We note many puzzles and raise many issues for future research. We have attempted to cover the major domains of sexual behavior as we have recorded them in our survey questionnaire. An effort has been made to provide a cohesive framework in which the observed patterns of behavior can be organized and digested.

We have two secondary goals in this study. These involve persuasion and advocacy. One is directed toward our scientist colleagues. We wish to persuade others that our inquiry can and should be replicated, built upon, and advanced. We raise more questions in our research than we answer; we open more lines of investigation than we can ever pursue or settle. By our example, and by the intellectual challenges that we pose as we speculate about what we find, we hope to encourage others to join us in conducting research on sexual behavior. The other goal is directed toward the community at large. We as a nation are woefully ignorant about the social context of sexuality, and this ignorance promotes fear and creates dysfunction in both our private and our public lives. Open discourse, inquiry, and debate about important issues should be grounded on solid information, and that is what we have begun to provide here. We hope to persuade the reader, not that we know all the answers, or that we have all the facts right, but that the facts can be obtained through scientific inquiry, and that they should be pursued and encouraged, then debated, clarified, and interpreted. A healthy sex life and a healthy nation require it.

We must clarify two points as we begin. As social scientists, we report our findings and speculate about their meaning from the perspectives of, and in the language of, our sciences. For some readers, this may seem stilted. Some may find our discussions of what people do in their bedrooms to be offensive or embarrassing. Even other social scientists who are familiar with viewing human beings as objects of study rather than as individuals may be uncomfortable at first with the idea of extending explanations of social behavior to the domain of sex. Partly, this stems from the fact that, in our society, sex is generally so private that we do not talk about our sex lives directly; instead, we confront stylized and fictionalized representations in the media and in our literature. As a result, we are each encouraged to think of our own sex lives in terms of highly personalized and individualized decisions rather than as being affected by those around us and by our culture. As we will demonstrate in this book, sexual behavior and sexual preference exhibit surprisingly persistent social regularities that imply that social factors play a strong role in shaping sexual expression.

Also, a second impediment to discussing sexuality in a scientific manner is that for many it is difficult to separate the empirical phenomenon of sexuality from the moral or religious considerations that attend it. Indeed, for many people, such considerations are a fundamental part of how they perceive sexual issues and how they behave sexually. It is important to recognize, however, that philosophical and theological perspectives on sexuality are not necessarily inconsistent with a scientific approach. As scientists, we are interested in describing as accurately as possible what people do sexualiy and in formulating and evaluating explanations for why they do as they do. We make no assumptions and offer no judgments about what people "should" do sexually. Ethics is not our expertise; our sciences do not provide insight about that. Ultimately, of course, this is a question that each person must answer for himself or herself.

We do suggest that accurate information about the realities of sexual activity can be instructive in formulating and evaluating theological and philosophical positions on the subject, and, for this reason, we hope that the information in this volume will be of interest both within and outside the scientific community.

Outline of the Book

Part I contains the theoretical foundations and the substantive rationale for our study. While presenting no survey results, it is a lengthy section that treats critical issues of central importance to understanding the substantive implications of those results. Readers already knowledgeable about modern survey techniques and their rationales may elect to skip chapter 2 on the study design.[1] But even readers quite familiar with certain aspects of our theoretical approach are likely to find chapter 1's integrated treatment essential for understanding the logic and significance of the survey results. The sheer volume of results has necessitated a reportorial style that does not always highlight the relevance of a particular finding to our theoretical perspective. The reader's familiarity with the theoretical perspective will be helpful in understanding that relevance. In chapter 1, we describe the basic elements of our theoretical approach: social scripting theory, social network theory, and choice theory. We show that each of these can be applied to the study of sexuality, and we note how each complements the other. Chapter 2 describes the context of our inquiry. Both political and funding circumstances have influenced our research strategy. It is useful, we believe, for the reader to understand the development of our study design, our survey questionnaire, our field strategy, and so on. Chapter 2 reviews these decisions briefly and places them in context.

In part II, we report findings about sexual behavior. Chapter 3 addresses sexual practices and preferences and describes these by key socioeconomic characteristics. The manifold patterns in which individuals simultaneously express their sexuality in fantasy and other forms of autoeroticism and partnered sexual activities are described in the concluding section. Chapter 4 discusses the subjective appeal of a broad spectrum of sexual practices and partnering relationships and how these preferences interact with social factors to produce different sexual outcomes. Chapter 5 discusses the number of sex partners over the adult lifetime and within the past twelve months. We report many patterns by sociodemographic characteristics of the respondent and begin to identify some of the major social forces that affect this key dimension of sexuality. Chapter 6 presents our analysis of the all-important social network of sexual partners. In this chapter, we investigate the hypotheses suggested in the theo-

---

1. Briefly, the National Health and Social Life Survey (NHSLS) is based on personal interviews in 1992 with 3,432 respondents who were randomly drawn from the noninstitutionalized civilian population of the United States by an area probability design, with supplementary samples of black and Hispanic residents.

retical chapter, chapter 1, and explore the systematic patterns of partner selection. Chapter 7 then uses what we have learned about sexual networks to address central issues in the epidemiology of sexually transmitted infections and diseases. Chapter 8 presents information about homosexuality, raising questions about its definition and the closely related matters of its incidence and prevalence in the population at large. Concluding this section of the book, chapter 9 reports on childhood and adolescent sex and sexual victimization.

Part III presents information about the consequences of sexual behavior. Chapter 10 focuses on health consequences, examining indicators of happiness and of physical health. Chapter 11 provides a detailed analysis of the incidence and prevalence of sexually transmitted infections in the population at large. Chapter 12 looks at the relation between sexual behavior and fertility, in terms of numbers of children born and also of contraceptive practices and reported abortions. Chapter 13 explores the relation between sexual behavior and the stability of marriage and cohabitational partnerships. Chapter 14 discusses data on attitudes toward sexual issues and investigates how these attitudes—say, regarding the impropriety of extramarital sexual affairs—correlate with respondents' own sexual behavior. In a more speculative vein, the epilogue briefly revisits our theoretical agenda and then highlights several policy implications of our research findings.

The book contains an extensive appendix section. In appendix A, we report the sampling procedures and more technical information about our sample. In appendix B, we compare the character of our sample to other high-quality samples in recent years in order to determine the representativeness of our sample. Appendix C contains our survey questionnaire.

PART I

In part I, we set the stage for our study, describing the perspectives that we use to organize and interpret our survey data in later chapters. Facts and figures have no meaning unless they are placed in a context, so in this section we discuss several overarching ideas and ways of thinking about sexual behavior that help us make sense of the patterns we find. Theoretical concepts and ways of thinking (or paradigms) help us all understand the empirical world around us. Typically, these are so ingrained and informal as not even to be noticeable. When we approach a topic like sexual behavior about which scholarly discourse has been so limited and marginalized, it is more important than usual to attempt to offer some organizing principles and ideas for the task of studying that behavior. In chapter 1, we provide that discussion.

Our survey questionnaire emphasizes certain aspects of sexual behavior, such as the importance of the choice of a partner, how that choice gets made, and the character of the sexual relationship with that partner; of necessity, the questionnaire does not emphasize other important topics about sexual behavior. How we selected these featured topics, how we framed them, how we asked about them, and how we interpret the answers we received are decisions that we made on the basis of the theoretical perspectives described in chapter 1. In chapter 2, we describe the design of our survey and the reasons we made the decisions we did regarding its implementation.

These two chapters, then, provide the background for our inquiry.

CHAPTER I

Theoretical Background

Human sexual behavior is a diverse phenomenon. It occurs in different physical locations and social contexts, consists of a wide range of specific activities, and is perceived differently by different people. An individual engages in sexual activity on the basis of a complex set of motivations and organizes that activity on the basis of numerous external factors and influences. Thus, it is unlikely that the tools and concepts from any single scientific discipline will suffice to answer all or even most of the questions one might ask about sexual behavior. This chapter introduces the several approaches that we have found especially helpful in formulating what we hope will prove to be a more comprehensive social scientific understanding of sexuality.

1.1 A Social Scientific Approach to Sexuality

Much of the previous scientific research on sexuality has been conducted by biologists and psychologists and has thus focused on sexual behavior purely as an "individual level" phenomenon. Thus, such research has defined sexual activity to be the physical actions that a person performs (or the thoughts and feelings that a person experiences) and has sought to explain individual variation in these actions in terms of processes endogenous to the individual. A good example of this approach is the study of sexual "drives" or "instincts." In drive theories, people are assumed to experience a buildup of "sexual tension" or "sexual need" during periods of deprivation or during particularly erotic environmental stimulation. When sexual activity is experienced, the drive is satiated and the need reduced. Such cycles of increased drive and its resultant satiation are often used to explain hunger and thirst and, by analogy, sexual conduct. Differences in drives across individuals are generally assumed to result from underlying biological or psychological differences in those individuals.

The major shortcoming of such studiously individualistic approaches is that they are able (at most) to explain only a very small part of the story. This is because, unlike the sexual behavior of certain animal species (e.g., salmon, who are genetically programmed to swim upstream at the appropriate time to spawn), human sexual behavior is only partly determined by factors originating within the individual. In addition, a person's socialization into a particular culture, his or her interaction with sex partners, and the constraints imposed on him or her become extremely important in determining his or her sexual activities. This observation—that an individual's social environment affects sexual behavior—is perhaps obvious, yet research on social processes represents a disproportionately small amount of the extant scientific literature on human sexuality.

This does not mean that there have been no social scientific studies of sexual behavior. One prominent researcher, Ira Reiss (see, e.g., Reiss 1967, 1986, 1990), recently enumerated more than a dozen national surveys of sexual attitudes and practices since Kinsey and his associates' work appeared in the late 1940s. Previous national studies of sexual behavior have targeted specific subpopulations or have focused on a relatively narrow range of sexual conduct. For example, Zelnik and Kantner (1972b, 1980; Zelnik, Kantner, and Ford 1981) conducted three national studies of pregnancy-related behavior among adolescents. Subsequently, Sonenstein, Pleck, and Ku (1991) conducted a more comprehensive study of sexual practices among adolescent males, and the CDC (1992b) reported on a limited number of sexual behaviors among a national sample of high school students. With regard to adults, the first nationally representative data were collected by Reiss in 1963. Later, Klassen, Williams, and Levitt (1989) conducted a study of adults age twenty-one and older (the data were collected in 1970) that focused primarily on sexual attitudes. In addition, the National Survey of Family Growth (Mosher and McNally 1991) asked its fifteen- to forty-four-year-old female respondents a limited number of questions about sexual behavior, and Tanfer's 1983 study of twenty- to twenty-nine-year-old women (see Tanfer 1992) focused on a much broader range of sexual behaviors, relationships, and attitudes. These studies were followed in 1991 by a well-publicized study conducted by the Batelle Institute of twenty- to thirty-nine-year-old men that collected data on a wide range of sexual conduct (Billy et al. 1993). Finally, the National AIDS Behavioral Surveys (Peterson et al. 1993) collected behavioral data relevant to the transmission of AIDS from respondents in twenty-three "high-risk" U.S. cities. While these studies provide information on several important issues, few have attended seriously to the fact that sexual activity occurs in the context of a relationship (see, e.g., Blumstein and Schwartz 1983) or the epidemiological consequences of the structure of sexual networks. (For recent reviews of these and other studies of human sexual behavior, see Turner et al. 1989; Miller, Turner, and Moses 1990, 401–19; Schwartz and Gillmore 1990; McKinney and Sprecher 1989; and Laumann et al. 1994b).

We thus have in hand a number of important indications of where to look for the effects that social factors have on sexual behavior. One example is the persistent finding that a person's social class ("working" vs. "middle") is correlated with certain aspects of sexual behavior (e.g., Weinberg and Williams 1980), although there is some evidence that the strength of this association is diminishing with time (DeLamater 1981). Another persistent finding comes from the relatively large literature on adolescent sexuality (Brookman 1990).

Sociologists have found that adolescents involved in religious activities tend to delay first intercourse longer than those who are not (DeLamater and MacCorquodale 1979a). These and other essentially descriptive findings are certainly interesting, yet, without a systematic theoretical framework within which to interpret them, they cannot help us understand how and why specific social processes or circumstances affect sexual behavior.

Biological and psychological studies of sexual behavior focus solely on the individual as the relevant "unit of analysis." That is, the objective of such research is to answer questions about why an individual exhibits certain sexual behaviors. But this line of inquiry can reveal only part of the story. Most sexual behavior is not performed by an individual alone and in the absence of others. Instead, sexual behavior is social in the sense that it involves two people (or more). Sex involves negotiation and interplay, the expectation and experience of compromise. There is competition; there is cooperation. The relationships between the partners and between their mutual actions make the sexual partnership or dyad an essential analytic unit in the study of sexuality. This focus on the social, the external, the relational, and the public dimensions is what distinguishes our inquiry from the psychological and biological orientations that have characterized much sex research in the past.

Although little progress has been made in the social sciences toward developing systematic *theories* about the social processes involved in sexual behavior, social psychology, sociology, and economics have each developed persuasive theories explaining other spheres of social behavior. Therefore, it seems sensible to draw on such theories in attempting to formulate a social scientific theory of sexual conduct. We have begun with three theoretical traditions—scripting theory, choice theory, and social network theory—each addressing certain aspects of sexual behavior. Together, these theories allow us to move toward the construction of a more comprehensive theory of the social dimensions of sexuality.

1.2 Scripting Theory: Explaining Sexual Content

Previous researchers have generally adopted the perspective that there is an inevitable negative conflict between the biological nature of human beings and the cultures in which they are reared. With regard to sexual behavior, this implies that social factors function solely to inhibit or constrain people's intrinsic sexual desires and urges. For example, it is assumed that biologically mature adolescents will naturally have intercourse (that they both want to and have the opportunity to do so) and that those who do not are simply better at "controlling their urges." We reject this perspective, not because it allows for the influence of biological effects on sexual behavior, but because it takes a narrow view of the role of social processes as merely constraining sexual conduct. In contrast, along with Ortner and Whitehead (1981a, 1981b), Herdt and Stoller (1990), and others, we argue that sociocultural processes play a fundamental role in determining what we perceive to be "sexual" and how we construct and interpret our sexual fantasies and thoughts. Thus, although biological factors may indeed affect sexual behavior, they play at most a small role in determining what those specific behaviors will be and how they will be interpreted.

Scripting theories of sexual conduct address exactly these types of questions. The starting point for these theories can be expressed in terms of several assumptions about the ways in which specific sexual patterns are acquired and expressed. First, they assume that patterns of sexual conduct in a culture are locally derived (i.e., that what is sexual and what *sex* means differs in different cultures). Second, they assume either that human beings possess no biological instincts about how to act sexually or that the effects of such instincts are minor in comparison with the effects of an individual's socially determined scripts for conduct. People may vary biologically in activity level and temperament, but there are no *direct* links between this variation and what they will do sexually as adults. Third, they assume that, through a process of acculturation lasting from birth to death, individuals acquire patterns of sexual conduct that are appropriate to their culture (including those patterns that are thought to deviate from the norms of the culture). Fourth, they assume that people may not enact the scripts provided by their culture exactly but instead may make minor adaptations to suit their own needs. In complex and contradictory cultures, such individual adaptations will be very diverse.

On the basis of these four principles, sexual scripts specify with whom people have sex, when and where they should have sex, what they should do sexually, and why they should do sexual things. These scripts embody what the intersubjective culture treats as sexuality (cultural scenarios) and what the individual believes to be the domain of sexuality. Individuals improvise on the basis of the cultural scenarios and in the process change the sexual culture of the society. In this way, individual sexual actors as well as those who create representations of sexual life (e.g., the mass media, religious leaders, educators, and researchers) are constantly reproducing and transforming sexual life in a society. For example, introducing condoms into sexual activity as part of an AIDS education and prevention program requires changing scripts for sexual conduct on the part of individuals. If large numbers of individuals adopt this new script, they will change the effects that sexual activity has on health by reducing unwanted pregnancies, abortions, and the spread of sexually transmitted diseases.

The scripting perspective distinguishes between cultural scenarios (the instructions for sexual and other conduct that are embedded in the cultural narratives that are provided as guides or instructions for all conduct), interpersonal scripts (the structured patterns of interaction in which individuals as actors engage in everyday interpersonal conduct), and intrapsychic scripts (the plans and fantasies by which individuals guide and reflect on their past, current, or future conduct) (Gagnon and Simon 1973; Simon and Gagnon 1987; Gagnon 1991). Sexual conduct involves a reflective individual interacting socially with others, guided in part by a meaningful system of individually interpreted cultural instructions. Thus, for example, a female adolescent considering whether to have intercourse for the first time with her boyfriend is responding both to her perceptions of what women who "do it" are like and to her own personal understanding of what the event would mean to her. At the same time, she and her boyfriend may feel as though the sexual interactions that they currently have involving fondling and mutual masturbation are not a complete enactment of what "lovers do." The strength of the scripting model is that it brings together the two levels of meaning (the intersubjective or cultural and the intrapsychic) and links them to a system of interpersonal action.

Several studies provide evidence for the importance of sexual scripts in shaping both perception and behavior (Geer and Brussard 1990; Castillo and Geer 1993). For example, in one study, male subjects listened to one of two different narratives, during which time their level of sexual arousal was monitored. Both narratives began with identical stories describing a young woman getting into her car and driving to a building, where she goes into a room, closes the door, and removes her clothes. At this point, a man enters the room; he is identified in the first narrative as the woman's gynecologist, in the second as her boyfriend. Predictably, subjects hearing the first narrative experienced significantly less arousal than those who heard the second, despite the similarity of the two narratives. Since the physician was not part of the subjects' sexual scripts, they had to reevaluate their perceptions of the situation.

With regard to the effects of scripts on actual behavior, research among adolescents has repeatedly demonstrated the existence of a general pattern of activities that young people follow as they acquire sexual experience (Brady and Levitt 1965; DeLamater and MacCorquodale 1979a; Simon and Gagnon 1967). The pattern begins with kissing, proceeding first to necking and then to the male fondling the female's breast (first over the clothing, then underneath). Next occurs fondling of each other's genitals, first by the male, then by the female. This is followed by genital-genital contact and then by vaginal intercourse. Only after intercourse do adolescents go on to try oral sex, again first by the male, then by the female. What this means is that those who have had vaginal intercourse are also likely to have engaged in kissing, necking, fondling, and apposition. Similarly, those who have not yet engaged in "heavy petting" are unlikely to move directly to intercourse. Of course, not all adolescents complete the entire program or, to use the especially apt euphemism, "go all the way." Moreover, any single interaction is subject to practical considerations (such as being restricted to the backseat of a car) that may result in temporary deviations from the script.

Studying scripts directly is difficult since it requires detailed data not only on what activities occur during a sexual encounter but also on the order in which those activities occur. One group of researchers has trained couples to record their sexual interactions in a diary, using an elaborate coding scheme to distinguish among various activities and positions (Coxon 1986, 1993). This and similar approaches are impossible to implement in a national, cross-sectional survey. Instead, in our national survey we relied on asking several detailed questions about the occurrence of specific activities during respondents' last sexual encounter. Our approach is to use patterns in the co-presence of these activities to make inferences about the nature of the scripts being used.

1.3 Choice Theory: Sexual Decision Making

While scripting theories are useful in explaining the range of activities (or scripts) available to an individual, they tell us little about how the individual chooses among these various possibilities. For example, an individual may have different scripts for how to act toward different partners (e.g., a new partner, a "one-night stand," and a spouse) and in different situations; however, the content of these scripts alone tells us little about why that individual may choose to pursue certain types of relationships to the exclusion of others. In order to address this important issue, we turn to an economic approach to decision making. Essentially, economic choice theory is concerned with how people utilize the resources available to them in the pursuit of one or more specific goals. Since one's resources are generally limited, choices arise regarding how these resources should be apportioned among various activities leading to one or another goal. Were there no scarcity of the necessary resources, there would be no constraint on the achievement of one's goals and no need for choices to be made. However, the necessary resources (i.e., time, money, emotional and physical energy, personal reputation) required to engage in sexual behavior are limited, and choices must therefore be made.

It is important to recognize that an economic approach presumes the existence of a goal or a set of goals. Thus, in order to utilize this approach, we must first identify what those goals (or at least some of them) are. For example, the goals of sexual behavior may include sexual pleasure itself, the emotional satisfaction that results from being intimately involved with someone toward whom one feels affection, having children, and acquiring a "good reputation" among one's friends. So we have listed four goals that may motivate a person to use his or her limited money, time, and energy to achieve one or another of these goals.

People differ in the importance that they accord these various goals and in their capacities to achieve them. Choice theory focuses on how these goals and capacities influence behavior. Invariably, the efforts of one person to achieve his or her goals affect the efforts of others. That is what makes this a social science—people's efforts do not take place in isolation. When it comes to selecting a sex partner, for example, if one person succeeds in attracting a partner, that person is "taken," or "spoken for," and is no longer available to anyone else—or at least can be won away only through competition. This social dimension of sexual behavior is less obvious but no less real when it comes to most other activities, from using contraception to selecting a "sexy" outfit to wear to a party.

In order to make our discussion more concrete, suppose that we are interested in explaining why people have the number of sex partners that they do. Chapter 5 shows that 71 percent of adults (aged eighteen to fifty-nine) report having only one sex partner during the previous year and that 53 percent report having only one sex partner over the previous five years. These data suggest that most people change sex partners relatively infrequently, choosing instead to remain in long-term, sexually exclusive relationships. Ignoring for a moment the details surrounding this conclusion (these are addressed in chapter 5), consider how an economic framework might be used to interpret this finding. As we stated above, we will assume that most people desire some amount of sexual stimulation and that this, together with other goals, leads them to pursue sexual relationships with one or more partners. Yet securing partners is not without cost; one must expend time, money, emotional energy, and social resources in order to meet people and negotiate a sexual relationship. Solely on the basis of this consideration, it would seem to be more cost effective to fulfill one's sexual needs by remaining in a long-term relationship than by constantly searching for new partners. One might "look around" and perhaps even fantasize about potential partners, but the costs involved in actually pursuing them relative to simply maintaining one's current relationship may be too high. Only those whose objectives explicitly include having sex with many partners (perhaps because of the excitement and uncertainty) will frequently choose to incur such costs.

In this example, an individual spends resources and engages in activities for the purpose of achieving sexual pleasure, in much the same way as an industrial firm manufactures a product in order to make a profit; both may be described as *productive* activities. And, like most productive activities, both can involve the creation of unintended by-products, desirable and undesirable. In the case of the manufacturer, toxic waste from the manufacturing process, hazardous working conditions for employees, and higher incomes and lower unemployment in the community are all potential by-products. In the case of having sex with a partner, an unwanted pregnancy, a sexually transmitted infection or disease, a happier, more pleasant personality, and a greater ability to concentrate are examples of possible by-products. Much of the complexity of life's choices arises in dealing with these by-products since it requires resources to avoid or eliminate the negative ones.

The number of sex partners that a person has may also be affected by by-products other than those resulting from sexual activity itself. Consider, for instance, an individual who chooses to cohabit with his or her sex partner in order to share living expenses and to enhance the level of companionship. One by-product of most arrangements such as this is the expectation of sexual exclusivity[1]—an expectation so important that failing to adhere to it normally

---

1. One might argue that sexual exclusivity is not a by-product but an objective in itself; more specifically, one might argue that the mutual trust and certainty that come from being in a sexually exclusive relationship are potential objectives.

leads to the termination of the relationship. This by-product clearly impinges on the number of sex partners that an individual may have, encouraging monogamy as long as the primary relationship lasts. An individual confronted with this situation must make a decision, weighing the value of the primary relationship and the value of honesty and dependability against the value of experiencing an additional sexual relationship and exploring a potentially preferable partnership.

These decisions are often made in the face of uncertainty. In the case that we are discussing—an individual living with one sex partner who must decide whether to pursue another—the individual faces uncertainty about detection, about the nature of the new partnership, and about the risk of disease, pregnancy, and harm. The more information one has about the outcome of a choice, the wiser will be the choice, of course, but then there is the decision about how much information to acquire before making the choice. Acquiring that information itself is costly, however, in terms of both time and possibly money.[2]

Like so many choices we make, choices regarding sexual behavior are often made under uncertainty. It is the case that people have different attitudes toward risk; some enjoy taking risks, while others prefer to avoid risk.[3] One can spend resources reducing risks—finding out about the likely outcome or reducing the likelihood of some by-product—and one can reduce the adverse effect of a bad outcome through insurance. One reason that couples discuss their views and their prior sexual histories is to share information about the probabilities of good and bad eventualities from having sex together. Similarly, people use contraception to avoid pregnancy and disease, travel to distant places to carry on affairs in order to avoid detection, and generally treat their decisions about sexual behavior with some degree of strategy and purpose that characterizes their choices in other domains.

While formal models of behavior often assume that risks are perceived accurately, research in psychology has shown that people do a rather poor job of estimating not only the absolute sizes but even the relative sizes of the risks that they encounter. For example, in a recent study of possible determinants of self-perceived risk for AIDS, Prohaska et al. (1990) found that respondents in those demographic subgroups with the highest prevalence of HIV infection (singles, males, blacks, and Hispanics) were not more likely to perceive themselves as at risk than other respondents. The study did, however, show higher perceptions of risk among respondents with multiple partners during the past

2. We use the terms *risk* and *uncertainty* interchangeably here. More formally, the distinction is sometimes made between risk as a circumstance where probabilities are known (or knowable) but outcomes are not (tossing a coin, e.g.) and uncertainty as a circumstance where the probabilities themselves are not knowable (the probability of reincarnation, e.g.). For the classic statement of the distinction and its implications, see Knight (1921).

3. Ask yourself which of these two alternatives you prefer: option A will provide you with $100 outright; option B will provide you with a fifty-fifty chance of either $200 or no money at all. These two alternatives have the same "expected payoff" of $100, but some people strongly prefer A and others B.

five years as well as among those who knew little or nothing about the previous sexual behavior of their partners. Finally, respondents who reported that they would be ashamed if they contracted AIDS were less likely to perceive themselves as being at risk. Although it is difficult to interpret this last finding, it suggests the possibility that people's emotional and moral reactions to the disease—factors that may have nothing to do with objective risk—may affect their subjective risk assessment.

In addition to risk management, another conceptual tool from economics that can be useful in understanding sexual behavior is that of human capital. Just as the manufacturing firm invests in equipment and raw materials in order to produce a specific product to be sold for profit, so do individuals invest in education and skills in order to achieve their objectives. This is obvious in the case of people preparing to enter or reenter the job market. However, there are also types of human capital that facilitate the pursuit of sexual objectives. One example is the skills necessary to attract potential sex partners. These might include a healthy and attractive appearance, good conversational skills, and the like. Clearly, such human capital is most valuable to those who are actively searching for a partner, so these people should be expected to invest more highly in these skills than others who are involved in long-term monogamous relationships. Since skills tend to deteriorate with disuse, people who have been out of the market for a period of time are likely to find their skills rusty on returning. Moreover, new expectations and protocols in dating may require learning the new "rules of the game."

Another type of human capital used to secure sexual activity is the skills necessary for maintaining an existing relationship. These might include the ability to satisfy one's partner physically as well as the ability to accommodate his or her personality and interests, to get along with his or her family and friends, and so forth. Such skills have been the focus of studies that seek to understand why married couples choose to remain married or to divorce. In a marriage (or in any long-term sexual relationship), each partner acquires specific skills that are beneficial in the couple's interactions. Yet these skills are valuable only as long as the couple remains together. This loss of value associated with dissolution provides incentive for couples to remain together. Furthermore, those couples who have made greater investments in partner-specific skills will have more incentive to remain together than those who have made fewer investments.

Thus far, our discussion about choice theory has been oriented around an individual decision maker. However, the decisions of one person (or institution) often impinge on others through the marketplace in which people acquire the resources to achieve their goals. The key factor in determining an item's value in the market is desirability relative to scarcity. Without desirability, scarcity alone does not provide much value, as seen by considering the value of last month's local newspaper—copies may be scarce, but they are not very valuable since few people are interested in reading old news. In contrast, the air that we breathe is highly desirable, but little value is placed on it since it is typically quite abundant. Thus, value is determined by the competitive forces of demand (reflecting desirability) and supply (reflecting availability), while it is measured by the commodity's unit price relative to other goods.

Perhaps the most obvious example of a market in the context of sexual behavior is the market for sex partners. In most cases, this market does not involve a product being exchanged for money but consists instead of a barter exchange in which each person both seeks (i.e., demands) a sex partner and offers (i.e., supplies) himself or herself as a partner in exchange. Each prospective partner offers his or her own physical attributes, personality, skills, etc., in exchange for those of a partner of interest to him or her. This exchange is made explicit in advertisements that appear in the personals column of the newspaper, such as "SWM, gd looking, seeks F undr 30 for fun/companionship."

Anyone who has participated in the market for sex partners knows that those possessing more of the traits most valued in a particular culture have more opportunities for exchange than those possessing fewer. The majority of these opportunities are likely to involve similarly or less attractive potential partners, from among whom each individual is expected to choose the "best deal" that he or she can get.[4] This mechanism of competition generates partnerships in which the two partners are likely to have similar "values" on the partner market. If there is a disparity between the numbers of males and females on the market, those who are least desirable are likely to be left without a partner altogether. An example of this is the often talked about "marriage squeeze" in which middle-aged and older women lose out to younger women in the competition for an insufficient number of eligible men (this topic will be discussed in detail in chapter 5).

An important aspect of selecting a sex partner is that it involves little prior knowledge of the other's sexual competence. Like many other "products" acquired in the marketplace, one does not know all about the partner's sexual interests, capabilities, and limitations before a match is made. That, of course, is true of the book or the car you buy, the job you accept, even the sweet corn you select at the grocery. Consequently, one relies on reputation, on what you can tell from looking and talking, on the reliability of the broker or grocer, and so forth. In short, buyers invest in information about the product: they choose to spend some resources of time and effort and maybe money obtaining as much information as seems worth paying for before making a selection, whether of a book, a car, or a sex partner. Likewise, sellers invest in presentation and persuasion: they choose to expend resources of time, energy, and

---

4. Although it has been known for some time that there is a moderate correlation between the attractiveness of sexual partners, there has been debate over whether this similarity is the result of a market mechanism in which each person seeks the best partner he or she can find or the result of a process by which people select partners similar to themselves (Kalick and Hamilton 1986).

probably money looking good, being personable and intelligent, maintaining a good reputation, being active in the right circles, and so forth. Different strategies attract different buyers: markets are coupled and differentiated.

In a day when one shunned sexual contact before marriage, the information that partners had about their sexual compatibility was probably far less at the time of the wedding than is the case in a day when most couples have sex with each other before they form marriage bonds. You would think that this more "intensive searching" would lead to more compatible matches and thus lower divorce rates, but that surely has not been the case in the United States over the past three decades. The explanations for the higher divorce rates lie elsewhere, and there is an extensive literature on that subject (e.g., see Becker, Landes, and Michael 1977; Michael 1988; Becker 1991; Cherlin 1992).

It is around the time that one is thinking about buying a new car that interest is piqued and discussions are held with friends about how they like their new Saturn or how good the service is on their new Mazda. Similarly, in the marketplace for sex partners, there is a time of considerable searching and exploring and a time after a selection is made and a partnership formed when the searching stops or is at least greatly diminished. Just as interest in the new car market is renewed when the current car needs to be replaced, interest in a new sex partner can be renewed when divorce or separation occurs, and it is during these times of more extensive searching that additional sex partners are more likely to be acquired. Over the lifetime of an individual we should expect to see certain periods of relatively extensive exploration of the sex partner marketplace and other times with little involvement in that marketplace. Most people probably retain at least a little interest in those markets in which they are not active, both from intellectual curiosity about how the market is going generally and from the realization that they might find themselves back in the market unexpectedly since, after all, accidents do happen—a traffic accident or a stolen car or, analogously, an unexpected marital disruption or the death of a partner, for example.

When we think about the market for sex partners, despite the strangeness of the concept to some, there are many parallels to other more familiar marketplaces. We noted above that individuals surely differ in their goals or objectives as they choose a sex partner—recreational sex, an intense companionship, a partner for raising children, for example. Not surprisingly, then, those active in the market will surely place different values on different attributes in prospective partners—some men might value companionship more than physical attractiveness, while others might value earning power or a strong sense of family loyalty in a prospective sex and marriage partner more than any other attribute. The same diversity of interests and valuations exists on the other side of the market, and this is as true in the sex partner market and the marriage partner market as in the employee/job market. Jobs, like partners and employees, bundle many characteristics into a single opportunity, and one's judgment about the attractiveness of a particular job often hinges on the importance of one or another of these characteristics—for example, the opportunity to learn, or to be intellectually challenged, or to get a high salary, or to have security in employment, or to travel, or to have a safe environment in which to work, and so on. These same complexities of first weighing the importance of diverse attributes and then ascertaining the characteristics of the prospective job or partner or employee are what makes the marketplace so challenging. Some people are more capable of sorting through these complexities than others; most people expend considerable resources—time, energy, and money— attempting to make better choices.

Another aspect of markets is that they have physical dimensions. Geographic distance adds costs to matching just as much as acquiring information does. Most people search in local markets, and the partitioning of the market into the jobs or the sex partners in the local community—even in the local social networks in which a person is active—reflects the costliness of searching more widely. That, like the fact that information about options is costly, is a reality in most markets.

Markets are surely not "perfect" if by that one means that full and accurate information is available instantly and costlessly. Nevertheless, markets are extraordinarily effective in facilitating search and selection of a relatively good match.

We have used the example of the marketplace for sex partners to illustrate the application of economic theory to one aspect of sexual behavior, the choice of sexual partners. Scarcity, imposed by limited resources and by competition, characterizes many personal sexual choices. The fundamental logic of goal-oriented behavior, investments in resources and avoidance of costs, and the perception and management of personal risk can explain a wide range of sexual expression. As we shall indicate below, this economic framework is largely consistent with both scripting and network theory, and many of our explanations will be based on a combination of these.

Before moving on, we consider briefly one additional aspect of sexual behavior that economic choice theory can help address. As individuals, most of us are accustomed to thinking of sexuality in highly personal terms, consisting of our own thoughts and what we do with our partners. For this reason, our choices about which sexual activities to pursue are based on our personal assessments of the benefits and costs involved. However, the private choices that we make about sexual behaviors and attitudes can also have consequences at a collective or societal level. There can be both benefits and costs to society as a whole that are not immediately visible to the individual. Such benefits or costs are called *externalities*. Since prices and market values of products affect the choices that people make, it stands to reason that, in circumstances where prices are incorrectly perceived or where part of the price is not known to the decision maker, a wrong decision is likely to be made, in which case we say that the market has failed. That is what happens with externalities—they are not taken into account when choices are made, and the "wrong" choice often results. When that occurs, governments frequently step in to cause decision makers to take account of the "correct" cost or benefit of a decision.

An excellent example of the externalities involved in sexual behavior is the situation surrounding China's decision to impose regulations on the fertility of its citizens. Although having several children may have been rational from the perspective of individual parents, the opinion of the Chinese government was that the resulting increase in population would continue to impose costs on the country as a whole—costs that would eventually be felt by its citizens. Thus, the government chose to intervene by prohibiting parents from having more than one child and imposing penalties on and mandatory sterilization of those who fail to comply.

In the United States, an externality resulting from fertility, many would argue, is the burden on the welfare system of children whose parents are either unable or unwilling to support them financially. While many couples determine how many children they can afford to support and plan their fertility accordingly, other couples bear children they did not plan or plan children they subsequently cannot afford. Child welfare programs in effect lower the cost of raising a child to the natural or custodial parents and impose these costs on the taxpayer. Congress addressed this issue in 1988 by passing the Family Support Act, a bill that set up child support enforcement offices in each state to identify noncustodial parents and legally garnish their earnings in order to help pay for the support of their children.

Another externality associated with sexual behavior is the possible transmission of diseases such as gonorrhea, chlamydia, and HIV. Such diseases not only threaten an individual's health but also contribute to collective costs such as the provision of subsidized medical care and research and the increased risk of being exposed to the infection as it becomes more widespread.

The choices that individuals make about sexual behavior that exposes them to the risk of unwanted pregnancy or disease are made in the context of the costs of avoiding these outcomes. Since there are negative externalities associated with these outcomes, it seems a sensible strategy to subsidize the costs of avoiding them. That is one rationale for government support of programs that distribute contraceptives and information about how to avoid pregnancy and sexually transmitted disease or infection. People do not infallibly make the correct choice, and sexual behavior may not be the best example of rationality in action, but there is much strategy in our sexual behavior and much purposiveness in what we choose to do and not do sexually. Lowering the cost of avoiding outcomes that are socially undesirable because they involve negative externalities is surely wise.

Note how a brief discussion of externalities can quickly become a discussion of government policy or an advocacy of collective action. Choice theory promotes discussion of this nature since it facilitates an articulation of the relation between private choices and public repercussions, between individual and collective action. We will return to this set of issues later in the book.

1.4   Network Theory: The Sexual Dyad

So far, we have said little about how the sexual partnership (or dyad) is theoretically significant. Both scripting and choice theories focus on what individuals do, explaining it on the basis of the experiences, circumstances, and decisions of those individuals. However, sexual activity is fundamentally social in that it involves two or more persons either explicitly or implicitly (as in the case of sexual fantasy and masturbation). This simple fact has three important implications. First, since sexual partnerships are a special case of social relationships, we may expect these partnerships to conform to certain regularities that have been observed regarding social relationships more generally. This provides a theoretical framework within which to study the dynamics of sexual partnerships—who becomes partners with whom, how these partnerships are maintained, and why some of them eventually dissolve. Second, since sexual activity is negotiated within the context of a social relationship, the features of the relationship itself become important in determining what activities will occur. This may seem obvious at first; however, such thinking represents a subtle but major departure from previous research on sexuality (see esp. Blumstein and Schwartz 1983; Sprecher and McKinney 1993). Finally, sexual dyads do not exist in a vacuum but are instead embedded within larger networks of social relationships. Thus, individual dyads are affected by the social networks surrounding them, and this in turn influences the sexual activity of their members. We now turn to a more detailed discussion of each of these implications.

One of the most persistent empirical regularities that has been observed among social relationships is the tendency toward *equal status contact,* meaning that people tend to initiate and maintain relationships with others who have the same or similar social characteristics as they themselves do. This general pattern of same-status contact has been observed in studies of friendship (Laumann 1966, 1973; Verbrugge 1977; Fischer 1982; Hallinan and Williams 1989), professional relationships (Heinz and Laumann 1982; Baker 1991), and relationships among discussion partners (Marsden 1988). Specifically, these studies have shown that such relationships are more likely to exist among persons of the same gender, age, race, education, and religion. Several factors account for these findings, including the fact that our society is geographically and socially segregated in ways that greatly reduce an individual's opportunities to interact with people unlike himself or herself. In addition, some authors have suggested that people prefer to interact with similar others in order to reinforce their own self-identity, to validate their own behaviors and attitudes, and, most obviously, because they are more likely to share common interests with such people. Finally, a person's family, friends, and other associates maintain control over the kinds of people with whom that person forms relationships, often decreasing the likelihood that he or she will interact with dissimilar others. Such control may be exercised in the form of an outright admonishment for interacting with a particular person or merely through a refusal to admit the unwanted other person fully to their "group." These reactions are often due to the perception that the dissimilar person will threaten the cohesiveness of the group.

For similar reasons, we also expect sexual relationships to occur more frequently between people with the same or similar characteristics. Research on similarity among married couples seems to confirm this general hypothesis, identifying large amounts of both educational (Mare 1991) and religious (Kalmijn 1991) homogamy (in other words, marriage partners share similar characteristics). More recently, the same has also been found among cohabiting couples (Schoen and Weinick 1993). Since we may assume that the majority of marriages and cohabitational relationships begin as noncohabiting sexual relationships, these results imply at least a moderate degree of homophily among more narrowly sexual relationships.[5] Our study is the first to gather the data necessary to examine this issue, an examination that has potentially powerful consequences for determining the pathways through which sexually transmitted infections and diseases spread (Anderson and May 1992; Morris 1989).

For nonsexual relationships such as friendship (especially those that are particularly close and intimate), the theories that we have identified are limited to predictions of pure homophily (or similarity between ego and alter). More specifically, they treat friendship as symmetrical in that the logic of their arguments does not distinguish between the two parties.[6] Such reasoning only partially explains the patterning of sexual relationships. This is because most sexual relationships incorporate asymmetrical elements that may make homophily with respect to certain characteristics difficult to achieve or undesirable. The most obvious example is the case of gender; while friendships and collegial ties often occur among people of the same gender, most sexual relationships do not. On the contrary, most people's basic understanding of sexual activity is restricted to opposite-sex relationships. This point may seem obvious, yet, in combination with the existence of gender homophily among other types of relationships, it implies that sexual relationships provide a unique social bridge between the two genders.

5. This assumption is certainly valid for the younger cohorts in our sample, but, among the oldest cohorts, the majority of married couples had not engaged in premarital sex.

6. It is important to note that, while ego and alter may be *theoretically* indistinguishable, there are important differences that arise in the data collection process. This is because the data used to measure homophily are typically collected by asking a sample of persons to describe themselves *and* those with whom they share a relationship (e.g., their three best friends). Respondents are thus free to select which alters to report, and, since people generally desire to be associated with others of similar or higher status than themselves (Laumann 1966), these methods generally yield data in which certain types of nonhomophilous relationships—those in which the alter has a higher social prestige than the ego—are more likely to be reported. While this effect is an important indicator of the asymmetrical character of "social distance," it is not part of theories attempting to explain the objective reality of friendship patterns.

Another important example of asymmetry in sexual relationships is the division of labor within marriages. The traditional arrangement in which the husband is the main breadwinner and the wife is responsible for household tasks creates incentives for women to marry men with high levels of educational achievement and, thus, a high value in the job market. By the same token, because educational achievement is less tied to the successful completion of household tasks, men do not have the same incentives to marry highly educated women. This difference in incentives, together with the historical fact that men have had greater educational opportunities than women, the delay between leaving school and marriage, and the social taboo against wives earning more than their husbands (Brines and Joyner 1993), has resulted in a considerable proportion of nonhomogamous marriages in which the husband has more education than the wife. However, this trend is changing as more women pursue higher levels of education and as their value in the labor market increases (Oppenheimer 1988). For example, educational parity among couples, particularly among those who are college educated, has increased (Mare 1991).

Just as the nature of these asymmetries has changed over time, we also expect them to differ across different types of sexual relationships. More specifically, we expect the patterns of racial, age, educational, and religious similarity that have been observed in marital relationships to be different in noncohabitational sexual partnerships. For example, since noncohabitational relationships do not involve the pooling of incomes and expenses, we hypothesize that such relationships are perhaps more likely to occur among persons of different educational backgrounds than are marriages. Moreover, since noncohabitational relationships involve less commitment and social recognition, we predict that characteristics such as race and religion will also be less important. In fact, certain types of sexual relationships might be *more* likely to occur among dissimilar persons. An individual interested in pursuing an extramarital relationship, for example, might intentionally locate a socially dissimilar person in order to minimize the possibility of being discovered by his or her spouse, family, and friends.

In sum, sexual relationships differ markedly from other types of relationships with respect to the types of exchanges that occur within them, and these differences lead to different predictions about the occurrence of sexual relationships between persons with different social characteristics. Moreover, we expect the pattern of sex partner choice to differ across the different types of sexual relationships. In chapter 6, we discuss these issues in greater detail and present several illustrative analyses using our data.

Why should we be interested in how social characteristics structure the occurrence of sexual partnerships? From a public health perspective, this structuring is important because it restricts the pathways through which sexually transmitted diseases can be spread. As a result, the epidemiological models that have been developed to predict the spread of diseases that can be transmitted through casual contact (e.g., tuberculosis) cannot predict the spread of diseases such as AIDS. Such models are based on a fundamental assumption of "random mixing"—that each person has the same opportunity to come into contact with every other—which, we shall show, is completely false in the case of sexual partnering. Models that do take into account the structured nature of partnerships predict very different trajectories for the spread of AIDS. In general, assortative mating (that is, selection of mates who are similar to each other) slows the overall spread of the disease and creates a "multipeaked epidemic as the infection spreads from the higher to the lower risk groups" (Anderson and May 1992, 64). What becomes critical in this process are the sexual partnerships linking persons in high-risk groups to those in low-risk groups. For example, part of the reason why AIDS has not spread as rapidly as was originally predicted is that the majority of the early cases occurred among male homosexuals, a group whose members have few outside sexual contacts (i.e., few homosexual men are also currently having sex with women). Instead, it was largely through heterosexual intravenous drug users—a group whose members have many outside sexual contacts—that the infection began to spread to the larger population. And, as we shall show, the network of heterosexual relationships in the larger population is so fragmented that it is unlikely that the infection will spread very rapidly there.

In addition to the epidemiological consequences, the social composition of sexual relationships also affects the type of behavior that occurs within them. These effects are distinct from those that are due to the individual characteristics of the partners; hence, they can be examined only by studying the dyad as a whole. This point can be illustrated best with an example. Suppose that we are interested in explaining why only certain people engage in oral sex. The standard way of proceeding is to ask a sample of individuals whether they have oral sex and then to measure a variety of other attributes of those individuals that are believed to be causally related to having oral sex. Following this approach does generate results—for example, age, education, and race are all correlated with whether respondents report having oral sex. These factors are, however, only part of the picture. For example, in chapter 3, we show that oral sex is a largely reciprocated activity, which implies that it is more likely to occur in those relationships where both parties are willing to perform the act. In addition, other characteristics of respondents' sexual partnerships are likely to affect whether they engage in oral sex. Thus, while more educated people are more likely to have oral sex, it may also be the case that there is something about the types of sexual relationships that these more highly educated respondents have that increases the likelihood that oral sex will occur within them. Clearly, such effects would be missed entirely by focusing only on the respondents themselves.

There are several elements of sexual relationships that might plausibly affect which sexual behaviors occur within them. We have already identified one of these as being related to the characteristics of the partners involved. This is the nature of the exchange between the two partners. Relationships that, in addition to sexual interaction, involve the exchange of items, such as economic resources, companionship, and other types of support, may place certain constraints on the types of sexual services that one partner can (or is willing to) extract from the other. For example, if a woman perceives that she is getting more from her partner than she is giving, she may feel obligated to correct this imbalance by performing sexual activities that her partner enjoys. Similarly, if a man perceives himself to be dependent on his partner, he might be willing to forgo his own sexual interests in order to please his partner (Emerson 1981). Conversely, people who perceive themselves as giving more than they receive or as being less dependent on their relationships than their partners might be more likely to ask their partners to perform certain activities or refuse to comply with their partner's wishes. Many authors have analyzed traditional marital relationships within this framework, assuming that, since the husband generally earns all or most of the family income, he therefore retains an advantage in the bedroom. By the same logic, we would expect those relationships in which both partners contribute equally or in which economic resources are not pooled to exhibit a more even exchange of sexual services.[7]

The exchanges that occur within a relationship are not the only features of that relationship that can affect sexual behavior. Another important feature is the way in which the relationship is socially defined and perceived by the participants. Some common examples of socially defined sexual relationships are "high school sweethearts," "lovers," "boyfriend and girlfriend," "husband and wife," and "one-night stand." Clearly, these may be interpreted differently by different people, and it is also possible that culturally distinct subgroups use a different set of definitions. Nevertheless, such definitions structure the way in which we think and talk about the sexual behavior of people around us as well as our own. Consequently, we learn and make decisions about what is and is not appropriate sexual behavior within the context of a specific type of relationship, rather than solely in terms of the individual performing the behavior. Thus, some men force their wives to have sex with them because they believe that, within marriage, a husband is owed sex by his wife whenever and however he wants it, even though the same man might consider the exact same behavior directed toward a stranger or even a girlfriend to be rape. Similarly, a married couple might refrain from engaging in certain activities because they consider them to be degrading and therefore not something to do with one's spouse, even though they may have engaged in those activities with previous partners. Finally, understandings about what is appropriate within a given relationship can also be linked to understandings about "types" of individuals, as illustrated

---

7. While it is likely that many husbands have traditionally used their status as primary breadwinner to justify asymmetries in their sexual relationships with their wives, we should be careful about concluding that recent advances toward equality in earning potential will necessarily result in greater sexual "equality." For example, recent research has shown that, although the earnings gap between men and women has been consistently decreasing, women still do a majority of household work (Brines 1994).

by the traditional idea that there are two types of women: those "who will" and those "who won't."

These last two points regarding how features of the sexual dyad affect behavior within it begin to illustrate the way in which both scripting and choice theories combine with a network approach to generate more comprehensive explanations of sexual conduct. Although the network approach emphasizes the properties of *relationships* rather than persons, it cannot by itself be used to explain what goes on within a specific relationship. This requires an understanding of what motivates the individuals in that relationship, such as that provided by scripting and choice theory. Understandings about what is appropriate within the context of a specific relationship are nothing other than scripts—scripts that are specific not only to the persons involved but also to the relationship between those two people. Similarly, exchanges between partners result from the strategically motivated interests of both partners, implying that, if a relationship costs a partner more than it benefits him or her, he or she will withdraw from the exchange. Nevertheless, regardless of people's cultural understandings and their motivations, sexual activity can occur only when two people come together in a relationship. The fundamental contribution of the network approach is in showing how the social networks in which people are embedded affect whether two people will get together to form a sexual relationship and, if they do, which cultural understandings and economic motivations they will bring to that relationship. The first part of this section focused on the former issue; we turn now to a discussion of the latter.

Sexual scripts are learned through interaction with others, and this interaction is clearly shaped by the networks in which we are embedded. Most research on this subject has focused on the sexual behavior of adolescents and has generally found that sexually active adolescents tend to have friends who are also sexually active (Billy, Rodgers, and Udry 1984), although it is unclear which causes which. Similarly, the legitimacy of oral sex in youthful sexual relationships is dependent on gendered support networks that supply different legitimations for these forms of conduct to both male and female adolescents (Gagnon and Simon 1987). Another less common but still convincing illustration of the role of networks is provided by reports among young boys of "circle jerks," an activity in which a group will masturbate to orgasm, often in some competitive fashion (to see who will ejaculate the soonest, who has the largest penis, or how far the semen travels on ejaculation).

We also expect social networks to be important in determining the sexual behavior of adults. To understand these influences, we must specify the interests that third parties have in the occurrence (or nonoccurrence) of certain activities within specific types of partnerships. By *third parties* we mean people connected to either or both members of a focal sexual dyad by one or more types of social relationship. Thus, parents have interests in the sexual experiences of their children, such as wanting them to refrain from sexual activity until they are "ready," wanting them not to date people whom they consider to be "poor" influences, etc. Similarly, children of divorced parents also have interests in the sexual relationships of their parents since these can claim part of the parent's attention and lead to remarriage. Third-party interests are not limited to relatives; friends too can be interested in each other's happiness in a relationship and be wary of the threat that that relationship might pose for the stability of the friendship. Even those connected to an individual by instrumental relationships, such as that between an employer and an employee, can attempt to constrain that individual's sexual activities. An example of this is the recent regulation imposed by WalMart department stores on their employees prohibiting married employees from dating in order to preserve the family-oriented image of the store.

Probably the best organized of all groups that have an interest in sexuality are stakeholders in reproductive activity. They range from individual parents to large-scale organizations such as Planned Parenthood that supply services, participate in political lobbying, and seek private and government resources and support for their programs. Control of reproduction involves the control of sexual activity, necessarily a complicated relationship. Morally conservative stakeholders attempt to control both sexuality and reproduction through moral instruction, policing the content of school curriculum and of the media, limiting information about contraception and the availability of contraceptive devices, limiting the access of the potentially sexually active to services for the prevention of sexually transmitted infection and disease (including HIV), and so forth. In contrast, liberal stakeholders seek to provide most of these services while remaining (somewhat) indifferent to the sexual expressions of consenting adults over the age of sixteen.

Other highly organized and politically active stakeholders are those who seek either to facilitate or to limit the acceptance of same-gender sexual relationships and the legal provision of the same rights and privileges for these couples as are enjoyed by heterosexual couples (e.g., allowing them to raise children, to show affection in public, etc.). Friends, relatives, and even parents often admonish or outright reject gay individuals because they do not know how to behave or are uncomfortable around them and, more important, because they are forced to justify or deny the individual's behavior in front of their own friends and associates. In fact, intolerance of homosexuality is so ubiquitous in this country that many homosexuals are forced either to conceal their sexual preference or to move to one of the few social environments where being gay is accepted.

An example of a less organized but still powerful third-party interest is that in maintaining exclusivity in established sexual partnerships, especially marriages. Part of this interest stems from the belief that extramarital sex is morally wrong, a belief that is almost universally accepted (roughly 90 percent of adults believe that extramarital sex is either "always wrong" or "almost always wrong"). In keeping with this attitude, our data suggest that the annual incidence of extramarital sexual activity is modest. Although we do not deny the fact that one's own moral and religious beliefs strongly influence the decision to limit oneself to a single partner at a time, we do argue that these beliefs are legitimated and reinforced through interaction with others who share such beliefs and who have concrete interests in the couple's sexual exclusivity. For example, in their attempts to support one spouse, the relatives and friends of that person are likely to regard any extramarital activity on the part of the other spouse as unjustifiable. For this reason, those who are interested in pursuing extramarital sexual activity often do so outside their own social networks (e.g., at an out-of-town convention) in order to minimize the possibility of being discovered by someone who knows their spouse, relatives, or friends.

In addition, there are those who have an interest in the stability of the couple and therefore resist extramarital activities that might threaten it. Relatives perhaps have the strongest interest in the stability of a married couple. Here, the interest in stability overlaps with the interest in reproduction; dissolution of a marriage not only has potentially negative effects on the children but also, depending on the children's age, can create additional responsibilities for relatives. For the same reason, children clearly have interests in the stability of their parents' relationship and are likely to react negatively if they perceive that one parent is turning away from the other. Friends, especially friends who are themselves married, are also likely to have an interest in the couple's stability and therefore refuse to sanction extramarital activities. This interest may be due in part to their own beliefs, but it is almost certainly also due to the fact that they themselves are engaged in maintaining and legitimating their own marital relationship. To acknowledge the potential for extramarital activity, even if only by discussing it with a friend, risks both personal temptation and the possibility of being labeled by others as a potential "cheater." This fact increases people's reluctance to address the topic in conversation, thus decreasing the possibility of locating potential partners or social approval for the behavior.

Opportunities to pursue extramarital sexual activity are also limited by the very large proportion of individuals in the society who are already in relationships. Especially after age thirty, the number of uncoupled individuals is small. This is exacerbated by the fact that marriage accustoms a couple to the conversations and activities of the other married couples to whom they usually restrict their associations. Presumably, some fraction of these married individuals might be willing to engage in extramarital sex; however, this number is almost certainly quite small and, more important, very difficult to identify for the reasons discussed above.

Sexual activity is not unique in being motivated and constrained by the interests of third parties. However, unlike other spheres of activity, sexual activity almost always occurs in private and is usually talked about in highly routine and nonrevealing ways. This fact makes the surveillance of the sexual dyad by outsiders remarkably difficult—third parties are privy only to the testimony of the individuals themselves about what happened. This has both positive and negative social consequences—sexual encounters may be conducted entirely by trial and error and independently of regulation, leading to sexual experimentation, or they may be occasions on which the participants deliberately or ignorantly exploit or violate each other.

Not only are most explicitly sexual activities conducted in private, but the formation of most affectionate/sexual dyads are marked by what Slater (1963) has called *dyadic withdrawal.* In adolescence particularly, but later in life as well, an important phase in affectionate/sexual dyad formation is withdrawal from other social responsibilities (Surra 1990). Thus, young people withdraw not only from parents but also from peers during intense love relationships that may or may not involve sexual activities. Similar patterns occur later in life, although they may become problematic for certain bystanders, such as children from a prior relationship. Such withdrawal signals the increased sexual potential of the relationship but at the same time reduces the interactions that partners have with members of their personal networks. This reduced rate of interaction curtails the amount of both negative and positive commentary on the choice of partner. There is some evidence that there may be more withdrawal among couples of dissimilar status, although the research on this point is only suggestive.

1.5   Interrelations among the Theories

As we have indicated, each of these three theories is intended to answer different types of questions about sexual activity. However, since these questions are interrelated, so are the theories used to explain them. In most cases, these interrelations take the form of consistent or complementary predictions by the different theories. For example, we have already shown how both scripting and choice theories may be used to explain what occurs within specific relationships identified by the network approach. Occasionally, however, there are inconsistencies in what the theoretical approaches would predict and no clear way of reconciling these differences on the basis of theoretical arguments alone. In this section, we explore some of these interrelations with the goal of constructing an integrated and more comprehensive set of theoretical arguments.

First, we consider the mutual relevance of scripting and network theories. These two approaches complement each other well; scripting theory addresses the structure of events, while network theory addresses the structure of relationships among persons. Since joint participation in an event often implies the existence of a relationship between the participants (e.g., those who attend a family gathering have kinship ties), these two structures are necessarily linked. This fit between the two structures may be described in terms of the diagram in figure 1.1 (for a more extended discussion of this approach, see Laumann and Knoke 1987).

Figure 1.1 shows a rectangular matrix, in which the first m rows (and columns) represent m distinct social "events" and the remaining n rows (and col-

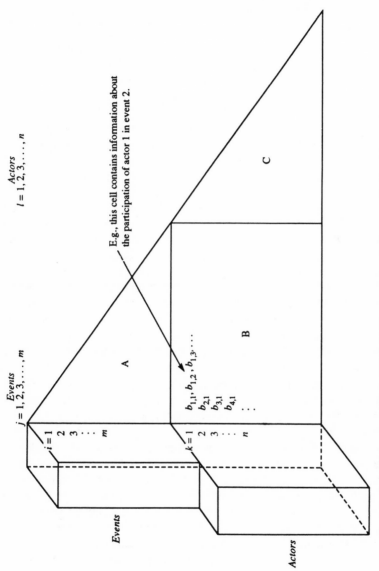

Fig. 1.1 A matrix representation of the interface among events, actors, and actors/events.

umns) represent n social "actors." Leaving aside for the moment the question of how the m events and the n actors are to be selected (to be taken up below), look first at submatrix C. This matrix is formed by the intersection of the n rows and the n columns representing actors (or persons) and provides a convenient way of representing the network of relationships among these actors. For example, the cell at the intersection of the fifth row and the first column might contain a number representing the strength of the relationship between the first and the fifth persons. For simplicity, we begin with the assumption that all relationships are reciprocal—that is, if person 1 has a particular relationship to person 5, it is also true that person 5 has the same relationship to person 1. The advantage of making this assumption is that we need consider only the lower triangular half of submatrix C (as pictured) since the information contained in the upper half is redundant.

Next, consider submatrix B, formed by the intersection of the n rows representing actors and the m columns representing events. The cells in this submatrix contain information about the presence of particular actors at specific events. This is the form in which our data were often collected; for example, people's narratives provide accounts of who was present at particular events. Since the information contained in this matrix is identical to that contained in the upper-right submatrix (not pictured), the upper-right submatrix is not necessary. Finally, submatrix A contains information about the intersection between events. This intersection can be defined in different ways; however, we define it in terms of overlapping participation. More formally, two events will be said to intersect if one or more persons are co-present at the two events, and the strength of the intersection will be proportional to the number of persons co-present.

We have already said that submatrix C represents the network of relationships among the actors in our model. In contrast, submatrix A represents the relationships among the different events or the scripts used by the actors in that particular population.[8] Thus, this submatrix can be thought of as a kind of cultural map, describing how specific events are combined by people into larger portfolios of action. The fundamental point of the model is that submatrices A and C are necessarily related through B—changes in one imply changes in the other. In fact, B contains all the information required to construct both A and C (for an elaboration of this point, see Breiger 1988). Thus, this theoretical model provides a framework within which the relations between cultural scripts and social networks can be examined.

To illustrate the model, consider as an example a woman who is married and has children. In general, we would expect those to whom she is socially

---

8. Note that the concept of script is being used here to refer to a sequence of events that might occur over a period of days or even weeks, as opposed to scripts that are enacted during a single sexual encounter. For our purposes, these are essentially the same, the fundamental aspect being that scripts are portfolios of action comprising a set of culturally connected "events" or "activities."

connected (e.g., coworkers, friends, neighbors, family) to know that she is married and has a family and therefore to include her in events and activities that take this into account. Other married couples might invite her and her husband to join them for a visit, other parents might invite her and her children to participate in various activities, etc. At the same time, participation in such events (intentional or otherwise) will provide her with opportunities to form new social ties based on her statuses as wife and mother. Together, these two mutually reinforcing processes will result both in the woman being connected to others who either are married themselves or will treat her in a manner appropriate to her marital status and in her participating in events that mainly involve other married people.

Now suppose that this woman gets divorced and becomes interested in searching for a new male partner. To do so, she must use a script for interaction that allows her to signify to potential partners that she is available—perhaps wearing different clothing, being more willing to engage in small talk with new acquaintances, expressing interest through various gestures—what we might call flirting. However, such behavior is not generally appropriate at the types of events that she has previously attended, in large part because there are so few participants who would be eligible partners (i.e., not married or in a steady relationship). This presents a dilemma: in order to participate in the "dating scene," the woman must begin to go to bars, singles clubs, or other activities with a significant number of potential partners; however, this is not easy since her friends and acquaintances are not eligible for or interested in such activities. In fact, newly divorced or separated people often report having difficulty "getting back into the game," in large part because the activities in which they participate and the social ties that they have developed do not support such behavior. This example demonstrates the important fact that people's social networks determine the types of scripts that they are able to enact.

Before this model can be effectively applied to a specific case, the set of relevant actors and events must be carefully identified. This issue has been referred to as the *boundary specification problem* by Laumann, Marsden, and Prensky (1983). As we have already argued (and will continue to argue throughout), identifying the set of relevant people with respect to an individual's sexual behavior is especially tricky since many third parties have nonobvious interests in what is normally considered to be private behavior. In our case, constraints on the length and complexity of the questionnaire prohibited us from asking respondents about the full range of network members and events that we would define as theoretically relevant. We did, however, inquire about a broader set of people and activities than that studied by previous national surveys.

Just as the network approach complements scripting theory, it can also be viewed as complementary to choice theory. Social networks may be viewed as shaping, facilitating, and constraining purposive decision making on the part of the individual. For example, an individual's network can affect the costs and benefits of a particular course of action and even determine whether certain alternative courses of action are perceived to be viable. In some cases, network ties can actually create these alternatives, as in the case of using friends as contacts to find a job (Granovetter 1982) or to locate a sexual partner. These are specific instances of what Coleman (1990) has called *social capital*. Like human capital (discussed above), each person possesses certain social ties that can be useful in pursuing certain interests. A person may "invest" in his or her social capital as in the case of a newly married man endearing himself to his in-laws so that he might call on them in the future for household assistance (Wellman and Wortley 1990). It is likely that a person's social capital is an important determinant of his or her ability both to meet new sex partners and to achieve a stable relationship with a current partner.

This latter point can be seen best in terms of investments in what might be called *partner-specific* social ties. These consist of those relationships that an individual initiates solely because of his or her partner, such as getting to know the partner's family and friends. Such investments are often reciprocal, both partners coming to know family and friends of the other. The ties represent an important type of social capital since they act to promote stability within the relationship. When a couple announces that they are considering terminating their relationship, friends of the couple often try to keep it intact by emphasizing its positive elements and providing other types of social support. In contrast, people who are friends with only one person in the couple may not perceive their remaining together as desirable and might therefore encourage them to end the relationship. In either case, the couple's decision is not only affected but also shaped by the structure of the networks in which both parties are embedded.

Another example in which network structure and choice theory intersect is in the analyses of the marketplace for sex partners. Here, choice theory emphasizes that each individual will attempt to locate the most desirable partner possible. But social network theory emphasizes that the search for a partner is highly constrained by the structure of the network in which that individual is embedded. Thus, the fact that an individual interacts mostly with people of a similar age and social background who live nearby means that he or she will have relatively few opportunities to meet and become acquainted with potential sex partners outside this set. In the language of choice theory, the costs of searching within one's own social network are substantially lower. Even if such potential partners are encountered, perhaps in a store, at a bar, or during a trip, the interests of others who are connected to that individual are likely to prevent him or her from pursuing a partnership with such people. This mechanism strengthens the tendency toward homophily among sexual partnerships by dividing the market for sex partners into a set of smaller, local markets. It is within these local markets that choice theory can be most helpful.

Notice how these two theories complement each other. Choice theory emphasizes the fact that strategic decisions are made and that they involve weighing a number of different and competing goals and assessing the different attributes of each potential sex partner. Social network theory, in contrast, emphasizes how important the context is in which the individual makes decisions and reminds us how constrained the choices really are for the individual who is effectively embedded in a network of family, friends, coworkers, and community. Both perspectives contribute to our understanding of the sexual behavior that we observe; neither is sufficient to provide a full understanding of all that we observe.

This general logic—that the pursuit of a set of predetermined goals provides the "engine" for behavior and that the effect of social networks is merely to constrain this behavior—is the way in which choice theory and network theory have usually been combined (e.g., Marsden and Laumann 1977; Marsden 1983; Granovetter 1985; Coleman 1990). One implication of this approach is that, while eliminating the network might increase the efficiency with which people can pursue their objectives, the behaviors themselves would not fundamentally change. Thus, the structure of the network is viewed as determining where and when specific behaviors might occur but not the nature of the behaviors themselves. In contrast, we would propose a somewhat broader conception of the role of social networks. Specifically, we would point out that networks orchestrate, at a very basic level, the various social situations with which we, as individuals, are confronted. And, since much of our behavior is precipitated by or fashioned in response to these situations, we may argue that an individual's position in the network is not merely constraining but also facilitative.

The sharpest inconsistency among the three approaches is between scripting and choice theories. As we have already noted, a fundamental assumption in choice theory is that individuals act strategically or rationally in the pursuit of goals. Actions that do not fit this description cannot be accounted for by economic principles, and, in extreme formulations of the theory, the existence of such irrational behavior is denied. In contrast, scripting theory suggests that individuals model their actions on the basis of a predetermined (although somewhat flexible) set of cultural scenarios. Given the small number of scenarios relative to the number of different circumstances that people encounter, it is likely that certain people will be unable to locate a scenario that represents what would be considered "rational behavior" in their particular case. In such instances, the predictions of the two theories would conflict. Yet there is a more fundamental difference between scripting and choice theories than the existence of discrepant predictions. The two theories assume very different mechanisms underlying people's behavior. Choice theory assumes that individuals are constantly evaluating their situations and making choices, whereas scripting theory assumes that individuals are constrained by a script that they learned from those around them.

Here again, we suggest that there is an element of truth in each of these perspectives and that, carried to an extreme, neither is very helpful. Thus, an individual who is presented with the opportunity for a one-time sexual encounter with a stranger might intentionally pursue a "wild and passionate" script in the pursuit of sexual pleasure, despite the fact that such a script does not include using a condom—a behavior that by itself might be considered risky. Moreover, we also recognize that people may improvise from the basis of a particular script in order to accommodate their particular needs. Indeed, this possibility was acknowledged and built into the theory in its initial formulation (Gagnon and Simon 1973). If people use scripts not as rigid programs but rather as rough guides, then we might look toward choice theory to explain some of the change in various scripts over time. A good example of this would be the significant changes in behavior in the gay community that have occurred in response to AIDS. Here, the scripts for sexual conduct have not been completely replaced, but they have surely been modified and some of the "riskiest" behaviors eliminated.

1.6   Master Statuses and Master Relationships as Social Signals

At this point, the reader might be wondering how these general theoretical approaches can be used to inform and interpret analyses of the actual data collected in this study. After all, using a survey instrument limits the researcher to asking only those questions that are easy to understand and to answer. Thus, for example, we were unable to measure sex scripts directly since doing so would require a complicated series of questions about numerous specific activities and the order in which they occurred. More important, the fact that ours was a national survey prohibited us from tailoring certain questions to particular locations or subpopulations. This meant that much fine-grained cultural (and, to some extent, regional) variation in these scripts was beyond our grasp. Similarly, our ability to measure people's networks was also quite limited; we could not ask them about specific places or events where they socialized, nor could we ask them about their relationships with specific persons other than their sex partners. For example, it would be very useful to know something about the larger network structures in which respondents are embedded since these structures certainly affect the structure of their sexual networks. Since such structures are unique to particular locations, however, they are beyond the scope of this type of study. Finally, the methods used to study rational decision making also require an intensive set of questions (such as those designed to determine an individual's preference ordering) targeted to a specific situation. These limitations are important ones, forcing us to relegate focused examinations of specific issues to future projects. However, a national study such as this one is a necessary precursor to more specialized work (for a thorough discussion of the rationale for the present study, see chapter 2).

Given these limitations, we have adopted a primarily inductive approach using the types of information that are easier to collect accurately with large surveys, such as information about the respondent's gender, race (and ethnic background), age, education, marital status, and religious affiliation. Each of these characteristics or "statuses" is a basic component of the self-identity of the individuals who possess them, organizes the patterning of social relationships, and organizes people's understanding of the social world around them. Of course, many other characteristics also possess these features; however, this basic set is both universally recognized and, in many cases, arguably most salient—hence the term *master statuses*. These three features imply that differences in master statuses are likely to be associated with differences in the scripts to which people are exposed, in the types of choices that people perceive as viable as well as the costs and benefits that they associate with these choices, and in the structure of the social networks in which people are embedded. In short, our approach is to focus on differences across the "status groups" defined by the master statuses in sexual behaviors, attitudes, and partnering activity in an attempt to infer the existence of different scripts, choices, and network structures.

Before exploring the usefulness of master statuses for explaining patterns of sexual conduct, it is important to note some of the empirical properties of these statuses that determine how they are implicated in specific social processes. For example, these statuses differ in the extent to which they can be recognized socially. Gender is an attribute that cannot escape even the most cursory face-to-face encounter, while religious affiliation is generally a latent characteristic that is more difficult to determine, even for those with whom one has considerable interaction. Another property of these statuses is that people who possess them vary in the degree to which they consider them to be important. Thus, an individual who is a devout Catholic is likely to take that label more seriously than an individual who does not attend church and is Catholic by default (i.e., his or her parents are Catholic).

Yet another property of master statuses is that they are not implicated in a homogenous manner throughout the population. Thus, being Catholic in New England, and probably of Irish or French descent as well, means something different than being Catholic (and of German or Italian descent) in St. Louis, and, consequently, people expect different behaviors of Catholics in New England than they do in St. Louis. Similarly, being a woman means different things in different places; one might expect that a woman college student has more opportunity than a middle-aged woman living in a small southern town to pursue a male sex partner actively without being considered deviant. Not only do the meanings attached to specific statuses vary, but, in most cases, a specific status does not operate in isolation. Instead, each individual embodies several statuses simultaneously and must manage the expectations associated with each of these statuses at the same time.

Because of these latter two properties—that specific statuses have different meanings in different segments of the population and that they do not operate alone but in concert with each other—we are less interested in differences based on a particular status in isolation and focus instead on the set of social positions consisting of specific combinations of status characteristics. This will be especially true with regard to gender: almost all the analyses that we present have been conducted separately for men and women.[9] Not only is sexual activity physiologically different for men and women, but our sexual interactions and our very understanding of sexuality are fundamentally organized around our concept of gender (cf. Ortner and Whitehead 1981b). Thus, it seems reasonable to hypothesize that men and women express themselves sexually in fundamentally different ways.

One final property of the master statuses is the inherent complexity in the ways in which they affect sexual activity. An important example concerns gender and age (and perhaps also race). While these statuses possess the three social features described above, they are also associated with biological differences that may have important consequences for sexual expression. Since we were unable to collect any biological data (and since, in many cases, it is unclear what type of biological data would be relevant), we are not able to differentiate analytically between the effects of social factors and those of biological factors. In fact, even with both types of data, it turns out to be quite difficult to separate the two effects (for a discussion of some of the relevant issues, see Udry 1988 and Udry and Campbell 1994). In some cases, we will, however, identify where biological effects may be present. Moreover, we hope that the national baselines for behavior established by this study will help those investigators researching biologically related topics with clinical or otherwise specially selected samples evaluate the sexual activity of those samples relative to the population.

Another example of the complexity with which the master statuses affect sexual behavior concerns age. As we have said, an individual's age may be associated with various sexual behaviors as a result of factors related to biological maturity, social expectations concerning what conduct is "appropriate" at a given age, and various age-related experiences such as having children, becoming divorced, entering retirement, etc. This set of factors has become the basis for a new approach to social research called the *life-course perspective,* an approach that is especially useful in studying sexual behavior (cf. Laumann, Gagnon, and Michael 1989). In addition, however, it is likely that the social environment experienced by an individual during puberty (especially the latter stages involving first sexual experiences) is especially important and that the effects of these experiences will persist throughout the individual's lifetime. Such effects (called *cohort effects* by demographers) are impossible to distinguish from the other type of age effects using cross-sectional data; thus, in making our interpretations, we consider both types when appropriate. However, our data on sexual partnerships are historical (i.e., we know the dates throughout the respondent's lifetime when specific partnerships began and ended) and therefore provide an important exception. We use these data in

---

9. In other words, we allow the associations between master statuses and sexual behavior to vary across gender.

chapter 5 to separate age and cohort effects on the number of sex partners that people have.

Our strategy of relying on certain individual characteristics as master statuses may be extended by using certain, observable characteristics of sexual *relationships* to identify fundamental differences in the social and behavioral aspects of those relationships. One such characteristic is whether the relationship involves marriage. Among nonmarital relationships, we will also want to distinguish between those relationships in which the partners live together and those in which they do not. Both these characteristics—being married and living together—reflect important cultural, legal, and interpersonal distinctions between sexual relationships. In addition, cultural wisdom suggests that there may be a distinction between those nonmarital and noncohabitational relationships in which one or both partners have some intention of pursuing the relationship further and those that the partners explicitly view as short term. This possibility is evinced by the various social labels that people use to describe their own partnerships and those of their acquaintances: *boyfriend/girlfriend, one-night stand, lover,* etc. This third distinction is less objective than the first two and, as such, is more difficult to measure with a survey instrument. For our immediate purposes, we have used the convention of identifying short-term relationships as those that consist of only one or a very few sexual events. We are planning to direct future efforts toward measuring respondents' own intentions regarding these relationships in order to distinguish more precisely between them.

Just like the master statuses discussed above, these master relationships can also be part of the participants' self-identities, can affect the participants' locations in the surrounding social network, and serve to organize people's understandings of the sociosexual world. And, like the master statuses, these relationships also vary in the degree to which they are socially visible or, in other words, in the extent to which people other than the partners themselves are aware of the relationship and consider it to be significant. Clearly, marriage is the most socially visible of the four relationship types, short-term relationships the least. Long-term relationships and those in which the partners are living together are in the middle, although it is unclear which is more visible than the other. On the one hand, the mere fact of sharing a household may result in cohabiting relationships being more socially visible than those in which partners do not live together; however, certain long-term partnerships, such as those in which the couple is engaged to be married, are also likely to be quite visible. A related issue that intersects with visibility is the extent to which a relationship is considered to be socially legitimate. This becomes important because relationships not considered to be legitimate are more likely to be concealed by the partners or ignored by those around them. Thus, a young woman may not tell her family and friends that she is living with her boyfriend in order to avoid criticism or a reputation as being sexually permissive; consequently, her family and friends may underestimate the significance of the relationship.

The significance of a relationship's degree of social visibility is twofold. First, and most obviously, people who are not aware of a particular relationship are unable to comment on its appropriateness or the lack thereof. For example, the members of an interracial couple may choose to tell only their closest friends about their relationship, thus avoiding potential criticism. As a result, the couple also forgoes the potential social support that can facilitate maintaining the relationship. Consistent with this reasoning are a few studies showing that, among dating couples, perceptions of negative third-party reactions are negatively associated with level of romantic involvement and stability of the relationship (Eggert and Parks 1987; Parks and Adelman 1983).

Also important is the fact that social visibility can often be used to predict the degree to which various third parties will be "interested" in the relationship. For example, consider parents whose daughter decides to date a man whom they (and others around them) consider to be somehow inappropriate. Although they may disapprove, the parents may tolerate the boyfriend in the interests of maintaining a positive relationship with their daughter. However, if the couple decides to live together, the parents are then forced to speak about and justify the boyfriend in front of family members and friends. Doing so may cause the parents to reevaluate their initial position on the relationship and perhaps to remind their daughter of their disapproval.

In addition to differences in social visibility, our four master relationships also differ in the motivations that they are likely to reflect on the part of the participants, providing considerable analytic leverage in explaining between whom certain relationships will occur and how those relationships will be conducted. For example, a short-term relationship is likely to result from purely sexual motivations, whereas marriage clearly results from a complex set of motivations of which sexual interests may be only a small part. On the basis of the theoretical arguments presented above, we expect these differences in motivation to correspond to observable differences in sexual conduct.

The master statuses and relationships that we have just described provide a continuity throughout the analyses presented in the following chapters. Our primary intention in pursuing this broad approach is to provide a rough picture of both the frequency with which people engage in specific sexual activities and the patterns by which these frequencies vary throughout the population. As we have indicated, we are keenly aware that this approach ignores a tremendous amount of local variation in sexual activity. For this reason, we must view this study as a necessary first step in developing a more in-depth program of research into the social causes and consequences of sexual behavior.

CHAPTER 2

The Study Design

Most people with whom we talked when we first broached the idea of a national survey of sexual behavior were skeptical that it could be done. Scientists and laypeople alike had similar reactions: "Nobody will agree to participate in such a study." "Nobody will answer questions like these, and, even if they do, they won't tell the truth." "People don't know enough about sexual practices as they relate to disease transmission or even to pleasure or physical and emotional satisfaction to be able to answer questions accurately." It would be dishonest to say that we did not share these and other concerns. But our experiences over the past seven years, rooted in extensive pilot work, focus-group discussions, and the fielding of the survey itself, resolved these doubts, fully vindicating our growing conviction that a national survey could be conducted according to high standards of scientific rigor and replicability.

When we began working on the design of the survey in 1988, the only comprehensive American study of sexuality based on a large cross section of the population was the famous two-volume Kinsey Report (Kinsey, Pomeroy, and Martin 1948; Kinsey et al. 1953) published almost forty years before; but Kinsey's sampling design, essentially volunteer and purposive in character, failed to meet even the most elementary requirements for drawing a truly representative sample of the population at large (Cochran, Mosteller, and Tukey 1953; Institute of Medicine 1986). Surprisingly, instead of serving as the beginning of a series of population-based sexual behavior studies, little of note followed Kinsey's pioneering work. There was one major attempt to survey a fairly large sample (about 3,000 people) of the U.S. population, which was funded by the National Institute of Mental Health in 1970, but the results of that study were not published until the late 1980s (Fay et al. 1989; Klassen, Williams, and Levitt 1989). From the late 1960s on, but before the advent of AIDS, there were surveys of selected, limited segments of the population, such as young people, primarily college students (Gagnon and Simon 1973; Jessor and Jessor 1975; DeLamater and MacCorquodale 1979a), women, primarily younger women (Zelnik and Kantner 1972b, 1980; Zelnik, Kantner, and Ford 1981; Hofferth and Hayes 1978; Forrest and Singh 1990; Mosher 1990; Mosher and McNally 1991; Tanfer and Horn 1985; Tanfer 1987), and sexual partnerships in various relationships like marriage or cohabitation (Blumstein and Schwartz 1983). For the most part, these studies asked few questions about sexual practices, focusing instead on social issues or problems related to sex such as adolescent, primarily premarital sex, contraception, and fertility (both planned and unplanned). In most cases, vaginal intercourse was the only sexual behavior asked about. Studies covering a wider range of sexual behaviors, such as *American Couples* (Blumstein and Schwartz 1983), or studies of gay men and lesbians, such as *Homosexualities* (Bell and Weinberg 1978), did not use probability samples and therefore could not be used to estimate population rates. Still, this research proved to be of value in planning our project.

This monograph is the product of a long and arduous process. Completing a research project such as this was not merely a scientific and technical challenge; it provoked a protracted political battle conducted in the national and local press, in the Congress, and in the federal agencies that ultimately set many limitations and constraints on what we were able to do (for a detailed political history of the project see Laumann, Gagnon, and Michael 1994a). In this chapter, we sketch the broad context out of which the present study grew because we believe that it provides the rationale for the current study, which represents a compromise among a variety of conflicting goals and objectives.

The society in which we live treats sex and everything related to sex in a most ambiguous and ambivalent fashion. Sex is at once highly fascinating, attractive, and, for many at certain stages in their lives, preoccupying, but it can also be frightening, disturbing, or guilt inducing. For many, sex is considered to be an extremely private matter, to be discussed only with one's closest friends or intimates, if at all. And, certainly for most if not all of us, there are elements of our sexual lives never acknowledged to others, reserved for our own personal fantasies and self-contemplation. It is thus hardly surprising that the proposal to study sex scientifically, or any other way for that matter, elicits confounding and confusing reactions. Mass advertising, for example, unremittingly inundates the public with explicit and implicit sexual messages, eroticizing products and using sex to sell. At the same time, participants in political discourse are incredibly squeamish when handling sexual themes, as exemplified in the curious combination of horror and fascination displayed in the public discourse about Long Dong Silver and pubic hairs on pop cans during the Senate hearings in September 1991 on the appointment of Clarence Thomas to the Supreme Court. We suspect, in fact, that with respect to discourse on sexuality there is a major discontinuity between the sensibilities of politicians and other self-appointed guardians of the moral order and those of the public at large, who, on the whole, display few hang-ups in discussing sexual issues in appropriately structured circumstances. This book is a testament to that proposition.

The fact remains that, until quite recently, scientific research on sexuality has been taboo and therefore to be avoided or at best marginalized. While there is a visible tradition of (in)famous sex research, what is, in fact, most striking is how little prior research exists on sexuality in the general population. Aside from the research on adolescence, premarital sex, and problems attendant to sex such as fertility, most research attention seems to have been directed toward those believed to be abnormal, deviant, criminal, perverted, rare, or unusual, toward sexual pathology, dysfunction, and sexually transmitted disease—the label used typically reflecting the way in which the behavior or condition in question is to be regarded. "Normal sex" was somehow off limits, perhaps because it was considered too ordinary, trivial, and self-evident to deserve attention. To be fair, then, we cannot blame the public and the politicians entirely for the lack of sustained work on sexuality at large—it also reflects the prejudices and understandings of researchers about what are "interesting" scientific questions. There has simply been a dearth of mainstream scientific thinking and speculation about sexual issues. We have repeatedly encountered this relative lack of systematic thinking about sexuality to guide us in interpreting and understanding the many findings reported in this book.

While we entered relatively uncharted waters in choosing the sexual content to be included in our survey, we found that we faced many of the same problems that any major survey research enterprise confronts (cf. Bradburn, Sudman et al. 1979; Miller, Turner, and Moses 1990; Catania et al. 1990; Catania et al. 1993). We discovered that the techniques that work in other domains work just as well when studying sexuality. For example, most of the problems involved in securing the participation of respondents in a survey are the same whether one is conducting a general purpose survey of political opinions, a study of labor force participation, or one of sexual behavior. Respondents must be convinced that the research has a legitimate purpose, that it is not some attempt to trick them into buying something, that their confidentiality will be protected, etc. (For an extended discussion of the issues raised in protecting the privacy, confidentiality, and security of individual respondents' disclosures to the interviewer, see section 2.2 below.) Answering questions about sexual experiences involves the same cognitive tasks—understanding the question, searching one's memory, and reporting the result—as are raised in any other survey about life experiences.

But this is perhaps to anticipate ourselves. In order to understand the results of our survey, the National Health and Social Life Survey (NHSLS), one must understand how these results were generated. To construct a questionnaire and field a large-scale survey, many research design decisions must be made. To understand the decisions made, one needs to understand the multiple purposes that underlie this research project. Research design is never just a theoretical exercise. It is a set of practical solutions to a multitude of problems and considerations that are chosen under the constraints of limited resources of money, time, and prior knowledge.

To understand the purpose of this research, one might first ask why there were no major follow-up studies to the Kinsey Report for over thirty-five years, why only in the 1980s more sexual behavior surveys began to appear. The simple and incontrovertible answer is, in short, AIDS.[1] The identification of a rapidly spreading fatal disease, associated primarily with sexual transmission, eventually produced major public health responses in research and intervention programs (Shilts 1988). It is beside the point whether these responses were well conceived, well directed, or of sufficient scope and depth. The point is that, by the mid-1980s, it was clear that there was a major public health crisis and that the knowledge and techniques available for combatting it were woefully inadequate. In particular, there was no current information about the sexual practices of the population, let alone any information about why, how, and in what contexts people might engage in them. It was becoming increasingly obvious that AIDS was an infectious disease and that among its major routes of transmission were particular sexual activities, especially anal intercourse. There was much confusion about AIDS in advanced Western industrial societies because initially most of those who contracted the disease were gay men. For a while, it was an open question whether AIDS was somehow specifically associated either with being a gay man or with some other environmental factor associated with gay male culture. As the biology of the disease became better understood, and, in particular, as it became increasingly evident that a medical "cure" or "prevention" would take a long time to develop, it was realized that changes in behavior would be the most effective means of halting the further spread of the disease (see, e.g., Institute of Medicine 1986; Coyle, Boruch, and Turner 1991).

From a public health perspective, two major issues loomed large: epidemiological projection and educational intervention. Questions such as the likely direction and extent of spread, what groups were most at risk, and what the barriers were to behavior change needed to be answered. These questions, however, involved related questions about the distribution and social organization of sexual behavior and attitudes in the population as a whole. One quickly discovered that there were practically no data with which to answer these questions. The major source of existing data, the Kinsey studies of males and females, had two major drawbacks: they were forty or more years out of date, and they were not based on representative samples of the U.S. population.

It was in this context that a push for a major survey of the sexual behavior

1. Under the press of AIDS, a number of studies were undertaken, both large and small, in the United States and internationally. Among the national probability sample surveys that contained at least some sexual behavior questions motivated by the need for data to combat the spread of AIDS were the addition of a small sexual behavior self-completion supplement to NORC's annual General Social Survey (GSS) of the U.S. adult population from 1988 to 1991 and again in 1993 (Michael et al. 1988; Smith 1991b); the cross-national comparative Project Hope Survey (see Wells and Sell 1990); the National AIDS Behavioral Survey (NABS), a telephone survey of U.S. adults (see Catania et al. 1992b); the National Survey of Men (NSM), a national household-based survey of twenty- to thirty-nine-year-old men (see Billy et al. 1993); a large-scale telephone survey in France of adults eighteen to sixty-nine (Spira et al. 1993); a large-scale British survey (Wellings et al. 1994); as well as surveys in Norway (Sundet et al. 1988), Denmark (Melbye and Biggar 1992), Finland (Kontula and Haavio-Mannila 1993), and the Netherlands (Sandfort et al. 1991).

of the U.S. population asserted itself. Elements of this story are instructive because they help explain both the design of the current survey and its limitations. Our purpose here is not to tell this story with an eye toward identifying heroes, culprits, and victims but rather to help explain why certain decisions were made in designing our current survey. Contrary to certain textbook impressions, research design is not a simple optimization process where, given a few simple objectives, one makes a set of nonambiguous choices. It is a continuing process of compromise, attempting to balance competing objectives in the context of limited resources of personnel, time, and money. Almost always, one must make design choices when one does not know the grounds on which to prefer one design over another, and it is often impractical to test various options in advance.

The AIDS crisis thus provided the critical impetus for a coalition of interested federal agencies—including the Centers for Disease Control (CDC), the National Center for Health Statistics (NCHS), the National Institute of Child Health and Human Development (NICHD), the National Institute on Aging (NIA), and the National Institute of Mental Health (NIMH), to name a few—to express support for a national survey of sexual practices. To be sure, some, like the NICHD, had since the early 1970s been interested in supporting research on sexual behavior as part of their responsibilities in supporting research relevant to population growth, family formation and stability, fertility, contraception, and child health. But the formation of this coalition did not occur overnight. It was only after a number of independent scientific blue-ribbon panels (e.g., Institute of Medicine 1986) had decried the lack of data on sexual behavior and the crucial nature of this information for designing a reasonable response to AIDS that a request for proposals (RFP) for the design of a national survey of adult sexual behavior was finally issued by the NICHD in July 1987. A parallel RFP to design a national survey focused on adolescent sexuality was announced by the NICHD at the same time.

The RFP for the adult survey nicely reflects a number of the tensions inherent in the project. The title of the RFP itself, "Social and Behavioral Aspects of Fertility-Related Behavior," is almost charming in its indication of the government's ambivalence about the whole matter. The frank Anglo-Saxon term *sex* appears nowhere in the title or in the introductory statement of purpose. Moreover, the RFP was not actually a request for data collection; rather, it offered support only for a year of design work done under contract, with the government agency an active co-participant in the process. Only after the design work had been accepted by the agency would a subsequent RFP to conduct the survey be issued. It was an open secret that whichever team was awarded the design project would have an advantage in the subsequent competition to conduct the survey itself. The point of designing the study under contract was to permit active government supervision of the content and execution of the survey project in light of the known political sensitivities to engaging in research of this kind under government auspices and in light of the agencies' interests in targeting the research in substantive directions consistent with their missions. Our team won the competition to design the adult sexual behavior survey project and began full-scale work on such a design in January 1988. A design for a large-scale national survey of adults was completed by the end of that year. However, even before we had completed that work, the contract was augmented to include collecting data from a 2,000-person national survey that was also to implement a number of methodological experiments. It was hoped that this survey would demonstrate the feasibility of and test various options for a much larger national survey as well as rapidly provide some basic parameters about U.S. adult sexual behavior needed in the government's public health efforts to combat AIDS.

It is important to note here that, while the appearance and spread of AIDS explains the availability of government funding, AIDS itself was not the sole focus of the RFP or the project therein envisioned. Key personnel in agencies such as the NICHD had long wanted to launch major studies of human sexuality; the public policy and public health needs coalescing around AIDS finally made it possible. The two goals of supporting research to secure critical information relevant to intervention programs for sexually transmitted infections like HIV and of securing comprehensive knowledge of human sexuality in its manifold forms are not particularly compatible or consistent with one another. The first goal is considerably more narrow and limited in scope, given current thinking about sexually transmitted infections by medically oriented disease-prevention experts.[2]

Since we were convinced that effectively addressing the second, more comprehensive goal would transform our understanding of the first goal, we fully embraced both in our original design project and in our current project. In our successful response to the RFP, we argued that a broadly conceived, socially informed perspective on human sexuality along the lines sketched in chapter 1 was essential to constructing effective intervention strategies that targeted the appropriate population subgroups most at risk. In choosing our team to carry out the design work for a national survey, the NICHD and, through its peer-review process, the various health-related professions endorsed this dual approach. During the political struggles that ensued, this broader commitment

---

2. Consider, e.g., the matter of interrogating respondents about their masturbatory practices and attitudes. The issue elicited heated and protracted debates between government officials and our research team. From a strict consideration of possible vectors of disease transmission, it is obvious that masturbation can play no role as a vehicle of infection. Some officials who regarded masturbation as an especially private/intimate and presumably problematic activity did not want to ask any questions about it and justified their opposition on those grounds. But, from the larger perspective of an individual's sexual economy, one would like to know how masturbation fits into the entire range of an individual's repertoire of sexual expression. Is it complementary or supplementary to a respondent's partnered sexual activities, serving to enhance sexual arousal or to avoid premature ejaculation? Is it performed strictly as a substitute for partnered sexual activity when suitable partners are unavailable? In some important sense, it is the "safest sex" of all so far as disease transmission and fertility control are concerned. Yet no one has produced empirically grounded data to address these questions. It struck us as especially foolhardy to prejudge such matters.

to a comprehensive treatment of the life course and the social nature of human sexuality was compromised in favor of the narrower, more behavioristic inventory of individual sexual practices. Senior government scientists hoped that such a strategy would secure approval from the Reagan and Bush political appointees at the highest administrative levels in the Department of Health and Human Services (HHS). But this strategy was to no avail because even a heavily modified interview instrument that focused more narrowly on presumed disease pathways was never given approval throughout the four years of the Bush administration, nor was funding for a large-scale national survey of adult sexual practices authorized by the Congress during this period. Indeed, as of this writing (May 1994), despite the change in administration, the National Institutes of Health (NIH) reauthorization bill for fiscal year 1994 again explicitly prohibits funding SHARP (Survey of Health and AIDS-Related Practices), our version of the national survey of adult sexual practices, and the American Teen Sex Survey to be conducted by a University of North Carolina (Chapel Hill) research team, although language elsewhere in the bill permits the NIH to conduct research on these topics, subject to certain guidelines.

Once it became clear by the fall of 1991 that government inaction would doom our planned survey, we were able to secure funding from a consortium of major private foundations, an arrangement that allowed for a more comprehensive approach to the survey instrument on sexual practices on a modest-sized representative sample of the U.S. population.[3] Ironically, our failure to secure government funding freed us to abandon the overly compromised, narrowly targeted survey instrument in favor of the much more comprehensive approach that the government had originally contracted with us to provide. The time spent waiting in vain for the approval of the instrument was not wasted. We continued pilot work on the interview instrument throughout the waiting period, including conducting detailed cognitive interviews in order to probe and debrief respondents about how they understood our questions and a number of focus groups with men and women, African-Americans, Hispanics, and whites in a continuing effort to refine the survey instrument.

The breadth and scope of this project differentiates it from other recent

3. Because we had hit an apparent dead end in securing funding for the national survey, the research team decided to adopt another strategy: propose a regular NIH scientific grant request to conduct a study of sexual practices in two mid-sized cities that would investigate the local structure of sexual markets through a combination of ethnographic and survey techniques informed by a more comprehensive view of human sexuality than could be reflected in a study dominated by disease-prevention concerns. The study proposal received a very high priority rating for funding by the scientific review panel in February 1991 and concurrence on its utility and desirability by the NICHD Advisory Council in June 1991, with an indication that funding would begin in October 1991 at the onset of the new fiscal year. In mid-September, we were informed that the funding of the grant would be "political suicide" in light of the Senate vote earlier in the month in response to an amendment proposed by Senator Jesse Helms that forbade the funding of the national survey of adult sexual practices. His amendment had secured a vote of 66 in support and 34 opposed. (For a more extended discussion of the political events surrounding this and other congressional actions taken over the past seven years, see Laumann, Gagnon, and Michael 1994a.)

national surveys of sexual behavior (cf. Catania et al. 1992b; Billy et al. 1993) and even from the French (Spira et al. 1993), and British (Wellings et al. 1994) studies. In order to produce scientific data helpful in fighting AIDS, preventing unwanted pregnancies, avoiding other sexually transmitted infections, understanding the conditions of stable and unstable sexual partnerships over time, and even investigating the features of emotionally and physically satisfying sexual relationships, we were convinced that our study needed to be more rather than less inclusive. If it is the case that few scientifically reliable and valid data on sexual behavior are available, then it behooves us to be catholic in our approach. Surely it makes sense to employ a broad social scientific perspective that treats sexual behavior or sexual conduct as a social phenomenon subject to the same kinds of theories and models as other types of social behavior rather than as something sui generis. The first chapter of this volume sketches the essential elements of our theoretical perspective, providing the scaffolding for all that follows.

2.1 Major Issues in Designing a Study of Sexuality in the Age of AIDS

Turning to the research design of the NHSLS itself, we divide the discussion into three parts: the sample design, the selection and training of the interviewers, and the interview itself (both the construction of the questionnaire and the mode of administration).[4] As mentioned earlier, many final design decisions were made without the benefit of as much prior experience and pretesting as we had hoped. We will, of course, note unresolved methodological issues that await further experimentation and field experience. Since we hope that our experience will be helpful to subsequent researchers in the field, we have included methodological appendixes that address many of these issues in greater depth. Appendix A treats issues of sampling and sampling error as well as potential sources of measurement error inherent in the interview situation itself. Appendix B compares the realized NHSLS sample with other comparable studies. In the absence of any means to validate directly the data collected in a survey of sexual behavior, these analyses assess data quality by checking for bias in the realized sample that might result from potential respondents' unwillingness to participate because of the subject matter as well as by comparing results with other surveys. In every case, the results have greatly exceeded our initial expectations about what would be possible. They have gone a long way toward allaying our own concerns and skepticism about the potential data qual-

4. This division roughly corresponds to the two major sources of error in survey results. Sampling issues are related to *sampling error,* i.e., how representative a given sample is. Both the selection and the training of interviewers and all the design issues related to the interview itself can be subsumed under what is usually called *response* or *measurement error,* i.e., how well the answers given reflect the experience or attitude that is of research interest. There is no research measurement without error. The goal is both to randomize and to minimize the error that enters into the process. Appendix A explores these issues in greater detail and with a more technical vocabulary.

ity problems that might have been involved in a survey that explicitly focused on sexual behavior. Appendix C contains the full text of the questionnaire used to collect the data reported here. The reader can see the exact wording used as well as the context of the questions in the overall flow of the interview.

At the outset, we remind the reader that there are many limitations that were imposed on this design. We view this work as a major step forward in the application of modern survey technology to the study of sexuality, but it still needs to be expanded and improved on. We are only too aware that the NHSLS is a much-scaled-down project from the one that we originally designed for the U.S. government. That design (Laumann, Gagnon, and Michael 1989) called for a much more adequate sample size of between 10,000 and 20,000 persons and was estimated to cost between $10 and $20 million, depending on certain design options. (To put this cost in some perspective, it is not at all uncommon for NIH-sponsored clinical trials establishing the clinical efficacy of certain drugs in a disease process afflicting only a modest number of patients nationally to cost in excess of $30 million.) It will thus be instructive to see how the cutbacks and design changes necessitated by the curtailed funding for our project (approximately $1.6 million) for a sample size of only 3,432 cases has imposed major compromises in the capacity of our survey to generate reliable and accurate estimates of certain population parameters and to address certain analytic questions of central importance to our understanding of the social organization of sexuality.

Sample Design

The sample design for the NHSLS is the most straightforward element of our methodology because nothing about probability sampling is specific to or changes in a survey of sexual behavior. For many people, however, probability sampling seems mysterious and is regarded with skepticism. Although a full discussion of survey sampling is well beyond the scope of this book, we do address a number of issues in greater technical detail in appendixes A and B. (The reader unfamiliar with the concepts of sampling frames, population universes, and statistical inference is referred particularly to appendix A for some helpful orientation to these matters.) We stress here the importance of probability sampling in realizing our research goals and then note several specific sampling design decisions of importance to understanding the limitations of our sampling frame.

Probability sampling, that is, sampling where every member of a clearly specified population has a known probability of selection—what lay commentators often somewhat inaccurately call random sampling—is the sine qua non of modern survey research (see Kish 1965, the classic text on the subject). There is no other scientifically acceptable way to construct a representative sample and thereby to be able to generalize from the actual sample on which data are collected to the population that that sample is designed to represent. Probability sampling as practiced in survey research is a highly developed practical application of statistical theory to the problem of selecting a sample. Not only does this type of sampling avoid the problems of bias introduced by the researcher or by subject self-selection bias that come from more casual techniques, but it also allows one to quantify the variability in the estimates derived from the sample.

There seems to be greater confusion around this issue in sex research than in other fields. Several reasons may account for this. First, sex research is closely associated with and often derives from medical and psychological research, in which sampling issues are deemphasized or ignored. While neglect of sampling in medical research can occasionally have negative consequences, it is not nearly so problematic as in areas like demography and other kinds of research oriented toward large populations where systematic variability in traits and behaviors of interest is an essential feature of the population being studied. As long as members of a population are identical or very similar in terms of the features of research interest, then it is appropriate to study only a small number of population members, even purposively sampled, because there is no relevant variability across the population at large. In effect, looking at a few members tells you all you need to know about all members of that population.

For instance, Masters and Johnson's (1966, 1970) research on human sexual response and the physiology of arousal and orgasm was based on patients and volunteers studied in the laboratory. The key assumption made was that the physiological processes being studied vary little across human populations, once obvious differences in gender, age, and relevant physiological conditions are properly taken into account. What variability there is in physiological response is presumably rooted in the biological organism and is likely to be uncorrelated with most social distinctions among people. In our view, even such assumptions about the sources of biological variability in human populations are quite problematic and need to be demonstrated, and thus the generalizability of Masters and Johnson's findings to populations not represented in their purposive samples remains an open question. In sharp contrast to these conventional assumptions about biological variability in human populations, issues related to behavior, such as rates of occurrence of specific sexual techniques and practices, were thought to vary a great deal and in systematic ways across the U.S. population, let alone across the whole human race. As soon as interest shifts to these highly variable, socially organized phenomena, one ignores sampling issues at great peril to research validity and generality.

The second reason that debate about the usefulness of probability samples persists among sex researchers is that the font of population-oriented sex studies, the work of Alfred Kinsey and his colleagues (Kinsey, Pomeroy, and Martin 1948; Kinsey et al. 1953), did not use probability sampling and explicitly rejected its feasibility. Kinsey was convinced that one could not conduct sex history interviews with randomly selected strangers. And he believed that the various techniques he devised that were intended to increase the variability among the volunteers he recruited could compensate for this lack of probability-based sampling. These convictions were mistaken, with respect to both theory and practice. While Kinsey's research represented a major advance on earlier work, the total lack of probability sampling undermined his ability to generalize from his sample to the population at large. This point was clearly made in a very thorough and sympathetic critique of his work (Cochran, Mosteller, and Tukey 1953) by a committee of eminent statisticians shortly after its publication. Despite this well-known criticism, up until the mid-1980s, when we began this project, only one attempt had been made to use modern survey research methods, including probability sampling, in a study that had adult sexual behavior as its primary focus in the United States. Unfortunately, even though the study had been successfully completed in the early 1970s, it was not published until the late 1980s (see Fay et al. 1989; Klassen, Williams, and Levitt 1989).[5]

The public's continuing fascination with sex was assuaged over the years by the appearance of any number of studies using some form of convenience sampling and falsely claiming the power to describe the population at large from such data: for example, studies based on the readers of *Psychology Today* (Athanasiou, Shaver, and Tavris 1970) and *Redbook* (Tavris and Sadd 1978) or questionnaires distributed through various organizations and drop-off points such as the work of Shere Hite (1979, 1981) and Janus and Janus (1993). Researchers such as Hite and the Januses present themselves as following in Kinsey's footsteps. Like Kinsey, they have contended that one can go from their samples to generalizations about the U.S. population at large through some quota-based adjustment process (see Smith 1989; Greeley 1994).[6] No survey researcher or statistician would accept such claims. In fact, these studies were quite clearly much worse in this regard than Kinsey's. Such studies, in sum, produce junk statistics of no value whatsoever in making valid and reliable population projections. Their estimates are very likely to be strongly biased in

5. Ironically, even though the 1970 study had been organized by the Kinsey Institute and was somewhat timid in terms of the extent of the sexual behavior information that it attempted to gather and the methods that it used (the bulk of the questionnaire focused on sexual attitudes rather than on behavior, and the sexual behavior questions were asked only on a self-administered form), there was nothing to indicate that modern survey research methods had in any way failed to obtain reasonable information on a representative sample (cf. Fay et al. 1989). As late as 1988, the then director of the Kinsey Institute could argue, in what was basically a rehash of Kinsey's arguments of forty years before, against the applicability of modern survey research to the study of sexual behavior (Reinisch, Sanders, and Ziemba-Davis 1988).

6. Magazine reader–based surveys are a perfect illustration of the distinction and confusion of sample size and sample quality. While in probability sampling, all other things being equal, larger sample sizes always bring improved precision of estimates, in the absence of probability sampling no such benefit accrues. One can get amazingly high numbers of questionnaires filled out by magazine readers: 20,000 in the case of the *Psychology Today* survey and over 100,000 in the case of the *Redbook* survey. Even so, these usually represent ludicrously low response rates of well under 10 percent of the readership, which already constitutes a highly preselected population. Reported statistics based on these samples demonstrate how far they differ from the general population in terms of liberalism and education (cf. the discussion in Klassen, Williams, and Levitt 1989, 12–14).

an upward direction (i.e., overestimating the incidence of certain behaviors) because the samples are highly self-selected on the very variables of interest—specifically, strong interest in sexual matters.

Greeley (1994), for example, systematically compared results reported in the "Janus Report" (Janus and Janus 1993), which were based on a convenience sample of some 8,000 cases gathered over a number of years using a variety of casual means ranging from volunteers who came to the offices of sex therapists to friends and acquaintances recruited by the original volunteers, with results from the General Social Survey (GSS), which was based on a national household-based probability sample of adults conducted annually by the National Opinion Research Center over the past twenty years with the support of the National Science Foundation. Table 2.1 provides some highlights of this comparison.

From table 2.1, the reader can readily see that the Januses' estimates are frequently two to ten times higher than the GSS estimates. What might have been excusable and understandable for Kinsey and his associates working in the late 1930s through the early 1950s, when many of these issues about sampling were only beginning to be given serious attention, becomes inexcusable—a willful blindness—by the 1970s, when statistical practice and teaching have rapidly developed both in depth and in diffusion of the relevant knowledge and techniques. Unfortunately, we suspect that the public's perception of the sexual practices of the population at large has been greatly shaped over the years by such studies—quite understandably since no better information was readily available.

The NHSLS and other current serious efforts to study sexual practices in heterogeneous populations (e.g., the other major national studies mounted around the world in response to AIDS, such as Spira et al. 1993 in France, Wellings et al. 1994 in Great Britain, Kontula and Haavio-Mannila 1993 in Finland, and Billy et al. 1993 and Catania et al. 1992b in the United States) all use probability samples. But the decision to use probability sampling is only

| Table 2.1 | Comparison of Percentages of People Having Sex at Least Once a Week Estimated by the Janus Report and the GSS, by Age and Gender |

	Men		Women	
Age	Janus	GSS/NORC	Janus	GSS/NORC
18–26	72	57	68	58
27–38	83	69	78	61
39–50	83	56	68	49
51–64	81	43	65	25
Over 65	69	17	74	6

Source: Greeley (1993).

the first design decision. How large should the sample be? From what population should the sample be drawn? Should certain groups be oversampled? Let us look at these questions in turn (for a general treatment of these and related issues, see Kish 1965).

SAMPLE SIZE

How large should the sample be? There is real confusion about the importance of sample size. In general, for the case of a probability sample, the bigger the sample, the higher the precision of its estimates.[7] This precision is usually measured in terms of the amount of sampling error accruing to the statistics calculated from the sample. The most common version of this is the statement that estimated proportions (e.g., the proportion of likely voters planning to vote for a particular candidate) in national political polls are estimated as being within ± 2 or 3 percent of the overall population figure. The amount of this discrepancy is inversely related to the size of the sample: the larger the sample, the smaller the likely error in the estimates. This is not, however, a simple linear relation. Instead, in general, as the sample size increases, the precision of the estimates derived from the sample increases by the square root of the sample size. For example, if we quadruple the sample size, we improve the estimate only by a factor of two. That is, if the original sample has a sampling error of ± 10 percent, then the quadrupled sample size will have an error of ± 5 percent.

Some further thought will make it obvious that, while increasing sample size will increase precision, after rather modest increases proportionate increases in further precision can be achieved only by very large increases in sample size.[8] For almost all political polling where the goal is to derive estimates of proportions for the U.S. population as a whole, samples of no more than 1,000–1,500 work quite well. In fact, such samples produce estimates with no more sampling error than ± 3 percent for any given estimate.

In order to determine how large a sample size for a given study should be, one must first decide how precise the estimates to be derived need to be. To illustrate this reasoning process, let us take one of the simplest and most commonly used statistics in survey research, the proportion. Many of the most important results reported in this book are proportions. For example, what proportion of the population had more than five sex partners in the last year? What

7. This proposition, however, is not true when speaking of nonrandom samples. The original Kinsey research was based on large samples. As noted earlier, surveys reported in magazines are often based on very large numbers of returned questionnaires. But, since these were not representative probability samples, there is no necessary relation between the increase in the sample size and how well the sample estimates population parameters. In general, nonprobability samples describe only the sample drawn and cannot be generalized to any larger population.

8. Another myth or mistaken intuition about sampling is that it depends on the proportion of the population included. In fact, when sampling from relatively large populations, certainly anything over a million, this makes almost no difference. It is only the size of the sample itself that matters.

proportion engaged in anal intercourse? With condoms? Estimates based on our sample will differ from the true proportion in the population because of sampling error (i.e., the random fluctuations in our estimates that are due to the fact that they are based on samples rather than on complete enumerations or censuses). If one drew repeated samples using the same methodology, each would produce a slightly different estimate. If one looks at the distribution of these *estimates*, it turns out that they will be normally distributed (i.e., will follow the famous bell-shaped curve known as the Gaussian or normal distribution) and centered around the true proportion in the population. The larger the sample size, the tighter the distribution of estimates will be.

One way to get a sense of how the precision of estimates depends on sample size is to look at a method that statisticians use to emphasize the variability involved in a given estimate from a sample. Instead of merely computing a single proportion (or mean), statisticians often use "95 percent confidence intervals"; that is, an interval or range of values is estimated that will contain the true value in the population 95 percent of the time if one repeats the process over and over. Two factors determine the size of these confidence intervals or bands: the size of the sample and the value of the true proportion in the population. It turns out that the bands are largest for estimates based on traits that are true for 50 percent of the population. As traits become rarer (or more common, since the finding that a trait is true for 60 percent of cases studied is equivalent to its opposite being true for 40 percent of the cases), the confidence bands are somewhat narrower. This can readily be seen by examining table 2.2. The first column in the table shows the width of a 95 percent confidence interval around the estimated proportion of .50 for various sample sizes. For example, assume that the true proportion of people who had intercourse for the first time by the

Table 2.2   **Width of One Side of a 95 Percent Confidence Interval for the Estimate of a Proportion (1.96 times the standard error of a proportion)**

	Population Proportion					
Sample Size	.50	.30	.20	.10	.05	.01
25	.196	.180	.157	.118	.085	.039
100	.098	.090	.078	.059	.043	.020
200	.069	.064	.055	.042	.030	.014
400	.049	.045	.039	.029	.021	.010
800	.035	.032	.028	.021	.015	.007
1,000	.031	.028	.025	.019	.014	.006
1,500	.025	.023	.020	.015	.011	.005
2,000	.022	.020	.018	.013	.010	.004
3,000	.018	.016	.014	.011	.008	.004
5,000	.014	.013	.011	.008	.006	.003

age of seventeen in the U.S. adult population is 50 percent. If we were trying to gauge the precision of an estimate of this proportion given various sample sizes, we find that 95 percent of the samples of size twenty-five would be between (50 percent − 19.6 percent =) 30 percent and (50 percent + 19.6 percent =) 70 percent. However, if we used a sample size of 100 (i.e., four times as large), 95 percent of our samples would produce estimates between (50 percent − 9.8 percent =) 40 percent and (50 percent + 9.8 percent =) 60 percent. Quadrupling the sample size again to 400 would decrease the size of the interval by half and would produce an interval of approximately ± 5 percent.[9]

This analysis applies to an estimate of a single proportion based on the whole sample.[10] In deciding the sample size needed for a study, one must consider the subpopulations for which one will want to construct estimates. For example, one almost always wants to know not just a single parameter for the whole population but parameters for subpopulations such as men and women, whites, blacks, and Hispanics, and younger people and older people. Furthermore, one is usually interested in the intersections of these various breakdowns of the population, for example, young black women. The size of the interval estimate for a proportion based on a subpopulation depends on the size of that group in the sample (sometimes called the *base* "*N*," i.e., the number in the sample on which the estimate is based). It is actually this kind of number that one needs to consider in determining the sample size for a study.

When we were designing the national survey of sexual behavior in the United States for the NICHD, we applied just these sorts of considerations to come to the conclusion that we needed a sample size of about 20,000 people. First, we identified the size of the smallest groups that we wanted to be able to characterize. As can be seen from table 2.2, a reasonable minimum sample size for such a group is about 400. This will allow one to derive estimates for such a group that have 95 percent confidence intervals of ± 5 percent. For example, we wanted to draw a large enough national sample to be able to compare homosexuals and heterosexuals. A rough estimate of the proportion of the population that were gay men that was being used at the time was 4 percent. This implied that, in order to draw a sample that would contain 400 homosexual men, we would need 400/.04 or 10,000 men in our sample. For the sample

---

9. Note that the intervals are widest at .50. As the true proportion declines, the intervals become smaller. Since we often do not know the true proportion, it is common practice to report the interval width for 50 percent as the most conservative, knowing that it cannot be larger than this for a given sample size. This produces the commonly reported error rate of ± 3 percent that one often sees in national news and political polls since these are based on samples of about 1,000 people.

10. A similar analysis can be performed for a single mean (arithmetic average). In this case, the inverse square root relation between various sample sizes will work exactly the same way. However, the width of the confidence interval will depend, not on the size of the mean, but on its variance in the population. A trait that has little variation will have a smaller confidence interval around its estimate.

to reflect the proportion of men and women in the population (i.e., about 50/
50) would imply an overall sample size of about 20,000.[11] Our basic design
recommendations for a national survey were based on this number.[12] It is also
worth noting that British and French researchers both have independently
completed surveys of about this size (18,876 and 20,055, respectively).

The logic of the discussion presented above assumes a given true proportion
in the population and a known sample size. This is the type of thinking that
one uses in determining the necessary sample size for a survey in advance of
the data collection. A very similar logic, but operating in reverse, is used to
compute confidence intervals for statistics computed from a sample. In this
case, we do not know the true population parameter; we are trying to estimate
it from our sample. The proportion estimated from our sample respondents'
data is our best guess of the true value. Even though we do not know the true
value, we do know something about the variability involved in our estimation
process. As pointed out above, this has to do with the sample size and the
magnitude of the value in the population. We can use table 2.2 to estimate a
confidence interval around our estimated proportion. Since the cells of the
table tell us that 95 percent of the samples (of a given size) will produce estimates within a given range of the true value, we can be confident that the true
value will be within a range of similar size placed around any one of the observed estimates generated 95 times out of 100. For example, suppose that in
fact 5 percent of the adult men aged eighteen to fifty-nine living in households
in the United States have had at least one sexual experience with another man
since turning eighteen. If we repeatedly draw samples of 1,000 men and ask
them if they have had such an experience (and if they are perfectly frank with
us, i.e., there is no measurement error to worry about, only error due to sampling), 95 percent of our estimates of the prevalence of same-gender sex among
men since age eighteen will be in the range from 3.6 percent (.05 − .014) to
6.4 percent (.05 + .014).

Now think about the process in reverse. We have a single sample of 1,000
men. We compute a statistic based on this sample of the proportion of men
who have had sex with another man since turning eighteen. Say we get 4.4
percent. (The chances are practically nil that we will get the exact same value

11. A similar analysis could be conducted with any number of other subgroups. The general
point is that we needed to be able to have a sample that would be large enough so that relatively
rare groups and behaviors (e.g., on the order of 1–5 percent) would still produce enough cases that
we would be able to look at these groups with some level of precision. Even so, we realized that
some further subclassifications (or breakdowns) of the sample that might be of theoretical and
substantive interest would be impossible. The cost of sample sizes larger than 20,000 just did not
appear to be reasonable.

12. In fact, we recommended a basic sample size of about 14,000. This number was based on a
more complex sample design that involved oversampling younger, more sexually active segments
of the population while maintaining a gender split of 50 percent. This scheme would produce a
sample with a power (precision) equivalent to that of a simpler sample of 20,000 while costing
somewhat less. The details behind the reasoning are described in detail in Laumann, Gagnon, and
Michael 1989.

as the "true" population value. However, we have just seen that we are very likely to get a value within a narrow range around the true value.) We can then calculate a 95 percent confidence interval for this statistic. A very reasonable approximation of this can be produced by using table 2.2 to find the width of an interval for a proportion of .05 (the closest approximation to .044) and a sample size of 1,000—.014. This produces an interval of 3.0–5.8 percent. (If we use 4.4 percent as our best guess of the population value for our calculation, our estimate of the width of the confidence interval will be .013. This produces an interval of 3.1–5.7 percent, extremely close to our approximation from the table.) In this case, we do not know the true value. We know only that we have a very precise degree of confidence, 95 percent, that the true value is somewhere in the range 3.0–5.8. Making assertions like this, we will be in error five times out of a hundred. (One can construct wider intervals that will provide higher degrees of confidence, e.g., 99 percent, but the 95 percent level is most common.) We hope this extended discussion will help the reader in interpreting the proportions reported later in this book. We always provide the number of cases from our sample on which our statistics are based. The reader can get a rough estimate of the degree of precision of the estimated proportions following this example and using table 2.2.

The U.S. government's political inability to go forward with the proposed survey led us to seek private-sector support to undertake even a modified version of the study. We found that it was simply not feasible to secure sufficient private funding to mount a study on the scale originally proposed. We thus developed a greatly downsized version of the study that was designed to demonstrate the feasibility of conducting sexual behavior research using modern sampling and interviewing techniques and to provide at least some limited basic information about the sexual patterns found in the U.S. population. Funding was sufficient to permit interviewing a sample of 3,432 (of which 3,159 constitute a straightforward cross-sectional sample of English-speaking adults in households and 273 are derived from oversampling blacks and Hispanics).[13] This sample size is much larger than necessary to get precise national estimates on many population parameters of interest and to begin examination of basic relations in the data. It is clearly inadequate for in-depth analyses of the smaller

---

13. Further discussion of the sample can be found in appendix A. The basic sample design is a stratified, multistage area probability sample of clusters of households in the United States. It was drawn from the NORC 1980 national sampling frame. This frame is described in detail in Davis and Smith (1991, app. A). For the cross-sectional component of the sample, households in the United States have an equal probability of selection. One adult between the ages of eighteen and fifty-nine per household was randomly selected using a Kish table (Kish 1965). This person had to be proficient enough in English to understand the questions and respond to them. In the oversample component, a replicate sample of households was selected in the same way as the cross section, but respondents were selected only from households with either black or Hispanic residents. Unless otherwise stated, all analyses in this book that do not explicitly include race/ethnicity as a variable were based on the cross-sectional sample of 3,159 adults. Tabulations using the race/ethnicity variable include all 3,432 respondents.

subpopulations of interest. The NHSLS is not the ultimate study but rather a major step forward that needs to be followed up in greatly expanded form.

SPECIFYING THE TARGET POPULATION: HOUSEHOLD, AGE RANGE, AND LANGUAGE

Many other decisions about the population to be sampled had to be made in designing the sample for the NHSLS. All these decisions were shaped and constrained by the limited and uncertain funding for the project.[14] Since our goal was to undertake a broad investigation of sexual conduct in the age of AIDS rather than a narrowly focused AIDS-risk study, we wanted our sample to represent as much of the U.S. adult population as possible. We resisted temptations to narrow the population focus in various ways. For example, we thought it best to focus equal attention on men and women despite some who correctly argued that men were much more likely than women to have sex lives involving many partners. A standard strategy is to oversample those parts of the population with the greatest variability on the dimensions of interest. Others argued that we should focus on the big cities where presumably riskier sexual behavior is concentrated. Again we resisted. One area where we faced a more difficult choice was in terms of the age range to cover. When we were designing a large-scale national survey with adequate government funding, we spent a good deal of effort investigating ways to include the full adult age range in the study.[15] Once we were faced with a greatly reduced sample size, we decided that we should narrow the age range somewhat. From preliminary data, it was clear that many measures of the amount of and variation in sexual behavior decline with age. We initially narrowed the age range to eighteen to sixty-five, but unanticipated higher costs induced us to narrow the range to people between eighteen and fifty-nine years of age, inclusively.

Several other limitations were placed on the sample. We interviewed only people who are currently living in households. This excludes people living in institutions or group quarters, such as college dormitories, prisons, nursing homes, and military barracks. This decision grew out of the way in which probability sampling is conducted for most face-to-face surveys. While it is possible to include nonhousehold populations in the sampling frame, it involves

14. In the acknowledgments, we express our appreciation to the seven private foundations that provided support for this study. The reader can readily appreciate the problems of coordinating so many independent sponsors. While the bulk of the funding was in hand early in our planning effort, a substantial part of the funding was not known to be available until we were already in the field. Uncertainty of funding required that we have contingency plans for many phases of the fieldwork, should funding not become available in a timely fashion.

15. The question of including adolescents raises a different set of issues. From the beginning, two separate government studies were being designed: one a study of adults and the other a study of teenagers. Partially for historical reasons, then, our team focused only on adults eighteen and older. In addition, we were reluctant to pursue the inclusion of people under eighteen years of age because we would have needed to obtain their parents' consent in order to interview young people about sexual matters. This raises a whole set of costly logistic problems that we could avoid by excluding the young.

special (and costly) procedures. We also believed that the sexual experiences and sex lives of many people living in group quarters would be affected by that fact and that it would therefore be better to study them as special populations. In the original design report, we had proposed options for studying people in prisons, the military, and college dormitories as part of an expanded national research effort. In the present study, this simply was not feasible. Overall, people not living in households represent less than 3 percent of the adult population.[16]

The other segment of the population that we felt compelled to exclude from the NHSLS but that we had planned to include in the full design is the Spanish-speaking part of the non-English-speaking population residing in the United States. These people represent less than 2 percent of the adult population. Some survey researchers use Spanish-speaking interviewers to conduct such interviews without a special Spanish-language instrument. On the basis of focus interviews with Hispanic men and women and extensive pilot work, we are convinced that a special effort must be made to construct a culturally neutral Spanish translation of a sex questionnaire. We had begun the process of translation, but we could not afford to complete it in time for use in the NHSLS. Moreover, having Spanish-speaking interviewers available wherever we encountered such a household would have substantially increased costs.

Appendix A examines many of these population coverage issues in much greater detail. In summary, the sampling frame for the NHSLS includes over 95 percent of the adult population aged eighteen to fifty-nine. It is to this population that our results are meant to be generalized, that is, to adults eighteen to fifty-nine living in households in the United States between February and October 1992 and conversationally competent in English. We turn now to the issue of what proportion of the people sampled actually completed interviews.

GAINING COOPERATION: THE RESPONSE RATE

To many people, probability sampling is like magic or an incomprehensible scientific fetishism. This suspicion of its claims is accentuated when it is applied to a topic like sexuality, which is usually treated as a complex, unmeasurable, mysterious, even irrational matter. As a practical matter, however, probability sampling is clearly the correct methodology when variation in large populations is to be studied. The intricacies of probability sampling are well understood by specialists and widely applied. The fact that probability sampling is routinely used by governments, economists, sociologists, political pollsters, demographers, epidemiologists, product quality control engineers, and other scientists and technicians should be reassuring.

Certain problems arise in probability sampling of human populations that

---

16. According to an analysis reported in Davis and Smith (1991, 697) using 1980 census data, this rate varies by age. Among those eighteen to twenty-four years old, 9.4 percent were not living in households. Most of these were living in college dorms or in military quarters. For persons twenty-five to sixty-four, only 0.8–1.4 percent lived outside households.

do not arise in other applications. And it is possible that sexuality as a specific subject matter poses new problems or accentuates others. As noted before, Kinsey believed that it would be impossible to draw a probability sample of potential respondents, approach them more or less out of the blue, and convince them to participate in an interview about their sex lives. This widely shared belief may well have been the major contributing factor to the lack of sex research on populations using probability sampling during the intervening years between the publication of the Kinsey volumes and the appearance of AIDS. Many social scientists and laypeople with whom we talked when we began this project still felt that it would be impossible to get sufficiently high rates of participation, let alone answers one could trust as valid and reliable.[17] These are two crucial elements that go beyond the question of drawing a representative sample of the U.S. adult population and speak to the credibility and generalizability of the findings reported in this book. We need to address them in turn.

First, let us consider the cooperation or response rate. No survey of any size and complexity is able to get every sampling-designated respondent to complete an interview. Individuals can have many perfectly valid reasons why they cannot participate in the survey: being too ill, too busy, or always absent when an effort to schedule an interview is made or simply being unwilling to grant an interview. While the face-to-face or in-person survey is considerably more expensive than other techniques, such as mail or telephone surveys, it usually gets the highest response rate. Even so, a face-to-face, household-based survey such as the General Social Survey successfully interviews, on the average, only about 75 percent of the target sample (Davis and Smith 1991). The missing 25 percent pose a serious problem for the reliability and validity of a survey: is there some systematic (i.e., nonrandom) process at work that distinguishes respondents from nonrespondents? That is, if the people who refuse to participate or who can never be reached to be interviewed differ systematically in terms of the issues being researched from those who are interviewed, then one will not have a representative sample of the population from which the sample was drawn. If the respondents and nonrespondents do not differ systematically, then the results will not be affected. Unfortunately, one usually has no (or only minimal) information about nonrespondents. It is thus a challenge to devise ways of evaluating the extent of bias in the selection of respondents and nonrespondents. Experience tells us that, in most well-studied fields in which survey research has been applied, such moderately high response rates as 75 percent

---

17. Skepticism about the possibility of studying sex using survey research was not universal. Many people in the field of sex research were skeptical, although far from all. The one group that was confident that this research could be conducted without much difficulty and at a high level of quality were the professional survey researchers, especially those who managed field operations, many of them experienced interviewers themselves.

do not lead to biased results. And it is difficult and expensive to push response rates much higher than that. Experience suggests that a response rate close to 90 percent may well represent a kind of upper limit.

Because of our subject matter and the widespread skepticism that survey methods would be effective, we set a completion rate of 75 percent as the survey organization's goal. In fact, we did much better than this; our final completion rate was close to 80 percent. We have extensively investigated whether there are detectable participation biases in the final sample. These comparisons are documented in appendixes A and B. To summarize these investigations, we have compared our sample and our results with other surveys of various sorts and have been unable to detect systematic biases of any substantive significance that would lead us to qualify our findings at least with respect to bias due to sampling.

One might well ask what the secret was of our remarkably high response rate, by far the highest of any national sexual behavior survey conducted so far. There is no secret. Working closely with the NORC senior survey and field management team, we proceeded in the same way as one would in any other national area probability survey. We did not scrimp on interviewer training or on securing a highly mobilized field staff that was determined to get respondent participation in a professional and respectful manner. It was an expensive operation: the average cost of a completed interview was approximately $450.

We began with an area probability sample, which is a sample of households, that is, of addresses, not names. Rather than approach a household by knocking on the door without advance warning, we followed NORC's standard practice of sending an advance letter, hand addressed by the interviewer, about a week before the interviewer expected to visit the address. In this case, the letter was signed by the principal investigator, Robert Michael, who was identified as the dean of the Irving B. Harris Graduate School of Public Policy Studies of the University of Chicago. The letter briefly explained the purpose of the survey as helping "doctors, teachers, and counselors better understand and prevent the spread of diseases like AIDS and better understand the nature and extent of harmful and of healthy sexual behavior in our country." The intent was to convince the potential respondent that this was a legitimate scientific study addressing personal and potentially sensitive topics for a socially useful purpose. AIDS was the original impetus for the research, and it certainly seemed to provide a timely justification for the study. But any general purpose approach has drawbacks. One problem that the interviewers frequently encountered was potential respondents who did not think that AIDS affected them and therefore that information about their sex lives would be of little use.

Gaining respondents' cooperation requires mastery of a broad spectrum of techniques that successful interviewers develop with experience, guidance from the research team, and careful field supervision. This project required extensive training before entering the field. While interviewers are generally trained to be neutral toward topics covered in the interview, this was especially important when discussing sex, a topic that seems particularly likely to elicit emotionally freighted sensitivities both in the respondents and in the interviewers. Interviewers needed to be fully persuaded about the legitimacy and importance of the research. Toward this end, almost a full day of training was devoted to presentations and discussions with the principal investigators in addition to the extensive advance study materials to read and comprehend. Sample answers to frequently asked questions by skeptical respondents and brainstorming about strategies to convert reluctant respondents were part of the training exercises. A set of endorsement letters from prominent local and national notables and refusal conversion letters were also provided to interviewers. A hotline to the research office at the University of Chicago was set up to allow potential respondents to call in with their concerns. Concerns ranged from those about the legitimacy of the survey, most fearing that it was a commercial ploy to sell them something, to fears that the interviewers were interested in robbing them. Ironically, the fact that the interviewer initially did not know the name of the respondent (all he or she knew was the address) often led to behavior by the interviewer that appeared suspicious to the respondent. For example, asking neighbors for the name of the family in the selected household and/or questions about when the potential respondent was likely to be home induced worries that had to be assuaged. Another major concern was confidentiality—respondents wanted to know how they had come to be selected and how their answers were going to be kept anonymous.

A number of techniques were used to deal with reluctant respondents, but none of these were unique to this survey. One technique that interviewers are especially fond of, but that survey research and funding organizations are less happy about, is the use of incentive fees. We did use such fees in this effort—in a careful and targeted way. Initially, respondents were not offered any money, and fees, usually of $25.00, were reserved to convert refusals when needed. In some areas, known to be difficult, respondents were offered a fee of $10.00 immediately. As time went on and it became clear that sufficient funds were available, all respondents were offered $35.00: $10.00 to complete the household enumeration and $25.00 to complete the interview. (Enumerations can be completed by any adult in the household, interviews only by the one randomly selected member of the household.) As the sample in an area began to be used up and response rates were still low, incentive fees given to selected respondents were used carefully and in close consultation between field management and field interviewers. Fees of up to $100 were offered for interviews. This was done rarely, and analyses partially presented in appendix A show no relation between respondent fee and quality of the information provided. Especially in a household area probability design, the judicious use of incentive fees is cost efficient since so much of the expense is due to interviewer travel time and costs incurred returning to residences.

Other techniques that were used included interviewers who specialize in respondent conversion. Some of this work was successfully conducted on the telephone. Close coordination between the field management staff, the central office staff, and the researchers helped orchestrate the very successful fielding of this study. There was a moment in the field period when it appeared as if we might not be able to get our target response rate. Increased interaction between the various levels of management and between field managers and their interviewers turned the tide. Often trying different specialized tactics proved successful. For example, a second set of conversion letters was tailored to address specific issues that respondents seemed to be raising. In one case, a local professor at a state university was asked to write the letter. Our sense is that no specific tactic was a magic bullet but rather that the attention paid to local problems and the constant combination by managers of pressure to persist and support for interviewers' creative application to the task eventually paid off.

Data Quality Issues Related to Interviewing and Field Operations

Methodological issues concerning the quality of the data collected fall into two broad categories: those relating to the mode and context of the interview and those relating to the design of the interview instrument itself. An extensive tradition in survey research methodology exists on these topics, but often with spotty and inconclusive results (see, e.g., Bradburn, Sudman, et al. 1979; Rossi, Wright, and Anderson 1983) (for reviews of this literature with a focus on sexual behavior, see Catania et al. 1990, Miller, Turner, and Moses 1990, and Catania et al. 1993). In particular, it remains an open question whether the methodological findings already in hand can be generalized to surveys on such sensitive topics as ours. In practice, survey research methods, like many specific scientific laboratory techniques, remain more an art than a science.

Recently, the spate of major modern sex surveys has spawned a small cottage industry of methodological research where some of these topics have been explicitly addressed (cf. Catania et al. 1990; Coates et al. 1986). For example, a British survey group undertook a pilot study in which they explored the effects of different linguistic formulations (e.g., vernacular or "street language" vs. more formal English) of the questions about sexual practices and beliefs (see Spencer, Faulkner, and Keegan 1988). A French research team (see Spira et al. 1993) compared face-to-face and telephone interviewing and examined the effect of advance letters in securing respondents' cooperation.

Ironically, our political problems with the government-funded project had mixed effects on our own methodological investigations. On the one hand, the delays caused by political opposition to the research gave us much more time to pursue some methodological research in greater depth than we might have otherwise, while, on the other, the opposition simply stopped us from carrying out several important experiments that we had planned. The methodological work that we did undertake between 1988 and 1992 was primarily qualitative in nature and focused largely on issues related to the content and construction of the questionnaire.[18]

The important experiments that we could not conduct addressed a number of key issues related to the mode and context of the interview, including gender and/or race matching of interviewers with respondents and comparisons of the effects of different interviewing modes (e.g., telephone vs. face-to-face vs. self-administered) and of different interviewing contexts (e.g., being interviewed at home vs. being interviewed at a "neutral site" outside the home where greater privacy could be guaranteed). These questions were to be investigated experimentally in a national feasibility survey of about 3,000 cases. This survey, similar in size to the NHSLS as finally completed, was seen as a precursor to the much larger national survey. Government scientific professionals at the NICHD, the CDC, the NCHS, and the NIMH entertained doubts about the feasibility and the design of the national survey while still wanting data and national estimates as soon as possible. To resolve these doubts, we proposed to conduct a moderately sized survey to test the various alternative designs and methods experimentally right away. The results of the pretest would have provided a much more informed basis for selecting the appropriate design for the national survey. But this was not to be. We never secured the authorization to proceed with the pretest. In the absence of the pretest results, we had to exercise our best professional judgment in choosing among the various methodological alternatives. A simple logic guided these judgments. We chose the less expensive alternative unless there was a compelling reason to believe that it would seriously compromise the quality of the data.

MODE OF ADMINISTRATION: FACE-TO-FACE, TELEPHONE, OR SELF-ADMINISTERED

Perhaps the most fundamental design decision, one that distinguishes this study from many others, concerned how the interview itself was to be conducted. In survey research, this is usually called the *mode* of interviewing or of questionnaire administration. We chose face-to-face interviewing, the most costly mode, as the primary vehicle for data collection in the NHSLS. What follows is the reasoning behind this decision.

A number of recent sex surveys have been conducted over the telephone, including the French national survey (Spira et al. 1993) and the CAPS (Center for AIDS Prevention Studies) National AIDS Behavior Survey (NABS) (Catania et al. 1992b; Dolcini et al. 1993). The principal advantage of the telephone survey is its much lower cost. Its major disadvantages are the length and complexity of a questionnaire that can be realistically administered over the

---

18. A variety of methodological research strategies were followed: culturally diverse focus groups; various sorts of pilot interviews at all stages of questionnaire development, including, in addition to regular pilot tests of the questionnaire, intensive pilots called *cognitive interviews* as well as open-ended reinterviews; and work on a Spanish translation. These are discussed in greater detail below.

telephone and problems of sampling and sample control. The French survey, by far the most ambitious sex survey conducted over the telephone, reflects these problems. Two versions of the questionnaire—short and long—were used. The long version, given to only 24 percent of the total sample (4,820 of 20,055), lasted about forty-five minutes, while the remainder of the sample was given the short version, which took about fifteen minutes. For comparison, the NHSLS, cut to its absolute minimum length, averaged about ninety minutes. Extensive field experience suggests an upper limit of about forty-five minutes for phone interviews of a cross-sectional survey of the population at large.

In addition, the French researchers thought it necessary to use an advance letter to get a sufficient response rate on the telephone. Unfortunately, in order to do this, they had to use only listed phone numbers, for which they could get addresses, rather than random digit dialing, which is more common in telephone research because it allows the inclusion of households with unlisted numbers as well. This is a much more severe limitation for the French survey, whose population of inference (see the discussion of this concept in appendix A) is based exclusively on a sample of people with listed telephone numbers. The probable effect of this strategy is disproportionately to exclude people at both ends of the income or social class spectrum. Poor people are less likely to have telephones at all, and upper-middle-class people are more likely to have unlisted phone numbers. Another disadvantage of phone surveys is that it is more difficult to find people at home by phone and, even once contact has been made, to get them to participate. The French researchers report their response rate as 72.0 percent (Spira et al. 1993, 92). But this number excluded households that were not contacted at all (2.7 percent of the original 40,000 telephone numbers) as well as those where they were never able to talk to the selected respondent (9.1 percent of 30,157 contacted households). In a face-to-face survey, both types of nonresponse would be counted *against* the final response rate. Even if we ignore the 2.7 percent who were not contacted at all, the French response rate is 65.5 percent when calculated in the more conservative fashion common to face-to-face surveys. One further consideration in evaluating the phone as a mode of interviewing is its unknown effect on the quality of responses. Are people more likely to answer questions honestly and candidly or to dissemble on the telephone as opposed to face to face? Nobody knows for sure.

The other major mode of interviewing is through self-administered forms distributed either face to face or through the mail.[19] When the survey is conducted by mail, the questions must be self-explanatory, and much prodding is typically required to obtain an acceptable response rate. The British sex survey employed a "mixed mode" of face-to-face interviewing combined with the use

---

19. We ruled out the idea of a mail survey because its response rate is likely to be very much lower than any other mode of interviewing (see Bradburn, Sudman, et al. 1979).

of extensive self-administered forms. This procedure has been shown to produce somewhat higher rates of reporting socially undesirable behaviors, such as engaging in criminal acts and substance abuse. We adopted the mixed-mode strategy to a limited extent by using four short, self-administered forms, totaling nine pages altogether, as part of our interview. When filled out, these forms were placed in a "privacy envelope" by the respondent so that the interviewer never saw the answers that were given to these questions. The first form consisted of a single page of questions about personal and family income: for many respondents, this—not sex—constituted the most sensitive set of questions in the interview. The second form basically replicated the self-administered form that had been used in the General Social Survey during the past four years (two pages), the third included four questions about masturbation in the last year (two pages), and the fourth asked about twenty questions (four pages) (for the actual questions asked, see appendix C). This fourth self-administered module was given at the very end of the interview and covered some of the most sensitive and important information about lifetime sexual experiences and AIDS-risk behaviors.

The fundamental disadvantage of self-administered forms is that the questions must be much simpler in form and language than those that an interviewer can ask. Complex skip patterns must be avoided. Even the simplest skip patterns are usually incorrectly filled out by some respondents on self-administered forms. One has much less control over whether (and therefore much less confidence that) respondents have read and understood the questions on a self-administered form. The NHSLS questionnaire (discussed below) was based on the idea that questions about sexual behavior must be framed as much as possible in the specific contexts of particular patterns and occasions. We found that it is impossible to do this using self-administered questions that are easily and fully comprehensible to people of modest educational attainments.

To summarize, we decided to use face-to-face interviewing as our primary mode of administration of the NHSLS for two principal reasons: it was most likely to yield a substantially higher response rate for a more inclusive cross section of the population at large, and it would permit more complex and detailed questions to be asked. While by far the most expensive approach, such a strategy provides a solid benchmark against which other modes of interviewing can and should be judged. The main unresolved question is whether another mode has an edge over face-to-face interviewing when highly sensitive questions likely to be upsetting or threatening to the respondent are being asked. As a partial control and test of this question, we have asked a number of sensitive questions in both formats so that an individual's responses can be systematically compared. The results of these comparisons will be reported in the appropriate substantive chapters. Suffice it to say at this point that there is a stunning consistency in the responses secured by the different modes of administration.

GENDER MATCHING OF INTERVIEWERS AND RESPONDENTS

A key design decision that we would have pretested via a controlled experiment had we been able is the issue of matching interviewers to respondents by gender and/or race. The question of gender matching in a survey on sex looms especially large. Most professional interviewers are women. This is largely a historical artifact related to the fact that interviewing is part-time work rather than steady employment. Women have other advantages as interviewers as well. There is no question that women have an easier time gaining access to a household because they are regarded as less threatening and viewed with less suspicion as to their motives. Remember that the initial approach to a household in a survey such as the NHSLS is for the purpose of selecting a respondent and involves enumerating all who live in the household and their ages. But the question does arise as to what effect the gender of the interviewer has on the interaction with the respondent during the actual interview. Will men and women respondents be affected in similar or different ways? Will people who have engaged in socially disapproved activities (e.g., same-gender sex, anal sex, prostitution, or extramarital sexual relations) be equally likely to tell this to a male as to a female interviewer? At present, these questions remain unresolved empirically. What slim evidence there is suggests that there is no difference or that women interviewers are preferable.[20] Although this issue is certainly important enough to evaluate in an experimental design where respondents have been assigned at random to an interviewer of one gender or the other, we did not expect the effect of gender matching to be especially large or substantively noteworthy. The experience and belief among NORC survey research professionals was that the quality of the interviewer was important but that it was not necessarily linked to gender or race. Quality is a complex product of personality, training, and experience. Although many laypeople have worried that women interviewers might be viewed as mother figures to whom respondents would be less likely to admit socially disapproved sexual behavior, it seems just as plausible that they might be seen as a generalized version of the sympathetic, nurturant professional, such as a nurse or social worker, to whom one may unburden all of one's problems.

RACE MATCHING OF INTERVIEWERS AND RESPONDENTS

Similar considerations apply to race. Slightly more evidence may exist for race effects in interviewing, although most of this research has been on topics specifically related to racial themes (e.g., Schuman and Converse 1971; Sudman and Bradburn 1974). Again, there are arguments on both sides of the issue. In practice, there is a somewhat greater chance of race matching than gender matching (given that most women will be interviewed by women, as

---

20. In their study of college students' sexual behavior, DeLamater and MacCorquodale (1979a) found that women were preferred as interviewers by both men and women.

will most men). Since, in a national survey, interviewers are recruited from the local area where the interviewing will take place, they often reflect the racial/ ethnic makeup of the area. Because neighborhoods are often predominantly of one race/ethnicity, there is inevitably some matching that is done in making interviewing assignments. But, as with gender, we were not convinced that compulsory matching was necessary. We knew that it would be more expensive, probably necessitating the use of outside interviewers, and its benefits were not proved. Instead, we concentrated our time and money on recruiting and training the best possible interviewers we could find, regardless of gender or race.

RECRUITING AND TRAINING INTERVIEWERS

We firmly believed that it was very important to recruit and train interviewers for this study very carefully. In particular, we worried that interviewers who were in any way uncomfortable with the topic of sexuality would not do a good job and would adversely affect the quality of the interview. We thus took special steps in recruiting interviewers to make it clear what the survey was about, even showing them especially sensitive sample questions. We also assured potential recruits that there would be no repercussions should they not want to work on this study; that is, refusal to participate would not affect their future employment with NORC. None of these steps seemed to hinder the recruitment effort. In general, interviewers like challenging studies. Any survey that is not run of the mill and promises to be of current public relevance is regarded as a good and exciting assignment—one to pursue enthusiastically. In short, we had plenty of interviewers eager to work on this study. Of course, a few interviewers did decline to participate because of the subject matter.

We especially wanted experienced interviewers whose training on the survey would be as extensive as possible. In-person training is extremely expensive. Many NORC surveys are conducted without such training for that reason, relying instead on extensive written materials for "home study." At first, it appeared that a large-scale personal training session in Chicago for the national survey staff (ultimately numbering around 220 interviewers and their field supervisors) would be prohibitively expensive. Happily, the MacArthur Foundation was willing to commit the necessary funds on very short notice. As a result, personal, study-specific training was conducted in Chicago over a three-day period (with an additional two days of general training for the new hires). While we have no empirical evidence to prove it, we believe that this training played a key role in making the study a success. The collective training sessions communicated a heightened sense of commitment and enthusiasm for the study that carried over to the day-to-day operations in the field. Interviewers became comfortable with discussing sexuality in a variety of ways, but always in a neutral, professional manner. The importance of being neutral and nonjudgmental, always important in survey interviewing, was emphasized. Ways of dealing with the interviewers' own fears and anxieties were discussed by a professional psychologist, Dr. Richard Carroll, who at the time was the director of the Sex and Marital Counseling Clinic at the University of Chicago Hospitals and had served as a consultant to the research project from its inception. We were also concerned about the possibility of interviewers being threatened or arousing the wrong kind of interest from some respondents. Interviewers were instructed to take every precaution in protecting themselves. They were told that, should they feel uncomfortable or in danger, they should terminate the interview and leave immediately. In fact, very few such occasions arose, and no extraordinary incidents occurred. Throughout the field operations, such problems were carefully monitored. The provision of interviewer assistance (e.g., escorts) and the identification of appropriate local and national counseling services for those respondents who might request advice from an interviewer were arranged in advance of field operations in a given local area.

The Questionnaire

The questionnaire itself is probably the most important element of the study design. It determines the content and quality of the information gathered for analysis. Unlike issues related to sample design, the construction of a questionnaire is driven less by technical precepts and more by the concepts and ideas motivating the research. It demands even more art than applied sampling design requires.

Before turning to the specific forms that this took in the NHSLS, we should first discuss several general problems that any survey questionnaire must address. The essence of survey research is to ask a large sample of people from a defined population the *same set of questions*. To do this in a relatively short period of time, many interviewers are needed. In our case, about 220 interviewers from all over the country collected the NHSLS data. The field period, beginning on 14 February 1992 and ending in September, was a time in which over 7,800 households were contacted (many of which turned out to be ineligible for the study) and 3,432 interviews were completed. Central to this effort was gathering comparable information on the same attributes from each and every one of these respondents. The attributes measured by the questionnaire become the variables used in the data analysis. They range from demographic characteristics (e.g., gender, age, and race/ethnicity) to sexual experience measures (e.g., numbers of sex partners in given time periods, frequency of particular practices, and timing of various sexual events) to measures of mental states (e.g., attitudes toward premarital sex, the appeal of particular techniques like oral sex, and levels of satisfaction with particular sexual relationships).

The basic problem in writing a questionnaire thus becomes the construction of a formal protocol that combines the specific wording of questions as well as instructions and skip patterns that allow the interviewer to take all the respondents over the same material. As much as possible, each respondent should be asked the same questions in the same words and in the same order since variations in wording and order are known to affect the responses that one gets (cf. Bradburn, Sudman, et al. 1979; Groves 1989). There are two ways to approach this problem. One approach is to make the questionnaire very simple, treating each question as a separate summary statement that can be answered independently of all other questions. This is what one must do in a self-administered questionnaire. It is also almost always the practice in questionnaires that focus on attitudes.

The approach that we took is quite different. As discussed in chapter 1, this research treats sexuality as socially and temporally organized thoughts, behaviors, and experiences. Our real interest is not in simple isolated facts but rather in the more complex concatenations and contextualizations of behavior. Scripts imply a set of ordered or interrelated behaviors; social networks focus on experiences within specific partnerships and the multiplicity and timing of an individual's partnering activities over the life course; and choice models imply choosing among ordered sets of alternative partners and behaviors. However, because individual lives differ greatly, the same basic material must be covered with each respondent, but with provisions for skipping those questions that simply do not apply to that respondent. Certain questions must thus act as filters for later questions. If a respondent had a particular experience (e.g., being married, living with a partner, or having at least one sex partner in the past year), then he or she would be asked a series of follow-up questions. Sometimes earlier questions help organize the respondent's thinking; for example, the timing of marriages discussed early in the interview served to organize later questions about lifetime partners.

When we began this project seven years ago, there were almost no examples of in-depth surveys of sexual behavior using a standardized questionnaire. Our problem was to marry practical knowledge and skills in the art of survey questionnaire construction with our theoretical and conceptual framework for studying sexuality. We were fortunate in working closely with a wide range of staff from NORC who brought with them many years of experience conducting complex face-to-face surveys on a vast array of topics. Much of this knowledge is not written down but exists as individual expertise. In particular, the field staff of experienced interviewers and field managers were invaluable and extremely generous in their contributions. Each of the authors had extensive survey research experience as well, but the NHSLS was a unique venture that went well beyond our past experience. This was to be an innovative survey rather than a simple application of a well-established formula. We also benefited from the eager, dedicated research assistants, mainly social science and public policy graduate students from a number of departments at the University of Chicago.

Since the first step in this project was to design a survey rather than to collect data, our initial effort was to gather advice from a wide variety of experts in the fields of survey research, demography, social networks, epidemiology, sexually transmitted infections, drug use, adolescence, fertility, sexual dysfunction, and poverty and race. These experts served as an advisory panel for the original design work that we performed under a contract with the National Institute of Child Health and Human Development. The guiding principles for the basic framework of the questionnaire were worked out in conjunction with this group.[21]

Writing the questionnaire for the NHSLS was an extremely complicated and prolonged process. Once again, the checkered political history of this project took its toll. The instrument that we finally used is much closer to our original effort than an interim bowdlerized version that we concocted as a compromise in an attempt to appease the political Right.[22] Because of the much more limited funding available for the NHSLS, we decided to cut and simplify the original draft questionnaire in ways that seriously narrowed the information collected. This was particularly true in terms of the detail sought on sexual techniques. While we did resist the "medicalized" AIDS focus that many (including the Right) wanted to impose on the project, to conserve time and money we ourselves restricted the focus to only a few sexual techniques: oral, vaginal, and anal, or what is sometimes called *penetrative sex* in the AIDS-risk literature. In the original version, we had asked about a much more comprehensive range of physical acts, including hugging, kissing, and a wide range of manual and oral stimulation. Similarly, to keep the questionnaire under ninety minutes in length, we reduced the number of questions about contraceptive behavior, sexual attitudes, and several other topics.

A number of fundamental decisions were made in designing the questionnaire. The basic problem was to construct an instrument that would collect information in a way that would minimize reporting bias and error. There are at least two sources of reporting problems: cognitive and normative. Cognitive problems exist in any questionnaire. Questions must be clear and unambiguous so that all respondents understand them in the same way. In a behaviorally oriented interview calling for extensive retrospection, care must be taken to minimize the cognitive tasks of recollecting and summarizing (see, e.g., Bradburn, Rips, and Shevell 1987). The second major challenge to reporting accuracy is normative. In a survey about a subject as personally sensitive as sexuality, it is essential that every tactic be employed to reduce underreporting and other forms of response bias due to "social desirability," that is, respondents giving answers calculated to be socially acceptable and approved rather than being frank and honest.

---

21. See the acknowledgments for a list of the members of the advisory panel. The proposed design for a large-scale national survey can be found in *The Design Report of the National Health and Sexual Behavior Project,* completed in April 1989 (Laumann, Gagnon, and Michael 1989).

22. In that version of the questionnaire, besides a narrowing of the sexual techniques to be considered and the deletion of questions about sexual fantasies and masturbation, the government reviewers had insisted that we insert a set of filter questions before asking about sexual practices that in effect would have eliminated anyone who had been monogamous and married for ten years or more. Only those people thought to be at some risk of contracting AIDS were to be asked about their sexual practices. This would, of course, have limited our understanding of both nonmonogamous and (self-proclaimed) monogamous respondents.

Another set of issues needing resolution is related to how best to think about the subject matter itself, that is, what definition of sex and sex partner would be most appropriate and what language should be used in discussing various aspects of sexuality with the respondents. More generally, what are the most important things we need to know about sexuality from a national sample of adults? Without clear standards of relevance and priority, we have no basis for selecting items to be included or dropped from the interview. Even though ninety minutes on the average is a fairly generous interview time for general survey work, we quickly found it to be quite constraining in light of what we thought we needed to learn about our subjects' sexuality. We found that we had to drop many topics and questions because of time constraints and our fear of overburdening respondents and inducing break-offs in the interviews. As it turned out, these fears were unfounded. Once the interview began, respondents almost never discontinued it.

The final instrument is far from perfect. But we believe that it is an important first step in conducting comprehensive population research on sexuality. Appendix C contains the interview schedule. Readers can see for themselves exactly how the questions were asked and in what context.

As pointed out several times, there are very few successfully executed questionnaires to use as models for our study and none that have attempted to gather a complete picture of adults' sex lives. Instead, there are bits and pieces of prior experience that could be drawn on. John Gagnon is one of only a few people who has been trained to conduct and has actually conducted the Kinsey sex history interview. But that interview is very different from the kind of survey that we proposed to do. The Kinsey instrument was to be memorized and used as a protocol or interview guide rather than as a survey interview. It consisted of a large number of items, but the interviewer was allowed to vary the order and wording of questions for every respondent. The Kinsey method was to use a small number of highly trained interviewers to conduct all the interviews. The interviewers were the researchers themselves.[23] This allowed greater flexibility in interviewing since it assumed that the interviewers understood exactly the purpose of each question and could judge answers and reformulate the question as necessary. We do not know whether these assumptions are correct and whether this tactic produces better or worse data. While it may be the case that the questionnaire as a flexible measurement instrument may well improve the quality of the answers in some cases by facilitating narrative flow, it may do so at the price of incomparability across respondents.

The problem that we faced in writing the questionnaire was figuring out how best to ask people about their sex lives. There are two issues here that

23. This is, of course, a very slow and laborious process. Kinsey and his colleagues had taken nine years to collect data on 12,000 respondents when the first volume of their report was published in 1948. Kinsey himself had conducted 58 percent of the interviews ("histories" as he called them), or 7,036 interviews. All but 4 percent had been conducted by three people (Kinsey, Pomeroy, and Martin 1948, 10–11).

should be highlighted. One is conceptual, having to do with how to define sex, and the second has to do with the level or kind of language to be used in the interview.

Very early in the design of a national sexual behavior survey, in line with our goal of not reducing this research to a simple behavioral risk inventory, we faced the issue of where to draw the boundaries in defining the behavioral domain that would be encompassed by the concept of sex. This was particularly crucial in defining sexual activity that would lead to the enumeration of a set of sex partners. There are a number of activities that commonly serve as markers for sex and the status of sex partner, especially intercourse and orgasm. While we certainly wanted to include these events and their extent in given relationships and events, we also felt that using them to define and ask about sexual activity might exclude transactions or partners that should be included. Since the common meaning and uses of the term *intercourse* involve the idea of the intromission of a penis, intercourse in that sense as a defining act would at the very least exclude a sexual relationship between two women. There are also many events that we would call sexual that may not involve orgasm on the part of either or both partners.

For these reasons, in the key section of the questionnaire where we ask respondents to enumerate their sex partners in the past twelve months, we use the following definition of sex: "Here, by 'sex' or 'sexual activity,' we mean any mutually voluntary activity with another person that involves genital contact and sexual excitement or arousal, that is, feeling really turned on, even if intercourse or orgasm did not occur." (For the full context of the question, see section 4 of appendix C.) This definition serves to elicit a broader list of partners and events than some more common definitions. In the description of the sexual relationship, the specific content in terms of sexual techniques and outcomes such as orgasm are collected. This definition also excluded forced sex. This was dealt with separately in a later section of the questionnaire. This was done to protect respondents from emotional upset earlier in the questionnaire and also because forced sex seems to define a partially separate domain.

Another major issue is what sort of language is appropriate in asking questions about sex. It seemed obvious that one should avoid highly technical language because it is unlikely to be understood by many people. One tempting alternative is to use colloquial language and even slang since that is the only language that some people ever use in discussing sexual matters. There is even some evidence that one can improve reporting somewhat by allowing respondents to select their own preferred terminology (Blair et al. 1977; Bradburn et al. 1978; Bradburn and Sudman 1983). Slang and other forms of colloquial speech, however, are likely to be problematic in several ways. First, the use of slang can produce a tone in the interview that is counterproductive because it downplays the distinctiveness of the interviewing situation itself. An essential goal in survey interviewing, especially on sensitive topics like sex, is to create a neutral, nonjudgmental, and confiding atmosphere and to maintain a certain professional distance between the interviewer and the respondent. A key advantage that the interviewer has in initiating a topic for discussion is being a stranger or an outsider who is highly unlikely to come in contact with the respondent again. It is not intended that a longer-term bond between the interviewer and the respondent be formed, whether as an advice giver or a counselor or as a potential sex partner.[24]

The second major shortcoming of slang is that it is highly variable across class and education levels, ages, regions, and other social groupings. It changes meanings rapidly and is often imprecise. Our solution was to seek the simplest possible language—standard English—that was neither colloquial nor highly technical. For example, we chose to use the term *oral sex* rather than the slang *blow job* and *eating pussy* or the precise technical but unfamiliar terms *fellatio* and *cunnilingus*. Whenever possible, we provided definitions when terms were first introduced in the questionnaire—that is, we tried to train our respondents to speak about sex in our terms. Many terms that seemed clear to us may not, of course, be universally understood; for example, terms like *vaginal* or *heterosexual* are not understood very well by substantial portions of the population. Coming up with simple and direct speech was quite a challenge because most of the people working on the questionnaire were highly educated, with strong inclinations toward the circumlocutions and indirections of middle-class discourse on sexual themes. Detailed reactions from field interviewers and managers and extensive pilot testing with a broad cross section of recruited subjects helped minimize these language problems.

In writing the questionnaire, numerous attempts were made to convey to respondents the general framework within which we were working. We tried to avoid normatively loaded or sensational language. Much of the questionnaire is devoted to behavior and experience. We consciously decided to defer questions about attitudes until late in the questionnaire after the questions about behavior. In striving to be matter of fact in the way we asked questions, we discovered that respondents found it very difficult to come up with language of their own to talk specifically about sexual practices. It was much easier for them to answer the direct, simple questions we posed that asked for yes or no answers or simple indications of the frequency with which some behavior had occurred. We avoided having respondents repeat sexual terms in their answers or being asked to come up with them on their own.

---

24. Interviewers are not there to give information or to correct misinformation. But such information is often requested in the course of an interview. Interviewers are given training in how to avoid answering such questions (other than clarification of the meaning of particular questions). They are not themselves experts on the topics raised and often do not know the correct answers to questions. For this reason, and also in case emotionally freighted issues for the respondent were raised during the interview process, we provided interviewers with a list of toll-free phone numbers for a variety of professional sex- and health-related referral services (e.g., the National AIDS Hotline, an STD hotline, the National Child Abuse Hotline, a domestic violence hotline, and the phone number of a national rape and sexual assault organization able to provide local referrals).

In addition, we worked very hard to craft the questionnaire as a whole so that it would flow logically and naturally from topic to topic. We started out with nonthreatening questions about background, moved to major sexual relationships such as marriages and cohabitations lasting a month or more, and then to fertility. Only after this gentle preparation did we begin to ask detailed questions about sex partners and sexual practices.[25] We began with the past year's sexual events and sex partners because we believed that the time period was short and recent enough to facilitate accurate recall. Central to the social network perspective is the careful enumeration of sex partners, the collection of basic information about their social and personal characteristics, and the identification of the sexual practices within specific relationships. Of course, this is a very time-consuming process when there are many partners. We thus collected detailed information on no more than two partners in the last year and then asked for more aggregated information on partners in excess of these two. Information on the sexual techniques practiced with these two (or fewer) partners was followed by a description of the last sexual event. (Since the vast bulk of the population—some 80 percent—has only one or no sex partner in a given year, this strategy effectively covers the population at large in a cost-effective way.) From there, we turned to a review of the number of partners since age eighteen, but phrased in such a way as to determine partners before, during, and after major relationships (marriages and cohabitations). This technique was an effort to assist recall in reporting partnerships and also served as a way to describe sexual relationships over the life course by organizing the respondent's acquisition of partners around entries and exits from relationships.

Masturbation was generally felt to be the most sensitive topic of any we discussed, making both respondents and interviewers the most uncomfortable. We thus adopted a form to be filled out by the respondents themselves in an effort to increase the accuracy of the report of the practice. The forms were administered in such a way that the interviewer did not see the answers. On completion, the form was put immediately into an envelope, which was then sealed before it was returned to the interviewer. This technique, often used in surveys asking about a respondent's participation in criminal behavior, has been shown to produce higher rates of reports of socially disapproved behaviors (see Bradburn, Sudman, et al. 1979). A short set of questions about the extent of one's thinking about sex and the sexual techniques and fantasies that respondents find appealing followed. The next section took up early sexual experiences and learning, including being touched sexually by older children

25. A short self-administered questionnaire (SAQ) covering basic sex partner information for the past year, for the past five years, and since age eighteen was included earlier, just after the first section of the questionnaire (see appendix C). This SAQ replicated questions used in a national survey that had been conducted annually from 1988 to 1991. It was intended to collect basic information for comparison purposes and to serve as a methodological check on the face-to-face answers.

or adults and first vaginal and first same-gender experiences. This section also introduced questions about forced sex. All the inquiries until this point had asked about voluntary or consensual sexual encounters. Forced sex was treated late in the interview when the respondent was presumably more comfortable with the interview process. A section on health issues followed that covered sexual dysfunction, experience with sexually transmitted infections, and factual knowledge about sex. The final face-to-face section contained a small number of attitude items. Finally, the respondent was given a self-administered questionnaire (SAQ) with questions about lifetime sexual experiences, some of which were already covered in the preceding sections and some of which introduced new material. Again, extremely sensitive questions were asked there to facilitate reporting.

Occasionally, we used another technique designed to enhance reporting that was originally developed by Kinsey.[26] He believed that many people were reluctant to admit certain behaviors. He argued that one could increase reporting by assuming that respondents would have done something. Asking someone a simple yes or no filter question about whether he or she engaged in a particular practice (e.g., performed oral sex on a woman) leads, in his view, more frequently to denials, whereas asking how often or when was the first time a certain practice was performed has the effect of implicitly giving a respondent permission and approval for having done it. This distinction is quite subtle, and demonstration of its efficacy has not been compelling. We suspect, however, that many behaviors in the questionnaire are underreported to varying degrees, despite our varied efforts to encourage full disclosure.

As this brief description conveys, writing the questionnaire for the NHSLS involved a complex balancing of competing considerations. While it is easy to point out the many limitations inherent in the data collected, there is really no other methodology for collecting information on the sex lives of a large representative sample of the population. Our experience strongly indicates that a very high-quality sample in terms of response rate (see appendix A) and representativeness (see appendix B) was achieved. We are reassured by many elements of our experience and that of others. We find highly consistent results across major surveys of this type (for some systematic comparisons, see appendix B). In the following chapters, we report high levels of consistency across the answers provided by individual respondents in our own survey. In short, we have every reason to believe that our respondents were trying to be as truthful and forthcoming as they could in response to our interrogation. Almost certainly there is underreporting of certain practices and behaviors, but there

---

26. This technique is closely related to a standard technique of survey research using open-ended questions. Interviewers are taught to probe by saying, "What else?" rather than, "Is that all?" The latter is more likely to elicit a simple affirmative response. The former places a slightly higher burden on respondents to indicate that they have mentioned everything. This technique is commonly used in delicatessens (and other stores), where the salesperson will never say, "Is that all?" but will rather use the prompt, "What else?"

is also considerable systematic and interpretable variation and patterning to the distributions of activities and beliefs reported, as we shall see. Further research must test our findings, and continued methodological improvements are necessary to improve the quality of the data collected. Ultimately, readers will have to decide for themselves how credible and persuasive our findings are.

2.2   On Privacy, Confidentiality, and Security

Major issues associated with protecting the privacy, confidentiality, and security of our respondents' replies were, for the most part, avoided by the simple expedient of destroying all identifying information about the respondent as soon as possible after the interview, given a brief interval to permit verification by the NORC central office that an interview had, in fact, taken place. Such a procedure, of course, eliminates the possibility of a longitudinal study design—a highly recommended feature of the proposed national survey design that our research team had originally proposed to the government (see Laumann, Gagnon, and Michael 1989, esp. pp. 5.1–5.7). We were convinced, however, that the legal safeguards currently available for privately funded research are wholly inadequate in protecting the confidentiality of our respondents' answers for any length of time. We could not, in good conscience, offer guarantees of confidentiality that independent legal counsel had advised us were flimsy and unreliable.

Issues of respondent confidentiality are at the very heart of survey research. The willingness of respondents to report their views and experiences fully and honestly depends on the rationale offered for why the study is important and on the assurance that the information provided will be treated as confidential. We offered respondents a strong rationale for the study, our interviewers made great efforts to conduct the interview in a manner that protected respondents' privacy, and we went to great lengths to honor the assurances that the information would be treated confidentially. The subject matter of the NHSLS makes the issues of confidentiality especially salient and problematic because there are so many easily imagined ways in which information voluntarily disclosed in an interview might be useful to interested parties in civil and criminal cases involving wrongful harm, divorce proceedings, criminal behavior, or similar matters.

In a recent paper on protecting privacy and confidentiality in research, Boruch (1989) offers two premises germane to our project with which we are in wholehearted agreement. The first premise is that diminution of individual privacy can be minimized without needlessly abridging the quality of research. The second premise is that no single action adequately safeguards confidentiality, that reasonable safeguards require multiple solutions to the problems of privacy. We have adopted Boruch's definitions of three key terms: *privacy, confidentiality,* and *security. Privacy* is a property of the individual (in survey research, the respondent), notably a right or interest in controlling disclosure of information about oneself. *Confidentiality* is a characteristic of the information that has been disclosed. As such, it refers to the degree to which the information about the individual is revealed to a third party. Finally, *security* is a physical property of the system used to process and store information. Each of these three concepts poses distinctive policy issues when designing survey procedures that will adequately implement and protect individual respondents' legitimate expectations about trustworthy and appropriate use of their personal disclosures and the investigators' and the survey organization's responsibilities and liabilities in this regard.

Privacy

Issues of privacy are inherent in the design of any survey. All surveys that focus on the individual depend on the willingness of individuals to reveal information, however innocuous, about themselves. In the NHSLS, the network design requires respondents to reveal information not only about themselves and the characteristics of their sexual relationships but also about the characteristics of their sex partners. Although we may have the informed consent of the individual respondents, we run the risk of violating the privacy of the respondents' partners, who are nonconsenting and perhaps identifiable. Furthermore, as Laumann (1989) suggests in his response to Boruch (1989), individuals may believe that, although they have the right to disclose information about themselves, in so doing they may reveal information about social groups to which they belong and thus violate the privacy of the group. Because the NHSLS explores social behaviors, about which we know little, it is difficult to anticipate the extent to which the exercise of the right to reveal information may unintentionally abrogate social allegiances.

Confidentiality

If we had pursued our initial interest in a longitudinal design, we would have faced special challenges in protecting confidentiality. Such a design would require the research firm to maintain complete sets of identifiers, both external and internal to the data set. The external identifiers, such as names, addresses, telephone numbers, and preassigned identification numbers, would be necessary for locating and contacting respondents in subsequent rounds of the survey. The internal identifiers, which are limited to the preassigned identification or case numbers, are requisite to accessing records from different rounds of data collection. Thus, until the final round of the survey is complete and the links destroyed, it would be possible, through subpoena, for example, to link the data record to a named, identifiable respondent. There are several legal protections against judicially ordered disclosure of respondent records that are available to specially determined federally sponsored health studies, for example, the issuance of a certificate of confidentiality from the secretary of health and human services under a provision of the Public Health Service Act. Obviously such protection is not readily available to nongovernment studies. It was this consideration that led us to abandon any plans for longitudinal work with the NHSLS respondents and to impose special procedures for removing all identifying materials from the interview schedules as soon as practicable.

Security

Any survey on the scale of the NHSLS requires large numbers of people in the survey organization to be involved in physically handling interview records, and this poses considerable scope for intentional or inadvertent disclosure of an individual's answers. Special procedures were imposed to minimize the number of people who could, in principle, know the personal identity of respondents at the same time that they had access to the interview record. Interviewers worked with two separate (and distinctly colored) sets of forms, which were designed to segregate personal identifiers from the interview record itself. Each set of forms was returned under separate cover to the central office for processing. Workers at the central office responsible for logging in a completed interview did not see the forms that had personal identifier information, and vice versa. Only the senior study director had a master file permitting the linkage of the assigned respondent interview number with the preassigned sample number identifier that contained information on a person's identity. Once interview verification by the central office had been completed, all sheets containing information on the personal identity of the respondent were systematically destroyed, using a specially designed and supervised procedure. At this time, we no longer have any information whatsoever on the personal identities of our respondents—they are truly anonymous. Because of concerns about deductive disclosure (i.e., if one knows a handful of personal items about an individual, such as marriage date, number of children and when they were born, local residence, and so on, and also knows that the individual was interviewed, one can deduce the identity of a respondent with a considerable likelihood of being correct), we have eliminated all codes of interviewee residence below the level of census region from the public use tape.

PART II

In chapters 3–9, we present our findings about adult sexual behavior based on the National Health and Social Life Survey (NHSLS). We first consider sexual practices in detail. Here we add information about the subjective appeal of those practices as well. The number of sex partners acquired within the year, over a five-year period, and over the adult's lifetime is the subject of chapter 5. We then focus more closely on the choices that people make regarding their sex partners, emphasizing the importance of the social network from which these partners are selected and discussing how these networks affect the spread of infection and disease. We also present information about the gender of the sex partners and the complexity of identifying and measuring same-gender preferences and identity. We end this section with a discussion of the onset of sexuality and the measures of the prevalence of sexual victimization among adults in our survey.

CHAPTER 3

Sexual Practices and Profiles of Sexual Expression

Of all the topics we consider, the content of sexual action and interaction has received the least scholarly attention. What people do sexually—alone or with others—and how they think about their sex lives are subjects that have rarely entered the mainstream of social scientific discourse. Despite its marginal status as a research topic, however, sexual practices have by no means been ignored. Indeed, despite formidable barriers, sociological research on sexual behavior has made considerable progress since the initial efforts of Kinsey and his colleagues (Kinsey, Pomeroy, and Martin 1948; Kinsey et al. 1953). Nevertheless, with some significant exceptions (e.g., Reiss 1960, 1967; Blumstein and Schwartz 1983), research prior to the HIV/AIDS epidemic did not emphasize the character of sexual partnerships or even numbers of partners as an all-important dimension of one's sex life. The traditional concern that women remain virgins until marriage focused on the difference between no partners and one or more, and sexual promiscuity (often ill defined numerically) was condemned, although rarely analyzed. More often, sex researchers focused on a variety of behaviorally oriented measures in which either the number of partners or the characteristics of partners were glossed over.

These tendencies found initial expression in the work of Kinsey and his associates. In both *Sexual Behavior in the Human Male* (1948) and *Sexual Behavior in the Human Female* (1953), these researchers partitioned the sex lives of their respondents into classes of sexual activities measured primarily in terms of incidence, prevalence, and frequency. The key measure in the first volume on men was whether an orgasm occurred during the sexual encounter, although this was expanded to include experiences without orgasm in homosexual encounters, a measure that was more frequently used when Kinsey and his associates faced the sex lives of women, where orgasm was not always associated with sexual activity. The "outlets," as Kinsey labeled them, were the frequencies of orgasm in such sexual practices as masturbation, nocturnal sex ("wet") dreams, petting and intercourse with opposite-gender sex partners, petting and intercourse with same-gender sex partners, and animal contacts. The

We gratefully acknowledge Christopher Browning's critical contributions in helping with the data analysis and drafting the chapter. Kristen Olson and Fang Li provided valuable assistance in all phases of the data preparation, analysis, and interpretation of results reported in this chapter. The chapter was prepared under the direction of John H. Gagnon and Edward O. Laumann.

sum of all these orgasms constituted an individual's "total sexual outlet" in a specific time period.

For Kinsey and his colleagues, the profile of sexual activities and the total number of orgasms from any outlet represented the complex outcome of a tension between biological sexual possibility and cultural constraints. Both how many orgasms or sexual experiences there were and what specific sexual practices were enacted (e.g., masturbation, oral sex, sex with same-gender partners) represented an unstable compromise between biology and society. What was critical to Kinsey's work was an emphasis on the individual sexual actor, his or her biological potential, and the relation of that potential to social and cultural forces. While all the independent variables in the Kinsey studies were social (e.g., class, generation, religion, gender), the differences between the behaviors of individuals and, most particularly, the differences between women and men resided in biological factors (except for homosexuality, which he treated as learned [Kinsey et al. 1953]). Kinsey, of course, is not alone in claiming that modes of sexual expression have fundamental roots in individual level biological or psychological characteristics (cf. Jones and Kelley 1984; Udry et al. 1985; Udry 1988; Udry and Campbell 1994; Rossi 1994a; Posner 1992).

While fully recognizing the significance of biological factors, particularly physiology, maturation, and aging, on sexual expression, we suggest that sexual behavior is fundamentally structured by social factors. Accordingly, we highlight the social nature of selected sexual practices. In introducing this shift in theoretical emphasis, we want to take account of the fact that all sexual practices are determined primarily by social factors. This includes masturbation (which is practiced in a complex environment of condemnation and elicitation and is often accompanied by socially scripted fantasies) as well as those practices that occur at the level of the partnership or dyad. These latter should be seen as a result of an explicit or tacit negotiation between two (or more) people who embody specific social locations and cultural understandings.

From this perspective, sexual behavior is structured by the social and personal characteristics of the partners, the relevant resources and strategies for realizing the sexual preferences/goals that they bring to a given transaction, and the set of expectations engendered by the various networks in which the partners are respectively embedded. Our approach generates both a different way to interpret more traditionally posed questions and a different class of questions based on an attention to partnership- or network-level interpretations or data. Thus, the traditional question of how a specific background variable affects a specific sexual practice (e.g., "What effect does ethnicity have on the lifetime occurrence of oral sex?") can be treated as measuring how individuals occupying a specific social status behave. In our view, a more fruitful interpretative approach is to ask how the category membership (being a member of one or another specific ethnic group) shapes the opportunities for particular kinds of partnerships in which oral sex is possible. With data on the social characteristics of partners or relationships, we can ask a different kind of question (e.g., "How do well-established marriages enmeshed in dense, cross-cutting social networks differ sexually from shorter-term, socially isolated sexual partnerships?"). Our attention shifts from "master status variable" to "master relationship," be it a marriage, a live-in relationship, a longer-term non-live-in relationship, or a shorter-term partnership. Each type of sexual relationship will have different implications for the ways in which sexual transactions will play themselves out.

The range of topics examined in previous studies is broadened to include not only information on the incidence and frequency of specific sexual techniques but also consideration of the different contexts and outcomes of sexual activity. Section 3.1 reports data on autoerotic sexual activity (masturbation) and the overall frequency of partnered sex and partnered sexual techniques (specifically, vaginal, oral, and anal sex). In section 3.2, we report measures of the outcomes of sexual activity, including rates of orgasm and reported levels of physical and emotional satisfaction within specific partnerships. In section 3.3, we report rates of drug and alcohol use before and during sexual activity in different types of partnerships. Finally, adopting a holistic perspective on individual sexual conduct, section 3.4 examines how different facets or aspects of sexual expression, including levels of autoerotic activity and partnered sexual behavior (consisting of the amount and range of partnering behavior and specific sexual practices), are simultaneously combined by individuals into characteristic profiles of sexual conduct that describe their current sex lives. Here we compare those individuals who report low levels of autoeroticism and partnered sexual activity of any sort with those who report generally high levels of sexual activity on all facets of sexual expression and with others who combine the facets in various permutations. Discussion of the subjective appeal of a broad variety of sexual practices and partnering relationships and how these preferences interact with social factors to produce different sexual outcomes is deferred to chapter 4.

Since the NHSLS study was designed, in part, to fill significant gaps in our knowledge of sexual behavior associated with the acquisition of the AIDS virus, our inquiries were slanted toward those sexual practices that could be demonstrably related to the transmission of infection. This disease-centered emphasis led us to omit significant nongenital sexual practices that are often independent sources of human physical and emotional pleasure and satisfaction, such as hugging, kissing, and body stroking, as well as more detailed reports of subjective responses to these events. In addition, we did not gather sufficient data on the negotiations that elicited these sequences of physical activities and subjective responses. We view this as a serious limitation of our study and plan to incorporate a more inclusive list of sexually relevant techniques in future work.

3.1   Sexual Practices

Masturbation

Masturbation has had a troubled history in Western cultures. For nearly two centuries, many physicians believed it to be the source of a wide variety of physical and mental illnesses ranging from tuberculosis to neurasthenia. The expenditure of vital bodily fluids in all sexual activity, but most especially in masturbation, was believed to be debilitating to the point of degeneracy. Even today masturbation is considered variously as a sin, as a sign of social or psychological incompetence, as evidence of a lack of willpower, or as appropriate only for adolescents and people who do not currently have sex partners (Hare 1962; Gagnon 1977, 1985; Money 1986).

Popular orientations toward autoeroticism include the assumption that rates of masturbation in the absence of a sex partner are an index of the sex drive of an individual as well as the notion that the capacity to suppress the impulse to masturbate is a measure of an individual's ability to control a powerful drive. These views focus on the individual actor and the sex drive as crucial to explaining masturbation. Following from these views is the belief that rates of masturbation rise and fall with the availability of sex partners, suggesting that each individual has a given level of "sex drive" that needs to be expressed in one way or another. Partnered sex is viewed as superior to masturbation, and, in the absence of partnered sex, masturbation becomes a plausible, if socially stigmatized, alternative.

In our view, masturbation is driven primarily by a variety of social factors both in adolescence and in adulthood, and it can have complementary, supplementary, or independent status with reference to partnered sex. The limited body of earlier evidence on masturbation has largely focused on masturbation in adolescence and the differential patterns of initiation, incidence, and frequency among girls and boys, although Kinsey did report on masturbation among adults. The increased incidence of masturbation reported by young men nearing adolescence has often been construed as the result of biological forces, but the failure to examine environmental factors closely has oversimplified this process. Anecdotal data suggest that young men often attribute to internal forces feelings and urges that are actually responses to the external environment and that first orgasms and ejaculations are often experienced as frightening, painful, or dysphoric. Further biosocial research on this portion of the life course is clearly needed to disentangle the variety of effects of biological and social psychological change.

We have not explored this period in the life course largely because of our doubts about the validity of retrospective data on a period of rapid change, often many years in the past. We have gathered data on masturbation in adulthood, focusing on the frequency of masturbation, whether orgasm was associated with masturbation, and whether respondents felt guilty about masturbating. We asked respondents to report on these matters for the last year. The information was gathered using a self-administered questionnaire (SAQ), which was placed about two-thirds of the way through the face-to-face questions (for the instructions and items used, see appendix C). We chose this method when interviewers expressed anxiety about asking questions about masturbation. These were interviewers who had not indicated any difficulty in asking questions about anal sex or sex with same-gender partners. The items concerning masturbation also prompted significant negative responses from the government officials who were responsible for reviewing a variation of this survey instrument when we were working on a pretest version; they insisted that questions on masturbation be removed from the study. These experiences accord with a classic study of responses to survey questions (Bradburn et al. 1978) that found masturbation to be the most sensitive of the several topics studied (see also Catania et al. 1986).

The anxiety about masturbation is remarkable given that masturbation differs from other sensitive subjects in one major respect—its prevalence. While we knew that, if asked directly, questions about forcing others to have sex or taking drugs would tend to elicit responses biased toward more normative or socially approved behavior, those practices share the characteristic of being extremely rare. Masturbation has the peculiar status of being both highly stigmatized and fairly commonplace.

The first four columns of table 3.1 display the percentages of respondents reporting either that they did not masturbate at all in the last year or that they did so at least once a week. Most immediately striking are the differences between the genders. While the percentage of men in these marginal or "edge" categories of the distribution differs by only 10 percentage points (with 37 percent of men reporting that they did not masturbate at all last year and 27 percent reporting a frequency of at least once a week), the equivalent discrepancy for women is over 50 percentage points (58 and 8 percent, respectively). Masturbation appears to be, in general, a less salient form of sexual expression for women. Nevertheless, close to half of all women and more than six out of ten men did report masturbating in the past year—relatively large proportions when compared with other "sensitive" practices.

Age is also significantly related to the frequency of masturbation. Interestingly, young adults, often thought to be the most autoerotically active, were less likely to have masturbated in the past year than those slightly older (the twenty-four to thirty-five-year-olds). Of eighteen- to twenty-four-year-olds, 41 percent of men and 64 percent of women said that they did not masturbate at all last year. The distribution is slightly U shaped for both women and men, the proportion not masturbating falling in the next two age groups and then stabilizing at about one-third of the men and half the women until age fifty. For people over fifty, half the men and seven of ten women report no masturbation.

When we consider the relation between masturbatory activity and marital status, an interesting and counterintuitive finding emerges. Conceptions of masturbation as moral lapse fit within a broader normative orientation toward

Table 3.1 **Frequency of Masturbation, Orgasm during Masturbation, and Felt Guilt, by Master Status Variables[a] (% distributions)**

Master Status	Frequency of Masturbation (%)				% "Always" or "Usually" Having an Orgasm during Masturbation		% Who Felt Guilty after Masturbation	
	Not at All		Once a Week					
	Men	Women	Men	Women	Men	Women	Men	Women
Total population[b]	36.7	58.3	26.7	7.6	81.5	61.2	54.0	46.8
Age:								
18–24	41.2	64.4	29.2	9.4	73.2	50.8	58.6	56.4
25–29	28.9	58.3	32.7	9.9	81.9	55.8	59.8	52.7
30–34	27.6	51.1	34.6	8.6	85.1	64.9	52.1	38.4
35–39	38.5	52.3	20.8	6.6	81.9	65.7	53.2	48.8
40–44	34.5	49.8	28.7	8.7	84.9	64.0	49.2	45.7
45–49	35.2	55.6	27.2	8.6	88.2	70.6	48.2	35.4
50–54	52.5	71.8	13.9	2.3	83.0	56.9	56.7	53.3
55–59	51.7	77.6	10.3	2.4	71.4	55.0	48.9	50.0
Marital status:								
Nev. marr., not coh.	31.8	51.8	41.3	12.3	80.3	53.7	59.6	48.1
Nev. marr., coh.	15.8	54.9	36.8	12.7	89.6	61.5	42.6	51.4
Married	42.6	62.9	16.5	4.7	82.1	61.2	55.1	49.2
Div./sep./wid., not coh.	30.2	52.7	34.9	9.6	80.7	68.5	47.3	41.3
Div./sep./wid., coh.	41.2	50.9	17.6	12.7	80.0	63.6	†	35.5
Education:								
Less than HS	54.8	75.1	19.2	7.6	59.6	45.6	42.2	44.2
HS grad. or eq.	45.1	68.4	20.0	5.6	81.9	54.9	56.3	46.1
Some coll./voc.	33.2	51.3	30.8	6.9	81.4	60.4	58.1	49.8
Finished coll.	24.2	47.7	33.2	10.2	87.5	69.7	53.4	49.0
Master's/adv. deg.	18.6	41.2	33.6	13.7	94.7	87.3	50.0	34.9
Religion:								
None	32.6	41.4	37.6	13.8	85.9	78.7	37.4	51.1
Type I Prot.[c]	28.9	55.1	28.2	7.4	86.1	66.8	56.8	43.9
Type II Prot.[c]	48.4	67.3	19.5	5.8	76.1	52.9	56.4	46.8
Catholic	34.0	57.3	24.9	6.6	80.8	54.7	57.1	50.7
Jewish	†	†	†	†	†	†	†	†
Other	22.2	52.9	41.7	17.6	71.0	†	58.1	†
Race/ethnicity:[d]								
White	33.4	55.7	28.3	7.3	84.0	66.6	54.3	47.7
Black	60.3	67.8	16.9	10.7	64.7	45.8	50.6	35.6
Hispanic	33.1	65.5	24.4	4.7	78.5	49.4	54.4	51.4
Asian	38.7	†	31.3	†	†	†	†	†
Native Am.	†	†	†	†	†	†	†	†
Total N	1,320	1,649	1,320	1,649	921	845	895	760

Note: Nev. marr.,/not coh. = never married, not cohabiting; nev. marr., coh. = never married, cohabiting; div./sep./wid., not coh. = divorced/separated/widowed, not cohabiting; div./sep./wid., coh. = divorced/separated/widowed, cohabiting; less than HS = less than high school; HS grad. or eq. = high school graduate or equivalent; some coll./voc. = some college/vocational school; finished coll. = finished college; master's/adv. deg. = master's/advanced degree; Type I/II Prot. = Type I/II Protestant; Native Am. = Native American. † indicates that the base N for the cell was under thirty cases.

[a]All respondents regardless of sexual orientation.

[b]Cross section N = 3,159.

[c]For an explanation of categories of Protestants, see appendix 3.1A.

[d]With oversample, N = 3,432.

sexuality that traditionally prohibited any form of sexual expression that did not lead to procreation. Masturbation's associations with sexual failure, however, are uniquely related to its status as an uncoupled sexual practice. Although what characterized this failure varied somewhat across different social groups—particularly for men and women—one common element was the absence of a sex partner, either temporarily or over a longer period of time. The imagery was cast in research form by Kinsey. In his view, masturbation was one of several outlets resulting ultimately in orgasm. Although he dispensed with the evaluative aspects of the popular theory, he retained the notion that sexual energy was channeled to autoerotic or coupled sexual outlets in a kind of zero-sum complementarity.

The obvious hypothesis to be culled from Kinsey's theory is that the frequency of masturbation decreases in the context of a stable sexual relationship with an available partner. This appears to be the case among the married, more dramatically for men than women, although both genders show the same effects. More people do not masturbate, and fewer people masturbate one or more times per week. However, this is not the entire story since a large portion of the reduced incidence of masturbation among the married is a result of being older. Note that many of the men among those never married but living with a partner, a rather youthful group, are masturbating frequently. Independent analyses have demonstrated that there is no difference in the incidence or frequency of masturbation among young women living with a partner, older women living with a partner, and women who have never married. Cohabiting individuals, then (and probably younger married respondents as well), are characterized by comparatively high rates of both masturbation and coupled sexual activity. The point is not to argue that Kinsey's observations are incorrect but rather to suggest that the frequency of masturbation has no set quantitative relation to other partnered sexual activities. The frequency with which an individual masturbates is as likely to be a function of social factors as it is of the availability of alternative outlets.

Indeed, such social factors as education, ethnicity, and religion all play important roles in organizing rates of autoerotic activity. The effect of education is particularly dramatic. Eighty percent of men who have graduate degrees report masturbating in the past year, and this incidence declines in a stair-step fashion to 45 percent of those who have not completed high school. A similar pattern occurs among women, with 60 percent of those who have attended graduate school having masturbated in the past year, a proportion that declines to 25 percent among women who have not finished high school. This pattern is less sharp in terms of the frequency of masturbation, but the better educated are also masturbating more frequently than the less well educated. There is an interaction between education and race, with blacks, both women and men, less likely to masturbate than whites. For instance, one-third of white men and 56 percent of white women reported that they had not masturbated at all in the past year. Black men, however, were almost twice as likely to report that they did not masturbate at all last year. Interestingly, although 68 percent of black women did not masturbate last year, they were also most likely (of all racial and ethnic groups) to say that they masturbated at least once a week (11 percent compared with roughly 7 percent of whites and 5 percent of Hispanics). These findings, along with the differences found between religious and secular respondents, demonstrate quite clearly that the incidence and frequency of masturbatory activity are functions of variations in social location.

One of the traditional assumptions about masturbation is that it is an activity that always leads to orgasm (or, in Kinsey's terms, outlet), at least among men. Given that women often report sexual activity without orgasm, it seemed plausible to ask in what proportion of self-masturbation a respondent experienced orgasm. There is evidence from an earlier study of the sexual conduct of a national sample of college students (Simon, Gagnon, and Berger 1972; Gagnon 1977) that both women and men had engaged in genital self-stimulation without orgasm. We do not view the absence of orgasm as a behavioral failure; rather, we sense that sexual pleasure is often unrelated to orgasm.

About 80 percent of men and 60 percent of women reported that they usually or always experienced orgasm when masturbating. These rates followed the pattern of effects found in the examination of the incidence and frequency of masturbation (e.g., blacks report lower orgasm rates than whites, and the religiously conservative report lower rates than those with no religion). The lower the incidence of masturbation in a group and the fewer the number of people who masturbate frequently, the lower the proportion of people who experience orgasm every or almost every time they masturbate. The effect was again dramatic in terms of education: the best educated among both women and men were very likely to report orgasm all or nearly all the time (95 percent for the men and 87 percent for the women with at least some graduate education).

These effects of education parallel Kinsey's findings that the better educated are more likely to masturbate, masturbate more often, and, from our findings, are more likely to find pleasure in masturbation. How can we account for this effect? It is likely that the better educated have more secular views in general, have more liberal views of sexual activity in particular regardless of their religious affiliation, and are more likely to consider pleasure a major goal of sexual activity. (For an extended examination of sexual attitudes and their association with the master statuses, see chapter 14.)

The relation between frequency of masturbation and frequency of orgasm when masturbating is direct. The more often people masturbate, the more likely they are to report experiencing orgasm when masturbating (see table 3.2). The strongest difference can be found between those who masturbate rarely (one to five times per year) and those who masturbate more often. A fifth of men and a third of women who masturbate one to five times a year report having orgasm never, rarely, or only sometimes. The difference between

Table 3.2   Frequency of Orgasm in Masturbation, by Frequency of
             Masturbation for Men and Women (% distributions)

| | Frequency of Orgasm in Masturbation | | | |
| | Men | | Women | |
Frequency of Masturbation	Never to Sometimes	Usually or Always	Never to Sometimes	Usually or Always
One to six times a year	20	80	33	67
Once a month	12	88	16	84
Two to three times a month	7	93	16	84
Once a week or more	6	94	19	81
Total N		833		682

women and men remains, with fewer women reporting orgasm usually or always, even with similar rates of masturbation.

Despite secular trends in the amount and frequency of masturbation among younger cohorts, about half the women and men who masturbate report feeling guilty about it. An examination of the age data in this survey indicates that age is not necessarily related to guilt, that more guilt about masturbation is not necessarily found in older groups than in younger groups. The difficulty with this analysis is that it may well be that those who feel guilty are those who are more likely to stop masturbating, leaving only those who do not feel as guilty. Another factor may be that the proportion of those who feel guilty declines as masturbation becomes a more routine part of adult lifestyles.

In addition to asking about feelings of guilt, we asked respondents to tell us why they masturbated in the past year (see table 3.3). They could choose as many responses as they wished. The largest proportion chose "to relieve sexual tension" (three-quarters of the men and 63 percent of the women), while the next most common choice was "physical pleasure" (chosen by an equal percentage of men and women). This response was particularly characteristic of the college educated (half the college-educated men and a larger number of college-educated women chose this reason for masturbation, while only about one-third of the less well educated did). Responses similar to the release of sexual tension—"to relax" and "to get to sleep"—were more rare: about a quarter of the men and a third of the women chose relaxation as the reason for masturbating, while a smaller number chose the desire to sleep. Support for Kinsey's view of the complementarity of masturbation and partnered sex can be found in the proportions who chose the unavailability of a sex partner as the reason for masturbation (an equal proportion of women and men—one-third—chose this response). A minority reported that one reason for masturbation was that their current partner did not want sex, a choice made by three times as many men as women.

Table 3.3　　　　　　　**Reasons for Masturbation, by Gender**

		Gender of Respondent (%)	
Reasons for Masturbation		Men	Women
To relax		26	32
Relieve sex tension		73	63
Partners unavailable		32	32
Partner doesn't want sex		16	6
Boredom		11	5
Physical pleasure		40	42
Go to sleep		16	12
Fear of AIDS/STD		7	5
Other		5	5
Total N		835	687

Further exploration of the factors that influence participation in masturbation and that set the rates of masturbation (both the act and the orgasm associated with the act) will be undertaken. However, it should be obvious that variations in these phenomena are profoundly influenced by a variety of master status variables, including marital status, education, and ethnicity. Drawing attention to the social nature of masturbation—typically understood largely in terms of individual level factors—highlights the even greater effect of social factors on sexual practices requiring two people. Accordingly, we now turn to a consideration of the frequency of sex with a partner (including partners of both genders) as well as specific sexual techniques involved in sex between women and men (discussion of same-gender practices is deferred to chapter 8).

The Frequency of Partnered Sex

Of the topics considered in this study, the level of an individual's sexual activity, however indexed over time, is perhaps the most lore ridden of all. While little popular musing occurs about the practice of particular sexual techniques, nearly every social group is subject to myths about the nature of their sex drive. Sexual stereotyping of racial minorities, the elderly, the working classes, and the religiously inclined, for instance, has been a historically pervasive component of American sexual ideology. Folk or even academic theories about the sexual nature of particular groups, such as those that assign blacks or Native Americans an inherently sexually uninhibited character, are simplified versions of drive theory that merely shift the unit of analysis (that for which a hypothesized level of drive could be discussed) from the individual to the social group. Such group-based theories of sex drive are unpopular now, at least among academics. As we have noted, however, theories that look toward a biologically based sex drive as an explanatory framework at the individual level are still quite prominent, especially among the general public. While our perspective emphasizes the importance of social groups in shaping sexual conduct, we view their role not in terms of shared biological properties but rather in terms of mechanisms through which common conceptions of appropriate sexual behavior are produced and reinforced.

Our measure of the frequency of partnered sex in the last year is an aggregate estimate made by the respondent covering all partners, both women and men, in the last year. The item was included in a self-administered questionnaire (SAQ) that respondents filled out on their own early in the interview. The question on frequency of partnered sex was the same item on the frequency of partnered sex included in the SAQ that was part of the General Social Survey (GSS) for 1988, 1989, 1990, 1991, and 1993. We included a version of this SAQ in our survey (its place in the sequence of items can be determined from appendix C) in order to continue collecting these data on an annual basis as well as to determine the reliability of the data that we were gathering in our survey.[1]

Recent popular commentators on the sexual state of the nation have noted—with either consternation or applause, depending on their angle of vision—a widespread sexualization of American society. From fragmentary data and inferences from an increasingly sexually oriented media system, it was inferred that actual rates of sexual activity had increased. While there can be no scientific standard about how much partnered sex is good or bad in moral terms, what is striking about our data at a general level are the modest rates of partnered sex that characterize most of our respondents, at least in contrast to the frequency of other everyday activities and the expectations created by media representations.

Table 3.4 reports the frequency of sex in the past year by the master status characteristics discussed in chapter 1. These frequencies are based on all the people in the sample, including those who had no partner in the past year. For the total population (see the row in table 3.4 so labeled), roughly 8 percent of men and 7 percent of women reported having had sex four or more times a week. Indeed, the modal frequency of sex for our respondents was "a few times per month" (36 percent of men and 37 percent of women), and roughly 10

1. The General Social Survey (GSS) is conducted by the National Opinion Research Center (NORC) and is funded by the National Science Foundation. From 1972 to 1991, the survey was conducted practically every year on a probability sample of individuals living in households. The annual sample size is approximately 1,500 respondents aged eighteen and over, and the survey has a response rate of about 75 percent. From 1988 to 1993, in response to the AIDS epidemic, the GSS included questions about attitudes toward AIDS and about whether respondents knew people with AIDS (and other relevant index questions that could be used to calibrate numbers of people with AIDS from network information) and an SAQ that asked about numbers and types of sex partners and frequency of partnered sex. In the years 1988–91, there were some limited methodological experiments in question order and wording, but, by 1991, the design of the SAQ had been standardized. It was this standard design that was included in the NHSLS and repeated in the 1993 GSS. From 1993 on, the GSS will be conducted on a biannual basis with a sample size of over 3,000. Our additions to the GSS were funded by the NORC Director's Fund and the Rockefeller Foundation.

Table 3.4 **Frequency of Sex in the Past Year, by Master Status Variables (% distributions)**

Master Status Variables	Frequency of Sex in the Past Year (%)					
	Not at All	A Few Times per Year	A Few Times per Month	Two to Three Times a Week	Four or More Times a Week	Total N
Men						
Total population[a]	9.8	17.6	35.5	29.5	7.7	1,330
Age:						
18–24	14.7	21.1	23.9	28.0	12.4	218
25–29	6.7	14.8	31.0	36.2	11.4	210
30–34	9.7	16.7	34.7	31.5	7.4	216
35–39	6.8	12.6	40.0	35.3	5.3	190
40–44	6.7	16.9	44.4	26.4	5.6	178
45–49	12.7	19.8	33.3	27.8	6.3	126
50–54	7.8	19.6	45.1	22.5	4.9	102
55–59	15.7	24.7	41.6	16.9	1.1	89
Marital status:						
Nev. marr., not coh.	22.0	26.2	25.4	18.8	7.6	382
Nev. marr., coh.	0.0	8.5	35.6	37.3	18.6	59
Married	1.3	12.8	42.5	36.1	7.3	687
Div./sep./wid., not coh.	23.8	22.5	28.5	20.5	4.6	151
Div./sep./wid., coh.	0.0	8.3	36.1	44.4	11.1	36
Education:						
Less than HS	14.8	20.2	28.4	29.5	7.1	183
HS grad. or eq.	10.1	15.1	34.4	31.7	8.7	378
Some coll./voc.	8.7	19.9	33.5	28.8	9.1	427
Finished coll.	9.0	15.8	43.9	25.8	5.4	221
Master's/adv. deg.	7.0	15.8	42.1	30.7	4.4	114
Religion:						
None	12.6	25.1	24.6	26.8	10.9	183
Type I Prot.[b]	8.1	18.9	38.1	27.0	7.8	307
Type II Prot.[b]	10.9	14.5	35.6	32.1	6.9	421
Catholic	7.9	17.3	36.5	30.6	7.6	353
Race/ethnicity:[c]						
White	9.7	17.3	35.6	29.6	7.8	1,053
Black	8.3	16.5	37.6	30.4	7.2	194
Hispanic	8.5	14.7	34.1	28.7	14.0	129
Women						
Total population[a]	13.6	16.1	37.2	26.3	6.7	1,664
Age:						
18–24	11.2	16.1	31.5	28.8	12.4	267
25–29	4.5	10.3	38.1	36.8	10.3	223
30–34	8.1	16.6	34.6	32.9	7.8	283
35–39	10.8	15.7	37.8	32.5	3.2	249
40–44	14.6	15.5	46.1	16.9	6.8	219
45–49	16.1	16.1	41.0	23.6	3.1	161
50–54	19.3	20.7	40.0	17.8	2.2	135
55–59	40.8	22.4	29.6	4.8	2.4	125

Table 3.4   (continued)

Master Status Variables	Not at All	A Few Times per Year	A Few Times per Month	Two to Three Times a Week	Four or More Times a Week	Total N
Marital status:						
Nev. marr., not coh.	30.2	23.5	26.0	13.3	7.0	315
Nev. marr., coh.	1.4	6.9	31.9	43.1	16.7	72
Married	3.0	11.9	46.5	31.9	6.6	905
Div./sep./wid., not coh.	34.3	23.2	21.9	16.8	3.7	297
Div./sep./wid., coh.	0.0	9.4	39.6	39.6	11.3	53
Education:						
Less than HS	18.7	14.5	36.2	22.6	8.1	235
HS grad. or eq.	10.8	15.9	37.7	29.6	6.0	483
Some coll./voc.	13.5	15.9	37.7	25.2	7.7	571
Finished coll.	12.5	18.3	33.5	29.7	6.1	263
Master's/adv. deg.	17.8	15.8	44.6	17.8	4.0	101
Religion:						
None	10.1	18.9	36.5	25.7	8.8	148
Type I Prot.[b]	12.9	17.4	39.8	25.1	4.7	402
Type II Prot.[b]	14.8	14.3	36.0	26.0	8.9	608
Catholic	14.4	15.6	37.0	27.5	5.4	443
Race/ethnicity:[c]						
White	12.8	16.4	38.1	26.2	6.7	1,277
Black	17.0	18.3	32.5	25.1	7.1	323
Hispanic	11.4	10.2	35.2	33.0	10.2	176

Note: For abbreviations of master status variables, see the note to table 3.1.

[a]Cross section $N = 3,159$.

[b]For an explanation of categories of Protestants, see appendix 3.1A.

[c]With oversample, $N = 3,432$.

percent of the sample reported having had no sex at all in the last year. While the frequency of sex did not vary significantly by gender, women are slightly more likely to have been sexually inactive in the past year than men (14 percent of women compared with 10 percent of men). To summarize the overall pattern, American adults fall roughly into three levels of activity in partnered sex. About 35 percent of the total have sex with a partner at least two or more times a week, and nearly 30 percent have partnered sex only a few times a year or not at all. The remaining 35 percent have partnered sex once or several times a month.

Contrary to the historically popular stereotypes of group differences in rates of sexual conduct, we found only minor variations in frequency of partnered sex across race and ethnicity, religious affiliation, and level of education.

Blacks, whites, and Hispanics reported broadly similar rates, with Hispanic men being somewhat more likely to report higher frequencies of sex. The current religion of the respondents was not related to frequency of sex. While men reporting no religion were slightly more sexually active than men reporting a religious affiliation, women who reported no religion were just as likely to report high frequencies of sexual activity as were conservative Protestants (see the row in table 3.4 labeled "Protestant Type II"; see appendix 3.1A at the end of this chapter for explanations of the terms "Type I" and "Type II" Protestants.) Finally, although respondents who did not complete high school were somewhat more likely to report having had no sex last year, a respondent's level of education generally appeared to have little effect on reported frequency, at least for the broad middle ranges of educational attainment in the United States, which include high school graduates through college graduates and constitute 79 percent of the population eighteen to fifty-nine years of age. The data indicate that highly educated women (i.e., those with master's or other advanced degrees) have relatively lower rates of partnered sex. Part of the explanation may be found in the fact that these women are less likely to have had a sex partner in the past year than are less highly educated women.

Social characteristics that did relate strongly to reported frequencies of partnered sexual activity were age and marital status. We found the largest gender discrepancies in frequency of sex when controlling for age. For instance, for both genders, age was curvilinearly related to having had no sex partner in the past year, but with markedly different patterns for men and women. Younger respondents (eighteen- to twenty-four-year-olds) were more likely to have had no partnered sex in the last year, with 15 percent of the men and 11 percent of the women reporting no sociosexual (i.e., partnered) activity. This should not be surprising since this is the period during which people change partners frequently and during which many young people are just beginning to have sex. Rates of sociosexual inactivity drop rapidly for twenty-four- to twenty-nine-year-olds and increase slightly for respondents in their early thirties (perhaps because this age group encompasses a higher number of divorcing couples, whose patterns of sexual activity are likely to be disrupted). At this point, gender-based patterns of sociosexual inactivity begin to diverge. While rates for men stabilize at around 7 percent without a partner and begin to increase moderately for respondents in their late forties, rates of sociosexual inactivity for women increase steadily from the early thirties (8 percent) to the early fifties (19 percent) and increase dramatically in the late fifties (41 percent).

Since this overall pattern of the interaction of gender and age with sexual inactivity is of critical importance in understanding the social organization of sexuality in the United States, we graph the data reported in table 3.4 in figure 3.1. We are able to extend the age range covered in the figure to those aged eighty-five and over by estimating the percentages of the sexually inactive from pooled data gathered by the GSS in 1988, 1989, 1990, and 1991 for adults

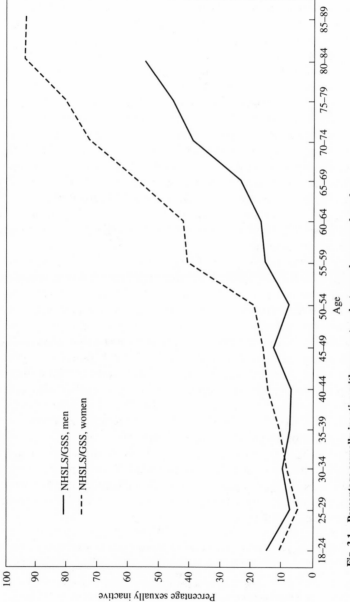

Fig. 3.1 Percentage sexually inactive with any partner last year, by age and gender.
Note: Frequency data for ages sixty to eighty-nine are taken from the General Social Survey (GSS).

aged sixty years and older.[2] The GSS used the same sampling frame that the NHSLS used, but it did not impose an upper age limit on the selection of sample respondents. The same question on number of partners was asked in the GSS as was used in our survey (for an extended analysis of the GSS data, see Michael et al. 1993).[3] The over-sixty age groups show a continuing discrepancy between the genders in their likelihood of being sexually inactive in the past year. By ages seventy to seventy-four, over 70 percent of the women are sociosexually inactive, while only 35 percent of the men in that age group, half the number of women, report that they are sociosexually inactive.

While biologically based changes brought on by the process of aging certainly play a role in sexual activity among those over sixty, we believe that such an explanatory framework cannot account for the particular patterns revealed by our data. A more complete framework for understanding the divergent gender-based experiences of our respondents would take into account the normative effect of aging. How do culturally sanctioned conceptions of the sexuality of older women affect their likelihood of having sex? Put differently, what resources—sexual, social, economic—can older women bring to the sexual marketplace that can overcome the deeply ingrained cultural prejudice against their participation?

The patterns that we see revealed by age, however, may also represent veiled relations with another crucial factor in explaining differential rates of sociosexual activity—marital status. A widespread myth about sociosexual activity is that it becomes routinized, dull, and progressively less frequent in the context of marriage—popularly felt to be one of the least favorable methods of ensuring an active and exciting sex life. In fact, what we find is that married respondents are among the more sociosexually active individuals in our sample (cf. Blumstein and Schwartz 1983). While their rates are below those of never-married partners who are living together—by far the most sociosexually active, with 19 percent of the men and 17 percent of the women having sex four or more times a week—the latter are, at any given moment in time, a very small proportion of the population (some 7 percent) and heavily concentrated among the youngest age groups. Much of the sociosexual activity noted for respondents in their mid-twenties is no doubt due to the rapid rate at which marriage occurs during this period. When age is controlled, the frequency of marital sex more nearly approximates (but still does not equal) that of cohabitational sex (data not shown).

2. We were able to pool the four annual surveys into one grand sample because, after very careful examination, we were unable to detect any significant differences between the sample years—i.e., there is no time trend in these data. Such a change might have been anticipated because of the growing concerns about the AIDS epidemic in the population at large. One response could have been a reduction in the number of sex partners in the past year. This was not observed.

3. We compared the GSS estimates for the eighteen- to fifty-nine-year-old age groups with those of NHSLS and found only negligible differences between them. Figure 3.1 plots only the NHSLS estimates (from table 3.4) and uses the GSS estimates for the over-sixty age groups. No estimate is given if the base N is fewer than thirty respondents.

When marital status is viewed as a feature of a sexual partnership, however, neither the high frequency of marital sex nor the decline of sociosexual activity with age comes as a great surprise. Although we delve more deeply into the characteristics of partnerships and their significance later in this chapter, it is important to establish at the outset how marital status, in particular, functions at the level of the dyad to structure sexual practices. At the most obvious level, marriage provides (as does cohabitation) easier physical access to a person who is expected to be a willing sex partner. Living with a partner ensures that the option of sex, at least, may be available on a fairly regular basis. Over time, the very predictability and routinization of sex that marriage facilitates may contribute to its decreased incidence, especially as it becomes increasingly competitive with child-care responsibilities and growing work and financial responsibilities and stresses as the family grows (Goldscheider and Waite 1991).

Declining frequencies of sexual activity for older couples may have as much to do, then, with the length and nature of their interpersonal relationships and other network obligations (to children, aging parents, etc.) as they do with the physiological effect of aging per se. Divorce, the death of a spouse, and social proscriptions of sexual assertiveness will leave a significant proportion of middle-aged women without access to a sex partner (see fig. 3.1). Not subject to the same cultural sanctions, middle-aged men acquire new partners at a much higher rate and will, in turn, experience frequencies of sexual activity that approach those of younger people. Note again, however, that both the proximity of partners and the length of a sexual relationship are characteristics of partnerships, not individuals.

The Duration of Partnered Sex

The character of the partnership in which sexual activity occurs also influences the amount of time invested in typical sociosexual events. One interpretation of the data presented in table 3.5 on the duration of the respondent's last event might be that the length of the average sexual transaction is a function of age.[4] Age appears to be associated with both an increase in the percentage of shorter sexual events and a decline in the proportion of extended sexual encounters. We have defined events that respondents reported as lasting fifteen minutes or less as *shorter sexual events* and those lasting an hour or more as *extended sexual events*. We have not used the times given because of the well-known inability of individuals to recall actual times of events and people's equally well-known tendency to overestimate times of events. We therefore

4. We do not propose to treat people's reports of the length of time that their last sexual event took as being especially precise with respect to the number of minutes elapsed. People are focused on other things than keeping track of the time, and there are inherent and unresolved ambiguities in defining the beginning and the end of a sexual event. We do believe, however, that people can provide reasonable indications of the relative amounts of time spent involved in sexual activity, and we have therefore focused on people's sense of the event being very brief (less than fifteen minutes) or quite long (over an hour).

Table 3.5   **Duration of Last Event[a] by Master Status Variables**
(% distributions)

Master Status Variables	Duration of Last Sexual Event (%)					
	Fifteen Minutes or Less		One Hour or More		Total	
	Men	Women	Men	Women	Men	Women
Total population[b]	11.0	14.7	19.7	14.8	45.3	54.7
Age:						Total N
18–24	4.8	7.3	30.7	22.6	189	248
25–29	6.7	10.2	26.4	19.0	193	216
30–34	6.8	13.1	23.7	15.4	190	260
35–39	11.5	16.7	20.9	10.1	182	228
40–44	10.3	12.2	13.3	15.3	165	189
45–49	18.8	17.9	12.0	10.5	117	134
50–54	21.9	25.9	6.3	9.3	96	108
55–59	21.3	35.9	4.0	2.6	75	78
Marital status:						
Nev. marr., not coh.	3.5	6.6	38.0	32.8	287	229
Nev. marr., coh.	7.3	17.7	25.5	11.8	55	68
Married	15.9	16.1	9.3	7.8	690	900
Div./sep./wid., not coh.	3.2	16.5	32.3	25.8	124	194
Div./sep./wid., coh.	13.2	13.7	18.4	13.7	38	51
Education:						
Less than HS	19.2	25.9	19.9	14.2	156	197
HS grad. or eq.	12.3	16.7	18.6	14.0	349	443
Some coll./voc.	8.1	12.3	22.3	16.1	385	496
Finished coll.	8.8	9.0	17.2	14.1	204	234
Master's/adv. deg.	9.3	8.4	16.7	13.3	108	83
Religion:						
None	8.8	13.2	26.3	20.2	160	129
Type I Prot.[c]	9.9	14.2	17.7	12.0	282	359
Type II Prot.[c]	14.1	16.9	18.8	14.4	383	524
Catholic	10.4	13.7	18.6	15.8	328	393
Race/ethnicity:[d]						
White	9.7	14.1	19.4	13.5	959	1124
Black	15.2	17.5	25.0	21.5	184	274
Hispanic	13.3	18.2	15.9	15.6	113	154

Note: For abbreviations of master status variables, see the note to table 3.1.

[a]*Last event* refers to the respondent's most recent sexual event ocurring in the twelve months prior to the interview.

[b]Cross section $N = 2,703$.

[c]For an explanation of the categories of Protestants, see appendix 3.1A.

[d]With oversample, $N = 2,936$.

treat the time of the event as an ordinal rather than an interval scale. Of eighteen- to twenty-four-year-old respondents, 31 percent of men and 23 percent of women reported having extended sexual events (an hour or more). However, the proportion of fifty-five- to fifty-nine-year-olds reporting extended sexual events was under 5 percent.

There are at least three general interpretations of these data. First, age may be seen to influence one's energy or physical stamina for sexual activity. Yet, while age may have some effect on the capacity to mobilize sexually specific physical resources (on the association of physical sexual dysfunction with age, see chapter 10), differences in reported duration of sexual events may be more effectively explained through reference to variation in the social circumstances and cultural constructions of sexual interaction. For instance, different age cohorts may have different typical understandings of what constitutes a sexual event. As we will see, older respondents are less likely to engage in such practices as oral sex, tending to focus almost exclusively on vaginal intercourse. To the extent that the practice of oral sex is associated with other forms of foreplay or non–genitally oriented sexual techniques, older respondents will tend to have considerably shorter sexual encounters.

Third, older respondents are also more likely to be engaged in long-term stable relationships in which the duration of sexual events may be defined as the length of sexual intercourse itself. Younger respondents are more likely to be involved in short-term or relatively new relationships in which sexual activity is more salient. Time spent together, say on a date, may be seen to revolve more explicitly around sexual activity than day-to-day interaction in a shared household. In addition to sexual intercourse itself, the perceived length of a sexual event for these partnerships may include kissing and petting, disrobing, and extended foreplay—activities that are less likely to form a major component of sexual events with a familiar partner.

Indeed, significant discrepancies are found when considering the relation between the length of the last sexual event and marital status. Of the never-married noncohabiting respondents, only 4 percent of men and 7 percent of women said that their last sexual event lasted only a short time, while 38 percent of men and 33 percent of women reported extended sexual events. The proportion of cohabiting respondents reporting extended sexual events declined to 26 percent of men and only 12 percent of women, and the equivalent proportion of married respondents was under 10 percent for both genders. These fairly dramatic declines in reported length of sexual event indicate that the third explanation discussed above may be of particular import in understanding the organization and perception of time spent on sexual activity.

While understanding the variation in the frequency and duration of partnered sexual activity affords considerable insight into people's sex lives, it is only one facet of the whole spectrum of sexual expression. In the next section, we move beyond the undifferentiated notion of sexual activity employed thus far to examine the actual substance of sexual behavior.

3.2 Sexual Techniques with Opposite-Gender Partners

What actually occurs during sex with a partner is an extremely private matter, but one with important social consequences, whether entangling alliances, pregnancy and birth, violence, or disease. As with many other "private" behaviors, one can find a host of social consequences for what two consenting adults agree to do in private. However, what consequences will be counted as of interest to the state or society remains a complex and divisive matter. The advent of HIV/AIDS brought home once again how costly the ramifications of sexual behavior can be. Yet, at the same time as specific sexual techniques have become an increasingly important focus of concern, it has become ever more apparent how limited our knowledge of them is. Answers to basic questions like who does what, how often, and with whom have simply been unavailable until the recent spate of work has begun to fill in some of the answers (e.g., Billy et al. 1993; Sonenstein, Pleck, and Ku 1989a, 1989b; Catania et al. 1992b).

We were concerned, however, with questions relevant not only to the AIDS epidemic but also to our broader understanding of sexuality (for earlier work taking this perspective, see Blumstein and Schwartz 1983). To address these needs, our interviews elicited information on the occurrence and incidence of four basic sexual techniques utilized in sex between women and men—vaginal intercourse, fellatio, cunnilingus, and anal intercourse—in the most recent sexual event, during the past year, and over the life course.[5] We also gathered information on sexual techniques in same-gender sexual partnerships but have chosen to analyze these data in chapter 8.

The extent and rapidity of sexual transformations in the United States have been, and continue to be, subjects of great debate. Many commentators have been quick to use the term *revolution* to characterize poorly documented changes in certain aspects of sexual activity in the United States. What is meant—when the "revolution" began (if it did), to whom it applied, and what changes it wrought—remains contested. As we see in chapter 5, patterns of sexual partnering underwent significant change in the 1960s, and it is this shift away from "monogamous" sexuality that is usually associated with the "sexual revolution." (For contemporary discussions of these changes, see Athanasiou

---

5. The reader will note a shift in data presentation in subsequent tables in this chapter from that of table 3.4, which presented the complete distributions of responses to the frequency of partnered sex by master statuses. There is simply not the space—or, we suspect, the reader patience—to inspect detailed frequency distributions for each sexual practice and outcome. We have adopted the strategy of presenting selected features of the frequency distribution for a particular practice that, in our judgment, best conveys in abbreviated form the nature of the overall distribution of responses. Most of the distributions on sexual practices are not well-behaved normal distributions with a well-defined mean or central tendency and symmetrically infrequent outliers on either side of it. Typically, they are highly skewed, with most respondents falling into one category and a rapid tailing off in one direction. The number of partners (discussed in chapter 5) exemplifies the pattern.

1973; Bartell 1970; Cannon and Long 1971; Cherlin 1978; Chilman 1978; Clayton and Bokemeier 1980; Ferrel, Tolone, and Walsh 1977; Goldscheider and Waite 1991; Reiss 1986; Scanzoni et al. 1989; Schwartz and Gillmore 1990; Westoff and Ryder 1977.) Yet equally significant changes were occurring in mainstream notions of the appropriate content of sex acts between women and men. The menu of appropriate sexual "techniques" (discrete forms of physical interaction oriented toward either mutual or one-sided sexual pleasure) began to expand during this period, providing both new options and new responsibilities.

To gain more insight into these trends, we asked our respondents to report whether they had ever experienced any of four sexual techniques practiced by opposite-sex couples—vaginal, oral (active and receptive), and anal sex. Excepting vaginal intercourse, table 3.6 presents these lifetime percentages by the master status variables alongside the proportion reporting the occurrence of the specified technique in the last sexual event. These two analyses are based on different populations: the former on all respondents regardless of current partnership status, the latter on those respondents with an opposite-gender last-event sex partner. This juxtaposition provides some indication of the extent to which the practice in question constitutes a regular, an episodic, or an isolated occurrence in the sex life of the respondent.[6]

Vaginal Intercourse

Vaginal intercourse was excluded from the table owing to the lack of notable variation in its distribution across the master status variables. Ninety-five percent of men and 97 percent of women reported a lifetime incidence of vaginal intercourse, with only marginally fewer respondents reporting its occurrence in the last sexual event. These findings confirm the near universality of vaginal intercourse as a defining sexual technique of heterosexuality. The small proportions of the population who have not had vaginal intercourse at least one time in their lives (5 percent of men and 3 percent of women) represent both respondents who have not yet begun having partnered sex with the opposite gender and those respondents who have not engaged in vaginal sex owing to a persistent lack of desire or opportunity. This former population is, of course, concentrated in the younger age categories, for whom either lack of opportunity or beliefs have limited premarital sexuality. For example, 12 percent of eighteen- to twenty-four-year-old men had never had vaginal intercourse. The proportion reporting experience with vaginal intercourse continues to increase in successive age categories, stabilizing (at around 97–99 percent) for men in their mid-thirties or older. While on average men report an earlier age at first

6. We also have reports on how regularly these practices occur over the course of the past year (see appendix C, section 4, questions 29–34). Because of space limitations, we do not include this information in these tables, although we have carefully inspected these data to discern patterns and have used them in interpreting the results for lifetime and last event.

Table 3.6   **Selected Sexual Practices, by Master Status Variables (% distributions)**

	Mean Frequency of Sex per Month[b]		Sexual Practices[a]							
			Occurrence of Active Oral Sex (%)				Occurrence of Receptive Oral Sex (%)			
			Men		Women		Men		Women	
Master Status Variables	Men	Women	Life	Last Event	Life	Last Event	Life	Last Event	Life	Last Event
Total population[c]	6.5	6.3	76.6	26.8	67.7	18.8	78.7	27.5	73.1	19.9
Age:										
18–24	7.2	7.4	72.4	27.7	69.1	19.1	74.2	28.9	74.7	24.2
25–29	7.6	7.5	84.8	32.0	76.2	23.8	84.8	33.7	79.8	24.3
30–34	6.7	6.8	78.9	29.6	76.6	19.1	78.9	32.2	83.1	22.3
35–39	6.6	6.1	82.3	30.4	71.3	21.0	87.5	29.8	73.7	23.3
40–44	5.9	5.5	84.0	31.2	72.7	16.9	85.7	28.9	76.8	12.6
45–49	6.2	5.5	73.4	21.2	65.2	21.6	77.4	22.1	72.7	18.3
50–54	5.5	4.6	60.0	16.1	48.5	11.7	66.0	13.8	59.4	12.6
55–59	4.4	3.5	58.4	9.9	38.9	5.5	58.0	14.1	44.3	6.9
Marital status:										
Nev. marr., not coh.	5.6	5.3	66.7	28.9	59.4	21.0	70.3	32.8	67.7	26.8
Nev. marr., coh.	8.6	8.8	85.7	30.2	72.2	21.5	89.3	34.0	76.4	22.7
Married	6.9	6.5	79.9	25.2	70.7	16.9	80.4	23.0	73.9	16.9
Div./sep./wid., not coh.	5.4	5.1	81.5	30.1	64.1	25.4	88.1	34.5	73.1	24.2
Div./sep./wid., coh.	8.0	7.6	80.0	29.7	79.6	16.3	80.0	37.8	85.2	20.4
Education:										
Less than HS	6.5	6.3	59.2	16.4	41.1	10.1	60.7	16.4	49.6	13.2
HS grad. or eq.	6.9	6.3	75.3	30.1	59.6	16.4	76.6	25.3	67.1	18.5
Some coll./voc.	6.6	6.3	80.0	31.3	78.2	20.7	84.0	31.0	81.6	22.2
Finished coll.	6.0	6.4	83.7	23.7	78.9	22.9	84.6	31.1	83.1	20.7
Master's/adv. deg.	6.1	5.1	80.5	20.6	79.0	28.8	81.4	30.4	81.9	27.0
Religion:										
None	6.7	6.3	78.9	33.8	77.9	29.2	83.2	35.2	83.3	30.6
Type I Prot.[d]	6.2	5.8	81.9	26.9	74.5	19.6	82.8	23.5	77.4	18.7
Type II Prot.[d]	6.8	6.7	67.1	22.4	55.6	12.9	70.2	24.3	64.8	16.1
Catholic	6.6	6.2	82.4	27.2	73.6	21.5	82.1	29.2	76.6	21.8
Jewish	†	†	†	†	†	†	†	†	†	†
Other	5.6	†	65.8	†	65.7	†	73.7	†	65.7	†
Race/ethnicity:[e]										
White	6.6	6.3	81.4	28.3	75.3	21.0	81.4	28.7	78.9	21.2
Black	6.4	6.2	50.5	16.9	34.4	9.3	66.3	18.2	48.9	13.1
Hispanic	7.7	7.8	70.7	23.5	59.7	18.7	73.2	25.5	63.7	22.0
Asian	5.9	†	63.6	†	†	†	72.7	†	†	†
Total N[f]	1,200	1,437	1,321	1,109	1,661	1,380	1,038	1,109	1,660	1,384

Table 3.6   (continued)

	Sexual Practices							
	Occurrence of Anal Sex (%)[g]							
	Men			Women			Total	
	Life	Last Year	Last Event	Life	Last Year	Last Event	Men	Women
Total population[c]	25.6	9.6	2.3	20.4	8.6	1.2	44.6	55.4
Age:							Total N	
18–24	15.8	7.4	1.8	16.2	10.1	.9	226	276
25–29	22.4	11.2	1.2	20.3	11.9	2.4	224	234
30–34	30.2	10.3	2.8	21.2	8.1	1.2	228	291
35–39	32.3	11.9	1.7	27.5	9.5	0.0	203	266
40–44	40.1	13.0	3.8	23.2	8.3	.5	186	229
45–49	23.8	10.3	2.8	26.1	9.5	3.2	140	168
50–54	14.0	3.1	1.1	14.4	1.9	0.0	109	143
55–59	18.6	4.0	4.2	9.2	2.5	1.4	91	140
Marital status:								
Nev. marr., not coh.	17.7	8.9	2.1	19.1	11.8	2.0	406	339
Nev. marr., coh.	30.4	9.1	1.9	18.1	7.4	3.0	61	73
Married	27.1	9.7	2.3	21.3	7.3	1.0	724	949
Div./sep./wid., not coh.	35.2	10.5	3.5	20.0	10.2	.6	165	310
Div./sep./wid., coh.	25.7	10.5	2.6	22.2	13.5	0.0	38	56
Education:								
Less than HS	21.0	8.9	1.4	12.7	8.5	.5	190	246
HS grad. or eq.	23.1	8.0	3.4	16.6	7.4	1.7	403	512
Some coll./voc.	25.7	9.2	1.1	24.6	10.2	1.1	450	588
Finished coll.	30.5	12.0	3.1	21.8	7.2	.9	239	281
Master's/adv. deg.	29.2	12.7	2.9	28.6	8.3	1.3	121	109
Religion:								
None	34.1	9.2	.7	36.1	16.7	2.5	194	152
Type I Prot.[d]	22.1	7.3	1.5	20.4	7.7	.6	324	422
Type II Prot.[d]	21.0	7.2	1.7	16.8	5.9	1.2	444	631
Catholic	28.1	13.0	3.6	19.8	9.8	1.1	377	476
Jewish	†	†	†	†	†	†	26	29
Other	29.7	27.3	†	25.7	†	†	41	37
Race/ethnicity:[e]								
White	25.8	8.3	1.8	23.2	8.4	1.2	1114	1338
Black	23.4	9.7	3.0	9.6	6.0	1.5	208	342
Hispanic	34.2	18.9	3.9	17.0	12.5	0.7	137	184
Asian	15.2	†	†	†	†	†	35	30
Total N[f]	1,309	1,236	1,124	1,658	1,477	1,383	1,407	1,747

Note: † indicates that the base N for that cell was under thirty cases. For the abbreviations of master status variables, see the note to table 3.1.

(continued)

Table 3.6   (continued)

aPercentages are calculated on the basis of three time periods: over the life course, over the past year, and during the last sexual event. The relevant sample varies over the different time periods. Lifetime inquiries are based on the entire cross section; the last event and the last year include only those respondents who engaged in opposite-gender partnered sex in the last year.
bAverage frequency of sex is calculated for those respondents who experienced any partnered sex in the last year regardless of the gender of the sexual partner.
cCross section $N = 3,159$.
dFor an explanation of the categories of Protestants, see appendix 3.1A.
eWith oversample, $N = 3,432$.
fTotal N for column category (i.e., each sexual practice variable by gender—the three-way subtables by age, marital status, etc.) may be slightly reduced depending on the number of cases missing from each master status variable. Column N's also do not take into account the inclusion of the oversample used to calculate percentages by ethnicity ($N = 3,432$). Row N's, however, do take into account the inclusion of the oversample.
gQuestions concerning the occurrence of anal sex in the last year are partner specific—we ask only whether anal sex occurred within the "primary" or "secondary" partnership last year. To the extent that respondents experienced anal sex in partnerships other than primary or secondary, the percentages reported may slightly underestimate the true sample proportion of respondents who experienced anal sex in the last year.

intercourse than women, there is a substantial proportion of both women and men who do not start intercourse until their late teens or early twenties, deferring their initial experience of intercourse until marriage (for a more extended discussion of age at first intercourse, see chapter 9). After the teenage years, those women who have not experienced intercourse tend to become sexually active earlier than men who have not. Thus, only 6 percent of eighteen- to twenty-four-year-old women had not experienced vaginal intercourse. And, of those women who will have vaginal intercourse at all during their lifetime, most have done so by their late twenties.

The salience of vaginal sex as the defining technique in sex between women and men is reflected in the data on the incidence of vaginal sex in the last sexual event for opposite-gender couples. Recall that these data are based only on those who had an opposite-gender last-event partner. Ninety-five percent of the last events reported by men and 96 percent of those reported by women included vaginal intercourse. The conventional sex script still seems to terminate in vaginal intercourse in most sexual encounters (i.e., although postcoital petting may ensue, no other discrete genitally oriented acts occur). These proportions are stable across all the master statuses with only a few groups reporting an incidence lower than 95 percent. These differences are small but include those who are never married and not living with a partner (14 percent of men and 13 percent of women report a sexual event that did not include vaginal intercourse), and the most-educated women (11 percent). The view in popular sexual practice and belief that vaginal intercourse *is* sex tends to be confirmed by these data, although a significant minority of sexual events between women and men do not involve vaginal intercourse.

Oral Sex

The apparent consensus surrounding the central role of vaginal intercourse in the sexual event may be contrasted with the far more ambiguous status of oral sex. The proportion of men reporting any lifetime incidence of fellatio performed on them by a woman was roughly the same as the equivalent figure of women reporting cunnilingus performed on them by a man—approaching three-quarters. Yet the proportion for whom oral sex is a current activity (as measured by its occurrence in the last sexual event) is roughly 50 percentage points lower, at around one-quarter. Oral sex, then, is a technique with which most people have at least some familiarity, but it has in no sense become a defining feature of sex between women and men (as vaginal intercourse or, perhaps, kissing is). Indeed, the relatively high incidence of lifetime experience with oral sex means that a variety of responses to oral sex are likely—some may find it acceptable and legitimate, others offensive. Those who find oral sex an acceptable or legitimate practice may or may not also find it appealing. Although we consider the appeal of oral sex and other sexual techniques in the next chapter, it is important to establish at the outset the ambiguity of oral sex in the repertoire of sexual techniques.

The uncertainty surrounding oral sex has the most immediate implications for relations between the genders. The term *oral sex* refers to two discrete practices—fellatio and cunnilingus—which are often viewed as oriented primarily toward the sexual pleasure of the receptive sexual partner. Unlike vaginal intercourse, which, according to one cultural ideal, should produce mutual, genitally oriented sexual pleasure with a single act (if not in time, at least in space),[7] fellatio and cunnilingus are often performed independently of one another, as "before vaginal intercourse play." This fact should not preclude a recognition that the person who receives oral sex is not the only person who is experiencing pleasure. Performing oral sex is often as arousing as receiving it. While we did not ask whether respondents found performing oral sex arousing, we did ask whether they found it appealing. These items are analyzed in chapter 4. In addition, mutual or simultaneous oral sex between women and men does occur in some proportion of sexual encounters, but we did not ask about this in our study.

The typically sequential performance of the two acts implies an ongoing potential problem of reciprocity and the differential symbolic meanings of oral sex. The problem is not merely one of mutual reciprocity but the issue of what kind of man or woman performs oral sex and in what kind of relationship. Oral sex is fraught with symbolic ambiguity. Should "good" women do it? What kind of man would do it?

7. Such radical feminist writers as Dworkin (1987) have argued that the centrality of vaginal intercourse is a patriarchal construct that serves to reproduce the sexual domination of women by men while denying the former sexual pleasure.

With these issues in mind, we wanted to compare the two genders in terms of both active and passive participation in oral sex. Focusing on the last event, 27 percent of men reported performing cunnilingus on their partner, and 28 percent reported receiving fellatio. While the way in which these percentages are computed does not permit us to infer that the same men practiced both forms of oral sex,[8] we can say that, in general, men report receiving oral sex as often as they perform it on their partners. Equal percentages of women received and performed oral sex during the last sexual event as well; however, both proportions are roughly 8 percentage points lower than the figures reported by men. This discrepancy poses a problem similar to the one we encounter in chapter 5 regarding the gender discrepancy in reporting number of sex partners. It may be that men are slightly overreporting the incidence of oral sex in the last sexual event, or that women are underreporting its occurrence, or both. It may also be that men are engaging in oral sex with women who are underrepresented in the sample. The latter option, however, seems unlikely since the vast majority of our respondents are currently involved in longer-term stable relationships and few have more than one partner—either simultaneously or sequentially. In any case, within gender, reports of the occurrence of fellatio and cunnilingus in the last event appear to be equal.

The emergence of oral sex as a widespread technique practiced by opposite-gender sex partners probably began in the 1920s, and over the past seventy years it has become more common in various social contexts and among most social groups. If there has been any basic change in the script for sex between women and men, it is the increase in the incidence and frequency of fellatio and cunnilingus. Kinsey and his colleagues reported that about 70 percent of the white, middle-class, and well-educated married couples who volunteered to be interviewed in his studies (these individuals' marital lives were spent between 1925 and 1945) reported that they had had oral sex at least one time. These were clearly the avant-garde of the sexual revolution in our society. Our data suggest that this proportion is now to be found in nearly all sections of society, not just the better-educated and middle-class groups.

The trend that has brought oral sex to its contemporary prevalence is illustrated when age is controlled. It is useful to think of the effect of age, however, not in terms of the effect of advancing years, but rather as an indication of when the respondent became sexually active. Figure 3.2 displays the percentages of men and women who have experienced either cunnilingus or fellatio in their lifetime by birth cohort. This combined measure does not reveal a significant increase in lifetime experience over the independent measures reported in table 3.6, indicating that the occurrence of cunnilingus and that of fellatio are highly mutually correlated. However, roughly 8 percent of both

8. Since the data refer to the last act, we can calculate how many respondents reported that their last event included both fellatio and cunnilingus. Men reported that 18 percent of their last sexual events included both forms of oral sex, women 12 percent.

A. Men

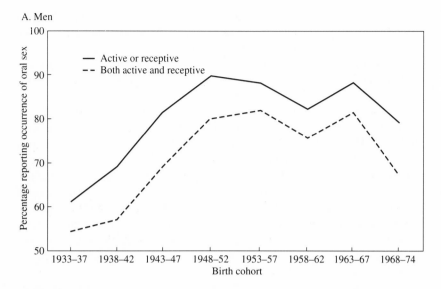

B. Women

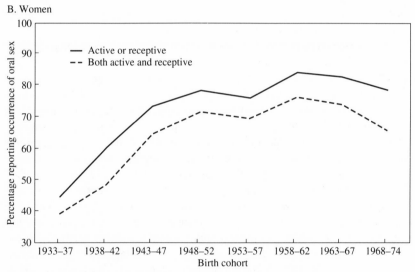

Fig. 3.2   Lifetime occurrence of oral sex, by cohort. A, Men. B, Women.

men and women have experienced only one type of oral sex. Independent analyses (not presented) demonstrate that the majority of these respondents have experienced only receptive oral sex and that these respondents are concentrated in the earlier birth cohorts.

The overall trend of figure 3.2, however, reveals what we might call a rapid change in sexual techniques, if not a revolution. The difference in lifetime experience of oral sex between respondents born between 1933 and 1942 (who would have been age eighteen in the decade 1951–60) and those born after 1943 (who became age eighteen in the 1960s and after) is dramatic. The proportion of men experiencing oral sex in their lifetime increases from 62 percent of those born between 1933 and 1937 to 90 percent of those born between 1948 and 1952. The significant increase in lifetime experience occurs for cohorts coming of sexual age (twenty to twenty-four) just prior to 1968. Indeed, no further increase in lifetime experience occurs for respondents born after 1948–52. The timing of changes in sexual techniques appears to have been responsive to cultural changes in the late 1950s, changes that peaked in the mid- to late 1960s, when they approached saturation level in the population. The lower rates among the youngest groups in our survey are not necessarily evidence of a decline in oral sex; these groups simply have not yet engaged in sexual relationships in which oral sex has become likely, if not normative.

These data seem to confirm the possibility that, prior to the mid-1960s and perhaps even as early as the 1950s, oral sex was being practiced more widely outside marriage and in groups in which it had previously been relatively uncommon (although it is also possible that many older cohort members may have experienced oral sex after their initial period of sexual socialization in response to the changes of the 1960s).

The broader significance of these findings, however, is their demonstration of the importance of sociohistorical factors in producing and changing sexual practice—certainly not an obvious perspective for sex researchers prior to the 1980s.[9] Kinsey, for instance, felt that stimulation of the genitals by the mouth was a form of "oral eroticism" rooted, along with most sexual techniques, in the mammalian heritage. Oral sex was simply another "biological potential urge" of the human animal, and its relative absence from the typical repertoire of sexual techniques was a function of civilized repression.

Yet it is hard to imagine that the increased prevalence of fellatio and cunnilingus is due to the removal of normative barriers to a "natural" mammalian sexual practice. Although our data cannot directly address hypotheses concerning the emergence of particular sexual techniques, we nevertheless stress the importance of social factors in facilitating change in sexual practice. For instance, the growth in rates of lifetime experience of oral sex for older cohorts may be attributable in part to the development in the late 1950s and early 1960s of a sizable population of young single people in urban centers. The prolifera-

9. The view that sexuality is culturally conditioned was widespread among such anthropologists as Margaret Mead and Ruth Benedict in the 1930s, and it is now widespread among cultural anthropologists today (see, e.g., Ortner and Whitehead 1981a, 1981b; Herdt and Stoller 1990). Since the 1980s, many historians have focused on the cultural and social construction of sexuality and gender, in part influenced by the French philosopher/historian Michel Foucault (1978) and social constructionist approaches to sexuality developed in sociology in the late 1960s and early 1970s (Gagnon and Simon 1973). Such a constructionist perspective is not common among many sex researchers, who specialize in research on contemporary sexual practices.

tion of clerical and secretarial positions generated by the expansion of the corporate sector in most major cities provided new opportunities, especially for young unmarried women, to live and work in urban centers (D'Emilio and Freedman 1988; Ehrenreich 1986). This demographic shift resulted in the development of a distinct urban "singles" culture in which multiple partnering was a more common occurrence and sexuality was the object of an increasingly widespread consumerism. The nonmarital and recreational nature of sexuality in this population may have initiated a rapid and eventually far-reaching diffusion of increasingly elaborate sexual practices such as fellatio and cunnilingus. These demographic and economic factors undoubtedly interacted with emerging movements toward "sexual liberation" to encourage certain social groups to incorporate oral sex into their sexual routines. However, it appears that the politically oriented movements salient during the latter half of the 1960s did not *initiate* the increased incidence of oral sex. Rather, this period appears to mark a *leveling off* of the trend. From this perspective, new forms of sexual practice were simply socially diffused and not the products of some newly released biological propensity.

Testament to the socially organized nature of sexual techniques is the fact that growth in rates of lifetime occurrence of oral sex has by no means been uniform across social categories. Both the youth-oriented urban cultures of the early 1960s (cf. Lofland 1970) and their more politically oriented counterparts of the late 1960s were confined largely to white middle- and upper-middle-class populations. To the extent that sex partner choice within these groups was homophilous (see chapter 6), sexual practices that gained popularity within them would not tend to spread beyond their boundaries. A consideration of such social characteristics as education and race confirms that growth in rates of lifetime experience with oral sex has not been uniform. For instance, less-educated respondents are significantly less likely to have experienced oral sex in their lifetime. The same proportion of men—roughly 60 percent—with less than a high school degree have ever experienced fellatio as cunnilingus. Both proportions, however, increase significantly—by 15 percentage points—for men with a high school degree and exceed 80 percent for higher education levels. A similar but even more pronounced leap in lifetime oral sex experience is found among women with higher levels of education. The proportion of women with less than a high school education who have performed fellatio on a partner is only 41 percent, and only 8 percent more have experienced cunnilingus. Yet women with a high school degree reported rates of lifetime experience of both forms of oral sex that are 17–19 percentage points higher, and women with at least some college education were just as likely as men to have ever experienced fellatio or cunnilingus (around 80 percent).

Analysis of the effect of race on lifetime experience of oral sex also reveals significant differences. White respondents have considerably higher rates than all other racial or ethnic groups. Of white men, 81 percent have experienced fellatio, and the same proportion have performed cunnilingus on a partner.

White women are only slightly less likely to have engaged in oral sex (75 percent have fellated a partner, and 79 percent have received cunnilingus). Comparable proportions for black respondents, in particular, are markedly lower. Blacks are some 30 percentage points less likely than whites to have engaged in the two forms of oral sex (excepting the percentage of black men reporting the occurrence of fellatio—66 percent—which was 15 percentage points below that of white men). While these differences are due in part to the significant discrepancies in education level between the two races, multivariate analyses confirm the independent effect of race on the lifetime incidence of oral sex. Previous studies have pointed to the discrepancy in the proportion of whites and blacks performing oral sex (e.g., Hunt et al. 1974), but with little explanation.

Finally, religion is also associated with lifetime incidence of oral sex. Its effect, however, may be minimal owing to the confounding effects of other factors—principally education. One immediate indication that education may be behind some of the differences between religious groups is the fact that religious affiliation alone is not associated with any systematically different behavior. Those respondents who reported having no current religious affiliation were not, on the whole, more or less likely to have experienced oral sex than mainstream Protestants or Catholics (although they were more likely to participate in oral sex regularly). Religiously conservative Protestants (Protestant Type II; see appendix 3.1A for an explanation), however, were much less likely than any of the other three groups to have had oral sex. Sixty-seven percent of conservative Protestant men, for instance, had performed cunnilingus—12 percentage points less than respondents reporting no religion and 15 percentage points less than mainstream Protestants or Catholics. The equivalent discrepancies for lifetime experience of fellatio were 13 and 12 percentage points, respectively. Type II Protestant women reported even lower relative rates of lifetime oral sex experience. While men and women claiming no religion do not differ in their reports of experience with fellatio and cunnilingus, Type II Protestant women were 11 percentage points less likely to have performed oral sex and 5 percentage points less likely to have received it. The distribution across religious groupings corresponds roughly to the distribution of education among them. Type II Protestants tend to have somewhat lower levels of education than Type I ("mainstream"; see appendix 3.1A) Protestants or those without religious affiliation. Catholics are, however, on average less educated but have relatively high rates of lifetime oral sex experience, indicating that Catholics are more accessible to those forces in the society that facilitate rather than inhibit the practice of oral sex.

The current prevalence of oral sex in the United States is the product of a sociohistorically based shift away from the traditional script of the sexual event between women and men as involving a minimum of precoital stimulation and a rapid move to vaginal intercourse. Beginning in the 1920s, the sexual script for opposite-gender sex has become increasingly elaborated to include more kissing, more caressing of the body, more manual genital contact, and, more recently, more oral sex. At the same time, the ultimate goal has largely remained vaginal intercourse. However, as we have seen, the growth in the proportion of the population having experienced oral sex at any time in their life has not been a uniform social phenomenon. While oral sex has become a nearly universal technique for the vast majority of people (the better educated, those under fifty, those belonging to majority religious sects), that oral sex has not become more predominant for other groups has, we think, to do with both a lingering normative constraint on their sexual practices as well as the structure of the sexual networks through which individuals acquire partners. The highly socially structured nature of sexual networks bounds the diffusion of sexual practices. The possession of certain constellations of social characteristics affects the likelihood that a potential sex partner will have experienced oral sex and will in turn encourage or facilitate its occurrence. Indeed, separate analyses (presented below) reveal the strong relation between number and type of sex partners and the occurrence not only of oral sex but of other sexual techniques (e.g., anal sex) as well.

Anal Sex

Unlike oral sex, anal sex has not entered into the repertoire of regular sexual practices for most women and men in the United States, although its prevalence is larger than one might have expected from the limited discussion of the topic in the pre-HIV/AIDS era. Table 3.6 above reports the incidence of heterosexual anal intercourse over the life course, in the past year, and in the last sexual event. We included the figures for the past year to demonstrate the pattern of participation in heterosexual anal sex—one that is peculiar to anal sex as a sexual technique practiced by opposite-gender partners. Rates of participation in oral sex between women and men for the past year were very similar to rates over the lifetime, indicating that those who have experienced oral sex at all are likely to continue to engage in it at least on an occasional basis over the rest of the life course. In contrast, anal sex, which one-quarter of men and one-fifth of women have experienced, is far less frequent in any given year of life. The proportion of respondents who had heterosexual anal intercourse in the last year was 9 percent (recall that this is restricted to people who had a sex partner in the last year). In the last sexual event, only 2 percent of men and 1 percent of women engaged in anal sex (this is based on those with a sexual event in the past year regardless of the character of the partner). Anal intercourse, then, is not only far less frequently experienced over the life course but also far less likely to become a common or even an occasional sexual practice once it has been experienced. However, an annual rate of anal sex of around 10 percent is larger than most observers would have expected, as is the rate of over 1 percent in the last event.

Controlling for cohort membership again reveals a somewhat different pattern of lifetime incidence of anal intercourse when compared with oral sex.

While a fairly steady increase in the proportion of those ever experiencing anal sex occurs for those born from the 1933–37 (people aged fifty-five to fifty-nine) through the 1948–52 (people forty to forty-four) cohorts—from 19 to 40 percent for men and from 9 to 23 percent for women—the proportion declines for the younger cohorts rather than remaining stable (as was the pattern for oral sex). While these lower rates of anal sex among more youthful cohorts may be a result of the role of anal sex in HIV transmission, it could as likely be that experiences with anal sex require a longer engagement in partnered sex and a larger number of sex partners among whom an interested partner might be found. This latter hypothesis is supported by the fact that the decline in lifetime experience with anal sex occurs for cohorts that were sexually active in the 1970s and early 1980s before the onset of the HIV/AIDS epidemic.

Given the evidence about the relation between oral sex and education, we might expect education to be positively correlated with the experience of anal intercourse. To the extent that an experimental sexual ideology is associated with higher levels of education, it would seem reasonable to expect more educated individuals to be inclined to try anal intercourse. We find that level of education is positively associated with lifetime experience with anal intercourse—a pattern similar to those found for cunnilingus and fellatio. However, it is also the case that education is positively related to number and type of sex partners, indicating that more education would be associated with relatively high levels of experience with anal sex. Indeed, what we find is that more education increases the likelihood that an individual will have ever experienced anal sex; however, education is unrelated to the incidence of anal sex in the last year or the last sexual event. Individuals with more education, then, are more likely to experience anal sex but are less likely, once they have, to incorporate it into their regular sex life.

Although new cultural orientations toward sexuality have probably had an effect on the practice of anal sex, older aversions, sometimes based in religious values, no doubt continue to play a role. In contrast to fellatio and cunnilingus, anal sex remains offensive to large segments of the population. While having a religious affiliation was not associated with lifetime incidence of oral sex, it is strongly related to the occurrence of anal sex. Of respondents reporting no religious affiliation, 34 percent of men and 36 percent of women said that they had engaged in anal intercourse at least once in their lifetime. Type I and Type II Protestant men converged in their lifetime reports of anal intercourse at 22 and 21 percent, respectively. Only 20 percent of Type I Protestant women had experienced anal sex—about 3 percentage points more than Type II Protestant women. Religious affiliation is not uniformly associated with lower rates of anal sex, however. Catholic men are somewhat more likely to have had anal sex in their lifetime (28 percent) than Protestants and are almost twice as likely to have experienced it in both the last year and the last sexual event. Oddly, comparable proportions for Catholic women are considerably lower—at around the same level as Protestant women.

These religiously based differences are, to some extent, confounded with ethnicity. Analysis of the distribution of anal sex experience across racial categories reveals significant discrepancies. Hispanic men, in particular, reported considerably higher rates of lifetime anal sex experience than did any other racial or ethnic category (34 percent, as opposed to 26, 23, and 15 percent for white, black, and Asian men, respectively). Although their reported incidence of anal intercourse in the last sexual event did not differ significantly from other groups, the proportion of Hispanic men who had anal sex in the past year was one of the highest of any social category, 19 percent—well over twice that of either black or white men. The high rate of experience with anal sex among Hispanic men may be attributable to the tradition of Latin American machismo, which emphasizes the masculine aspects of penetrative sex, be it vaginal or anal (Parker 1991; Carrier 1989).

The practice of anal intercourse, then, is not limited to the randomly distributed sexual eccentric but is, like the other techniques we have considered thus far, a highly socially structured phenomenon. As we have seen, the better-educated members of the white majority in their thirties and forties (along with Hispanic men) are most likely to have had an experience in their lifetime with anal sex. These characteristics, however, do not appear to structure the incorporation of anal sex into regular sexual repertoires, except among Hispanic men, indicating that lifetime experience with anal sex may for most people be an isolated experimental incident associated with multiple partners. Through expanding opportunities for nonmarital sexual interaction and a more open sexual climate, the sexual transitions of the 1960s undoubtedly facilitated more widespread exposure to the idea of anal sex for cohorts who came of age in this period, as it did for oral sex. However, the apparently persistent effects of religious proscriptions against the practice of anal sex have contributed to its relatively limited popularity.

To his credit, Kinsey was in no way ignorant of the heavily socially structured character of the array of sexual techniques that he studied. In fact, much of the actual presentation of his data was organized around social categories. Yet, despite his inclination to view data through a social matrix, he remained wedded to a simplistic, biologically based conception of sexuality. Kinsey consistently maintained that the social organization of sexual techniques clearly revealed by his own data was a product of variously powerful normative barriers to the expression of basic biological urges. Recognizing the limitations of our data, our objective has been to demonstrate that the techniques that characterize the sexual event, somewhat artificially represented by the four techniques discussed above, have no natural or biologically given order or end state. The recent period of rapid change in sexual practices should be seen, not as a result of unleashed biological proclivities confronting attenuated cultural prohibitions, but as an active process of social construction and transformation.

Sexual Relationships and Sexual Pleasure

The elements of sexual interaction (e.g., hugging or oral sex) do not exist in behavioral isolation. In the case of partnered sex, these acts occur in clusters along with other sexual acts that are generated in interaction with another individual. Together, these acts constitute what we refer to as a *scripted sexual event*. This implies an ordered sequence of events in which actors usually have some knowledge of what is to be expected. This foreknowledge may not exist in cultures where there is widespread ignorance of what constitutes sexual interaction prior to first partnered sex or where violent introductions to sex are common. Even in the United States, large numbers of young people enter sexual interactions with very limited knowledge of what happens after hugging and kissing.

As with the acts that constitute them, sexual events are embedded within a broader setting of activities, interactions, and outcomes, both sexual and nonsexual. The relationship in which the sexual event is produced and the web of relationships surrounding the individuals are major forces shaping the content of the event itself. In this section, we expand our explanatory framework to include not only the social features of the individuals involved but the relevant characteristics of the sexual relationship as well. From a focus on the set of individual attributes brought to bear on sexual acts, we move to a consideration of the social and behavioral context of sexual relationships.

We wish to examine, from the perspective of the kinds of relationships in which individuals are embedded, two sets of practices that may or may not occur in sociosexual relationships. The first of these practices is the experience of sexual satisfaction as measured in terms of either orgasm or subjective reports of physical or emotional satisfaction. The notion that sexual satisfaction is a "social practice" as well as a biological event may be somewhat surprising, especially in a discussion of orgasm. Usually, sexual satisfaction is viewed as the "natural" outcome of the application of correct sexual techniques. As we will see, orgasm is not a "natural" or universal outcome of sexual interaction, no matter how well intended, nor are the senses of physical and emotional well-being that are supposed to accompany sex. The second practice is whether individuals engaged in a sexual interaction consume alcohol or drugs just prior to or during the sexual event. Drinking is complexly related to sexuality: in some encounters it facilitates sociability, in others it is a source of violence, and in still others it enhances or impedes sexual performance.

We will consider the distributions of these practices across master status attributes, but only within a specific sexual partnership. In most cases, the data presented will refer to these practices within heterosexual relationships of various durations within specific levels of personal and social commitment. Thus, the relationships are classified as marriages, cohabitations, longer-term noncohabitational relationships, and shorter-term noncohabitational relationships.

Our method of gathering information on partnerships put the focus on getting information on relationships involving higher levels of social commitment. Time constraints on the interview process and research decisions about what data were important to gather shaped the final distribution of relationships about which we have information. Because of time constraints, we were able to gather detailed information on only two sexual partnerships in the last year. Given that most of our respondents had only one or two sex partners, this did not involve any difficulty of coverage. However, for those with more than two partners, we had to decide which to include in the more detailed questioning. We decided always to include the partnership that had the highest levels of personal and social commitment. Thus, if a person were married and had two other partnerships, we always included the married partner and selected the most recent of the other two partnerships. Similarly, we always chose a cohabitational relationship over others and again selected the most recent of other partners, for those that had two or more additional partnerships. Those respondents who were not living with a partner or married who had two or more partners, we asked whom they viewed as their primary partner. Persons who were not married or living with a partner who had only one partner were not asked who their primary partner was. These decisions mean that our data underrepresent short-term and more casual relationships and make those data less interesting from a public health point of view than they might otherwise be. The data that we present for this discussion (see table 3.7 below) are based on only one of the partnerships for those who reported two or more (as was the case for the data on the last year in table 3.6 above). The data are thus on individuals reporting a single relationship, privileging relationships that involve higher levels of social commitment.

It is important to keep these constraints on the distribution of relationships in mind when interpreting the data presented. For instance, individual level measures of reported incidence of oral sex over the lifetime, which refer to behavior across sexual partnerships, should not be confused with a report of the occurrence of oral sex within a single partnership. While an individual might have a great deal of experience with oral sex, the practice may have been absent from a particular sexual relationship, for whatever reason. Consequently, the following data should be seen as descriptive of individuals' reports on specific sexual relationships.

Outcomes: Sexual Satisfaction

Satisfaction is a nebulous term. Historically, *satisfaction* referred to proper reparation or atonement for a sin. To satisfy, then, consisted of adequately repairing a loss that one had imposed on another—in the sinner's case, on God. We do not normally think of sexual desire as a "loss" requiring "repair" by a sex partner. Nevertheless, *sexual satisfaction,* a term well established in the popular vocabulary of sexuality, does connote obligation. It can be seen as a good, produced in a sexual dyad, with a resulting distribution of variable equity. Unlike some goods, however, no currency exists by which the fairness of the distribution of sexual satisfaction can be measured. Despite this uncertainty and incommensurability, however, individuals nevertheless judge the equity of a sexual relationship partly on the basis of perceptions of the relative distribution of sexual satisfaction. These subjective assessments, in turn, inform the ongoing process of sexual negotiation and exchange.

Recognizing the inherently ambiguous nature of sexual satisfaction, we chose to include both subjective and objective measures of sexual satisfaction. We asked our respondents to rate how emotionally and physically satisfying their sexual relationships were on a five-point scale from "not at all" to "extremely" (see appendix C, section 4, questions 36–37, 50–51). We also asked (as an objective measure of satisfaction) how often respondents experienced orgasm during sex with these same partners (see appendix C, section 4, questions 33–34, 47–48). In the following discussion, however, we limit our analysis to sexual satisfaction experienced within a specific relationship during the past year.

The Practice of Orgasm

The psychobiological experience of orgasm as the ultimate goal of sexual activity has been known to many cultures even though it has been differently named, understood, and valued in different societies and cultures across history. With the rise of medical science in the West, orgasm has had a very ambiguous status. The differences in the behavioral expression of orgasm and the reported changes in consciousness and involuntary movements associated with orgasm in some individuals led to an unease about its potential for harm, both morally and biologically. During the nineteenth century, there was a complex debate, primarily centered in the medical profession, about who should have orgasm and how often. While there were minority voices arguing for the right to sexual pleasure for both women and men, the majority viewed female sexual pleasure as particularly suspect, and male sexual pleasure was viewed in a guarded manner as well.

By the end of the nineteenth century, orgasm ceased to be problematic either to most physicians or to the new "sexologists," although many still condemned excessive sexuality as dangerous to men's health. However, orgasm among women assumed a more convoluted role in the scientific understanding of sexuality. In psychoanalysis, a distinction was made between the clitoral orgasm and the vaginal orgasm, treating what appeared to be the anatomical locus of the event as a measure of developmental maturity. Clitoral orgasms were viewed as infantile in terms of psychobiological development, although natural in the prepubescent female. As the female became adult, the site of excitement was to move from the clitoris to the interior of the vagina, where the mature orgasm was to be experienced. This confused theory of the migration of sensation from one portion of the female genitals to another simply mapped the Freudian view that masturbation was the mark of immature psychological development and vaginal intercourse (and reproduction) the mark of psychological maturity onto the woman's body.

It is a measure of the level of repression of female sexual pleasure that these disastrously incorrect ideas could have been welcomed by many; at least they made a place for women's orgasm, even if restricted to the deepest recesses of the vagina. The psychoanalytic was not the only point of view taken about women's orgasm, and a number of women (e.g., Marie Stopes and Margaret Sanger) regularly espoused women's right to sexual pleasure, in oral sex as well as in intercourse, but these remained minority voices for many years.

This inheritance of ideas that opposed sexual pleasure for women or specified the proper locus for that pleasure has shaped much of the discussion of women's orgasms until the present day. Arguing that all orgasms were clitoral, Masters and Johnson (1970) prescribed clitoral stimulation for the treatment of the disorder that came to be labeled *anorgasmia* (formerly called *frigidity*). This argument proceeded from the anatomical evidence that there were no surface nerve endings in the vagina and a high concentration of nerve endings in the clitoris. This solution did not address the fact that women subjectively report orgasms that are sited in the clitoris and at various sites in the interior of and around the entry to the vagina. Indeed, in the 1970s, a debate erupted about a new female pleasure center, the Grafenburg-spot (G-spot), which is on the upper vault of the vagina and which can be stimulated most easily during rear-entry intercourse. This debate includes such issues as whether this anatomical "spot" exists and why it remained secret for so long. What is not debatable is that some women report orgasms, the site of which is reported to be in this region.

Our view is that orgasm is a complex response to socially contextualized physical and mental stimuli and that, in any specific individual, there will be a variety of sources of effective stimulation, both physically and mentally. This is true among both women and men; however, orgasm among women is a form of experience that is poorly taught and has limited sources of social support. As a consequence, many women report having orgasm infrequently, and many clinicians and activists have tried to work out programs that improve the frequency of orgasm. These have involved talking as well as behavioral therapies and educational efforts either with women alone or with women and their partners. Instruction in how to achieve orgasm implies the right to orgasm as well as suggesting better techniques or relationships to produce those orgasms.

In the context of the transformations of sexual and gender roles during the 1960s, women's orgasm became a highly politicized issue that involved feminists, researchers, and clinicians. Our contribution to this debate is simply to report the frequency of own orgasm and that of a sex partner as experienced by a sample of women and men in current relationships. What it is, how to achieve it, how to recognize it, and other questions concerning female orgasm are not addressed in this study. Our concern was to establish some parameters for one aspect of sexual pleasure and to attempt to account for these parameters from the social circumstances of individuals in various types of sexual relationships.

With this background in mind, we turn to table 3.7, wherein data on the proportion of respondents reporting that they "always" had an orgasm with a specific partner in the last year are presented. (Recall that these specific partners may be marital partners, cohabitational partners, partners selected as "primary" by those who had two or more partners and no marital or cohabitational partner, or the partner of those with only one partner who is not a marital or a cohabitational partner. Each individual respondent is represented by only one partnership. For the sake of brevity, we refer to this as the *primary* partnership.)

Three-quarters of the men report that they always have orgasm during sex with this specific partner, a far lower figure than the 100 percent that would be expected by those who view sexual events as equivalent to orgasm for men. However, there remains a major difference between the genders. At 29 percent, the proportion of women who said that they always have an orgasm with this specific partner was 46 percentage points lower than that of men. To the extent that female orgasm is now considered both a right (for women) and a responsibility (for men), this discrepancy undoubtedly constitutes a source of considerable intergender/interpersonal tension.[10]

The proportion always having an orgasm has only a limited relation to the master status variables for both women and men. A band of ± 5 percent around the proportion for women and men contains nearly all the different percentages reported by age, marital status, education, and religion. Only the youngest groups of women and men report frequencies of orgasm that are lower than older groups. These differences are not large, but they probably reflect relative inexperience with partnered sex. There may be difference in the reasons for women and men—the former may be first achieving orgasm, while the latter may be more anxious about sexual performance in their first sexual encounters. Among men, more Hispanics report always having orgasm than do other ethnic groups. Although the proportion of older men who said that they always had an orgasm did not drop systematically, older women did report slightly reduced rates of consistent orgasm. This decline could be either a cohort, an age, or a partner's age effect. Similarly, while there are other differences in the experience of orgasm on the part of women, none of these is easily interpreted. For instance, there is variability among women of different education levels but no systematic and direct effect of education. Indeed, women who might be expected to have more frequent orgasm—the better educated—have slightly lower rates. Given the level of oral sex among these women and the increased levels of experimentation with techniques, we might expect the rates to be higher.

---

10. This is not, however, to suggest that orgasm is necessarily always the primary "goal" of sexual interaction.

Religion may also have an independent effect on rates of female orgasm in sexual relationships. However, the highly discrepant educational (and ethnic) backgrounds of the different religious groupings must be kept in mind when interpreting rates of orgasm by religious background—figures that might otherwise appear counterintuitive. For instance, women without religious affiliation were the least likely to report always having an orgasm with their primary partner—only one in five. On the other hand, the proportion of Type II Protestant women who reported always having an orgasm was the highest, at nearly one-third. In general, having a religious affiliation was associated with higher rates of orgasm for women (27 percent of both Catholics and Type I Protestants reported always having an orgasm with their primary partner). Women with lower levels of education are overrepresented among Type II Protestants, as are more highly educated women among secular respondents. The discrepancies, however, between the two groups are of sufficient magnitude to suggest that religion may be independently associated with rates of female orgasm.

An ambiguity concerning orgasm is highlighted by our respondents' reports of their sex partners' experience of orgasm. Table 3.7 reports the proportion of men and women who said that their partners always had an orgasm during sex. Recall that these comparisons are between people sharing the same background attributes, not partners in the same relationship. The assumption is that these individuals are likely to have sex partners who have a similar background status and that this correlation is more robust among certain master status variables than among others (e.g., people of the same race are more likely to be married to each other than are people of the same age). While women's estimates of how often their male partners experience orgasm were very close to the reports of our male respondents (78 and 75 percent, respectively), the proportion of men who claimed that their partners always had an orgasm was 15 percentage points higher than women's own reports (44 and 29 percent, respectively). Some groups reported even larger differences, and, in the case of education, these differences were systematic. Among those men whose education ranged from less than high school to entry into college, the difference between men's estimates of women's orgasm and the self-reports of orgasm of women who were at the same education level was 20 percent and higher. This difference falls to 4 percent among those with advanced degrees. This suggests that better-educated men have more accurate perceptions of how often their partners achieve orgasm. It is also interesting that men in cohabitational relationships substantially overestimate the proportion of partners always having orgasm when compared to reports by women in cohabitational relationships (the difference is 27 percentage points).

A more detailed multivariate analysis would be needed to determine these differences more precisely. However, there are several possible explanations that might be advanced for this discrepancy. Men may be overreporting how often their partners experience orgasm because it is a socially desirable outcome of sexual interaction. Men may also have more difficulty identifying the

Table 3.7 Percentage of Sexual Satisfaction/Substance Use in Self-Reported "Primary" Partnerships Last Year[a]

	Satisfaction								Alcohol and Drug Use											
	R Always Had an Orgasm with P		P Always Had an Orgasm with R		R Extremely Physically Satisfied with P		R Extremely Emotionally Satisfied with P		Frequently Drank before or during Sex—R or P[b]		Alcohol Users[c]				Any Drug Use before Sex		Total	
											R Alone		R and P					
Master Status Variables	M	W	M	W	M	W	M	W	M	W	M	W	M	W	M	W	M	W
Total population[d]	75.0	28.6	43.5	78.0	46.6	40.5	41.8	38.7	8.6	6.2	30.3	5.8	64.8	72.3	1.1	.5	45.7	54.3
Age:																	Total N	
18–24	70.2	21.5	44.6	79.7	43.9	44.3	41.0	39.4	8.6	4.1	26.9	3.4	70.4	71.7	1.1	.4	194	247
25–29	72.8	31.1	42.6	76.1	50.3	38.6	46.4	40.0	9.2	3.7	22.7	2.9	72.7	68.8	1.5	.5	203	224
30–34	76.3	29.1	39.0	78.8	42.7	42.4	36.5	38.5	6.3	8.9	31.9	7.3	62.2	70.9	1.0	1.2	206	265
35–39	77.8	28.3	46.6	82.7	47.5	39.3	40.7	36.5	7.7	3.9	31.9	8.0	63.7	73.9	0.0	.9	186	234
40–44	77.8	33.2	42.8	77.2	48.5	45.8	38.1	44.0	11.8	9.3	26.0	5.6	68.3	69.2	3.0	0.0	172	194
45–49	81.0	34.3	45.9	76.1	39.7	38.8	37.1	40.0	11.2	9.6	39.3	9.0	52.5	77.6	.9	0.0	120	138
50–54	69.1	25.9	44.9	72.2	48.0	35.2	50.0	37.0	4.1	4.6	50.0	8.0	47.7	82.0	0.0	0.0	99	110
55–59	75.3	24.7	43.1	74.4	57.5	28.8	54.8	26.3	9.5	5.1	32.4	†	62.2	†	0.0	0.0	75	81
Marital status:																		
Nev. marr., not coh.	74.9	25.7	45.6	72.1	38.8	39.8	32.4	31.4	14.0	8.4	18.2	3.4	77.3	76.0	1.4	.4	312	235
Nev. marr., coh.	75.9	23.5	49.1	83.6	44.4	45.6	35.2	44.1	9.3	8.8	24.4	2.2	70.7	73.3	3.7	1.5	61	72
Married	75.3	28.9	40.6	79.5	51.6	41.1	48.9	42.1	5.2	4.0	36.0	7.6	58.8	69.6	.3	.2	705	913
Div./sep., not coh.	73.2	33.9	51.7	77.8	35.0	36.3	23.0	27.4	12.2	12.1	30.4	4.1	64.1	76.9	3.3	1.6	126	198
Div./sep., coh.	73.7	19.2	48.6	67.3	57.9	42.3	52.6	36.5	10.5	7.7	†	2.4	†	73.2	2.6	0.0	38	55

Education:																		
Less than HS	77.3	30.1	50.3	81.3	46.8	37.8	42.9	32.1	9.7	8.2	42.0	4.1	58.0	60.2	1.9	0.0	159	199
HS grad. or eq.	75.9	34.5	45.3	80.0	49.7	42.0	45.4	40.7	10.0	5.4	33.8	5.9	60.1	71.6	1.1	.7	358	449
Some coll./voc.	72.0	24.9	44.9	77.5	45.6	41.1	41.3	38.6	6.5	5.4	28.1	5.5	66.7	72.7	1.3	.8	407	506
Finished coll.	77.2	23.8	38.2	74.0	44.2	38.3	36.5	38.3	6.3	6.4	24.1	7.7	70.8	78.9	0.0	0.0	214	242
Master's/adv. deg.	73.6	29.6	33.0	70.4	45.8	43.4	42.6	45.8	11.9	8.4	26.9	5.9	68.7	78.4	.9	0.0	112	88
Religion:																		
None	75.3	21.5	44.3	73.8	43.8	34.6	36.9	30.0	10.5	9.2	26.8	7.1	67.0	78.8	2.5	.8	171	135
Type I Prot.[e]	72.6	27.4	36.6	76.3	48.1	39.0	41.3	39.6	7.8	5.6	26.3	4.8	67.6	78.6	0.0	0.0	295	363
Type II Prot.[e]	74.8	32.6	46.2	82.9	48.7	43.8	45.9	40.0	6.8	6.0	35.7	7.2	59.7	62.0	1.0	1.0	393	532
Catholic	78.6	26.5	47.4	75.8	44.2	38.5	40.1	38.9	9.2	6.1	31.3	5.3	64.3	74.7	.9	.3	337	404
Jewish	†	†	†	†	†	†	†	†	†	†	†	†	†	†	†	†	23	28
Other	65.6	†	35.5	†	42.4	†	39.4	†	18.2	†	31.6	†	68.4	†	6.1	†	35	29
Race/ethnicity:[f]																		
White	75.2	26.2	41.0	76.7	47.0	40.1	42.7	38.3	8.2	6.0	27.3	5.6	68.1	75.1	.6	.6	998	1,148
Black	75.0	37.8	54.4	84.4	43.1	43.7	40.0	39.9	12.8	8.5	48.5	9.2	44.7	60.3	1.7	.4	188	280
Hispanic	83.9	34.0	56.9	79.6	50.9	38.6	43.4	39.2	8.0	6.6	47.5	3.7	47.5	59.3	3.5	.7	119	164
Asian	†	†	†	†	†	†	†	†	†	†	†	†	†	†	†	†	29	24
Native Am.	†	†	†	†	†	†	†	†	†	†	†	†	†	†	†	†	13	24
N	1,208	1,450	1,193	1,452	1,212	1,461	1,214	1,464	1,215	1,461	735	838	1,215	1,458	1,215	1,451	1,257	1,493

Note: R = respondent; P = partner; M = men; W = women; † indicates that base N is under thirty cases. For the abbreviations of master status variables, see the note to table 3.1.

[a] Sample restricted to those respondents who report having a "primary" sex partner last year. Primary was defined as the respondent's current spouse or live-in partner. If not currently cohabiting at the time of the interview, the respondent was asked to choose a primary partner from all partners last year.

[b] Frequently is defined as a response of "always" or "usually" to the question, "How often (do/did) either you or your partner drink alcohol before or during sex?"

[c] Of respondents who drank at all in the last year before or during a sexual encounter with the primary partner.

[d] Cross section N = 2,750.

[e] For an explanation of the categories of Protestants, see appendix 3.1A.

[f] With oversample, N = 2,988.

occurrence of female orgasm. The desirability of orgasm, coupled with the fact that it is not always easily identified, may lead men to misinterpret certain events occurring during sexual interaction as signs of orgasm. Finally, some women may feign the occurrence of orgasm during sex if it is unlikely to happen and the sex partner involved is highly invested in his capacity to induce orgasm.

Physical and Emotional Satisfaction

Orgasm, however, is only one dimension of sexual satisfaction. The frequency with which orgasm is experienced may be of highly variable significance in assessing the degree of sexual satisfaction felt from a particular event or in a particular partnership. Acknowledging the impossibility of constructing a truly comprehensive "objective" measure of sexual satisfaction, we inquired into our respondents' subjective evaluations of the levels of both physical and emotional satisfaction that they experienced in their partnerships.

It should be clear that the relation between the physical and the emotional dimensions of sexual satisfaction is complex. In attempting to differentiate between physical and emotional satisfaction, we were trying to gauge the extent to which sexual activity in a given relationship was oriented toward the physical aspects of sexual pleasure, emotional satisfaction, or some combination of the two. We believe that one can usefully draw an analytic distinction between the two aspects of satisfaction, even as we recognize that the two are likely to be highly interdependent. Indeed, the relation between physical and emotional satisfaction is a heavily scripted one in our culture. For instance, what we have called the *relational script* (see chapter 14) emphasizes the importance of a loving and intimate relationship to physically satisfying sexual relations—especially for women. In order not to violate this script, a relationship that has become sexual may be interpreted as an intimate and emotionally satisfying one simply because sexual activity has occurred.

Despite these limitations, we believed that a broad measure of the sexual satisfaction of our respondents is useful in helping us understand how different sexual lifestyles and their social circumstances are evaluated. Accordingly, table 3.7 reports the proportions of men and women who said that their primary sexual partnerships were "extremely" physically pleasurable or "extremely" emotionally satisfying. Considering the former first, we find that a fairly large proportion of both men (47 percent) and women (41 percent) felt that these specific partnerships could be accurately characterized as "extremely" physically pleasurable.

Somewhat fewer women were extremely satisfied with the physical dimension of their sexual relationships than were men. Differences in rates of orgasm experienced by men and women may play a role in this discrepancy, but only within the context of a set of expectations associated with a sexual script. That is, if women do not expect orgasm to be a regular outcome of sexual activity, they are less likely to consider its absence a deprivation. Similarly, a sexual partnership in which orgasm frequently occurs may not necessarily be considered satisfying if other scripted interactions do not typically take place as well. The gender and sexual transformations of the 1960s and 1970s engendered new sexual scripts that emphasize not only the mutual right to orgasm but equality throughout the sexual process as well. Thus, if orgasm is not associated with (or the product of) reciprocal and mutually attentive sexual action, it may not be considered sufficient to assign high satisfaction to a sexual event. This example further highlights the complexity of the relation between physical and emotional satisfaction and the potential for sexual response and its evaluation to be highly dependent on the scripts that frame a sexual event or relationship. This new set of scripts is, of course, only a subset of a much broader and more diverse collection of socially organized symbolic resources and expectations used to construct sexual interaction. As we have pointed out, these scripts may generate different sexual expectations and contribute to variation in felt satisfaction.

In general, other than gender, most of the master status variables are not systematically related to differences in the level of physical pleasure experienced for young and middle-aged respondents. There are some differences that may be indicative of larger social processes. While age has no significant effect on younger adults, dramatic gender-based divergence occurs for respondents in their fifties. While the proportion of men reporting extreme physical satisfaction in partnered sex is generally under (and does not exceed) 50 percent for respondents under fifty, it increases to 58 percent for respondents in their late fifties. On the other hand, the proportion of women reporting extreme physical satisfaction in sex remains around 40–45 percent for those under fifty and drops to 29 percent for fifty-five- to fifty-nine-year-olds. This may have to do with differences in patterns of sexual partnering for men and women as they age. As men age, they become increasingly more likely than women to acquire new partners. Consequently, rates of sexual satisfaction for older men may be driven by the acquisition of new, and most likely younger, sex partners. Women, on the other hand, are more likely to be reporting on relationships of long duration in which sexual activity may be subsiding. Alternatively, this rise in reported rates of physical satisfaction for older men may indicate not only that some older men are acquiring new partners but also that men who remain in long-term marriages are not experiencing significant declines in felt satisfaction.

Related to our discussion of the scripts that emerged with the gender and sexual transformations of prior decades are rates of satisfaction by level of education. Since the movement to promote sexual equality was largely confined to middle- and upper-middle-class groups, we might expect sexual scripts emphasizing equality to have had the most effect on those groups. Despite the fact that levels of education are associated with divergent sexual scripts, however, they do not appear to be associated with differences in reported physical satisfaction. Indeed, excepting gender, age, and, for men, marital status, none of the master status characteristics is associated with reported physical satisfaction, suggesting that broader social factors may not relate directly to the degree of sexual pleasure that respondents are willing to assign to primary sexual partnerships.

Despite the high correlation between physical and emotional satisfaction, it is nevertheless the case that some respondents felt that their primary partnerships were highly pleasing physically but less satisfying emotionally. Simply comparing the aggregate rates of extreme physical satisfaction with the corresponding rates of emotional satisfaction indicates that at least some of our respondents are reporting higher physical than emotional satisfaction. Although some reported higher emotional than physical satisfaction, this was a substantially smaller proportion of the sample. While the data in table 3.7 do not permit more detailed comparisons between physical and emotional satisfaction, they do reveal the similarities and differences in distribution between the two categories. For instance, the proportion of men and women reporting extreme emotional satisfaction with their partner is somewhat smaller than the equivalent discrepancy for physical satisfaction. (Also see chapter 10.)

One significant parallel between the two dimensions of satisfaction concerned the distribution of respondents reporting extreme emotional satisfaction by age. We noted earlier that age did not appear to relate to physical satisfaction for respondents aged eighteen to fifty but that gender-based discrepancies began to emerge for older cohorts. The distribution of emotional satisfaction follows the same pattern, while the proportion reporting extreme emotional satisfaction with their primary partner remains relatively stable until age fifty at around 40 percent; this proportion increases to 50 percent of fifty- to fifty-four-year-old men and 55 percent of those between fifty-five and fifty-nine. Roughly the same proportion of women and men reported extreme emotional satisfaction in this specific partnership (about 40 percent) until age fifty. However, the equivalent proportion of fifty-five- to fifty-nine-year-old women plummets to 26 percent. The comparability of the distribution of emotional satisfaction by age with that of physical pleasure further indicates that a significant divergence in felt sexual satisfaction in primary partnerships occurs for older respondents. We have suggested that different patterns of sexual partnering for men and women of this age group may account, in part, for this discrepancy. It may also be the case that conflict between the scripts brought to bear on sexual interaction by men and women may be more pronounced for older respondents. Changes in sexual and gender values may have affected the expectations or entitlements that older women bring to sexual events but not the felt obligations of the men—primarily husbands or long-term partners—with whom they have sex.[11]

---

11. Multivariate analyses performed to determine the independent effects of the master status variables on sexual satisfaction indicate that the effect of age (for women) is to reduce the odds of reporting either extreme physical or extreme emotional satisfaction. The decrease in rates of physi-

In general, respondents in marriages were more likely to report high degrees of emotional satisfaction. The proportion of married men who reported extreme emotional satisfaction from sex was 49 percent—nearly 17 percentage points higher than the proportion of never-married, noncohabiting men. Similarly, the proportion of married women who reported high levels of emotional satisfaction was 42 percent, compared with 31 percent of never-married, noncohabiting women.[12] There are at least two possible explanations for this discrepancy. First, marriage is a normatively distinct relationship involving a number of assumptions about the prior commitments and understandings of marital partners. To marry implies that judgments have been made about the capacity of an intimate partner to provide emotional fulfillment and physical satisfaction (at least this has been the case in the past several decades). On the other hand, a certain amount of ambiguity is normatively appropriate for individuals in relationships that are more recently formed or that do not involve some explicit commitment like marriage or cohabitation. Consequently, it may be easier to recognize and admit dissatisfaction in these types of relationships than in marriages. Second, commitment in relationships tends to be, in large part, a reciprocal function of emotional and physical satisfaction. Although popular representations of marriage often portray the dulling of mutual affection over time, the relative security that marriage provides may be a significant source of emotional satisfaction as well as a comfortable context in which to pursue physical pleasure.

Emotional satisfaction, like physical pleasure, did not exhibit any noteworthy associations with race or religion. These broader social characteristics may not relate directly to the process of framing and evaluating sexual events in these partnerships. This may be a function, however, of the population of sexual partnerships to which our analysis has thus far been restricted. The strong relations between marital status and both physical and emotional satisfaction indicate that characteristics of the sexual dyad itself—the level of commitment or "investment" characterizing it, its normative "status," and the types of sexual scripts typically associated with it—play powerful roles.

3.3 Sexual Relationships and Contextual Action

Alcohol and Drug Use

Patterns of alcohol and drug use are important dimensions of the context of sexuality for at least three reasons. The first is related to our interest in the

---

cal *and* emotional satisfaction indicates that the decline in sexual satisfaction reported by older women is not likely to be merely a function of physiological or health-related changes.

12. These discrepancies between men's and women's levels of satisfaction by marital status are consistent with a literature that has documented the relatively more favorable effect of being married on men's health (with respect to rates of morbidity and mortality) than on women's (see, e.g., Gove, 1972, 1973; Gove and Tudor 1973; Clancy and Gove, 1974).

communication of sexually transmitted infections and successful fertility planning. Substance use can impair judgment, increasing the likelihood that prophylactic and contraceptive measures will be neglected. Second, alcohol and certain types of drugs enhance sexual desire in both men and women. However, substance use can also produce physiological side effects, especially for men, that result in reduced sexual capacities. In this sense, substance use may become an aspect of the process of sexual negotiation. Third, excessive alcohol or drug use is often associated with sexual violence, especially among men. For these reasons, we asked the frequency with which our respondents used alcohol or drugs before or during sex in this specific relationship and, if respondents reported any use of alcohol or drugs, whether they used the substance alone or with their partner and how strongly it affected either of them.

Returning to table 3.7, we see that the proportion of partnerships in which frequent alcohol use occurred before or during sex by either the respondent or his or her partner was around 9 percent for men and 6 percent for women.[13] Men report slightly more frequent alcohol use in their partnerships than do women. This pattern holds true across most age categories except for those respondents in their early thirties and fifties. Despite the small discrepancy between the two genders, however, the pattern of frequent drinking by age is fairly consistent for sexual partnerships, whether reported by men or by women. Both men and women are somewhat more likely to experience frequent alcohol use before or during sex in their forties than in any other period of the life course. This may be due to the increases of stress in midlife. However, when compared with other age periods, these differences are modest. What is perhaps most important to point out is that frequent drinking associated with sex occurs in one partnership in ten during this age period.

Higher rates of drinking are associated with differences in marital status. Those never married are more likely to drink frequently prior to or during sex than are those who are divorced or separated. The higher rates among primary partnerships were found among never-married noncohabiting respondents (14 percent of men and 8 percent of women) as well as divorced or separated respondents (12 percent of both men and women). By facilitating sexual contact, however, co-residence may function simply to decrease the proportion of sexual events involving alcohol rather than the absolute number of such events.

Given our orienting interests, it is also important to distinguish between joint and individual alcohol consumption in primary partnerships. The relevant data presented in table 3.7 take as the population of concern all primary relationships that reported any use of alcohol in the last year (rather than just frequent users) in order to give a more comprehensive picture of alcohol use as well as to increase the number of cases analyzed in the body of the table. Large

---

13. *Frequent* is here defined as a response of "always" or "usually" to the question "How often (did/do) you or your partner drink alcohol before or during sex?" (see appendix C, section 4, question 27).

and consistent gender differences are found when we consider the percentage of respondents who reported usually drinking alone.[14] Over 30 percent of men reported drinking alone before or during sex (of all those who reported drinking at all in association with sexual events), while only 6 percent of women did so.

Drinking alone prior to or during sex shows no systematic pattern by age, although there is an inconsistent drift toward high rates with age. These data suggest that a respondent's age, and possibly the length of the partnership, may be related to a decrease in the incidence of sociable presex alcohol consumption. Men report decreasing rates of joint alcohol use before sex with increased age—a pattern consistent with this suggestion. However, comparable proportions for women remain relatively stable (at around 70 percent) and actually increase for the older age groups. In other words, the proportion of women who reported that their partners usually drank alone before or during sex was considerably lower than the reports of our male respondents about their female partners' alcohol use. However, when we add the percentages of individual and joint alcohol consumption—leaving us with the residual proportion of partnerships in which the partner drank alone—for the two genders, we find that the proportion of women drinking alone as estimated by men is, in fact, much closer to women's own reports than are the equivalent estimates of men's behavior by women.

Since "casual" alcohol use is considered more appropriate for men, women may not note its consumption prior to sex—unless, of course, it is excessive. For respondents in their late forties and early fifties, however, the gender-based discrepancies are extreme. While between 40 and 50 percent of men in this age group who drank reported usually drinking alone before or during sex with their partner, only about 10–12 percent of women reported that their partner usually drank alone before or during sex. (While the question here concerned drinking both before and during sex, in this case we would assume that most of this drinking by men occurs before since women would note whether their partners were drinking during sex.)

Indeed, a look at alcohol use before sex for the different categories of marital status supports the hypothesis that partnership type is an important determinant of alcohol consumption patterns. While marriage decreases rates of frequent alcohol use before sex, it increases the likelihood that presex alcohol consumption will occur alone. The proportion of married men who reported usually drinking alone before sex was 10 percentage points higher than the proportion of men living with their partners who reported doing so and 18 percentage points higher than the figure for never-married men living alone. Similarly, the proportion of married women who reported usually drinking alone before sex was more than double (8 percent) that of women either living

14. *Drinking alone* is defined as a response of "respondent only" to the question, "[When you drank,] was that usually you, your partner, or both?" (See appendix C, section 4, question 27a).

with partners or living alone. Here there is probably a joint effect of age and marital status, with the more youthful among those living together and never married drinking together.

Our other social variables—education, race, and religion—are also associated with sociable alcohol use prior to sex. Education is positively associated with joint alcohol use for men but not for women. Of men with less than a high school education, 42 percent reported usually drinking alone before sex. This figure declines fairly steadily to around one-quarter of men with at least a college degree. This education effect may explain, in part, the relations that we find between solitary drinking before sex and religious affiliation. The same proportion (26–27 percent) of Type I Protestant men and men reporting no religious affiliation (groups with relatively high levels of education) said that they usually drank before having sex. However, religious groups with lower average levels of education reported higher rates of solitary drinking—36 percent of Type II Protestants and 31 percent of Catholics. As with education, religious affiliation was not associated with sociable drinking patterns for women. Finally, black and Hispanic men were roughly 20 percentage points more likely to report drinking alone before sex (49 and 48 percent, respectively) than were white respondents. Again, this relation may be a function, in part, of disparities in levels of education among racial categories.

The use of alcohol in the context of sexual association is a highly variable and heavily socially structured phenomenon. However, as table 3.7 reveals, rates of drug use by the various master status characteristics are harder to interpret. Unlike alcohol consumption, the rarity of drug use in the context of sexual activity renders its analysis across social categories of questionable value. The extremely low incidence of drug use among our respondents is itself a significant finding, however. Only 1.1 percent of men and 0.5 percent of women said that they used drugs before sex at any time in the last year with these specific partners. Rates of drug use may be more profitably examined, however, when we turn later in the chapter to an analysis of "master relationships," where we clarify and supplement the data gleaned from current relationships in this section.

Relational Dimensions of Sexual Behavior

In the following discussion, we describe a theoretical framework that highlights ways in which sexual practices may be structured by features of a sexual relationship and, in turn, the social context in which that relationship is embedded. Three claims organize the discussion. First, we argue that "stakeholders" in a sexual relationship—interested third parties as well as the participants in the relationship itself—shape and reinforce conceptions of appropriate sex partners. Second, these expectations may have a considerable effect not only on the choice of a sex partner but also on the course and character of the sexual relationship once it has begun. The social context of a sexual partnership may influence the level of "commitment" or "investment" in that relationship. Finally, sexual relationships involving low levels of investment may have certain features that affect their sexual character. Differences between these types of relationships should not be attributed solely to the individuals who compose them but rather to differences in the nature of the partnerships themselves.

It is important to explore the choice of concepts that we have introduced to characterize these relationships. Commitment and investment come from different intellectual traditions and imply different measurement properties. *Commitment* is a more social or psychological concept, one that expresses both the culture's and the individual's sense that relationships can be scaled on the relative irreversibility of the promises that have been made or the obligations that have been assumed. Greater commitment implies increased obligation through an enhanced affective bond. *Investment* is a concept from human capital economics that allows one to specify the amount of resources to be invested in a relationship. While it suggests a smoother and more calculated commitment of resources (a twenty-dollar vs. a fifty-dollar gift), it can cope with the lumpiness of resource allocation that occurs when there are relationship transitions. Part of the power of the investment model is its ability to specify various resources that are being allocated at various stages of relationships. Affection, time, sex, money, and external social support can all be viewed as resources that have differential allocation requirements at various stages of "commitment." We shift from one usage to another recognizing the common terrain that they map and in some cases use the phrase *commitment/investment* to suggest their commonalities.

Individuals bring socially structured sets of expectations and resources to sexual partnerships. Sexual relationships, however, are only one of many relationships that constitute social networks. Most people maintain sexual partnerships in the midst of a broader set of familial, friendship, and work-related social commitments. While these other relationships are external to a sexual partnership, they may influence both its formation and its stability as well as its nature. In chapter 1, we referred to third parties who are invested in the outcome of a sexual relationship as a key subset of *stakeholders*. These individuals reinforce expectations about the characteristics of appropriate sex partners. An individual who violates these expectations risks alienating key stakeholders on whom he or she may rely for other rewards.

Of course, sexual partnerships vary in the degree of mutual commitmen/investment that they involve. An individual who may be an acceptable "short-term" sex partner (according to the standards and expectations of relevant stakeholders) may be considered entirely "out of the question" for marriage. As we shall see in chapter 6, the master status characteristics serve as a kind of social filter through which the pool of appropriate sex partners is narrowed. Different constellations of social characteristics may be appropriate or inappropriate, depending on the level of commitment characterizing a relationship. Beyond these broad social criteria, stakeholders may have certain independent interpersonal requirements that influence an individual's choice of sex partner or the trajectory of particular relationships.

We suggest that a sexual relationship's relative stability and level of commitment/investment are not simply functions of factors related specifically to the sexual dyad itself. In addition, stakeholders' expectations exert an independent effect on these features of sexual relationships. In an effort to capture the meaningful variation in these levels of commitment/investment, in part engendered and supported by third-party stakeholders, we have constructed a four-category measure of sexual partnering. At the lowest level of current commitment are what we call *shorter-term partnerships*—those that have lasted under one month.[15] Relationships that have lasted longer than one month but that are not cohabitational we categorize as *longer term*. The third and fourth levels are categories with which we are already familiar—*cohabitation* and *marriage*. It is important to note that these are fuzzy sets. Some of our shorter-term relationships may evolve into longer-term relationships, cohabitations, or marriages. Indeed, a shorter-term relationship may become a marriage within a thirty-day period (recall the whirlwind romance). We are limited by the cross-sectional character of our data to a snapshot of these relationships. There may be differences among shorter-term relationships that transform some into more committed relationships; indeed, we are sure that there must be, given our view that shorter-term relationships that become more committed relationships receive social support from a variety of stakeholders. However, we are also sure that we have a sample of relationships at various stages of increasing and decreasing commitment/investment (i.e., some of the marriages that we have captured in our survey are in the throes of dissolution) and that we can reasonably assume that our primary concerns about levels of commitment can be found in this categorization.

In claiming that each relationship type represents an increased level of investment or commitment, we do not mean to suggest that the differences between each of these relationships represent steps on an ordinal scale. The difference between a shorter-term and a longer-term relationship is one of duration, while the step to cohabitation or the step to marriage requires passing other tests or crossing other thresholds of commitment or investment. Each relationship type is in some sense qualitatively distinct while at the same time occupying a place on a scale of investment. (For a related discussion of the differing commitments in cohabitational and marriage partnerships, see Willis and Michael 1994.)

Yet what constitutes "investment" in sexual partnerships? We consider increased investment in a relationship to mean not only an increase in the quan-

---

15. In choosing one month to define short-term partnerships, our intention was to include not only one-night stands—sexual relationships involving only one sexual event—but relationships that may have extended over a number of discrete sexual events but that are nevertheless considered fleeting or transitory.

tity of resources exchanged but also a proliferation of the types of resources exchanged between sex partners. While shorter-term sexual relationships may be more oriented toward sexual exchange, relationships of longer duration inevitably involve exchanges of emotional, social, and perhaps financial resources as well. It is in this sense that the expectations of stakeholders are implicated in a sexual relationship as a potential dimension of exchange (in addition to influencing the choice of a sex partner). If a sex partner is rejected by an individual's broader social network, maintaining the relationship will involve higher social costs. In turn, these costs will enter into ongoing transactions with that sex partner, perhaps even affecting the balance of sexual resources exchanged.

This discussion highlights some ways in which stakeholders may shape the nature of a sexual relationship. In turn, features of a sexual partnership may operate independently of other social factors to produce certain characteristic sexual outcomes.[16] To the extent that other dimensions or avenues of exchange are not as well developed (or nonexistent) in shorter-term relationships, we might expect interaction in them to be more oriented toward sexual exchange than it is in their longer-term counterparts. For instance, rewards may be more likely to be sexual in nature, or problems may be resolved sexually in the absence of other established forms of reconciliation. Shorter-term relationships, then, may be more sexually oriented not because of the personal proclivities of the partners involved but because of factors that characterize the relationship itself.

We employ these insights as a framework for understanding how the various sexual techniques and measures of sexual pleasure and contextual actions are distributed over the relationship types discussed. But, before considering these data, we need to report on how they differ from data presented in earlier sections on these same topics. The numbers of cases in these tables are based on partnerships, not individuals. In the course of the interview, we asked respondents to tell us how many people they had sex with in the past year. For those who had sex with only one or two people, we inquired in detail about the character of the relationship. Since well over 90 percent of our sample had no, one, or two partners in the last year, there was no difficulty. However, for those who reported three or more partners, we had to make a decision about whom to select. We always chose marital or live-in partners if they existed; when they did not, we asked respondents to tell us who their primary partner was. The second partner chosen from those remaining was the most recent. In cases in which a respondent did not or could not choose a "primary" partner, we selected the two most recent partners.

These selection procedures bias the data toward marriages and cohabita-

---

16. The effects of relationship type, independent of the master status characteristics (excepting marital status, of course), on the sexual variables discussed below have been confirmed through individual level multivariate analyses.

tional and longer-term relationships if they were characterized by the respondent as primary (respondents were more likely to choose longer-term relationships as primary). The distribution of shorter-term relationships is therefore truncated. By using all the relationships, those respondents with two partners in the past year are overrepresented in these tables, and there is a lack of statistical independence between the categories. Suitable caution should be taken in interpreting them.

Table 3.8 reports percentage distributions of the sexual variables thus far considered over shorter-term, longer-term, cohabitational, and marital relationships.[17] Respondents were asked how often they had sex with a given partner only if sex occurred within the relationship more than ten times. Consequently, we do not report data on the frequency of sex for short-term relationships. This limitation renders any assessment of the extent to which short-term relationships differ from more committed relationships in terms of frequency of sex impossible. However, when we consider long-term relationships in comparison with cohabitational and marital relationships, both men and women report more frequent sex in live-in relationships, and long-term partnerships were also marked by a considerably higher frequency of sex than were marriages and, at least for women, did not differ markedly in this respect from cohabitational partnerships. Of respondents in long-term partnerships, 38 percent of men and 40 percent of women reported having sex three to six times a week or more, compared with 54 and 46 percent of cohabiting men and women, respectively. The equivalent proportion of married respondents was around one-quarter. This is a plausible order for a number of reasons. Those in marriages are, on the average, older and in relationships of longer duration, while those cohabiting both are younger and have equivalent access to their partner. The lower rate for those in longer-term relationships is a function of a decreased sexualization of the relationship and the lack of access structured by not living together.

Oral sex was complexly related to relationship type, and this relation was different for women and men. A number of comparisons can be made from these data answering the questions, Do men and women reporting on their own relationships report equal rates of oral sex (both receptive and active)? (That is, do men and women report that they give and receive oral sex at similar rates?) How do the reports of women compare with those of men on the same behaviors? (Do women report cunnilingus at the same rates that men report cunnilingus?) Do these rates differ across relationships?

In terms of the first question, men in cohabitational relationships report that they usually/always give and receive oral sex in about the same proportion, married men and men involved in long-term relationships report that they are

---

17. The findings discussed below about the associations between relationship type and sexual practices were found to be significant (in multivariate analyses not presented here) when controlling for the effects of other master status variables.

more likely (by about 5 percent) to give than to receive oral sex, and men in short-term relationships report that their partners are twice as likely usually/always to perform fellatio on them as they are usually/always to perform cunnilingus on their partners. The difference in usually/always receiving oral sex differs substantially between marriages and other relationships (12 percent in comparison to 30 percent). In part, these differences are a result of differences in cohort membership between these relationships, but they are also linked to the differing erotic definitions of these relationships.

The picture of reciprocity in their relationships reported by women is similar to that reported by men, although the absolute rates are lower, except among the married. Women report lower rates of giving oral sex to than receiving it from their cohabitational or longer-term male partners, but the differences are modest (similar to the men). Women agree with men that in shorter-term relationships they are more likely usually/always to perform oral sex than are their male partners.

If we directly contrast the women's and the men's reports (men reporting fellatio with women reporting fellatio and men reporting cunnilingus with women reporting cunnilingus), the difference between the genders' reports are usually dramatic, except for the married. Men report that they experience fellatio at a far greater rate than women report providing it. Thirty-one percent of men and 15 percent of women in cohabitational relationships, 26 percent of men and 16 percent of women in longer-term relationships, and 29 percent of men and 23 percent of women in shorter-term relationships report fellatio usually/always. Reports of cunnilingus by gender differ as well, with women generally reporting lower rates than men. However, the pattern is reversed for shorter-term partnerships, with women reporting higher rates than men (29 vs. 15 percent).

How can we summarize this complex picture? Shorter-term relationships involve high rates of fellatio. Oral sex was least likely to occur usually or always in marriages. In nearly all cases, men reported higher rates of oral sex than women.

Independent of the characteristics that an individual brings to a relationship, such as age, education, religion, and race, the character of the partnership is associated not only with the frequency of sexual activity but with the content of sexual behavior as well. It might be argued that people who are more "sexually inclined" seek brief partnerships in order to engage in a greater variety and frequency of sexual activity. However, when (in analyses not presented here) we controlled for features of an individual that might capture this inclination, such as the number of sex partners since age eighteen and even the appeal of oral sex itself, shorter-term relationships were more likely to involve more frequent oral sex for men. The lower rate of cunnilingus suggests that sexual interaction may be more male centered in the context of brief relationships.

Given that oral sex is more likely to occur in shorter-term relationships, it is somewhat surprising that anal sex occurs least often in these relationships.

Table 3.8A   **Frequency of Heterosexual Activity and Techniques, by**
                      Master Relationships[a]

| | Percentage Reporting the Specified Frequency of Occurrence of Selected Sexual Technique | | | | | | | | |
| | Had Sex Three to Six Times a Week or More[b] | | Always Had Vaginal Intercourse | | P Always/ Usually Performed Oral Sex on R | | R Always/ Usually Performed Oral Sex on P | | Any Occurrence of Anal Intercourse Last Year | |
Master Relationships	Men	Women	Men	Women	Men	Women	Men	Women	Men	Women
Marriages	26.6	24.7	79.5	81.1	12.1	11.9	16.9	9.9	9.5	7.6
Cohabitations	53.7	45.5	81.4	77.1	30.6	19.6	29.4	14.7	9.3	13.2
Long-term partners	37.7	40.4	77.8	74.6	26.3	19.8	22.0	16.3	7.4	7.1
Short-term partners[c]	†	†	81.3	86.2	29.1	29.9	15.2	23.0	5.3	4.6
N	1,045	1,266	1,465	1,611	1,460	1,607	1,458	1,606	1,472	1,608

Table 3.8B   **Selected Heterosexual Outcomes, by Master Relationships**

| | Percentage Reporting Specified Sexual Outcome | | | | | | | |
| | R Always Had an Orgasm | | P Always Had an Orgasm | | R Extremely Physically Satisfied | | R Extremely Emotionally Satisfied | |
Master Relationships	Men	Women	Men	Women	Men	Women	Men	Women
Marriages	75.0	28.6	40.2	79.7	51.1	40.0	48.1	41.5
Cohabitations	77.2	24.0	52.2	75.9	44.4	41.7	35.2	34.6
Long-term partners	73.8	31.0	48.2	74.9	34.8	37.8	26.4	29.0
Short-term partners[c]	80.5	43.0	69.3	82.6	15.9	16.1	10.6	12.6
N	1,467	1,610	1,441	1,610	1,474	1,622	1,475	1,625

While the differences are not large, the finding is consistent that marriages, live-in relationships, and longer-term relationships have a higher incidence of anal sex. This finding supports the master status variable analysis in which those who are older and who have more sex partners were identified as most likely to have anal sex.

The level of satisfaction experienced in shorter-term relationships also differed significantly from that reportedly experienced in other relationships. Women reported being more likely always to experience orgasm during sex in shorter-term relationships, while men reported their usual high levels of or-

Table 3.8C   **Selected Contextual Practices, by Master Relationships**

Percentage Reporting Specified Frequency of Occurrence of Contraceptive/Drug or Alcohol Use

| Master Relationships | Always Used Condom During Vaginal Intercourse | | Always Used Other Birth Control during Vaginal Intercourse | | Always Used Condom During Anal Intercourse | | Always or Usually Drank Alcohol before or during Sex | | Who Drank Frequently? | | | | Always or Usually Used Drugs before or during Sex | |
| | | | | | | | | | R Alone | | R and P | | | |
	Men	Women	Men	Women	Men	Women	Men	Women	Men	Women	Men	Women	Men	Women
Marriages	7.7	7.6	34.3	44.1	13.2	13.0	5.3	4.3	44.7	5.0	47.4	55.0	.3	.2
Cohabitations	13.3	10.8	40.6	50.0	18.8	11.1	9.3	10.2	46.7	†	53.3	61.9	3.1	2.4
Long-term partners	26.2	20.0	42.5	51.3	39.4	21.4	16.2	12.0	11.1	4.2	84.7	79.2	1.8	1.8
Short-term partners[c]	47.7	51.9	21.4	41.6	62.5	50.0	47.7	40.7	4.2	5.7	88.7	82.9	6.0	2.3
N	1,424	1,583	1,419	1,579	125	128	1,622	1,476	196	144	196	144	1,476	1,619

Note: R = respondent; P = partner; † indicates that base *N* is under thirty cases. For a discussion of condom use, see chapter 11.

[a]*Heterosexual* defined by act rather than identity. Analysis of the effect of master relationships is based on all sexual partnerships on which we have sexual data. Consequently, respondents with more than one sex partner will be overrepresented in these analyses — a methodological issue that we treat in more detail in chapter 6.

[b]Respondents were asked how often they had sex with a given partner only if sex occurred more than ten times (excluding most short-term partnerships).

[c]*Short-term* partnerships defined as noncohabitational partnerships lasting under one month. Information on sexual techniques was collected on short-term relationships only if sex occurred more than once.

gasm during sex regardless of the type of relationship in which they were involved. However, both men and women in shorter-term relationships reported considerably lower rates of both physical and emotional satisfaction than those in all other relationships. The sexual focus of short-term relationships as well as the anxiety about the future of the relationship may operate to reduce the more generalized physical and emotional satisfactions that derive from sexual relationships. Indeed, in the case of both men and women, physical and emotional satisfaction declines as they are participants in less and less committed relationships. Individuals in longer-term relationships, in which sex is only one of many avenues of exchange, may focus less on the benefits received from sexual interaction and may therefore be more inclined to evaluate their level of experienced physical satisfaction positively.[18] Finally, as we would expect from the previous discussion, shorter-term relationships would be less likely to have established methods of emotional communication and support.

An analysis of alcohol and drug use by type of relationship clarifies some difficulties in the analysis by master statuses. Always or usually drinking is dramatically related to the type of relationship in which the respondent is participating. Forty percent of women and nearly half of men in shorter-term relationships report usually or always drinking before or during sex. This falls to 5 percent among the married. This is clearly related to the social conditions under which people in new relationships meet and socialize. Going out often involves alcohol consumption as part of the sociability prior to sex. As the relationship stabilizes and expectations of the other party's conduct are shared, alcohol use declines.

However, when we turn to the question of who drinks, it is clear that a far larger proportion of men in marriages and cohabitational relationships drink alone prior to sex, while those in less invested relationships are more likely to drink with their partner. It appears that, among women, drinking is more often a form of sociability both in and out of relationships while solitary drinking on the part of men is more linked to the sexual performance itself. The small amount of nonalcohol drug use that we detected is clearly situated among people in shorter-term relationships and, to a lesser extent, among those people living with a partner.

These insights highlight the importance of features of the sexual dyad in generating sexual behavior. Although we downplay the simple notion that finding a particular sexual technique or practice appealing will unproblematically lead to its occurrence, we nevertheless recognize that individuals do have different sexual preferences. These inclinations exist as components in scripts for appropriate sexual behavior that serve as reference points for the subjective

18. Yet another explanation is provided by the discussion in chapter 1 that, through practice, couples become more skilled at satisfying each other sexually and that these skills help bond the couple together and represent an important form of partner-specific human capital. These skills enhance sexual satisfaction.

evaluation of sexual action and in the partner-specific explorations of what practices and skills are effective in pleasing one's partner sexually. In chapter 4 we present the distribution of sexual preferences across social categories and some discussion of their relation to sexual behavior.

3.4 Profiles of Sexual Expression

In this section, we wish to examine ways in which the sexual practices of individuals can be considered together as a profile of sexual expression. From the orientation of this volume it is obvious that we do not view the assembly of sexual practices exhibited by individuals to be the result of random processes or merely the outcome of individual proclivities. What we wish to do here is examine a variety of salient sexual practices that can be treated as analytically separable to form the basis for distinct profiles of sexual action.

Kinsey's concept *total sexual outlet*—which refers to the distribution of the individual's orgasms over a range of outlets such as masturbation, marital and nonmarital heterosexual activity, homosexual activity, and so forth—exemplifies a previous attempt to summarize an individual's pattern of sexual behavior. Although this concept allowed Kinsey to characterize patterns of sexual behavior as a simple additive phenomenon of the experience of orgasm, the notion of varying levels of sex drive distributed over a range of possible outlets, or the "hydraulic" theory of sexuality, is, we suggest, a misleading metaphor for an individual's sex life as a whole.[19] On the contrary, we argue that distinctive configurations of the facets of an individual's sexual conduct depend on the cultural meanings of sexual behavior transmitted through social interaction.[20]

We have chosen a variety of individual and partner-driven sexual practices to capture both relations within these domains and the relation between the public and the private (or the interpersonal and the intrapsychic) dimensions of sexual action. We discuss the organization of autoerotic facets of sexual expression (sexual fantasy, masturbation, and the use of autoerotic materials such as sexually explicit videos, books, or magazines) and how they are related to facets of partnered sexuality. This allows us to confront the notion, suggested by the hydraulic metaphor, that autoerotic activity compensates for lack of partnered sex. Finally, we present characteristic profiles of sexual conduct that highlight the socially structured nature of the many manifestations of sexual expression.

19. This theory is called *hydraulic* because the sex drive is compared to the force of overflowing water and the ways in which the drive is satiated are related to a given number of possible "outlets." For each individual, some of these outlets may be "blocked" by the influence of social norms or customs. Kinsey postulated that the blockage of one outlet will cause a greater level of flow in the unblocked outlets, thereby suggesting that the various forms of sexual expression are compensatory.

20. Of course, interpersonal interaction is not the only way in which the cultural meanings of particular sexual practices are transmitted to individuals. Positive or negative evaluations of oral sex, e.g., may be in large part related to the treatment of oral sex in movies, novels, and sex manuals. (For a discussion of the role of popular sex manuals in creating sexual ideologies, see, e.g., Seidman 1989).

Autoerotic and Partnered Dimensions of Sexual Activity

Autoeroticism is the dimension of the sex life defined by sexual desire and/or gratification experienced by an individual without the direct participation of another person. As we have argued earlier, it should not be concluded from the absence of a specific partner that autoerotic activities are without social content or social origins. On the contrary, sexual fantasies almost always incorporate the imagined presence of others who conform to cultural scenarios for an appropriate sex partner doing appropriate sexual things in a social context appropriate to sexual activity, even if the actual enactment of the fantasy is highly unlikely or impossible. Autoerotic activities differ from partnered activities in that they do not require coordination with another and in that they can avoid many of the other reality-centered features of partnered sex through the flexible resources of the imagination. Let us point out that the sexual imagination is not "infinitely" flexible but rather depends on social sources for its form and content. Indeed, the repetitive content of pornography may suggest how limited the erotic imagination is.

We attempted to measure three facets of autoerotic activity in the interview instrument: sexual fantasy, masturbation, and the use of erotic or pornographic material. The highly socially structured character of masturbation has already been discussed earlier in this chapter. Sexual fantasy and the use of erotic materials are also socially structured, and in remarkably similar ways (although, unlike masturbation and the use of erotica, sexual fantasy is unrelated to religious affiliation). For present purposes, the use of erotica includes watching an X-rated movie or video, going to see erotic dancers at a club, reading a sexually explicit book or magazine, using sex toys, or calling a phone sex service. Regrettably, we did not ask respondents whether they did these activities alone or in the company of a sex partner. Nevertheless, we have treated them as autoerotic because they do not require the participation of another person. (For the marginal distributions of these items for men and women, see table 3.9.) The consistent patterning of these measures of autoerotic activity with respect to salient social categories and the strong (Pearson) intercorrelations among the three measures, as described in table 3.10, indicate that the use of erotic material is likely to be accompanied by masturbation and frequent sexual fantasy. Similarly, frequent masturbation is likely to be accompanied by frequent sexual fantasy, and those who never or rarely think about sex are very unlikely to masturbate frequently or use erotica. This allows us to combine the three measures into a more parsimonious scale of autoerotic activity.[21]

21. Each individual has a score of 0, 1, or 2 on each facet of autoerotic activity. These scores are added together to create a new variable with a range between 0 and 6. Because of the small number of cases at the two extremes, we combined categories 1 and 2 and categories 5 and 6. Thus, the individual who never or rarely thought about sex and never masturbated or used erotica is assigned a score of 1. The individual who had sexual fantasies and masturbated more frequently and had also used more than one kind of erotic material is assigned a score of 5.

Table 3.9   **Sexual Fantasy and Use of Autoerotic Materials (% distributions)**

	Men	Women
Thinking about sex:		
More frequently	54	19
Less frequently	43	67
Never or rarely	4	14
Autoerotic material:		
X-rated movies or videos	23	11
Go to a club that has nude or seminude dancers	22	4
Sexually explicit books or magazines	16	4
Vibrators or dildos	2	2
Other sex toys	1	2
Sex phone numbers	1	0
Any of the above	41	16

Note: Rarely or never refers to "less than once a month" or "never"; *less frequently* refers to "a few times a month" to "a few times a week"; and *more frequently* refers to "every day" or "several times a day." *Fantasy* is measured by the frequency with which the respondent reported thinking about sex.

Table 3.10   **Intercorrelations of Selected Indicators of Autoerotic Activity**

	Fantasy	Masturbation	Erotica
Men:			
Fantasy			
Masturbation	.25***		
Erotica	.27***	.34***	
Women:			
Fantasy			
Masturbation	.22***		
Erotica	.22***	.22***	

$***p > .0001$.

Clearly, the most important finding is the great disparity between levels of autoerotic activity for men and women (see fig. 3.3). Also notice that the relation between masturbation and fantasy and between masturbation and the use of erotica is somewhat stronger among men than women, which suggests that the articulation between these facets of autoerotic activity is much greater for men. Levels of autoerotic activities are, however, also strongly correlated with every one of our master statuses, strongly indicating their distinctive embeddedness in different social settings and circumstances. Both the salience and the desirability of autoerotic activity may vary considerably among gender, racial, religious, or educational subcultures. For example, Gagnon and Simon (1973) argued that, within subcultures of men and women, the differential level of masturbatory activities in adolescent men and women can be attributed to

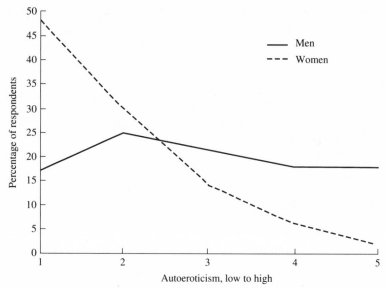

Fig. 3.3   Distribution of autoeroticism by gender.

participation in gender-segregated peer groups. They point out that masturbation is a salient concept in the adolescent subculture of young men whereas it
is completely absent in the adolescent subculture of young women.[22] Similar
processes may occur in subcultures centered around other social characteristics. For example, certain highly religious respondents evaluate the practice of
masturbation or the use of erotica as a symptom of moral failure, whereas such
an understanding is unlikely among secular individuals. On the other hand,
more secular individuals entertain a very different objection to masturbatory
activities—regarding individuals who engage in them as lacking competence
in their adult gender roles, roles that include expectations of success in securing sex partners. As another instance, preliminary research conducted during
the development of the survey instrument suggested that masturbation is both
less salient and more stigmatized among black men than among other social
groups.

Although autoerotic activities are socially considered sexual, sex and sex
life are almost always considered to involve partnered sex in general and intercourse in particular. Other activities tend to be understood as substitutes for

22. The discrepancy between men and women might also be an artifact of the questions that we
asked. If these questions were oriented toward autoerotic practices more common among men
than women, such a bias could be responsible for the observed differences. This may not, however,
be a reflection on the design of our questionnaire so much as an artifact that most of the pleasurable
aspects of sexuality are socially defined in contemporary Western culture from a male point of
view. Sexually pleasurable activities that are commonly experienced only by women are less likely
to be considered sexual or autoerotic.

penetrative sex. Our data strongly suggest, however, that this is not the case. Across individuals, most Americans do not use autoerotic activity to compensate for a lack of partnered sex. In fact, higher levels of autoeroticism are associated with higher levels of partnered sexual activity. Men do not masturbate to compensate for the lack of a partner, and women without partners are actually less likely to masturbate. Figure 3.4 shows that both men and women who are highly autoerotic are more likely to have multiple partners in the last year. Women with low levels of autoeroticism are more likely to have no partner, and the relation shows no trend for men.

Autoerotic activity is, in some sense, imaginative tutelage in a diversity of sexual scripts. In fact, individuals with higher levels of autoerotic activity are more likely to find a broader range of activities appealing than individuals with lower levels of autoerotic activity. As we discuss in greater detail in the next chapter, we asked respondents to rate various sexual techniques, forms of visual stimulation, and types of sex partners or sexual relationships from "very appealing" to "not at all appealing." Individuals who engage in little or no autoerotic activity found, on average, only about one of the items—usually vaginal intercourse itself—very appealing. By contrast, individuals who frequently engage in autoerotic activity find three to four of the items very appealing. As depicted in table 3.11, the number of items that respondents found very appealing increases monotonically with the level of autoerotic activity.

The individual who develops a more elaborate sexual script through sexual fantasy, masturbation, and the use of erotica/pornography is also more likely to enact a more diverse set of practices. Autoeroticism is highly correlated with the incidence of such sexual techniques as fellatio, cunnilingus, and anal intercourse. As depicted in figure 3.5, both men and women with higher levels of autoeroticism are more likely to engage in oral and/or anal sex in spite of the fact that men consistently report engaging in these practices more often than women (see section 3.2 above).[23] This finding suggests that interest in more elaborate sex scripts (possibly developed during autoerotic activity) could be a factor underlying the propensity to engage in a more diverse repertoire of partnered sexual practices. Although men are more likely to engage in autoerotic activities than women and to engage in a more elaborate set of practices, women with high rates of autoerotic activity engage in similarly elaborate scripts.

---

23. Unfortunately, our "diverse" repertoire is limited to only three practices: active and receptive oral sex and anal intercourse. Although the addition of certain other practices (such as vaginal intercourse, kissing, and hugging) would not be particularly enlightening because of their virtual universality, others, such as body stroking and manipulation of the genitals, do represent distinctive scripts. If we had included these items, we would be able to present a more finely grained picture of the diversity of repertoires—the small pilot surveys that were fielded during the process of constructing the questionnaire indicate that there is a great deal of variability in the presence or absence of such events in sexual repertoires. Although these items were included in a version of the pilot questionnaire for the NHSLS, they were dropped because of limitations on the length of the interview.

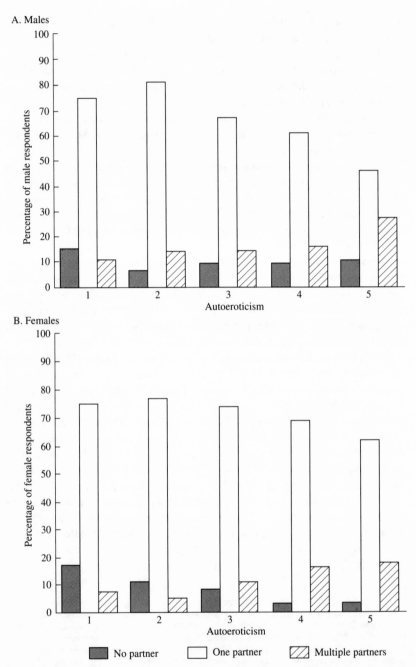

Fig. 3.4 **Number of partners and autoeroticism in the last year. A, male respondents. B, female respondents.**

Table 3.11   Scores on Autoeroticism Scale by Mean Number of Sexual Preference
                    Items Rated "Very Appealing"

	Autoeroticism: Low to High				
	1	2	3	4	5
Mean number of sexual preference items rated "very appealing"	1.22	1.91	2.44	2.86	3.66

The exploratory analyses in the preceding section suggest fairly monotonic relations between autoerotic activity, preferences for a more diverse set of sexual techniques, number of partners, and the enactment of more elaborate sexual scripts. Those who engage in relatively little autoerotic activity are less likely to prefer a wider range of sexual techniques, are less likely to have a partner, and, if they have a partner, are less likely to have sex frequently or engage in oral or anal sex. Similarly, individuals who engage in different kinds of autoerotic activity more often find a wider range of practices appealing and are more likely to have had at least one partner with whom they have sex frequently. Individuals who frequently think about sex, masturbate, and have used some type of pornography/erotica within the last year are much more likely to report enacting more elaborate interpersonal sexual scripts.

Given this evidence for the association between partnered sexual activity and autoerotic activity, we selected four patterns of sexual expression based on the two levels of autoerotic activity, the number of partners (none, one, or two or more), and frequency of partnered sex in the last year for closer examination.[24] For reasons of space and clarity, we chose only four of the twelve possible configurations as illustrative examples, but these four sexual profiles include 44 percent of our men and 55 percent of our women respondents. The four types to be discussed include (1) individuals with little autoerotic activity and no partnered sexual activity, (2) individuals with little autoerotic activity and infrequent sex with one partner, (3) individuals with more autoerotic activity and frequent sex with one partner, and (4) individuals with more autoerotic activity and frequent sex with two or more partners.

These profiles represent a selection of the diversity of sexual scripts that individuals enact. The profiles are intended to capture the content rather than the quality of an individual's sex life. Our data suggest that those individuals who participate in autoerotic activities are more likely to prefer and enact more elaborate sex scripts. This bears on the content of sex scripts and has no obvious implications for the quality of the individual's sociosexual life. In order to

24. We divided respondents into two categories of autoerotic activity on a scale of 1–5: "little" (1 or 2) and "more" (3, 4, or 5). Number of partners in the last year was collapsed into zero, one, or multiple partners. Finally, frequency of sex was dichotomized into respondents who had sex once a week or more ("more frequent partnered sex") and those who had sex less than once a week ("less frequent partnered sex").

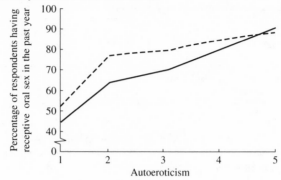

A. Receptive oral sex and autoeroticism

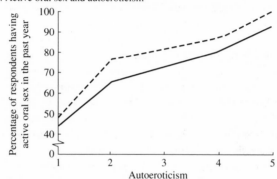

B. Active oral sex and autoeroticism

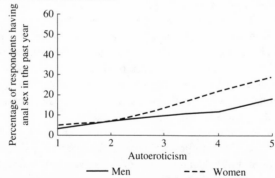

C. Anal sex and autoeroticism

——— Men   - - - Women

Fig. 3.5   Sexual practices and autoeroticism. A, Receptive oral sex and autoeroticism. B, active oral sex and autoeroticism. C, anal sex and autoeroticism.

Table 3.12   **Profiles of Partnered and Autoerotic Sexual Activity for Men and Women, by Likelihood of "Always" Having Orgasm**

	Little Autoerotic Activity and Less Frequent Partnered Sex with One Partner (%)		More Autoerotic Activity and More Frequent Sex with One Partner (%)		More Frequent Autoerotic Activity and More Frequent Sex with Multiple Partners (%)	
	Men	Women	Men	Women	Men	Women
Always had an orgasm with primary partner	70	27	76	30	75	26

emphasize this point, table 3.12 gives the rates of orgasm by sexual profile for those respondents with a partner last year. There is no significant association between sexual profile and sociosexual satisfaction (as measured by percentage of respondents who report always having an orgasm).

Although levels of sexual satisfaction are not captured by these profiles, the particular configurations of the facets of sexual expression are. We propose that the configurations of sexual activities are shaped by social processes that differ, depending on the individual's social location. The profiles are presented in table 3.13 to highlight the socially structured character of sexual expression and to suggest the extent to which an individual's social location (in terms of the master statuses) might serve to facilitate or inhibit the level of sexual interest and expression. Social location affects the ways in which individuals experience and understand their sex lives. It affects the extent to which they consider sex an important part of life and whether they view certain practices as desirable or unappealing. Social location is also a proxy for the level of resources (cultural, social, and economic) that an individual can mobilize to achieve the fulfillment of his or her sexual wants. Different location in the social order is the primary force that allocates individuals to different profiles of sexual activity.

Low Autoerotic Activity and No Partnered Sexual Activity

Individuals with this profile have engaged in very little autoerotic activity and partnered sexual activity in the last year. They are predominantly women, some 78 percent of the total in the category. Over 60 percent of these women are over the age of forty, and nearly 50 percent are divorced, widowed, or separated and living alone, thus lacking access to a regular sex partner. Women at both extremes of the distribution of educational attainment are overrepresented here. The minority of men characterized by this least sexually active profile are more likely to be in either their early twenties or their late fifties and either to have never been married or to be widowed, separated, or divorced. The men are more likely to have less than a high school education, and 45

Table 3.13   Sexual Profiles and Master Statuses (% distributions)

	No Partner, Low Autoeroticism		One Partner/ Less Often, Low Autoeroticism		One Partner/ More Often, High Autoeroticism		Two or More Partners/More Often, High Autoeroticism		Sample Distribution	
	Men	Women	Men	Women	Men	Women	Men	Women	Men	Women
Overall	22	78	31	69	60	40	77	23	45	55
Age:										
18–24	26	13	10	11	19	18	26	29	16	16
25–29	13	4	8	11	19	24	29	18	16	13
30–34	9	9	11	15	20	18	18	29	16	17
35–39	9	11	15	15	12	18	11	7	14	15
40–44	4	13	17	17	15	11	9	11	13	13
45–49	13	12	9	11	7	9	3	7	10	10
50–54	7	14	14	11	5	1	1	0	8	8
55–59	19	25	16	9	3	1	2	0	6	8
Marital status:										
Nev. marr., not coh.	64	38	11	12	13	7	44	26	29	20
Nev. marr., coh.	0	0	1	2	8	9	14	11	4	4
Married	11	12	79	72	69	64	24	26	52	55

Div./sep./wid., not coh.	25	49	6	11	5	13	16	22	12	18
Div./sep./wid., coh.	0	1	3	3	5	6	2	15	3	3
Education:										
Less than HS	24	19	17	13	11	10	13	7	14	14
HS grad. or eq.	31	24	31	32	29	28	29	21	29	29
Some coll./voc.	31	32	28	34	34	41	32	46	32	34
Finished coll.	11	15	16	14	14	14	23	18	17	16
Master's/adv. deg.	2	10	9	6	12	6	3	7	9	6
Religion:										
None	16	6	9	7	13	13	18	19	14	9
Type I Prot.[a]	16	26	29	26	26	17	25	27	23	24
Type II Prot.[a]	45	37	36	36	24	37	27	23	29	34
Catholic	24	28	22	28	34	32	28	27	27	27
Race/ethnicity:										
White	70	72	78	75	82	77	69	68	74	70
Black	21	21	15	15	9	12	15	19	14	18
Hispanic	9	8	7	9	9	10	16	13	9	10
N	54	190	273	613	202	136	96	28	1407	1747

Note: For the abbreviations of master status variables, see the note to table 3.1.

[a]For an explanation of the categories of Protestants, see appendix 3.1A.

percent are Type II Protestants. Thus, the social profiles of the men and women with this sexual pattern are strikingly different; this reflects the different social circumstances in which a lack of interest in autoerotic matters is defined as socially appropriate for men and women. The majority of women with this profile are older, and nearly a majority of men are Type II Protestants. These individuals are associated with groups in which the practice of autoerotic activities would be considered aberrant or morally undesirable.

However, the different social characteristics of the men and women in this category may also reflect the different kinds of resources that men and women are expected to bring to sexual transactions. Men prefer partners who are younger and more attractive than themselves, whereas women are more willing to marry men who are older or not physically attractive but less willing to become involved with men who are not financially secure (South 1991). Following this social logic, older women and younger men would be relatively disadvantaged in sexual transactions. Similarly, men with little education (which is moderately associated with income) would be disadvantaged, as would women with high levels of education (because of the small number of men with equal or higher levels of education). In sum, individuals are more likely to have this sexual profile by virtue of both the interests and the resources associated with their social location.

Low Autoerotic Activity and Less Frequent Sex with One Partner

Individuals who have partnered sex with one partner relatively infrequently and little autoerotic activity are also likely to be women (69 percent of the category). This profile includes the largest number of respondents (about 28 percent of the total sample) and thus tends to reflect the distribution of the characteristics in the sample fairly closely. Married people, however, are over-represented (79 percent of the men and 72 percent of the women). In some sense, this profile may represent a "silent majority" of people for whom a modest amount of sexual activity is a routine part of life but for whom sex is neither especially salient nor problematic. These men and women may be preoccupied with other aspects of life, such as family or career responsibilities or both, and have little time or energy to devote to elaborating their sexual activities. It is worth recalling that this may well reflect an accommodation to a stage of life; these people were not always married or burdened with child care and work responsibilities. They may well have conducted their sex lives according to other sexual profiles in other periods of their lives.

More Autoerotic Activity and Frequent Sex with One Partner

Individuals with this profile had both the interest and the opportunity to engage in substantial autoerotic and partnered sexual activity with one partner in the past year. Men, married people, and those never married but living with a partner are overrepresented in this profile, while never-married men and women who live alone are underrepresented. Catholics are somewhat overrepresented and female Type I Protestants underrepresented. Individuals with this profile are likely to be involved in a live-in relationship in which sexual exclusivity is almost universally expected and in which mutual monitoring of behavior will be facilitated. Both expectations and circumstances will militate against engaging in more than one relationship simultaneously, and the fact that people are married or in cohabitational relationships makes rapid turnover of relationships less likely.

More Autoerotic Activity and Frequent Sex with Multiple Partners

Individuals with this profile manifest high levels of generalized interest in autoerotic and partnered activities and were also involved with two or more partners in the last year. They are predominantly men, some 77 percent of the category as a whole. These highly active people are much more likely to be men in their twenties to mid-thirties or women between eighteen and thirty-five. People over forty-five are almost wholly absent from this profile. About 44 percent of the men and 26 percent of the women have never been married and are living alone. Men and women who have never been married but are living with a partner are also overrepresented in this profile. Individuals with low levels of education are underrepresented in this profile, while women who are not religious are overrepresented. Sexuality is thus highly salient and less routine for people having this profile. The fact that a majority of individuals with this profile are younger and never married suggests that they are searching for a partner or at least occupying a social position in which a high level of sexual activity with multiple partners is not strongly sanctioned. It also appears that individuals with this profile have significant levels of social, economic, and cultural resources with which to pursue nonroutine sexual interactions successfully.

3.5 Conclusion

Overall, these profiles of sexual expression suggest that the interests and resources associated with specific social locations lead to diverse manifestations of sexual expression. With cross-sectional information referring only to the current period (i.e., the past twelve months), we cannot examine with any precision the dynamics of individuals passing from one profile to another over time in response to changing life circumstances. It is obvious that individuals do have sexual histories that, on the whole, are orderly and predictable, even if they entail major personal discontinuities in the character and extent of sexual conduct from one stage to the next and are unwanted. Chapter 13 describes some features of this orderliness in marital and cohabitational history as functions of age and cohort, but we can only infer the associated changes in sexual conduct since we did not ask for comparable detail on sexual activities in periods at some remove from the present. The point here is to underline the fact that a person's sexual profile describes a limited cross section of his or her activities at the current moment. How stable or changeable that profile is over time can be expected to exert substantial effects on how individuals think about their own and other people's sex lives, past, present, and future.

APPENDIX 3.1A:
CONSTRUCTION OF THE RELIGION VARIABLE FOR PROTESTANT RESPONDENTS

The Protestant Church in the United States is composed of a diverse population of well over 200 distinctly named denominations and sects (Gaustad, 1962). The genealogy of these groups is a convoluted one. While all denominations have evolved since their emergence in the United States, some have remained relatively intact (theologically, socially, and demographically) while others have been marked by a history of conflict, division and subdivision. Consequently, any classification system applied to Protestantism oversimplifies the inevitable intradenomination variability in religious and political orientation. For instance, both Southern Baptists (generally conservative) and American Baptists (a more mainstream, even liberal, wing concentrated in the Northeast) may code themselves as "Baptists" while maintaining very different religious world views. No coding system that seeks parsimony as well as conceptual clarity can hope to take account of each and every distinction within or between Protestant sub-groups.

While the coding scheme we have employed is certainly no exception, we feel it captures the theological and political "center of gravity" of the major Protestant groups. Our questionnaire asked of each respondent what his or her current religion was (see appendix C, section 1, questions 15–18). If the respondent reported "Protestant," he or she was asked "what specific denomination is that, if any?" with "Baptist," "Methodist," "Lutheran," "Presbyterian," "Episcopalian" or "Other" as possible responses. In the last case, the respondent was asked to name his or her specific denominational affiliation. These verbatim responses were recoded along with the initial denominational categories to produce 52 distinct groups. We then created a variable for Protestant religious affiliation that sorted denominations by their modal religio-political orientation. We identified this modal orientation based on the General Social Survey's threefold scheme (each denomination is coded as "liberal," "moderate," or "conservative") and with reference to Roof and McKinney's excellent descriptive overview of contemporary American religion (Roof and McKinney, 1987; see also Roof 1985, 1993).

We decided on a two-category variable that would differentiate between the mainstream and fundamentalist strains of contemporary Protestantism. Type I Protestants comprise liberal and moderate denominations, including, e.g., Methodists, Lutherans, Presbyterians, Episcopalians, and United Church of Christ. These groups are generally more mainstream in orientation and are typically older, more well established denominations (excepting Baptists, who are coded as Type II Protestants). Type II Protestants (including, e.g. Baptists, Pentecostals, Churches of Christ, and Assemblies of God) are politically conservative and are more likely to have an evangelical or fundamentalist religious world view. Because doctrinally and demographically marginal groups such as Mormons and Jehovah's Witnesses share a more conservative/fundamentalist orientation, we included them within this category. For Type II Protestants, religious considerations may simply be more important or salient in organizing sexual action than they are for Type I Protestants. One expression of this key distinction between Type I and II Protestants is the relative percentage of respondents in both groups who report having had a "born again" religious experience. One third of Type I Protestants reported such an experience, while fully two-thirds of Type II Protestants did so. In addition, as a brief glance at the findings from this chapter will reveal, our variable construction holds up quite nicely to a variety of conceivable tests of external validity.

CHAPTER 4

The Social Organization of Subjective Sexual Preferences

What a given individual finds sexually appealing is often represented as highly idiosyncratic. A person's sexual thoughts, fantasies, and preferences are conventionally seen as expressing his or her distinctiveness or singularity in a way that few other realms of personal knowledge and experience can. Yet subjective preferences are as much a product of social factors as are the sexual behaviors that we examined in chapter 3. In this chapter, we consider the social organization of preferences for a variety of sexual acts and practices. Although presented in isolation from their behavioral context, these practices must be seen as moments in the various sex scripts that render them meaningful. It is through reference to such intrapsychic sex scripts that questions concerning the appeal of certain sexual practices are framed, interpreted, and answered. Indeed, scripts organizing the normative relation of particular social categories to the realm of sexuality in general may channel responses to questions concerning sexual preferences. For instance, women over age forty-five, particularly those with lower levels of education, may frame their own desire with reference to scripts that assign different levels of sexual drive to men and women. In consequence, they may be more oriented, on a general level, toward response categories that describe their level of appeal for sex acts as moderate. In addition to intrapsychic scripts, we also recognize the importance of interpersonal scripts and their reciprocal influence on constellations of sexual preferences. Sexual partnerships and social contexts provide resources through which sexual scripts and proclivities are constructed and negotiated over time.

We also examine the relation between actual behavior over the life course and sexual preferences for certain key sexual techniques. Whether a particular sexual practice has occurred in the lifetime of an individual has important implications for the interpretation of its reported appeal. Finally, we consider the relation between the appeal of sexual techniques (e.g., oral sex) and their occurrence in the last sexual event. The degree to which the two are correlated for an individual gives us some measure of his or her capacity to influence sexual outcomes in a relationship. Assessments, for instance, of the relative

We gratefully acknowledge Christopher Browning's help in data analysis and drafting. The chapter was prepared under the direction of Edward O. Laumann and John H. Gagnon.

power of men and women in sexual interaction cannot be made effectively without reference to the desires that individuals bring to sexual events.

Of course, the universe of possible sexually related tastes expands far beyond the scope of our study. Unfortunately, time constraints limited our inquiry into sexual preferences to a core set of fourteen practices. These practices fall under three general preference categories. First, we consider preferences for particular sexual techniques. Included in this category are vaginal, anal, and oral sex as well as manual stimulation of the anus and the use of vibrators. Second, we inquire into preferences for certain types of visual stimulation, including watching a partner undress or seeing other people engage in sex acts. Finally, we examine the appeal of different types of sex partners or sexual relationships: same-gender sex, sex with a stranger, group sex, and relationships involving force.

Before looking at these subjective preferences for sexual practices in greater detail, we should note several important limitations of the data. The first has to do with the selection of the items to be included. They were not chosen by starting with a large universe of items that were then presented to a well-defined sample of judges, a procedure that would have allowed us to select practices with well-known response properties. To the contrary, we proceeded in a somewhat ad hoc manner, selecting a range of practices that seemed to tap various dimensions of sexuality, some more popular, some less. Other items (e.g., hugging, kissing, breast fondling) could have been included in their stead. As a result, the list may be biased to an unknown degree, including more items of greater appeal to certain groups of respondents (men or women, younger or older, less or more educated, etc.). Second, it is possible that the response category that we have chosen to characterize this variable, the proportion who found it "very appealing," may have too high a threshold of "appeal" for various groups (for the text of the item, see appendix C, section 7, questions 4–5). Thus, men might find it easier to respond that an item is "very appealing" than women (who might more often have chosen "somewhat appealing"), and young people might have found it easier than those who are older to make a similar choice. Such presumptions would lead us to predict that men, or young people, will find more sexual practices to which they can respond with "very appealing" than women, or older people, will.

Our hunches are strongly borne out, as depicted in table 4.1. Men and women are strongly distinguished in their relative willingness to find practices in our list "very appealing." To be sure, even the men managed to find, on the average, only 2.6 items "very appealing," and, in four out of five cases, one of them was vaginal intercourse. Appeal displays a more complex pattern by age, within genders; there is little change across age categories between eighteen and forty-four, and then there appears to be a distinct "break" in the number of items found to be very appealing. One suspects that this may be more a period than an aging effect since only the age cohorts having come of sexual age before 1965 show the decline and it is essentially uniform across the subse-

Table 4.1   **Mean Number of "Very Appealing" Responses to the Appeal Items, by Social Characteristics**[a]

Social Characteristics	Mean Number of "Very Appealing" Responses	
	Men	Women
Total population	2.57	1.64
Age:		
18–24	2.50	1.61
25–29	2.84	1.89
30–34	2.68	1.86
35–39	2.76	1.75
40–44	2.82	1.59
45–49	2.19	1.71
50–54	1.94	1.25
55–59	2.08	1.04
Education:		
Less than HS	2.27	1.27
HS grad. or eq.	2.40	1.56
Some coll./voc.	2.70	1.67
Finished coll.	2.79	1.87
Master's/adv. deg.	2.60	2.13
Race/ethnicity:		
White	2.60	1.68
Black	2.47	1.49
Hispanic	2.38	1.65
Asian	2.65	1.50
Native Am.	1.80	1.08
N	1,410	1,749

Note: Nev. marr., not coh. = never married, not cohabiting; nev. marr., coh. = never married, cohabiting; div./sep./wid., coh. = divorced/separated/widowed, cohabiting; div./sep./wid., not coh. = divorced/separated/widowed, not cohabiting; less than HS = less than high school; HS grad. or eq. = high school graduate or equivalent; some coll./voc. = some college/vocational school; finished coll. = finished college; master's/adv. deg. = master's/advanced degree; Type I/II Prot. = Type I/II Protestant (see appendix 3.1A); Native Am. = Native American.

[a]Means are based on fourteen appeal items in the case of women and fifteen in the case of men (an additional item on the appeal of active anal sex was included for men).

quent fifteen years of age. Educational differences seem to exert little influence on men's responses, with the exception of men with more than a college degree. For women, increasing education appears to exert a positive effect on the willingness to express the strong appeal of sexual practices. Finally, for both men and women, the differences by racial/ethnic groups are statistically significant, suggesting the possibility of important differences in the sex scenarios associated with these different groups.

With these caveats on the limitations of the scale of subjective preferences in mind, we can turn to table 4.2, which reports the percentage of respondents who said that a given sexual practice was "very appealing."[1] Practices are listed in the order of their popularity in the sample as a whole, not broken down by gender. In general, the sexual techniques that we asked about were more appealing to our respondents than were the practices that involved varied features of partnerships. Even such less conventional sexual techniques as those involving anal stimulation were more popular than having sex with a stranger or a person of the same sex and considerably more appealing than forced sex. Similarly, the highly discrepant appeal of the two visually oriented practices could be a function of the nature of the sex partner involved. Watching a "partner" undress was a relatively appealing practice, second only to vaginal intercourse in overall popularity. Seeing "other people" do sexual things, however, was considerably less popular, ranking with other practices that involved unconventional sexual partnerships. The limited number of practices included in this analysis precludes drawing any strong conclusions from this tendency. However, the data suggest that the type of relationship within which a sexual practice is imagined may organize the assessment of its relative appeal.

Of the techniques that we considered, only vaginal intercourse commands almost universal appeal. Roughly eight out of ten respondents consider vaginal intercourse very appealing. The highly normative character of vaginal intercourse undoubtedly contributes not only to the size of the proportion of respondents who find it very appealing but also to the closer correspondence (compared with other practices) of the proportions reported by men and women (84 and 77 percent, respectively).

Although gender was not as important a factor in structuring the appeal of vaginal intercourse, other master status characteristics were clearly associated. Age, for instance, was curvilinearly related to the appeal of vaginal intercourse: younger and older respondents were somewhat less likely to report it as highly preferable. The decline is more significant for older women. From a peak of 81 percent of women in their twenties, the percentage remains stable through the middle-aged cohort and declines abruptly (to 67 percent) for women in their late fifties. As we have suggested, this may be less a function of declining sexual interest or experienced pleasure with age than of the implicit

1. For the questions asked, see appendix C, section 7, questions 4–5. Respondents were asked whether they found a given sexual technique or practice "very," "somewhat," "not," or "not at all" appealing. The seemingly redundant labeling of the negative categories ("not" and "not at all") was intended to distinguish between those acts found generally distasteful or tedious from practices considered exceptionally repellent to our respondents. We considered it very likely that we would find that people's assessments of practices that are highly repellent to them follow distinctive social and psychological principles that are not merely the mirror or reverse image of those used to explain people's strong attractions to certain practices. Recall the literature on work satisfaction (e.g., Herzberg, 1973) that shows that aspects of jobs that are intrinsically rewarding and satisfying are quite different from those features of jobs that serve as sources of dissatisfaction. Further work will clearly be needed to sort out these and other issues pertaining to subjective preferences for sexual practices.

Table 4.2   The Social Organization of Sexual Preferences[a] (percentage who found selected techniques/practices "very appealing")[b]

Selected Social Characteristics	Vaginal Intercourse		Watching Partner Undress		Receiving Oral Sex		Giving Oral Sex		Group Sex		Anus Stimulated by Partner's Finger		Stimulate Partner's Anus		Active Anal Sex, Men
	Men	Women	Men	Women	Men	Women	Men	Women	Men	Women	Men	Women	Men	Women	
Total population	83.8	76.8	47.8	26.8	45.0	28.8	33.5	16.5	13.3	1.1	5.6	4.1	6.2	2.4	4.1
Age:															
18–24	77.3	70.2	49.8	30.8	46.7	35.4	31.6	14.6	17.8	1.8	3.6	2.6	4.0	.7	2.7
25–29	82.1	81.1	51.1	34.3	55.9	36.1	44.3	21.1	14.8	.4	6.3	3.9	7.2	2.6	4.7
30–34	82.9	81.2	45.3	33.1	45.3	35.9	35.9	22.0	14.6	.7	5.4	3.8	5.9	1.4	5.6
35–39	87.2	78.8	54.5	26.7	50.5	35.0	34.5	19.6	12.8	1.9	6.9	4.2	7.5	2.7	5.6
40–44	89.1	77.7	50.5	24.0	51.6	21.8	39.6	14.8	10.9	1.3	8.2	3.5	9.9	3.1	6.8
45–49	87.1	78.4	40.3	25.1	33.3	24.6	27.5	18.6	12.1	1.8	2.9	6.0	2.9	3.6	1.5
50–54	85.3	75.7	40.4	14.9	26.9	12.2	21.1	7.2	8.3	‡	2.8	5.8	2.8	4.3	‡
55–59	82.0	66.7	40.0	12.5	26.7	9.5	15.6	4.4	8.9	‡	7.8	5.1	7.8	2.9	2.4
Marital status:															
Nev. marr., not coh.	74.1	62.9	49.1	31.4	49.4	32.8	33.5	15.8	14.4	1.2	5.7	2.7	5.7	1.8	4.6
Nev. marr., coh.	85.0	79.2	60.0	34.2	56.7	42.5	43.3	21.9	31.1	2.7	11.7	6.8	13.6	2.7	6.9
Married	88.0	81.5	45.2	25.4	39.8	25.4	30.1	15.0	11.0	.8	5.2	3.7	5.9	2.3	3.8
Div./sep./wid., not coh.	87.2	77.3	51.8	26.1	47.6	30.5	39.6	19.5	11.6	.6	4.9	5.2	6.1	2.6	3.8

Div./sep./wid., coh.	86.8	73.2	52.6	17.9	59.5	32.1	48.6	19.6	23.7	3.6	7.9	5.4	7.9	3.6	2.7
Education:															
Less than HS	72.7	65.7	46.3	22.5	32.3	16.9	23.1	12.8	13.2	.8	4.8	3.3	7.0	3.3	4.4
HS grad. or eq.	83.9	75.5	47.6	25.0	39.0	25.8	30.8	13.2	11.4	1.2	5.2	4.7	6.3	2.6	3.0
Some coll./voc.	84.0	78.6	46.8	27.1	49.9	31.0	37.9	16.5	15.2	.9	6.3	3.3	5.7	2.4	4.7
Finished coll.	87.7	83.1	52.3	29.4	54.7	36.5	36.9	21.7	15.5	1.4	5.9	4.0	5.9	1.4	3.9
Master's/adv. deg.	92.4	83.2	45.4	37.0	47.1	37.7	35.3	27.4	8.3	1.8	4.2	7.5	6.7	2.8	5.4
Religion:															
None	79.4	75.5	47.9	29.8	57.2	47.0	43.3	27.8	17.0	2.0	6.2	4.7	8.8	2.7	4.2
Type I Prot.	84.8	81.1	48.4	25.3	47.2	27.9	34.3	14.2	11.8	1.0	5.3	4.1	4.7	2.6	2.9
Type II Prot.	85.3	75.8	48.3	26.1	36.0	20.4	25.2	10.9	10.0	.8	5.1	4.8	5.8	3.4	4.0
Catholic	84.2	75.0	47.5	28.5	44.5	32.5	34.1	20.2	15.7	1.1	5.6	2.8	5.9	1.1	3.6
Jewish	†	†	†	†	†	†	†	†	†	†	†	†	†	†	†
Other	75.0	69.4	45.0	27.0	47.5	44.4	42.5	22.2	22.0	2.7	12.5	5.6	7.5	†	7.9
Race/ethnicity:															
White	84.6	78.2	47.6	26.7	47.8	30.6	37.1	18.2	13.4	.9	4.5	4.0	5.2	2.3	3.9
Black	85.4	73.7	51.5	34.7	30.6	19.2	17.5	7.6	13.0	1.2	7.3	3.5	7.3	3.2	3.1
Hispanic	80.9	67.8	46.3	20.2	38.5	31.9	26.9	18.1	10.9	1.6	5.9	4.4	8.1	2.8	3.0
Asian	71.4	73.3	28.6	20.7	37.1	26.7	28.6	16.7	17.1	†	25.7	6.9	22.9	3.4	11.4
Native Am.	†	†	†	†	†	†	†	†	†	†	†	†	†	†	†
N	1,396	1,730	1,398	1,733	1,391	1,728	1,391	1,727	1,403	1,739	1,393	1,726	1,391	1,727	1,350

(*continued*)

Table 4.2 (continued)

	Using a Dildo or Vibrator		Watching Other People Do Sexual Things		Same-Gender Partner		Sex with a Stranger		Passive Anal Intercourse		Forcing a Sex Partner		Being Forced by a Sex Partner	
	Men	Women	Men	Women	Men	Women	Men	Women	Men	Women	Men	Women	Men	Women
Total population	4.4	2.9	5.3	1.5	3.2	2.9	4.1	.9	2.8	1.0	.3	.2	.1	.1
Age:														
18–24	3.1	.7	4.0	1.1	4.0	1.4	4.9	1.1	1.9	.4	‡	.4	.4	.4
25–29	5.0	1.7	6.3	3.0	3.1	3.4	2.7	.4	2.3	2.2	‡	‡	.5	‡
30–34	4.6	3.8	7.5	1.7	7.1	3.4	8.0	.7	4.6	.7	.9	.3	‡	‡
35–39	6.0	3.4	4.9	.8	1.5	4.2	3.4	1.1	2.5	.4	‡	‡	‡	‡
40–44	6.0	3.5	5.4	1.3	2.2	3.5	3.8	1.7	3.9	1.3	‡	.9	‡	‡
45–49	2.9	5.4	3.6	1.8	3.6	4.8	1.4	.6	2.2	1.8	‡	‡	‡	‡
50–54	.9	2.9	5.5	1.4	.9	1.4	‡	.7	‡	1.4	‡	‡	‡	‡
55–59	4.4	2.2	3.3	1.4	‡	‡	6.6	.7	3.4	.7	2.2	‡	‡	‡
Marital status:														
Nev. marr., not coh.	4.5	3.4	7.2	2.1	6.7	3.9	6.2	.6	3.6	1.2	.5	.3	.2	‡
Nev. marr., coh.	5.1	1.4	13.1	‡	6.4	6.8	8.2	1.4	3.4	‡	‡	‡	‡	1.4
Married	4.2	2.6	3.9	1.5	.7	1.8	2.8	.8	2.6	.5	.3	.2	.1	‡
Div./sep./ wid., not coh.	3.7	2.6	4.8	1.0	1.2	2.3	3.0	1.3	1.9	1.6	‡	.3	‡	‡
Div./sep./ wid., coh.	7.9	7.1	5.3	1.8	‡	10.7	2.6	‡	‡	7.1	‡	‡	‡	‡
Education:														
Less than HS	4.3	.8	7.9	1.2	2.1	.4	7.9	.4	2.7	.8	1.1	‡	.5	‡

HS grad. or eq.	3.8	2.6	4.0	1.2	2.0	2.4	2.0	1.2	1.8	1.4	.2	.6	.2	‡
Some coll./voc.	6.3	2.4	5.4	2.2	4.7	2.7	3.8	.5	3.2	.7	.2	‡	‡	‡
Finished coll.	3.0	3.6	5.4	.7	3.8	4.6	4.6	1.1	3.0	1.1	‡	.4	‡	.2
Master's/adv. deg.	2.5	8.5	5.8	1.8	2.5	6.4	4.2	1.8	4.3	1.0	‡	‡	‡	‡
Religion:														
None	7.2	4.0	10.3	2.0	5.7	5.3	6.7	1.3	3.7	1.3	.5	‡	1.0	.7
Type I Prot.	4.3	1.9	4.3	1.2	3.4	1.2	2.5	.7	2.2	1.0	.3	.2	‡	‡
Type II Prot.	2.8	2.7	4.5	1.4	2.5	2.4	2.7	1.0	2.1	1.1	‡	.5	‡	‡
Catholic	5.4	3.2	4.5	1.9	1.9	3.6	4.8	.4	1.9	.8	.5	‡	‡	‡
Jewish	†	†	†	†	†	†	†	†	†	†	†	†	†	†
Other	2.6	5.6	4.9	2.7	9.8	10.8	7.5	5.4	15.0	‡	‡	‡	‡	‡
Race/ethnicity:														
White	4.1	3.2	5.0	1.6	3.3	2.7	4.0	.9	2.6	.9	.2	.1	.2	.1
Black	5.9	2.4	7.7	1.8	2.9	3.5	3.4	1.5	2.0	1.8	‡	.9	‡	‡
Hispanic	3.0	2.2	2.2	.5	2.9	4.4	3.6	‡	2.2	1.6	1.5	‡	‡	‡
Asian	5.9	0.0	8.6	3.3	‡	‡	2.9	0.0	14.3	‡	‡	‡	‡	‡
Native Am.	†	†	†	†	†	†	†	†	†	†	†	†	†	†
N	1,387	1,723	1,404	1,742	1,404	1,743	1,403	1,742	1,370	1,724	1,404	1,742	1,402	1,743

Note: For variable definitions, see the note to table 4.1. † indicates that base *N* is under thirty cases. ‡ means zero observations.

[a] Regardless of sexual orientation.

[b] Respondents were asked whether they would rate a given sexual practice as "very," "somewhat," "not," or "not at all" appealing.

desexualization of older women in our culture, a condition that has important implications for the way in which women view and present their own sexuality.

Partnership type is of importance in evaluating the appeal of a sexual technique. This is indicated by the differences found between respondents who were living with a sex partner at the time of the interview and those who were not. Never married and noncohabiting respondents were less likely to report vaginal intercourse very appealing than either cohabiting or married respondents. Of respondents without a live-in partner, 74 percent of men and 63 percent of women reported vaginal intercourse as very appealing, compared with percentages that were ten to fifteen points higher for respondents living with their sex partners. The latter group, on average, has considerably higher levels of investment in their sexual partnerships than does the former. Indeed, respondents in relatively long-term and highly committed relationships may tend to consider the appeal of certain sexual techniques in the context of a specific partner rather than across partnerships. Married individuals may be more likely to say that they find vaginal intercourse very appealing because of its central—if not defining—role in the sexual event. For these respondents, reporting vaginal intercourse as anything less than very appealing may evoke more fundamental or possibly partner-specific sexual dissatisfactions that are at odds with the script defining intimate relationships. In other words, to say that vaginal intercourse is only somewhat appealing may, for some, be tantamount to saying that their spouse or even sex is only somewhat appealing.

It is worth noting, however, that some 20 percent of the population did not regard vaginal intercourse as very appealing despite its near ubiquity as a sexual practice.[2] As we have seen, age and marital status may play some role in this tendency. Less education, however, may lead to the predominance of more traditionally oriented scripts that frame sex not in terms of health—either psychological or relational—but in terms of more traditional categories, such as the distinction between mind and body, or that between human and animal, or even religious categories. For these individuals, sex may be seen more as a drive to be conquered and contained. Consequently, the extreme categories of appeal are more likely to be avoided. As we saw in table 4.2, men with less than a high school education were nearly 20 percentage points less likely to report vaginal intercourse as very appealing than were men with advanced degrees (73 compared with 92 percent). The equivalent discrepancy for women was 17 percentage points.

Much of our speculation concerning the distribution of the appeal of vaginal intercourse draws on the more fundamental sexual scripts that are likely to be conceptually linked to so common a sexual practice. Thus, we focused on the implications of responses to questions concerning its appeal for general satisfaction with a sex partner or one's essential relation to sexuality—all of which

---

2. Recall that, on various behavioral queries, some 95 percent of the population indicated vaginal intercourse as having occurred in the last event or in the last year if they had a partner.

depend on the assumption that, for most people who prefer sex with people of the opposite gender, vaginal intercourse is, in fact, an (if not the) act that defines an event as sexual. Although oral sex is next in popularity as a sexual technique, it does not occupy the essential and defining role that vaginal intercourse does in the sexual event for heterosexuals. Indeed, as we stated earlier, oral sex may be the most contested of the sexual practices that we consider. Its potential as a cause of conflict in sexual relationships (a topic that we consider below) renders the distribution of its appeal of particular interest.

Compared with vaginal intercourse, the discrepancies between men and women with regard to the appeal of both giving and receiving oral sex were considerably larger. Keeping in mind the possible tendency for women to view the appeal of sexual practices with reference to less extreme categories, we nevertheless observed significant gender-based differences in the preference for oral sex. While 45 percent of men found receiving oral sex (fellatio) very appealing, only 17 percent of women found giving oral sex very appealing. On the other hand, gender-based reports of the appeal of cunnilingus were markedly closer. Only 5 percentage points separated the proportions of women (29 percent) and men (34 percent) who said that they found cunnilingus very appealing—and notice here that the proportion of men is actually larger. Contrary to the popular construction of oral sex as a sacrifice for the performing partner, the proportion of men who report cunnilingus to be very appealing is not radically different than the proportion reporting the same level of preference for fellatio. For women, the proportion preferring to receive oral sex was more than 10 percentage points higher than the proportion preferring to perform it, indicating that fellatio may be viewed as an obligation for women in a way that cunnilingus is not for men. Again, we examine these discrepancies in more detail and with reference to their behavioral correlates below.

Preferences for both giving and receiving oral sex exhibited many of the same distributive tendencies that we observed for vaginal intercourse. Older respondents were less likely to report high levels of preference for both giving and receiving oral sex. Older women, in particular, were highly unlikely to report giving oral sex (4 percent) or receiving it (10 percent) as very appealing. Younger respondents did not find receiving oral sex to be less appealing than older cohorts did, but they did appear to find giving it somewhat less appealing. This may reflect higher rates of inexperience and unfamiliarity with the practice.

While we found no apparent differences between married respondents and those living together with respect to the appeal of vaginal intercourse, the latter reported both giving and receiving oral sex as very appealing at higher rates than did respondents of any other marital status. These discrepancies may be due, in part, to the youth and the higher average level of education of the cohabiting population. As with vaginal intercourse, education was associated with an increase in the reported appeal of oral sex. Men with advanced degrees, however, were somewhat less likely than college-educated men to prefer receiving oral sex and were no more likely to prefer giving oral sex. Finally, the strong association between race and the incidence of oral sex held for its appeal as well. Blacks, in particular, were noticeably less likely to find either giving or receiving oral sex very appealing. The discrepancies between men and women with regard to fellatio were extreme. The proportion of men who reported fellatio as very appealing was four times the comparable proportion of women.

The other practices that we considered—primarily anal eroticism—were uniformly less popular than either oral or vaginal sex or watching one's partner undress. We asked about both anal intercourse and manual stimulation of the anus. The population of interest in our discussion of appeal includes respondents who reported both same- and opposite-gender partners. Consequently, comparisons of the proportions finding the various sexual techniques discussed here appealing—especially those involving anal stimulation—with the behavioral figures reported earlier should be interpreted with these differences in population composition in mind. For instance, the overall proportion of men who reported active anal intercourse very appealing (4.1 percent) was nearly twice that reporting its occurrence during a last heterosexual event (2.3 percent). Similarly, the considerably smaller proportion of women who find the compatible technique—receptive anal intercourse—very appealing (1 percent) may not necessarily indicate discrepant levels of appeal in the heterosexual population. Rather, differences in sexual orientation (among men) may account for some of the discrepancy. The proportion of men who report receptive anal intercourse very appealing (2.8 percent) may be predominantly representative of a population more oriented toward same-gender partnerships.[3]

Techniques involving manual stimulation of the anus (by the partner or the respondent) were only slightly more popular than anal intercourse. The proportion of men reporting either as very appealing was around 6 percent. Women were somewhat more inclined to report receiving anal stimulation as very appealing than they were either anal intercourse or stimulating a partner's anus. In general, however, anal eroticism has not been incorporated into the sex scripts, either intrapsychic or interpersonal, of most Americans. Neither has the use of dildos or vibrators. To the extent that the popularity of these devices is representative of the appeal of other, similar ones, we can also conclude that supplementary sex "aids" or "toys" have not made significant inroads into the imaginative sex lives of men and women.

It is worth noting that our inquiry concerned the general appeal of "using a dildo or vibrator"—we allowed the respondent to determine whether the ques-

3. Compared with the percentages of men who report any same-gender desire, identity, or behavior (same-gender partners), the proportion of men reporting receptive anal intercourse to be very appealing is surprisingly high (for an extended discussion of these data, see chapter 8). We suspect that some men may have interpreted the question to mean heterosexual anal intercourse performed in a "passive" position (e.g., with the woman on top).

tion referred to use with a partner or without. Presumably, men would be more likely to refer to their use in interaction with a partner, whereas women might consider the appeal of dildos or vibrators as masturbatory devices. Thus, the question was likely to evoke different interpretative frames for the two genders. Men were, however, still more likely to find their use more appealing than women—excepting women with advanced degrees, 9 percent of whom reported using a dildo or vibrator to be very appealing, 6 percentage points higher than the mean for all women (3 percent).

Despite their low popularity, techniques involving anal eroticism still held greater appeal than practices involving unconventional sex partners or sexual relationships. Of the five practices that fell into this category, only group sex commanded a relatively high level of popularity. The appeal of group sex, however, was based largely on the significant proportion of men who found this practice very appealing (13 percent). The ratio of the proportion of men who found group sex very appealing to that of women was by far the largest of any practice that we considered. Only 1 percent of women found group sex appealing, indicating that men have a far greater likelihood of including this practice in sexual fantasy than do women.

Why this is so undoubtedly relates to the very different narratives that are likely to be evoked for men and women by the image of sex with more than one person. For heterosexual men, in particular, group sex may be imagined as an enactment of typically masculine scripts emphasizing sexual prowess, conquest, and domination. Gay men, on the other hand, may regard group sex as "hot sex"—not domination sex. Women, however, often (and correctly) view group sex as a male sex partner's attempt to increase the number of his sex partners by exchanging his primary partner with other men. Given women's preferences to have sex of all kinds (marital and extramarital) in affectional contexts, their aversion to group sex should be expected. (See table 4.3 below, where over 75 percent of the women in all four age and racial subgroups reported finding group sex "not at all appealing.")

Other relationship or partner-oriented practices, however, had limited appeal for both genders. Having a sex partner of the same gender was considered very appealing by roughly 3 percent of the population. Interestingly, the proportions of men and women who report having a sex partner of the same gender as very appealing are far closer than are comparable reports of actual same-gender sexual behavior. Of the women who report having sex with another woman as very appealing, less than half had a same-gender partner in the last year, compared with nearly 85 percent of the equivalent proportion of men. Reporting a same-gender partner as very appealing was also more highly associated with level of education for women than for men. These discrepancies may relate to differences in the construction of the script organizing same-gender sexual orientation for men and women. A more extended discussion of these and other issues relating to same-gender sexuality can be found in chapter 8. On a general level, however, it is clear that sexuality is envisioned through a man/woman frame by the vast majority of Americans.

Anonymous sexual interaction was also highly unpopular. Only 4 percent of men and 1 percent of women said that they found having sex with a stranger very appealing. Responses to this question may have been driven, in part, by its indirect associations with "unsafe" sex. Knowledge of the personal histories of sex partners has become highly salient in the context of the AIDS crisis. Apart from the influence of AIDS and other sexually transmitted diseases on the appeal of anonymous sex, however, we may surmise that, even for men, personal intimacy enriches both fantasized and actual sexual interaction. Indeed, as we report in chapter 8, the occurrence of sexual partnerships based on little or no previous interaction is relatively rare.

Finally, forced sex was the least appealing form of sexual association of the practices that we examined. Despite the fact that domination has been posited as a central element of heterosexual sexual relations by certain branches of feminism (MacKinnon 1989; Dworkin 1987) as well as sexual subcultures that celebrate the potent—even archetypal—nature of sexual domination, the proportion of men and women who found either forcing another or being forced to have sex very appealing was less than 0.5 percent. This is especially interesting in light of the fact that the proportion of women who report having been forced to do something sexual is nearly one in five. In chapter 9, we discuss the prevalence of forced sex in greater detail.

The low proportion of men who report forced sex to be very appealing in contrast to the rate at which women report being forced has at least two possible explanations. First, this is a very difficult form of conduct to admit finding very appealing, and we would normally expect that many of the men who recognized their sexual conduct as involving force would deny its appeal. Even when it is the force that is salient in generating sexual desire, men may view the interactions as essentially sexual and the force as a secondary necessity. Second, it is undoubtedly the case that some men view women's resistance to sexual advances as "no meaning yes" and view their acts of force and coercion as simply overcoming conventional forms of feminine resistance. Indeed, the contemporary debate over sexual harassment and date rape is an example of the reconstruction of a sex script. Concern about men's conventionalized misinterpretation of women's sexual intentions resulting in abuse has now led to efforts at altering the script that labels verbal protest as merely an obligatory appeal to the traditionally reactive sex role for women and girls. Despite these efforts at change, a substantial proportion of men may still consider sexual events during which they have encountered verbal resistance as "unforced" and would not report that "force" was appealing.

The relative popularity of those practices involving visual stimulation can also be seen, in part, as a function of the type of relationship within which they occur. Watching a partner undress was second only to vaginal intercourse in overall popularity. The appeal of this practice is due not only to the fact that undressing or "stripping" is a highly eroticized act that symbolically anticipates (but does not involve) physical interaction but also to its place in a set of conventional sexual narratives involving a legitimate relationship. The imagined partner is assumed to be normatively appropriate—spawning a variety of possible sexual scenarios. Significant gender differences, however, characterized the reported appeal of watching a partner undress. The proportion of men reporting this practice to be very appealing (48 percent) was nearly 20 percentage points higher than the equivalent proportion of women. The figure for women also declined significantly with age—from roughly 30–35 percent of women in their twenties and early thirties to 13 percent of women in their late fifties.

On the other hand, watching "other people doing sexual things" was relatively unpopular among our respondents. Only 5 percent of men and 2 percent of women reported this practice as very appealing. Again, the explanation may lie in the conception of the sexual relationship typically evoked by such a question. The implicit associations between this practice and voyeurism, the observation of a sexual transaction to which the respondent is imagined to be an unknown third party, render the conceived relationship illicit.

As is clear from table 4.2 above and table 4.3 (which permits more precise delineation of population subgroups by gender, age, and race simultaneously), population subgroups entertain decidedly different preference orderings among the various sexual practices. If sexual activity is generally a voluntary and consensual activity, then a major problem confronting the population at large is to match pairs of individuals with compatible sexual tastes.[4] Since individual sexual preferences are not typically revealed during the presexual stages of a relationship, it is likely that considerable mismatching on the most preferred activities is the usual feature of sexual partnerships.

How do we come to such a conclusion? Consider, first, a matching system where pairings of sex partners are arranged by a random process. Under this assumption, we need only multiply the probability that person A possesses a certain strong preference (here we use the proportion reporting that a practice is very appealing as a proxy for a strong preference) for a given sexual practice by the probability that person B also possesses such a preference. Using the percentages of men and women as estimates of the probability of preferring a given practice, we can obtain rough estimates of the likelihood of encountering a sex partner with compatible tastes.[5] In the case of vaginal intercourse, a random mixing process would result in only 64 percent of the pairs being matched on their shared strong preferences for vaginal intercourse (i.e., from table 4.2, the 84 percent of the men who find vaginal intercourse very appealing

---

4. This is an instance of decision making under uncertainty, as discussed briefly in chapter 1.

5. For the purposes of this exercise, we assume heterosexual partnering. Estimates based on percentages reported in table 4.3 would be inaccurate to the extent that respondents with preferences for same-gender sex partners have different preferences.

Table 4.3   Appeal of Selected Sexual Practices, by Gender and Age (% distributions)

Selected Sexual Practices	18–44				45–59				
	Appeal of Sexual Practice				Appeal of Sexual Practice				
	Very	Somewhat	Not	Not at all	Very	Somewhat	Not	Not at all	Total N
White men									
Vaginal intercourse	84.4	11.4	1.3	2.8	84.5	11.0	1.1	3.4	1,087
Watching partner undress	50.1	44.3	2.9	2.7	40.0	49.4	6.8	3.8	1,089
Receiving oral sex	53.4	34.2	4.5	7.9	30.7	35.2	10.2	23.9	1,083
Performing oral sex on a partner	40.8	41.3	7.6	10.4	25.7	35.5	12.1	26.8	1,084
Group sex	14.8	33.3	20.7	31.3	9.8	18.9	24.5	46.8	1,092
Anus stimulated by partner's fingers	4.6	18.0	24.6	52.7	4.5	13.6	25.7	56.2	1,085
Stimulating partner's anus with fingers	5.7	21.6	21.6	51.0	3.8	16.6	21.5	58.1	1,083
Using a dildo or vibrator	4.9	21.0	26.8	47.3	1.9	18.2	26.9	53.0	1,082
Watching others have sex	5.6	36.3	21.9	36.3	3.4	27.1	21.8	47.7	1,093
Same-gender sex	3.6	1.6	5.3	89.5	2.3	.8	5.6	91.4	1,093
Having sex with a stranger	4.5	29.3	25.1	41.2	1.9	22.6	24.1	51.5	1,092
Receiving anal intercourse	2.7	8.1	14.6	74.6	1.9	5.4	10.0	82.8	1,067
Forcing someone to have sex	.2	1.9	13.5	84.3	0.0	1.5	11.3	87.2	1,093
Being forced to have sex	.2	2.7	13.8	83.3	0.0	2.3	9.4	88.3	1,091
Active anal intercourse	4.7	9.2	14.1	71.9	1.2	7.1	9.5	82.2	1,054
Total N^a		844				268			

White women

									Total N[a]
Vaginal intercourse	79.2	17.3	1.2	2.3	75.3	18.9	1.7	4.2	1,302
Watching partner undress	30.0	53.0	10.0	7.1	18.3	50.6	15.8	15.3	1,304
Receiving oral sex	35.5	37.4	11.5	15.7	17.5	26.7	14.4	41.4	1,299
Performing oral sex on a partner	20.5	43.1	15.6	20.9	11.9	21.9	17.5	48.6	1,298
Group sex	.9	8.2	14.0	76.8	.8	4.2	6.9	88.1	1,309
Anus stimulated by partner's fingers	3.1	16.0	18.8	62.2	6.4	12.2	15.0	66.4	1,298
Stimulating partner's anus with fingers	1.6	12.0	17.8	68.6	3.9	12.5	12.8	70.8	1,300
Using a dildo or vibrator	3.0	15.7	25.0	56.4	3.6	15.3	18.4	62.7	1,296
Watching others have sex	1.6	20.2	15.7	62.5	1.7	11.3	13.3	73.8	1,311
Same-gender sex	3.1	3.2	9.6	84.2	1.9	2.2	5.5	90.3	1,312
Having sex with a stranger	1.1	9.3	11.6	78.1	.6	4.1	5.5	89.8	1,311
Receiving anal intercourse	1.0	3.9	8.8	86.3	.8	2.5	8.1	88.6	1,297
Forcing someone to have sex	.1	1.6	5.8	92.5	0.0	.6	3.9	95.6	1,311
Being forced to have sex	.1	1.9	5.2	92.8	0.0	.8	4.1	95.0	1,312
Total N[a]		966							

Black men

Vaginal intercourse	85.1	9.3	.6	5.0	86.4	9.1	2.3	2.3	205
Watching partner undress	55.9	31.1	5.0	8.1	34.1	38.6	13.6	13.6	205
Receiving oral sex	34.2	28.6	8.7	28.6	15.9	9.1	13.6	61.4	205
Performing oral sex on a partner	19.9	26.7	19.3	34.2	6.8	15.9	11.4	65.9	205
Group sex	14.3	32.9	13.7	39.1	6.7	8.9	11.1	73.3	206
Anus stimulated by partner's fingers	8.1	8.1	23.0	60.9	2.3	6.8	15.9	75.0	205

(*continued*)

Table 4.3   (continued)

Selected Sexual Practices	18–44				45–59				Total N
	Appeal of Sexual Practice				Appeal of Sexual Practice				
	Very	Somewhat	Not	Not at all	Very	Somewhat	Not	Not at all	
Stimulating partner's anus with fingers	7.5	13.0	19.9	59.6	4.5	11.4	15.9	68.2	205
Using a dildo or vibrator	6.3	6.3	25.8	61.6	2.3	13.6	9.1	75.0	203
Watching others have sex	8.7	28.0	13.0	50.3	2.2	13.3	11.1	73.3	206
Same-gender sex	3.7	.6	5.0	90.7	0.0	0.0	0.0	100.0	206
Having sex with a stranger	3.7	30.4	21.1	44.7	2.2	15.6	11.1	71.1	206
Receiving anal intercourse	1.9	5.7	14.6	77.7	0.0	0.0	9.1	90.9	201
Forcing someone to have sex	0.0	3.7	13.0	83.2	0.0	2.2	11.1	86.7	206
Being forced to have sex	0.0	1.2	13.0	85.7	0.0	0.0	6.7	93.3	206
Active anal intercourse	4.0	7.9	8.6	79.5	0.0	0.0	9.3	90.7	194
Total N[a]		162				45			
Black women									
Vaginal intercourse	73.9	20.1	2.4	3.6	72.7	14.8	1.1	11.4	337
Watching partner undress	40.8	36.8	12.8	9.6	18.2	39.8	13.6	28.4	338
Receiving oral sex	23.2	24.4	10.0	42.4	6.9	11.5	14.9	66.7	337

								Total N[a]
Performing oral sex on a partner	8.8	21.5	15.1	54.6	3.4	6.9	16.1	73.6	338
Group sex	1.6	7.6	16.0	74.8	0.0	4.5	15.9	79.5	338
Anus stimulated by partner's fingers	3.6	9.2	15.1	72.1	3.4	11.5	9.2	75.9	338
Stimulating partner's anus with fingers	3.2	10.0	13.6	73.2	3.4	6.9	9.2	80.5	337
Using a dildo or vibrator	2.4	5.6	17.9	74.1	2.3	9.2	12.6	75.9	338
Watching others have sex	2.0	13.5	15.9	68.5	1.1	12.5	13.6	72.7	339
Same-gender sex	4.0	2.0	8.8	85.3	2.3	3.4	8.0	86.4	339
Having sex with a stranger	1.6	6.4	10.8	81.3	1.1	3.4	8.0	87.5	339
Receiving anal intercourse	.8	2.8	8.1	88.3	4.5	2.3	8.0	85.2	336
Forcing someone to have sex	1.2	1.2	11.2	86.5	0.0	0.0	9.1	90.9	339
Being forced to have sex	0.0	0.0	11.6	88.4	0.0	0.0	6.8	93.2	339
Total N[a]			251				89		

[a]Figures do not take into account missing values for individual appeal items.

multiplied by the 77 percent of the women who share this same level of enthusiasm). But only 8 percent of the pairs would match on their shared enthusiasm for fellatio, and only four in 10,000 pairs would share a strong preference for anal sex.[6]

It is obvious that, if partners choose each other on the basis of similar master status characteristics (as they typically do; see chapter 6), they can somewhat improve their chances of finding a match on their most preferred practices. (Readers can work out for themselves the matches for different combinations of gender, age, and race for each partner from table 4.3.)[7] Yet, even if partners

6. The argument can be elaborated by taking into account not only the probability of agreement or match with respect to a given preference but also the likelihood of clashing preferences or mismatch. Mathematically, agreement can be defined as the sum of the products of the "matching" proportions for men and women on a given sexual practice. The degree of mismatch for a given practice can be defined as the sum of the "nonmatching" proportions for men and women.

In general, let P equal the percentage of men who prefer a given sexual practice, and let Q equal the percentage of women who prefer the same practice. Then, the expected percentages of matched and mismatched couples are given by, respectively,

$$PQ + (1 - P)(1 - Q) = 1 - P - Q + 2PQ,$$
$$(1 - P)Q + P(1 - Q) = P + Q - 2PQ,$$

assuming random mating with regard to preference for practices. Taking partial derivatives with respect to P (i.e., $[\partial(\%\ \text{matched/mismatched})/\partial P]$) yields $-1 + 2Q$ for matched couples and $1 - 2Q$ for mismatched couples. Thus, the percentage of matched couples rises as P rises if $Q > 1/2$, and the percentage of mismatched couples rises as P rises if $Q < 1/2$. If $Q = 1/2$, half the pairs are matched and half mismatched for every value of P. An even split (50:50) by either gender maximizes mismatch. From the standpoint of matching mixed-gender dyads on a particular sexual preference, it is functional to have "lopsided" preferences (either quite high, like 75 percent, or quite low, like 6 percent).

We consider the degree of match of sexual preferences (by gender alone) for vaginal intercourse, fellatio, and cunnilingus in the following table, which shows the preference match/mismatch for mixed-gender dyads under the random mixing model ("liking" a given practice refers to a "very appealing" response; "disliking" refers to any other response on the scale provided):

Practices by Gender	Proportions Liking/ Disliking Practice		Match (%), Both Prefer	Mismatch (%)	
	Like	Dislike		Neither Prefer	Disagree
Vaginal intercourse			64	4	32
Men	84	16			
Women	77	23			
Fellatio			8	46	46
Men	45	55			
Women	17	83			
Cunnilingus			9	47	44
Men	34	66			
Women	29	71			

Under this specification of the random mixing model, then, greater potential for conflict lies in the practice of oral sex than of vaginal intercourse.

7. To be sure, thinking of matching preferences in this fashion presents an overly static description of what is, after all, a highly dynamic process in which a complex sequence of events unfolds

could be selected on the basis of prior information regarding sexual preferences, discrepancies between partners in the overall appeal of particular techniques would inevitably result in some degree of preference clashing within many sexual dyads. The relative appeal of oral sex highlights this potential for mismatching. While the percentages of men and women who said that they found cunnilingus very appealing were nearly equivalent, the percentage of men who said that they found fellatio to be very appealing was nearly three times that of women. The arithmetic also suggests that further matching problems will arise when whole sets of preferences are considered.

Depending on the nature of the relationship and the extent to which preference profiles clash, one or both parties may have strong incentives to decline future transactions with that partner. However, the level of prior investment in a relationship may render the costs of extricating oneself from it and the subsequent search for a new partner greater than the sacrifices involved in remaining with a sexually "incompatible" partner. The extent to which this condition prevails for a given partnership will have different implications for the character of the sexual exchange within it. Whose preferences are realized during a given event may give us some insight into the way in which power infuses sexual relations between men and women.

We focus here on the gender-based likelihood of engaging in preferred oral sexual activities during the last sexual event. Specifically, we examine the incidence of fellatio and cunnilingus during the respondent's most recent sexual event for those men and women who reported these acts to be very appealing. The highly discrepant reports of the appeal of fellatio indicate that the potential for conflict over its occurrence is higher than for conflict over that of cunnilingus. Cunnilingus, however, has particular salience—especially for younger women—in light of the debates of the 1960s and 1970s that brought its relationship to female orgasm to the attention of the broader public. Although equivalent proportions of men and women report finding cunnilingus appealing, we wanted to know whether these reports translated into actual behavior during a typical sexual event. In other words, men may have reported cunnilingus as appealing but performed it relatively rarely.

We found no significant differences between men and women, however, with regard to their likelihood of experiencing preferred oral techniques. Of men who found cunnilingus very appealing, 49 percent performed it during the last sexual event. The proportion of women who found fellatio very appealing and who also performed it during the last event was 51 percent. The proportions of men and women who found receiving oral sex very appealing and who also received it during the last event were equal at 44 percent. Although

---

between two partners engaged in a sexual transaction who perform more or less preferred acts contingent on what has already happened or is about to happen in the present or a possible future event. The data requirements for describing such a time-dependent process were too severe for it to be attempted in our survey context.

only half those respondents who found oral sex very appealing performed that act in the last event, women do not appear to receive oral sex less frequently than men do. We do not, however, draw any conclusions regarding the "fairness" of the typical sexual event from these data. The apparently reciprocal practice of oral sex has no necessary relation to the subjective experience of sexual equity. For instance, although men may perform oral sex on women as often as they receive it, we have no information on how long cunnilingus typically lasts or whether orgasm regularly occurs during it. We can say, however, that women are not systematically deprived of the occurrence of receptive oral sex relative to men.

Although examining people's preferences for specific activities is informative, it does not address the question of how preferences for these activities are jointly distributed in the population, or, in other words, how people combine preferences for several activities into an overall preference profile. The simplest way to approach this question is to count the frequency with which people express preferences for particular combinations of activities. Although there is a large number of possible combinations with which people could respond to the different items, we have chosen to begin with only a few combinations that either occur frequently or are of particular substantive interest. These are presented in table 4.4. (To simplify our interpretations, we have excluded from the table those who identified themselves as homosexual, and have excluded from the activities sex with a same-gender partner and receptive anal intercourse for men. Because of the low frequency with which people judged them to be appealing, we also excluded forcing someone and/or being forced to have sex.)

Looking at the first row of table 4.4, we see that 2.6 percent of the "heterosexual" cross-sectional sample found none of the activities to be appealing— a profile of responses that might be interpreted as revealing a lack of interest in sex altogether. The second group consists of respondents who found only vaginal intercourse to be appealing, while the third comprises respondents who reported watching a partner undress to be appealing in addition to vaginal intercourse. Together, these two groups represent nearly one-fifth of the heterosexual population, and reflect a preference for relatively simple and unelaborated sexual interactions.[8]

The fourth group consists of those who find vaginal intercourse, watching a partner undress, and oral sex (either active or receptive) to be appealing. This is an interesting category, both because it represents approximately one-fifth of the sample and because it consists of activities that can be considered fairly "conventional." The last two categories reflect elaborations on the fourth. Interestingly, each of these groups also represents approximately one-fifth of the

8. Of course, it is possible to vary both the location in which one has sexual intercourse and the physical positions one uses; however, we did not have space to inquire about people's preferences for these.

Table 4.4   Cross-Classification of Respondents According to the Number of "Heterosexual" Activities Judged to Be Appealing and Selected Master Status Attributes (respondents who identified themselves as homosexual are excluded)

Number of items judged to be appealing	Total %[a]	White 18–29 Men	White 18–29 Women	White 30–44 Men	White 30–44 Women	White 45–59 Men	White 45–59 Women	Black 18–29 Men	Black 18–29 Women	Black 30–44 Men	Black 30–44 Women	Black 45–59 Men	Black 45–59 Women
1. None	2.6	1.4	1.9	0.6	1.3	1.1	4.9	4.8	1.9	2.1	4.2	0.0	7.9
2. Only vaginal intercourse (VI)	6.0	1.4	6.1	1.0	6.2	2.3	12.7	0.0	9.4	1.0	13.9	20.0	22.5
3. VI and watching partner undress (WPU)	13.0	5.8	10.5	4.8	10.9	16.2	24.1	3.2	25.5	18.8	23.6	28.9	24.7
4. VI, WPU, and active or receptive oral sex (OS)	19.7	15.7	32.5	16.9	27.1	15.0	13.2	15.9	21.7	6.3	15.3	6.7	2.2
5. VI, WPU, OS, and 1 or 2 additional items[b]	22.6	32.2	24.5	27.9	22.9	22.9	16.5	28.6	18.9	17.7	15.3	0.0	5.6
6. VI, WPU, OS, and 3 or more additional items	17.6	29.0	9.9	35.4	13.9	20.7	5.7	23.8	3.8	20.8	6.9	11.1	5.6
N	3,122	345	363	480	595	266	370	63	106	96	144	45	89

[a]Oversample excluded from this column. Percentages in this column add to 81.4 percent; the remaining 18.6 percent did not fall into one of the six categories.

[b]These include having sex with a stranger, sex with multiple partners, watching others have sex, using a dildo or vibrator, stimulating a partner's anus with your fingers, having a partner stimulate your anus with his or her fingers, passive anal intercourse (women), and active anal intercourse (men).

sample, indicating that 40 percent of the population have somewhat elaborated preference profiles, at least with respect to the set of activities about which we inquired.

Of course, table 4.4 represents only one simple way to examine respondents' overall preference profiles; more detailed analyses are beyond the scope of this chapter. We may conclude, however, that the unidimensional models often used by psychometricians are unlikely to provide an adequate characterization of these items. Such models would postulate that each person builds his or her preference profile in the same manner, so that if one person finds more activities appealing than does a second person, for example, those found appealing by the second will be among those found appealing by the first. That our data violate such a model can be seen from the fact that 18.6 percent of the sample could not be placed into one of the six categories. This was because these individuals did not report either oral sex or watching a partner undress to be appealing but did find other activities (in addition to vaginal intercourse) appealing. The implication is that there are multiple ways of constructing one's profile of sexual preferences—ways that are likely to be associated with particular cultural understandings about sexuality.

Also shown in table 4.4 is the incidence of each of the six response profiles within population subgroups defined on the basis of gender, race, and age. (Hispanics are omitted owing to the relatively small number of cases.) These percentages reveal three persistent patterns. First, in almost all cases, the percentages of women exhibiting each of the first four preference profiles are greater than the corresponding percentages of men, often by a factor of two. Conversely, the percentages of men with the last two profiles are higher than those of women, especially for the last profile. In fact, more than one-third of white men ages thirty to forty-four reported seven or more activities to be appealing. This suggests that, at least in terms of the specific set of activities about which we inquired, men are considerably more likely than women to find large numbers of the activities appealing.

The effect of age is somewhat weaker, and in most cases appears to be nonlinear. For example, the percentages of those who find only vaginal intercourse to be appealing are roughly similar for the first two age groups, but increase considerably among the third. In contrast, among both white men and women, those in the middle age category exhibit the highest incidence of the sixth response profile. Among blacks, the likelihood of being in each of the last three categories appears to decline monotonically with age.

Finally, comparing across racial groups, we see that black men ages forty-five to fifty-nine are more likely to exhibit profiles two and three than are white men of similar age, and the reverse is true for profiles five and six. Similar comparisons can also be made between white and black women. This finding is consistent with behavioral evidence reported earlier that sexual interactions among blacks consist of fewer distinct activities than those occurring among whites.

The information in table 4.4 is important because it moves us closer to the theoretical objectives outlined in chapter 1. Recall that, according to scripting theory, the fundamental units of sexual behavior are not individual activities but "scripts" that specify both a series of activities and a context in which those activities are to be performed. We believe that the expressed preferences reported in this chapter are reflective of people's "ideal" scripts. From the data presented in table 4.4, we may conclude that for approximately 40 percent of the population, the ideal sexual script is limited to vaginal intercourse, watching a partner undress, and some type of oral sex. Another 40 percent report ideal scripts that include these as well as additional activities. And of the remaining respondents, the majority fall somewhere in between (mostly excluding oral sex but including other activities), with only a small percentage reporting that nothing that we asked about was appealing.

Also especially noteworthy is the substantial association between gender, race, and age on the one hand, and the incidence of particular profiles of sexual preferences on the other. To the extent that these profiles reflect distinct ideal scripts, we may expect them to exert a substantial effect, when matched or mismatched, on the selection, retention, and relative satisfaction of sex partners over time. In particular, we see that an individual can increase his or her chances of locating a partner with similar preferences by choosing a partner from the same racial or age group, a fact that may serve to maintain some of the differentiation in the market for sex partners. At the same time, we also observe a major disjuncture between the stated preference profiles of men and women.

The Number of Partners

This chapter discusses the number of sex partners of adults in the United States. No other measure of sexual behavior has been more often studied in recent years. This is primarily because the number of partners has been identified by epidemiologists and public health officials as a key indicator of the risk of contracting and transmitting AIDS. Also, no other single feature of one's sex life more succinctly reflects the broad social dimension of sexual behavior; it reflects the breadth of sexual experience and provides some indication about the nature of the person's social relationships. The material in this chapter provides continuity with earlier studies by focusing on the number of sex partners. It delves in considerable detail into the nature and correlates of this important measure of sexual behavior.

Important as it is, however, we want to stress that number of sex partners is a quite limited measure of sexual behavior. Its parsimony comes at a price. It is a highly simplified characterization of sexual behavior since it captures in a single number a complex history of individual maturation and change and cannot reflect the highly variable process by which one selects sex partners at different stages of the life course. Before exploring this measure in detail, however, we first emphasize some of its limitations.

There are many ways in which a person may accumulate a particular number of partners, and these can have radically different social implications. For instance, the experience of having two partners in a given year is likely to be very different for people of the same age, race, and other salient social characteristics, depending on whether they are married. Consider two twenty-five-year-old white men, one married with a young child and a job that requires extensive travel, the other a single graduate student. If the married man intends to have sex with someone other than his wife, he may engage in an extensive covert search for a partner who is likely to be recruited from a population wholly unrelated to his primary circle of acquaintances—picking up someone in a distant city to which he travels for business reasons, for example, in order to minimize the chances that his illicit relationship will be discovered. The other man may have had a steady partner for the last few months of the school

The empirical analysis in this chapter was prepared by Rita Butzer (section 5.2), Joel A. Feinleib (sections 5.1 and 5.4), and Kara Joyner (section 5.3). Robert T. Michael directed their work and wrote the chapter.

year, broken up over the summer, and begun a new partnership in the fall, both partners being women he met in the day-to-day activities of his academic life. Both have had two partners within a year's time, but the implications of this fact for these two men and their two partners are very different.

The choice about number of partners is not made in isolation; rather, we should expect that choice to be affected by circumstances such as marital status. A married person who is committed to sexual exclusivity with a spouse faces a wholly different set of incentives and circumstances than an unmarried person. Over a short time period such as a year, we should expect these differing circumstances to have a major influence on the reported number of sex partners. However, notice that, interviewed at different times and under different circumstances, the same individual would probably report quite different behavior. If current circumstances have a substantial effect on current behavior, then the number of partners over a long time period, or over the whole adult lifetime, may tell us more about the length of time that an individual spent in one marital status or another than it tells us about any other attribute.

This is what we mean by placing sexual behavior in its social context—by knowing the social, demographic, and economic circumstances in which a person has one or two or four partners and knowing whether these partnerships occurred simultaneously or sequentially, whether they are long-term or one-time only, etc., we can be far better informed about the reasons for, and the likely consequences of, that behavior.[1] Knowing only the number is not knowing very much.

Were we interested only in a measure of the risk of disease from an individual's sex life, even then the number of sex partners is only a crude proxy. The residential college student who reports two partners in the past year recruited from among his fellow classmates is a participant in a very different sexual marketplace than a private in boot camp who also reports two partners in the past year, one his old high school sweetheart, the other a prostitute. Knowing only the number of partners is not knowing very much. Whether partners are simultaneous or sequential, what the social networks are from which they are recruited, the frequency of sex, the practices engaged in, the protection employed—all can dramatically affect the likelihood of infection. We suggest that, despite the importance of knowing more about sexual behavior as it relates to disease transmission, the nearly exclusive focus on number of sex part-

---

1. Consider another example. People in their late adolescence are involved in a peer culture that accepts and may even promote promiscuity, with the expectation that entry into a cohabitational relationship or a marriage will end such permissive behavior. The number of times one moves from one primary relationship to another might effectively drive the accumulation of lifetime partners. Another social context that is especially conducive to raising the number of lifetime partners, as we show below, is service in the military. Here again, we would expect men to accumulate partners more rapidly, both because of peer group support and because of the peculiarities of living on military reservations with few heterosexual opportunities except for off-base weekends. In sum, the highly stereotypical simplifications in the discussions of numbers of partners that are often found in the literature need to be more adequately contextualized so that meaningful interpretations can be made.

ners that is sometimes found in the public health literature provides a very limiting and potentially distorting lens through which to view sexual conduct and the risk of disease.

This chapter, nonetheless, does focus on the number of sex partners, and attempts to look at this variable in its social context. Knowing how many different people an individual has had sex with does provide a useful and succinct measure that can be used to characterize adult sexual behavior, especially if it is examined within a broader array of measures of sexual conduct. It reflects, at least in part, the breadth of sexual experience and provides some indication of the nature of the person's social relationships. There are, of course, many other dimensions of amount and content of sex—including the frequency of various sexual practices, the range of sexual activities engaged in, the intensity or meaning of sexual activity to the individual, and the quality and character of the sexual experience and sexual relationships over time—and we have already begun to examine them in the preceding two chapters. Although we must consider each of these aspects of an individual's sexual life one at a time owing to the dictates of narrative exposition, it is useful to keep in mind their inherently interrelated and interdependent character.

Throughout the chapter, we feature the shape of the whole distribution of the number of partners instead of focusing on the average number. The average number of partners over various time periods for one group or another turns out to be rather uninteresting. That is because one gets the same number of partners for almost every group as the distribution's mean (the numeric average), or as its median (the number of partners of the person who would be exactly in the middle of the distribution if all the observations were lined up from the fewest to the most partners), or as its mode (the number of partners more people had than any other number). The central tendency of nearly all the distributions of number of partners within the past year and over the past five years, as we show below, is *one* partner. Only when we look at the distributions over the whole adult lifetime, or over large segments of the lifetime, is there much noticeable variation in the mean or the median value from one group to another. Consequently, we feature here the shape of the whole distribution rather than simply reporting the average.

Also, it is important to note that the distribution of the number of sex partners in a short period of time like the past year is highly skewed, or nonsymmetrical, with a long tail to the right end of the distribution. Typically, a very large majority (around 80 percent) of the respondents have no or only one partner, and a mere 3 percent report five or more partners. An equally large majority (about 80 percent) of those who do have more than one partner have either two, three, or four partners in the past year, so the distribution of partners of the subset of persons with two or more is also dramatically skewed to the right.

In this chapter, we look at the proportions of people who report having had specific numbers of sex partners for three time periods. For the last year, we examine the proportion who had no partners, one partner, two to four partners, and five or more partners. For the past five years and for the lifetime (i.e., between age eighteen and the age at the interview), we divide this distribution into none, one, two to four, five to ten, eleven to twenty, and twenty-one or more.

The chapter has four sections. The first describes the distribution of the number of sex partners over these three time periods (the past twelve months, the past five years, and the adult lifetime since age eighteen) and distinguishes these distributions by the basic demographic and socioeconomic characteristics called *master statuses* in chapter 1—gender, age, current marital status, education, ethnicity/race, and religion. Sections 5.2 and 5.3 describe the number of sex partners within key segments of the lifetime (i.e., by specific ages) and specific segments of time (e.g., before the first marriage, during the first marriage, etc.). Section 5.4 offers a very brief multivariate analysis of these several measures.

5.1 The Number of Partners over Specific Time Intervals

Measuring the Number of Sex Partners

On first impression, one might think that number of sex partners is a simple and straightforward concept and therefore quite easy to measure. Even so, there are simplifications that we need to impose on the concept in order to describe it. We have chosen, for example, to count partners of both genders without distinction in this chapter, although later in the volume we do distinguish between heterosexual and homosexual partners. Initially, as well, we do not delve into the nature or importance of the sexual partnership and simply count the number of partners; we count a lifetime spouse and a casual one-time sex partner each as one partner. Later, we go into detail about the relationship.

The National Health and Social Life Survey (NHSLS) asked respondents in several ways and in several time frames about the number of sex partners they had had. Here we summarize the number within the past twelve months prior to the survey in 1992, within the past five years covering the period 1987–92, and over the respondent's whole adult lifetime since turning eighteen. As some of our respondents were young adults (as young as eighteen) while others were much older (as old as fifty-nine), we capture the behavior of adults of all ages from eighteen to fifty-nine in these specific time period reports. As chapter 2 described, some questions about number of partners were asked both in a self-administered questionnaire (SAQ), which assured respondents that the interviewer would not know their answers, and in the face-to-face interview. Thus, we have the same information twice for several measures and have combined the information here for analysis.

Respondents were asked how many sex partners they had had in the past twelve months in both the SAQ and in the interview. In the SAQ (see appendix

C), the question was asked, "How many sex partners have you had in the last 12 months?" The respondent was given nine categories from which to choose: 0, 1, 2, 3, 4, 5–10, 11–20, 21–100, and more than 100 partners. The definition of *sex partner* was not made explicit in the SAQ, so the respondent had to come up with his or her own. Subsequently, in the face-to-face interview, the respondent was asked in detail about each and every sex partner in the twelve months preceding the interview, including information about that partner's age and education and the dates of the first and last sexual encounter. *Sex or sexual activity* was explicitly defined there as "mutually voluntary activity with another person that involves genital contact and sexual excitement or arousal, that is, feeling really turned on, even if intercourse or orgasm did not occur."

Despite our expectation that the implied definition of *sex* in the self-administered questionnaire would be more restrictive than in the face-to-face interviews, the responses from these two methods were very close. In the vast majority of the observations (i.e., in 86 percent of the cases), the same answer was given in both the self-administered section and the face-to-face section. This is a reassuring finding about the accuracy of the questionnaire itself—there is much internal consistency in the answers provided. Where differences existed, we attempted to reconcile them and were able to do so in most cases; there were some cases (162) with an answer to only one of the two questions, so we used that one answer. When differences could not be reconciled, we chose the higher number reported in the two places so as to err on the side of overestimation. (For the specific method and implications of our imputation and reconciliation procedures, see chapter appendix 5.1A.)

The number of partners over the past five years was determined solely from responses to the self-administered questionnaire. No analogous direct question was asked in the face-to-face interview. The number of partners since turning eighteen was available from the SAQ and can also be gathered by combining answers to a series of face-to-face questions about the number of partners the respondent had before, during, and after each period of marriage or cohabitation with a sex partner, so this question is by far the most complex in terms of its cognitive demands on the respondent and of its piecing together from different places in the questionnaire. The variable that we use here is a composite from these two sources (for details, see chapter appendix 5.2A).

The Distributions of Sex Partners by Six Master Statuses

Table 5.1 reports the percentage distribution of the number of sex partners for several specific social groups for each of the three respective time spans (twelve months in table 5.1A, five years in table 5.1B, and the whole adult lifetime in table 5.1C). Before we focus on the important substantive findings in the table, we describe in detail how to read the table. Look first at the top row of table 5.1A. It indicates that, for all respondents taken as one group, 11.9 percent report having had no sex partners within the past twelve months, 71.1 percent report having had only one sex partner, 13.7 percent report having had

Table 5.1A   **Number of Sex Partners in Past Twelve Months, by Selected Social Characteristics (% distributions)**

Social Characteristics	No. of Partners (%) 0	1	2–4	5+	Total %	N
Total population	11.9	71.1	13.7	3.2	100	3,155
Gender:						
Male	9.9	66.7	18.3	5.1	100	1,407
Female	13.6	74.7	10.0	1.7	100	1,748
N						3,155
Age:						
18–24	10.8	57.0	23.7	8.6	100	502
25–29	5.5	72.0	16.8	5.7	100	457
30–34	8.7	72.8	16.2	2.3	100	519
35–39	9.6	77.3	10.7	2.4	100	467
40–44	11.3	74.7	12.8	1.2	100	415
45–49	15.3	74.7	8.8	1.3	100	308
50–54	15.1	79.3	5.2	.4	100	251
55–59	31.6	64.9	3.5	0.0	100	231
N						3,150
Marital status:						
Nev. marr., not coh.	25.3	38.0	27.6	9.0	100	742
Nev. marr., coh.	.7	74.6	20.1	4.5	100	134
Married	2.3	93.7	3.4	.7	100	1,673
Div./sep./wid., not coh.	30.8	40.5	26.0	2.7	100	474
Div./sep./wid., coh.	1.1	79.8	16.0	3.2	100	94
N						3,117
Education:						
Less than HS	16.3	66.5	14.7	2.5	100	436
HS grad. or eq.	10.7	74.3	12.5	2.5	100	913
Some coll./voc.	10.9	70.9	14.2	4.0	100	1,036
Finished coll.	11.9	69.2	15.4	3.5	100	520
Master's/adv. deg.	12.6	73.9	10.4	3.0	100	230
N						3,135
Religion:						
None	11.0	66.5	16.8	5.8	100	346
Type I Prot.	10.9	74.4	12.6	2.4	100	745
Type II Prot.	12.6	70.4	14.0	3.0	100	1,072
Catholic	12.7	72.0	12.7	2.7	100	853
Jewish	3.6	78.2	14.6	3.6	100	55
Other	15.4	62.8	15.4	6.4	100	78
N						3,149
Race/ethnicity:						
White	11.6	73.3	12.3	2.7	100	2,449
Black	12.8	60.1	21.1	6.0	100	549
Hispanic	10.6	69.5	17.4	2.5	100	321
Asian	15.4	76.9	7.7	0.0	100	65
Native American	11.9	76.2	9.5	2.4	100	42
N						3,426

Table 5.1B **Number of Sex Partners in Past Five Years, by Selected Social Characteristics (% distributions)**

Social Characteristics	No. of Sex Partners (%) 0	1	2–4	5–10	11–20	21+	Total %	N
Total population	8.0	53.3	25.8	8.6	2.7	1.7	100	2,999
Gender:								
Male	7.1	45.7	27.7	12.0	4.2	3.3	100	1,330
Female	8.7	59.4	24.3	5.9	1.4	.4	100	1,669
N								2,999
Age:								
18–24	11.8	21.5	38.1	18.4	6.0	4.1	100	483
25–29	4.4	38.0	36.6	11.5	6.5	3.0	100	434
30–34	5.2	53.2	28.9	9.8	2.2	.8	100	502
35–39	7.3	62.1	21.2	6.6	1.1	1.6	100	438
40–44	5.8	65.2	22.0	5.2	1.2	.5	100	400
45–49	9.4	66.4	17.8	4.2	.7	1.4	100	286
50–54	8.9	75.4	14.4	1.3	0.0	0.0	100	236
55–59	15.2	74.7	8.3	1.8	0.0	0.0	100	217
N								2,996
Marital status:								
Nev. marr., not coh.	19.2	16.0	34.8	19.7	6.4	3.9	100	699
Nev. marr., coh.	.8	31.0	43.4	15.5	5.4	3.9	100	129
Married	2.4	78.6	14.8	2.6	.9	.7	100	1,598
Div./sep./wid., not coh.	13.3	32.1	41.1	9.9	2.5	1.1	100	445
Div./sep./wid., coh.	4.4	34.1	47.2	12.1	2.2	0.0	100	91
N								2,961
Education:								
Less than HS	11.1	53.5	24.7	8.0	1.0	1.7	100	413
HS grad. or eq.	9.0	54.0	27.5	6.8	1.9	.9	100	858
Some coll./voc.	6.6	51.4	25.6	10.6	4.2	1.7	100	1,002
Finished coll.	6.6	52.2	26.4	9.2	2.5	3.1	100	488
Master's/adv. deg.	7.8	62.1	20.6	6.4	2.3	.9	100	219
N								2,980
Religion:								
None	5.5	40.6	34.1	11.9	6.1	1.8	100	328
Type I Prot.	7.5	54.8	25.9	8.2	2.1	1.4	100	717
Type II Prot.	9.0	55.7	24.0	7.4	2.0	1.8	100	1,027
Catholic	8.3	54.6	24.9	8.8	1.9	1.6	100	799
Jewish	0.0	52.1	31.2	10.4	6.2	0.0	100	48
Other	13.5	54.0	14.9	9.5	6.8	1.3	100	74
N								2,993
Race/ethnicity:								
White	7.4	55.4	24.8	8.1	2.6	1.7	100	2,341
Black	9.3	42.7	30.7	11.3	3.5	2.5	100	515
Hispanic	10.9	52.5	23.1	10.9	2.0	.7	100	303
Asian	11.7	60.0	21.7	5.0	1.7	0.0	100	60
Native American	15.0	50.0	30.0	0.0	5.0	0.0	100	40
N								3,259

Table 5.1C **Number of Sex Partners since Age Eighteen, by Selected Social Characteristics (% distributions)**

Social Characteristics	No. of Sex Partners (%)						Total	
	0	1	2–4	5–10	11–20	21+	%	N
Total population	2.9	26.1	29.5	21.7	10.6	9.2	100	3,126
Gender:								
Male	3.4	19.5	20.9	23.3	16.3	16.6	100	1,394
Female	2.5	31.5	36.4	20.4	6.0	3.2	100	1,732
N								3,126
Age:								
18–24	7.8	32.1	34.1	15.4	7.8	2.8	100	499
25–29	2.2	25.3	31.3	22.2	9.9	9.0	100	454
30–34	3.1	21.3	29.3	25.2	10.8	10.3	100	516
35–39	1.7	18.9	29.7	24.9	14.0	10.8	100	465
40–44	.7	21.9	27.6	24.2	13.7	12.0	100	410
45–49	2.0	25.7	23.8	25.1	9.6	13.9	100	303
50–54	2.4	33.9	27.8	18.0	9.0	9.0	100	245
55–59	1.3	40.0	28.3	15.2	8.3	7.0	100	230
N								3,122
Marital status:								
Nev. marr., not coh.	12.3	14.8	28.6	20.6	12.1	11.6	100	734
Nev. marr., coh.	0.0	24.6	37.3	15.7	9.7	12.7	100	134
Married	0.0	37.1	28.0	19.4	8.7	6.8	100	1,660
Div./sep./wid., not coh.	.2	11.1	33.4	28.7	14.7	11.9	100	470
Div./sep./wid., coh.	0.0	0.0	31.9	44.0	12.1	12.1	100	91
N								3,090
Education:								
Less than HS	4.2	26.7	36.0	18.6	8.8	5.8	100	431
HS grad or eq.	3.4	30.2	29.1	20.0	9.8	7.4	100	900
Some coll./voc.	2.1	23.9	29.4	23.3	11.9	9.3	100	1,033
Finished coll.	2.1	24.1	25.8	23.9	11.1	13.0	100	515
Master's/adv. deg.	3.5	24.6	26.3	22.8	9.6	13.2	100	228
N								3,107
Religion:								
None	2.6	16.2	29.0	20.3	15.9	15.9	100	345
Type I Prot.	2.3	22.8	31.2	23.0	12.4	8.3	100	736
Type II Prot.	2.9	29.8	30.4	20.4	9.5	7.0	100	1,066
Catholic	3.8	27.2	29.2	22.7	8.1	9.1	100	843
Jewish	0.0	24.1	13.0	29.6	16.7	16.7	100	54
Other	2.6	41.6	19.5	15.6	7.8	13.0	100	77
N								3,120
Race/ethnicity:								
White	3.0	26.2	28.9	22.0	10.9	9.1	100	2,427
Black	2.2	18.0	34.2	24.1	11.0	10.5	100	544
Hispanic	3.2	35.6	27.1	17.4	8.2	8.5	100	317
Asian	6.2	46.2	24.6	13.8	6.2	3.1	100	65
Native American	5.0	27.5	35.0	22.5	5.0	5.0	100	40
N								3,393

Table 5.1D   **Sex Partners since Age Eighteen**

Social Characteristics	Median	Min.	Max.	N
Total population	3	0	1,016	3,126
Gender:				
Male	6	0	1,016	1,394
Female	2	0	1,009	1,732
Age:				
18–24	2	0	256	499
25–29	4	0	178	454
30–34	4	0	250	516
35–39	4	0	400	465
40–44	4	0	1,016	410
45–49	4	0	1,009	303
50–54	2	0	604	245
55–59	2	0	150	230
Marital status:				
Nev. marr., not coh.	4	0	900	734
Nev. marr., coh.	3	1	53	134
Married	2	0	604	1,660
Div./sep./wid., not coh.	5	0	1,016	470
Div./sep./wid., coh.	6	2	519	91
Education:				
Less than HS	3	0	150	431
HS grad. or eq.	3	0	1,016	900
Some coll./voc.	4	0	604	1,033
Finished coll.	4	0	1,009	515
Master's/adv. deg.	4	0	323	228
Religion:				
None	5	0	900	345
Type I Prot.	4	0	604	736
Type II Prot.	3	0	1,016	1,066
Catholic	3	0	403	843
Jewish	6	1	1,009	54
Other	3	0	323	77
Race/ethnicity:				
White	3	0	1,009	2,427
Black	4	0	1,016	544
Hispanic	2	0	142	317
Asian	1	0	323	65
Native American	3	0	25	40

Note: Nev. marr., not coh. = never married, not cohabiting; nev. marr., coh. = never married, cohabiting; div./sep./wid., not coh. = divorced/separated/widowed, not cohabiting; div./sep./wid., coh. = divorced/separated/widowed, cohabiting; less than HS = less than high school; HS grad. or eq. = high school graduate or equivalent; some coll./voc. = some college/vocational school; finished coll. = finished college; master's/adv. deg. = master's/advanced degree; Type I/II Prot. = Type I/II Protestant (see explanation in appendix 3.1A).

two, three, or four partners, and 3.2 percent report having had five or more. The last column indicates that 3,155 of the total 3,159 survey respondents provided sufficient information to be included in this row.

Look next at the top row of table 5.1C. There we see that, over the lifetime since age eighteen, only 2.9 percent of all respondents report having had no sex partners, 26.1 percent had only one, 29.5 percent had two, three, or four, and, adding the remaining three groups together, 41.5 percent had five or more (21.7 percent had five to ten, 10.6 percent had eleven to twenty, and 9.2 percent had twenty-one or more). Of course, the cumulative number of sex partners over the adult lifetime is much higher than the number in a single year. For example, it is much rarer for any individual to have had no partners over the adult lifetime than over the past twelve months (3 vs. 12 percent) and much more likely to have had five or more partners over the lifetime than over the past twelve months (41 vs. 3 percent).

The categorical representation of the number of partners in the columns of table 5.1 (i.e., focusing on the percentage of a group who had no partners, one, two to four, and five or more over the past twelve months) was not constructed haphazardly. We suggest that each of these four categories represents a distinct and substantively important level of sexual behavior from both a social and a public health perspective.

Having no sex partners over a given time period may indicate intentional abstinence for any of several reasons, from ill health to physical separation from one's sex partner (e.g., being in jail or being away from home on a job assignment). A person with no sex partners will be exposed to neither the pleasure nor the dangers associated with partnered sex. If this circumstance has existed throughout the lifetime, the person has remained a virgin, and, as table 5.1C shows, 2.9 percent of the adults in our survey report having had no sex partner since turning eighteen. (In a later section of this chapter, we refine this percentage of the population who are virgins by taking account of any sex partners during adolescence as well.)

A person with only one sex partner may be intentionally conforming to the social norm of fidelity within a relationship. Having only one sex partner is by far the most prevalent behavior when we look over the past twelve months (table 5.1A), and it remains the modal number of partners when we look over the past five years (table 5.1B) or the whole adult lifetime (table 5.1C) as well. (This latter statement is true if we consider the numbers above one partner in single units, not shown in the tables.)

A person with two or more partners may have had a series of exclusive sexual relationships or several partners concurrently. Depending on the circumstances and on the belief system of the interpreter, the number of partners may have religious and ethical implications as well as social and public health ramifications. For simplicity of presentation, we combine two, three, and four partners into a single category in many of the tables in this chapter, but, as other tables show, there is in fact gradation even within this narrow range.

The upper category that we use is five or more partners in the past year and twenty-one or more partners over the adult lifetime, with intermediate categories of five to ten and eleven to twenty. These are prompted by the small number of cases found in these higher orders of magnitudes. Moreover, five or more partners within the year or more than twenty partners over the lifetime is probably a good indicator of limited commitment to any particular relationship.

We have explored a few specific aspects of the sexual experience of those with different numbers of sex partners within the past twelve months, and these suggest why partitioning the numbers as we have is illuminating. Consider the issue of concurrent partners. If one has sex with four people in a year, say, and does so sequentially, with no overlap, both the social interpretation of these partnerships and the likely rate of disease transmission are quite different than if all four relationships occur simultaneously.[2]

We looked at the issue of concurrent partners for those who reported two or more within the past twelve months. As table 5.2 shows, as the number of partners goes up, the likelihood that some are concurrent goes up as well. For those with five partners or six or more partners, it is very likely that some of those relationships were being conducted concurrently. What may be more surprising is that this table tells us that about half of those with two partners, about 40 percent of those with three partners, and one-quarter of those with four partners within the past twelve months have only one partner at a time.

A second aspect of sexual experience that varies with the number of partners is the likelihood of a one-time or one-sex-event partner.[3] Someone with whom one has sex only once is probably much more likely to be a pickup, or someone who is not very well known to the subject. (Of course, it may just be that the sex was not satisfying and the partnership therefore never renewed.) Table 5.2 also shows that the likelihood of at least one one-time partner in the year rises dramatically as the number of partners increases.

A third aspect of sexual experience that varies with the number of partners is the proportion of time spent with a partner or with more than one partner.

2. To make this point about disease transmission simply and concretely, suppose that our respondent has sex with four different people and that initially one of the four has a sexually transmittable infection. For simplicity, suppose that the infection is transferred with certainty if sex occurs. Now, if our respondent has sex with each of the four in sequence and with none simultaneously—i.e., if he has sex with Sally in January, with Susie in March, with Sarah in June, and with Samantha in November—then the expected number of the five of these people (including our respondent) who will have the infection by the end of the year is 3.5. That is, if it was Sally who had the infection initially, all five will get it, but, if it was Samantha, only she and the respondent will have it by the end of the year. On the other hand, if our respondent has sex with all four partners concurrently—i.e., has sex with one, then another, then the first again, back and forth—then, by the end of the year, all five will be expected to have the infection. In this important sense, the sequencing of partners as well as the number of partners is of critical importance in the spread of a sexually transmitted infection.

3. A *one-time sex partner* is defined here as one whose first and last dates of sex are in the same month and with whom the frequency of sex is one.

Table 5.2 **Aspects of Sexual Experience, by the Number of Partners in the Past Twelve Months**

No. of Partners	% with Any Simultaneity	N
2	51	246
3	61	104
4	75	52
5	83	30
6+	85	59

	% with Any One-Time Partners	N
1	1	2,262
2	25	246
3	54	104
4	60	52
5	67	30
6+	71	59

	No. of Months in the Past 12 with 0, 1, or 2+ Partners			
	0	1	2+	N
1	1.2	10.8	. . .	2,262
2	2.8	6.7	2.5	246
3	2.4	6.7	3.0	104
4	2.2	5.5	4.3	52
5	1.8	4.3	5.9	30
6+	1.6	2.8	7.6	59

	% Ever Having an STI, by Number of Partners since Age 18[a]	
	Men	Women
0	1	0
1	3	5
2–4	6	13
5–10	14	33
11–20	27	48
21+	37	55

[a]See table 11.6.

Table 5.2 also looks at respondents with a specific number of sex partners over the past twelve months; in it, we calculate, on average, how many months in that twelve-month period were spent with no sex partners, with one, and with two or more. For example, respondents who had three partners over the past twelve months spent on average 2.4 months with no sex partners, 6.7 months with one, and 3.0 months with two or more. So even those who had three partners over the year spent about nine months having sex with only one partner or no one at all. This illustrates yet again why the number of partners within a year is only a crude indicator of the amount of sex or the extent of exposure to risk.

A fourth aspect of sexual experience is the risk of a sexually transmitted infection (STI). While this is investigated in detail in chapter 11, table 5.2 shows the percentage of men and women who report ever having had an STI, by number of sex partners over the adult lifetime.

KEY FINDINGS FROM TABLE 5.1

Table 5.1 contains many interesting facts about the numbers of sex partners that adults have and how these differ by the several master statuses. The proportions in the table are calculated from the survey sample, and the standard deviation for that proportion is suggested in table 5.3, on the assumption of independence for each cell in the table *and* assuming wholly random (i.e., nonclustered) sampling. So, for example, if the value of the estimated proportion is .10 with a sample size of 100, a 95 percent confidence interval around that .10 spans the interval .04–.16. (A more complete table describing the standard deviations of the proportions by sample size is provided in table 2.2.)

We highlight below a few of the more important findings in table 5.1 but leave to the reader a full review of the table.

In a given year, over 80 percent of all adults aged eighteen to fifty-nine have no sex partners or only one; only about 3 percent have five or more partners. Few adult Americans are currently having sex with large numbers of people within the short time interval of a year. This pattern confirms that observed in the annual General Social Surveys (GSS) from 1988–91, the National Survey of Family Growth (NSFG) in 1988 for women age fifteen to forty-four and the National Survey of Men age twenty to thirty-nine (see Smith 1991b; Greeley 1991; Michael, Laumann, and Gagnon 1993; Billy et al. 1993). As the time period over which we observe the number of sex partners expands, the number of partners increases, of course. Over the past five years, about 60 percent of adults still report having had no sex partners or only one, but the upper tail of the distribution is considerably larger: over the five years, about 13 percent of adults have had five or more partners, including about 4 percent who report having had more than ten. Expanding the time frame further to cover the whole period since turning eighteen, only about 30 percent of adults have had no sex partners or only one, while over 40 percent have had five or more, a figure that includes nearly 20 percent who have had more than ten.

Men are significantly more likely than women to report having had several partners, and, correspondingly, they are significantly less likely to report having no sex partners or only one than are women, a pattern that persists for all three time periods. Cumulated over the lifetime, these differences by gender are quite large—over half the men but only about 30 percent of the women report having had five or more sex partners since turning eighteen.

Table 5.3   **The Standard Deviation of the Proportion, for Three Sample Sizes.**

	Sample Size		
Proportion	30	100	1,000
.05	.040	.023	.007
.10	.055	.030	.009
.50	.091	.050	.016

Now, there is a basic adding-up constraint that these gender differences seem to violate. Logically, men should have the same number of female sex partners as women have male sex partners, but the men, here, seem to report more partners than the women. We note that this inconsistency has been found, as well, in several other surveys in recent years in the United States, the United Kingdom, France, Finland, and elsewhere. The inconsistency constitutes an important puzzle for which we, like others, have no good answer. This is the first of many puzzles that we note in this volume that deserve much more research attention.

There are several logical explanations for this gender inconsistency, and we list them here in no particular order: (1) The men may be having sex with other men with more frequency than the women have sex with other women; this can reconcile the two total volumes. (2) The men may be having sex with women outside the age range that we included—eighteen to fifty-nine. (3) The men may be having sex with women outside the sample frame that we used— either with women living outside the continental United States or with women who do not reside in households. (4) The men and women may differ in what they consider a sex partner—the men may consider a quick act of sex as counting, while women may not count a brief, inconsequential event. (5) There may be a few women who have very many male partners, and, since we do not ask specific numbers above 100, it is possible that these few very sexually active women balance off the volume reported by men. (6) Either men may exaggerate or women may understate. (7) There are, in fact, about 8 million more adult women than men in the United States, so a somewhat smaller average number of male partners for women than female partners for men can be reconciled.

We have not attempted to reconcile how much of the discrepancy that we observe can be explained by each of these seven logical possibilities, but we conjecture that the largest portion of the discrepancy rests with explanation 6. (For an exploration of this issue based on the NORC GSS data, see Smith 1991a.)

Age is strongly associated with number of sex partners. In the current short run of the past twelve months (see table 5.1A), age is strongly negatively related to number of partners. Over 30 percent of eighteen- to twenty-four-year-olds have had two or more partners, and nearly 9 percent have had five or more.

These proportions decrease steadily for older age groups. Conversely, at older ages, the proportion reporting having had no sex partners rises from a low of only about 5.5 percent for those aged twenty-five to twenty-nine to a high of 31.6 percent for those aged fifty-five to fifty-nine. The reverse holds, however, when we consider the accumulated number of partners over the adult lifetime (see table 5.1C). Here, there is a steady increase in the proportion with, say, eleven or more partners from the youngest group through those in their forties; then it falls off again, reflecting the trend in sexual behavior over time, as we explore in a later section of this chapter.

Marital status is also quite strongly related to number of sex partners. In the past twelve months, currently married individuals are far more likely to have had only one sex partner than those in any other marital status category. We have identified in table 5.1 those who are currently cohabiting, and they too are more likely to have had only one sex partner than their counterparts who are currently living alone, although they have more partners than those who are formally married.

Cohabitation apparently implies less of a commitment to sexual exclusivity than formal marriage, but a stronger commitment than for those who are living alone. The relation with current marital status is weaker when we look at the number of sex partners over the past five years (table 5.1B), but this is presumably because not all those current marriages were in force over the whole five-year period. The relation is weaker still looking over the entire adult lifetime (table 5.1C), and again remember that we are simply sorting adults by their current marital status category here. Even for these categories, however, those who were married at the time of the interview have discernibly fewer sex partners over their whole adult lifetime than those who were not married. We organize the data to look at the number of sex partners during the whole interval of the marriage in a later section. Here, we emphasize the strong relation between current marital status and the short-term number of sex partners.

Neither education level nor current religious affiliation has a pronounced relation with number of sex partners in the recent past. There are no notable relations with education level seen in tables 5.1A or 5.1B (number of partners in the past twelve months or over the past five years). There are two interesting points in the relation between number of partners and religious affiliation. Jews report a far lower incidence of having had no sex partners than respondents in other religion categories, and those who report no religious affiliation have a higher incidence of having many sex partners.

Considering the accumulation of partners over the whole adult lifetime, there is a pattern of rising number of partners with higher levels of education. Regarding religion, neither of the two facts noted for the recent past holds up over the whole adult lifetime. Jews do appear to have substantially more partners than any other religious group (as seen in table 5.1C), but no other patterns of note are in evidence. (Notice, however, that the information on Jewish behavior is based on only about fifty observations in tables 5.1B and 5.1C.)

Regarding race/ethnicity, a larger proportion of blacks report having more than one sex partner in the past year, and substantially fewer Asians report more than one partner. The differences in the pattern for blacks and whites in the numbers of partners are less pronounced over the five-year period and still less so over the whole adult lifetime. Both blacks and whites report more partners over the adult lifetime than Hispanics, Asians, or Native Americans.[4] (Here as well, the information base is only sixty observations for Asians and only forty for Native Americans. A sample of size 3,500 seems large, but, by the time one focuses on a small minority of that number, the cases dwindle quickly. This is the key rationale for conducting much larger surveys.)

Table 5.1D is another representation of the information contained in table 5.1C. It shows the central tendency and range in values of the number of sex partners in the adult lifetime. Remember that each panel of this table contains the same 3,126 respondents and that each panel divides them into different categories. You will notice in this table that the range in number is very great, often from no partners to several hundred or even a thousand or more (there are in fact only five respondents in our data set who report having had more than 500 partners). Notice, however, that the central tendency of the distribution—the median number of partners—is three overall and never exceeds six. (We do not report an arithmetic mean as the mean is highly volatile and excessively affected by the one or two extreme cases in each cell.)

So table 5.1D tells us that the median adult in the United States in the age range eighteen to fifty-nine has three sex partners—men report having six and women two. The maximum numbers are really quite large, we note. The shape of the distribution is where much of the story lies: there are many who report having quite a small number of partners (half the sample has three or fewer), and there are very few who report having a large number (say, several dozen or more). But there are some—and not an insignificant number in the whole population—with a very large number of sex partners. They are not made up. We found them in our sample, but they are not typical of most Americans.

Table 5.1 tells us a great deal about the patterns of numbers of sex partners by the master status categories that we identified in chapter 1. Gender, age, and marital status are key factors distinguishing adults by number of sex partners. While education appears to be a factor correlated with number of partners over the adult lifetime, those with more education are on average somewhat younger, so this relation partially reflects the same phenomenon as age. The more educated also tend to marry later, so they have a longer period of sexual

4. The reader may notice a larger number of cases in the table reporting behavior by race/ethnicity. For this and all comparisons that are conducted separately for whites, blacks, and Hispanics, the oversampled cases of blacks and Hispanics are added in.

maturity prior to marriage, and this longer period "at risk" of many partners may help explain some of the higher incidence of many partners by education observed in table 5.1C. The differentiated patterns of behavior by Jews, by blacks, and by Asians deserve far more careful scrutiny in subsequent research, but this will require a larger sample than ours.

The Distributions by Gender, Age, and Marital Status Combined

Table 5.4 more succinctly summarizes the salient findings in table 5.1A and does so by separating out the relations among numbers of partners and all three important master statuses: age, marital status, and gender. Table 5.4A presents a set of nine "cells" defined by age and current marital status, shown separately for men and women. Within each cell is shown the distribution of partners in the four categories previously discussed. The top left cell, for example, describes the distribution of partners for young (eighteen to twenty-nine), never-married women: among these women, 12.9 percent report having no sex partners within the past twelve months, 56.6 percent report one, 24.2 percent two to four, and 6.2 percent five or more. One sees in this table the tremendous influence of age and marital status on reported sexual behavior defined in terms of number of partners for each gender: those who are younger and single (either never married or no longer married) are far more likely to report having five or more partners within the past twelve months; this is especially so for the men. Those who are older and single are far more likely to report having no sex partners within the past twelve months.

Table 5.4B is organized in a similar manner, except that the columns are defined for three categories of current living arrangement instead of current marital status. Here the columns are unmarried and living alone, unmarried and living with a sex partner, and married (which implies living with a spouse).

KEY FINDINGS FROM TABLE 5.4

A few of the more important relations seen in table 5.4 are the following.

Married individuals of all age groups and across genders are dramatically more likely to have had only one partner in the past twelve months. Among those who are married, the young (eighteen to twenty-nine) and middle-aged (thirty to forty-four) men are noticeably more likely to have had two or more partners than are older (forty-five to fifty-nine) men or women of any age. Cohabiting but unmarried adults are much more likely to have had more partners than their married counterparts but much less likely to have had many partners than their noncohabiting counterparts. Commitment to sexual exclusivity is clearly closely linked to the nature of the partnership—those formally married are more sexually exclusive than those who are cohabiting, and they, in turn, are more exclusive than those who are not involved in a cohabitational relationship.

Table 5.4A **Number of Sex Partners in the Past Twelve Months, by Age, Gender, and Current Marital Status (% distributions)**

	Marital Status		
Age and Partner Status	Never Married	Married	Formerly Married
Women[a]			
18–29:			
No partners	12.9	0.0	2.0
1 partner	56.6	96.0	58.8
2–4 partners	24.2	3.0	33.3
5 or more partners	6.2	1.0	5.9
N	256	201	51
30–44:			
No partners	37.3	1.3	18.9
1 partner	42.4	96.4	58.3
2–4 partners	17.8	2.1	21.7
5 or more partners	2.5	.2	1.1
N	118	473	180
45–59:			
No partners	64.9	7.3	54.1
1 partner	27.0	91.3	36.1
2–4 partners	8.1	1.4	9.0
5 or more partners	0.0	0.0	.8
N	37	275	133
Men[b]			
18–29:			
No partners	14.6	.8	†
1 partner	40.7	90.9	†
2–4 partners	30.5	5.8	†
5 or more partners	14.2	2.5	†
N	302	121	21
30–44:			
No partners	23.1	.6	14.0
1 partner	34.0	93.3	40.2
2–4 partners	35.4	5.6	39.2
5 or more partners	7.5	.6	6.5
N	147	356	107
45–59:			
No partners	†	3.7	30.1
1 partner	†	91.5	45.2
2–4 partners	†	3.7	23.3
5 or more partners	†	1.2	1.4
N	15	246	73

[a]*N* = 1,734.
[b]*N* = 1,398.
†*N* = fewer than thirty cases.

Table 5.4B   **Number of Sex Partners in the Past Twelve Months, by Age, Gender, and Current Cohabiting Status (% distributions)**

	Cohabiting Status		
Age and Partner Status	Not Cohabiting	Cohabiting, Unmarried	Married
Women[a]			
18–29:			
No partners	14.3	0.0	0.0
1 partner	51.3	76.8	96.0
2–4 partners	27.7	18.8	3.0
5 or more partners	6.7	4.4	1.0
N	238	69	201
30–44:			
No partners	30.4	2.2	1.3
1 partner	45.8	86.7	96.4
2–4 partners	21.7	11.1	2.1
5 or more partners	2.0	0.2	
N	253	45	473
45–59:			
No partners	61.3	†	7.3
1 partner	29.7	†	91.3
2–4 partners	8.4	†	1.4
5 or more partners	.6	†	0.0
N	155	15	275
Men[b]			
18–29:			
No partners	16.1	0.0	8
1 partner	35.8	67.3	90.9
2–4 partners	33.2	24.5	5.8
5 or more partners	15.0	8.2	2.5
N	274	49	121
30–44:			
No partners	22.7	0.0	.6
1 partner	30.1	73.7	93.3
2–4 partners	39.4	23.7	5.6
5 or more partners	7.9	2.6	.6
N	216	38	356
45–59:			
No partners	42.1	†	3.7
1 partner	35.5	†	91.5
2–4 partners	22.4	†	3.7
5 or more partners	0.0	†	1.2
N	76	12	246

[a]*N* = 1,721.
[b]*N* = 1,390.
†*N* = fewer than thirty cases.

Table 5.4C   **Number of Sex Partners, Selected Studies (% distributions)**

Data Set	In the Past 12 Months				
	0	1	2–4	5+	N
Men					
NHSLS	9.9	66.8	18.3	5.1	1,408
U.K.	13.1	73.0	12.3	1.5	8,384
France	11.1	77.5	10.3	1.0	8,942
Finland	4.5	78.4	18.2	4.5	897
GSS 1988–91	9.7	67.7	17.1	5.4	1,746
NSM	8.7	67.7	14.5	9.2	3,317
Women					
NHSLS	13.6	74.6	10.0	1.7	1,747
U.K.	13.9	79.4	6.4	0.0	10,492
France	17.3	78.0	4.5	.2	11,104
Finland	8.3	78.6	10.7	0.0	881
GSS 1988–91	12.7	75.5	11.1	.6	2,175
	Over the Lifetime				
Men					
NHSLS	3.4	19.5	20.9	56.2	1,394
U.K.	6.6	20.6	29.0	43.8	8,384
France	4.5	21.4	29.1	45.0	8,772
Finland	2.9	12.4	24.9	59.8	980
GSS 1988–91	3.8	16.6	24.3	55.7	1,148
NSM	5.0	26.5	46.6	21.9	3,317
Women					
NHSLS	2.6	31.4	36.4	29.6	1,732
U.K.	5.7	39.3	35.1	19.8	10,492
France	5.7	46.1	34.4	13.7	10,449
Finland	3.8	27.6	35.0	34.2	1,046
GSS 1988–91	4.2	34.7	34.4	26.7	1,401

Sources: United Kingdom: Wellings et al. 1994; Johnson et al. 1994. France: Spira et al. 1993. Finland: Kontula and Haavio-Mannila 1993.

Note: There are many differences in definitions in these studies: *Differences in the period of time:* The NHSLS and the GSS use the adult lifetime (i.e., over age eighteen); others use the whole lifetime including ages younger than eighteen. *Differences in the categories of numbers:* The French categories are 2–5, not 2–4, and 6+, not 5+; the NSM categories are 1–3, 4–19, 20+ over the lifetime and 2–3 and 4+ over the past eighteen months. *Differences in ages:* The NHSLS includes ages eighteen to fifty-nine; the U.K. survey includes ages sixteen to fifty-nine; the French survey includes ages eighteen to sixty-nine; the Finnish survey includes ages eighteen to seventy-four; and the NSM includes ages twenty to thirty-nine only. The GSS for 1988–91 has been calculated for ages eighteen to fifty-nine.

The proportion of adults with many partners in a given year decreases dramatically with age, and the proportion with no partners increases with age. With respect to the proportion with no partners, never-married men and women are quite similar; however, men who have been but no longer are married are significantly more likely than comparably aged women to have had at least one partner.

The group with the highest proportion having had five or more partners within the past year is young, unmarried men. Table 5.4A shows that 14 percent of young unmarried men report more than five partners, and table 5.4B similarly shows that 15 percent of the young men who are not currently married or cohabiting report having had five or more partners. The groups with the next highest rates of having had five or more partners are the other unmarried men under age forty-five—6.5–7.5 percent of these groups report having had five partners. The female groups reporting the highest rates of five or more partners are also young, unmarried, and living alone, but the rates for the women are decidedly lower than those for the men. From a health perspective, these men and women with five or more partners within the past year are those at greatest risk of exposure to STIs, as we show in detail in chapter 11.

Let us recap the most important facts revealed in tables 5.1 and 5.4. Over the twelve months preceding our survey in 1992, the vast majority of adults aged eighteen to fifty-nine had no more than one sex partner, and, over the adult lifetime by that date, and averaging over the young and older respondents in our study, about one in four men and about one in ten women reported having had sex with as many as ten partners. The men reported more partners than did the women, and that is a puzzle for which we have no convincing explanation. Age is dramatically negatively related to number of current partners and, of course, positively related to the accumulation of partners over the lifetime, at least up to the mid-forties. After that age, even the accumulated numbers of partners appear to decline with age, reflecting a longer-run trend that we explore in greater depth in the next section. Marital status is the third demographic variable that is closely linked to number of partners; married men and married women exhibit substantially higher rates of sexual exclusivity than do people in other marital statuses. Cohabitation, interestingly, appears to be a halfway step to marriage in the sense that the rate of sexual exclusivity among cohabiting respondents is much higher than among those not cohabiting, but also noticeably lower than among the formally married.

We find the relations between number of partners and education level, religious affiliation, and race/ethnicity, to be much less compelling or substantial. This is not to suggest that these important social characteristics do not affect sexual behavior, but, in comparison to age, gender, and marital status, their gross correlations with numbers of partners are distinctly secondary.

The broad patterns of numbers of partners over the lifetime and over the past twelve months reported in our survey are quite similar to those reported in other recent, scientifically valid national surveys such as the GSS for the period 1988–91 (see Michael, Laumann, and Gagnon 1993; Smith 1991b; and Greeley 1991), the National Survey of Men (see Billy et al. 1993), and the British (Wellings et al. 1994; Johnson et al. 1994), French (Spira et al. 1993), and Finnish surveys (Kontula and Haavio-Mannila 1993). Table 5.4C shows the comparisons by gender for the number of partners within the past twelve months and over the lifetime from these several surveys.

While there are surely some differences in these distributions, the general patterns of number of partners are remarkably similar from one study to another. Look, for example, at the NHSLS and the U.K. study. Over the adult lifetime, the men in these two surveys have extremely similar numbers of partners, and the women in the U.K. study have slightly fewer partners than women in the U.S. study do. The same broad pattern is observed in the most recent twelve months in this U.S.-U.K. comparison. Similarly, the French distributions practically mirror the U.K. distributions, even though the French study is based on a phone survey while the U.K. study is a face-to-face survey like our NHSLS. These two U.K. and French studies are based on quite large samples of nearly 20,000 observations each.

The important points about this comparison are these. (1) In each of these independent surveys, the general character of the distributions of number of partners is the same—the U.S. distributions from our NHSLS sample are not in any way exceptional. (2) A generalizable scientific sample that reflects the behavior of the whole population in these several developed nations in very recent years shows that 80 percent or so of adults have had no sex partners or only one within the past year. (3) These surveys show substantially higher rates of lifetime partners reported by men than by women in each of these societies.

The first of these points is reassuring. As we delve more deeply into the details about sexual behavior, and go into topics not previously investigated and on which we cannot make comparisons, it is important to keep in mind that this key summary variable about sexual behavior does in fact conform very closely with the equivalent information from other data sets. The respondents in our survey appear to be answering our questions accurately and truthfully. It is most unlikely that anything but a basically similar pattern of behavior and a basically honest set of answers to these questions could have produced so similar a set of distributions as we see in table 5.4C. Like other survey researchers, we have confidence in the capacity of surveys such as this to yield important and accurate information. Those who would doubt the general accuracy of such surveys must explain how such similar findings can be produced by any other mechanism than similarity of actual behavior and honest reporting of that behavior.

The second point (that 80 percent or so of adults have had no sex partners or only one within the past year in each of these populations) raises the interesting question of why this is so. Why are all these Western industrialized societies so similar in this important respect? We suggest that these several societies have common structural features and similar incentives to marry and form two-adult, at least moderately stable partnerships and that, within that environment, the incentives to have only one sex partner are very strong and are reinforced by personal investments in the partnership, by pressure from peers or stakeholders, and by overt social policies.

As we indicated above, we do not have a satisfactory answer to the question implied by the third point (that men report having more sex partners than women do).

5.2 The Cumulative Number of Partners, by Age and Time Period

The purpose of this section is to examine two aspects of the passage of time—of dynamics—in the formation of sexual partnerships. These two aspects are distinct but intertwined in a way that makes it difficult to separate them. The one notion is that of aging or passage through the life course. Here, we are interested in the influence of age on the number of partners, that is, the accumulation of partners by a given age. To get at this notion, we can calculate the number of partners that a respondent reported having had by age twenty, say, and again by age thirty. From this information, we can infer how many new partners the respondent acquired during his or her twenties (from age twenty to age thirty), and we can see how that number changes as the respondent ages further from age thirty to age forty, and so forth. Of course, we know only the behavior up to the time of the interview, so we have many more respondents who report behavior in their twenties than those who report behavior in their fifties. We have progressively less data on the behavior of older men and women, and we end our observations at age fifty-nine.

The other notion of time on which we focus in this section is that of calendar time. The oldest respondents in our data set were fifty-nine in 1992 (the time of the survey), so they were born in 1933 and turned, say, eighteen in 1951. Since we asked about sexual behavior over the whole adult lifetime (meaning age eighteen and over), we have information on the sexual behavior of adults over the period from 1951 to 1992, but we know only about the behavior of those age eighteen in 1951, of those age eighteen and nineteen in 1952, etc.; we know the behavior of adults from age eighteen to age fifty-nine only for the year 1992. By organizing these data in a particular way—by specific age for those born at a particular time—we can track the behavior of, say, twenty-year-olds from the 1950s through the 1960s, 1970s, and 1980s. From data organized in this way, we can study the *trend* over time in sexual behavior of, say, twenty-year-olds. We can also see whether we can discern any patterns of behavior that seemed to change at specific points or periods of time. For example, we look to see whether we can discern any evidence of a greater rate at which people accumulated sex partners in the late 1960s and 1970s that might be evidence of the supposed "sexual revolution." Similarly, we look to see whether we can discern any evidence of a decline in the rate of acquiring additional sex partners after, say, 1985. If so, one might interpret that decline as a

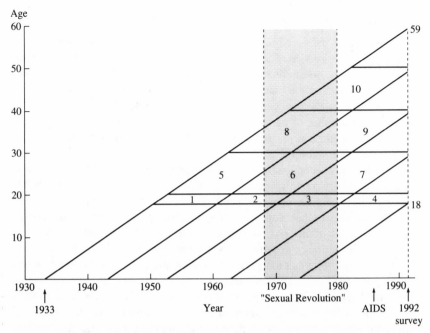

Fig. 5.1 Schematic diagram showing the age at each year for respondent born in a specific year.

reaction to the fear of the spread of AIDS. These period effects, as well as age effects, are the focus of attention in this section.

These notions and the discussion of the findings in this section are better understood with reference to figure 5.1. The horizontal shows years beginning in 1930 and going out to 1992; the vertical shows age beginning with birth and going up to age sixty. The left-most upward-sloping line depicts the year in which the oldest cohort in our survey was any given age, so the line begins in 1933, when that birth cohort was born, and extends upward to age fifty-nine in 1992. That line, for example, lets us know that this cohort turned twenty in 1953. Similarly, the parallel lines to the right depict the year in which other birth cohorts were each a given age. Now, if for illustrative purposes we think that there was a sexual revolution that began in 1968 and ended in 1980, then the vertical shaded band covering that twelve-year time interval was experienced by the different birth cohorts at successively younger ages, and the figure helps us sort that out. For example, that shaded vertical time period of the alleged sexual revolution occurred about age thirty-five for our oldest cohort but long before adolescence for our youngest cohorts. We will use this figure in the discussion below to help keep age and period effects clear; the little numbers in the various segments will be discussed later.

Measurement of the Key Variables

The concept measured here is the cumulative number of sex partners by a given age. The ages used are twenty, thirty, forty, and fifty. Because of the way in which the questionnaire asked about number of partners—by important intervals of the lifetime that varied in length, not by specific ages or specific calendar dates—the data cannot easily be reconstituted for this analysis. The data on the number of partners over the lifetime were collected for specific periods of the life course, such as the time period prior to the formation of the first marriage or live-in relationship, or that of that first union, or that between the first and any second marriage or cohabitational union, and so forth. Consequently, we know only how many *new* partners were acquired during each of these periods (and we obtained information about those new partners), but we do not know just when during the interval those partners were acquired. So, for the analysis in this section, it has been necessary to assume a uniform or an even distribution of new partners over that segment of the lifetime.

Let us describe this procedure by giving some examples. Suppose that we had a man respondent who had married at age twenty-two, and suppose that he reported having had four sex partners prior to his marriage. The time between becoming an adult (age eighteen) and his first union lasted four years, and, since he reported four partners during that interval, we assume that he added one new partner in each of those four years. So we would calculate that he had *two* partners during his adult lifetime up to age twenty.

Consider a second example, a married, thirty-five-year-old woman who had married at age twenty-three and who reported having had three partners before she married, one of whom became her spouse, and reported having had one other new sex partner other than her spouse while she was married, up to the date of the survey. We would consider her to have had one partner by age twenty, four partners by age thirty, and four partners during her adult lifetime up to the date of the survey. (Since she said that she had had three partners in the five years prior to marriage, we assume that she acquired partners during that interval at the rate of three in five years, or three-fifths of a partner each year. We calculate that she acquired $2 \times 3/5$ or 1.2 partners by age twenty, so we call that one partner. By age thirty, she had acquired all her premarital partners—three of them—and had acquired partners during her marriage at the rate of one in twelve years, or seven-twelfths by age thirty. This totals four partners by that age and, of course, four by her current age thirty-five as well.

You can see that, by assuming a uniform distribution in the rate of acquiring the partners reported for each segment of the life course, we have had to engage in estimation that is unbiased and neutral but that is not fully accurate. The fact is that we have compromised in our survey. We have maximized, as best we know how, the chance that the respondent would know the answer to the question asked and be able and willing to answer it, but, in going after that accuracy, we have had to forgo obtaining data fully compatible with all the analytic concepts we knew we would want to analyze. The concept with which we are working here is one that is rather severely compromised. By contrast, the accuracy of the information about the total number of partners each respondent had over the adult lifetime is, we believe, enhanced by this questioning strategy. This is just one of the trade-offs that we faced in crafting our survey.

As in the earlier section of this chapter, number of partners is reported here in four categories: no partners, one, two to four, and five or more. The data are reported here by birth cohorts, and these are defined in ten-year intervals—respondents born from 1933 to 1942, from 1943 to 1952, from 1953 to 1962, and from 1963 to 1972 (only those who were at least twenty years old at the survey are considered in this section).[5]

The Acquisition of New Sex Partners, by Birth Cohort and Gender

Table 5.5 shows the estimated number of sex partners by specific ages—age twenty, age thirty, age forty, and age fifty in successive panels—by birth cohort for men and women separately. Let us first describe how to read this table. The first row applies to men who were born between 1933 and 1942; it reports the number of sex partners as adults by their twentieth birthday, that is, during the time they were eighteen or nineteen. The table tells us that 1.0 percent of this birth cohort of men reported no sex partners during that two-year interval, 42.9 percent reported only one, 34.0 percent reported two to four, and 22 percent reported five or more. The number to the right tells us that there were 191 men in that group of respondents in our survey. If you refer back to figure 5.1, that time interval for this group of men is represented by the area marked "1." The location of that area in the figure helps us see that this time interval took place between about 1951 and 1962.

KEY FINDINGS FROM TABLES 5.5 AND 5.6

Studying the top panel of table 5.5—for men age twenty for four separate ten-year birth cohorts—we see two quite interesting patterns. First, notice that the 1933–42 cohort has a substantially lower rate of having had five or more partners by age twenty than is the case for all three of the other cohorts. The 1933–42 cohort has about 22 percent with five or more partners by age twenty, but the other three cohorts have about 30 percent with that many sex partners by age twenty. Look once again at figure 5.1. Let us hypothesize that men of most adult ages acquired sex partners at a more rapid rate after 1967—after the advent of the alleged sexual revolution. Then the behavior reported in this top panel in rows 2 and 3 reflects the pattern of sexual behavior after 1967, but

---

5. We have chosen to report data by ten-year birth cohorts in this and several other chapters. These equal length intervals do not, of course, conform precisely to the historical periods that we discuss here—e.g., the pre–World War II cohorts, the baby boom and subsequent baby bust cohorts, the period of alleged rapid sexual change in the 1970s, the post-AIDS period, etc. We think that the common use of these same four cohort intervals across chapters facilitates comparisons.

Table 5.5   **Number of Sex Partners by Specific Ages, by Gender and Birth Cohort (% distributions)**

Cohort	No. of Partners				
	0	1	2–4	5+	N
Age 20					
Men:					
1933–42	1.0	42.9	34.0	22.0	191
1943–52	1.6	32.7	34.0	31.7	303
1953–62	7.0	26.9	36.3	29.8	402
1963–72	10.3	28.0	31.1	30.6	350
N	71	387	426	367	1,246
Women:					
1933–42	5.8	78.0	15.1	1.1	259
1943–52	4.7	59.7	27.4	8.3	362
1953–62	4.0	48.0	36.6	11.5	506
1963–72	8.8	40.0	37.9	13.3	398
N	87	821	477	144	1,525
Age 30					
Men:					
1933–42	1.2	32.8	28.1	38.0	171
1943–52	1.2	26.3	25.9	46.7	255
1953–62	4.7	18.4	28.0	49.0	343
N	21	186	213	353	769
Women:					
1933–42	4.7	67.2	25.5	2.6	235
1943–52	1.9	45.7	34.6	17.8	315
1953–62	2.0	35.6	39.9	22.4	441
N	26	460	347	163	991
Age 40					
Men:					
1933–42	1.3	30.8	20.1	47.8	159
1943–52	1.2	20.6	20.2	58.1	248
N	5	101	83	220	407
Women:					
1933–42	2.6	58.9	29.9	8.7	231
1943–52	1.6	36.0	36.0	26.4	314
N	11	250	183	103	545
Age 50					
Men:					
1933–42	1.3	30.3	18.7	49.7	155
N	2	47	29	77	155
Women:					
1933–42	2.6	54.3	31.2	12.1	232
N	6	127	73	28	232

the behavior of the men in row 1 does not involve that time period. (In the figure, the areas marked "2" and "3" are directly in the shaded band that depicts the sexual revolution, but the area marked "1" is not.) So the lower rate of having many partners in the very top row of that first panel seems to be consistent with the hypothesis of a higher rate of sex partner acquisition beginning sometime after the mid-1960s.

Looking at the panel that reports the behavior of women by age twenty—the second panel in table 5.5—that same pattern is again in evidence. For the women, the more recent birth cohorts appear to have successively more partners by that age.

This is, then, we suggest, very real (albeit somewhat blurry) evidence of a period effect, with a higher rate of acquiring many sex partners after the mid-1960s, holding age constant. It would seem reasonable to call that period effect a sexual revolution.

The second intriguing finding in that same top panel of table 5.5 is seen by studying the column reporting the percentage with no partners. Notice that, for the men, only a very small percentage of those born in the 1933–43 and 1943–52 cohorts report no partners by age twenty. (They came of age in the 1950s and 1960s, when the age at first marriage was quite low, compared to later cohorts, so a large percentage of them were in fact married by age twenty.) But compare that to the 1963–72 cohort, which came of age in the early 1980s. Of those men born in the 1960s, over 10 percent reported no partners by age twenty, compared to only about 1 percent of their earlier cohort counterparts. Look at figure 5.1 once again, this time from the point of view of how the AIDS scare of the mid-1980s might be revealed in this top panel. Notice that AIDS was discovered midway through the time interval reported in this top panel for the 1963–72 cohort. If those eighteen- and nineteen-year-olds reduced their sexual activity and therefore their risk of infection, cutting back on numbers of sex partners, that behavior would show up in table 5.5 as more of them having fewer partners at ages eighteen and nineteen compared to the birth cohorts who came of age at an earlier date. That is precisely what we see in that top panel for these men. Again, this same pattern is exhibited by the women in the second panel of table 5.5.

Therefore, there is at least suggestive evidence in the behavior of the youngest birth cohort of a noticeable reduction in the rate of acquiring sex partners by age twenty, and that behavior is consistent with a behavioral response to the fear of AIDS.

The time period covered by the panels of table 5.5 that report behavior by age thirty is represented in figure 5.1 as the areas marked "1" and "5" for the top row of data, as the areas marked "2" and "6" for the second row of data, and so on. Here too we can see that the period effect that commenced in about 1968 did not have much influence on the 1933–42 cohort by age thirty. Again, we see that a much smaller proportion of these men and women report having had five or more sex partners. Nearly half the men in the 1943–52 and 1953–62 birth cohorts report having had five or more partners by age thirty. The women also exhibit quite different proportions of having many partners, with only 2.6 percent of the 1933–42 cohort, nearly 18 percent of the 1943–52 cohort, and over 22 percent of the 1953–62 cohort having had five partners. Here again, there is quite compelling evidence of a period effect on number of sex partners that can indeed be considered a sexual revolution.

It is interesting to notice that, in the panels reporting behavior by age forty, the 1933–42 cohort never did "catch up" with the later cohorts in terms of the high proportions who had five or more sex partners. Presumably, by the late 1960s, when the revolution in sexual behavior was beginning, that 1933–42 cohort had married and settled down. As a result, many in that cohort—a third' of the men and nearly 60 percent of the women—report having had no more than one sex partner by age forty. Nearly half the men and only 8.7 percent of the women report having had five or more partners by that age. For the younger cohort—the 1943–52 group—the rates of having many partners were still substantially higher by age forty.

Table 5.6 rearranges the same data as are presented in table 5.5 to facilitate comparisons at different ages within a single ten-year birth cohort.[6] Figure 5.2 shows these same data for the final column only, the proportions of each group who report having had five or more sex partners by that age.

One sees here the expected increase in the accumulated number of partners at older ages; as figure 5.2 depicts, the rate of accumulation (the steepness of the line) declines dramatically as age advances. This is in large part because respondents search for a mate, and, when one is found, they form cohabitational or marriage unions and acquire very few additional sex partners thereafter, as we discussed in the previous section. The flattening of the line as the cohort ages in part reflects the fact that more of the cohort members have formed stable partnerships and are no longer "searching" for new partners, at least not at the same pace or with the same intensity. Notice, also, that one sees substantially lower rates of accumulation of partners by women than by men in either the table or the figure.

Sex Partners before and after Age Eighteen

Estimating the rate of virginity from these data raises one of the complications of our study, as we mentioned in passing in an earlier section of this

6. The reader may notice that there are a few instances in table 5.6 in which an illogical thing happens: a higher percentage of the cohort has, say, had no partners by age forty than at age thirty. Of course, one can only accumulate partners, not subtract from the number of partners that one has *ever* had. The explanation for this apparent error in the table is that the number of people in the cohort changes slightly from one cell to another. Those who have dropped out for any reason can affect these proportions, so there is no error here so far as we are aware.

Table 5.6   **Number of Sex Partners by Birth Cohort, by Gender and Specific Ages (% distributions)**

	No. of Partners				
Age	0	1	2–4	5+	N
1933–42 cohort					
Men:					
Age 20	1.0	42.9	34.0	22.0	191
Age 30	1.2	32.8	28.1	38.0	171
Age 40	1.3	30.8	20.1	47.8	159
Age 50	1.3	30.3	18.7	49.7	155
Women:					
Age 20	5.8	78.0	15.1	1.1	259
Age 30	4.7	67.2	25.5	2.6	235
Age 40	2.6	58.9	29.9	8.7	231
Age 50	2.6	54.3	31.2	12.1	232
1943–52 cohort					
Men:					
Age 20	1.6	32.7	34.0	31.7	303
Age 30	1.2	26.3	25.9	46.7	255
Age 40	1.2	20.6	20.2	58.1	248
Women:					
Age 20	4.7	59.7	27.4	8.3	362
Age 30	1.9	45.7	34.6	17.8	315
Age 40	1.6	36.0	36.0	26.4	314
1953–62 cohort					
Men:					
Age 20	7.0	26.9	36.3	29.8	402
Age 30	4.7	18.4	28.0	49.0	343
Women:					
Age 20	4.0	48.0	36.6	11.5	506
Age 30	2.0	35.6	39.9	22.4	441

chapter. We asked respondents to tell us about their sex partners since turning age eighteen in some detail, as we are interested in adult sexual behavior. We also, but briefly, asked respondents in another later section of the questionnaire about their sexual experiences prior to their eighteenth birthday. We found out how many partners they had had prior to that time, but we did not ask them to clarify for us whether the partners they had before turning eighteen were the *same* ones they reported for the period after turning eighteen. Moreover, we asked the questions about the period after age eighteen earlier in the interview than we asked about adolescent behavior, as we anticipated that the latter might, for some respondents, be more sensitive and we wanted therefore to build up a good rapport before asking those more sensitive questions. Consequently, we have no way of adding the two numbers of partners together. That

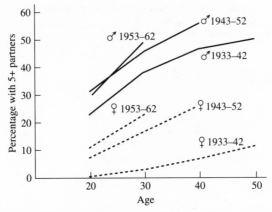

Fig. 5.2 Percentage of respondents who reported having five or more sex partners by a specified age, by gender and birth cohort.

is the primary reason that we focus on the number of partners during adulthood (i.e., after turning eighteen) in this chapter.

One of the few instances in which we can unambiguously add the partners before and after turning eighteen is when there were none in one of the two time periods. Table 5.7 lets us look at the issue of virginity with more precision than earlier tables allowed. It takes each of the birth cohorts of men and women separately—the groups defined in the top two panels of table 5.5—and shows the number of sex partners reported prior to age eighteen as compared to the number reported by age twenty.

FINDINGS FROM TABLE 5.7
Of those who had had no sex partners as an adult by age twenty, over 80 percent had also had no sex partners prior to age eighteen. Table 5.7 reveals that, across all four cohorts, of the seventy men and eighty-six women who reported having had no partners by age twenty, sixty of the men and seventy of the women also had had none before turning eighteen.

In general, sexual behavior prior to age eighteen appears to mirror the behavior in subsequent years; those men and women who report relatively many partners at eighteen and nineteen years also report relatively many partners in the period prior to age eighteen. We can now return to the point raised earlier in this chapter about the 2.9 percent of the sample who reported having no sex partners in their *adult* lifetime (i.e., since turning age eighteen). With the additional information about partners before age eighteen, we find that, of the forty-seven men and forty-five women in the sample who reported having had no partners since age eighteen, forty-four of those men and forty-four of those women also had none before age eighteen. (Only one of the women had one partner before eighteen, two of the men had one partner, and one man had two to four partners.) So the adjustment in the estimate of the proportions of adults aged eighteen to fifty-nine who are virgins yields the following estimates: 3.2 percent of men (instead of the 3.4 percent listed in table 5.1C), 2.5 percent of women (no change from table 5.1C), and 2.8 percent overall (instead of 2.9 percent).

5.3   The Number of Sex Partners before, during, and following First Union

In this section, as in the preceding one, we look at the accumulation of sex partners over the lifetime. The preceding section focused on accumulation by specific ages. Here, we focus on accumulation during successive intervals of time defined by heterosexual marriage or cohabitational episodes. That is, here we look at the accumulation of new sex partners in three successive time intervals—from age eighteen to first marriage or cohabitational union; during that first union; and from the end of that first union to the beginning of the next, if a second occurred. Both these ways of organizing our analysis have certain strengths, and each reveals different behaviors.

Looking at specific ages over the lifetime is a simple, easily understood way of characterizing the life course. All respondents pass through specific ages in a uniform manner. Thinking about the lifetime in segments defined by important events such as cohabitation, marriage, and divorce, however, organizes the time into potentially more relevant segments, although the duration of the intervals will differ from person to person. Because of the relevance of these life-course segments in their lives, we believe that respondents find it easier to recall the number of sex partners in these marital or cohabitational segments, so our survey questionnaire was organized around these time intervals (defined by starting and ending dates of these partnerships). We anticipated that the rate of accumulation of sex partners would differ in these segments, with relatively many before a union, fewer during a union, relatively more again after the union ended (if it did), and few again during a second union (if there was one). If it exists, this punctuated pattern should be observable in our data.

Because our data on numbers of sex partners were collected by life-course segments, it is easier for us to analyze the data in this form—that is, we need to make no special assumptions of a uniform rate of acquiring partners for this analysis, as we had to do for the analysis in the previous section, which is organized by age. But there are difficulties here as well.

As in the two previous sections, we count partners of both genders here without distinction, and we report behavior separately for men and women and by birth cohort.[7] We include only heterosexual unions here, so we exclude from

---

7. One minor difference between this section and the preceding one is that here we include in the most recent birth cohort a twelve-year span covering those born between 1963 and 1974, whereas in the previous section we used a ten-year interval covering the period 1963–72 and did

Table 5.7

Table 5.7 **Distributions of Number of Sex Partners before Age Eighteen by Number between Ages Eighteen and Twenty, by Gender and Birth Cohort**

No. of Partners between 18 and 20	No. of Partners before Age 18				
	0	1	2–4	5+	N
Women					
1933–42 cohort:					
0	100.0	0.0	0.0	0.0	2
1	85.2	9.9	1.2	3.7	81
2–4	49.2	20.0	26.2	4.6	65
5+	19.1	9.5	33.3	38.1	42
N	111	25	32	22	190
1943–52 cohort:					
0	100.0	0.0	0.0	0.0	5
1	72.7	11.1	5.0	11.1	99
2–4	52.9	18.6	22.6	5.9	102
5+	33.3	11.8	18.3	36.6	93
N	162	41	45	51	299
1953–62 cohort:					
0	85.7	3.6	10.7	0.0	28
1	62.9	20.0	10.5	6.7	105
2–4	34.5	26.9	29.7	8.9	145
5+	30.2	13.4	30.2	26.0	119
N	176	77	93	51	397
1963–72 cohort:					
0	82.9	5.7	11.4	0.0	35
1	58.8	17.5	14.4	9.3	97
2–4	33.9	20.2	36.7	9.2	109
5+	13.1	15.0	25.2	46.7	107
N	137	57	85	69	348
Women					
1933–42 cohort:					
0	80.0	20.0	0.0	0.0	15
1	71.8	24.3	2.0	2.0	202
2–4	56.4	28.2	12.8	2.6	39
5+	100.0	0.0	0.0	0.0	3
N	182	63	9	5	259
1943–52 cohort:					
0	100.0	0.0	0.0	0.0	17
1	73.0	22.3	2.8	1.9	215
2–4	68.7	16.2	14.1	1.0	99
5+	53.3	30.0	13.3	3.3	30
N	258	73	24	6	361
1953–62 cohort:					
0	94.7	5.3	0.0	0.0	19
1	61.0	27.8	8.3	2.9	241
2–4	43.2	29.7	20.5	6.5	185
5+	46.6	24.1	17.2	12.1	58
N	272	137	68	26	503

Table 5.7   (continued)

No. of Partners	No. of Partners before Age 18				
between 18 and 20	0	1	2–4	5+	*N*
Women					
1963–72 cohort:					
0	65.7	22.9	11.4	0.0	35
1	51.3	28.5	15.2	5.1	158
2–4	36.0	22.0	34.0	8.0	150
5+	28.3	18.9	28.3	24.5	53
N	173	96	94	33	396

this analysis those who formed homosexual partnerships as their first union as well as those who did not form any partnership. As a vast majority of both men and women form a marriage or a cohabitational union, we include about 75 percent of the sample in this section. As in the preceding section, we count only new partners here. We are unable to add to this number any partner with whom the respondent began having sex in an earlier interval and whom he or she kept as a sex partner because of the way in which we asked the questions in our survey.[8]

The Form of Partnership and the Age of Entry

Traditionally, formal marriage was overwhelmingly the most common form of union, but in recent decades many adults form informal cohabitational unions, at least initially. Studies have shown that these cohabitational relationships are typically of short duration in the United States, with a half-life of only about one year, and with the majority of these unions converting into formal marriages (for details about patterns of cohabitation in the United States, see Bumpass and Sweet 1989, Thornton 1988, and Willis and Michael 1994).

We conjecture that the patterns of sexual partnerships formed prior to the

---

not include those born in 1973 or 1974 in that one section only since they had not yet reached age twenty, the focus of that section.

8. In section 6 of our questionnaire (see appendix C), we asked only about the *additional* partners the respondent had in each segment of time, and then we asked if the respondent continued to have sex with any of the previous partners already reported to us. But we asked this last question only if the respondent had at least one new partner in this interval, and we asked only if he or she had sex with any of the previous partners, not the number of those previous partners with whom he or she had sex in this interval. Consequently, we cannot know the total number of sex partners in any of these intervals unless the respondent happened to have had at least one new one and only one previous one or none concurrently. The sample censoring here is excessive, so we consider only the new partnerships. We note that, of those with at least one new partner in each of the three intervals considered in this section, only about 20 percent reported any concurrent partners, and it is likely that those with no new partners had fewer concurrent partners than did those with new partners. Therefore, the number of partners that we do not include here is probably not great, but we cannot be certain of this.

union may be quite different for those who first enter into a formal marriage than for those who first enter into an informal cohabitation. Accordingly, we separate those two groups in the analysis here. Furthermore, some respondents initially formed a cohabitational union and later converted it into a formal marriage; for our analysis, we treat these groups separately as well. As the pattern of sex partner accumulation may also differ from decade to decade, we display the data by birth cohort, and, as always, we show the patterns for men and women separately.

Our NHSLS data cover the behavior of respondents aged eighteen to fifty-nine, and we observe in these data the growing tendency in the post–World War II period to form cohabitational unions. Table 5.8 shows, by birth cohort, the percentage of each gender whose first union was a formal marriage, not a cohabitation. One sees here the dramatic shift over time toward cohabitation as the initial form of partnership. For example, 93 percent of the women born in 1933–42 first formed their partnerships by marriage, while only 36 percent of the women born in 1962–74 did so, with the others—7 percent of the 1933–42 cohort and 64 percent of the 1963–74 cohort—forming cohabitational unions instead.

The age of entry into the first partnership is, of course, likely to influence the number of partners accumulated by the start of that partnership, so let us first look at the age at first union in our data (see again table 5.8). One sees a slight decline in the age at the start of the first partnership and a more dramatic decline in the age if the first partnership was a cohabitational union. The third column shows the age at first marriage regardless of whether it was the first union or not, and one sees a slight rise in the age at the start of the first formal marriage across the first three cohorts. We note that our youngest cohort includes those aged eighteen to twenty-nine, so some of these men and women will form their first partnership later. Thus, we have a truncated view of their median age at entry into a union at this time. Our data are not structured to reveal the dramatic rise in period-specific median age at first marriage found in national data.[9]

The Accumulation of Sex Partners by Interval

Table 5.9A shows the percentage distributions of number of new sex partners acquired between age eighteen and first marriage, during the marriage, and in the interval between the first marriage and the start of a second partnership, if one occurred, all by gender and birth cohort. The top row of the table tells us, for instance, that, of the men whose first union was a formal marriage and who were born in the decade 1933–42, 41.9 percent had no sex partners

9. The most recent Current Population Survey data, e.g., show the median age at first marriage rising for both men and women from 1960 to 1992: 22.8 and 20.3 in 1960, 23.2 and 20.8 in 1970, 24.7 and 22.0 in 1980, and 26.5 and 24.4 in 1992 for men and women, respectively (*Current Population Reports,* ser. P-20, no. 468 [December 1992], table B, p. vii).

Table 5.8   **Percentage of First Unions That Were Formal Marriages, and**
                   Median Age at First Union or Marriage

Cohort	% of First Unions That Were Formal Marriages, by Birth Cohort and Gender	
	Men	Women
1933–42	83.6	93.1
1943–52	69.7	78.2
1953–62	46.9	57.6
1963–74	34.3	36.0

	Median Age at First Union or First Marriage[a]		
	First Union	First Union as Cohabitation	First Marriage
Men			
1933–42	22.5	23.0	22.9
1943–52	22.3	22.0	22.8
1953–62	22.0	21.5	23.5
1963–74	21.1	20.6	22.3
Women			
1933–42	20.2	†	20.2
1943–52	20.7	21.9	21.0
1953–62	20.5	20.7	21.2
1963–74	19.9	19.7	21.0

[a]The first marriage is not necessarily the first partnership. †Fewer than thirty cases.

from age eighteen to the time of their marriage, 9.0 percent had only one, 20.6 percent had two to four, and over one-quarter (28.4 percent) had five or more. The right-hand end of that row also tells us that the median duration of that interval from age eighteen to marriage for that group of men was 4.7 years and that this information is based on 159 respondents. Table 5.9B shows the same information for respondents whose first union was a cohabitation. Here we distinguish the period "during" the cohabitation in terms of those whose co-habitation did not convert into a formal marriage ("during1") and those whose cohabitation was converted into a formal marriage ("during2").

FINDINGS FROM TABLE 5.9

There are several important patterns revealed by table 5.9. Let us first com-pare the behavior within each of the four panels of the table, that is, the married men, the married women, the cohabiting men, and the cohabiting women, sep-arately.

Each cohort and each gender group shows a remarkably similar pattern of acquiring relatively many partners in the short intervals before a union is formed and after a union dissolves but of acquiring very few partners during that union. The pattern is captured in table 5.10, which is constructed from

Table 5.9A Percentage Distribution of Number of New Sex Partners in Three Life Segments—before, during, and after Formal Marriage—and Median Duration of the Segment (by gender and birth cohort)

Cohort	Distribution of No. of Partners				Median Duration	N
	0	1	2–4	5+		
Men whose first union was marriage						
1933–42:						
Before	41.9	9.0	20.6	28.4	4.7	159
During	77.1	5.2	11.1	6.5	27.0	163
After	45.0	15.0	25.0	15.0	5.4	63
1943–52:						
Before	36.8	12.3	17.6	33.3	4.5	209
During	79.8	5.8	11.1	3.4	15.1	216
After	33.7	17.3	26.9	22.1	4.5	107
1953–62:						
Before	38.7	9.0	21.9	30.3	4.6	157
During	84.2	7.0	3.8	5.1	9.7	166
After	45.6	21.1	17.5	15.8	3.3	63
1963–74:						
Before	46.3	13.4	19.4	20.9	4.0	76
During	90.1	4.2	4.2	1.4	2.8	81
After	†	†	†	†	†	18
Women whose first union was marriage						
1933–42:						
Before	81.7	9.9	7.3	1.0	2.8	195
During	91.9	6.8	.9	.4	29.4	243
After	56.6	24.6	9.0	9.8	5.8	130
1943–52:						
Before	66.5	15.5	12.2	5.7	2.9	246
During	88.4	6.2	4.3	1.1	18.0	290
After	53.1	17.2	19.3	10.3	5.3	158
1953–62:						
Before	57.3	19.1	16.7	6.9	3.0	250
During	91.7	5.4	2.2	.7	10.2	292
After	48.8	20.8	20.8	9.6	3.1	129
1963–74:						
Before	64.9	7.2	19.6	8.2	3.1	106
During	93.8	4.4	1.8	0.0	3.9	127
After	†	†	†	†	†	27

†Fewer than thirty cases.

table 5.9A. Look at the pattern for the earliest two birth cohorts of men: before they married, *half* these men had two or more sex partners, and, after they divorced, separated, or were widowed, again nearly *half* acquired two or more new sex partners. While they were married, in contrast, only about *16 percent* of these men had two or more extramarital partners. This pattern is observed for the other cohorts and for the women as well, and to a lesser extent it is also seen in the patterns of those who cohabited (see table 5.9B).

Table 5.9B **Percentage Distribution of Number of New Sex Partners in Three Life Segments—before, during, and after Cohabitation—and Median Duration of the Segment (by gender and birth cohort)**

Cohort	Distribution of No. of Partners				Median Duration	N
	0	1	2–4	5+		
Men whose first union was cohabitation						
1933–42:						
Before	23.3	13.3	20.0	43.3	5.1	31
During1	†	†	†	†	†	8
During2	†	†	†	†	†	24
After	†	†	†	†	†	8
1943–52:						
Before	20.9	3.5	26.7	48.8	4.2	89
During1	64.3	9.5	23.8	2.4	.8	44
During2	76.6	14.9	2.1	6.4	10.5	50
After	43.6	7.7	17.9	30.8	6.7	43
1953–62:						
Before	11.2	14.8	25.4	48.5	3.7	172
During1	80.4	10.8	7.8	1.0	1.0	108
During2	75.6	6.4	15.4	2.6	9.0	81
After	32.0	13.0	33.0	22.0	4.2	105
1963–74:						
Before	20.4	11.5	31.9	36.3	3.2	135
During1	75.8	11.0	6.6	6.6	.9	112
During2	83.7	7.0	4.7	4.7	4.3	45
After	34.7	18.7	22.7	24.0	1.6	84
Women whose first union was cohabitation						
1933–42[a]						
1943–52:						
Before	23.3	20.5	31.5	24.7	4.1	77
During1	80.0	10.0	6.7	3.3	1.4	33
During2	72.7	18.2	4.5	4.5	11.4	48
After	†	†	†	†	†	29
1953–62:						
Before	24.1	18.4	36.2	21.3	3.3	183
During1	83.5	11.8	4.7	0.0	2.0	96
During2	89.7	7.8	1.7	.9	9.5	119
After	45.5	16.9	24.7	13.0	4.6	87
1963–74:						
Before	32.4	23.0	25.0	19.6	2.8	178
During1	88.7	7.2	3.1	1.0	1.0	128
During2	91.0	5.6	3.4	0.0	4.2	101
After	48.7	27.6	18.4	5.3	1.6	91

Note: "During1" is the period of time during a cohabitation that did not convert into a marriage; "During2" is the period of time during a cohabitation that did convert into a marriage.

[a]Only seventeen cases in all.

†Fewer than thirty cases.

Adults acquire sex partners at a rapid rate before and after marriage but at a very low rate during marriage. This pattern is all the more notable when we see that the two intervals before and after marriage are quite short in duration (about four years) while the length of the marriage is quite long (over twenty-five years at the median for the earliest birth cohort). So the length of time "at risk" of acquiring new partners is much longer in the marriage period, and still the rate of acquiring new sex partners is dramatically lower. Table 5.10, better than almost any other in the book, depicts the importance of the life-course or life-cycle perspective on sexual partnering. Age itself is an important determinant of sexual activity, but here we see that, when one exits from a marriage, the rate of acquiring new sex partners is again quite high. There is not a uniform decline in this behavior with age; it is altered dramatically once a marriage ends.

Again, men report acquiring many more partners than do women. This pattern is evident in each interval and for every cohort.

Except for the shift toward cohabitation instead of formal marriage, there are no important trends in evidence in table 5.9 for either gender.

For both men and women, those who cohabit in their first union acquire more sex partners before that union than those who first marry, are far less likely to have had no sex partners in that interval (compared to those who marry), and are far more likely to have had five or more partners in that interval. This pattern is seen for both men and women. This result is congruent with those of Newcomb (1986), who also finds that, before the union, those who cohabit have more partners than those who marry.

Let us step back for a moment and reflect on this last finding. To be concrete, let us focus on a small piece of information in table 5.9. Take, for instance, the 1953–62 cohort since it has the most balanced percentages of marriages and cohabitations. This is a group born in the Eisenhower years mostly, the core of the baby boomers, and they entered their first union in the decade

Table 5.10   **Percentage with Two or More Sex Partners among Those Whose First Union Was a Formal Marriage**

	Men			Women		
Cohort	Before Marriage	During Marriage	After Marriage	Before Marriage	During Marriage	After Marriage
1933–42	49	18	40	8	1	19
1943–52	51	14	49	18	5	30
1953–62	52	9	33	24	3	30
1963–74	40	6	†	28	2	†

†Fewer than thirty cases.

Table 5.11   **Percentage with No Sex Partners and with Five or More Sex Partners Before Forming a Union among Those Whose First Union Was Either a Formal Marriage or a Cohabitation**

	No Sex Partners Before		Five or More Sex Partners Before	
	Marrying	Cohabiting	Marrying	Cohabiting
Men	~40	~10	~30	~50
Women	~60	~25	~7	~20

between 1974 and 1984, before AIDS was recognized as a widespread problem. The proportions of each group who had *no sex partners* before forming their union, according to table 5.9, are shown in table 5.11. Here we see a big difference—those who married were far more likely to have had no partners before the union was formed than were those who cohabited. The reverse is true in terms of those who had had five or more partners before forming their first union. From table 5.9 we obtain the proportions shown as well in table 5.11. Again, we see a substantial difference between those who married and those who cohabited.

What should we make of this? How might we explain it? One explanation is that there is a range of sexual interest in the population and that those who are interested in a breadth of sexual experience have many partners quickly and tend to form informal unions (ones that are more tentative and involve a lesser degree of commitment, i.e., cohabitational unions). Others, in contrast, happen to be more interested in a more intensive emotional or psychological commitment to a partner. The latter group is more cautious about sexual experimentation, acquires fewer partners along the way, and forms more formal, more enduring unions (i.e., marriages).

Another explanation may be that those who cohabited began to have sex at an earlier age. Maybe the fact is that those who start having sex earlier remain more active in terms of acquiring more partners and then choose to remain relatively more active and thus form less restricting and shorter duration cohabitational unions.

These data bring up a more interesting question as well. What causes individuals to choose either a wide breadth of sexual experience with many partners or a deep involvement with a single person? What causes individuals to begin to have sex at earlier ages? Is it upbringing? Is it circumstances encountered early in life? Does education, religion, or cultural heritage play any role in the process? These are questions that we want to explore and want to encourage others to explore as well because we do not think that these patterns are best interpreted as just happenstance. We need to understand the social and cultural factors that can explain, at least partially, the systematic differences among people's sexual commitments and interests. That can help us target

people when distributing information about the risks associated with their behavior. Only by understanding behavior and its correlates and consequences
can informed choices be made and harmful behavior avoided.

Another way to see the different rates at which sex partners are acquired by
those who marry or cohabit is shown in table 5.12 according to median number
of partners. We see that, for those who marry, the number is no partners for
women and one or two for men whereas, for those who cohabit, the number is
one or two for women and three or four for men.

Finally, for the subset of those who were still residing with their first partner
at the time of the 1992 survey, we asked specifically whether the respondent
engaged in sexual activity with that partner prior to marriage. That highly
sample-truncated information is also displayed in table 5.12. There, we see that
many more of the men and women in later birth cohorts report having had sex
with their partner prior to marriage than was so in earlier cohorts. (We do not
show this information for those who cohabit as there are few of them still in
that first partnership at the time of the survey.)

This suggestive result is consistent with the result shown in table 5.13,
which is not truncated. It indicates that more recent cohorts are more likely to
have had vaginal intercourse with someone prior to marriage. The proportions
who report *not* having had intercourse before marriage (here unconditioned by
the current status of that marriage) exhibit a strong downward trend for both
men and women, but especially strong for women in the early cohorts. Fewer
men than women report being virgins at marriage, but that gender difference
is much smaller for the 1953–62 cohort than for the earlier cohorts. The higher
proportion in the most recent cohort may be a behavioral response to the risk
of AIDS, but it also may be caused by sample censoring.

Table 5.13 also shows the median age at first intercourse, by gender and by
whether the respondent's later first partnership was a formal marriage or an
informal cohabitation. There is a slight indication here of a younger age at first
intercourse over time, and in most of the comparisons one sees an earlier age
for those who cohabited than for those who formally married. The results in
this table are consistent with previous studies showing an earlier age at first
intercourse for those who cohabit (see, e.g., Newcomb 1986).[10]

Extramarital Sex

Table 5.9A above shows the percentage distribution of numbers of extramarital sex partners, and table 5.9B shows the same information for those involved in cohabitational relationships. Table 5.14 indicates the percentage with

10. These median values belie considerable variation. For the final column in the bottom panel
of table 5.13 showing the same median age (eighteen) for married women across all four cohorts,
the *mean* age at first vaginal intercourse was 18.9, 18.8, 18.5, and 18.1, the range in age was nine
to thirty-four, eleven to thirty-six, thirteen to thirty-six, and twelve to twenty-five, and the number
of observations on which that median age of eighteen is based is 241, 290, 289, and 127, respectively, for the 1933–42, the 1943–52, the 1953–62, and the 1963–74 cohorts.

Table 5.12   **Median Number of Sex Partners before Marriage or Cohabitation and Percentages Having Sex with Spouse before Marriage**

| | Median No. of Sex Partners Before | | | |
| | Marriage | | Cohabitation | |
Cohort	Men	Women	Men	Women
1933–42	1	0	4	†
1943–52	2	0	4	2
1953–62	2	0	4	2
1963–74	1	0	3	1

| | % Who Had Sex with Spouse before Marriage[a] | |
	Men	Women
1933–42	32.6	30.7
1943–52	48.6	51.1
1953–62	56.3	55.9
1963–74	69.8	57.7

[a]This includes only those who were still in their first marriage at the time of the survey.
†Fewer than thirty cases.

at least one extramarital (or extracohabitational) partner, holding the duration of the union fixed (in columns 1–4) and partitioning into two categories (in columns 5–6), those whose union is and is not still intact at the time of the survey interview.

Let us first describe how to read table 5.14. The top row shows, for example, that for men born in the years 1933–42 whose first union was a marriage that lasted at least sixteen years, almost 20 percent—19.8 percent—reported having an extramarital affair some time during that marriage.[11] One might expect that those whose unions have extended over a longer period of time have been "at risk" of acquiring an extramarital partner for a longer period of time, and we might therefore expect to see higher rates of extramarital partnerships the longer one remains in a union. Another explanation for this pattern would be that the rate of extramarital affairs is higher in those marriages that end sooner in divorce. Far more inquiry is required here before we have enough information to choose among various explanations.

The final two columns of table 5.14 show the percentage who had affairs divided into those whose first union was still intact at the time of the survey and those whose first union was not. We caution that this table is not one that can be interpreted as revealing a causal relation between having an extramarital sex partner and having a more or less stable union. To explain just one reason why, consider that, while it could be the case that an unexpected and unplanned

11. This first union may either have ended before or have been ongoing when the interview was conducted.

Table 5.13   **Percentage Who Did Not Have Vaginal Intercourse before Marriage (by gender) and Median Age at First Vaginal Intercourse (by gender and type of first union)**

	No Vaginal Intercourse before Marriage (%)	
Cohort	Men	Women
1933–42	26.4	55.1
1943–52	19.0	33.8
1953–62	18.6	27.4
1963–74	22.0	30.2

	Median Age at First Vaginal Intercourse			
	Cohabitation		Marriage	
	Men	Women	Men	Women
1933–42	16.5	†	18	18
1943–52	17	19	18	18
1953–62	17	17	17	18
1963–74	16	16	17	18

†Fewer than thirty cases.

sexual encounter that happened to result in an affair did in fact adversely affect the stability of a person's marriage, it could just as logically be the case that a person who was unhappy in his or her marriage and was convinced that it would soon end went looking for another sex partner while still married. The evidence that we have presented in this table cannot distinguish between these two cases, and we would probably want to conclude that the first case is one in which the extramarital sex affected the stability of the marriage and that the second case is one in which it did not. Since we cannot here distinguish one case from the other, we cannot make inferences about causality.

KEY FINDINGS FROM TABLES 5.9 AND 5.14

The findings about extramarital affairs seen in tables 5.9 and 5.14 include the following.

The proportions who report having had extramarital or extracohabitational affairs are seldom greater than 25 percent. The vast majority of men and women report that they are monogamous while married or living with a partner. Over 90 percent of the women and over 75 percent of the men in every cohort report fidelity within their marriage, over its entirety.

There is a tendency, but not an overwhelming one, for those in cohabitational unions to report higher rates of affairs when the duration of the union is controlled. (The uncontrolled comparisons are not very interesting since the cohabitational unions are so much shorter than the formal marriages.)

Table 5.14　　　　**Percentage with Extramarital or Extracohabitational Sex Partners, by Gender, Type of Partnership, and Birth Cohort**

Cohort	Duration of Union (years)				Union Intact	
	0–3	4–6	7–15	16+	Yes	No
Men						
Married						
1933–42	†	†	†	19.8	15.7	34.4
1943–52	29.0	†	19.6	15.5	14.4	27.2
1953–62	22.2	†	15.1	†	13.4	21.0
1963–74	10.0	†	†	†	6.1	†
Cohabiting						
1933–42	†	†	†	†	†	†
1943–52	32.4	†	†	†	†	34.1
1953–62	20.2	†	†	†	†	20.2
1963–74	22.9	†	†	†	†	29.0
Cohabitation to marriage						
1933–42	†	†	†	†	†	†
1943–52	†	†	†	†	†	†
1953–62	†	†	33.3	†	16.7	34.2
1963–74	†	†	†	†	†	†
Women						
Married						
1933–42	†	†	†	5.8	3.7	12.4
1943–52	11.9	†	18.5	9.3	7.1	15.2
1953–62	4.5	19.2	7.5	6.0	2.2	16.0
1963–74	7.6	6.2	†	†	4.0	†
Cohabiting						
1933–42	†	†	†	†	†	†
1943–52	†	†	†	†	†	†
1953–62	16.4	†	†	†	†	16.7
1963–74	8.4	†	†	†	†	13.0
Cohabitation to marriage						
1933–42	†	†	†	†	†	†
1943–52	†	†	†	†	†	†
1953–62	†	†	11.5	†	5.1	15.1
1963–74	5.6	5.9	†	†	8.1	†

†Fewer than thirty cases.

Those whose union is intact are far less likely to report having had an extramarital or extracohabitational affair than those whose union has ended. Here, the caution noted above about inferring causality is quite important.

We have an additional piece of information in the data set that also addresses the issue of extramarital sex. In the SAQ administered early in the interview, we asked each respondent, "Have you ever had sex with someone other than your husband or wife while you were married?" Notice that this question applies only to formal marriage and applies to all marriages should there have been more than one. This information is therefore not identical to that contained in table 5.14. Nonetheless, it pertains to the same basic behavior, and it is useful to see whether it corroborates or conflicts with the behavior seen in that table. The percentage responding yes to this question, by gender and birth cohort, is reported in table 5.15. The same question was asked in the 1991 GSS survey in an SAQ format as well; in that sample of adults in the age range eighteen to fifty-nine, 21.7 percent of the men and 13.4 percent of the women responded yes.

5.4   Multivariate Analysis of the Number of Partners

We have seen that the most important social factors that distinguish adults in terms of number of sex partners are marital status, gender, and age. To conclude this chapter, we present, briefly, a more sophisticated statistical analysis of the factors that are correlated with the choice about the number of sex partners over the past twelve months and over the adult lifetime. Here, we again look at four categories of number of partners—no partners, one partner, two to four partners, and five or more partners within the past twelve months and no partners, one, two to ten, and eleven or more over the adult lifetime—and we treat these categories as distinct, with each adult choosing to have a given number of partners in each time frame. We look at the relations among the six master status variables that were introduced in chapter 1 and that were used in table 5.1 above. We also include a few more variables to see whether they have any influence on the number of sex partners.

The nature of the statistical procedure is that it estimates the relations simultaneously for all the variables and for all four categories at once, taking account of the separate and pairwise relations, and yielding an estimate of the influence of each variable holding all the others constant at their average level in the data set. It is called a *multinomial logistic statistical model,* and table 5.16 is derived from its estimation. The rows in this table are deceptively simple, but they are based on this rather complex estimation process over all the approximately 3,000 respondents. The rows here are estimates that control for all the other variables in the table; the asterisks indicate that the accompanying value is statistically different from that of the italicized row, which is the comparison group.

In table 5.16A, for example, the top row shows that 12.3 percent of men are

Table 5.15   **Percentage Reporting Extramarital Affairs**

	Cohort	Men	Women
	1933–42	37.0	12.4
	1943–52	31.4	19.9
	1953–62	20.5	14.5
	1963–74	7.1	11.7
	Total	24.5	15.0

Table 5.16A   **Multivariate Analysis of Partners in Past Twelve Months: Predicted Probabilities Controlling for All Other Characteristics in Table, NHSLS 1992**

	No. of Partners (% distributions)					
	0	1	2–4	5+	%	N
Men	12.3	69.2	14.8*	3.7*	100	3,081
Women	*12.7*	*74.5*	*10.9*	*1.9*	*100*	*3,081*
Age 18–29	8.0*	73.2	14.0	4.8*	100	3,081
Age 30–44	*11.3*	*73.3*	*13.8*	*1.6*	*100*	*3,081*
Age 45–59	21.8*	69.2	8.4*	.7	100	3,081
Not cohabiting	30.9*	41.7	23.2*	4.2*	100	3,081
Cohabiting	*1.5*	*83.6*	*12.7*	*2.2*	*100*	*3,081*
Married	2.7	93.4	3.0*	.8*	100	3,081
Less than HS	18.4*	69.9	9.7	2.0	100	3,081
HS grad./some coll.	*12.0*	*73.0*	*12.3*	*2.7*	*100*	*3,081*
Coll. grad. or more	10.7	68.6	16.9*	3.9*	100	3,081
White	*16.7*	*70.8*	*10.4*	*2.0*	*100*	*3,081*
Black	15.2	67.1	13.3*	4.4*	100	3,081
Hispanic	16.5	69.1	11.8	2.6	100	3,081
Other	20.3	70.2	8.7	.9	100	3,081
Sexual activity:						
Guided by religion	20.4*	71.3	7.2*	1.1*	100	3,081
Not guided by religion	*13.6*	*70.2*	*13.3*	*2.8*	*100*	*3,081*
Virgin at 18	22.5*	69.2	6.6*	1.6	100	3,081
Not virgin at 18	*11.2*	*72.3*	*13.9*	*2.5*	*100*	*3,081*
Ever in jail	12.9	70.7	13.7*	2.7	100	3,081
Never in jail	*17.6*	*70.2*	*10.1*	*2.1*	*100*	*3,081*
Touched before puberty	19.5*	63.1	13.5	3.8*	100	3,081
Not touched before puberty	*16.7*	*71.5*	*10.1*	*1.8*	*100*	*3,081*

Note: Dummy variable comparison group in italics.

*Statistically significant difference from comparison group (at 5 percent).

estimated to have had no sex partners within the past twelve months; the absence of an asterisk indicates that this value is not different statistically from that for women. We also see that 69.2 percent of the men are estimated to have had one sex partner and 14.8 percent two to four; the asterisk on the latter tells us that this is a significantly different percentage than that for women. All these percentages control for the age, marital status, education level, race/ethnicity, and other descriptive variables in this analysis.

There are four additional variables in this estimation model in table 5.16A that we have not previously introduced. One indicates that the respondent answered that he or she agreed or strongly agreed with the statement, "My religious beliefs have shaped and guided my sexual behavior." About 54 percent

Table 5.16B **Multivariate Analysis of Partners since Age Eighteen: Predicted Probabilities Controlling for All Other Characteristics in Table, NHSLS 1992**

	No. of Partners (% distributions)					
	0	1	2–10	11+	%	N
Men	3.3*	25.2	46.8	24.8*	100	2,927
Women	*2.3*	*28.1*	*56.0*	*13.5*	*100*	*2,927*
Age 20	2.6	35.9*	53.2	8.3*	100	2,927
Age 30	2.7	24.2*	54.3	18.7*	100	2,927
Age 40	2.9	21.1*	50.3	25.7*	100	2,927
Age 50	3.5	26.2*	46.1	24.1*	100	2,927
Never cohabited	19.0*	15.6*	42.7	22.7*	100	2,927
1 cohabitation	*0.0*	*41.7*	*44.7*	*13.6*	*100*	*2,927*
2 or more cohabitations	0.0	0.0	73.4	26.6	100	2,927
Less than HS	5.3*	29.2	52.6	12.9*	100	2,927
HS grad./some coll.	*2.8*	*27.7*	*50.4*	*19.0*	*100*	*2,927*
Coll. grad. or more	1.8	23.3*	50.3	24.4*	100	2,927
White	*3.0*	*27.2*	*50.7*	*19.1*	*100*	*2,927*
Black	1.7*	18.6*	56.3	23.4	100	2,927
Hispanic	2.6	31.3	46.6	19.5	100	2,927
Other	3.0	33.1	47.1	16.8	100	2,927
Sexual activity:						
Guided by religion	3.7*	29.9*	50.3	16.0*	100	2,927
Not guided by religion	*1.3*	*21.9*	*54.1*	*22.6*	*100*	*2,927*
0 partners before 18	4.2	27.8*	51.5	16.4*	100	2,927
1 partner before 18	.9	27.6*	53.4	18.0*	100	2,927
2 partners before 18	.1	26.6*	53.8	19.4*	100	2,927
5 partners before 18	0.0	22.8*	53.4	23.8*	100	2,927
Ever in jail	1.4	22.4	49.7	26.4*	100	2,927
Never in jail	*2.8*	*27.1*	*51.9*	*18.1*	*100*	*2,927*
0 years in military	2.8	27.1	51.1	19.0*	100	2,927
2 years in military	2.0	26.2	51.6	20.1*	100	2,927
10 years in military	.3	22.4	52.5	24.7*	100	2,927
20 years in military	0.0	17.3	51.4	31.2*	100	2,927
No sex without love	3.0	29.9*	53.7	13.4*	100	2,927
Sex without love	*2.0*	*17.7*	*52.2*	*28.0*	*100*	*2,927*
Touched before puberty	3.1	21.0*	49.5	26.3*	100	2,927
Not touched before puberty	*2.7*	*27.6*	*51.6*	*18.1*	*100*	*2,927*

Note: Dummy variable comparison group in italics.

*Statistically significant difference from comparison group (at 5 percent).

of the respondents did agree with this statement, and the table tells us that those who agreed are substantially less likely to have had two to four or five or more sex partners within the past year, holding constant age, gender, education level, etc. The second added variable indicates that the respondent was a virgin at age eighteen—about 51 percent were so. Here, we see that those who were still virgins at age eighteen are also dramatically more likely to have had no sex partners in the past twelve months and far less likely to have had two to four partners than those who were not still virgins at age eighteen.

The third added variable indicates whether respondents had ever spent a night in jail—about 13 percent have—and those who have are a little more likely to have had two to four sex partners within the past twelve months. The final added variable indicates whether the respondent said that he or she had been touched sexually before puberty—16 percent said that they had been— and this variable is discussed at some length in chapter 9. We see in the table that those who said that they had been are more likely to have had several sex partners within the past twelve months.

Now these final four variables are included here partly to illustrate that one can investigate specific relations between a belief or an experience early in life and the number of sex partners currently. Without going into detail about an analytic model in which these patterns might be interpreted, they are little more than illustrative. We note that we have shown here a few variables that are in fact statistically related to the number of sex partners, and we caution that we have selected them partly because they do have statistical significance. We considered several other variables as well that turned out not to have a statisti- cally significant relation with the number of sex partners, and, since we se- lected these on the basis of their significance, one cannot put much weight on these findings. The reason is that, at a 95 percent level of confidence (which is the level we are employing in this book), one of every twenty nonsignificant coefficients will in fact be incorrectly considered significant; therefore, if one looks widely enough, one is bound to find a few spuriously "significant" fac- tors! Factors that we looked at that failed to show any relation with number of sex partners in this multinomial logistic model are of some interest; they were residential location (i.e., living in the suburbs, in town, or in the country), polit- ical identification (Republican, Democrat, or independent), military service, household income, and family structure (i.e., whether the respondent lived with both parents at age fourteen, was the youngest or the only child in the family). The relations observed in the table are best viewed as suggestive of factors that deserve to be investigated more rigorously in subsequent work.

Table 5.16B shows an analogous statistical model run on the number of sex partners over the entire adult lifetime (i.e., since turning eighteen). Here, the estimation was conducted a little differently for three of these variables. Age was included in the model as a continuous variable assumed to have a quadratic relation; then the rows of the table were evaluated at specific ages. We see that the proportion of respondents estimated to have ten or more partners rises with age up to forty or so and then turns down. Similarly, the number of sex partners before age eighteen and years in the military are both included in the model as continuous variables and then depicted in table 5.16B evaluated at specific values such as one partner or ten years in the military.

Substantively, the results shown in table 5.16 mirror in large measure the patterns that we saw in table 5.1, but here they are estimated holding constant the several other demographic and experiential factors listed. We again see that men tend to report more partners; naturally, the number of partners grows with age, but older respondents have fewer partners in the past year and are far more likely to have none currently. The currently married are far more sexually exclusive, and, in the short time interval, those not cohabiting are much more likely to have several partners, while, over the adult lifetime, those who have never lived with a partner have a much more diffuse distribution of numbers of partners—many more have had no partners, and many have had ten or more. Regarding education level, within the past twelve months and over the adult lifetime, those who have graduated from college appear to have had more partners than others. Blacks appear to have had more partners in the short time interval of the past twelve months, but, over the adult lifetime, they are less likely to have had no partners or just one but are not more likely to have had a large number of partners.

The illustrative co-factors that we report in this table suggest that those guided by their religion systematically have fewer sex partners while the number of sex partners before age eighteen is systematically related to the number acquired after that age as well. Ever spending a night in jail has a slight relation to the number of sex partners, but not a major one, while length of time in the military does appear to be highly associated with the likelihood of having eleven or more sex partners over the adult lifetime. Disturbingly, there is a strong and persistent link between those who reported being touched sexually before puberty and the likelihood of having a relatively large number of partners as adults, both cumulatively and within the past twelve months. We have added here a variable defined by agreement with the statement, "I would not have sex with someone unless I was in love with them," which is in fact statistically related to lifetime number of partners. Those who did agree with the statement are estimated to be among the least likely to have had a large number of partners (ten or more) over the adult lifetime, so the statement and the associated behavior are in fact closely linked.

We note in closing that the model shown in table 5.16 can be used to calculate the probability that a particular respondent has, say, ten or more sex partners over the lifetime, and that estimation ability allows us to characterize each respondent by that probability. Armed with that analytic tool, we will be able to link this particular aspect of one's sex life—number of partners—with other aspects described in the chapters that follow.

APPENDIX 5.1A:
CONSTRUCTION OF THE VARIABLE PART12 (Number of Partners in the Last Twelve Months)

During the interview, respondents were asked in two different places and in two different ways about the number of sex partners that they had had in the last twelve months. The question was first asked in the self-administered questionnaire (SAQ) (see appendix C, SAQ no. 2, questions 1–2; for the point in the interview when the SAQ was administered, see appendix C, section 1 [the very end]). Later, in the face-to-face interview (see appendix C, section 4), *sexual activity* was defined as "mutually voluntary activity with another person that involves genital contact and sexual excitement or arousal." The question was then asked, "Over the past twelve months, how many people . . . have you had sexual activity with . . . ?" This response took on particular values (not categorized) and was followed up with questions on each partner.

Ideally, once we categorize the questionnaire response, the number of sex partners given in response to each question should have been the same. The actual correlation between the variables was .89, with 86 percent of the cases giving identical responses to the two questions. There are several plausible explanations why responses might differ. (1) Respondents may have estimated the number of partners in the SAQ before being asked actually to recall each one and give more detail. (2) Once *sexual activity* has been so defined, more acts may be considered sex acts than would have been previously. (3) Respondents may consider their partner (spouse) to be a sex partner, but, because of, say, ill health, no sexual activity may have occurred during the period in question. The variable PART12 was constructed to attempt to reconcile these differences in the hope of getting a more "accurate" response.

One of the questions lacked a response in 162 cases. In these cases, whichever response existed was used. Four cases had no valid response for either question. For cases where the reported numbers of partners differed by one or two, an attempt was made to determine whether there was an unambiguous reason for this and which response was more "accurate."

In nineteen cases in which a current spouse or live-in partner existed, the respondent claimed one partner and a frequency of sex at least once in the last twelve months in the SAQ but no partners in the face-to-face interview. These cases may be the result of a misunderstanding of the question in the interview, insufficient probing by the interviewer, or an unwillingness to discuss these sex questions openly. In these cases, the seemingly more accurate response was one partner.

In twelve cases in which a current spouse or live-in partner existed, the respondent claimed one partner but no sexual activity in the last twelve months in the SAQ. This explains why in the face-to-face interview the response was no partners. In most cases, during the interview the respondent at first claimed one partner last year and started telling about this partner, but, when the frequency of sex with this partner and the timing of the last sexual event were inquired about, it became clear that no sexual events had happened in the last twelve months. The interviewer corrected the response, but the SAQ was not changed at all. In these cases, the correct response was no partners.

There were four cases in which the respondent claimed one partner and a frequency of sex once or twice in the last twelve months in the SAQ but no partners in the interview. On probing, comments were made to the effect that no sex actually occurred in the last twelve months. In one case, the spouse had actually passed away thirteen months before (and the spouse was the only partner that the respondent had ever had). In these cases, the correct response was no partners.

Some of the cases in which the respondent claimed more partners in the last twelve months in the SAQ than during the interview were due to a sort of "telescoping" effect. That is, a response is obtained to the question about number of partners in the last twelve months, but the reported dates of these events make it clear that some took place more than twelve months ago. The interviewer correctly omitted these from the reply roster. In eight cases in which there is no doubt that this happened, the response from the interview was used.

There were cases in which the interviewer noted in the margins that the current spouse or live-in partner was unable to have sex for health reasons but the respondent included this person in the number of partners in the last year in the SAQ anyway. In these cases, the response from the interview was used.

There were forty-five cases in which the respondent claimed no partners in the SAQ but one partner in the interview. Also, there were forty-nine cases in which the respondent claimed one partner in the SAQ but two in the interview. These discrepancies seemed to be explained by two factors: (1) some respondents do not consider a spouse or live-in partner to be a "sex partner" despite having sexual relations with this person; (2) when asked the number of sex partners in the SAQ, the definition of *sex* is left to the respondent's discretion, whereas, in the interview, an explanation of what we mean by *sex* is given. In these cases, the response from the interview is used.

In cases in which the differences are irreconcilable, the greater number is used. This is done to add credibility to our results concerning the small number of partners. This way, if anything, our numbers are biased upward.

The correlation of the new variable, PART12, and the original variable, PLY12CAT (from the face-to-face interview), is 0.96 (based on 3,424 observations); the correlation of PART12 and PARTNERS (from the SAQ) is 0.95 (based on 3,278 observations).

APPENDIX 5.2A:
CONSTRUCTION OF THE VARIABLE PART18 (Number of Partners since Age Eighteen)

Data on the number of partners since age eighteen are gathered in two distinct parts of the NHSLS. First, as part of the self-administered questionnaire (see appendix C, SAQ no. 2, questions 8–10), the respondent is asked separately for the number of male and female partners since his or her eighteenth birthday. No categories are specified, and no temporal references are suggested other than the respondent's eighteenth birthday and "the recent past you have already told us about," which refers to previous questions in the SAQ asking for the number of sex partners in the past twelve months and the past five years. The respondent must record a specific number of partners. Second, in the sixth section of the face-to-face interview (see appendix C) (i.e., prior to extended sections on the number of spouses and live-in partners over the life course, sex partners in the last year, etc.), respondents are queried as to the number of partners over stages of the life course from age eighteen until twelve months before the interview date. They are asked about the number of sex partners other than spouses or live-in partners in the duration before, during, and after periods of cohabitation mentioned in section 2 of the face-to-face questionnaire. The number of partners since age eighteen is calculated by cumulating the number of partners in each of these periods, adding the number of spouses/live-in partners and the number of sex partners in the last year (who are not also spouses or live-in partners prior to the past twelve months).

Ideally, the number of partners since age eighteen from both sources would agree. Practically, however, we expect that the responses in the SAQ are more prone to memory lapse, to rounding, and to misinterpretation as to just who should be included. (Several respondents, for example, did not include their current spouse or live-in partner.) In contrast, during the face-to-face questioning, the individual periods of cohabitation are offered as reference points; also, respondents are shown a time line ("life history calendar") visually illustrating the time period in which partners were acquired. It is our assumption that the more carefully elucidated method used in the face-to-face questionnaire yields a more accurate measure of the true number of partners that the respondent has had since age eighteen.

The correlation between the discrete distributions measured in the SAQ and questionnaire was 0.86 (N = 2,700). This may be expected since responses range from none to just over 1,000 and SAQ responses tend to be clumped at round numbers (e.g., twenty, thirty, fifty) while the questionnaire measure is somewhat smoother (see table 5A.1.)

Reconciling the two measures into a single variable (P18, the discrete distribution, or PART18, the categorical representation) followed two straightforward rules. First, for all respondents for whom adequate data existed (2,992 of 3,159), the face-to-face derived version was used. Although our data do not allow us to reconcile the source of all the discrepancies in the two measures, in those particularly noticeable forty-nine cases in which the SAQ reported no partners and the questionnaire reported some number of partners, the questionnaire provided adequate information to confirm the measure of at least one partner. This particular discrepancy accounted for the major difference in the categorical distribution of the two measures (see table 5A.2). The second rule

Table 5A.1   **Categorical Distribution of SAQ versus Questionnaire Measures of Sex Partners since Age Eighteen—NHSLS**

	PRT18S (SAQ)							
PRT18Q (Questionnaire)	Missing	0	1	2–4	5–10	11–20	21+	N
Missing	**33**	*4*	*19*	*40*	*40*	*17*	*14*	167
0	12	**74**	2	0	0	0	0	88
1	83	38	**582**	69	17	6	2	797
2–4	92	8	65	**637**	71	7	2	882
5–10	48	1	10	99	**440**	32	8	638
11–20	28	1	2	3	112	**140**	28	314
21+	29	1	0	1	7	43	**192**	273
N	325	127	680	849	687	245	246	3,159

Note: Cases affected in construction of PART18 in italics. Cases with same response in SAQ and interview in bold.

Table 5A.2   **Comparison of Percentage Distributions, SAQ (PRT18S), Questionnaire (PRT18Q), and Constructed Measure (PART18)—NHSLS**

	% Distributions		
Partners	PRT18S	PRT18Q	PART18
0	4.5	2.9	2.9
1	24.0	26.6	26.1
2–4	30.0	29.5	29.5
5–10	24.2	21.3	21.7
11–20	8.6	10.5	10.6
21+	8.7	9.1	9.2
N	2,834	2,992	3,126
Mean	10.35	10.11	10.33
S.D.	35.26	39.48	39.69
Median	3	3	3

was that, for all cases where the questionnaire was missing data (167 of 3,159), the SAQ response was substituted (134 of the 167 cases were filled this way).

Guide to Variables

P18	Discrete version of constructed number of sex partners since age 18
PART18	Categorical version of constructed partners since age 18
P18S	Discrete version of SAQ partners since age 18
PRT18S	Categorical version of SAQ partners since age 18
P18Q	Discrete version of questionnaire partners since age 18
PRT18Q	Categorical version of questionnaire partners since age 18

CHAPTER 6

Sexual Networks

As portrayed in literature, movies, and daily conversation, selecting a sex partner is often motivated by such factors as the right "physical chemistry" or being "in love." These states are assumed to arise within the individual and are frequently described as both spontaneous and irrational. Two implications are often drawn from this popular view of the partnering process. First, choosing a partner is viewed as a highly personal decision; hence, our negative reactions toward arranged marriages and well-meaning relatives and friends intervening in our personal life. In fact, people usually act as "matchmakers" for a friend only when that person is perceived to be having trouble locating a partner on his or her own. A second implication is that, in selecting a partner, we focus primarily on that person's immediate physical appearance and personality rather than on such features as social class, age, ethnic background, and institutional affiliations. For this reason, sexual relationships are assumed to have the potential to transcend these conventional social boundaries.

Contrary to this cultural image, we demonstrate in this chapter that the vast majority of sexual partnerships originate within tightly circumscribed social settings, resulting in relatively few partnerships between people with sharply different social characteristics. This is not to say that there is no element of personal choice involved. This choice is, however, strongly motivated and constrained by one's family, friends, and acquaintances and by the social situations, such as school and work, in which one participates. Thus, while we may as individuals focus on that part of the process that appears to be within our immediate control, our choice of sex partner is ultimately constrained by the same factors that determine with whom we become friends, colleagues, and acquaintances.

Several studies have documented the extent to which certain social relationships are "structured" by attributes such as race/ethnicity, age, educational background, and religious affiliation (e.g., Laumann 1966, 1973; Fischer 1982; Heinz and Laumann 1982; Marsden 1988; Hallinan and Williams 1989). By saying that a particular attribute *structures* a type of relationship, we mean

L. Philip Schumm drafted this chapter and generated the tables and figures, ably assisted by Kristen Olson and Ezra Zuckerman. The chapter was prepared under the direction of Edward O. Laumann.

that the likelihood of such relationships occurring between two people depends on whether they are similar or dissimilar with respect to the attribute in question. In general, relationships are more likely to form among those with similar characteristics (we refer to this as *homophily*).[1]

To the extent that people recruit their sex partners as they do their other associates, we may expect sexual networks to exhibit a similar structure. In addition, the structure of sexual networks may reflect that of other social networks because people are likely to meet potential partners through network contacts, and are thus likely to have partners who reflect the social composition of their networks, and because partnerships that are more easily integrated into one's social network (i.e., are socially similar to or perceived as appropriate by the members of one's network) are more likely to persist through time. Finally, the fact that previous studies of marriages have shown significant amounts of homophily with respect to ethnicity (Pagnini and Morgan 1990), education (Rockwell 1976), and religion (Johnson 1980) suggests that the same should be true of sexual partnerships more generally. (For an introduction to social network analysis, see Wellman and Berkowitz 1988.)

Of course, there are certain unique features of sexual relationships that result in structural differences between these and other types of social networks. Perhaps the most obvious difference is gender. Since the majority of people in modern Western cultures restrict their search for sex partners to the opposite gender, the proportion of partnerships involving two men or two women is quite small (for a discussion of the incidence of same-gender partnerships, see chapter 8). As a result, one can think of the sexual networks in these societies as composed of two groups (males and females), with most relationships between them and very few within.[2] We discuss additional features unique to sexual relationships and their implications for the structure of sexual networks in both this chapter and the next.

The fact that sexual networks are structured according to certain social attributes has at least two significant consequences. The first has to do with the way in which sexual partnerships are implicated within more general social processes. For example, sexual partnering can be synonymous with the decision to marry or, more frequently, lead to the decision to marry (or live together) and/or have children. In this way, the structure of sexual relationships can affect the flow of resources among individuals and, at a more macro level, between social groups and from one generation to the next.

---

1. Of course, this is not always true, and, even when it is, there are important differences across types of relationships in the exact manner and extent to which they are structured according to specific attributes. Nevertheless, the fact that most relationships that have been studied have exhibited some degree of homophily (i.e., a tendency toward equal status contact) makes this general observation a useful point of departure.

2. More formally, a network composed solely of heterosexual relationships is analogous to what is known in graph theory as a bipartite graph (for an introduction to graph theory, see Harary, Norman, and Cartwright 1965; Harary 1969).

A second consequence of the structure of sexual partnering is that it greatly affects the rate at which sexually transmitted infections (STIs) can spread throughout the population, a matter of particular concern with respect to the AIDS virus. Although the technical details required to show exactly how patterns of partnering can affect the spread of STIs are quite complicated (we address some of these in the following chapter), the basic point is a simple one. Leaving aside other issues (such as how efficiently an infection is transmitted by various types of sexual contact), an infection spreads most quickly when partnering is random, that is, when no social attributes and processes or any other factors structure partnering. Deviations from randomness tend to slow the overall spread of an infection and, depending on the nature of the deviation, may prevent it from reaching certain subgroups altogether. One reason that early predictions overestimated how rapidly the AIDS virus would spread among heterosexuals is that they relied on mathematical models that assumed that sexual partnering *was* random, largely because there were no data available on how partnering (especially outside the context of marriage or cohabitation) is organized in the society at large. The present study is the first to gather such data at the national level, and we discuss its implications for the spread of STIs in the following chapter.

The first section of this chapter provides a brief theoretical discussion of the major factors determining who is likely to become sex partners with whom, focusing primarily on those factors that have implications for the structuring of sexual networks according to master statuses. Following this, we examine what our data have to say about the actual *process* by which people initiate their sexual relationships. This information consists of responses to questions about where respondents met their partners, who (if anyone) introduced them, and the length of time between first meeting the partner and first having sex. The latter piece of information is important because it allows us to distinguish between those relationships that began as sexual relationships and those that may have initially had nonsexual motivations and only subsequently become sexual. In addition to these questions, we also asked respondents whether certain partners got to know their family and friends. This allows us to compare the extent to which different types of partnerships become integrated into an individual's existing social network.

Next, we examine an important consequence of the partnering process, namely, the extent to which sexual partnerships occur between individuals with the same or similar social attributes. Specifically, we present data on the proportion of partnerships in which both respondent and partner are similar with respect to age, race/ethnicity, educational attainment, and religious affiliation. These are not the only attributes that structure sexual partnering (see, e.g., the discussion of attractiveness below); however, as we argue, they are particularly relevant to understanding the social processes that both facilitate and impinge on partnership formation. In addition, the fact that they are easily recognized means that respondents are generally able to describe their partners with respect to these attributes (an obvious requirement for this type of survey research).

Three analyses allow us to relate homophily directly to the partnering process as described by our data. First, we compare the incidence of homophily across marital, cohabitational, and both long- and short-term sexual relationships. Second, we examine differences in homophily across relationships in which the partners were introduced by a family member or a friend or in which they introduced themselves. Third, we compare homophilous to heterophilous relationships in terms of the likelihood that partners become incorporated into each other's larger social networks.

Finally, we present the complete data on respondents' attributes and those of their partners, showing not only the proportion of partnerships involving those of similar status but also the proportions of each type of heterophilous partnership (e.g., black/white, white/Hispanic, etc.). We briefly describe the patterning among these heterophilous partnerships and some of its implications. However, owing to the complexities involved in working with these data, we are forced to relegate in-depth analyses to future work.

6.1 Master Statuses and the Partnering Process

Sexual partnering is a complex process consisting of several stages, each of which is affected by a different set of factors. Some of these factors directly involve the social attributes of the partners, while others are indirectly affected by or simply associated with these attributes. The fact that social attributes are implicated in so many different ways in the partnering process makes it difficult to draw inferences from attributional data on partnering outcomes—that is, data on the attributes of respondents and of their previous and current partners. Therefore, before presenting data on the structure of sexual networks, we briefly discuss the process of partnering and some of the ways in which social attributes are involved in it.

The Composition of the Pool of Eligible Potential Partners

Before addressing the issue of how individuals select sex partners, it is necessary to describe the pool of eligible people from which a partner is to be drawn. Perhaps the most obvious factor affecting this pool is the composition of the population as a whole. For example, one might begin with the hypothesis that the likelihood of contact with people from different groups is positively related to the relative size of those groups (a condition that would be true if the set of people with whom an individual came into contact represented a random subset of the population). To the extent that this is true, it implies, for example, that members of a racial or ethnic minority will have more opportunities to interact with members of the majority than the reverse and that, as the size of the minority group increases relative to that of the majority, its opportunities for contact with the majority will decrease (Blau 1977).

Of course, those with whom we come into contact are not a random subset of the population but rather a highly selected subset. Consider, for example, those sexual partnerships that begin with one partner introducing himself or herself to the other. Since a logical prerequisite for introducing oneself is an awareness of the other person, self-introductions are most likely to occur among people who attend the same school, work at the same location, are members of the same church or social organization, or frequent the same bars or social events. Not only do these situations bring people together physically, but they also facilitate the acquaintance process by creating shared interests and experiences. And, since such situations generally involve participants who are socially similar, they increase the likelihood that acquaintanceships, and thus sexual partnerships, will occur between socially similar people (cf. Mc-Pherson and Smith-Lovin 1987).[3] (While this is not true for computer dating services or "singles" ads, our data indicate that only a small fraction of respondents met their partners in this manner.)

Three basic mechanisms ensure that the social situations (or events) in which people participate are composed of socially similar individuals. The first is that certain settings, such as regional high schools, community colleges, churches, and neighborhood bars, primarily draw participants who live nearby. Thus, since geographic areas are segregated by attributes such as race (Massey and Denton 1993), income, and in some cases age, they will be primarily composed of individuals who are similar with respect to these attributes.

A second mechanism has to do with the nature of the situations themselves. Schools, for instance, bring together people who have attained the same level of education; dance clubs bring together people who like the same type of music; and jobs often bring together people who have similar interests and abilities. Yet a third mechanism results from the link between participation in specific events and the structure of social networks (recall the discussion in chapter 1). Among the many reasons why people choose to participate in a specific event, one of the most important involves their network of relationships—relationships both to others who will be participating and to those who have certain interests in the outcome of the event (Laumann and Knoke 1987, 18–35). For example, people may attend a party or a cultural event because a friend or an acquaintance has invited them. Alternatively, a person may acquire a specific job by receiving information about the job or a critical endorsement from an acquaintance (Granovetter 1973, 1982). In these cases, social networks enhance the social homogeneity of a situation or an event because people's networks are generally homogenous with respect to certain socially recognized characteristics, a fact that has been consistently demonstrated in studies of

3. In some cases, events bring together people who are *different* with respect to certain social characteristics. For example, colleges that draw students from all over the country facilitate contact among students from different racial and cultural backgrounds. However, even though this situation may generate some sexual partnerships between dissimilar people, the overall number of such partnerships is likely to remain low owing to individual choice and to social dynamics within the school that highlight attributional distinctions among students.

studies of friendship (Laumann 1966, 1973; Fischer 1982), work relationships (Heinz and Laumann 1982; Frank 1993), and relationships among discussion partners (Marsden 1988).

Finally, social networks can also affect the meeting process in a more direct way when potential partners are introduced by a mutual acquaintance. In this case, an individual's set of potential partners is restricted to those people known to his or her own acquaintances, a fact that will increase the likelihood of partnerships occurring among similar persons. In addition, third-party introductions, especially those performed with the intention of initiating a sexual relationship, are often affected by the judgment of the intervening party about whether a specific couple will be appropriately matched. A woman trying to set her friend up with a date will try to select a man whom she believes will be compatible—a criterion that often implies that he has the same social attributes as her friend.

The Role of Individual Choice

Once we have acknowledged these limitations on the pool of eligible partners, we may consider the role of individual choice in determining which partnerships will be pursued. Specifically, we are interested in knowing why people select certain others as sex partners and what implications this has for the structure of sexual partnerships with respect to certain social attributes. Unlike the part of the process described above, the part involving individual choice has been extensively theorized about. Most of this work may be classified into three basic approaches.[4] The first, pursued mainly by psychologists, focuses on the importance of interpersonal attraction in the partnering process (for an excellent review and critique of this literature, see Feingold 1988). Much of this work has been directed toward explaining the persistent finding—both among dating and among married couples—that the physical attractiveness of one partner is moderately correlated (approximately .5) with the attractiveness of the other. Researchers initially interpreted this finding to mean that people intentionally selected a partner similar in attractiveness to themselves; however, Kalick and Hamilton (1986) have shown that this finding could also result from people searching for the most attractive partner available since those who are most attractive pick each other early on and drop out of the market. Although we were unable to measure the attractiveness of our respondents and their partners and therefore cannot address this issue directly, it is possible that the effects of attractiveness contribute to the structure of sexual partnerships by social attributes. This would occur if perceptions of attractiveness varied systematically according to race, age, and income.

---

4. A fourth approach that has been pursued by some biologists suggests that people select a mate in order to maximize their reproductive potential (Bancroft 1987). While we cannot disprove this evolutionary theory, we doubt that it can account for much of the current structure of sexual partnering.

A second approach to explaining the selection of sex partners asserts that people intentionally select partners who are similar to themselves with respect to certain social characteristics (Newcomb 1961). This behavior, sometimes referred to as *matching* or *assortative mating*,[5] is hypothesized to occur for several reasons. For example, people may be more likely to initiate and continue interactions with similar others owing to shared cultural understandings that allow them to communicate with each other effectively (DiMaggio and Mohr 1985). In addition, people may perceive such interactions as especially gratifying since those who are socially similar to themselves are likely to confirm their own worldview. Finally, many people either disapprove or are apprehensive of their friends or relatives becoming sexually involved with partners of a different racial background, religious upbringing, age, or education level. Since individuals are generally aware of the expectations of those around them and are likely to behave in accordance with those expectations in order to avoid possible sanctions, we expect perceived disapproval by others to act as a significant disincentive to becoming sexually involved with dissimilar others (Eggert and Parks 1987).

The third approach to explaining the selection of sex partners is based on viewing the sexual partnership as an exchange in which partners trade both sexual services and other resources (Becker 1991; England and Kilbourne 1990; Blau 1986; Waller and Hill 1951). The fundamental idea behind this work is that people will pursue those partnerships in which the perceived "value" of the resources that they receive from the other partner is greatest relative to the value of the resources that they are prepared to offer in return. This behavior has implications for how attributes such as race, education, and age structure partnering because these attributes are often associated with the types of resources that a partner is able to offer. Note that, unlike the cultural matching theory, this theory does not necessarily predict that partnerships will occur between similar persons. For example, it has traditionally been suggested that, when selecting a spouse, women exchange their attractiveness and homemaking skills for a man's earning potential, thereby explaining a tendency observed in some studies for women to marry more educated men (called *hypergamy*), even after taking into account differences in educational attainment between the genders (e.g., Mare 1991; Stevens and Schoen 1988).

An important consequence of thinking about sexual partnerships as a form of exchange is that it underscores the fact that choosing a sex partner is not a unilateral decision but rather must be negotiated between the two parties involved (with the exception of those partnerships that are coerced). This is an important point because it makes the task of securing a sexual partnership much more complex. In addition, it opens the possibility that certain market

5. Although the term *assortative mating* is often used specifically to refer to mating between individuals with similar attributes, it has also been used as a general way of referring to all observed patterns of mating. Given this ambiguity, we have decided not to use the term here.

forces may constrain the set of potential partners from which an individual may choose (for an illustration of this point, see chapter 1).

Different Types of Partnerships

We also expect the way in which individuals locate sex partners and the factors affecting their choices to vary according to the type of partnership in question, depending on whether the partnership is a marriage, a cohabitational relationship, or a long- or short-term sexual partnership.[6] There are three basic reasons for this. First, each type of partnership requires a different type and level of involvement from the participants. For example, marriage involves a formal agreement to live together, to share both resources and family of origin, and to raise children together. Thus, we would expect issues of cultural compatibility and parity in exchange to be particularly important, resulting in a relatively high proportion of within-group marriages. In contrast, short-term sexual partnerships require less time spent together and a more narrowly defined exchange; hence, the relative importance of physical attraction may increase, and we may expect a somewhat lower proportion of within-group partnerships. The same reasoning also applies to long-term partnerships and cohabitational relationships, although there is considerably more heterogeneity within these categories with regard to personal involvement.

A second difference among these four types of partnerships arises from differences in the participants themselves, some of which are revealed by the mere fact of being in a particular type of relationship. For example, previous research has shown that those who cohabit also tend to have more liberal attitudes toward family life and religion (Tanfer 1987; Newcomb 1986), and we might expect the same to be true of those who engage in short-term sexual partnerships. These more liberal attitudes may be associated with a greater willingness to brave social proscriptions against between-group partnerships, resulting in the lower proportion of within-group partnerships seen in cohabitational relationships and short-term partnerships than in marriages and long-term partnerships.

The third important difference among these relationships may be linked to the degree of social visibility associated with them. Marriages are necessarily the most visible since a spouse becomes a legal part of an individual's public identity. Nonmarital partners, in contrast, may be concealed from family, friends, and acquaintances, although doing so becomes more difficult the longer the relationship persists. What is important is that, by making a partnership publicly visible, one is opening that partnership to possible scrutiny about its appropriateness. Thus, we would expect norms proscribing between-group

6. We defined *short-term sexual partnerships* as those that lasted one month or less and involved no more than ten instances of sexual activity; all remaining partnerships are considered to be long term. A small number of partnerships that began within the month prior to the interview and had not yet ended were omitted since we do not know how long these partnerships will last.

partnerships to be more closely followed in marriages and other socially legiti-mated sexual partnerships (e.g., engaged couples, boyfriend/girlfriend) than in less visible partnerships. In fact, the very attempt to conceal a partner from one's acquaintances may increase a person's likelihood of acquiring a partner from a different social group.

Using these differences across partnerships to interpret our data is compli-cated by the fact that, while a person may select a partner in order to pursue a particular type of partnership with him or her, the four types of partnerships that we have identified also represent stages through which partnerships gener-ally develop. Thus, for example, people may pay less attention to proscriptions against between-group partnerships when selecting a short-term partner than when selecting a potential spouse, but it may also be the case that short-term partnerships involving socially dissimilar people are less likely to become long-term partnerships and lead subsequently to marriage. In reality, both pro-cesses probably occur. The only way to separate the two would be to use infor-mation on people's intentions when entering a partnership, on how those inten-tions affect the course of the partnership, and on whether and how those intentions change. Unfortunately, we were unable to collect such information.[7] However, we shall attempt to address this issue by examining where and how each of the four types of partnerships were initiated. Differences between the partnerships may suggest the existence of different strategies for meeting dif-ferent types of partners, and these strategies may affect the probability that between-group partnerships will occur.

6.2   Social Networks and the Partnering Process

In this section, we focus our attention on what our data reveal about the *process* by which sexual partnerships are generated. As we have already discussed, much of the theoretical (and experimental) literature has focused on those as-pects of the partnering process that involve individual choice, attempting to answer questions about why people select certain partners over others. Yet, while the answers to such questions are clearly important, they do not tell us much about the actual social processes by which real-world partnerships are initiated and maintained. This is because people do not simply select a partner from among eligible members of the population according to their own criteria but are instead limited to those with whom they come into contact. Moreover, it is likely that certain types of contact have greater potential for generating sexual relationships than others. And, once a partnership has begun, it does not become detached from the social environment but rather is continually ex-posed to the social expectations of others—a factor that can affect the durabil-

7. Collecting such data would be difficult, particularly since one would be depending on people's ability to recall their intentions accurately. An alternative way of approaching the problem would be to ask people about their willingness to engage in particular types of partnerships with people different than themselves (e.g., South 1991). However, the link between such answers and actual behavior is unclear.

ity of the relationship. Examining these factors is important not only to achieve a more complete understanding of the partnering process but also because they operate in conjunction with the choices of individuals to determine the structure of sexual partnerships.

Survey data do not allow us to observe the partnering process directly. Rather, we are limited to observing the *outcomes* of the process in the form of specific sexual partnerships reported by respondents. Moreover, we observe only successful outcomes, or those partnerships that actually occurred. Thus, we know nothing about partnerships that were available but never pursued or about intimate relationships that did not reach the point of sexual involvement. This fact, coupled with the fact that there was not sufficient time during the interview to inquire about respondents' intentions and motivations regarding specific partners, limits our ability to make inferences about certain aspects of the partnering process. This is an important point—one that will arise repeatedly in the discussion below.

Introductions and Meeting Places

Our information about the partnering process consists primarily of answers to two questions about how respondents met their sex partners: where they met a particular partner and who (if anyone) introduced them.[8] These data reflect, albeit indirectly, two fundamental aspects of the partnering process. The first is the structure of sexual opportunity. Put simply, knowing where people meet their partners reveals where (and therefore with whom) opportunities for partnering occur. These opportunities are determined in part by specific features of the locations themselves that facilitate the initiation of potential partnerships. However, to the extent that people are selective about which opportunities they pursue, these data also reflect the strategies that people use for locating sex partners. In some cases, the issues of strategy and opportunity are linked, as in the example of a young man who goes to a bar specifically because he knows that there will be unmarried women there. Because our data reflect only indirectly the effects of opportunity and strategy and preclude us from separating one from the other, we use these two aspects as alternative, yet complementary, ways of interpreting the data.

Table 6.1 shows the distributions of the different types of introductions and meeting places separately for each type of partnership. Looking first at the top panel, we see that roughly one-third of all partnerships resulted from an introduction by a friend and another third from introducing one's self. The

8. By beginning with meeting, we are neglecting those aspects of the partnering process that occur prior to actual meeting, such as one partner becoming aware of or attracted to the other. These factors are important not only in self-introductions but also in brokered introductions since an individual may become interested in a potential partner and subsequently request an introduction to that person from a friend. Although such factors are a potentially important aspect of those meetings pursued explicitly for sexual purposes, they are beyond the scope of a national, broadly based study such as ours.

Table 6.1   Type of Introduction and Place of Meeting, by Type of Relationship (% distributions)

A. Type of Introduction

Type of Relationship	Close Relationship		More Distant Relationship					
	Family Member	Friend	Coworker	Classmate	Neighbor	Self-Intro.	Other Intro.	N
Marriages	15[a]	35	6	6	1	32	2	1,278
Cohabitations	12	40	4	1	1	36	3	319
Partnerships	8	36	6	4	1	42	1	920
Short-term partnerships	3	37	3	4	2	47	2	251

B. Place of Meeting

Type of Relationship	High Social Preselection					Low Social Preselection				
	School	Work	Private Party	Church	Gym/Soc. Club	Bar	"Personals" Ad	Vacation	Elsewhere	N
Marriages	23	15	10	8	4	8	<1	<1	30	1,288
Cohabitations	10	18	14	2	5	12	1	<1	37	326
Partnerships	22	17	16	2	4	14	<1	1	23	923
Short-term partnerships	22	11	25	1	4	17	2	1	17	257

*Note: N*s are unweighted. Percentages across rows may not add to 100 percent because of a small number of respondents (1 percent) who reported multiple answers.

[a]Indicates weighted percentage of marriages in which respondent was introduced to spouse by a family member.

remaining third are divided among introductions by family members, coworkers, classmates,[9] and others. The fact that approximately 60 percent of all partnerships involved an introduction by some third party indicates the importance of a person's social network in determining his or her set of potential partners. Also, it appears that partners are not drawn randomly from one's network contacts but rather in disproportionately large numbers from contacts through friends and family.[10] In interpreting these percentages, however, one must be careful to take into account the limitations identified above. Specifically, since we know nothing about those relationships that were terminated before reaching the stage of sexual involvement, we cannot separate the effects of initial selection from those of selective attrition. For example, while people may meet many potential partners through self-introductions, such introductions may be less likely than brokered introductions to result in a consummated partnership. Similarly, introductions by friends may be more likely to result in consummated partnerships than introductions by more distant acquaintances.

There are at least two reasons why this may be the case. First, it is likely that a person has (or is able to acquire) more information about potential partners met through mutual acquaintances than about potential partners met through self-introduction. Such information may be useful in determining one's compatibility with a potential partner, resulting in fewer "false starts" among brokered partnerships. (We return to this issue of information about potential partners later.) A second reason is that a person met through a mutual acquaintance is often more easily integrated into one's network than a person met on one's own. Although several authors have suggested that those involved in romantic relationships withdraw from their own social networks (e.g., Slater 1963), it is unlikely that such withdrawal is ever complete or long lived. Rather, it is likely that partnerships that are less easily integrated into one's network are more difficult and less attractive to maintain.

Without being able to say for certain, it seems probable that both selection and selective attrition are being reflected in these data. However, regardless of the actual process by which they are generated, the data still provide an accurate description of the partnerships that exist in the population. We focus on this fact below in addressing certain consequences of the partnering process.

In addition to the overall distribution of introductions, the frequency of certain introductions appears to vary across the different types of relationships. Specifically, marriages are most likely to involve an introduction by a family

9. The overall percentage of relationships with introductions by a classmate is primarily a function of the percentage of the population in school, the average age at first marriage, and the average length of each type of relationship. A simpler way of saying this is that people in school are likely to meet partners through classmates while those not in school are not. This reasoning also applies to the category *school* in the lower panel of the table.

10. Introductions from friends and family account for the vast majority of brokered introductions, despite the fact that one's friends and family constitute only a small percentage of one's total network (Bernard et al. 1990; Pool and Kochen 1979).

member, while short-term partnerships are least likely to involve such introductions. Conversely, self-introductions are most common among short-term
partnerships and least common among marriages. In contrast, the percentages
of introductions through friends do not vary, except perhaps for the higher percentage among cohabitational relationships. We may apply the same dual logic
in interpreting these patterns as we did in interpreting the overall distribution
of partnerships. On the one hand, we may view the four types of relationships
in terms of a progression in which short-term partnerships are potential long-
term partnerships, partnerships potential cohabitational relationships, and all
potential marriages. This assumption leads to the conclusion that partnerships
involving family introductions are more likely to become marriages, those involving self-introductions less likely. On the other hand, it is also possible that
people use different strategies for locating partners and that an introduction by
a family member is a strategy used more often by those looking for potential
spouses and self-introductions a strategy used more frequently by those looking for noncohabitational partners.

Although our data do not allow us to address these two hypotheses directly,
it is important to note their implications for the partnering process. The first
hypothesis implies either that kinship networks are important in shaping one's
intentions regarding specific partners or that the partners that one meets
through one's family are more "marriageable" than those met through others
(a possibility that we examine below). A more general argument can be made
about friendship and acquaintance networks to explain the opposite pattern
for self-introductions. The second hypothesis implies that the four types of
partnerships are not a simple progression but that people primarily pursue one
of the four types of relationships. These implications suggest the need for future studies to collect information about respondents' intentions regarding specific partners and about how these intentions change during the course of the
partnership.

Looking now at the lower panel of table 6.1, we see that the majority of
partners were met in one of four locations: school, work, a private party, or a
bar. The capacity of both school and work for generating partnerships is due
in part to the ubiquity of these in people's daily lives. However, there are at
least two additional features of these settings that increase their potential for
generating partnerships. The first is that they provide repeated contact with
others, allowing more opportunities and flexibility for negotiating partnerships
than exist in a bar, where such negotiations are necessarily abbreviated. Second, both settings bring together a set of individuals who are preselected on
the basis of common interests and backgrounds, thereby facilitating the acquaintanceship process and increasing the likelihood that people will perceive
each other as suitable partners. Since not all work environments exhibit these
features, we expect variation across occupations in their capacity to generate
sexual partnerships. Moreover, although certain work environments can facilitate the acquaintanceship process, it is important to recognize that they can

also affect sexual partnering in other, sometimes deleterious ways. An example of this would be a supervisor using his or her position of authority to coerce a subordinate into having sex. In addition, sexual relationships with coworkers can negatively affect job performance, as when a person is perceived as favoring a sex partner by other, fellow employees. For these reasons, certain employers have policies designed to prohibit sexual activity among coworkers, and people often attempt to keep their professional and private lives separate. It is unclear whether such factors operate to limit the number of partnerships that arise out of contacts initiated at work.

Introductions at private parties and bars display the same pattern as self-introductions; that is, their frequency declines as the duration and the level of commitment of the relationship increase. As before, this likely results from the dual effects of selective attrition and variation in partnering strategies. For example, the types of interaction and expectations about one's conduct that occur at private parties and bars may facilitate the negotiation of short-term sexual transactions, yet these might be difficult to maintain owing to potential differences in interests and the fact that each partner has a different set of friends and associates. With regard to introductions made at church, however, it is likely that the relatively high percentage of marriages with such introductions is due primarily to the fact that people who attend church and use this as a strategy for meeting partners are less likely to approve of and therefore engage in nonmarital sexual partnerships.

Our treatment of type of introduction and meeting place as two analytically separate items is admittedly a bit artificial since in reality the two occur simultaneously and in an interdependent fashion. This is most obvious in the case of introductions by coworkers that occur at work, by classmates at school, etc. Yet other cases are more interesting. For example, one might hypothesize that self-introductions occurring at private parties are different than introductions by friends that occur at private parties, the presence of friends revealing information about the type of party involved.

Unfortunately, we have neither the space nor the data necessary to examine this issue in detail (the joint distribution of type of introduction and meeting place is quite sparse). However, one feature of the joint distribution of type of introduction and meeting place is worth noting. This is the set of partnerships resulting from self-introductions made in a bar, on vacation, or through a "personals" ad. These situations are presumably least dependent on the structure of people's social networks and the selection rules governing locations such as school, work, and church (we discuss the consequences of this below). Interestingly, only 4 percent of marriages fall into this category, and this figure rises to only 7, 8, and 13 percent among cohabitational relationships, long-term partnerships, and short-term partnerships, respectively. We view this 13 percent as a rough upper bound on the proportion of partnerships that begin under such conditions of relatively high heterogeneity and minimum informa-

tion about the other partner.[11] The relatively low frequency of these partnerships helps explain the high degree of social similarity among partnerships,
even short-term sexual partnerships.

Time between Meeting and First Sexual Involvement

In interpreting these data describing how and where respondents met their
partners, it is important to recognize that the point of first meeting does not
necessarily correspond with the point of first sexual involvement. This is because, in many instances, people may know each other for a considerable
amount of time before becoming romantically or sexually involved. As a result,
the "meetings" described in table 6.1 represent a heterogeneous set, some being initiated for the explicit purpose of sexual involvement (e.g., asking someone for a date), others being initiated without such motivations. One way to
distinguish crudely between these two is to separate partnerships according
to the length of time between meeting and first sex. Of course, it is difficult to
define objectively what constitutes first sexual involvement. Moreover, it is
likely that people differ in what they believe constitutes first sexual involvement and that these subjective definitions reflect the nature of the relationship
more accurately than any objective definition that an investigator may impose.
For this reason, we asked respondents, "How long did you know [specific part-
ner] prior to having sexual activity for the first time," thereby allowing them to
determine individually what constitutes first sex. This fact should be kept in
mind when interpreting the data below.

Table 6.2 presents the percentage of partnerships with intervals of one
month or less and longer than one year between meeting and first sexual
involvement. One of the most interesting features of this table is the relatively
small overall percentages of partnerships with an interval of one month or less
(from 10 percent for marriages to 37 percent for short-term relationships).
Moreover, these percentages drop substantially as the interval is narrowed; for
example, only 1.4 percent of marriages involved sex within two days of meeting, and this figure rises to only 13.7 percent among short-term partnerships.[12]
These figures suggest upper bounds for the frequency with which scenarios

---

11. This interpretation would clearly be inaccurate if the *elsewhere* category, representing nearly
one-third of the data, included responses such as "in the grocery store" or "on the subway." However, an inspection of the marginal comments written by the interviewers to explain this response
revealed that the majority of situations were dependent on a close, personal acquaintance, such as
"at a friend's house."

12. There is some discrepancy between the reports of male and female respondents with regard
to time before first sex. For example, 24.3 percent of all partnerships reported by males had an
interval of one month or less, while only 14.7 percent of partnerships reported by women fell into
this category. This discrepancy is greatest among short-term partnerships, where 16.7 percent of
men but only 5.5 percent of women reported an interval of two days or less. As with the gender
discrepancy regarding number of partners (see chapter 3), our assumption is that these discrepancies primarily reflect reporting biases that derive from the traditional "double standard."

Table 6.2   Time from Meeting to First Sex, by Type of Introduction and Place of Meeting (% distribution)

	Type of Introduction			Place of Meeting					
	Family Member	Friend	Self	School	Work	Private Party	Bar	Elsewhere	Total
Percentage shorter than one month									
Marriages	10[a]	9	12	6	11	12	24	11	10
Cohabitations	36	39	33	10	28	25	63	38	35
Partnerships	21	26	32	13	21	32	49	25	27
Short-term partnerships	. . .	35	42	22	41	39	46	33	37
Percentage longer than one year									
Marriages	54	44	45	69	34	37	20	43	47
Cohabitations	16	18	25	26	25	30	8	21	22
Partnerships	36	26	24	44	27	17	11	32	28
Short-term partnerships	. . .	31	18	44	27	18	18	27	26

Note: " . . . " indicates fewer than thirty unweighted cases.

[a]Indicates weighted percentage of those marriages in which respondent was introduced to spouse by a family member with an interval between meeting and first sex of one month or shorter.

such as "sex on the first date" and the "one-night stand," so often portrayed on television and in movies, actually occur. For example, only those short-term partnerships involving sex within two days of meeting could be considered "one-night stands" in the classic sense, and these represent only 6.5 percent of nonmarital, noncohabitational partnerships occurring during the past year and an even smaller percentage of nonmarried, noncohabiting individuals.

Our lack of information regarding the initiation of romantic involvement within partnerships complicates the interpretation of the percentages in table 6.2. This is because there is likely to be considerable heterogeneity in the length of the period between when people start dating and when they become sexually involved. However, this issue may be approached in the following way. Although we cannot say for certain that relationships with an interval of one month or shorter between meeting and first sex were initiated with the intention of pursuing a sexual partnership, it seems reasonable to assume that this interval is too short for a nonsexual relationship to be established and then evolve into a sexual one. Moreover, the fact that first vaginal intercourse is often preceded by a trial period of kissing and petting implies that, in many cases, first sexual involvement occurs even earlier than first sexual intercourse, effectively reducing the maximum possible period between first meeting and first romantic activity. Thus, we might interpret the percentages in the top panel of table 6.2 as capturing a particular subset of partnerships—those in which the relationship began with romantic intentions and in which sexual intercourse was initiated within one month or less of meeting. Note that these conditions specify not only a subset of relationships but also a subset of individuals, namely, those willing to initiate sexual intercourse within one month or less of the beginning of a new relationship.

Now consider those partnerships with an interval of one year or more between meeting and first sex. Our intention in using this cut off is to capture those partnerships that began as nonsexual relationships and subsequently became sexual. Unfortunately, however, partnerships may also fall into this subset if the couple chose to abstain from sexual intercourse for a period of one year or longer (e.g., until marriage, engagement, or perhaps some other mark of commitment). Yet, while this situation certainly occurs among marriages, we would expect it to be less frequent among nonmarital partnerships, especially among cohabitational relationships and short-term partnerships. This is because abstaining from sexual activity is likely to be associated with certain religious and moral tenets prohibiting nonmarital sexual activity altogether. And, although some individuals might be willing to violate this rule within the context of a long-term, stable relationship (e.g., during engagement), they would be less likely to do so by cohabiting (owing to its visibility and traditionally negative perceptions) or by engaging in a short-term partnership (regarded by some as promiscuous). Thus, we may interpret the percentages in the last three rows of the bottom panel of table 6.2, especially those referring to cohabitational relationships and short-term partnerships, as revealing primarily a subset of partnerships that began as nonsexual relationships.[13]

Armed with this interpretive strategy, we may now inspect the percentages more closely. Marriages exhibit a uniformly low incidence of sex within the first month after meeting and a uniformly high incidence of sex after the first year, reflecting in part the choice among many couples to abstain from sex until marriage (recall that our sample includes marriages that began up to forty years ago). In contrast, cohabitational relationships and short-term partnerships exhibit a much higher incidence of sex within the first month, owing in part to the more permissive orientation of those who pursue such relationships. Interestingly, the percentage of short-term partnerships in which sex was initiated after the first year is substantial, particularly among those introduced by a friend. This suggests that up to 26 percent of all short-term partnerships occur between people who have known each other for some time, perhaps even as associates, colleagues, or friends (although, unfortunately, we cannot say for certain).

Comparing across the three types of introduction, we find that the percentage of partnerships initiating sex within the first month is lowest among family introductions and highest among self-introductions. With regard to the percentage of marriages and partnerships initiating sex after a year, this pattern is reversed. Both observations are consistent with the hypotheses that those who use family contacts as a strategy for meeting partners are more likely to abstain initially from sex (perhaps until marriage) and that self-introductions are more likely to be made explicitly for romantic purposes and thus progress to sexual involvement more quickly. Yet such hypotheses cannot explain the lack of a difference between the marriages in the top panel of the table and, more important, the *opposite* pattern exhibited by cohabitational relationships. We do not attempt to explain these apparent anomalies here since we would be engaging in pure speculation. We shall, however, emphasize the fact that these results demonstrate the existence of differences between types of relationships (and presumably between the people who pursue such relationships) in the process by which partners meet each other and become sexually involved.

Unlike the types of introduction, the different meeting places reveal systematic differences in the time between meeting and first sex. For example, the percentages of partnerships started at school with an interval of one month or less before first sex are uniformly low, suggesting that students are no more permissive as measured in this way than are other adults, perhaps even less so. The uniqueness of the school setting is also reflected in the uniformly high percentages of partnerships in which first sex occurred after one year. In fact,

13. Since the numbers in both panels are percentaged out of the total number of relationships, the two are interdependent. This does interfere with our primary goal, which is to provide a sense of the overall distribution of partnerships. However, it is important to recognize that there is an overlap between the two panels in terms of the information that they reveal.

nearly half of all respondents (excluding those living with a partner) introduced to their partner at school knew that person a year or more before having sex with him or her. This suggests that the school setting is uniquely conducive to the conversion of nonsexual relationships into sexual ones, a phenomenon that is likely to have important consequences for the sexual partnerships that result from it.

Partnerships initiated in a bar also appear to be systematically different from those initiated at other locations, in a manner opposite to those initiated at school. Specifically, partnerships in which the couple met in a bar exhibited both a uniformly high incidence of sex occurring within the first month and a uniformly low incidence of first sex occurring after one year. This likely reflects the fact that people often attend bars for the explicit purpose of meeting potential partners; therefore, such meetings are likely to lead either directly to romantic relationships or to no further contact.

These data suggest that the social context in which an introduction occurs is more important than the person making that introduction for predicting the sexual potential of a relationship. Differences across meeting places are primarily due to both differences in the proportion of participants eligible for sexual partnerships and differences in the styles of interaction that allow people to make and accept sexual or romantic advances. However, it should be recognized that these data raise more questions than they answer, pointing to the need for gathering more detailed information about how romantic relationships begin and about how sexual activity is initiated within those relationships.

6.3 Homophily among Noncohabitational Partnerships

Given this image of the partnering process, we may now examine an important consequence of this process—namely, the extent to which partnerships are more likely to occur between persons with similar social attributes. Table 6.3 presents the percentages of noncohabitational heterosexual[14] partnerships in which both partners have the same (or similar) race/ethnicity, education, and religion (we look at marriages and cohabitational relationships in the following section). The rows labeled *race* differ from those labeled *ethnicity* owing to two different ways of classifying respondents as Hispanic. As discussed in chapter 5, in order to maintain comparability with previous studies, we measured the racial background of respondents using a two-part question in which the respondent was asked to indicate first his or her race (excluding "Hispanic" as an option) and then whether he or she were ethnically Hispanic. This presented us with two ways of designating Hispanic respondents; those who wrote in *Hispanic* in answer to the race question (5.8 percent) and a larger set of

14. By focusing here on heterosexual partnerships, we do not mean to suggest that the structure of homosexual partnerships is either uninteresting or unimportant. The problem, however, is that there are too few same-gender partnerships in our data to support corresponding analyses.

Table 6.3   **Estimated In-choice Rates and Homophily Bias Parameters among Nonmarital and Noncohabitational Partnerships, by Gender (same-gender partnerships excluded)**

	Men			Women		
Characteristic	% In-choice	Homophily Bias (τ_i)	% DK[a]	% In-choice	Homophily Bias (τ_i)	% DK[a]
Race:						
White	92	.73		87	.43	
Black	82	.77		97	.96	
Hispanic	54	.51		65	.63	
Ethnicity:						
White	94	.83		90	.60	
Black	82	.77		97	.96	
Hispanic	46	.39		56	.52	
Education:						
< 12 Years	45	.31	16	39	.28	14
HS grad.	51	.32	9	46	.24	11
Some college	44	.11	10	37	.02	1
4-year degree	30	.20	4	41	.31	2
Graduate school	27	.25	3	26	.22	3
Religion:						
None	27	.19	23	36	.21	15
Type I Prot.	32	.14	19	30	.13	17
Type II Prot.	61	.44	16	72	.62	16
Catholic	68	.52	15	67	.54	9

[a]Indicates percentage of partnerships in which respondent did not know the corresponding characteristic of the partner.

people who reported being ethnically Hispanic regardless of their previously stated race (9.9 percent). The former method was used to generate the first set of percentages (those labeled *race*), the latter to generate the second set (those labeled *ethnicity*). To the extent that the act of writing in *Hispanic* as an answer to the race question reflects an especially strong sense of Hispanic identity, we would expect the percentage of such people who have Hispanic partners to be greater than that of those who described themselves initially as either white or black. (In measuring the race of respondents' partners, we used only the race question but added an additional answer category labeled *Hispanic*. Thus, the designation of respondents' partners is the same for both sets of percentages.)

Two additional aspects of the way in which this table is constructed have consequences for how we may interpret the percentages. First, unlike other tables in this book that contain percentages of individuals, this table (and all others in this chapter) contains percentages of relationships. And, although our sample of respondents was selected to be representative of the adult population of the United States, we must ask ourselves of what our sample of partnerships—generated by asking respondents to report their own partners during

the past year—is representative. Put another way, we must ask what these percentages of partnerships describe.[15] For example, it is clear that these partnerships are not representative of the population of individuals since those with
many partners are overrepresented. Specifically, our sample of 1,766 nonmarital, noncohabitational, heterosexual partnerships was reported by only 897 respondents, of which 517 (58 percent) reported only one, 179 (20 percent) two,
and the remaining 22 percent three or more.[16] Thus, 71 percent of the sample
of partnerships were reported by respondents who had multiple partners.

A more useful alternative is to interpret our sample of partnerships as being
representative of a particular sexual network, in this case, the network of noncohabitational sexual relationships occurring among the national adult population during a single year. For our purposes here, we shall not go beyond this
rather loose interpretation since describing the formal relation between our
sample of partnerships and the sexual network from which it is drawn is beyond the level of this presentation. However, what is important to realize is that
it is precisely this sexual network whose structure determines how a sexually
transmitted infection such as HIV will spread throughout the population.

Another more obvious feature of the table is that we have computed the
percentages separately for partnerships reported by male and female respondents. At first glance, this may seem a bit strange; after all, since we are focusing here on heterosexual partnering, men and women are in principle reporting
on the same partnerships, and there should therefore be some correspondence
between what the two have to say. In fact, this logical correspondence is ex-
ploited in certain demographic models of marriage, where it is referred to as
the *two-sex problem* (Pollak 1986). This correspondence, however, cannot be
established directly from these percentages since the absolute size of each subgroup must also be taken into account. Moreover, combining the data from
men and women can obscure the fact that the men in a particular subgroup
may have a different view of the sexual network than the women in that same
subgroup (e.g., see the discussion below comparing the percentage of same-
race partnerships reported by black men and black women). It is primarily for
this reason that we have presented the data for men and women separately.

With these issues in mind, we may now examine the percentages in table
6.3. Among both whites and blacks, the percentages of same-race partnerships
are quite high. In fact, 91 percent of *all* noncohabitational partnerships reported (by blacks and whites) involved partners of the same race. This means
that, with the exception of roughly 10 percent of their partnerships, these two

15. A well-known example in which a sample of individuals fails to yield a representative sample of relationships comes from studies of occupational mobility between fathers and sons (see,
e.g., Blau and Duncan 1967). Data for such studies are often collected by selecting a sample of
adult males and recording both their occupations and those of their fathers. However, such samples
of father-son pairs clearly overrepresent those pairs that come from families with many sons.

16. These percentages differ between men and women: 50 percent of the men and 66 percent
of the women reporting noncohabitational partnerships reported only one.

racial groups may be thought of as "self-contained" with respect to sexual partnering, a situation that has been demonstrated to have a significant effect on the spread of sexually transmitted infections (Morris 1991). And, although we cannot relate this result directly to the process by which a person selects one partner over another (because of the highly segregated nature of social contact), we may speculate about the consequences of this relatively small number of interracial partnerships. Specifically, the rarity of such partnerships is in part responsive to the close attention paid to them, which creates pressure on those involved in interracial partnerships to "explain" their relationship. More important, the small number of interracial partnerships is part of a larger social process that functions to maintain social "distance" between racial groups since sexual partnerships (and to an even greater extent marriages) often create social bridges between families and groups of acquaintances.

In contrast to this high percentage of racial/ethnic in-choice among whites and blacks, the percentage of in-choice among Hispanics is considerably lower. Specifically, the proportions of same-race partnerships reported by both black and white respondents are 82 percent or higher, while those for Hispanic respondents are between 45 and 56 percent for men and women, respectively. Although part of this may be due to misclassification of the partners (as discussed above), it is unlikely that this factor accounts for the entire discrepancy. Rather, it appears that Hispanics as a group are less exclusive with respect to sexual partnering than are either whites or blacks.

As we have discussed already, it is not possible to draw direct inferences from these percentages about how people choose their partners. One of the reasons for this is differences in opportunity—we know that people simply do not have equal opportunities to meet and become involved with different types of partners. Although our data do not allow us to measure opportunity directly, there is one major component of opportunity that we can model. This involves the relative sizes of the three racial groups. For example, consider a hypothetical individual who is searching for a sex partner. Even if the choice made is entirely random, that individual will be more likely to select a white than a black or Hispanic partner simply because there are many more white people in the population. Thus, embedded in our observed row percentages are effects of group size, and by separating these out we can produce a measure that more closely approximates the effects of the process by which partners are selected. In addition, such a measure has the virtue of being comparable across tables based on different attributes.

The procedure that we use to model the effects of group size was first proposed by Fararo and Sunshine (1964) and has since been utilized by Laumann (1973), Laumann and Pappi (1976), and Glenn (1984). Briefly, the idea is to construct a measure (called a *homophily bias*) that captures the probability that an individual in one group will select another individual from the same group *over and above* his or her likelihood of doing so on the basis of the size of the group alone. This measure, represented by τ_i, can be calculated for a specific group using the following formula:

$$\tau_i = \frac{\delta_i - \dfrac{N_i}{N}}{1 - \dfrac{N_i}{N}},$$

where δ_i is the observed proportion of within-group choices by group i, N_i is the size of group i, and N is the total number of individuals in the population (N_i/N represents the expected proportion of within-group choices by group i if partnering were random.)[17] The denominator is equivalent to the maximum attainable value of the numerator and serves to normalize the measure between -1 and 1. Without it, the range of the measure would be dependent upon the relative size of the group (Glenn 1984).

In order to calculate homophily biases for the data in table 6.3, we must first estimate the expected percentage of in-choice. In situations where all people in the population are, in principle, eligible to be chosen, the expected percentage of in-choice for a specific group is equivalent to the percentage of the population represented by that group. However, in the case of sex partners, not all people in the population are eligible. In fact, most adults are married and are therefore not available as potential partners (given the high rate of sexual exclusivity among marriages). Thus, one method for estimating the expected percentage of in-choice for each group is to select only those respondents who are not currently married and calculate the proportions of this subsample that are white, black, and Hispanic. On the basis of similar logic, one could argue for excluding those respondents involved in long-term, exclusive, nonmarital partnerships. We have decided not to do this, however, since any decision about which partnerships were long term would be merely ad hoc. Moreover, it is unlikely that introducing this complexity would alter our findings at a substantive level.[18]

Look back now at the homophily bias estimates given in table 6.3. Those for both Hispanic men and women computed using race are higher than those computed using ethnicity, reflecting the fact that those who wrote in *Hispanic* as their race were, as we had anticipated, more likely to report having Hispanic

17. Fararo and Sunshine's approach expressed the proportion of within-group choices by group i (δ_i) as the sum of two components: τ_i and $(1 - \tau_i)N_i/N$. The first component is called the *biased component* and may be thought of as the probability of occurrence of a hypothetical "event" by which an individual from group i selects another member of the same group. In cases where this does not happen (which occur with probability $1 - \tau_i$), the individual selects members from group i according to their proportion in the population (N_i/N). Rewriting this equation in terms of τ_i yields the formula presented in the text above.

18. For example, eliminating all current nonmarital cohabitors changes the homophily scores either slightly or not at all.

partners than those who designated themselves as white with Hispanic ethnicity. In contrast, the bias estimates for whites are lower, a necessary result given the fact that a large percentage of respondents who designated themselves as white with Hispanic ethnicity reported having Hispanic partners. In either case, however, the main result—that Hispanics are less likely to select other Hispanics as sex partners than are whites to select whites or blacks to select blacks—remains the same.

Comparing the data for men and women, we see that the homophily bias for black women is uniquely high; in fact, only 3 percent of black women who reported sexual partnerships reported having a nonblack partner, compared to 18 percent of black men. This finding is consistent with previous studies demonstrating that more black men than black women are involved in interracial marriages, even after accounting for the effects of composition (e.g., Schoen and Wooldredge 1989). Without additional information, we cannot determine how much of this is due to the effects of selection (i.e., the desirability of black women to potential nonblack partners) and how much is a reflection of the preference of black women for black sex partners. The important point, however, is that, as a group, black men occupy a somewhat different position in sexual networks than do black women.

Also included in table 6.3 are the rates of within-group choice and the corresponding homophily bias parameters for education and current religious orientation. Although these bias parameters are not as large as those for race/ethnicity, they nevertheless indicate a substantial tendency toward homophily among sexual partnerships with respect to both education and religion. Moreover, this tendency is distributed unevenly across the various categories. For example, the estimated homophily biases for Catholics and Type II Protestants are more than twice as large as those for Type I Protestants and for those who reported having no religious affiliation.[19] Part of this is likely due to the fact that these groups are not distributed evenly throughout the population but are instead concentrated in certain geographic locations and absent from others. For example, 70 percent of respondents from the states classified as East South Central (Kentucky, Tennessee, Mississippi, and Alabama) meet our definition of Type II Protestant, whereas only 17 percent of those from New England (Massachusetts, New Hampshire, Vermont, Maine, Connecticut, and Rhode Island) do.

Of course, it is also likely that certain religiously based differences are partly responsible for differences in homophily across religious groups. Those

19. Unfortunately, our sample contained too few partnerships reported by Jewish respondents (twenty-one altogether) to produce reliable estimates of within-group choice and homophily bias. Previous studies (e.g., Glenn 1984) have found Jews to have a higher tendency toward homophily in marriage than either Protestants or Catholics, and it seems reasonable to assume that this would be true of nonmarital partnerships as well. The reader should note also that, although religious homophily among marriages can be affected by people converting to the religion of their spouse, this is much less likely to affect homophily among nonmarital sexual partnerships.

most often discussed relate directly to marriage and can therefore be invoked to explain partnering only under the assumption that a significant number of people view their sex partners as potential spouses and choose them accordingly. For example, the Catholic church still discourages interfaith marriages and stipulates that the children from such marriages be raised Catholic. Also, relatives and perhaps close friends (especially those who are devout) are likely to object to interfaith marriages. Such factors may act as disincentives to enter an interfaith marriage and, by implication, may also limit the number of interfaith sexual partnerships.

A more convincing explanation of the observed differences in homophily bias involves differences in the salience of religious beliefs and activities in people's lives. For example, our data indicate that Type II Protestants are more likely to attend church several times a week than are either Catholics or Type I Protestants (see also Laumann 1973; Roof 1985, 1987, 1993; Carroll and Roof 1993). Type II Protestants are also more likely to view their religious affiliation as a primary part of their self-identity, allowing it to determine their attitudes and using it to justify their behavior. Many "born-again" Christians, for example, look at the world as composed of two types of people: those who are "saved" and those who are not. Such commitment to any religious faith, but especially to one that singularly emphasizes a fundamental distinction between people, would make it difficult to maintain an intimate relationship with a partner who did not share the same beliefs and experiences. This argument may also explain the higher bias among Type II Protestant women than men, if we assume that women are more likely to take their religious commitments seriously and that they are less able to impose these commitments on their partners.

These explanations are clearly speculative, the next step being to look more closely for evidence supporting them in the data. Nevertheless, even these basic results extend previous research on religious homophily in two fundamental ways. The first is that, despite evidence that religious homophily in marriage has declined during this century (Kalmijn 1991), our data indicate that among sex partners it remains quite strong for Catholics and Type II Protestants. This result is particularly surprising given our prior assumption that homophily should be weaker among sexual partnerships than among marriages. It suggests that the factors that are responsible for marriage occurring within religious groups are linked not to the decision to get married but rather to earlier stages in the partnering process.

These results also extend past work by demonstrating an important distinction between Type I Protestants and Type II Protestants with respect to religious homophily. Past studies of religious homophily have not made such a distinction and, as a result, have found comparable tendencies toward homophily among both Protestants and Catholics (Glenn 1984). In contrast, our data suggest that Type I Protestants have a lower homophily bias than Catholics and that combining them with Type II Protestants may obscure this fact.

The bias estimates for education are, in general, smaller than those for race and religion, yet they exhibit a specific pattern, being smallest for the middle category and largest for the extreme categories (except for the high bias among women who received four-year college degrees). The small bias for those with some college or vocational training, particularly among women, partly reflects the relative heterogeneity of this category, which is composed of a whole range of tradespeople and other skilled workers as well as an increasing number of people with associates' degrees in fields such as business, electronics repair, and the like. Because of this diversity, there are no social labels (such as *high school graduate* or *college graduate*) for, or expectations of, those in this category and no uniform social "markers" for identifying them, making it both less important and more difficult for people in this category intentionally to target others in the category as sex partners.

We may also ask why the biases for the other educational categories, especially those on the ends, are as large as they are. Part of this is because, like people in a particular racial or religious group, people in a particular educational group are likely to select partners from their own group, owing to increased opportunities for contact and for sharing various interests and experiences. However, another important factor results from the fact that educational categories, unlike racial and religious categories, may be ordered along a single continuum according to the years of schooling that they reflect. Moreover, adjacent categories on this continuum are in some sense more similar than those that are not adjacent, suggesting that, when an individual does select a partner from outside his or her own category, that partner will be likely to come from an adjacent category. As a result, those in the middle categories have more opportunities for between-group choice than those on the ends, a phenomenon referred to in the literature as *edge effects* (for a discussion of edge effects, see Laumann 1966 or Verbrugge 1977).[20] And, because the opportunities for between-group choice are more restricted for those on the ends than for those in the middle, we can expect their bias toward within-group choice to be somewhat higher.

Owing to the small size and nationally representative nature of our sample, these estimates of homophily bias represent about all we can do to address the issue of composition.[21] They are, therefore, our best indication as to the effects of various social processes that lead to homophily with respect to race, education, and religion. Before moving on, however, we would like to discuss briefly

20. Edge effects can also be concentrated on only one end of an ordered set of categories. For example, in a study of friendships among adult men, Laumann (1966) found that respondents were more likely to report friendships with people of similar or higher-status occupations than themselves. This meant that those in lower-status occupations could in principle choose from the whole range of occupations while those in the highest-status occupations were restricted primarily to within-group choice.

21. We could measure compositional effects more accurately by looking at each state (or homogeneous sets of states) individually; however, this analysis would be limited by the relatively small size of our sample.

some of the most obvious limitations of these estimates. One of these concerns the accuracy with which respondents report the characteristics of their partners. The only way to address this issue directly is to consult the partners themselves, an impossible option given the need to maintain the anonymity of our respondents. However, we have no reason to believe that large numbers of respondents intentionally misreported their partners' characteristics. A more likely possibility would be that some respondents did not know their partners' educational background or religious affiliation and guessed incorrectly. The problem is that such guessing is unlikely to be random. For example, studies of respondents' reports on the political orientation of their friends demonstrated that, when in doubt, respondents were likely to ascribe their own orientation to their friends (Huckfeldt and Sprague 1988; Laumann 1973). If this occurred more often among certain educational and religious groups than among others, it might artificially inflate our estimates of the homophily in those groups.

Unfortunately, we have no way of assessing the extent to which respondents guessed the characteristics of their partners. Our only information regarding this issue is the percentages of different sets of respondents who reported that they did not know the characteristics of their partners (provided in table 6.3), proportions that varied from only 1 percent among women with some college to 23 percent among men with no religious affiliation. This variation makes sense; we would expect college graduates and those who have been to graduate school to be more likely to talk about their education and careers with their partners. Similarly, we would expect Type II Protestants (and perhaps also Catholics) to be more likely to reveal their religious orientation to their partners through references to religious topics or activities. Even the lower rates of nonresponse among women with some college or more are consistent with studies that have shown women to be more interested than men in their partners' occupation (and, by implication, educational achievement) (e.g., Buss 1989). These interpretations suggest that "guessing" is not responsible for the observed differences in nonresponse.[22] This issue points to the need in future studies to ask questions about how respondents came to know certain characteristics of their partners. Such information not only would help validate their reports but would also be helpful in understanding the process by which partners share information about themselves.

A second and more important limitation of these estimates of homophily bias is that they ignore the fact that partnering is also highly structured by age and that the proportion of available partners with a particular characteristic might vary across age groups. This structure is revealed in figure 6.1, which

22. One might also argue that nonresponse will be higher among heterophilous relationships since partners who do not share a particular characteristic might be less likely to discuss it. As a result, the true homophily biases might be somewhat lower, depending on the amount of nonresponse in each category.

Age of Respondent

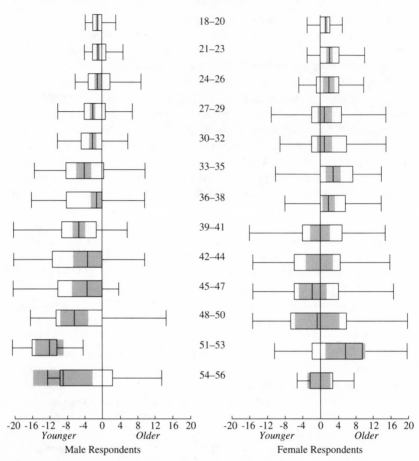

Fig. 6.1   Box plots of the difference (in years) between age of respondent and age of partner among all nonmarital and noncohabitational sexual partnerships, by gender. (Same-gender partnerships and oversample are omitted.)

shows the discrepancies between the ages of respondents and their sex partners. These box plots show that, although the range of partner ages for a given category of respondents is quite large, especially among the older age categories, the middle 50 percent of the data (contained within the box) lie within a much narrower interval—about ten years wide, on average. The mean structure of the data, revealed by the medians and their approximate 95 percent confidence intervals (indicated by the shaded areas), exhibit the typical pattern observed among marriages; on average, male respondents report partners slightly younger than themselves, and the number of years younger increases with the age of the respondent. As we would expect, the reverse is true for female respondents, although only for those under forty. In contrast, the partners reported by women over forty are about equally likely to be older or younger than the respondent. This is an interesting finding that might be interpreted in the following manner. If we assume that women desire sex partners somewhat older than themselves, then the failure of women over age forty in general to locate such partners may reflect the disadvantaged position of these women in the sexual marketplace. Note that this interpretation would be consistent with the data in figure 3.1 showing an increasingly larger proportion of women than men with no sex partners after age fifty.

There is much about these data that is likely to interest the reader. However, the fundamental point that we would like to emphasize is the importance of age in structuring sexual partnering. What this means is that, in principle, we may think of different homophily biases operating at different ages. In practice, these would be difficult to compute since we cannot split the sample into discrete subsamples by age so that partnering occurs only within each subsample. Schoen (1986) has developed a sophisticated method for analyzing the structure of intermarriage with respect to individual attributes that explicitly takes this into account, yielding estimates of the *magnitude of marriage attraction* between different age/attribute categories. Yet, while Schoen's method is superior in this respect, unfortunately it requires data in the form of a two-sex life table and thus cannot be applied to our data on sexual partnerships.

A third limitation of our homophily bias estimates is that they do not take into account the interdependence among the various attributes. Because race, education, and religion are empirically correlated in various ways, it is possible that part of the "bias" that we observe with regard to a particular characteristic might represent merely an unintended consequence of intentional bias with regard to another characteristic (for an example in which the effects of education and religion are modeled simultaneously, see Kalmijn 1991). Investigating this possibility among all three attributes would require working with sixty different categories (three race by five education by four religion) and would require special provisions to account for the fact that several of these categories would be empty.

Finally, the limitation that we view as most problematic is that the substantive relevance of these homophily bias estimates is largely dependent on the assumption that our expected rates of in-choice accurately capture people's opportunities for interaction with their own as opposed to other racial groups. Yet this is unlikely to be the case. Racial groups, for example, are not distributed evenly throughout the population but rather are present in high concentrations in certain areas and nearly absent from others. As a result, the amount of homophily that we observe is probably somewhat higher than would result if all people had equal opportunity to interact with each other. This fact, also true of religious groups, raises serious questions about the utility of national samples for characterizing the propensity of members of different groups to interact (Laumann and Schumm 1992). Moreover, even in situations where people with different characteristics live in relative proximity to one another, it is unlikely that they will have opportunities to interact in ways that would allow for the initiation of sexual partnerships. These problems are inherent in all attempts to use survey data to measure interaction between social groups. Yet, rather than dismiss the entire endeavor, we prefer to accept such national estimates with caution, recognizing that, although they may have no obvious connection to a controlled experiment in a laboratory, they nevertheless provide an accurate picture of what *is* going on in the population at the national level.

6.4   The Consequences of Specific Partnering Strategies

Differences in Homophily across Different Types of Partnerships

The results of the previous section—that sexual partnerships tend to occur between those of the same (or similar) racial/ethnic background, education level, and religious affiliation—make sense given the socially embedded character of the partnering process as described in sections 6.1 and 2. In this section, we go on to link certain aspects of that process more directly to homophilous outcomes. To begin, recall our observation that different types of partnerships may reflect different temporal stages in the partnering process *and* different intentions, on the part of the participants, regarding the status of the relationship. Both these have implications for differences across types of partnerships in the amount of specific types of homophily. For example, one might hypothesize that marriages will have the greatest degree of religious homophily since, for many people, religious issues become increasingly important when deciding to get married and raise children. In contrast, one might expect short-term partnerships to exhibit the lowest degree of homophily with respect to all attributes, assuming that purely sexual factors, as opposed to social considerations, are the sole motivation for such relationships.

Ideally, we would calculate homophily bias parameters for each of the four types of partnerships and compare them. Unfortunately, however, we are unable to do so because we have no way of estimating the composition of the set of eligible people from which to calculate expected percentages of in-choice. There are two reasons for this. First, the marriages and cohabitational relationships in our sample began at different times over an approximately forty-year interval, during which there may have been significant changes in the composition of the population. Although we might get around this problem by focusing only on partnerships that began during a period of a few years, our sample is not large enough to do so. Second, the fact that many disapprove of cohabitational or short-term sexual partnerships means that not all people are truly "eligible" for such partnerships, and there is no obvious way to identify which people are and which are not. For these reasons, we have chosen to compare

Table 6.4 **Percentage Homophilous, by Relationship Type: Percentage Distributions (includes only those marriages and cohabitational relationships that began during the past ten years)**

| Type of Homophily | Type of Relationship | | | |
	Marriages	Cohabitations	Long-Term Partnerships	Short-Term Partnerships
Racial/ethnic	93[a]	88	89	91
Age[b]	78	75	76	83
Educational[c]	82	87	83	87
Religious[d]	72	53	56	60

[a]Indicates weighted percentage of marriages that began within the past ten years and involved two people of the same race/ethnicity. Cases in which either partner was reported as Native American or "other" or had missing data are omitted.

[b]Age homophily is defined as a difference of no more than five years between partners' ages.

[c]Educational homophily is defined as a difference of no more than one educational category. The categories used were: less than high school, high school graduate, vocational training, four-year college, and graduate degree.

[d]Cases in which either partner was reported as "other" or had missing data are omitted.

the simple percentages of in-choice for each type of partnership, recognizing that these comparisons do not account for the effects of group size.

Table 6.4 presents the percentages of racial, age, educational, and religious in-choice separately for each of the four types of partnerships. On the basis of our earlier observation that a large number of partnerships differ in education level by a single category, we decided to include these partnerships as educationally homophilous. Similarly, age homophily is defined as a difference of no more than five years between partners' ages. In order to make the samples of marriages and cohabitational relationships more comparable to those of the other sexual partnerships, we have included only those marriages and cohabitations that began during the past ten years.[23] As expected, both racial and religious homophily are highest among marriages. In contrast, educational homophily is somewhat lower among marriages than among either cohabitational relationships or short-term partnerships. This finding is consistent with the hypothesis that, while it may be customary not to marry outside one's professed religious group (thus the low proportions of interracial and interfaith marriages), such a proscription does not appear to exist for education. Instead, the exchange of resources within marriage may function to keep the level of homophily lower than it might otherwise be.

Looking at the table as a whole, however, we see that the patterns of homophily within the different partnerships are essentially quite similar, most differences being only a few percentage points. The only exception to this is reli-

23. This is the smallest time interval that generated a sufficient number of partnerships.

gious homophily, which is substantially greater among marriages than among the other three types of partnership. An important implication of this is that, while factors related specifically to the institution of marriage (e.g., culturally prescribed endogamy, the influence of one's family, the exchange of resources, etc.) may strongly affect the amount of religious in-choice, such factors are much less important in determining the amounts of racial, age, and educational in-choice. Instead, these parameters on choice are already well established at the point of first sexual involvement. Put simply, with respect to race, age, and education, the people we date are generally similar to those we marry, while, with respect to religion, our choice of a spouse is somewhat more restricted. However, one should bear in mind that our estimate of religious homophily among marriages is likely to be slightly inflated owing to people switching faiths in order to match that of their spouse.

Comparisons among the percentages of age homophily should be interpreted with particular caution. This is because, as we know from figure 6.1, the degree of age homophily varies considerably with age.[24] Thus, the overall percentages in table 6.4 may be determined in part by the age distribution of the set of respondents reporting each type of partnership. In fact, the median ages of respondents reporting marriages, cohabitational relationships, and long- and short-term partnerships were thirty, thirty, twenty-nine, and twenty-five, respectively. This suggests that the higher degree of age homophily among short-term partnerships may be due in part to the fact that these partnerships are more likely to occur among younger individuals.

Finally, it is interesting that the proportions of homophilous short-term partnerships are, in general, similar or slightly larger than those of the other types of homophilous partnerships. Part of this, especially in the case of religion, may be due to the higher rate of nonresponse by people who did not know the religious affiliation of their short-term partner. If heterophilous relationships are disproportionately represented among these partnerships—a reasonable assumption since partners with different religious backgrounds may be less likely to discuss religion—then the actual amount of religious homophily among short-term partnerships may be somewhat lower. Another potential explanation might be that the occurrence of short-term partnerships is limited to specific racial, educational, or religious groups, thus reducing the possibilities for out-choice. Further analysis disconfirmed this possibility: the distribution of short-term partnerships across racial, educational and religious categories was quite similar to that for long-term partnerships.

Bearing in mind the problems involved in comparing across different relationships, it is important to note that these data appear inconsistent with our initial hypothesis that decreased social visibility among short-term partnerships and the search strategies employed in locating them would result in a lower degree of homophily. One possible explanation is that, while the rela-

24. In this case, we are really using age as a proxy for age at which the relationship began.

tionships that we have identified as short term had only a brief period of actual sexual activity, many do not represent our cultural notion of a one-night stand. For example, as shown in table 6.2 above, many respondents knew their short-term partners for a considerable amount of time before having sex with them.

Meeting Places, Introductions, and Homophilous Partnerships

Within each of the four types of partnerships, different strategies for meeting partners are also likely to be associated with differences in certain types of homophily. In simplest terms, the locations in which people meet their partners and the brokers who introduce them act as social "filters," increasing the likelihood of contact and subsequent interaction among individuals with similar attributes and experiences. Focusing first on location, there are two basic ways in which meeting places facilitate the creation of homophilous relationships. The first involves the purpose of the place and the restrictions that this imposes on who is allowed to be (or wants to be) present. For example, a school brings together students with the same level of education, a church practicing members of a particular faith. Since these patterns of contact are a result of the intrinsic nature of the location, we might refer to them as *structurally induced*.[25]

A less obvious, although perhaps more pervasive, manner in which specific locations structure patterns of interaction is through self-selection on the part of individuals regarding whether they will attend such places. These socially induced patterns are particularly important because they operate in locations that otherwise do not restrict attendance. Most bars and clubs, for example, do not explicitly restrict certain people from entering (other than those under the legal drinking age), yet their patrons select themselves on the basis of the type of bar and the people who frequent it. Other examples would be sports events or musical performances—few box offices would turn away a potential ticket purchaser, yet the average profile of those attending professional football games is quite different from that of those attending professional tennis matches, the profile of those attending the ballet quite different from that of those attending a rock concert, etc. The point is that the locations in which people meet their sex partners reflect boundaries on the types of partners that they are likely to encounter.

Table 6.5 presents the percentages of different partnerships within each category of meeting place that are homophilous with respect to each of the four attributes. Comparing across the columns, we see (as expected) that, while partnerships in which the couple met at school are most likely to be homophilous with respect to age and education, those in which the couple met at church are most likely to be homophilous with respect to religion. Other patterns are

---

25. Of course, not all structurally induced contact is among similar people. An important exception occurs in many work environments, where people with different skills and educational backgrounds often work together.

Table 6.5   **Percentage Homophilous, by Meeting Place**

Type of Homophily	School	Work	Private Party	Church	Gym/Soc. Club	Bar	Elsewhere
Marriages:							
Racial/ethnic	98[a]	95	94	94	93	94	96
Age[b]	97	71	88	88	80	73	80
Educational[c]	89	85	85	79	79	80	86
Religious[d]	81	72	78	96	63	75	80
Cohabitations:							
Racial/ethnic	83	90	87	. . .	. . .	95	92
Age[b]	86	70	72	. . .	. . .	53	71
Educational[c]	94	79	86	. . .	. . .	89	89
Religious[d]	. . .	55	64	. . .	. . .	40	56
Long-term partnerships:							
Racial/ethnic	88	85	94	. . .	81	87	91
Age[b]	99	64	71	. . .	58	64	73
Educational[c]	94	83	72	. . .	82	84	80
Religious[d]	56	48	56	. . .	51	53	60
Short-term partnerships:							
Racial/ethnic	95	92	87	. . .	. . .	94	97
Age[b]	97	75	74	. . .	. . .	71	78
Educational[c]	93	. . .	81	. . .	. . .	83	88
Religious[d]	. . .	. . .	. . .	. . .	. . .	. . .	. . .

Note: ". . ." indicates fewer than thirty unweighted observations.

[a]Indicates weighted percentage of those marriages in which partners met at school that involve two people of the same race/ethnicity. Cases in which either partner was reported as Native American or "other" or had missing data are omitted.

[b]Age homophily is defined as a difference of no more than five years between partners' ages.

[c]Educational homophily is defined as a difference of no more than one educational category. The categories used were less than high school, high school graduate, vocational training, four-year college, and graduate degree.

[d]Cases in which either partner was reported as "other" or had missing data are omitted.

not as systematic or obvious as these. For example, the lowest frequency of educational homophily (72 percent) occurs among partnerships in which the couple met at a private party, suggesting that such parties represent an important avenue through which partnering between different educational groups may occur. In contrast, the degree of educational homophily among partnerships in which the couple met at a bar is relatively high, reflecting in part the amount of self-selection with respect to education (or characteristics associated with education, such as occupation) that occurs among bar patrons. However, the percentage of age homophily among these relationships is uniformly low, a distinction also exhibited among all four types of relationships in which the couple met at work.

These simple observations are interesting because they provide us with a sense of the amount of homophily contributed by each meeting place to the homophily of the total set of partnerships described above (table 6.4).[26] However, these data might also be used to address two important theoretical issues. The first of these concerns the relation between the amount of contact between two (or more) groups and the number of heterophilous relationships that will result. To estimate this relation, we would view each category of meeting place as an observation consisting of two attributes: an amount of resulting homophily (the percentage from table 6.5) and a number reflecting the composition of the set of participants (unmeasured in our data).[27] Plotting these data should then tell us something about the association between composition and heterophilous partnering. This analysis would of course require more refined descriptions of the various meeting places than we have available and estimates of the composition of those places with respect to the attributes in question. Although difference in interaction across the different settings would strongly limit the interpretations of such an analysis, it would nevertheless provide some valuable clues about the nature of the partnering process.

A second issue concerns whether people select their partners differently depending on the type of partnership that they are interested in pursuing. The data in table 6.5 are better suited to answering this question than, say, those in table 6.4 because, as we have seen, there is considerable variation in the extent to which different meeting places generate the four types of partnerships. Therefore, if we assume, for example, that the private parties at which people meet potential long-term partners are the same as those at which people meet potential short-term partners, then the observed difference in racial homophily (94 as compared to 87 percent) is telling us something either about differences in selection criteria or about differences in the persistence of racially homophilous as opposed to heterophilous sexual partnerships.

Unlike meeting place, we found few differences in the percentage of homophilous relationships across the different types of introduction. Of course, this does not necessarily imply that the person making the introduction does not determine who is being introduced, only that our categories (i.e., family member, friend, etc.) are not appropriate for measuring such effects with respect to the four types of homophily. For example, among introductions by family members, it is likely that the nature of their relationship to the person being introduced is important, as would also be the case among introductions made by "close" friends as opposed to those made by more distant acquaintances.

Before going on, it is important to note that restrictions on the social composition of the pool of eligible people are not the only consequences of particular strategies used to identify sex partners. For example, another important

26. Of course, this is also dependent on the proportion of total partnerships resulting from each particular meeting place.

27. Although we were unable in this study to measure the social composition of specific social settings, there are data available that may be used to address this issue. For example, McPherson and Smith-Lovin (1987) have collected and analyzed data on the social composition of face-to-face groups.

consequence involves the amount of information that one partner has (or is able to obtain) about the other. As we have already mentioned, such information can accelerate the progression of a relationship, helping partners discover more quickly that they are either incompatible or that they share the same interests and attitudes. Both items that we have used to describe the meeting process—type of introduction and meeting place—are likely to be associated with the amount of information that two partners have or are able to infer about each other. With regard to the former, the major distinction is between "brokered" introductions involving a third party and "nonbrokered" or self-introductions. The presence of third parties who know both individuals provides an opportunity for one individual to inquire indirectly about the other. More important, brokered introductions often carry an implicit endorsement on the part of the broker, an obvious example being that in which the broker is acting as a "matchmaker" by introducing two people whom he or she believes will be compatible. Furthermore, it is reasonable to assume that the nature of an endorsement and the amount and accuracy of the information provided by a broker depend in part on the type of relationship between him or her and the individuals being introduced.

With regard to the latter, certain contexts provide more opportunities for discovering important information about potential partners than others. Schools, for example, provide not only a relatively dense network of friends and acquaintances through which information can travel but, as we have already seen, also opportunities for getting to know potential partners before becoming sexually involved with them. Other settings such as work, church, social clubs, and even private parties provide opportunities for inferring certain pieces of information about each other on the basis of the specific "rules" governing access to these activities. In contrast, bars, vacations, and "personal" ads are least likely to provide opportunities for discovering information about potential partners.

Homophily, Networks, and the Persistence of Partnerships

In addition to the manner in which partners meet each other, there is a second aspect of the partnering process that has consequences for the degree of homophily among current sexual partnerships. This is differential persistence: certain partnerships are likely to last a long time, and others are not. As a result, those partnerships with greater persistence are more likely to exist at any given point than are those with less persistence, thereby affecting the structure of current partnerships. And, to the extent that homophily is associated with greater persistence, this factor operates to increase the amount of homophily in the population.

We shall not present a direct analysis of the association between persistence (measured in terms of the duration of a partnership) and homophily because doing so would require more space and technical detail than we can afford here. Instead, we shall examine an important factor associated with persistence. This is the extent to which partners become acquainted with each other's family and friends. Such ties reflect a certain degree of commitment to the partnership on the part of the couple and therefore a willingness to establish the relationship as socially recognized. This suggests that such ties should be most likely among marriages and least likely among short-term partnerships. Yet commitment is not the only factor affecting one's decision to introduce a sex partner to family and friends; this decision is also affected by one's judgment about whether they will perceive that partner (and the relationship) to be "appropriate" and whether they will "get along" with him or her. For this reason, certain heterophilous relationships are likely to exhibit fewer such relationships than their homophilous counterparts. Cohabitational relationships are also likely to exhibit fewer of these ties (especially with family), owing to the traditional view of cohabitation as being morally and socially unacceptable. In addition to what the existence of such ties implies about the intentions and perceptions of the couple, these ties also reflect the potential degree of social pressure—both positive and negative—that may be brought to bear on the couple, thereby affecting the persistence of the partnership.

Table 6.6 shows the percentages of each type of partnership in which the partner "got to know" the respondent's family and friends, computed separately for homophilous and heterophilous partnerships. Those partnerships in which the respondent was introduced by a family member are excluded from the first two columns since, in these cases, the partner already knew the respondent's family; this was also done for the third and fourth columns with partnerships in which the respondent was introduced by a friend. The data clearly show that partners in homophilous relationships are more likely to get to know the respondent's family and friends than are those in heterophilous partnerships. This is especially true with regard to racial, age, and educational homophily while perhaps somewhat less so for religious homophily. Whether this is due to a conscious effort on the part of the respondent we cannot say. However, it is consistent with our hypothesis that dissimilar partners are, in general, more difficult to integrate into one's personal network. And, since the social support provided by this network is important in maintaining the partnership, we expect heterophilous partnerships to be shorter in duration than homophilous partnerships, other factors held constant.

There is also another way to interpret the percentages in this table. Looking *within* each column and comparing across the four panels, we see how each type of partnership differs in terms of the likelihood that the partners will know each other's family and friends. Since the percentages are computed separately for homophilous and heterophilous partnerships, these comparisons are not affected by variation in the rates of homophily among the different types of partnerships. As expected, the percentages consistently decline as we move from marriages through cohabitational relationships to long-term and then short-term partnerships. What is interesting, however, is the relative similarity between cohabitational relationships and partnerships. Although the percent-

Table 6.6   **Percentage of Homophilous versus Heterophilous Partnerships in Which Partner Knew Respondent's Family and Friends (excluding those introduced by family and friends, respectively)**

	Knew Respondent's Family		Knew Respondent's Friends	
Type of Homophily	Homophilous Partnerships	Heterophilous Partnerships	Homophilous Partnerships	Heterophilous Partnerships
Marriages:				
Racial/ethnic	100[a]	. . .	97	. . .
Age[b]	100	. . .	99	. . .
Educational[c]	100	. . .	95	. . .
Religious[d]	100	100	95	. . .
Cohabitations:				
Racial/ethnic	77	. . .	82	. . .
Age[b]	85	69	82	87
Educational[c]	79	. . .	82	. . .
Religious[d]	91	80	82	81
Long-term partnerships:				
Racial/ethnic	69	63	76	64
Age[b]	71	59	80	57
Educational[c]	71	54	77	63
Religious[d]	77	71	77	76
Short-term partnerships:				
Racial/ethnic	38	. . .	43	. . .
Age[b]	41	. . .	37	. . .
Educational[c]	37	. . .	42	. . .
Religious[d]	. . .	. . .	. . .	. . .

Note: ". . ." indicates fewer than thirty unweighted observations.

[a]Indicates weighted percentage of racially/ethnically homophilous marriages in which the respondent's spouse "got to know" his or her family, excluding those in which the spouse was introduced by a family member. Cases in which either partner was reported as Native American or "other" or had missing data are omitted.

[b]Age homophily is defined as a difference of no more than five years between partners' ages.

[c]Educational homophily is defined as a difference of no more than one educational category. The categories used were less than high school, high school graduate, vocational training, four-year college, and graduate degree.

[d]Cases in which either partner was reported as "other" or had missing data are omitted.

ages for the former are slightly higher, it appears that living together does not automatically result in greater integration into each other's personal networks. However, this result should be examined more closely, explicitly controlling for differences in the duration of the various partnerships.

6.5   The Structure of Between-Group Contact

The incidence of within-group partnerships, on which the calculation of homophily biases is based, is the most striking feature of the data on respondents' attributes and those of their partners. However, patterns in between-group contact are also important for understanding the spread of sexually transmitted infections and reveal, in fuller detail, the effects of social processes on the structure of sexual partnering. These patterns may be examined by referring to table 6.7, which indicates the racial/ethnic background of respondents (by convention, indicated by the row) and of their partners (indicated by the column). As in section 6.3, we are restricting our focus to those heterosexual partnerships in which the partners are not married and do not live together. The data for male and female respondents are tabulated separately. The percentages along the *main diagonal* (i.e., those cells in which the race/ethnicity of the respondent and that of the partner are the same) are identical to the percentages presented earlier in table 6.3; it is the off-diagonal cells, indicating partnerships between racial/ethnic groups, with which we are concerned here.

Like within-group choice, between-group choice may also be affected by the proportions of specific groups in the population. As a way of taking this into account, we have provided a second number in parentheses in the cells in table 6.7 (also in tables 6.8 and 6.9 below). This number is a residual, obtained by subtracting from the observed count the number that we would expect if between-group choice occurred randomly (i.e., in proportion to the size of each group).[28] Thus, positive residuals indicate cells with higher counts and negative residuals cells with smaller counts than would be expected. The residuals in the diagonal cells are all equal to zero; this is because we used a model to generate the residuals that essentially removes the effects of homophily so that we may concentrate solely on variations in between-group choice.[29]

Before examining these residuals, it is important to clarify what we mean when we speak about partner choice occurring randomly. In theory, we say that partner choice occurs randomly when the number of partners selected in each group is proportional to the number of available partners in each group. Yet determining the number of available partners in each group is a difficult matter. In calculating the homophily biases in table 6.3 above, we approximated this quantity by using the number of unmarried people in each group in the population. In contrast, in calculating the residuals, we approximated this quantity by the column totals from the table itself. The advantage of this latter procedure is that it perhaps better reflects the uneven manner in which the volume of partnering is distributed over the population. Unlike the former procedure, however, it cannot reveal the systematic over- or underreporting of certain types of partners by all respondents.

Looking now at the residuals in the top half of table 6.7, we see that the

28. Actually, these are Pearson residuals, obtained by dividing the residual by the square root of the expected cell count. Although this procedure is equivalent to standardizing the deviate under certain assumptions, we do not use this fact to make inferences about specific residuals. Rather, we make use of the fact that the Pearson residual represents the contribution of each particular cell to the table's overall χ^2, interpreting them as indicating places where the random model fails to fit the data.

29. We used a log-linear model with row and column effects and a unique parameter for each diagonal cell (sometimes referred to as a *differential homophily* model).

Table 6.7   **Race/Ethnicity of Respondents and Their Partners, by Gender (row percentages), Nonmarital and Noncohabitational Partnerships Only (same-gender partnerships excluded)**

| | | Partner's Race/Ethnicity | | | |
	White	Black	Hispanic	Asian	N
Male respondents					
Race/ethnicity:					
White	93.8	.6	2.1	1.9	677
	(0.0)	(.5)	(−1.1)	(1.3)	
Black	7.6	82.1	4.6	0.0	263
	(−.3)	(0.0)	(1.9)	(−1.8)	
Hispanic	42.4	1.2	45.9	5.9	85
	(.2)	(−.6)	(0.0)	(−.2)	
Asian	7.7	0.0	0.0	92.3	13
	(.3)	(−.2)	(−.5)	(0.0)	
Female respondents					
Race/ethnicity:					
White	89.5	6.4	1.6	.7	438
	(0.0)	(.1)	(−.4)	(.7)	
Black	1.0	96.9	1.0	0.0	192
	(−.7)	(0.0)	(1.7)	(−.4)	
Hispanic	26.0	16.4	56.2	0.0	73
	(.2)	(0.0)	(0.0)	(−.9)	
Asian	50.0	0.0	0.0	50.0	2
	(.6)	(−.6)	(−.3)	(0.0)	

Note: Figures given are percentage of choices within row. Percentages may not add to 100 percent owing to partners whose racial/ethnic background was not among those listed here (these cases are included in the table totals). Figures given in parentheses are Pearson residuals from log-linear model including row and column effects and a single parameter for each diagonal cell.

largest are concentrated in the upper-right-hand corner of the table, reflecting a potential difference between white and black respondents. Specifically, white men are more likely to report Asian partners and less likely to report Hispanic partners than would be expected under the model, while the reverse is true of black men. We should not make too much of the residuals in this table, however, because of the small number of between-group choices on which they are based. Furthermore, by statistical standards, almost all the residuals are quite small, suggesting that the random between-group choice model fits the data fairly well.[30]

In table 6.8, which classifies partnerships according to the education level of both respondents and their partners, the residuals are much larger, indicating a poorer fit of the random between-group choice model to the data.[31] Moreover, these residuals reveal a clear and systematic pattern. The positive residuals

30. For the top half of table 6.7 the log-likelihood ratio test is 14.1 on 5 *df,* for the bottom half 6.4 on 5 *df.* These values should be viewed as merely suggestive, however, given the small size of many of the cells in the table.

Table 6.8   **Education Level of Respondents and Their Partners, by Gender (row percentages), Nonmarital and Noncohabitational Partnerships Only (oversample and same-gender partnerships excluded)**

| | Partner's Education | | | | | |
	< High School	High School	Some College	4-Year College	Graduate Degree	N
Male respondents Education:						
< high school	44.6	33.7	16.3	3.3	2.2	92
	(0.0)	(2.4)	(−1.2)	(−1.8)	(−.1)	
High school	13.5	51.0	26.0	8.2	1.4	208
	(4.5)	(0.0)	(−.7)	(−1.5)	(−1.3)	
Some college	5.7	34.9	44.0	14.4	1.0	298
	(−.7)	(.7)	(0.0)	(.6)	(−2.3)	
4-year college	2.3	25.2	34.7	29.7	8.1	222
	(−2.4)	(−1.4)	(1.2)	(0.0)	(4.0)	
Graduate degree	0.0	18.3	28.3	26.7	26.7	60
	(−1.9)	(−1.4)	(.1)	(3.5)	(0.0)	
Female respondents Education:						
< high school	39.0	41.6	14.3	5.2	0.0	77
	(0.0)	(3.2)	(−.4)	(−2.3)	(−2.1)	
High school	16.9	46.3	15.4	14.0	7.4	136
	(3.7)	(0.0)	(−1.2)	(−1.3)	(.2)	
Some college	6.3	28.6	36.9	23.1	5.1	255
	(−.9)	(−.3)	(0.0)	(1.6)	(−1.1)	
4-year college	1.1	15.1	28.0	40.9	15.1	93
	(−2.2)	(−2.2)	(2.1)	(0.0)	(3.4)	
Graduate degree	0.0	29.0	16.1	29.0	25.8	31
	(−1.5)	(0.0)	(−.4)	(1.4)	(0.0)	

Note: See the note to table 6.7.

are located almost exclusively in the cells directly above and below the main diagonal, reflecting the fact that the majority of educational between-group choice is limited to differences of only one educational category. The only exception to this pattern occurs for relationships between high school graduates and those with some college education, a result that is partly due to a difference in the wording of the answer categories between the question asking about the respondent's education and the question asking about the education of his or her partner.[32]

We may also use these residuals to investigate the possibility that partner-

31. For the top half of table 6.8 the log-likelihood ratio test is 80.0 on 11 *df,* for the bottom half 74.7 on 11 *df.*

32. The question asking about the respondent's own education included the answer category "vocational/trade/business school," while the corresponding category in the question about the partner's education was "some college or vocational school." Our hypothesis is that the former was interpreted by respondents in a more inclusive manner than the latter, thus explaining the fact that, among respondents of *both* genders, the number of partnerships in which the respondent has some college and the partner is a high school graduate is greater than the number of partnerships with the reverse.

ships in which the man has more education than the woman are more likely to occur than those in which the woman has more education than the man. In the top half of table 6.8, the residuals below the main diagonal (those representing partnerships in which the respondent has more education than the partner) sum to 2.2, those above the main diagonal to −1.9, suggesting that, overall, male respondents are more likely to report female partners with less education than themselves. However, it is important to note that this difference is not distributed evenly throughout the table. In the bottom half, the sum of the residuals above the main diagonal (which correspond to those below the diagonal in the panel above) is 0, the sum of those below −.3. This difference also suggests that partnerships in which the man has more education are more likely to occur; however, the evidence is considerably weaker.

Finally, consider table 6.9, which classifies partnerships according to the current religious affiliation of respondents and their partners. The residuals in this table, like those in table 6.7 above, are generally small, reflecting a reasonable fit between the random between-group choice model and the observed data.[33] Given this, the residuals may indicate only random variation in the data, and we therefore make no attempt to interpret them.

Admittedly, this brief discussion of patterns among partnerships between different social groups only scratches the surface of what is an important topic, both from a sociological and from an epidemiological perspective. The next step will be to fit statistical models to tables 6.7–6.9 and then go on to examine simultaneously the effects of race, education, and religion in structuring sexual networks. Nevertheless, we hope that our presentation has given the reader a basic sense of what these data look like and of some of the issues involved in analyzing and interpreting them.

6.6 Conclusion

Our focus in this chapter has been twofold. First, we have examined various aspects of the actual process by which people meet their sex partners. Contrary to what one might think, our data indicate that this process is largely socially embedded even for short-term sexual partnerships; that is, it is directly mediated by an individual's social network and the particular events in which he or she participates. This means that the pool of eligible people from which one identifies potential sex partners is not a random subset of the population but rather a highly constrained subset. For this reason, it is a bit misleading to speak of a person *choosing* a partner on the basis of specific racial/ethnic, educational, or religious characteristics. Rather, we argue that the concept of *differential association* more accurately describes the process by which sexual networks become organized according to these social attributes. It is unlikely, however, that people are immediately aware of this phenomenon since, from

33. For the top half of table 6.9, the log-likelihood ratio test is 8.5 on 5 *df,* for the bottom half 8.2 on 5 *df.*

Table 6.9   **Religious Preference of Respondents and Their Partners, by Gender (row percentages), Nonmarital and Noncohabitational Partnerships Only (oversample and same-gender partnerships excluded)**

| | Partner's Religious Preference | | | | |
	None	Type I Protestant	Type II Protestant	Catholic	N
Male respondents					
Religious preference:					
None	26.9	21.2	11.5	28.8	52
	(0.0)	(.6)	(−1.2)	(.6)	
Type I Protestant	9.0	31.5	31.5	24.7	89
	(−.1)	(0.0)	(1.4)	(−1.2)	
Type II Protestant	4.3	8.6	61.2	19.8	116
	(−.2)	(−1.0)	(0.0)	(1.0)	
Catholic	5.8	14.2	10.8	67.5	120
	(.3)	(.5)	(−.7)	(0.0)	
Female respondents					
Religious preference:					
None	35.9	12.8	7.7	30.8	39
	(0.0)	(−1.1)	(−.8)	(1.9)	
Type I Protestant	14.6	30.3	23.6	23.6	89
	(−.3)	(0.0)	(1.0)	(−.6)	
Type II Protestant	6.7	12.5	71.7	8.3	120
	(.4)	(.3)	(0.0)	(−.6)	
Catholic	7.2	16.2	6.3	66.7	111
	(0.0)	(.6)	(−.8)	(0.0)	

Note: See the note to table 6.7.

the individual's point of view, he or she is simply responding to the opportunities for partnering that appear to be available.

Our data also indicate that, in the majority of partnerships, the partners knew each other for at least one month before initiating sexual activity and that, in roughly one-quarter of nonmarital partnerships, this interval between meeting and first sex was at least one year. As we noted in our discussion, the fact that we cannot determine at what point partners become romantically but perhaps not yet sexually involved makes it difficult to draw interpretations from these figures. Nevertheless, the data do suggest that the strategy of locating a sex partner from among one's current acquaintances is not uncommon. This has implications for how the choice of sex partner is made since knowing someone for a period of time affords the possibility of collecting information about that person that may be relevant in deciding whether to pursue a sexual relationship.

The second focus of this chapter has been to describe the structure of sexual networks with respect to race/ethnicity, age, education, and religion. We showed how one important aspect of this structure—the extent to which partnerships occur between those with the same social attributes—can be directly linked to different strategies for securing a sex partner, including which type of partnership to pursue, where to meet potential partners, and the decision about whether to incorporate a partner into one's existing social network by introducing him or her to friends and family. For example, we found that, as has been previously shown for marital partnerships, there are significant amounts of racial/ethnic, educational, and even religious homophily among noncohabitational sexual partnerships. This is an important finding because it suggests that what determines whom we marry, at least with respect to certain attributional features of the person, has already occurred at the point of first sexual involvement. Although we would stress the suggestive nature of this conclusion, the implication is that attempts to explain marital homogamy need to shift their focus to include factors affecting sexual partnerships.

Thus far, our inquiry into the structure of sexual networks has been motivated by what we can infer from this structure about the sociological factors that motivate and impinge on the decision to pursue particular types of sexual partnerships. And, as we have pointed out, making such inferences can be quite complicated. This is because data on those sexual partnerships that have actually occurred cannot tell us about other partnerships that were available, desired, or started but never sexually consummated. In addition, these data tell us nothing about respondents' own intentions regarding specific relationships. However, such data on partnering outcomes are sufficient for epidemiological purposes since in this case we are less interested in why sexual networks are the way they are than in describing that structure in ways appropriate for answering questions about the spread of sexually transmitted infections. It is these questions to which we now turn.

CHAPTER 7

Epidemiological Implications of Sexual Networks

In the preceding chapter, we demonstrated the fact that sexual networks are highly structured according to certain social characteristics, and we began to examine various aspects of the process by which this structure is generated. In this chapter, we shift our focus to the *consequences* of network structure for the spread of sexually transmitted infections. This single issue provided the most compelling rationale for collecting these data on sexual networks, for, although national level data are not entirely suited to studying the partnering process in detail, they are absolutely necessary for improving the accuracy with which we can predict the future impact of AIDS on the national population.

Despite considerable biological variation across sexually transmitted infections (STIs) (see chapter 11), all have one element in common: sexual networks form the pathways across which these infections are transmitted from one person to another. This fact may seem obvious, yet it represents a major distinction between STIs and other infectious diseases. Because infections such as measles or influenza can be contracted through casual or indirect contact, epidemiologists have been able to model their spread as being random with respect to the social features of the individuals involved—merely visiting a public place or having contact with someone who did creates the opportunity for infection. In the case of STIs, however, such models are clearly inadequate. Unlike casual contact, sexual partnering (and, by implication, the network that it generates) is highly nonrandom, a fact that has major consequences for both the rate with which and the extent to which an STI can spread (for a discussion of some of the ways that social structure can be incorporated into epidemiological models, see Morris 1993; for a formal introduction to mathematical models in epidemiology, see Anderson and May 1991 or Bailey 1975).

To see how a sexual network can affect the spread of STIs, consider the hypothetical sexual network pictured in figure 7.1. This figure is intended, not to be representative of the sexual network in any specific population, but rather to illustrate the various types of sexual relationships and the possible patterns among them. Each circle (referred to as a *node* in graph theory) represents an individual, and the lines (referred to as *ties* or *paths*) between them indicate sexual relationships (for an introduction to the mathematical theory of graphs,

L. Philip Schumm drafted this chapter, under the direction of Edward O. Laumann.

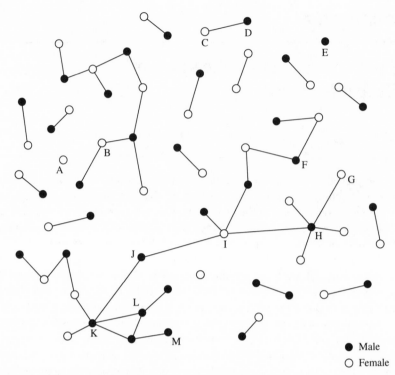

Fig. 7.1 A hypothetical sexual network. Each line indicates the presence of a sexual relationship.

see Harary, Norman, and Cartwright 1965; Harary 1969). The relationships pictured here represent those occurring during a specific period of time (e.g., one year); thus, nodes such as A and E represent individuals who have no sex partners during the period, C and G individuals who have only one sex partner, and H and L individuals who have several. In the case of an individual with several partnerships, these may be organized sequentially or concurrently, a distinction with significant implications for the spread of STIs (Morris and Kretzchmar 1994).

In order to simplify the discussion, we have drawn all the sexual ties to look alike. In reality, however, there is considerable variation across sexual ties in their likelihood of transmitting infection. This is especially true in the case of AIDS. For example, the probability of transmitting HIV associated with anal intercourse is significantly higher than that associated with vaginal intercourse, implying that partnerships in which anal intercourse occurs represent a "stronger" potential path of infection than partnerships in which it does not occur.[1] In fact, it has been estimated that, in the absence of co-factors such as the presence of genital sores resulting from other STIs, the transmission probability associated with vaginal intercourse is quite low (for a discussion of the effect of this on the spread of the infection, see Plumley 1992; for a discussion of the differential infectivity of STIs, see chapter 11). Moreover, there is evidence to suggest that the likelihood of transmission through vaginal intercourse from men to women is higher than that from women to men. Given these issues, it may ultimately be useful to think of a sexual network in terms of a graph in which each path is associated with a specific direction and strength (called a *valued, directed graph*). We do not have space here to consider this possibility further; however, we should note that the data on specific activities presented in chapter 3 may be used in conjunction with the data presented in this chapter to address this issue explicitly.

The epidemiological significance of our hypothetical network is most obvious for those individuals who have no partners (called *isolates*) or those who are members of unconnected dyads, such as the dyad composed of nodes C and D and the relationship between them. During short to moderate periods of time, these people constitute a much greater proportion of the population than is represented in our hypothetical network. For example, our data indicate that, during a given year, 12 percent of adults have no sex partners and that an additional estimated 72 percent[2] are members of unconnected dyads. The former clearly have no risk of becoming infected with an STI during the year, and the same is true of the latter, provided that their partner is uninfected at the beginning of the year. Thus, the existence of such individuals, some 84 percent of the total population, effectively reduces, for the period in question, the number of susceptible people in the population. Moreover, should any of these people have been previously infected, they will be able to transmit the infection to at most one other person.

A more systematic way of thinking about the effects of isolates and unconnected dyads, as well as other features of network structure, on the transmission of STIs is provided by the concept of *network* (or *graph*) *connectivity*. In introducing this concept, it is useful to begin by considering a pair of nodes. These two nodes, and the individuals represented by them, will be said to be *connected* if there is some unbroken path, either direct or indirect, linking them together. Thus, in our hypothetical network, nodes F and J are connected by a

1. Similarly, it is logical to assume that those ties that involve a higher frequency of sexual activity will have a greater potential for transmission, although the data available for HIV do not indicate a clear relation between the frequency of sex with a specific partner and the likelihood of transmission (Kaplan 1990).

2. This figure is estimated from a question asking respondents about how many partners *their partners* had during the past year. Although it is unclear how accurately respondents were able to answer this question, it is the only way to collect this piece of information, given the necessary constraints of confidentiality.

path of length 4, while nodes B and H are unconnected. At this point, the relevance of network connectivity to the spread of STIs should become evident since the only way for an STI to spread from one individual to another is if the two are connected.

We may extend this concept of connectivity to characterize an entire network in the following way. Consider selecting a random sample of nodes of size n_0 from a population of size N; we refer to n_0/N as the *starting fraction*. We then enumerate all the *new* nodes (those not in the original sample) to which those in the original sample are directly connected. Note that, if the starting fraction is small and the size of the population large, then it is unlikely that those in the starting fraction will be directly tied to one another (recall that they were selected randomly); thus, all the nodes to which they are tied will be new nodes. The sum of these new nodes and those in the original sample may then be divided by N to give the cumulative fraction of nodes reached (or contacted) at step 1. This process is then repeated, using those ties reported by the new nodes at step 1 to calculate the cumulative fraction of nodes reached at step 2. The *connectivity* of the network is defined as the average cumulative fraction of nodes reached as the number of steps approaches infinity, the average being calculated over the results obtained from several different starting samples (for further details on this tracing procedure, see Fararo and Sunshine 1964). From this definition, one can see that, as the connectivity of a network increases, so does the likelihood that two individuals (or sets of individuals) selected at random will be connected to each other.

Connectivity, as just defined, is relevant to the spread of STIs because it can affect the endemic prevalence of an infection or, in other words, the maximum proportion of the population that will become infected. This can be seen if we think of the set of people initially infected as analogous to the starting fraction described above. Those people in the population who are unconnected to this "starting fraction" will never become infected, assuming for the moment that the network is static and that they do not become infected through nonsexual means. Thus, we may think of the connectivity of a sexual network as providing a rough guide to the maximum prevalence of an STI, although in reality such reasoning is complicated by the fact that the initial set of people infected is unlikely to represent a random subset of the population.

In addition to this single measure of connectivity, however, we are also interested in the rate at which new nodes are added at subsequent steps of the tracing procedure. This rate may be related to the ultimate fraction reached, although this is not a mathematical necessity. We are interested in this rate because it limits, independent of other relevant biological and behavioral factors, the rate at which an STI can spread, measured in terms of the proportion of the population infected (Coxon 1993; Rapoport 1979). Although this rate is not included in the formal definition of *connectivity,* for the purposes of this discussion we speak of a *well-connected* network as one in which both the rate at which new nodes are added and the ultimate fraction reached are relatively high.

Unfortunately, despite the fundamental importance of network connectivity in either restricting or facilitating the spread of STIs, we are unable in most cases to measure connectivity directly. This is because it is impossible to implement the tracing procedure outlined above except in a few small, unique subgroups, owing to the enormous expense involved and the need to preserve the confidentiality of respondents and their partners. (For an example of a study in which all sexual relationships among a set of persons are enumerated, see Rothenberg et al. 1994.) This leads us to ask whether there are other features of a network that are related to its connectivity and can be measured using a standard survey instrument such as ours. In fact, there are several.

One of the factors related to a network's connectivity is the *density* of the network, defined as the proportion of all possible ties that actually occur. In general, if one network has a higher density than another, then that network will also have higher connectivity and a faster rate at which new nodes may be reached. This will always be true for random networks (Fararo and Sunshine 1964 provide a proof), and, although sexual networks are not random, it is likely that this result will still hold in many cases, particularly those where the discrepancies in density are large. Rather than calculate density directly, a procedure that is clearly impossible for networks of more than a couple hundred nodes, we may estimate it by using the fact that the density of a network may be written as an increasing function of the average number of ties (in this case, synonymous with the average number of sex partners) that each individual has (Granovetter 1976). This relation between average number of partners and density is one reason why AIDS spread rapidly among certain parts of the male homosexual community.[3] Owing to a relatively high average number of partners (McManus and McEvoy 1987; McKusick et al. 1985), the density, and thereby the connectivity, of these sexual networks was relatively high. In contrast, we know from the data reported in chapter 5 that the density of the sexual network in the national population is much lower.[4]

At any given point in time, most adults in the United States have only one sex partner (see the data in chapter 5 on the exclusivity of partnerships). Thus, the density of sexual networks—indeed, the very existence of any network structure beyond merely a collection of isolates and unconnected dyads—is dependent on the period of time over which the network is measured. This is an important issue because it highlights a fundamental difference between the

3. Another major reason was the high rate of transmission associated with anal intercourse.

4. In comparing the density of the sexual network among gay men to that of the network in the larger population, it is also important to note the large difference in size between the two. Since the number of possible ties in a network increases exponentially with the number of nodes while the number of actual ties increases only linearly, larger networks are almost always less dense than smaller networks.

analysis of sexual networks and that of other types of social networks. Most network studies have focused on social networks as they occur at a particular point in time. Even studies that have measured networks at multiple time points generally use conventional methods to characterize the network structure at each time point and then compare these results across the different periods. Yet the fact that sexual networks exist *only* through time means that we cannot study the link between these networks and the spread of STIs without explicitly confronting this inherently dynamic feature of these networks. Unfortunately, both network theory and methods have yet to address this issue.

The simplest epidemiological models address the inherently dynamic feature of sexual networks by incorporating a parameter that reflects the mean rate at which people change sex partners in the population per unit time (Anderson 1991). Heuristically, the effect of this parameter in the model is to determine, in conjunction with additional parameters measuring other behavioral and biological factors, the average number of secondary infections that are generated by a single individual during a specific period (formally referred to as the *basic reproductive rate*). The problem with this simple model is that it ignores the effects of variation in the number of partners that people have (see chapter 5 for a description of this variation). In network terms, the model fails to take into account the fact that certain individuals have large numbers of partners and thus are more likely both to become infected and to transmit that infection to others.

To remedy this deficiency, May and Anderson (1987; see also Anderson et al. 1986) have suggested that the effective value of the mean partner change rate for epidemiological purposes might be represented as the mean value, μ, plus the variance-to-mean ratio, σ^2/μ.[5] This says that increased variation in the number of partners that people have, assuming that other factors are held constant, will increase the reproductive rate of an STI. Thus, those people with the largest number of partners become very important in determining whether an STI will spread. Hethcote and Yorke (1984) coined the phrase *core group* to refer to such people, and this idea has motivated a considerable amount of subsequent research (e.g., Plummer et al. 1991; Rothenberg 1983).[6] Paradoxi-

---

5. Interestingly, Anderson and May (1988) have observed that, among a wide variety of populations, the mean (μ) and variance (σ^2) of the number of sex partners is related in the form $\sigma^2 = a\mu^b$, where b is approximately equal to 3. Blythe and Castillo-Chavez (1990) have formulated a stochastic model of pair formation to show how such a scaling law might arise.

6. In fact, there has been some debate over how *core group* should be defined. For example, several empirical studies have operationalized the concept of a core group in terms of geographic areas (Garnett and Anderson 1993; Potterat 1992)—those areas with the highest concentration of cases are referred to as the *core,* those with moderate concentrations are said to be *adjacent,* and those with low concentrations are referred to as the *periphery.* Because having more partners increases one's opportunities to become infected, core groups identified on the basis of high-prevalence areas are likely to overlap with those identified on the basis of high numbers of partners.

cally, however, simulations have shown that, while the existence of high variability in the number of sex partners increases the likelihood that an infection will spread, it also "results in a smaller fraction infected than a comparable situation with low variability in sexual activity" (Anderson 1991, 45). This result makes intuitive sense; while high variability implies the existence of a core group, it also implies the existence of many unconnected dyads (composed of people with only one partner) that are effectively shielded from infection.

In addition to variation across individuals in the rate at which they change sex partners, our data suggest a second dynamic feature of sexual networks that has not, to our knowledge, been examined within the context of models of STI transmission. In chapter 5, we showed that, although in any given year most people are likely to have only one partner, the number of partners since age eighteen is substantially higher. One hypothesis regarding this finding— what we call *punctuated equilibrium*—is that, for many people, the majority of sex partners are acquired during relatively brief periods marking the end of one long-term, exclusive relationship and the beginning of another. Unfortunately, the cross-sectional nature of our data on sex partners (recall that these were collected for only the past twelve months) does not allow us to examine this hypothesis in detail. Moreover, it is possible that this pattern does not describe those with the highest rates of acquiring partners since such people might be unlikely to have long-term relationships at all. However, to the extent that this hypothesis is correct, it may generate consequences for STI transmission since some people who would become infected during a more active phase of their life would then effectively "drop out" by acquiring a long-term partner, thereby reducing their ability to transmit the infection to others (except, of course, to their current partner).

Density is not the only factor determining connectivity in social networks.[7] A second, equally important determinant is the actual patterning of the ties that occur. For example, consider the structural location of the node H in our hypothetical network (fig. 7.1). This node has several partners; however, each of these partners, with one exception, has a direct tie only to H. Thus, were H to become infected, perhaps through his indirect tie to I, he could transmit that infection to at most four other people. By contrast, consider the location of K. If K becomes infected, he has the potential to infect many more individuals through his indirect connections with other parts of the network. From this example, it is evident that the mere existence of a subset of individuals who

7. In a random network, however, density alone determines connectivity. This fact led to the development of *biased net theory,* an approach to studying social networks in which the cumulative distribution of nodes reached at each step in an empirical network is compared with that expected from a random network in order to determine the extent to which the empirical network is "biased" or structured (Skvoretz 1990; Fararo and Sunshine 1964; Rapoport and Horvath 1961).

have many partners is not sufficient to guarantee that a disease will spread; it is also necessary that those partners be connected to the rest of the network.[8]

This issue has been the focus of several recent studies. Since in most cases it is not possible to enumerate the entire network (as we have done in our hypothetical figure), researchers have instead approached the problem by dividing the population being studied into "activity classes" based on each individual's number of partners and then attempting to measure the amount of mixing that occurs within and among these classes (Anderson, Gupta, and Ng 1990). In one set of data collected from a homosexual community (Haraldsdottir, Gupta, and Anderson 1992), it was found that mixing among activity classes was slightly dissortative or, in other words, that individuals in a particular activity class were somewhat less likely to select partners from the same activity class than would be expected by chance alone. (Note that this pattern is directly opposite to those that obtained for the various social attributes examined in section 6.3 of chapter 6.) However, it is unlikely that data from a small and unique subgroup such as this are of much value in characterizing the national population. Because we asked respondents not only about how many partners they had had but also about how many partners *their partners* had had, our data will make it possible, for the first time, to estimate the mixing patterns among so-called activity classes in the general population. These data are discussed and analyzed from an individual perspective in chapter 11.

As we might predict, simulation studies have shown that different rates of mixing within and between activity classes can have marked effects on both the rate at which an infection can spread and the maximum proportion that will become infected. Specifically, these studies show that, in situations where the overall mean rate at which people change partners is low (as it is in the general U.S. population), a strong bias toward within-class (assortative) mixing results in an increased likelihood that the infection will persist (Garnett and Anderson 1993). This is because assortative mixing increases the connectivity within the high-activity class, thereby increasing the likelihood that the infection will persist within this group. Since this group is directing relatively few of its sexual contacts to other groups, however, the vast bulk of the cases remain within this group (Anderson, Gupta, and Ng 1990).

In addition to differential association among activity classes, the homophily biases reported in table 6.3 also function to reduce the overall connectivity of the network (Fararo and Sunshine 1964, 72–82). The reason for this can best be understood by considering the extreme case in which the bias parameter is equal to 1. With regard to race, for example, this would correspond to a situa-

---

8. This idea is somewhat related to the epidemiological concept of an individual's *force of infectivity.* This is measured as the sum of the partners that an individual infects, each weighted by the length of time during which that partner has the opportunity to infect others (Rothenberg and Potterat 1988). Here is where an explicit consideration of the network could be helpful since what we really want to know is how many partners *those partners* had during the period in which they were infected.

tion in which there were no interracial partnerships. The effect on connectivity would be to reduce, independent of other factors, the maximum possible number of people to whom an individual could be connected from the entire set of nodes to the particular racially defined subset of which that individual is a member. Bias parameters less than 1, such as those we have estimated, reduce the connectivity of a network in essentially the same way.

With this in mind, let us return for a moment to the example of those parts of the male homosexual community in which the majority of AIDS cases were initially concentrated. In this instance, it is likely that the relative lack of substantial bias parameters operating on the sexual network was in part responsible for the speed with and the extent to which the disease spread. The most dramatic difference between these networks and heterosexual networks is the fact that the latter have a gender bias equal to 1 (i.e., ties between two persons with the same gender do not occur). In contrast, the fact that within a group of gay men or women, half of all possible ties are not automatically excluded increases the potential connectivity in their sexual network over that in an otherwise comparable heterosexual network. In addition, gay bathhouses and bars allow patrons to leave their social identities at the door and, once inside, to select partners solely on the basis of physical desirability. This suggests that biases with regard to various social attributes are smaller in gay networks than those that we have observed in the general population. This example is instructive, despite the fact that, because many persons with same-gender partners have also had opposite-gender partners, the sexual networks among heterosexuals and homosexuals cannot be entirely separated (see chapter 8).

As we have already discussed, an important limitation of individual bias parameters is that they provide only one possible view, with respect to a single characteristic, of the structure of a network. Real networks, however, reflect the effects of multiple biases operating simultaneously. The joint effect of these biases is to reduce the connectivity of the network considerably, making it even less conducive to the spread of STIs. To see how this occurs, look at table 7.1. This table is analogous to the differential association tables presented in chapter 6, section 6.5, except that we have used the combination of race, age, and gender to define the rows and columns. Including gender in table 7.1 means that the diagonal cells, which indicate same-gender partnerships, are relatively small. However, by including gender, we are able to represent the entire sexual network of the general population.

Two features of this table are of particular interest. The first of these concerns the large number of empty (or near empty) cells.[9] These represent "structural holes" in the network (Burt 1992)—instances in which there are no direct

---

9. Owing to our relatively small sample size, we have not attempted to make a statistical distinction between cells that represent "structural zeros" (i.e., a combination that logically cannot occur) and those that are simply small, although the effect of these on the transmission of STIs is likely to be similar. Our theoretically based hypothesis, however, is that several of these cells are in fact structural zeros because they represent combinations that are "socially impossible."

Table 7.1   Race, Age, and Gender of Respondents and Their Sex Partners (row percentages), Nonmarital Partnerships Only (oversample included)

	Partners																		
	White						Black						Hispanic						
	< 30		30–44		45+		< 30		30–44		45+		< 30		30–44		45+		
Respondents	M	F	M	F	M	F	M	F	M	F	M	F	M	F	M	F	M	F	N
White																			
18–29:																			
Male	2.4	79.9	1.3	10.1	...	...	.2	.2	...	.4	...	...	.2	1.8	...	...	...	...	552
Female	69.1	1.8	15.1	1.0	1.0	...	4.1	...	.8	...	...	...	3.1	...	1.3	...	...	...	392
30–44:																			
Male	1.9	21.5	4.9	60.6	1.2	3.7	...	.2	...	.5	1.0	...	...	.9	.4	1.2	.2	...	571
Female	7.8	1.2	60.5	4.2	15.7	...	.7	...	2.9	...	...	.2	...	.2	2.5	...	.2	...	408
45–59:																			
Male	.7	.7	3.4	40.9	.7	46.3	...	...	.8	...	...	...	...	...	...	1.3	...	1.3	149
Female	...	...	21.9	1.6	64.8	4.7	.8	...	.8	...	3.1	...	...	...	...	.8	.8	...	128

Black

												N
18–29:												
Male	7.5	...	1.2	...	.6	77.5	5.8	...	...	5.2	.6	173
Female	...	.7	...	...	68.5	25.3	...	.7	3.4	...	...	146
30–44:												
Male	1.0	1.4	6.7	2.9	.5	14.9	51.0	5.8	...	1.9	2.4	208
Female	1.4	...	.9	...	5.2	70.3	10.8	.9	...	.5	.5	212
45–59:												
Male	...	...	1.7	...	...	...	31.7	63.3	...	...	1.7	60
Female	...	...	...	...	1.8	19.3	71.9	3.5	...	...	3.5	57

Hispanic

												N
18–29:												
Male	3.7	31.7	4.9	2.4	1.2	1.2	...	...	...	31.7	4.9	82
Female	16.4	...	3.0	...	16.4	1.5	...	...	46.3	1.5	1.5	67
30–44:												
Male	13.6	7.6	27.3	1.5	...	...	...	...	1.5	10.6	28.8	66
Female	23.9	...	7.5	...	1.5	...	...	...	6.0	34.3	1.5	67
45–59:												
Male	21.1	...	...	15.8	15.8	...	...	...	...	...	31.6	19
Female	...	...	...	...	...	...	...	...	...	100	15.8	2

Note: Percentages may not add to 100 percent owing to partners whose racial/ethnic background was not among those listed here (these cases are included in the row totals). "..." indicates fewer than thirty cases.

ties between particular pairs of groups. One way to understand the effect of these structural holes on the spread of STIs is to think of the entire population as a building in which each of the eighteen subgroups is a room and each pair of rooms is connected by a separate door. Following this analogy, each empty cell in the table may be likened to a closed door. Now, let us simulate the presence of an STI by imagining a group of people beginning in one room and attempting to circulate into the various other rooms. The closed doors decrease the speed with which these people can get to certain rooms and, in some cases, may prevent people from getting to a room entirely. What is important to understand here is that this table represents a *conservative* estimate of the connectivity in the population since education, religion, and many other characteristics that we did not measure (e.g., political orientation, geographic location) are excluded.

Although two groups may have no direct ties between them, this does not necessarily imply that they are completely unconnected. For example, in our hypothetical network, the set of nodes consisting of K, L, and M has no direct ties to the set consisting of I, H, F, and G; yet the two are indirectly connected through node J. In this case, we say that J acts as a *bridge* between K and I. More generally, we may define a node as a bridge between two other sets of nodes if removal of that node results in the two sets being unconnected from each other. Similarly, we may extend this definition by defining a subpopulation as a bridge between two other subpopulations if removal of the first results in the latter two being unconnected. This concept may be used to explain why AIDS—a disease that originated within the male homosexual community— has remained concentrated within that community. Bisexuals provide the only sexual bridge between this community and the larger population, and, since the number of bisexuals is quite small,[10] this bridge is a rather ineffective one.

Just as bisexuals provide a bridge between homosexual and heterosexual populations, many of the subgroups represented in table 7.1 may act as bridges between two subgroups that are not directly connected. Unfortunately, this table does not provide sufficient information to determine whether this is the case. This is because, in order for a subgroup to act as a bridge between two others, the same people in that subgroup have to have sex with members from each of the other two groups, and this cannot be determined from an aggregate table such as table 7.1 We are currently working on ways to represent and analyze this rather complex information.

It is this issue of the *social* structure of partnering that epidemiological research has been slowest to address. There are two basic reasons for this. One of these has been the lack (until now) of empirical data on the social organization of sexual networks.[11] A second reason has to do with the complexities

---

10. Although many gay men have had some sexual interactions with women, such activity tends to be limited to certain periods of their lifetime (for a discussion of this point, see chapter 8).

11. For an exception, see Rothenberg and Potterat (1988).

associated with incorporating such data into specific models. The most common method for incorporating information about the structure of sexual networks into epidemiological models is to divide the population into a set of distinct groups and to introduce a "mixing matrix" describing the amount of sexual partnering within and between groups (Morris 1989, 1993; Blythe, Castillo-Chavez, and Palmer 1991). This mixing matrix is essentially equivalent to the differential association tables presented in chapter 6, with the row proportions being used to characterize each cell. The mathematical advantage of this approach is that it may be treated as a special case of the traditional *mass action model* in epidemiology, and, thus, much of the standard mathematical apparatus can be preserved.[12]

This approach, however, has several significant limitations. One of these has to do with estimating the elements of the mixing matrix from actual data. According to formal models, the mixing matrix must satisfy certain symmetry constraints, constraints that, as can be seen from tables 6.7, 6.8, and 6.9, are not likely to be satisfied by actual data. Although methods have been proposed for manipulating the data so that they obey these constraints, such methods are essentially ad hoc.

A more important issue concerns the fact that the size of the mixing matrix increases exponentially with the number of subgroups considered (e.g., simply adding three educational categories to table 7.1 would increase the number of cells from 324 to 2,916). As a result, the number of cases in each cell decreases rapidly, and, thus, so does the statistical precision with which we are able to estimate the true size of each cell in the population. Compounding this problem is the fact that, as we know from chapter 3, there is significant variation across these attributional subgroups in the extent to which members engage in specific sexual activities. As a result, the network ties reflected by the partnerships in a table such as 7.1 differ in their potential for transmitting specific STIs.

Using the information in sparse tables such as table 7.1 to construct and test models of the sexual network in the general population represents a formidable statistical task. However, we emphasize that a crucial part of such modeling efforts will involve developing a sociologically informed theory of how sexual networks are structured. For example, studies of adult friendship have shown that the likelihood of a friendship occurring between members of two different occupational groups is largely a function of the difference in social prestige between the two groups; the larger the difference, the less likely it is that the friendship will occur (Laumann 1973; Verbrugge 1977). Were such a model

---

12. This is generally referred to as a *compartmental* or *deterministic* approach within the epidemiological literature. There is another approach—labeled *stochastic*—in which the sexual network is modeled as a set of points located in either a continuous or a discrete space (e.g., Altmann 1993). In such models, the probability of contact (in this case, sexual activity) occurring between two individuals is determined by their proximity in the space. Although these models have the potential to capture more detail than do compartmental models, the data requirements are also considerably greater.

to apply in the case of sexual partnerships, it would provide a parsimonious description of tables such as table 7.1. It is likely, however, that even if such models are partially applicable to sexual relationships, they will have to be modified to take into account the many unique features of sexual relationships.

Finally, as we have already pointed out, aggregate tables such as those in chapter 6, section 6.5, and even table 7.1 fail to capture certain types of higher-order structure. Thus, bridging groups and other network features involving indirect ties are not explicitly represented. This is an important limitation that can be corrected only through modification of the existing models.

Clearly, much careful work will need to be done before the information contained in the data we have collected can be translated into formal models that will allow us both to explain the path that AIDS has taken in the population thus far and, more important, to predict the path that it will take in the future. On a less formal level, however, we believe that these data offer a convincing explanation of why AIDS has not achieved as high a prevalence in the general population as was originally thought. This, of course, is not meant to belittle the tragic effects of the infection. Nor are we denying the fact that many people will continue to become infected with the disease, many of these through heterosexual contact. We are suggesting, however, that the general lack of connectivity present in sexual networks among adults in the United States, together with the relatively low transmission probability of AIDS through vaginal intercourse, will significantly restrict the extent to which this disease will spread into the general population.

CHAPTER 8

Homosexuality

Perhaps no other single number in this study will attract greater public interest than our estimate of the prevalence of homosexuality.[1] Dramatic evidence of this popular interest is found in the recent protracted debates over President Clinton's proposal to eliminate the ban on gays in the military and the responses of the Congress and the military itself to such a proposition. Given the highly charged political atmosphere in which all sides adduced wildly contradictory statistics in support of their claims, we want to be especially careful that our data and interpretations are put forward in as responsible and straightforward a manner as possible. Of course, we have no way of controlling or even anticipating the ways in which our findings will be used, but we do want to avoid obvious misinterpretations wherever possible. In short, neither pedantry nor extreme scientific cautiousness leads us to assert that estimating a single number for the prevalence of homosexuality is a futile exercise because it presupposes assumptions that are patently false: that homosexuality is a uniform attribute across individuals, that it is stable over time, and that it can be easily measured.

Estimating the prevalence of various forms of sexual behavior is at the very heart of our research. In fact, the lack of data on the prevalence of men who have sex with other men was a major motivation for the original federally funded project that led to this study. By the mid-1980s, it was clear that the majority of AIDS cases involved men who had sex with men (Institute of Med-

---

We gratefully acknowledge the assistance with data analysis provided by Fang Li and Dawne Moon. The chapter was drafted and the bulk of the data analysis performed by Stuart Michaels.

1. We have used the terms *homosexuality* and *same-gender sex* or *sexuality* interchangeably in this chapter. We mean these terms to be taken as descriptive of specific partnerships, practices, or feelings. There are some problems with this usage. *Homosexual* and *homosexuality* (and, slightly later, *heterosexual* and *heterosexuality*) are late nineteenth-century creations and bear the mark of their development in a period of the medicalization of sexuality (Katz 1983; Foucault 1978; Chauncey 1983; and Halperin 1990). In particular, they are associated with the emergence of the notion of sexual types or beings defined in terms of the gender of their sex partners or related attributes. We have tried to avoid evoking these notions and to distance our discussion from inferences about etiology, associations, and consequences of the behaviors and feelings reported. *Gay* and *lesbian* as alternative terms referring to sexual patterns have the disadvantage of being associated with a particular historical moment and social (and often political) self-identification. The latter involves issues such as participation in a community and culture that are beyond the current research and its primary focus on the sexual. (For a related discussion in the context of the consideration of the work of Kinsey, see Gagnon 1990).

icine 1986; Shilts 1988). These early cases were men who had had many male sex partners recruited from the gay communities of a handful of major cities on the East and West Coasts (Klovdahl 1986). We also knew that the infectious agent (HIV) could be transmitted sexually and that certain practices, such as anal intercourse, were much more efficient routes of transmission than others. What we did not know was how many men engaged in these practices, the extent to which these men were concentrated in large cities, how they thought of themselves, how many partners they had, and so on. These data are needed to make projections about the spread of the disease, to identify the locations of the next phase of the epidemic, and to illuminate the social and attitudinal correlates of these behaviors.

The social stigma attached to homosexuality creates an added challenge for us. Homosexuality in Western societies has historically been viewed as a sin, a disease, or an aberration. These notions are still extremely widespread. During the twenty years prior to this survey, from 1972 to 1991, an overwhelming majority (over 70 percent) of the U.S. adult population has answered that homosexuality is always wrong in response to a question asked annually as part of the General Social Survey.[2] In spite of this apparent stability in public opinion over a long period of time, the past twenty-five years have seen a notable increase in the legitimation and visibility of homosexuality, in part the result of a growing political movement of lesbians and gay men.

The findings from our research need to be understood in this context. The widespread, strongly negative view of homosexuality shapes both behaviors and our attempts to measure them. While we have attempted to be nonjudgmental in our inquiries, many respondents are likely to have been reluctant to report behaviors and feelings that they think might reflect badly on them in the eyes of the interviewers or the researchers. The estimates derived from survey data on socially stigmatized sexual behaviors and feelings, whether they be masturbation, homosexual relations, anal sex, or extramarital affairs, are no doubt lower-bound estimates.

Independent of questions of valuation and judgment, recent writing and thinking about homosexuality can be divided into two major camps. These two basic views of homosexuality (and many minor variants of them) can be found both in popular thought and in more theoretical and scientific debates. These two perspectives have come to be called *essentialism* and *social constructionism* (Foucault 1978; Greenberg 1988; Halperin 1990; Stein 1992).[3]

---

2. The question asks specifically about whether "sexual relations between two adults of the same sex" are "always wrong, almost always wrong, wrong only sometimes, or not wrong at all." From 1972 to 1991, the most negative category of the four possible has averaged 73 percent. The exact wording of the question, repeated in the NHSLS, can be found in appendix C, section 10, question 4. During the same time, a substantial minority, and often even a majority, of Americans have opposed discrimination against homosexuals.

3. The basic division that will be described is quite independent of the valuation of homosexuality. People who accept one basic viewpoint or the other can hold either pro- or anti-gay beliefs. Social constructionism was mainly developed by pro-gay intellectuals. However, in denying the

Essentialism in various forms is probably the most widespread view, especially in popular thinking, although it also has many proponents among scholars and researchers. An essentialist view of homosexuality is closely related to perspectives that view sexuality through an individualistic, biological, or psychological lens. Those who explain sexuality as the expression of certain fundamental biological drives are likely to view homosexuality in such terms as well. In this view, homosexuality is thought of as defining a separate species of sexual being, the homosexual. The paradigmatic form of this thinking is a kind of biological or genetic causal model. The category *homosexual* describes an aspect of a person that corresponds to some objective core or inner essence of the person. Homosexuality is treated as analogous to similar views of gender or race, where, while the biological and social are seen as quite separate, the former is seen as producing a set of outcomes that, in turn, have social consequences and responses. All members of the categories in these various domains (be they men or women, heterosexuals or homosexuals, whites, blacks, or Asians) share an essential feature that is identical. Usually this essence is thought to be a single quality—for example, an X and a Y chromosome—that leads to external physical attributes (genitalia, etc.). Or this essence may be thought to be a range along a dimension—perhaps like skin color or levels of male hormone. People within this range are clearly to be distinguished from others.

Social constructionism, on the other hand, almost always involves a description and critique of essentialism. This is because elements of essentialism are so much a part of the "taken-for-granted," commonsense view that they need to be brought explicitly into focus. Constructionism examines the implicit assumptions of our thinking about sexual preferences and orientations and questions their universality. It emphasizes the historical and cultural variability of such sexual categories as *homosexuality* and *heterosexuality,* stressing how conceptions of sexual orientation and practices have changed over time and vary across societies. It raises questions about how the categories emerge, are maintained, and change.

We cannot adjudicate the conceptual and theoretical differences between these two opposing positions and their many variants. The data from a cross-sectional survey conducted in a single country at a given moment are simply inappropriate to resolve these issues. While our general theoretical framework is highly compatible with the social constructionist approach, the data themselves can certainly be treated from various points of view. A population-based survey lends itself to a continuous, multifaceted approach to defining and measuring homosexuality. It makes more sense to ask about specific aspects of

---

innateness of homosexuality, some of their arguments have recently been taken up by the right-wing anti-gay forces, who believe that homosexuality is a sin and want to argue that homosexuality is a choice. Views of homosexuality as a pathological condition or disease have traditionally sought its "cause," an essentialist notion, usually to cure or eradicate it. Ironically, today, many gay people are strong believers in some version of essentialism.

same-gender behavior, practice, and feelings during specific periods of an individual's life rather than a single yes-or-no question about whether a person is homosexual. This approach opens up the possibility of asking about the interrelation of these various elements. Rather than assuming that homosexuality is a single, uniform trait with the same underlying cause and the same outcome in all people, one can begin to look at variation in the aspects and extent of homosexual activity in different individuals.

As an underlying orientation, essentialist notions of homosexuality, on the other hand, correspond to widespread assumptions that many, if not most, of the respondents to our survey believe. Their answers are likely to reflect these conceptions, even if reality is more complex. For example, if respondents think that there are basically two types of people in the world, homosexuals and heterosexuals, they are likely to think about their own behavior in those terms. If those respondents see themselves as fundamentally heterosexual but have had on occasion homosexual feelings or experiences, they may simply not report such feelings or behaviors because they are not "real" or "truly indicative" of their underlying nature.

An essentialist view also pervades much of the discussion of the prevalence of homosexuality. Many of the questions and debates about the number and distribution of homosexuals in the population implicitly assume a clearly identifiable and easily quantifiable phenomenon. These questions also implicitly assume that the instances to be counted are all the same. We argue that these notions are incorrect.

8.1 Prior Research on the Prevalence of Homosexuality

Much public attention has been focused recently on the question of the prevalence of homosexuality. Much of this popular interest has been aroused by hotly contested debates about social control and civil rights. Passion runs high on all sides. Debates about how widespread homosexuality is, its causes, and its nature play key roles in arguments about public policies involving the extension, protection, or prohibition of certain rights. In the process, scientific exploration and hypotheses have been held hostage or used in inappropriate ways.

One of the many ironies of our research effort is that politicians such as Senator Jesse Helms and former Representative William Dannemeyer, who represented the extreme Right on these issues, led the attacks against the federal efforts to carry out national surveys of sexual behavior in large part because they were convinced that these studies would help legitimate homosexuality by demonstrating how widespread it was. At the time, 1988–92, while unwilling to accept the widely held notion that 10 percent of the population was homosexual, they feared that surveys might help promote this idea or even increase the estimated proportion to 20 percent. Yet all the recent population-based surveys of sexual behavior, including this one, have found rates that are much lower than 10 percent. Before considering the matter settled, however, there are a number of questions that need to be addressed. First, what was the empirical basis of the widely accepted figure of 10 percent? How much credence should it have been given? How should the results from a number of different surveys be interpreted? Are there other notions about homosexuality that should be revised in addition to the fairly widely accepted idea about its prevalence?

8.2 The Myth of 10 Percent and the Kinsey Research

It is beyond the scope of this chapter to explain why so many people, both the lay public and professional researchers, came to believe in a 10 percent figure so firmly, but it is worth discussing its probable origin. Strangely enough, both a strong argument against the notion that there is a single prevalence rate of homosexuality and a single estimate of 10 percent come from the same source, Alfred Kinsey (Kinsey, Pomeroy, and Martin 1948; Kinsey et al. 1953).

In chapter 2, we criticized the lack of probability samples in Kinsey's research, and we also acknowledged his important pioneering role in the study of human sexuality. He found, as we have, that, in order to ask people questions and expect reasonable and interpretable answers about their sexual experiences, one must be both direct and precise. In particular, one must specify clearly and simply the behaviors and the time period in which one is interested. The results of such queries, moreover, cannot be reduced to simple categorizations.

In particular, Kinsey argued strongly against the notion that the world can be split neatly into two classes, homosexuals and heterosexuals. To avoid this error, Kinsey reported many numbers rather than one. We do the same. It is in the nature of an empirical study of a complex pattern of behavior across a large and variable population to do so.

Let us briefly review Kinsey's numbers and see how they compare to the numbers reported in this research and other recent surveys. It is important to point out that much of the debate on prevalence has been about men, although sometimes this is only implicit.[4] In summarizing the rates of homosexuality among the white men he interviewed, Kinsey lists thirteen different statistics. A few of these numbers stand out either conceptually or because they have often been repeated. To provide a sense of the range as well as the specificity and style of Kinsey's statements, some are quoted here:

4. There are many reasons for this. Kinsey's figures for men appeared first (in 1948) and were presented more explicitly than the later discussion of women (1953). Kinsey's primary measure of sexual behavior was the orgasm, and this turned out to be a much easier measure to use with men than with women (see chapter 3). Historically, there has been a certain invisibility of lesbianism, and the debates about homosexuality have tended to reflect this. This can be seen in the terminology itself. *Homosexual* and *homosexuality* have no inherent gender reference—they denote sex between people of the same gender. Yet they have often been used to refer solely to men.

37 percent of the total male population has **at least some overt homosex-ual experience** to the point of orgasm between adolescence and old age. This accounts for nearly 2 males out of every 5 that one may meet. . . .

50 percent of all males (approximately) **have neither overt nor psychic** experience in the homosexual after the onset of adolescence. . . .

25 percent of the male population **has more than incidental homosex-ual experience** or reactions (i.e., rates 2–6) for at least three years between the ages of 16 and 55. In terms of averages, one male out of approximately every four has had or will have such distinct and continued homosexual expe-rience. . . .

10 percent of the males are **more or less exclusively homosexual** (i.e., rate 5 or 6) for at least three years between the ages of 16 and 55. This is one male in ten in the white male population. . . .

4 percent of the white males are **exclusively homosexual throughout their lives,** after the onset of adolescence. (Kinsey, Pomeroy, and Martin 1948, 650–51)

This section in the Kinsey volume on men, with its boldface type, has al-ways been easy to find and has been much quoted and cited.[5] Kinsey begins the list with 37 percent, which represents a measure of "any homosexual expe-rience," and ends with 4 percent, which represents a measure of "exclusive homosexuality." These seem to correspond to "folk" notions of what consti-tutes homosexuality. To many, homosexuality of any sort seems so foreign and deviant that any homosexual experience is enough to define someone as homo-sexual. On the other hand, exclusive homosexuality has often been treated as the expected state for the "true homosexual."[6] Of course, one reason for re-porting the data this way is to emphasize the variation in the mixture of hetero-sexual and homosexual experience, something that Kinsey was trying to do. (This seems a major function of the 50 percent figure that refers to the propor-tion of men who had not had any homosexual experience after puberty, whether or not it resulted in orgasm. Of course, that means that 50 percent of the men in Kinsey's sample had some sort of homosexual experience.)

Many people have pointed to the 10 percent figure in this passage and cited it as the source for the conventional population estimate of homosexual preva-lence. In fact, of course, this number refers only to men (white men at that), whereas 10 percent has been most commonly used to refer to the whole popu-

5. Kinsey and his colleagues did not report comparable numbers for women in their 1953 vol-ume. Instead, they found that women reported lower levels of homosexual activity, generally a half to a third the comparable levels for men (Kinsey et al. 1953, 474–75).

6. These notions are not confined to everyday life and folklore. In a recent short discussion of homosexuality, Billy et al. (1993) highlighted just such measures. Among their respondents, men between the ages of twenty and thirty-nine, 2.3 percent had at least one homosexual experience, and 1.1 percent had had exclusively homosexual experiences for the past ten years. (Note that this includes experiences of boys as young as ten years old.) The press devoted a lot of attention to this report, particularly to the second number of about 1 percent representing exclusively homosexual experience, often treating it as an estimate of the size of the gay population (Barringer 1993).

lation, male and female.[7] The choice of 10 percent as the single estimate to take from this list represents an interesting compromise. Its attraction seems to reside in the fact that it is a simple round number and one that is neither "too small" nor "too large." It avoids the extremes of counting someone as homosexual who engages in such activity only sporadically and not counting people with extensive homosexual experience who have also had heterosexual experiences.

Kinsey's figures are much higher than those found in all the recent population surveys, including ours. There are a number of reasons for this. As emphasized in chapter 2, the major difference between Kinsey and recent research is that Kinsey did not use probability sampling. Kinsey's respondents were all purposefully recruited rather than sampled with known probabilities of inclusion. This means both that they were volunteers who may have differed in systematic ways from those who did not participate (e.g., by being more open and comfortable about their sex lives and perhaps more sexually active) and that there is no statistically sound way to generalize from his sample to a population. In fact, Kinsey roamed far and wide in selecting his subjects. He was not averse to using institutional settings, including prisons and reform schools, from which to recruit his subjects. Kinsey also purposely recruited subjects for his research from homosexual friendship and acquaintance networks in big cities. Kinsey combined fantasy, masturbation, and sexual activity with partners in some of his calculations (e.g., the 50 percent figure). Experiences were collected retrospectively over the whole lifetime and almost as a matter of course were reported to include activity since puberty or since age sixteen. These devices would all tend to bias Kinsey's results toward higher estimates of homosexuality (and other rarer sexual practices) than those that he would have obtained using probability sampling.[8] Almost all the recent sexual behavior research, largely prompted by AIDS and the sexual transmission of disease, has focused on behavior, primarily penetrative sexual practices.

7. In fact, Bruce Voeller (1990) claims to have originated the 10 percent estimate as part of the modern gay rights movement's campaign in the late 1970s to convince politicians and the public that "We [gays and lesbians] Are Everywhere." At the time, Voeller was the chair of the National Gay Task Force. He says that, using Kinsey, he averaged a 13 percent number for men and a 7 percent number for women to come up with an approximate number of 10 percent for the whole population.

8. A reanalysis of a subset of the Kinsey data on men (Gagnon and Simon 1973, 131–32) demonstrated how much early experience contributed to the higher numbers. Analyzing the data from young men in college between 1938 and 1950, a group that was thought to be less subject to volunteer bias and other forms of selection that might have artificially increased the rate of same-gender experience (e.g., incarceration or being referred through homosexual networks), Gagnon and Simon found that about 30 percent had at least one homosexual experience (roughly comparable to the 37 percent quoted earlier). But, for over half these men (16 percent of the total), this experience was before the age of fifteen and not after, and, for another 9 percent, this experience was primarily in adolescence and had completely ended by age twenty. The remainder, about 5 or 6 percent, was equally divided between those who had exclusively homosexual experience and

There is one other fundamental difference between the Kinsey approach and contemporary surveys. Kinsey and a handful of highly trained colleagues conducted all the interviews. The structure of the Kinsey interview was a "sex history," and people were taken through their lifetime in segments. They were intensively questioned about a wide variety of forms of sexual activity, including fantasies. The focus seems to have been largely on numbers of orgasms achieved in various ways. Having no written and fixed questionnaire, the interviewers memorized the question order, and wording could be varied by the interviewer as he (or occasionally she) saw fit. These interviewers were not averse to challenging respondents who they believed were not admitting to stigmatized behaviors such as masturbation or homosexuality. The interview took respondents chronologically from their early childhood experiences to the time of the interview. It asked a lot about fantasy. The emphasis on ideation and the encouragement of subjects to describe homosexual thoughts and fantasies may have increased reports of other homosexual behaviors as well. It is possible that some of these techniques may have increased the disclosure and reporting of stigmatized activities.

8.3   Dimensions of Homosexuality

To quantify or count something requires unambiguous definition of the phenomenon in question. And we lack this in speaking of homosexuality. When people ask how many gays there are, they assume that everyone knows exactly what is meant. Historians and anthropologists have shown that homosexuality as a category describing same-gender sexual desire and behavior is a relatively recent phenomenon (only about 100 years old) peculiar to the West (Foucault 1978; Chauncey 1983; Katz 1983; Halperin 1990; Stein 1992). But, even within contemporary Western societies, one must ask whether this question refers to same-gender behavior, desire, self-definition, or identification or some combination of these elements. In asking the question, most people treat homosexuality as such a distinctive category that it is as if all these elements must go together. On reflection, it is obvious that this is not true. One can easily think of cases where any one of these elements would be present without the

---

those who had "substantial homosexual as well as heterosexual histories." One still wonders at the almost one-third who reported any homosexual experience compared to a maximal figure in our survey for a similar group of 10–12 percent (see table 8.2 below under *any sex*). One possibility suggested to us by our colleague George Chauncey is that this may in part reflect historical changes in the sex lives of American men. Remember that Kinsey was interviewing in the years surrounding World War II (1938–47) and that the sex lives being described would have extended back from then, whereas our oldest respondents were born in 1933. Changes in the structure of adolescence as well as the increasing visibility and labeling of homosexuality may inhibit the amount of adolescent sexual experimentation that goes on among young men more recently.

others and that combinations of these attributes, taken two or three at a time, are also possible.

Examples abound. Some people have fantasies or thoughts about sex with someone of their own gender without ever acting on these thoughts or wishes. And the holder of such thoughts may be pleased, excited, or upset and made to feel guilty by them. They may occur as a passing phase, only sporadically, or even as a persisting feature of a person's fantasy life. They may or may not have any effect at all on whether a person thinks of himself or herself as a homosexual in any sense. Clearly, there are people who experience erotic interest in people of both genders and sustain sexual relationships over time with both men and women. Some engage in sex with same-gender partners without any erotic or psychological desire because they have been forced or enticed into doing so. A classic example is sex in prison. Deprived of the opportunity to have sex with opposite-gender partners gives rise to same-gender sex, by volition or as the result of force. Surely this is to be distinguished phenomenally from situations in which people who, given access to both genders, actively seek out and choose to have sex with same-gender partners. Development of self-identification as homosexual or gay is a psychologically and socially complex state, something which, in this society, is achieved only over time, often with considerable personal struggle and self-doubt, not to mention social discomfort. All these motives, attractions, identifications, and behaviors vary over time and circumstances with respect to one another—that is, are dynamically changing features of an individual's sexual expression.

This discussion postulates no specific theory or viewpoint on the etiology and nature of homosexuality—another much contested terrain. Instead, we took as our starting point the need to collect good descriptive data on various features of same-gender practices and affect. For these descriptive purposes, we have identified three dimensions of homosexuality: same-gender sexual behavior (and its associated practices), same-gender desire and sexual attraction, and self-identity as a homosexual. We have paid most attention to behavior. Public health concerns about AIDS lent priority to questions about behaviors that place people at risk. Also, behavior seemed to be one of the least ambiguous elements of sexuality in general and homosexuality in particular. However, as soon as one thinks of the widely divergent meanings of a given sexual act to the participants, one begins to appreciate the oversimplification inherent in an exclusively behavioral approach. The prisoner in the state penitentiary who takes sex where he finds it and the young man cruising a city park, a known haunt of gay men, are engaging in meaningfully different, if superficially similar, behaviors.

We have broken the *behavioral* dimension itself into three separate aspects: the gender of sex partners, specific sexual acts or techniques, and the time frame within which sexual relationships or activities take place. We treat same-gender dyads and their sexual practices just as opposite-gender dyads and practices.[9] Rather than assuming that the world is made up of two very different types of sexual beings, homosexuals and heterosexuals, we make no assumption about inherent differences between various sexual practices and have let the distinctions, if any, emerge from the data.

Behavior is only one component of sexuality. It has been the focus of most of the recent discussions about the prevalence of homosexuality since these are the data emerging from AIDS-related surveys. While we, too, have emphasized sexual behavior, we have also investigated the *affective* or *cognitive* dimension. While these data are more limited, they allow us to ask some interesting questions about their relation to the behavioral aspect of same-gender sexuality. We cannot understand behavior without some sense of how the actor thinks about his or her actions and their relation to internal, psychological states and the actor's relation to others. The more psychological literature on homosexuality has emphasized internal states related to sexual desire. Especially before AIDS, homosexuality was viewed as an underlying sexual orientation, with desire for or sexual interest in people of the same gender treated as more fundamental than behavior (Marmor 1980). On the other hand, much of the sociological, historical, and social psychological work of the 1970s, following the dramatic emergence of the lesbian and gay civil rights movement, has emphasized the process of "coming out," the development of self-consciousness, and a relatively public sexual identity in the context of an emerging lesbian and gay community (Weinberg and Williams 1974; Levine 1979; Herdt 1992).[10]

8.4   Measurement and Prevalence of Same-Gender Behavior, Desire, and Identity

For the purpose of this analysis, we have divided the questions that relate to homosexual experiences and feelings into three basic dimensions: behavior,

9. It may surprise readers to realize that almost all the data reported in this book were generated without mention of the word *homosexual* or *heterosexual*. These words are used only once, late in the questionnaire, when we asked, "Do you think of yourself as heterosexual, homosexual, bisexual, or something else?" (see appendix C, section 8, question 49). All the behavioral data were generated from questions that asked only about specific partners or practices. In the case of partners, either the respondent had identified a partner and was then asked about the partner's gender (these questions always stated that all partners, whether men or women, should be included; e.g., see appendix C, section 2, question 1, and section 4, question 1), or the respondent was asked about how many male and female partners he or she had had of a given type in a given time period. At the very end of the questionnaire, respondents were asked whether they had ever engaged in specific sexual acts. These acts and questions were specified separately for male and female partners (appendix C, SAQ 4F and SAQ 4M).

10. Of course, there are any number of other aspects of personality and social interaction that one might consider. Historically, homosexuality was thought of as being associated with femininity in men and masculinity in women. Over time, the primary definitions of homosexuality have been separated from these notions, although incompletely (Green 1987). AIDS-related research, in particular, has ignored these dimensions almost completely. Issues related to social identity and its relation to an organized set of institutions or a community have also been neglected in surveys. Some have pointed to the need to investigate social and emotional preferences for people of one's own gender, sometimes called *homosociality* (Klein 1990).

desire, and identity. The questions that we asked about behavior always refer to partners or practices in specific time frames. Desire and identity are measured by questions about the respondents' current states of mind. Because of the many ways in which these three aspects of sexuality might be defined, we first explain how we operationalized them in our questionnaire and then compare their reported frequencies, before turning to an investigation of their interrelations.

Two quite different questions were asked to ascertain the presence of same-gender sexual "desire." The first asked about the appeal of sex with someone of the same gender, the second about the gender of the people to whom the respondent is sexually attracted. These questions appear toward the end of the interview after the main questions about partners and behavior. The first question was worded, "On a scale of 1 to 4, where 1 is very appealing and 4 is not at all appealing, how would you rate each of these activities: . . . having sex with someone of the same sex?" (see appendix C, section 7, question 4). For this analysis, the two answers "very appealing" and "somewhat appealing" are combined and treated as indicating the presence of homosexual desire. We call this measure *appeal.*

Later in the interview, at the end of a set of questions about early childhood and first sexual experiences, women were asked, "In general, are you sexually attracted to only men, mostly men, both men and women, mostly women, only women?" (see appendix C, section 8, question 47). Men were asked the same question (appendix C, section 8, question 48), except that the order of the answer categories was reversed. Respondents answering with any of the four categories referring to people of the same gender are treated here as expressing some level of homosexual desire. We refer to this variable as *attraction.*

Immediately following the question about attraction, a single question was asked about how respondents think of themselves: "Do you think of yourself as heterosexual, homosexual, bisexual, or something else?" (appendix C, section 8, question 49). This question yielded our measure of self-identification.[11] For the purpose of this analysis, we have treated respondents who said either "homosexual" or "bisexual" as having some degree of same-gender identity. Altogether, 2.8 percent of the men and 1.4 percent of the women reported some level of homosexual (or bisexual) identity.[12]

11. This question posed several problems. First, about 5 percent of the men and 6 percent of the women seemed to be uncertain about the meaning of these terms and gave answers that were coded by interviewers as equivalent to "normal or straight." In addition, under 1 percent of the respondents (thirteen men and ten women in the cross section) answered "something else" and were prompted to explain. A few of these (two men and four women) said "gay" or "lesbian" and have been included with those who chose "homosexual." Two respondents said that they did not distinguish partners on the basis of their sex (gender). They appeared to be defining themselves as bisexual, but we were hesitant to recode them as such until we checked their sexual experience. Since they had had both male and female partners, we included them with the bisexuals.

12. It would be interesting to compare and contrast homosexual (and gay/lesbian) identity with bisexual identity, but the numbers in a sample like ours are just too small. Fewer than 1 percent of

We have constructed five different measures of same-gender behavior. Figure 8.1 displays these measures for men and women as well as the affective measures described above. On the left in the figure are three measures based on the proportion of men and women who report same-gender sex partners in three different time periods: the past twelve months, the past five years, and since turning eighteen.[13] The rates for women are lower than the rates for men, varying from 1.3 percent of the sexually active women in the past year reporting at least one female partner to 4.1 percent reporting any female partners since turning eighteen. The rates for men vary from 2.7 percent in the past year to 4.9 percent with any male partners since age eighteen. The next two sets of bars labeled *any age* and *any sex* extend the period for same-gender sex back to puberty. Conceptually, they measure the same thing; however, they approach the measurement in different ways and produce different estimates, especially for the men.

Any age is a measure of the proportion of respondents who have had a same-gender partner at any time since puberty. It is constructed by combining responses from the previous three partner/time frame questions (past year, past five years, and since age eighteen) and the response to a question about the first sexual experience after puberty with a person of the same gender.[14] About 3.8 percent of the women and 7.1 percent of the men had had at least one same-gender partner since puberty according to this variable.

Any sex is based on questions asked on a self-administered questionnaire (SAQ) at the very end of the interview. The interviewer does not see the answers to these questions because the SAQ is placed in an envelope and sealed by the respondent before being handed back. These questions ask about ever having engaged in specific sexual activities with a man or woman since puberty. Both male and female respondents were asked about active and receptive oral sex and the question, "Have you ever done anything else sexual with another (woman/man)?" (see appendix C, SAQ 4F, questions 8–11, and SAQ 4M, questions 8–12). Male respondents were also asked about active and receptive anal sex with another man. *Any sex* is the proportion of respondents who completed the self-administered questionnaire who answered yes to any of the activities. Over 4 percent of the women and 9 percent of the men reported having

the men and women said that they were bisexual. Later in this chapter, we look at the mixture of male and female partners among the larger group reporting any same-gender partners, but without necessarily self-identifying as bisexual.

13. The base *N*'s for these rates include all people on whom we have information. In particular, they include the sexually inactive, who have no partners in a given time frame. In that sense, these are incidence and prevalence rates for partnering behavior.

14. The exact wording of the question is, "Now I would like to ask you some questions about sexual experience with (SAME SEX AS R; males/females) after you were 12 or 13, that is, after puberty. How old were you the first time you had sex with a (SAME SEX AS R; male/female)?" (see appendix C, section 8, question 40).

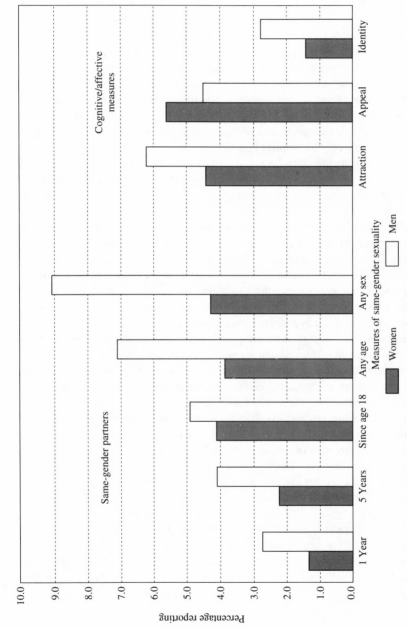

Fig. 8.1 Prevalence of various measures of same-gender sexuality, U.S. adults.

engaged in at least one of these sexual practices with a person of their own gender since puberty.

This last measure produced the highest reporting of same-gender sexual behavior. But the differences are slight for the women and dramatic for the men. There are a number of factors that help explain this pattern. Very few women (about 0.3 percent) who report having sex between puberty and age eighteen with a female partner do not also have sex with a woman after eighteen.[15] On the other hand, almost 2 percent of the men (comparing *any age* and *since 18*) report sex before eighteen but not after. However, when we look at *any sex,* the rate of women having a female partner since puberty increases another 0.5 percentage point, from 3.8 to 4.3 percent. But the rate for men increases another 2 percentage points, from 7.1 to 9.1 percent. If this higher number is correct, this implies that almost 4 percent of the men have sex with another male before turning eighteen but not after. These men, who report same-gender sex only before they turned eighteen, not afterward, constitute 42 percent of the total number of men who report ever having a same-gender experience.

But why should one measure be so much higher for the men than another conceptually similar measure? There are several possibilities. The increased privacy of the self-administered form may increase reporting of socially stigmatized behavior. Or the question may be understood somewhat differently by the respondent and may prompt a different answer. *Any sex* is based on questions about specific sexual practices rather than a question about sex partners. Some respondents may not have given an age for a first same-gender sex partner (the major component of *any age*) but might be prompted to remember a specific incident when a sexual act occurred. Some of these acts may not have been considered when reporting about a first same-gender partner. Finally, the questions about *any sex* are asked at the very end of the questionnaire, providing the fullest chance for recall. This measure produces a dramatically higher rate of same-gender partners than the other measures for men. However, it should be pointed out that, while this 9 percent is higher than any figure reported from the other recent surveys, and while it may be an under-report, it is still a far cry from the 37 percent that Kinsey reported.

How do these rates of same-gender partners compare with questions about attraction, appeal, and self-identification? The latter are displayed on the right-hand side of figure 8.1. The rates of reporting some degree of same-gender desire as a current state of mind are higher for both men and women than the rates of reporting same-gender partners for the more recent time frames (one and five years). The levels of reported sexual attraction to one's own gender and the appeal of same-gender sex are also much more comparable for women and men (varying around 5 percent). These different aspects of same-gender

---

15. The exact figures on which fig. 8.1 is based are reported in table 8.2 below.

sexual interest or desire are only moderately correlated. The relative levels of the two measures also differ for men and women, although this difference is not statistically significant. More men report being at least somewhat attracted to men (6.2 percent) than report finding sex with another man appealing (4.5 percent). In contrast, more women report finding the idea of sex with a woman appealing (5.6 percent) than report any sexual attraction to women (4.4 percent). In an analysis not shown, we found that 7.7 percent of the men and 7.5 percent of the women report one or the other form of same-gender sexual attraction or interest. About one-third of those (39 percent of the men and 34 percent of the women) reporting any same-gender desire expressed both forms, while the other two-thirds expressed only one form.

Our final measure, the self-reported same-gender sexual identity, has the lowest prevalence of any of these measures. About 1.4 percent of the women and 2.8 percent of the men report identifying with a label denoting same-gender sexuality. The ratio of homosexual to bisexual identification is about 2:1, slightly lower for women (1.8:1) and slightly higher for men (2.5:1). This result is discussed in some detail later in this chapter.

How do these simple rates compare with those found in other recent surveys? It is not our purpose to make an in-depth comparison, but overall we find that our results are remarkably similar to those from other surveys of sexual behavior that have been conducted on national populations using probability sampling methods. In particular, two very large-scale surveys were being carried out at the same time as we were designing and beginning to field such a survey in the United States, one in France (Spira et al. 1993) and one in Britain (Wellings et al. 1994). (These were discussed briefly in chapter 2.) There are many basic similarities and overlaps between the three surveys, but there are also many variations in methods and design. For example, the French survey interviewed 20,055 adults aged eighteen to sixty-nine over the telephone, and the British survey conducted 18,876 face-to-face interviews with people aged sixteen to fifty-nine living in England, Wales, and Scotland, but most of the sexual behavior questions were asked in a self-administered supplement. The British survey reports rates of same-gender sexual experience for men that range from 1.1 percent (in the past year) to 6.1 percent (ever having had any homosexual experience). The comparable figures for women are 0.4 and 3.4 percent (Wellings et al. 1994, 187). The French study results range from 1.1 percent of the men reporting at least one male partner in the past year and 4.1 percent reporting any male sex partners in their entire life (Spira et al. 1993, 138). These rates are somewhat lower than the rates that we found, but they are still quite close, especially compared to the rates found by Kinsey. The patterns of the findings in these recent surveys are also quite similar in terms of gender and age and elevated rates in large urban areas.[16]

16. Similar results have been reported regarding the homosexual experience of men in the United States (cf. Fay et al. 1989; Rogers and Turner 1991; and Billy et al. 1993).

8.5 The Interrelation of Same-Gender Sexual Behavior, Desire, and Identity

How are these three aspects of homosexuality interrelated? To answer this question, we first need to define a simple dichotomous variable denoting the presence or absence of each dimension. We sought relatively broad and inclusive summary measures for this analysis. However, we have excluded people who report their only same-gender sex partners before they turned eighteen. Thus, we have defined *behavior* in terms of a composite measure intended to tap the presence of any same-gender partner after age eighteen.[17] *Desire* combines the *appeal* and *attraction* measures defined above. For this purpose, any respondent who reported either being attracted to people of his or her own gender or finding same-gender sex appealing is considered to have some same-gender desire. Same-gender identity includes people who said that they considered themselves to be either homosexual or bisexual (or an equivalent).

Figure 8.2 displays the overlap among these three conceptually separable dimensions of homosexuality using Venn diagrams. These diagrams make use of overlapping circles to display all the logically possible intersections among different categories. While a Venn diagram distinguishes all possible combinations, it does not attempt to scale the areas in the circles to reflect the relative numbers of respondents in each category because of technical constraints in the geometry of representation. The latter is indicated by the numbers and percentages attached to each area.

The three circles each represent a dimension or component of same-gender sexuality. The totals of 150 women and 143 men, respectively, who report any same-gender behavior, desire, or identity are distributed across all the possible mutually exclusive combinations of the three categories. For example, the area of the circle labeled *desire* that does not overlap with either of the other circles includes only those respondents who reported some same-gender desire but reported neither same-gender partners since eighteen nor self-identification as a homosexual or bisexual. Desire with no corresponding adult behavior or identity is the largest category for both men and women, with about 59 percent of the women and 44 percent of the men in this cell. About 13 percent of the

17. There are four different sets of questions that were used to construct this composite: (1) questions about the number of male and female sex partners since turning eighteen asked on a self-administered form early in the interview (appendix C, SAQ 2, questions 8 and 9); (2) enumerated sex partners from cohabitational relationships and in the last year (appendix C, sections 2 and 4); (3) counts of sex partners of each gender during the life course since age eighteen (appendix C, section 6); and (4) respondents who report an age of first sexual experience with someone of the same gender as eighteen or older (appendix C, section 8, question 40). Not surprisingly, since these questions are asked in different places and in different ways (face-to-face vs. self-completion, directly vs. indirectly, etc.), there were some inconsistencies between responses. A respondent who answered that he or she had same-gender sex partners on *any* of these questions is treated here as having had an adult homosexual experience. According to this coding scheme, 5.3 percent of the men and 3.5 percent of the women had had at least one same-gender sex partner since their eighteenth birthday.

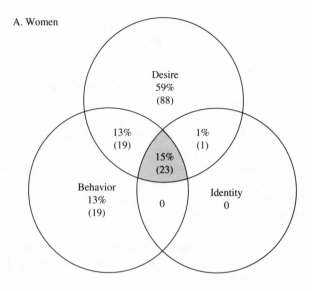

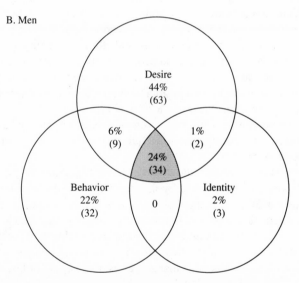

Fig. 8.2 Interrelation of components of homosexuality. A, For 150 women (8.6 percent of the total 1,749) who report any adult same-gender sexuality. B, For 143 men (10.1 percent of the total 1,410) who report any adult same-gender sexuality.

women and 22 percent of the men report a same-gender partner since turning eighteen, but no current desire or identity.[18]

No women reported homosexual identity alone. But there were three men who said that they considered themselves homosexual or bisexual even though they did not report desire or partners. This being an unlikely status, it is possible that these men simply misunderstood the categories of self-identification since none of them reported any same-gender experience or interest.

About 15 percent of the women and 24 percent of the men are found in the intersection of all three circles. This is practically all the women (twenty-three out of twenty-four) and the vast majority of the men (thirty-four out of thirty-nine) who identify as homosexual or bisexual. In order to see the relative proportions in each set of categories more clearly, pie charts based on the same data and categories are displayed in figure 8.3.

As it is measured here, sexual identity does not appear to represent an analytically separate dimension because it logically entails the existence of both desire and action. Desire, behavior, and the combination of desire and behavior seem to exist in at least a substantial minority of the cases, but identity independent of the other two is quite rare.[19] It is thus not surprising that no men or women reported behavior and identity without desire. Some sort of homosexual desire seems at the heart of most notions of homosexual identity. To report same-gender partners, *and* to say that one considers oneself to be homosexual or bisexual, *but* to deny any attraction or appeal of homosexuality, seems illogical. On the other hand, the idea of someone reporting desire and identity but no (adult) behavior does not seem so implausible since homosexuality is often thought of as an underlying sexual orientation understood in a psychological sense of fantasy or desire. One can at least imagine people who consider themselves to be homosexual (or bisexual) without necessarily having had any sex partners. In fact, this state appears to be quite rare, with only one woman and two men found in this category.

This analysis demonstrates the high degree of variability in the way that differing elements of homosexuality are distributed in the population. This variability relates to the way that homosexuality is both organized as a set of behaviors and practices and experienced subjectively. It raises quite provocative questions about the definition of *homosexuality*. While there is a core group (about 2.4 percent of the total men and about 1.3 percent of the total women) in our survey who define themselves as homosexual or bisexual, have

18. Even for the most current time period available, the past twelve months, 10 percent of the women and 11 percent of the men who had had a same-gender sex partner in the past year did not report either desire or identity. Please note the small number bases for these estimates.

19. The group of people who report behavior and desire but not identity is quite small among the men but fairly sizable among the women, comparable to the women who had sex partners but nothing else and to those who exhibit all three characteristics. This may indicate a slightly lower threshold of homosexual and bisexual identity among men than among women. This would fit with the historically greater visibility of gay men as opposed to lesbians.

A. Women

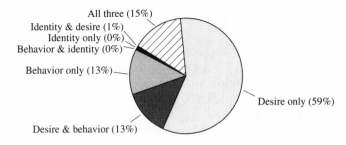

B. Men

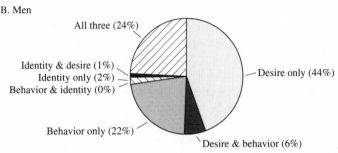

Fig. 8.3   Interrelation of different aspects of same-gender sexuality. A, For 150 women (8.6 percent of the total 1,749) who report any adult same-gender sexuality. B, For 143 men (10.1 percent of the total 1,410) who report any adult same-gender sexuality.

same-gender partners, and express homosexual desires, there are also sizable groups who do not consider themselves to be either homosexual or bisexual but have had adult homosexual experiences or express some degree of desire. Despite pervasive social disapproval, about 5 percent of the men and women in our sample express some same-gender desire, but no other indicators of adult activity or self-identification. A sizable number have had same-gender partners, but consider themselves neither as bisexual or homosexual nor as experiencing any current homosexual desire. While the measurement of same-gender practices and attitudes is crude at best, with unknown levels of underreporting for each, this preliminary analysis provides unambiguous evidence that no single number can be used to provide an accurate and valid characterization of the incidence and prevalence of homosexuality in the population at large. In sum, homosexuality is fundamentally a multidimensional phenomenon that has manifold meanings and interpretations, depending on context and purpose.

8.6   The Relation of Master Statuses and Same-Gender Sexuality

Modification of Master Status Variables

Tables 8.1 and 8.2 present the distributions of a number of measures of same-gender sexuality by various social and demographic variables. These tables use social and demographic variables similar to the master status variables introduced in the preceding chapters, but we have collapsed some categories because the relative rarity of same-gender sexuality made more fine-grained analysis statistically unreliable.[20] In addition, we took advantage of the replication of these measures in the General Social Survey (GSS) since 1988.[21] In particular, the three measures of gender of sex partners in different time periods (past year, past five years, and since age eighteen) appeared in the GSS.[22] In table 8.1, we pool the data from the GSS and the NHSLS to increase the sample size of U.S. adults aged eighteen to fifty-nine from a maximum of 3,159 for the NHSLS to a combined maximum of 8,744 for those variables that are in both the GSS and the NHSLS. Table 8.2 is based on the data from the NHSLS alone.

Three new variables are added to the list of master variables: urban/rural place of residence, both at the time of the interview and while growing up,[23]

20. Age was collapsed into four categories instead of the original eight five-year age intervals. In the new version, ten-year groupings are used. This has been done because the rates of reporting of same-gender sex are so low for many of these measures that the number of respondents within smaller subgroups of the sample as a whole can become vanishingly small.

21. Marital status has been collapsed into three categories: never married, currently married, and previously married (i.e., separated, divorced, and widowed). This was done both to have fewer categories and because cohabitational status is not available in the GSS. Since same-gender marriage is not legally recognized in the United States, we assume that all the marriages are between men and women; similarly, the separations, divorces, and deaths of spouses reported in the GSS refer to such unions.

22. In collaboration with our earlier work leading up to the NHSLS, the GSS began including a self-administered form with sexual behavior questions in 1988. It was modified slightly, mainly through the addition of items, in 1989 and 1990. The same basic form was used in 1991 and 1993, and that form was used in the NHSLS in 1992. (For the exact wording of the questions as used in the NHSLS, see appendix C, SAQ 2. In the NHSLS, these questions were actually presented to the respondent at the end of the first section of the questionnaire [demography] before any other sex questions. For a complete description of the GSS and the variations in question wordings, see Davis and Smith [1991]. In the GSS, the self-administered form with these questions was given to the respondent at the very end of the interview. For further comparisons of the GSS and NHSLS samples and other questions, see appendix B.)

For the purposes of this analysis, we have merged the NHSLS cross-sectional cases and the GSS cases aged eighteen to fifty-nine from 1988, 1989, 1990, 1991, and 1993 into a single data set. The sample sizes for these variables differ because not all questions were asked each year in the GSS. Only the gender of partners in the past year appears in every year of the GSS. The number of partners since age eighteen was added in 1989, and the number of partners in the past five years was added in 1990. We looked carefully for any effects of the year of the GSS survey on answers to the questions. Since no systematic patterns of temporal effects were detected, we feel justified in pooling the multiyear surveys into a single grand sample.

23. The GSS uses age sixteen as the reference age for the question. The NHSLS changed the age to fourteen to correspond to other surveys such as the National Longitudinal Survey. In both cases, the intent is to get an idea of where respondents were living while growing up and before

Table 8.1 **Percentage Reporting Any Same-Gender Sex Partners in Different Time Periods, by Selected Social/Demographic Variables (GSS and NHSLS combined)**

| | Partners | | | | | | | |
| | Last Year | | Past 5 Years | | Since Age 18 | | Total N | |
	M	W	M	W	M	W	M	W
Age:								
18–29	3.0	1.6	4.3	2.5	4.4	4.2	1,169	1,369
30–39	3.5	1.8	5.4	3.2	6.6	5.3	1,220	1,544
40–49	2.1	.8	3.0	1.3	3.9	3.6	968	1,141
50–59	1.4	.4	2.5	.9	4.2	2.2	558	773
Total	2.7	1.3	4.1	2.2	4.9	4.1		
N	3,493	4,376	2,223	2,838	3,072	3,853	3,915	4,827
Marital status:								
Never married	6.6	3.6	9.2	4.8	9.5	8.2	1,188	1,079
Married	1.0	.2	1.7	.8	2.4	2.1	2,153	2,588
Div./wid./sep.	1.0	1.3	2.2	2.7	4.9	4.5	560	1,138
Total	2.7	1.2	4.1	2.1	5.0	4.0		
N	3,479	4,354	2,209	2,816	3,058	3,831	3,901	4,805
Education:								
Less than HS	3.1	.9	3.0	2.2	4.5	4.9	592	770
HS grad.	1.4	.8	2.7	1.4	2.7	2.7	1,129	1,531
Some college	3.0	1.1	4.6	2.0	5.3	3.8	1,142	1,442
College grad.	3.5	2.5	5.4	3.5	6.9	5.8	1,039	1,066
Total	2.7	1.3	4.1	2.2	4.9	4.1		
N	3,481	4,363	2,214	2,826	3,061	3,839	3,902	4,809
Religion:								
Type I Prot.	3.0	1.7	5.0	2.2	5.3	4.0	1,019	1,308
Type II Prot.	1.8	.6	2.5	1.7	3.3	3.5	1,197	1,692
Catholic	1.7	.7	2.3	1.2	2.8	2.5	979	1,268
Jewish	4.5	2.7	8.7	2.0	5.0	6.7	74	83
None	5.9	4.0	8.1	5.7	10.7	9.7	504	356
Other	3.4	4.2	7.5	9.8	10.9	11.6	134	111
Total	2.7	1.3	4.1	2.2	5.0	4.1		
N	3,487	4,370	2,217	2,834	3,067	3,848	3,907	4,818
Religious attendance:								
Never	4.4	2.7	6.7	3.1	8.8	6.6	681	648
< 3 times per year	2.5	1.7	4.0	3.8	4.5	5.6	1,078	954
3–39 times per year	2.5	1.1	4.2	1.8	4.4	3.8	1,169	1,558
> 39 times per year	1.9	.7	2.2	1.3	3.4	2.6	951	1,621
Total	2.7	1.3	4.1	2.2	4.9	4.1		
N	3,462	4,337	2,206	2,811	3,043	3,816	3,879	4,781
Race:								
White	2.7	1.2	4.0	1.9	5.0	3.7	3,329	3,916
Black	3.6	1.3	5.4	2.9	5.0	5.4	423	692
Other	1.4	2.1	1.3	5.9	3.3	7.4	165	219
Total	2.7	1.3	4.1	2.2	4.9	4.1		
N	3,494	4,376	2,224	2,838	3,073	3,853	3,917	4,827

(continued)

Table 8.1   (continued)

| | Partners | | | | | | Total *N* | |
| | Last Year | | Past 5 Years | | Since Age 18 | | | |
	M	W	M	W	M	W	M	W
Place of residence:								
Top 12 central cities								
(CCs)	10.2	2.1	14.3	3.3	16.4	6.2	283	378
Next 88 central cities	3.6	1.2	5.2	2.5	5.7	5.5	433	607
Suburbs top 12 CCs	2.7	1.2	5.4	1.9	5.9	4.3	430	530
Suburbs next 88 CCs	1.6	1.3	3.5	1.7	3.4	3.6	635	773
Other urban areas	1.8	.8	2.5	1.7	4.1	2.9	1,446	1,659
Rural areas	1.0	.6	.9	1.0	1.5	2.8	422	529
Total	2.6	1.1	4.1	1.9	5.0	3.8		
N	3,255	4,054	1,983	2,512	2,829	3,530	3,649	4,476
Place of residence age 14/16								
Rural	1.2	.7	1.1	2.0	2.2	4.3	972	1,041
Town/med. city/suburb	2.5	1.3	3.5	2.0	4.8	3.7	1,783	2,376
Large city/metro. area	4.4	1.6	7.1	2.6	7.3	4.6	1,158	1,393
Total	2.7	1.3	4.1	2.2	4.9	4.1		
N	3,491	4,366	2,222	2,830	3,070	3,844	3,913	4,810

and frequency of religious attendance. The levels of urbanization of current and adolescent place of residence are included because we thought it relevant to reports and experience of homosexuality. The existence of highly visible gay and lesbian communities and neighborhoods in certain major cities like New York, San Francisco, Los Angeles, and Chicago led us to wonder whether place of residence would affect the incidence and prevalence of homosexuality (cf. Levine 1979; D'Emilio 1983; and Murray 1992). Urban-rural differences regarding sexual behavior were also reported in the Kinsey volumes. The type of place where respondents grew up (as measured at either fourteen or sixteen years of age) was added to help investigate whether the effect of current residence was due primarily to migration or to something else. Religious attendance is often used in place of or in addition to religious affiliation itself in explaining sexual behavior and attitudes because it is believed to index more adequately individuals' involvement in the social life of religious communities (cf. Lenski 1960; Laumann 1973; Schuman 1971; Glock and Stark 1965; Roof 1993).

leaving home to live independently. For the sake of brevity, and to have a comparable measure for all respondents, a single age for all respondents before the age of majority is used.

Table 8.2   **Percentage Reporting Various Types of Same-Gender (SG) Sexuality with a Partner (P), by Selected Social and Demographic Variables**

	Any Age, SG Ps since Puberty		Any Sex, SG Sex since Puberty		Attraction, SG Attraction		Appeal, SG Sex Appealing		Desire, Attract or Appeal		Identity, Homo/ Bisexual	
	M	W	M	W	M	W	M	W	M	W	M	W
Total	7.1	3.8	9.1	4.3	6.2	4.4	4.5	5.6	7.7	7.5	2.8	1.4
Age:												
18–29	5.1	2.9	6.4	4.2	7.4	4.4	5.6	4.7	9.1	6.7	2.9	1.6
30–39	8.8	5.0	10.6	5.4	6.3	6.0	5.4	6.8	7.2	9.2	4.2	1.8
40–49	8.0	4.5	10.9	4.6	6.7	3.3	3.7	7.3	8.6	8.3	2.2	1.3
50–59	6.5	2.1	8.8	1.9	2.5	2.8	1.5	2.5	4.0	4.6	.5	.4
Marital status:												
Never married	11.8	5.6	14.4	5.9	12.1	7.7	10.1	7.1	13.9	10.4	7.1	3.7
Married	4.1	2.6	6.1	2.8	3.5	2.1	1.7	4.3	4.7	5.2	.6	.1
Div./wid./sep.	6.9	4.1	7.7	5.5	3.0	6.4	1.5	6.6	3.9	9.6	1.0	1.9
Education:												
Less than HS	4.7	3.3	4.7	1.8	4.3	1.7	2.6	2.0	5.8	3.3	1.6	.4
HS grad.	5.2	1.8	7.3	2.3	4.8	1.6	2.2	4.1	5.5	5.3	1.8	.4
Some college/voc.	9.1	3.9	9.8	5.1	6.4	4.8	6.7	5.6	8.9	7.3	3.8	1.2
College grad.	7.8	6.7	12.0	7.3	8.3	9.3	5.0	9.2	9.4	12.8	3.3	3.6
Religion:												
None	12.4	9.9	15.4	11.3	10.9	12.8	8.2	12.6	12.9	15.8	6.2	4.6
Type I Prot.	7.7	2.1	9.5	2.0	7.7	3.3	4.6	2.8	8.3	5.2	3.1	.5
Type II Prot.	4.7	2.9	5.9	3.3	3.2	1.7	3.4	4.9	5.6	5.5	.7	.3
Catholic	6.4	3.4	7.9	4.2	4.3	5.3	2.4	5.9	5.3	8.4	2.1	1.7
Jewish	7.7	6.9	17.4	12.5	11.5	10.3	7.7	6.9	11.5	10.3	7.7	3.4
Other	9.8	18.9	17.1	14.7	14.6	8.1	12.2	13.5	19.5	16.2	7.5	5.4
Religious attendance:												
Never	10.9	4.4	13.2	5.7	6.4	4.4	6.3	7.0	7.6	7.4	4.7	2.2
< 3 times per year	5.3	6.4	7.2	7.2	8.2	7.9	3.8	7.3	9.6	10.1	2.6	3.1
3–39 times per year	6.5	3.7	8.1	3.2	5.5	4.5	6.3	5.7	7.9	8.0	2.9	1.1
> 39 times per year	7.5	2.2	9.7	3.0	4.5	2.2	1.8	4.1	5.1	5.5	1.5	.3
Race/ethnicity:												
White	7.6	4.0	9.6	4.7	5.9	5.1	4.8	5.7	7.4	7.8	3.0	1.7
Black	5.8	3.5	8.0	2.8	5.3	2.6	3.4	5.9	6.7	7.0	1.5	.6
Hispanic	8.8	3.8	7.5	3.5	13.3	3.9	4.4	6.0	13.9	7.6	3.7	1.1
Asian	0.0	3.3	3.2	0.0	14.3	0.0	2.9	0.0	17.1	0.0	0.0	0.0
Place of residence:												
Top 12 central cities (CCs)	14.2	6.5	15.8	4.6	15.8	5.9	10.8	8.4	16.7	9.7	9.2	2.6
Next 88 central cities	8.6	5.7	10.1	7.7	9.1	5.3	6.3	6.1	11.4	7.8	3.5	1.6
Suburbs top 12 CCs	10.3	5.7	11.9	4.1	7.6	4.8	5.6	6.7	10.3	9.0	4.2	1.9
Suburbs next 88 CCs	4.9	3.3	6.0	4.8	3.3	5.5	2.5	7.5	4.5	9.8	1.3	1.6
Other urban areas	6.5	2.7	9.7	3.4	4.6	4.1	3.4	4.7	5.3	6.9	1.9	1.1
Rural areas	2.5	2.1	2.7	2.2	4.4	.5	3.8	1.6	7.5	2.1	1.3	0.0

Urbanization of Place of Residence

One of the most striking relations in tables 8.1 and 8.2 is between the level of urbanization of the current residence of respondents and the various measures of same-gender sexuality. Men living in the central cities of the twelve largest metropolitan areas report rates of same-gender sexuality of between 9.2 and 16.7 percent (see the columns referring to *identity* and *desire*, respectively), as compared to rates for all men on these measures of 2.8 and 7.7 percent, respectively. And the rates generally decline monotonically with decline in urbanization.[24]

While the rates of reported same-gender sexuality for women generally follow a similar pattern to those for men, that is, they are positively correlated with degree of urbanization, this pattern is not nearly so marked as with the men. In general, the relation is not statistically significant for women, although it is quite consistent across the different measures of homosexuality.[25]

Before turning to a discussion of possible explanations for the relation between residence and same-gender sexuality, a few general comments on the interpretation and social effect of this relation seem appropriate. This relation is an illustration of the limitations of relying on a single number as a summary for a complete distribution. While we were writing this book in 1993, extensive media discussion and debate exploded over the low rates of homosexuality (however measured) found in various recent sample surveys, including the GSS. These debates focused on single estimates produced for the male population as a whole, numbers such as 1.1 percent of men between the ages of twenty and forty exclusively homosexual during the previous ten-year period and a 2.3 percent estimate of any homosexuality during the same time period (Billy et al. 1993; Barringer 1993) or a 2.5 percent figure of adult men reporting male sex partners in the last year (Rogers and Turner 1991; Rogers 1993). The NHSLS estimates are not so different from these. While the Billy

24. This measure of urbanization is taken from the GSS and is based on a coding of sampling point for the interview rather than a question asked of the respondent. See the discussion of the variable SRCBELT in Davis and Smith (1991).

25. In the combined NHSLS and GSS data, the only relation for women that is statistically significant is that between residence and same-gender partners since age eighteen. (The *p*-value of the chi-square with five degrees of freedom is .024.) As with any test of significance of a relation between two variables, statistical significance is a function of both the size of the sample and the degree ("strength") of the association or relation (i.e., the larger the sample, the more likely that a given degree of association will be found significant). This is based on a large sample size (3,530 women) and what appears to be a relatively marked association, with percentages varying from 6.2 percent for women living in the central cities of the twelve largest metropolitan areas to 2.8 percent among the women living in rural areas. In contrast, the relation for men is strongly significant for all three same-gender partner variables in the combined data set, with probabilities less than .001. However, a number of the patterns of association are as strong for the women as they are for partners since eighteen (cf. *any age, appeal,* and *any desire* in table 8.2), although the sample size is much smaller (about 1,750 women in NHSLS alone vs. about 3,500 in the combined GSS and NHSLS data set).

et al. estimates, especially the 2.3 percent, are quite low in comparison to our findings for this age group, the two are closer to each other than the 10 percent estimate widely accepted in the past.

While a single estimate is one of a number of possible summary measures for a whole population, it may not accurately reflect the situation of a specific subgroup within that population. A single number often masks very important differences. For example, in this book, we have generally avoided averaging the rates of various measures of sexual activity for men and women into a single estimate for the population as a whole because the consistent and obvious differences between men and women across almost all our measures seemed worth preserving. One could easily argue that other group differences are important. The only case where a single statistic completely represents a population characteristic is where a distribution is uniform across the whole population without regard to any social or other characteristic. The use of and debates about a single number as a measure of incidence of homosexuality in the population, be it 10 or 2 percent (or some other number), are based on the implicit assumption that homosexuality is randomly (and uniformly) distributed in the population. This would fit with certain analogies to genetically or biologically based traits such as left-handedness or intelligence. However, that is exactly what we do not find. Homosexuality (or at least reports about homosexuality) is clearly distributed differentially within categories of the social and demographic variables that are used in tables 8.1 and 8.2.[26]

One of the more interesting features of the distribution of same-gender sexuality by type of place is that it helps explain some of the disbelief expressed by members of the gay community in response to recent estimates of the prevalence of homosexuality. Even if one assumes that the distribution found by our research is accurate (rather than a lower bound or underestimate), our data indicate that about 9 percent of eighteen- to fifty-nine-year-old men living in the largest central cities in the United States currently identify as either homosexual or bisexual; a higher proportion (14 percent) have had male sex partners in the last five years; and an even higher proportion report some level of sexual attraction to other men (about 16 percent). For men living in gay communities in such cities as New York, San Francisco, Los Angeles, or Chicago, this implies that an even higher proportion of the men with whom they come in contact would be gay identified. Research implying that the "true" percentage was on the order of 1 or 2 percent would seem quite inaccurate to such people. Of course, the other side of the coin is that generalizing the experience of people living in the twelve largest cities (where about one-third of the U.S. population

26. There is a statistically significant relation between all the master status variables in table 8.1 and at least one of the same-gender partner measures for both men and women. There are two exceptions: urbanization while growing up for women and race for men. However, the relation between race and same-gender partners for women is due to the different (somewhat elevated) rate for "other" rather than any differences between whites and blacks.

lives) or in gay/lesbian networks to the rest of the country is equally inappropriate.[27]

What are the possible mechanisms that could explain the distribution of the various measures of same-gender sexuality by urbanization of place of residence that we observe? One obvious mechanism is migration. People interested in sex with people of their own gender move to more congenial social environments. Large cities are congenial in a number of ways. Large urban centers generally have more diversity and a greater tolerance of diversity, less familiarity among and scrutiny by neighbors, and an increased variety of work and leisure opportunities than smaller cities and towns. In the United States, many larger cities have substantial and visible gay and lesbian communities, which occupy residential areas with high concentrations of openly gay/lesbian people and institutions that cater to or are tolerant of them. Younger people living in smaller towns or rural areas who are interested in same-gender sex are likely to learn of these communities and may migrate to them, especially if they feel constrained by negative sanctions toward open homosexuality generally or in their local social networks of friends and family.

The migration model for explaining the increased proportions of same-gender sexual practice, interest, and identification among people in larger cities assumes that people discover their own inclinations more or less independently of their environment and then adjust their environment to their "inner nature." But there is another possibility. Large cities may provide a congenial environment for the development and expression of same-gender interest. This is not the same as saying that homosexuality is a personal, deliberate or conscious choice. But an environment that provides increased opportunities for and fewer negative sanctions against same-gender sexuality may both allow and even elicit expression of same-gender interest and sexual behavior.

To test these two models empirically is quite difficult. To do so, one would need longitudinal data. In any case, these two models or explanations are not mutually exclusive. Both might operate to varying degrees. We did not ask respondents about why they moved to their current residence, but migration seems plausible as at least one of the mechanisms by which the higher rates of same-gender sexuality among people living in big cities come about. It fits with many of the generally accepted notions about the "coming-out" process for gays and lesbians and historical work on gay communities (Levine 1979; D'Emilio 1983; Murray 1992).

The elicitation/opportunity hypothesis is the less obvious explanation. It runs counter to the more essentialist, biological views of homosexuality that

27. This may be similar to the mechanism that leads many to think that there is much more sexual activity and more variegated sexual practices throughout the society than the kinds of figures that research such as ours would imply. The images and contexts of sexuality with which we are usually presented in the mass media are often those of the young, the educated, the urban, the uncoupled, or those just beginning sexual relationships, just the places where we have found elevated levels of sexual activity and variety.

are so widespread. It implies that the environment in which people grow up affects their sexuality in very basic ways. But this is exactly one way to read many of the patterns that we have found throughout this research. In fact, there is evidence for the effect of the degree of urbanization of residence while growing up on reported homosexuality. This effect is quite marked and strong for men and practically nonexistent for women. Table 8.1 displays the relation between the urbanization of the place where respondents were living at age fourteen (sixteen for the GSS). We find a similar but much more moderated relation to current residence: among the male respondents, there is a clear monotonic relation between the level of urbanization and the proportion reporting same-gender partners in a given time period. Unlike current residence, residence at age fourteen or sixteen is very unlikely to be the result of a choice by the respondent based on sexual preference.

The relation of urbanization to same-gender sexuality is quite marked for men but much weaker for women. This is true for both current residence and residence while growing up. This suggests that homosexuality among men and women in the United States may be socially organized quite differently. It is even possible that the phenomena themselves (the various forms of same-gender sexuality) are different for men and women. (Of course, we have already demonstrated that the various forms of same-gender sexuality differ in substantial ways among men and among women as well.) Discussions of homosexuality often treat any same-gender sexual behavior or interest as fundamentally the same. These results challenge such easy conclusions.

Education and the Prevalence of Same-Gender Sexuality among Women

Most of the patterns in the relations between same-gender sexuality and the social and demographic master status variables observed in tables 8.1 and 8.2 are similar for men and women. Except for one variable, the appeal of having sex with someone of one's own sex, the rates for women are always lower than the rates for men in any particular category. Education, however, does seem to stand out for women in a way that it does not for men. Higher levels of education are generally associated with higher rates on any given measure of same-gender sexuality. But this pattern is more pronounced and more monotonic for women than it is for men. In general, women with high school degrees or less report very low rates of same-gender sexuality. The strength and consistency of the pattern for women is mainly due to the fact that women who have graduated from college always report the highest level of same-gender sexuality. In the case of the measures of desire or interest, the female college graduates' rates are higher than those of comparable men, even for sexual attraction, where the overall rate for women is lower than that for men. For the measures of appeal and desire, the women's overall rates are higher than or comparable to the men's rates, but this turns out to be largely due to the especially high rate among the college educated.

There does not seem to be an obvious explanation for this pattern. Higher levels of education are associated with greater social and sexual liberalism (see chapter 14) and with greater sexual experimentation (see Kinsey, Pomeroy, and Martin 1948; Kinsey et al. 1953; and chapter 3 above). Acceptance of nontraditional sexual behavior is likely to be higher among the more educated. This may facilitate higher rates of reporting among the better educated, even if behavioral differences across education levels are negligible. But it seems likely that both effects occur.

We have already observed some drop-off in heterosexual partners (and rates of sexual activity) among the more highly educated women (see chapters 3 and 5). On the one hand, more education for women may represent greater gender nonconformity. But it may also represent a higher level of personal resources (human capital) that can translate into more economic and social opportunities, which would, in turn, increase one's ability to please oneself rather than others. The fact that younger women (those under forty) report higher levels of same-gender partners in all three time periods but do not so clearly report higher levels of same-gender desire may be due to historical changes that affect the opportunities and norms for cohorts differentially. In particular, the expectation and need for women to work and the lowering of barriers to economic success have had a greater effect on younger women. A more general pattern of younger women's sexual experiences becoming somewhat more like men's seems to be emerging in terms of both same- and opposite-gender activity. Both the ideology of women's equality and the structural bases for its realization have been increasing in the postwar period, but with especially marked increases since the late 1960s.

The Mixture of Same- and Opposite-Gender Sex Partners

So far we have focused on the existence of any same-gender partners in given time periods or the expression of sexual interest in people of the same gender. Many of those who report same-gender sexual experience or interest also have sexual experiences with and interest in people of the opposite gender as well. Tables 8.3A and 8.3B show the gender breakdown of sex partners in various time periods and the distribution of sexual identification and sexual attraction for men and women.

First, let us look at the mixture of genders of sex partners in four different time periods: the past year, the past five years, since age eighteen, and since puberty. As would be expected, the longer the time period, the higher the proportion of people who report having had any same-gender partners. However, the relative proportion of people who have had only same-gender partners compared to the proportion who have had partners of both genders changes dramatically. While the overall proportions of men and women reporting any same-gender partners differ, the general pattern of how these are distributed between people having only same-gender partners and those having partners of both genders is quite similar. Beginning with the distribution of partners by gender in the last year, we find that 2.7 percent of the men had a male partner

Table 8.3A   **Prevalence of Same-Gender and Opposite-Gender Partners (Ps) (percentages)**

	Ps in Last Year		Ps in Past 5 Years		Ps since Age 18		Ps since Puberty	
	M	W	M	W	M	W	M	W
No partners	10.5	13.3	5.9	7.1	3.8	3.4	3.3	2.2
Opposite gender only	86.8	85.4	90.0	90.7	91.3	92.5	90.3	94.3
Both men and women	.7	.3	2.1	1.4	4.0	3.7	5.8	3.3
Same gender only	2.0	1.0	2.0	.8	.9	.4	.6	.2
Any same-gender sex (%):								
Both men and women	25.3	25.0	51.6	62.9	81.6	89.9	90.7	94.9
Same gender only	74.7	75.0	48.4	37.1	18.4	10.1	9.3	5.1
Total N	3,494	4,376	2,224	2,838	3,073	3,853	1,334	1,678

Note: Partner variables (last year, past five years, and since eighteen) are from combined GSS and NHSLS data (appendix C, SAQ 2, questions 4, 7, 8, and 9 cumulatively). Partners since puberty is based on age of first vaginal intercourse and age of first same-gender partner from NHSLS (appendix C, section 8, questions 20 and 40).

Table 8.3B   **Prevalence of Sexual Identity and Sexual Attraction, by Gender (percentages)**

Sexual Identity[a]	M	W	Sexual Attraction[b]	M	W
Other	.3	.1	Only opposite gender	93.8	95.6
Heterosexual	96.9	98.6	Mostly opposite gender	2.6	2.7
Bisexual	.8	.5	Both genders	.6	.8
Homosexual	2.0	.9	Mostly same gender	.7	.6
Any same-gender sex (%):			Only same gender	2.4	.3
Both men and women	28.2	37.5	Total N	1,404	1,731
Same gender only	71.8	62.5			
Total N	1,401	1,732			

[a]From appendix C, section 8, question 49.

[b]From appendix C, section 8, questions 47 and 48.

and 1.3 percent of the women a female partner. Of these, about three out of four report having only same-gender partners in the past twelve months, while the other quarter had at least one partner of each gender. In the past five years, 4.1 percent of the men and 2.2 percent of the women had at least one same-gender partner. About half these men had both male and female partners in this time period. The women are more likely than the men to have had sex with both men and women than only same-gender partners. Almost two-thirds of the women reporting a female partner in the past five years also report a male partner. The proportion of the men with male partners since age eighteen who report having had only male partners declines to about 20 percent of the total. For women, the comparable figure is about 10 percent. When the time period under consideration is extended to all partners since puberty, the proportion of men with *only* male partners declines again to 10 percent of the men with *any* male partners.[28] Translated to a prevalence rate for the men as a whole, this means that, since puberty, under 1 percent of all men (0.6 percent) have had sex only with other boys or men and never with a female partner. For women, the proportion is even smaller. About 5 percent of the women who have had female partners since puberty have never had sex with a male partner. This means that, overall, only 0.2 percent of all women have had sex only with women.

These findings based on measures of sex partners indicate once again just how normative heterosexuality is in our society. Over a lifetime, the vast majority of people who report sex with others include at least one opposite-gender partner. On the other hand, we have seen that there is a minority, about 9 percent of men and 4 percent of women, who have sex with someone of their own gender (see the *any sex* column in table 8.2). These data also indicate the importance of the life course in viewing issues such as the gender of sex partners as a dynamic process. Given the relatively low rates of same-gender partners and the small size of our sample, it is not possible to look at questions of the movement back and forth between partners of each gender over time. For many, no doubt, the pattern of the mixture of partners represents some experimentation early on and the settling into a fixed choice later, if for no other reason than the fact that most people have relatively few partners overall (see chapter 5). On the other hand, there are some people who have had both male and female partners in the past one to five years. Here again, men and women also appear to differ. Women are much more likely than men in any time frame longer than a year to have had male as well as female partners, given that they have any same-gender partners.

Let us now turn briefly to the questions of self-identification and sexual attraction (table 8.3B). The questions that we asked are in the present tense and refer to the respondents' self-assessment at the time of the interview. The distribution of the responses on sexual identification resembles the distribution of partners in the past year.[29] Does this mean that answers to a question about sexual orientation reflect a statement about current behavior, or do current behavior and orientation express relatively stable outcomes of a developmental process? In either case, the ratio of reports of a self-identification of homosex-

28. The measure used here for partners since puberty is based solely on the questions about the age of sex (after puberty) with first same- and first opposite-gender partner in the childhood and adolescence section of the questionnaire. This produces a slightly lower rate of same-gender partners than the *any same-gender partner* measure used in fig. 8.1 and table 8.2.

29. The major difference is that, while about 10 percent of the sample had no partners in the past year, practically everyone gave an answer that closely fit into one of the three major categories, heterosexual, homosexual, or bisexual. The distribution is consistent with the idea that the non–sexually active people had the same distribution on sexual identity as the sexually active people.

ual to one of bisexual is similar to the ratio of having only same-gender partners to having partners of both genders in the past year (between 2:1 and 3:1).

Responses to the question about sexual attraction display another interesting difference between men and women. If one looks only at the respondents
who report any sexual attraction to people of their own gender, one finds that,
whereas the men follow a bimodal distribution, the women's distribution is
monotonic. An equal proportion of men (2.4 percent) report being attracted
only to other men as report being attracted mostly to women (2.6 percent). The
other categories of same-gender attraction for men, that is, the men who report
equal attraction to men and women and the men who report mainly but not
exclusively being attracted to other men, are much lower, at 0.6 and 0.7 percent, respectively. For the women, the pattern is quite different. The largest
group of women who report same-gender attraction are those who report
mostly, but not exclusively, being attracted to men, 2.7 percent. As the degree
of sexual attraction to other women increases, the proportion of women reporting it declines. Only 0.3 percent of women report being exclusively attracted to other women. Now compare these rates with the rates of self-
identification (categories of sexual orientation). Slightly more men report being exclusively attracted to other men than report considering themselves to be
homosexual (2.4 vs. 2.0 percent), whereas more women consider themselves
to be homosexual than report exclusive same-gender attraction (0.9 vs. 0.3 percent). While the numbers here are very small, it appears that, whereas two-
thirds of the women who consider themselves to be homosexual report at least
some minimal level of sexual attraction to men, a much smaller minority of
the men who report attraction to men but none to women do not consider themselves to be homosexual. Again, there seem to be somewhat elusive (owing to
small sample sizes) but intriguing differences between the way that same-
gender sexuality is experienced by men and women in the United States.

Sex Partners, Frequency, and Practices

In this section, we return to some key measures of sexual behavior from
chapters 3 and 5 and compare their prevalence for people who do and do not
report same-gender partners. This is a preliminary analysis based on crude
summaries of means and proportions. We are limited by the fact that the rates
of reporting same-gender sexual behavior are so low and our sample size is
small. In chapters 3 and 4, we have already seen that the distribution of sexual
behaviors is related to a variety of social characteristics. We have also seen that
the distribution of same-gender sexuality is similarly differentiated. Ideally,
one would want to look at the differences between sexual behavior between
same- and opposite-gender couples, taking into account these other social statuses and contexts. However, we have barely thirty men and women in many
of these categories, the minimum that we have set for computing group estimates. In several cases, there are fewer than thirty women who had same-

gender partners in the past year or who consider themselves homosexual or bisexual. Still, it seems worthwhile to report these summary statistics where we have sufficient data as a preliminary indication of patterns that deserve further investigation when larger samples are available.

Table 8.4 displays data on the number of partners in various time frames: the past year, the past five years, and since age eighteen. Four different measures are used to divide respondents into two groups based on the presence or absence of same-gender sexuality: self-identification as homosexual/bisexual and having any same-gender partners in a given time frame. The mean number of partners includes all partners, both men and women, during the given time period. Only sexually active people are included in the calculation of the means.

We have included 95 percent confidence intervals for the means in this table to give a better sense of the variability in these distributions.[30] These lower and upper limits provide a sense of how large the range is within which the true means are likely to lie. When the intervals are overlapping, this implies that the differences between the means are not statistically significant.[31]

There is a clear overall pattern in this table. In all cases, when we dichotomize our sample, the group of people with same-gender partners (or who define themselves as homosexual or bisexual) have higher average numbers of partners than the rest of the sexually active people in the sample. In many, if not most, of the cases for the men, these differences are not statistically significant. Thus, the mean number of partners in the last year is just under two for men without any male partners and around three for men with at least one male partner. But the differences for the split based on identity and any partners since eighteen are clearly not statistically significant since the confidence intervals are overlapping. For partners in the past five years, the differences are larger and produce intervals that do not overlap and are more separated. Men with no male partners had a mean of about five partners in the past five years, as compared to means between twelve and twenty-one for the men with same-gender partners. Even though the discrepancies between the means for partners since age eighteen are quite large, in fact in only one case is the interval nonoverlapping. The pattern for the women is quite similar to that for the men, although the mean number of partners in the two longer time periods is gener-

30. The limits for these intervals are computed by adding and subtracting approximately two standard errors to and from the mean. Under the assumption that these variables are normally distributed, these calculated limits would include the true mean ninety-five times out of a hundred in repeated samples. Of course, number of partners is hardly normally distributed, but generally violation of the normality assumption still provides a reasonable approximation to more exact calculations. A major purpose of interval estimation is that it gives one a sense of the variability involved in the estimate. Variability of estimates is especially large for small sample sizes.

31. Even when the intervals do not overlap, the true means may still not differ. That is because the calculations used here assume that our methods produce more precision than we know they actually do. The point here is mainly to provide some guard against apparent differences, but additional caution against generalization is warranted.

Table 8.4   **Mean Numbers of Sex Partners, by Measures of Same-Gender Sexuality, Sexually Active Respondents Only**

	Time Frame								
	Partners in Last Year			Partners in Last 5 Years			Partners since Age 18		
		Confidence Interval			Confidence Interval			Confidence Interval	
	Mean	Low	High	Mean	Low	High	Mean	Low	High
Men									
Any same-gender identity:									
None	1.8	1.5	2.0	4.9	4.3	5.6	16.5	13.7	19.4
Homo/bisexual	3.1	1.9	4.2	18.0	9.3	26.7	42.8	12.4	73.1
Any same-gender partners since age 18:									
None	1.8	1.5	2.0	4.9	4.2	5.5	15.7	12.9	18.4
Some	2.3	1.7	2.9	12.2	7.2	17.2	44.3	22.2	66.5
Any same-gender partners in past 5 years:									
None	1.7	1.5	2.0	4.8	4.2	5.4	16.9	14.0	19.9
Some	2.9	2.1	3.8	16.7	9.9	23.5	26.6	15.1	38.0
Any same-gender partners in past year:									
None	1.8	1.5	2.0	4.9	4.2	5.5	17.1	14.1	20.1
Some	3.4	2.3	4.5	20.7	11.6	29.8	30.0	17.9	42.2
Women									
Any same-gender identity:									
None	a	a	a	a	a	a	a	a	a
Homo/bisexual	a	a	a	a	a	a	a	a	a
Any same-gender partners since age 18:									
None	1.3	1.2	1.3	2.2	2.0	2.4	4.9	4.4	5.5
Some	3.8	−.2	7.7	7.6	2.4	12.9	19.7	13.0	26.3
Any same-gender partners in past 5 years:									
None	1.3	1.2	1.3	2.2	2.0	2.4	5.2	4.6	5.8
Some	5.7	−1.5	12.8	10.1	1.0	19.2	19.9	9.4	30.4
Any same-gender partners in past year:									
None	a	a	a	a	a	a	a	a	a
Some	a	a	a	a	a	a	a	a	a

[a] Fewer than thirty cases.

ally less than half the rates for men. For the women, it is only the confidence intervals based on the number of partners since eighteen that clearly separate the two groups. Remember that the mean number of partners here is based on both male and female partners. Part of the difference in mean numbers of partners is due to the fact that the "same-gender" groups include many people who have both same- and opposite-gender partners.

The higher mean numbers of partners for respondents reporting same-gender sex corresponds to a stereotype of male homosexuals that is widespread in our society. It is thought to be both easier for men to find short-term male partners and harder for them to form long-term relationships. While some evidence in our data supports this general tendency, the differences do not appear very large in view of the higher variability in our measures that results from the small sample sizes of homosexually active men. From analyses not shown here, we estimate that over one-third of the men who had only male partners in the past year were living with a partner at the time of the interview. This compares with two-thirds of the men who only had female partners in the past year. Of course, for the latter this includes married as well as live-in partners. Lack of formal recognition of same-gender relationships and lack of social pressure and support to maintain them no doubt contribute to the lower rate of longer-term relationships and the higher rate at which new partners are acquired.

One stereotype about lesbians, on the other hand, holds that they form extremely strong bonds with each other, leading one to expect lower rates at which new partners are acquired. But our data do not fit that pattern. We already noted the large proportion of the women reporting female partners in our sample who also have sex with men. Analysis based on larger samples is necessary to sort out whether the lesbians' larger average number of partners is due to having relatively more female or male partners.

Is the comparison of people who report any same-gender sex partners with all those who do not the most appropriate? We have shown that the former are younger, more educated, more likely to live in large cities, and generally less religious. All these factors are also associated with having more sex partners. Again, we need a larger sample to pursue more refined and appropriate comparisons.

Frequency of Sex in the Last Year

In chapter 5, we pointed out that the relation between numbers of partners and the frequency of sex is nonlinear. Except for a very small proportion of people with many partners, the frequency of partnered sex generally declines with an increase in partners. This seems to be largely a matter of the inefficiencies of having to find new partners with whom to have sex rather than having sex with the same person, especially if that person shares living quarters with the respondent. This is a classic argument dating back at least to

Table 8.5   Mean Frequency of Sex per Month for Past Year, by Measures of Same-Gender Sexuality

	Men				Women		
		Confidence Interval				Confidence Interval	
	Mean	Low	High		Mean	Low	High
All men	6.5	6.2	6.8	All women	6.2	5.9	6.5
Any same-gender identification:				Any same-gender identification:			
None	6.6	6.3	6.9	None	a	a	a
Homo/bisexual	4.5	2.8	6.2	Homo/bisexual	a	a	a
Any same-gender partners since 18:				Any same-gender partners since 18:			
None	6.1	5.8	6.5	None	5.5	5.2	5.8
Some	5.7	4.4	7.0	Some	6.1	4.6	7.6
Any same-gender partners in past 5 years:				Any same-gender partners in past 5 years:			
None	6.3	6.0	6.6	None	5.8	5.5	6.1
Some	4.4	3.0	5.7	Some	5.5	3.4	7.7
Any same-gender partners in past year:				Any same-gender partners in past year:			
None	6.6	6.3	6.9	None	a	a	a
Some	4.3	2.6	5.9	Some	a	a	a

[a]Fewer than thirty cases.

Kinsey, Pomeroy, and Martin (1948), where it was applied to homosexually active men. Table 8.5 reports the mean frequency of sex per month (for the exact wording of the question, see appendix C, SAQ 2, question 5). We find practically no difference between the rates of sex per month for the different comparisons. The mean rates for men with male partners are consistently, but not significantly, lower than the rates for the rest of the men. The rates for women hardly differ at all between the two groups.

Selected Sexual Practices

In table 8.6, we turn to a preliminary investigation of the sexual practices of the people defined by several of our measures of same-gender sexuality. We add one group defined in terms of same-gender experience to the set that we have been using. We have included a category in table 8.6 labeled *any SG* [same gender] *sexuality, behavior, and desire.* This group includes all the people in the Venn diagrams and pie charts (figs. 8.2 and 8.3). This broad fuzzy set consists of all those one might consider labeling *homosexual* in almost any sense of that term during adulthood (i.e., since age eighteen), given the measures that we have in our survey. The measures of same-gender sexuality used

Table 8.6   **Percentage Reporting Selected Sexual Practices, by Various Measures of Same-Gender Sexuality**

| | Masturbation in Last Year | | | | Proportions Reporting Having Engaged in Practice since Puberty (on final SAQ) | | | | | | | |
| | Not at All | | Once per Week or More | | Active Oral Sex | | Receptive Oral Sex | | Active Anal Sex | | Receptive Anal Sex | |
	M	W	M	W	M	W	M	W	M	W	M	W
Total population	36.7	58.3	26.7	7.6	76.6[a]	67.7[a]	78.7[a]	73.1[a]	25.6[a]	N.A.	N.A.	20.4[a]
Any same-gender (SG) sexuality, behavior, and desire	24.4	29.5	49.6	18.7	32.3	26.7	39.9	34.6	27.3	N.A.	29.3	N.A.
Any SG partners (Ps) since age 18	15.3	29.8	55.6	19.3	58.9	61.8	69.9	72.2	50.0	N.A.	53.4	N.A.
Any SGPs in past 5 years	11.8	30.0	64.7	20.0	74.5	71.4	80.4	82.1	64.0	N.A.	62.8	N.A.
Any SGPs in past year	11.4	[b]	68.6	[b]	88.6	[b]	94.3	[b]	79.4	N.A.	77.1	N.A.
Any SG identity	7.7	[b]	74.4	[b]	89.5	[b]	89.5	[b]	75.7	N.A.	81.6	N.A.

Note: N.A. = not applicable.

[a]Proportion of respondents reporting practice with an opposite-gender partner (e.g., active oral sex reported by male respondents refers to ever having performed oral sex on a woman).

[b]Fewer than thirty cases.

in this table become more narrowly and exclusively defined as one moves down the columns.[32]

Table 8.6 includes masturbation in the past year, active and receptive oral sex, and active and receptive anal sex. The two tails of the distribution of masturbation are included: no masturbation in the past year and masturbating once a week or more. The proportion reporting each level of masturbation in the various groups defined by our measures of same-gender sexuality is displayed, as is the proportion for the total population. The rates of masturbation increase as one goes down the columns for both men and women. This appears as a decline in the proportion of people who say that they did not masturbate and an increase in the proportion who said that they masturbated frequently in the past year. The rates of masturbation for all these groups are much higher than the rates observed for the sample as a whole. We can only speculate why this might be the case. There is a compositional problem here similar to that for

32. This is not always true, although the exceptions are quite minor. The exceptions are that there are a few respondents who report same-gender partners in the past five years who did not have such partners since turning eighteen (i.e., among those under twenty-three at the time of the interview). Also, there were five men and one woman who did not have same-gender partners but who considered themselves to be homosexual or bisexual. These exceptions have only a very minor effect on the proportions in this table.

the comparisons made for numbers of partners. The same-gender sexuality groupings tend to be younger, more highly educated, more urbanized, and less religious. They are also less likely to be currently cohabiting or married. Perhaps they are also less subject to social taboos related to sexuality so that, in crossing a major line of sexual demarcation, they have lowered fears of breaching other barriers as well.

The sexual practices in this table refer to lifetime rates (i.e., since puberty) of ever having engaged in the specific practice with a person of the same gender (see appendix C, SAQ 4F [for females] and SAQ 4M [for males]). The comparison rates for the sample as a whole are based on reports of ever engaging in the equivalent practice with someone of the opposite gender. For example, the total population rate for active oral sex for men refers to men who performed oral sex on a woman (cunnilingus). The proportions below it for the various same-gender groupings refer to performing oral sex on another man (fellatio). For the women, the total population rate for active oral sex refers to fellatio performed on a male partner, and, for the same-gender groupings, the proportions are of women who performed oral sex (cunnilingus) on a female partner. The anal sex columns refer to anal intercourse and therefore were not asked of women in terms of other women. The total population rates are based on active anal intercourse by men with female partners and receptive anal sex reported by female respondents with male partners.

Similar to the pattern for masturbation, there are increasing proportions of the groups who report ever having engaged in a given practice as one moves down the columns in the table. In the first and, by far, the broadest grouping, about a third of the men report ever performing oral sex on another man, and about 40 percent report having had oral sex performed on them.[33] These proportions increase markedly in each of the next three rows as one moves down the column to the group of men who had sex with men in the past year. The highest level of active oral sex is close to 90 percent, receptive oral sex 94 percent, and 90 percent of those who identify as either homosexual or bisexual report receptive oral sex. For women, the rates and pattern of oral sex are quite similar. Unfortunately, there are fewer than thirty women in the two last categories, but, even for these groups (not shown here), the rates continue to increase. The highest rate for the women is 92 percent reported by the women identified as homosexual or bisexual. The rates of oral sex with same-gender partners for those who report a same-gender partner in the past year or who identify as homosexual or bisexual rise above those reported between opposite-gender partners for the sample as a whole. While, for these groups, oral sex becomes almost universal, approaching 90–95 percent, it is not so high among people

33. Many of the people in this set may never have had any sex with a person of their own gender. But this is not by definition or design. While 59 percent of the women and 44 percent of the men in this group reported only desire but no behavior and identity in adulthood, the sexual practice questions refer to activity any time since puberty.

reporting at least one same-gender partner since turning eighteen. Only 60–70 percent of these men and women report ever having oral sex with a same-gender partner.

Anal intercourse among men follows the pattern for oral sex, although at slightly lower rates. Anal sex increases from almost 30 percent to about 80 percent as one moves down the columns in the table. There is even more consistency between rates of reporting active and receptive anal intercourse. These rates are higher, even for the broadest definition of a same-gender category, than the lifetime rates for opposite-gender anal sex. On the other hand, while high, these rates are not as high as those for oral sex; 20–25 percent of the narrowest categorization of the men report never having had anal intercourse. They are also lower than the high rates of over 95 percent for vaginal intercourse reported in chapter 3.

8.7 Conclusion

In contrast to much of the literature on homosexuality, which draws sharp distinctions between people who identify socially and psychologically with the gay and lesbian experience and everyone else, we have not treated people who had same-gender experiences as being somehow fundamentally different. Following such reasoning, we have included the whole population in all the analyses (with a few exceptions) throughout the book. It was only in deference to the widespread interest in homosexuality per se that we decided to report our primary results on same-gender sexual practices and preferences in a separate chapter.

Our data, limited in some respects though they may be, represent the most varied and comprehensive measures of different aspects of homosexuality to be collected on a representative sample of U.S. adults. We have broadened the perspective of population-based sex research beyond a narrow focus on a small set of sexual behaviors between people of the same gender. Put simply, we contend that there is no single answer to questions about the prevalence of homosexuality. Rather, homosexuality is a complex, multidimensional phenomenon whose salient features are related to one another in highly contingent and diverse ways. For example, the highest rates of same-gender experience are found in the largest cities, with sharp declines across levels of urbanization. And there are marked gender differences in the report of same-gender experiences that also interact in complex ways with age and education. It is findings such as these that underscore the importance of understanding the social organization of sexuality throughout the life course.

CHAPTER 9

Formative Sexual Experiences

In this chapter, we discuss sexual experiences that are highly salient and emotionally charged: first vaginal intercourse and coercive or abusive sex. Although first intercourse and forced sex are at first glance disparate topics, in this chapter we have grouped them together under the rubric of formative sexual experiences. As we will see, all these experiences involve issues of consent and each has a special power to shape future sexual and nonsexual adjustment.

In our culture, first heterosexual intercourse usually represents the initiation into partnered sexual activity. This transition, or at least the age at which it occurs, has been the subject of extensive previous research that has been motivated in large part by changing policy concerns ranging from "sexual permissiveness" in the 1950s to more recent concerns with teenage pregnancy and sexually transmitted infections among young people. Our research also treats the topic of age at first intercourse, but we have expanded the discussion to a broader consideration of the changing quality of adolescents' sexual lives and how respondents characterize the social context of their early sexual experiences. In this way, we hope to get a sense of the qualitative aspects of how individuals experience a transition that has so much symbolic importance in our culture.

Coercive and abusive sexual experiences are also "formative" in the sense that they have, as we will see, important consequences for the happiness and well-being of those who experience them. Unlike research on age at first intercourse, research on forced sex has been limited by a lack of data from high-quality national samples. Our data include some of the first estimates of the prevalence of forced sex experiences based on a national probability sample of adult men and women as well as a broader treatment of the victims' relationships to their attackers and the physical and emotional consequences of forced sex.

Although our data include useful information about the social context of first intercourse and the prevalence of coerced sex, we must be sensitive to certain features of survey research methodology. We have gathered retrospec-

This chapter was drafted by Kristen Olson, with help from Nora Leibowitz, Fang Li, and Dawne Moon in data analysis and literature review. It was produced under the direction of Edward O. Laumann and John H. Gagnon.

tive accounts of highly salient and sensitive events. Individuals reinterpret the meaning and significance of *all* experiences—sexual or otherwise. Certain events considered "turning points" in personal biographies may be more susceptible to revision than others. Furthermore, individuals often reevaluate their sexual experiences in adolescence and coerced sex in light of the quality of their current lives as well as the current views of their own circles of friends, kin, and acquaintances, newspaper articles, television talk shows, and other vehicles of public opinion. Because of the ongoing social reconstruction of people's life experiences, survey data purporting to characterize the nature of first intercourse or to estimate the prevalence of prior coercive sexual experiences should be interpreted with caution. Nevertheless, we are confident that respondents give fairly accurate reports of facts such as the timing of first intercourse, even if they revise their accounts of how they felt about it at the time. Furthermore, because forced sex is undoubtedly underreported in surveys because of the socially stigmatized nature of the event, we believe that our estimates are probably conservative "lower-bound" estimates of forced sex within the population.

9.1 First Vaginal Intercourse and Youthful Heterosexuality

First intercourse, especially for women, has traditionally been a landmark event surrounded by a welter of moral strictures and normative concerns about the meaning of virginity, the loss of innocence, the transition to adulthood, and the assumption of responsibility for procreation and the next generation. Cultural proscriptions surrounding adolescent and premarital intercourse retain much of their potential to arouse public outcry, despite and because of the profound change in the numbers of young unmarried people engaging in sexual intercourse. As we see in greater detail in chapter 14, nearly 80 percent of the NHSLS sample still think that teenage sex is always or almost always wrong—even if the respondents themselves reported an early onset of sexual intercourse in their own lives. These views are, apparently, increasingly inconsistent with the actual pattern of behavior.

Cultural taboos about discussing sexuality limit the extent to which the mass media allow condom advertisements and public service announcements about "safe sex" and AIDS (Turner, Miller, and Moses 1989), although a recently announced federal initiative (in January 1994) to advertise condoms on television suggests some change. Beliefs about the morality of premarital sex and related issues, such as whether giving teenagers information about safe sex encourages them to have sex, cause many to oppose campaigns to distribute information about sexuality and contraception in high schools nationally.

Earlier Research on Youthful Premarital Sexual Activity

Popular belief holds that widespread premarital intercourse among young people as a common phenomenon is a fairly recent development, produced by the pervasive social decay afflicting modern society that expresses itself in rising rates of crime, licentiousness, and disorder. Evidence suggests, however, that premarital intercourse among young people, including many adolescents, was fairly common well before World War II.

In 1970, NORC conducted a survey for the Kinsey Institute that demonstrated a trend over the century of increasing numbers of premarital sexual relationships for American adults (Turner, Miller, and Moses 1989). While this trend was apparent for men, it was much stronger for women. Various studies showed a general trend through the 1960s of more women engaging in premarital sex, with more rapid increases during the 1970s (Zelnik and Kantner 1972a, 1980; Vener and Stewart 1974). Other studies focused on patterns of association among sexually active people, attitudes toward premarital sex, and the prevalence of premarital intercourse (Reiss 1960, 1967; Cannon and Long 1971; Chilman 1978).

Zelnik and Kantner (1980) collected data in 1971 and 1976 on the incidence of premarital intercourse among fifteen- to nineteen-year-old never-married women. They found that the lifetime prevalence of premarital vaginal intercourse increased from 21 percent in 1971 to 31 percent in 1976 for young white women and from 51 percent to 63 percent for young black women. They noted that there were increases in the percentages of sexually experienced respondents at each age between fifteen and nineteen for both races and that the increases for whites were two times greater than those for blacks. In 1970 and 1973, Vener and Stewart (1974) conducted cross-sectional surveys of thirteen- to seventeen-year-olds still attending school in Michigan. They found that the lifetime prevalence of vaginal intercourse for these adolescent men rose from 28 percent in 1970 to 33 percent in 1973. The respective proportions for adolescent women were 16 and 22 percent. Many of these surveys in recent decades provide accurate estimates of the age of first coital experiences, but they are limited because they targeted specialized populations. Even with these limitations, they were also important for suggesting problems and research strategies for later researchers.

Much of the research conducted on age at first intercourse during the mid- to late 1980s was motivated by an interest in contraceptive use and AIDS awareness among teenagers (cf. Sonenstein, Pleck, and Ku 1989b; Mosher and McNally 1991). The 1988 National Survey of Adolescent Males (NSAM) gathered data indicating that 60 percent of never-married young men aged fifteen to nineteen were sexually active (Sonenstein, Pleck, and Ku 1991). One-third of the fifteen-year-olds in their sample reported having had intercourse, as did half the sixteen-year-olds and almost two-thirds of those age seventeen. By age nineteen, 86 percent of the respondents reported having had sexual intercourse.

Using the 1970 survey data gathered by NORC for the Kinsey Institute, the authors of *AIDS: Sexual Behavior and Intravenous Drug Use* (Turner, Miller, and Moses 1989) came to much the same conclusion as earlier studies on the topic of premarital intercourse. Turner and his colleagues combined the 1970

Kinsey Institute data with the 1982 National Survey of Family Growth (NSFG).[1] Both surveys showed that, over time, more young people were having premarital sex (under age sixteen and under age nineteen, respectively). These surveys overwhelmingly suggest that there has been a significant change in the early heterosexual life of young women in the United States. In the Kinsey Institute study, fewer than 6 percent of American women born before 1911 reported that, before they were nineteen, they engaged in premarital sexual activity (including, but not limited to, intercourse) leading to orgasm. For the 1959–61 birth cohort, by contrast, in the NSFG (1982) more than 62 percent of women reported premarital sexual intercourse before age nineteen. Data on high school students gathered in 1991 indicate that 76 percent of young men and 66 percent of young women in the United States had first had intercourse by their senior year of high school.

Age at First Intercourse: NHSLS Results

Our data indicate that only 4.2 percent of the adult men and 2.7 percent of the adult women in the United States have never had vaginal intercourse. As one might expect, these numbers are slightly higher for the younger respondents (10.8 percent of the men and 6.2 percent of the women aged eighteen to twenty-four). Of the women and men who have ever had intercourse, somewhat fewer women respondents had their first vaginal sex before age eighteen than men, 46 percent compared to 57 percent.

In general, our data suggest a slight trend toward earlier experiences of first intercourse for both genders. Level of education is negatively associated with having intercourse before age eighteen, as is living with both parents. Not being religious is associated with having sex at a younger age, although it is also associated with never experiencing intercourse. Being religious not only acts as a constraint on early premarital sexual experience but may also facilitate early marriage and hence younger age at first intercourse.

Changes in the patterns of sexual practices among young people are evident in our data on the average age at first intercourse by cohort. Figure 9.1 divides the sample into four birth cohorts: those who were high school age between 1951 and 1960 (born 1933–42), between 1961 and 1970 (born 1943–52), between 1971 and 1980 (born 1953–62), and between 1981 and 1985 (born 1963–1967). We observe a small but discernible decline in mean age at first intercourse over these four decades for both men and women and for both whites and blacks. The mean age at first intercourse is higher for the women of each race, differing by nearly a year for the whites and by as much as two years for the blacks in some cohorts. These differences are nearly erased for

1. The proportion of respondents in the 1944–49 birth cohort in the NSFG who reported premarital intercourse by age twenty (46 percent) is lower than that of Kinsey Institute respondents who reported sexual activity to the point of orgasm (56 percent). This suggests that the respondents in the Kinsey study included in their responses sexual interactions that did not involve intercourse. The overall trend across birth cohorts appears fairly comparable in the two sources.

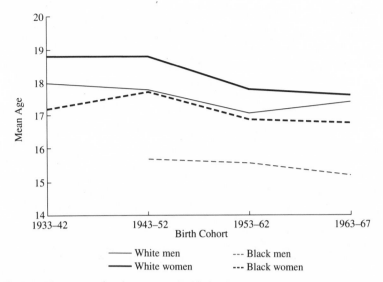

Fig. 9.1 Mean age at first intercourse, by birth cohort.

Note: This figure includes respondents who had vaginal intercourse no later than age twenty-five and who had reached their twenty-fifth birthday by the date of the interview. Missing line segments indicate an insufficient number of cases for a particular category (i.e., fewer than thirty). Figures for whites were computed from the cross section, those for blacks from the cross section including the oversample.

the whites in the youngest cohort. If one looks to figure 9.1 for evidence of a dramatic change that might be called a *sexual revolution,* it will not be found. There has, indeed, been a decline in the age at first intercourse, but, as is so often the case with social phenomena, that change has occurred gradually over a long period.

In general, it appears that mean age at first intercourse is declining among all ethnic groups, although this tendency appears to have started a cohort earlier for blacks than for whites and Hispanics. Overall, the difference between the mean ages of the different ethnic and racial groups has declined as the average ages have converged to between fifteen and eighteen years of age. Also notice that the difference between mean age at first intercourse between men and women has decreased over time for all racial/ethnic groups.

Figure 9.2 displays the cumulative incidence of age at first intercourse for men and women born between 1933 and 1952 (who were over forty at the time of the survey) and between 1953 and 1972 (who were under forty at the time of the survey). These data include all reports of first intercourse, whether it occurred before or at marriage. This figure shows that, within each age group, men have an earlier age at first intercourse than women. For men who came of age in the 1950s and 1960s, 35 percent had had intercourse by the age of sixteen, compared to only nineteen percent of women in the same cohort. The modal age is about seventeen for men and about eighteen for women in this

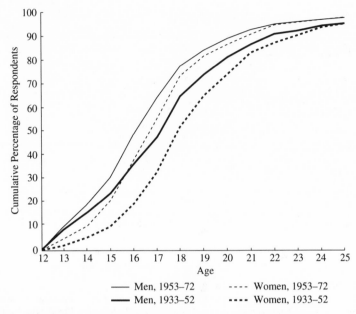

Fig. 9.2 Cumulative percentage of respondents by age at first intercourse.

age group. For those who came of age in the 1970s and 1980s, 48 percent of the men had had intercourse by the age of sixteen, compared to 37 percent of women. For the younger cohorts, the modal age is sixteen for men and nearly seventeen for women. For individuals who came of age in the 1950s and 1960s, 25 percent of the men and 45 percent of the women were still virgins at the age of nineteen, compared to only 15 percent of the men and 17 percent of the women who came of age in the 1970s and 1980s. Like figure 9.1, figure 9.2 indicates a trend toward earlier sexual experience over these four decades. In figure 9.2, one also sees evidence of a convergence in terms of the timing of men's and women's first experience with intercourse.

NHSLS Results Compared to Other Surveys

The patterns observed in various surveys that preceded the NHSLS are borne out in this survey. Data from the 1991 National Survey of Men (NSM) (Billy et al. 1993) allow the estimate that 90 percent of men aged twenty to twenty-four have had vaginal intercourse. The NHSLS estimate is identical to this. The NHSLS and NSM estimates for the proportion of respondents having had intercourse by other ages are consistent as well. The NHSLS data are also consistent with data from the NSFG (Pratt et al. 1984). The NSFG asked women aged fifteen to forty-four whether they had ever engaged in sexual intercourse. As the NSFG data were collected in 1982 and the NHSLS in 1992, we compared the responses of the women in the NSFG at the time they were interviewed to the responses of the NHSLS women at the comparable age. That is, we matched the NSFG women who were fifteen when they were asked about their current sexual experience with NHSLS women who were twenty-five when interviewed about what their experience had been when they were fifteen (ten years before, at the time the NSFG was being conducted). We similarly compared women who were nineteen when interviewed by the NSFG with women who were twenty-nine when they became part of the NHSLS, and so on for other ages. The similarity between the two data sets is striking. In the NSFG and NHSLS, respectively, 18 and 19 percent of female respondents reported having had vaginal intercourse by age fifteen. Seventy-four percent of the nineteen-year-old female NSFG respondents and 71 percent of the twenty-nine-year-old female NHSLS respondents reported having had sex by age nineteen. Because the NHSLS estimates are so close to those of the NSFG, we can be more confident of the accuracy of our estimates.

Number of Partners before Age Eighteen

The trend toward earlier experiences of first intercourse suggests another question. Given that adolescents are having intercourse earlier, how many sex partners are they accumulating during their teen years? We have seen that later cohorts of men and women had decreasing percentages reporting no partners before age eighteen. As the number of people abstaining from intercourse before age eighteen drops over the years, the number of people having more partners by that age increases, as can be seen in table 9.1. This change is particularly evident among women: only 2.5 percent of those born between 1933 and 1942 and about 10 percent born between 1963 and 1974 report five or more sex partners before age eighteen. Overall, a larger proportion of younger women had more partners before age eighteen, and considerably fewer women in the youngest cohort had no partners (about 42 percent) compared to women in the oldest cohort (about 68 percent). The other main point of interest is that the number of women and men with any given number of partners converges; gender differences in the number of partners before age eighteen are much more pronounced among older people compared to younger people.

Context of First Intercourse

Like many previous surveys about first intercourse, the NHSLS asked at what age the respondent first had vaginal intercourse; however, we also gathered more qualitative information about the experience. We asked whether first intercourse was something that the respondent wanted to happen at the time, something that he or she did not want but went along with, or something that he or she was forced to do against his or her will. If the first intercourse experience was not forced, we asked the respondent why he or she wanted to do it or went along with it. We also gathered information about respondents' relationship to their first vaginal intercourse partner and how many times they subsequently had sex with this partner (Carns 1975). We collected this information

Table 9.1   **Number of Opposite-Gender Sex Partners before Age Eighteen, by Birth Cohort and Gender (% distributions)**

| | Number of Partners | | | | | | |
	0	1	2	3	4	5+	N
1933–42:							
Men	57.5	12.5	4.5	6.5	5.0	14.0	200
Women	67.8	25.8	2.1	1.4	.4	2.5	283
1943–52							
Men	52.1	15.0	4.0	4.9	5.5	18.5	326
Women	70.0	20.9	3.8	1.8	1.5	2.0	397
1953–62							
Men	43.2	18.8	10.0	8.6	4.9	14.5	431
Women	52.4	27.6	7.7	5.2	1.6	5.5	557
1963–74							
Men	38.7	17.6	9.3	10.4	4.7	19.3	450
Women	41.8	22.9	11.6	8.0	6.1	9.6	510
All							
Men	45.8	16.6	7.6	8.0	5.0	17.0	1,407
Women	55.8	24.4	7.0	4.6	2.7	5.5	1,747

in order better to characterize how people view their first intercourse experience and to allow us to improve our understanding of the social nature of this transition, rather than simply to learn the age at which the transition occurred.

The respondents were asked whether their first experience of sexual intercourse was "something you wanted to happen at the time, something you went along with, but did not want to happen, [or] something that you were forced to do against your will" (see appendix C, section 8, question 21). As indicated in table 9.2, just over 92 percent of the men said that their first intercourse was something that they wanted to happen, but only 71 percent of the women answered that they wanted their first intercourse experience to happen when it did. Fewer than 8 percent of the male respondents reported going along with the experience without really wanting to, while more than three times as many women, or about one-fourth of all female respondents, reported that they did not want to have intercourse the first time. Just over 4 percent of female respondents reported being forced to have sex their first time, compared to less than 0.5 percent of male respondents. Analyses not presented here indicate that fewer of the women in the youngest cohorts report having wanted their first experience of vaginal intercourse to happen when it did than did women in the older cohorts, and, as we have seen above, more of these younger women were younger at the time of that sexual event. Many of the older women first had sex on their wedding night. A much larger percentage of black women report not wanting their first experience of vaginal intercourse to happen when it did than did women of other racial and ethnic groups, 41 percent compared to an average of 29 percent.

Among those who wanted their first vaginal intercourse to happen when it did, just over half the male respondents said that they were motivated by a curiosity about sex, and one-quarter did it because of their affection for their partner (see table 9.3). Almost half the female respondents cited affection for their partner as their reason for having intercourse the first time, and just under one-quarter of them reported curiosity about sex as their main motivation (48 and 24 percent, respectively). Only about 3 percent of the women said that physical pleasure was their main reason for having first intercourse, compared to four times as many men who said this (12 percent). Other analyses also show that, while 21 percent of the women reported having intercourse the first time on their wedding night, we do see an expected change from the older cohorts, in which about 45 percent of the women had intercourse the first time in marriage, to the youngest cohort, where only 5 percent of those who ever engaged in vaginal intercourse did not do so before marriage. This trend, although not as strong, is also apparent for the men; 17 percent of the men now

Table 9.2   **First Intercourse Wanted, Not Wanted, or Forced (percentages)**

First Intercourse	Men	Women
Wanted	92.1	71.3
Not wanted but not forced	7.6	24.5
Forced	.3	4.2
N	1,337	1,689

Table 9.3   **Reasons for Having First Intercourse, by Gender and Desire Status (percentages)**

Attributed Reasons	Wanted First Intercourse		Not Wanted but Not Forced	
	Men	Women	Men	Women
Affection for partner	24.9	47.5	9.9	38.5
Peer pressure	4.2	3.3	28.6	24.6
Curiosity/readiness for sex	50.6	24.3	50.5	24.9
Pregnancy	.5	.6	0.0	0.0
Physical pleasure	12.2	2.8	6.6	2.1
Under the influence of alcohol or drugs	.7	.3	3.3	7.2
Wedding night	6.9	21.1	1.1	2.7
N	1,199	1,147	91	374

fifty to fifty-nine years old had their first sex on their wedding night, while only 2 percent of the youngest cohort (eighteen- to twenty-four-year-olds) were married at the time.

As noted earlier, about 8 percent of male respondents and 25 percent of female respondents reported that they did not want to have vaginal intercourse the first time it happened but went along with it for any of a number of reasons. Among the men who went along with the experience, over half did so out of curiosity and more than 29 percent because of peer pressure. Of the women who went along with their first vaginal intercourse without wanting it to occur, 39 percent cite affection for their partner, 25 percent report curiosity about sex, and 25 percent report peer pressure. That such a large percentage of both men and women who did not really want to have intercourse did so because of peer pressure is an interesting commentary on the importance of peer approval in the youth culture.

Examining the relation between respondents and their first sex partner in table 9.4, we again note differences by gender. The vast majority of women report that they were in love with their first partner (55 percent were not married to this partner, and 22 percent first had intercourse with their spouse).[2] Most men report that their first partner was someone with whom they were not in love. The men's partners were friends or acquaintances about 49 percent and strangers and prostitutes only about 10 percent of the time.

Across age cohorts, there is a decline in the proportion of men who had their first sexual intercourse with a paid partner. Slightly less than 7 percent of the fifty-five to fifty-nine-year-olds, in contrast to 1.5 percent of the eighteen- to twenty-four-year-olds, report paying someone their first time. This represents a continuation of the earlier finding by Kinsey, Pomeroy, and Martin (1948) of this same decline among men coming of age before World War II.

If we examine the social relationships of women by their wanting their first intercourse to occur, we can see a dramatic contrast. Eight out of ten women who wanted the intercourse to occur when it did reported that they were in love with their partner; this falls to six out of ten among those who went along and 17 percent of those who were forced. A closer examination of those who were forced against their will to have their first vaginal intercourse allows us to specify more clearly what their relation to this man was. There were three spouses among the twelve men with whom the women reported that they were in love, while only ten men (14 percent) were strangers. Again, the vast majority of men who commit acts of violence against women are known to the women before the event.

Of the seventy-one women who reported being forced to have sex, 70 percent reported being physically forced, 8 percent reported the use of a weapon,

---

2. The data reported here refer only to respondents who wanted their first intercourse to occur when it did or who did not want it to occur but went along with it anyway. They do not include those respondents who report having been forced their first time.

Table 9.4   Relationship to First Sex Partner, by Gender and Desire Status
(percentages)

Relationship	Men	Women			
		All	Wanted	Not Wanted/ Not Forced	Forced
Spouse	10.4	21.8	28.6	5.1	4.2
In love	31.1	53.2	54.6	56.4	12.7
Knew well, not in love	36.5	17.3	13.4	26.5	26.8
Knew, but not well	12.3	5.3	2.5	9.2	28.2
Just met	4.9	1.0	.7	1.9	1.4
Paid	3.1	.1	.1	0.0	0.0
Stranger	1.0	.7	.1	0.0	14.1
Other	.8	.7	0.0	.7	12.7
N	1,328	1,663	1,178	411	71

and 25 percent reported that they were verbally threatened (these numbers cumulate to more than 100 percent because some women reported more than one level of force being used against them). Nine of the women reported that they were forced by a relative to have their first vaginal intercourse. In five of these cases, the offender was a father.

Included in the questions about first vaginal intercourse was a question about what techniques were used (kissing, touching genitals, oral sex, vaginal sex, and anal sex). As indicated in table 9.5, 95 percent of the respondents reported that vaginal intercourse occurred.[3] Eighty-five percent of men and 87 percent of women reported that kissing occurred; 79 and 74 percent, respectively, reported touching genitals. Very few people reported having anal sex as part of the first intercourse. The one major gender difference is that, while 16 percent of the male respondents said that oral sex occurred, only half as many women reported having had oral sex during this sexual encounter. From these data, first intercourse appears to be a relatively goal-directed experience for most people, without many of the other techniques that characterize later sexual encounters.

While the percentage of men and women who used birth control during first vaginal intercourse is fairly low (34 percent of men and 38 percent of women),

3. This is an anomalous finding because, by definition, first vaginal intercourse should include vaginal intercourse. We have two possible explanations for what led 5 percent of the respondents to answer in this way. The interviewer handed the respondent a card with the various practices written on it, each with a number. The respondent was asked to tell the interviewer the numbers corresponding to the techniques used during the first sexual encounter. One explanation is that some respondents assumed that, as the context for the question was the first time they engaged in vaginal intercourse, they did not need to, or were not supposed to, name it again. Another explanation is that some respondents did not understand the term in this context, were not literate enough to understand the written term *vaginal intercourse,* or were otherwise confused by the phrasing of the question.

Table 9.5   **Sexual Techniques and Use of Birth Control during First Intercourse, by Gender and Desire Status (coded all that occurred) (percentages)**

		Women			
	Men	All	Wanted	Not Wanted/ Not Forced	Forced
Sexual techniques					
Kissing	84.7	86.9	89.7	85.6	49.3
Manual stimulation of genitals	78.8	74.3	77.2	70.1	53.5
Oral sex	16.1	8.5	9.3	5.5	12.7
Anal sex	1.7	1.1	1.1	.7	2.8
Vaginal intercourse	95.1	95.9	95.9	96.3	95.8
N	1,295	1,651	1,175	402	71
Used birth control	33.8	37.9	43.1	28.4	7.1
N	1,268	1,653	1,175	405	70

there is an increase in the use of birth control from 25 percent in the older cohorts to 50 percent for the youngest group. Using birth control during first intercourse is positively associated with level of education. Jews and the nonreligious used birth control during first intercourse more than Protestants and Catholics. First intercourse that was part of a more serious, long-term relationship (sex with a spouse or lover) is positively associated with using birth control, suggesting that people are more likely to use birth control if the intercourse was a planned event.

One other question that we asked about first sexual partnership was the number of times the respondent subsequently had sex with the first partner. As shown in table 9.6, there are distinct gender differences here, with 28 percent of the male respondents and about half that number of women (14 percent) reporting that they had sex with their first partner only once. Conversely, twice as many women as men report still being sexually involved with their first partner (20 vs. 10 percent). This is a not unexpected finding, given the differences in these first encounters for women and men. Thus, more of the women reported first intercourse with a marital partner, and more reported being in love as the reason for their first intercourse.

Three main conclusions are to be drawn about first intercourse. First, over time, more people have their first experience with vaginal intercourse at younger ages. While average age at first intercourse is converging by gender and ethnicity, men historically had (and continue to have) sex somewhat earlier than women. Second, more and more people are having (premarital) sex earlier in their lives. Among the youngest respondents, the majority were no longer virgins by age eighteen: half had first intercourse between the ages of fifteen and seventeen. Third, gender differences are strong in adolescent sexuality. Men start earlier, have more partners, and are motivated by curiosity and self-

Table 9.6   **Number of Times Respondent Had Sex with First Intercourse Partner, by Gender and Desire Status (percentages)**

		Women			
Number of Times	Men	All	Wanted	Not Wanted/ Not Forced	Forced
One time	27.6	14.3	9.0	21.2	64.3
Two to ten	34.8	23.5	20.8	32.6	15.7
More than ten	27.7	42.1	44.5	38.9	17.1
Still having intercourse	9.9	20.2	27.5	7.3	2.9
N	1,330	1,683	1,199	411	70

interest; women begin later, have sex with spouses or more serious lovers, and use birth control more than men.

9.2   Forced/Coerced Sex in Adulthood

Forced sex, rape, sexual harassment, and violation of personal sexual boundaries are hotly contested and volatile issues in contemporary American society. Some theorists argue that rape is an act of uncontrolled passion or the result of a lack of female partners (Posner 1992), others that it is an extreme expression of male power (Brownmiller 1975).[4] For others, coerced intercourse is a biologically driven phenomenon in which men forcefully try to maximize the number of women with whom they procreate (Gelles and Wolfner 1994).

The definition of *rape* is controversial, and legal and moral definitions sharply differ.[5] Although many people argue about what defines the experience of rape, all recognize that it can have profound effects on people's lives. We asked respondents about forced sex, rather than specifically about rape, for two reasons. First, there was no reason to assume that the respondent would be able to characterize events that would be equivalent to rape in the legal sense. Second, we wished to cast a wider net for coerced sexual events, recognizing that meeting the legal standards for rape does not exhaust the category of women being coerced to have sex.

We asked about this topic in two separate ways, in the face-to-face interview and in the confidential self-administered questionnaire (SAQ). In the face-to-face questioning, we asked (appendix C, section 8, question 27), "After puberty, that is, after you were (AGE IN Q.1/12 or 13 years old), did a (OPPO-

4. Brownmiller (1975) was the first to suggest that rape is an expression of violence rather than of sex. Many later writers have also endorsed this view (see also MacKinnon 1989).

5. One difficulty in discussing data about a socially sensitive and publicly debated topic such as rape is that they do not in any way speak for themselves and are consequently easily interpreted in any number of partisan ways depending on one's agenda. While we cannot prevent willful or inadvertent misinterpretations of what we found, we want to be as clear as possible as to what the data do and do not represent. We have tried to limit our discussion to descriptions of the data, making further comments about relations when we felt that we had safe statistical grounds to do so.

SITE SEX OF R—male/female) force you to do anything sexually that you did not want to do?" (yes/no). If the answer was yes, we then followed up that question with a series of questions about other times this had happened, the number of different people with whom it happened, the relationship to the respondent of the person involved, the number of times it happened with that person, and specifically what had happened. These questions were asked of both the men and the women.

In the SAQ (appendix C, SAQ 4F, questions 5, 6, 13, and 14), following a series of questions about whether the women had ever had oral sex or anal sex or been paid by a man to have sex, we asked them, "Have you ever been forced by a man to do something that you did not want to do?" "Have you ever forced a man to do something sexual that he did not want to do?" "Have you ever forced another woman to do something sexual that she did not want to do?" and, "Have you ever been forced by a woman to do something sexual that you did not want to do?" Notice that we made a mistake in our questionnaire, inadvertently omitting the word *sexual* from the first question about being forced by a man. The context for this question is clearly a sexual "something," but the responses to that one question are nevertheless somewhat suspect.

We asked the men in the SAQ format (appendix C, SAQ 4M, questions 6, 15, and 16), "Have you ever forced a woman to do something sexual that she did not want to do?" "Have you ever forced a man to do something sexual that he did not want to do?" and, "Have you ever been forced by a man to do something sexual that you did not want to do?"

Respondents undoubtedly differ in how they understand our questions about forced sex. Some may have thought of our questions as pertaining just to violent, penetrative sex, while others probably understood the question in broader terms.[6]

Comparison of various studies of rape is difficult because the definitions of key terms like *rape, sexual assault, forced sex,* and *sexual victimization* vary (see Gelles and Wolfner 1994; Russell 1984; and Finkelhor 1979).[7] Similarly, there is disagreement in how respondents define *rape.* Thus, making valid estimates of the prevalence of rape and sexual assault is quite difficult. For examples of these difficulties, see Koss (1988) and Finkelhor (1984).

Clinical data also tend to have strong selection biases, thereby often providing inaccurate pictures of both the victims and the offenders. Victims of rape included in clinical samples are generally only those individuals able or willing

6. Current research suggests that the majority of rapes are committed by someone known to the victim, although some people think of rape as something that only a stranger does (for a discussion of marital rape, see Yllo and Finkelhor [1985] and Russell [1982]). Koss et al. (1988) found that, compared with those perpetrated by strangers, rapes by acquaintances were more likely to involve a single offender over several to many episodes and were less likely to be seen as rape or to be reported either to friends or to the police.

7. The legal definition of *rape* includes forced vaginal or anal penetration and forced oral-genital contact, but not other sexual experiences involving force or coercion.

to report their victimization. Biases in the way in which questions are asked as well as poorly conceived or written questions can affect the results of even those surveys that have representative samples.

Estimates of Coercive Sex

Table 9.7 reports the rates of forced sex by gender of the respondent and gender of the person forcing or forced. In the top panel, we see that 2.8 percent of the men in the survey report forcing a woman sexually and that 1.5 percent of the women surveyed report forcing a man sexually. Practically none of the respondents reported forcing sex on someone of their own gender.

In the bottom panel, we see the rates of the respondents being forced sexually, with 1.3 percent of the men reporting being forced by another man and nearly 22 percent of the women being forced by a man. Thus, overall, our data indicate that more than one in five women has experienced what she considers to be an incident in which she was forced to do something sexual that she did not want to do.[8]

We caution that, by the broad scope of the question that we asked, the reported experience involving force may not constitute rape in a legal sense or in the minds of the female respondents. Whatever the relation to rape, however, it is of considerable interest to find that as many as one in five women do consider themselves to have been forced against their will to do something sexually. Estimated rates of rape of women reported by other surveys vary from 5 percent (Kilpatrick et al. 1985) to 20–25 percent (Kanin 1957; Russell 1984).[9] Of the several logical possibilities of coercion by a person of one gender against another, table 9.7 shows that the only category with an incidence

8. We noted in the text that we asked questions about forced sex both in the face-to-face interview and in the self-administered questionnaire (SAQ). The results from the SAQ imply a much higher rate of occurrence of forced sex than the data from the face-to-face interview. For example, in the face-to-face interview about 15 percent of women respondents stated that they had ever been forced sexually, whereas in the SAQ over 20 percent of the women reported that they had ever been forced. We based our reports on the union of these reports. That is, any admission, whether in the face-to-face interview or in the SAQ, of having been forced sexually was counted as having experienced forced sex. We used a similar procedure to compute the rate of sexual coercion in men, although we neglected in the SAQ to ask men whether they had ever been forced sexually by a woman. Thus we can compare rates only for men who reported having been forced sexually by other men. In the SAQ, 2.1 percent of men reported that they had ever been forced sexually by a man; in the face-to-face interview, 1.7 percent reported ever having been forced by a man. About 1.5 percent of the men reported in the face-to-face interview that they had ever been forced sexually by a woman.

9. A brief review of some other surveys on rape and sexual assault puts the results of the NHSLS into a broader perspective. Kilpatrick and colleagues surveyed 2,004 randomly selected women in Charleston County, South Carolina (Kilpatrick, Veronen, and Best 1984; Kilpatrick et al. 1985). Fifteen percent of the women reported one or more attempted or completed sexual assaults. A third of these women described the assault as rape, and nearly another third described it as attempted rape. Only 29 percent of the women who reported having been raped told the police. Of the 930 women in Diana Russell's (1984) survey, 24 percent reported experiencing one or more forms of forced intercourse. Of the women who described such experiences, only 10 percent went to the police.

Table 9.7   Prevalence of Forced Sex, by Gender (percentages)

	Men	Women
Respondent ever forced a woman	2.8	.1
Respondent ever forced a man	.2	1.5
Never forced sexually	96.1	77.2
Forced by opposite-gender person	1.3	21.6
Forced by same-gender person	1.9	.3
Forced by both men and women	.4	.5
Missing/no answer	.3	.5
N	1,409	1,749

high enough to partition by master status and to investigate further is coercion by a man against a woman. Table 9.8 reports the rate of this coercion by master status variables. This partitioning by master status variables suggests that these variables only modestly structure the data on coercion. By age, there is a hint of lower rates at older ages, suggesting an upward trend in sexual assault since the FBI reports that the period of greatest risk of sexual assault on women is in the late teens and early twenties.

There is not a notable difference in the rate by education level. Catholic women report a rate of forced sex that is only half that of women who have no current religious affiliation. Asian and Hispanic women report notably lower rates than white women, with black women reporting rates between those extremes.

The most intriguing and unexpected pattern in table 9.8 may be the very low rate of sexual coercion reported by women living in central cities and the relatively high rate for those living in noncity urban areas. This latter pattern is not consistent with the perception that one has of the risks of sexual assault in big cities, but, as we show below, a vast majority of the reported forced sex occurs with someone well known to the respondent, not with someone un-known, which is the more typical circumstance thought to dominate in large cities.

Respondents were asked about their relationship to the people who forced

---

Many of the studies about rape and sexual assault have focused on college students, in part because the age of most college students puts them in a high-risk group for rape, and in part because, for a variety of reasons, college students are more accessible for study than nonstudents of comparable ages (who constitute nearly three-quarters of the age group eighteen to twenty-four [U.S. Bureau of Census 1980]). Unfortunately, these studies often use convenience sampling or have high rates of nonresponse, raising questions about validity. Reported rates of forceful attempts at sexual intercourse range between 10 and 25 percent (see Kanin 1957; Kirkpatrick and Kanin 1957; Rapaport and Burkhart 1984; Koss 1985, 1988; Koss and Oros 1982; Koss et al. 1985).

Table 9.8   **Distribution of Women Ever Forced Sexually by a Man,**
               by Master Status

	Respondent Ever Forced to Do Something Sexual by a Man		
	Yes	No	N
All women	22	77	1,749
Age:			
18–24	25	75	276
25–29	22	78	234
30–34	24	75	291
35–39	26	74	266
40–44	22	78	229
45–49	18	81	168
50–54	17	81	143
55–59	18	81	140
Education:			
Less than high school graduate	26	74	246
High school graduate or equivalent	17	83	512
Some college or vocational school	26	74	588
Finished college	22	77	281
Master's or advanced degree	23	77	109
Religion:			
None	31	68	152
Type I Prot.	21	79	422
Type II Prot.	25	74	592
Catholic	17	83	476
Race/ethnicity:			
White	23	76	1,338
Black	19	80	342
Hispanic	14	86	184
Asian	17	83	30
Size of place:			
Central city/12 largest SMSAs	16	82	154
Central city/100 largest SMSAs	29	71	244
Suburb/12 largest SMSAs	19	80	211
Suburb/100 largest SMSAs	19	81	307
Other urban	25	74	642
Rural	18	81	191

Note: Percentages do not add to 100 because of missing data and because women who were ever forced by a woman are excluded.

them sexually, and we found, as displayed in figure 9.3, that an overwhelming number of respondents knew their attackers, often very well. Of the women reporting forced sex, about 70 percent report being forced by one person. Of these women, a majority report that the person who forced them was either someone with whom they were in love or their spouse; an additional 22 percent of the aggressors were people the respondents knew well, another 19 percent

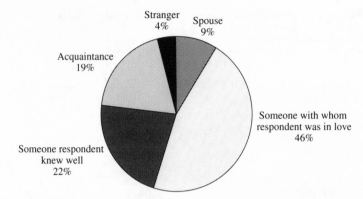

Fig. 9.3   The respondent's relationship to the person who forced him or her to have sex.
Note: N = 204. This figure includes female respondents who reported that they had ever been "forced to do something sexual that they did not want to do." Eighty-six women (or about 30 percent of all women who reported ever being forced) reported that they had been forced sexually by more than one person; they are not represented in the figure, but the distribution of the relationships to the people forcing them is similar.

acquaintances.[10] Thus, only 4 percent of the women forced to do something sexual were forced by a stranger.

Sexual assault is surely a traumatic event. How it affects the victim is not well understood. Independent of the questioning about forced sex, the NHSLS asked a series of questions about current and lifetime sexual functioning and practices and about current general health and happiness (see chap. 10). In table 9.9, we show the percentages of women who are not healthy, who are not happy, and who report one or another sexual practice, experience, or sexual dysfunction, partitioned by whether the woman reported being forced sexually. We note here again that while the partitioning by forced sex or no forced sex refers to the woman's entire lifetime, the selected features of the woman's sexual and nonsexual experiences may refer to either the past year only or to lifetime experience. Because the actual timing of the forced event(s) in the women's lives is not known, it is inappropriate to draw causal inferences from an observed pattern in the table.

About 15 percent of women who report ever having been forced sexually report not being healthy in the year preceding the survey, compared to 12 percent of women who report having never been forced. While that is a negligible difference, about 20 percent of the women forced to have sex said that they were not happy in the past year, and only 12 percent of the women who were not forced reported this. More women who were forced to have sex reported that their emotions interfered with sex than did those who had never been

10. These results concerning the relationships between the respondents and their attackers are broadly consistent with those reported in other studies (see Curtis 1976; Bureau of Justice Statistics 1984; Russell 1984; Koss 1988; Koss et al. 1988).

Table 9.9   **Comparison of Selected Features of Adult Women's Sexual and Nonsexual Experiences, by Forced Sex Status (percentages)**

	Not Forced	Forced
Not healthy last year	12	15[a]
Not happy last year	12	20
> 10 sex partners ever	6	21
Homosexual/bisexual identification	1	3
Ever performed oral sex	59	86
Ever received oral sex	64	91
Ever had anal sex with a man	15	38
Ever had group sex	2	10
Thought about sex often, last year	18	25
Lacked interest in sex, last year	31	41
Unable to experience orgasm, last year	22	33
Experienced orgasm too soon, last year	10	11[a]
Experienced pain during sex, last year	13	20
Sex was not pleasurable, last year	18	34
Was anxious about sexual performance, last year	10	17
Experienced difficulty lubricating, last year	17	26
Masturbated in the last year	37	60
Emotional problems interfered with sex, last year	42	57
N	1,285	326

[a]Not significant at the .05 level

forced (57 vs. 42 percent). Women who had never been forced reported less difficulty achieving orgasm and were also less likely to report pain during sex than were women who had been forced. Women who had been forced to have sex were more likely not to find sex pleasurable for a period of several months in the past year than those who had never been forced (34 vs. 18 percent). They also were more likely to have felt anxious about sexual performance than those who had never been forced (17 vs. 10 percent), and more likely to have had trouble lubricating (26 vs. 17 percent) than women who had not. They were also more likely to have thought about sex more often and to have masturbated in the past year than women who had never been forced. Regarding lifetime sexual experiences, women who had been forced reported higher incidences of active and receptive oral sex, anal sex, and group sex and were more likely to have had more than ten sex partners in their lifetime than women who had never been forced.

9.3   Adult and Adolescent Sexual Contacts with Children

Sexual contacts between adults and children are the most severely condemned of all the violations of the sexual rules of our society. The concern with child sexual abuse has always been significant, but in recent years there has been an escalation of both popular and scientific concern (cf. Browne and Finkelhor 1986; Kilpatrick 1987; Briere and Runtz 1993; Widom 1989a, 1989b, 1992;

Tsai et al. 1979). This has been, in part, a result of an increase in the awareness of the physical abuse of children, an awareness that sparked an increase in sensitivity to sexual abuse. This sensitivity has been sharpened by media attention to legal cases centering on allegations of mass child abuse in child-care facilities as well as allegations of sexual abuse by members of the clergy.

We asked all our respondents whether they had been touched sexually by anyone before puberty or when they were twelve or thirteen years of age (see appendix C, section 8, questions 3–19). By restricting our attention to sexual touching, we eliminated those cases of exhibitionism in which adults expose their genitals to children. We also eliminated all cases of child-child sexual contact by restricting this analysis to reported contacts between those *under* age twelve or thirteen and those *over* age fourteen. There is the possibility of a gray area that would include abuse by a fourteen- or fifteen-year-old of a thirteen-year-old in a conventional dating situation, but there are no cases of this kind reported in our data.

Sexual contacts by adolescents and adults with children are not rare in this study. About 12 percent of the men and about 17 percent of the women report that they had been sexually touched when they were children. But the incidence of being sexually touched as a child does not vary across the master status variables (data not shown). This experience is reported equally often by people of different ages (suggesting that there has not been an increase in rates in different years), of different ethnicities or races, or with differing levels of education. There is no social concentration of the experience that would suggest differential vulnerabilities to sexual touching by children in various social groups.

The women and men in the study had a variety of experiences of being touched sexually. Some were touched by women, others by men; some were touched by strangers, others by relatives; some had the experience a number of times, or extending over a long time period, or with a number of adults, while others reported only a single experience.

As can be seen in Table 9.10, the girls were primarily touched only by men, while the boys were touched more often by women but also by men. The female respondents reported that the men who had contact with them were more than twice as often likely to be over age eighteen, while the male respondents reported that they were more likely to have contact with a person who was an adolescent rather than an adult (two-thirds were between fourteen and seventeen). If one thinks about table 9.10 in terms of arraying the risk of sexual contact to children, the risk to girls is greatest from adult men, followed by adolescent men. The risk to boys is greatest from adolescent women, followed by adolescent and then older men.

Respondents were asked what happened sexually in these childhood contacts (see appendix C, section 8, question 3), and table 9.11 shows the percentage of contacts that involved the five specific activities that we asked about (counting all that apply). The table shows the results by the gender of both the

Table 9.10   **Age and Gender of Person Who Touched Respondent before Puberty: row percent (number of cases)**

	Touched by Men		Touched by Women		Touched by Both		
	14–17	18+	14–17	18+	14–17	18+	N
Women respondents	28 (79)	63 (180)	3 (9)	1 (3)	2 (6)	2 (7)	284
Men respondents	15 (25)	23 (38)	45 (74)	9 (15)	2 (4)	5 (8)	165

Table 9.11   **Percentage of Cases of Childhood Sexual Contact That Involved Specific Sexual Activities, by Gender of the Respondent and Gender of the Person with Whom Contact Occurred**

Respondent	Sexual Contact with a Male				
	Kissing	Touching Genitals	Oral Sex	Vaginal Intercourse	Anal Sex
Men	10	82	30	N.A.	18
Women	31	90	10	14	1
	Sexual Contact with a Female				
Men	64	82	10	42	0
Women	25	92	0	N.A.	N.A.

Note: N.A. = not applicable.

respondent and the adult involved. Touching genitals was by far the most common behavior, regardless of the gender of the respondent or the adult involved. There was more opposite-gender kissing. Vaginal intercourse is more common in contacts between boys and older girls or women. The contacts between boys and older girls or adult women appear less likely to be victim-offender situations than the behavior of sexually precocious boys with girls who are only somewhat older than they themselves are. The pattern of sexual activities is similar to that for activities that occur in opposite-sex adolescent and adult sexual contacts.

The age of the children when such contacts occur varies considerably. As indicated in table 9.12, the older men who touch girls or boys select a similar age profile, with the modal group those between seven and ten. The boys touched by women tend to be older, and the touchers tend to be young, as we noted above.

Given the small sample size, it is not possible to explore in detail the relation between the age of the older person and that of the younger, except in the case of girls touched by adolescent boys or men. In this case (data not shown), there is a modest effect, with more adolescent boys having contact with girls

Table 9.12   **Percent Distribution of the Age at the Time of the Sexual Touching, by Gender of the Respondent and the Adult Involved**

| | Touched by Male | | | |
Respondent	≤ 6 Years	7–10 Years	11–13 Years	N
Women	33	40	27	256
Men	30	46	24	63
	Touched by Female			
Women	. . .	. . .	. . .	26
Men	31	26	43	101

Note: ". . ." indicates fewer than thirty cases.

eleven to thirteen in contrast to girls six and younger, who are more likely to be touched by men over age eighteen.

As table 9.13 indicates, the vast majority of the people in our sample report an experience with only a single adult. However, the number of multiple events is not trivial. About one in three of the respondents report these events occurring with more than one person.

Perhaps the most significant element in the sexual touching of children by adolescents and adults is the prior relationship between the child and the older person. Since in our study we did not include reports of exhibitionism, we expected that far more of the adults would be known to the child. While there is a great deal of fear of sexual contact between strangers and children, unless the contact is coerced, not many strangers have the social skills to introduce themselves to a child and to create a situation in which they can impose physical sexual activity on the child, other than by force. While the child molester who is a stranger does exist, more often, at least according to our data, children are likely to be compelled to engage in sexual activities by people known to them. In addition, we would expect that, the closer the relationship, the more problematic the experience would be. What is clear from table 9.14 is that it is those who are close to the child that predominate as the adults who impose sexual activity on the child. Family friends and relatives are the primary offenders, with more of the former having sex with boys and more of the latter with girls.

Closely linked to this variable is the frequency with which our respondents reported being touched. About 34 percent reported that they were touched one time, 38 percent a few times, and 27 percent many times. These frequencies do not differ by gender.

As one might expect, only a small number of our respondents told someone about this sexual contact with an older person. Twenty-two percent of the respondents reported that they told someone else about their experience, with somewhat more women (26 percent) saying that they told than men (15 percent). Given the social relationships between these respondents and the adult,

Table 9.13   Number of Adolescents/Adults by Whom the Respondent Was Touched (% distributions)

	1	2	3+	N
Women	68	20	13	269[a]
Men	70	16	13	156[b]

[a]Twenty responses were not applicable.
[b]Ten responses were not applicable.

Table 9.14   Relationship to the Respondent of the Adult Who Had Sex with the Respondent as a Child (percentages)

	Women	Men
Stranger	7	4[a]
Teacher	3	4[a]
Family friend	29	40[a]
Mother's boyfriend	2	1[a]
Older friend of respondent	1	4[a]
Other relative	29	13[a]
Older brother	9	4[a]
Stepfather	7	1[a]
Father	7	1[a]
Other	19	17[a]
Number of cases	289	166

Note: The table adds to more than 100 percent because some respondents were touched by more than one adult.
[a]Difference between genders not significant at the .05 level.

this inability to report what was occurring is not surprising. The adults were often either valued by the respondent when they were children or valued by other adults important in their childhood lives.

We asked all our respondents who reported having been sexually touched by an adolescent or an adult whether this experience had affected their lives. There was a striking difference between the reports of women and men. Of the 166 men, only 134 responded to this item (about 20 percent nonresponse); of these, a little less than half (45 percent) reported that the experience had affected their lives. Many more of the women responded to this question (273 of 289), and 70 percent of them reported that the experience (or experiences) had affected their lives. Nearly all the responses to the follow-up question indicated that the experience had negative effects. Again, women were more likely than men to answer this open-ended question.

In addition to these self-reports, we have looked at a number of variables to examine how these early experiences affected the later sexual lives of these people in contrast to those who did not report such experiences (cf. Kilpatrick 1987; Browne and Finkelhor 1986; Widom 1989b; Briere and Runtz 1993).

Before considering the differences, it is important to pose some alternative explanations of any differences that might be found. These data are based on recollections of events by our respondents, events that are often in the distant past (i.e., in some cases, events may have occurred as long as forty years ago). The causal relation between these recollections of childhood experiences and current experience is complex. One interpretation of any differences found might be that accurately recalled earlier experiences have consequences for experiences in adulthood. An alternative hypothesis might be that the characteristics of adult experiences may influence what is remembered and how it is remembered. Both these hypotheses need to be entertained as we interpret our findings.

Those with early childhood sexual experiences, both women and men, were consistently *more* sexual in adulthood than those without such experiences. At the same time, in nearly every comparison displayed in table 9.15, more of those with childhood sexual experiences with adolescents or adults were likely to report difficulties with sexuality (cf. Browne and Finkelhor, 1986).[11]

While those with and without such contacts were equally likely to report not being in good health in the past year, a larger proportion of those with such contacts reported not being happy in the past year. While this does not represent a majority of either group, the differences are significant. In nearly all the comparisons dealing with sexual experience, more of those who reported sexual contact as children were likely to report more sex partners in their lives and to have participated in oral, anal, and group sex as well as to be thinking of sex more often. We do not treat these differences in adult sexuality as negative outcomes, but the early experience could be interpreted as triggering higher levels of sexual activity in adulthood.

In some of the comparisons, the differences are very substantial. Among both women and men, there are dramatic differences in the numbers of partners in a lifetime and in the prevalence of anal sex with an opposite-gender partner. Among the women, there are substantial differences in giving and receiving oral sex. Among men, there are large differences in the proportion who think about sex once a day or more.

At the same time, more of those who reported sexual contacts with adults or adolescents in childhood are somewhat more likely to report troubles in their recent sexual lives than those without such contacts. These differences are not as large as those found for the sexual practice variables, but are all in the same direction of somewhat higher rates of sexual troubles. It may well be that those people with higher rates of sexual activity are also those with a greater probability of sexual difficulties simply on the basis of multiple exposure to untoward outcomes; however, it is also plausible that those with childhood sexual encounters may find sexual adjustment more problematic in adulthood.

11. We find it remarkable that the patterns in tables 9.9 and 9.15 are so similar.

Table 9.15　　**Comparison of Selected Features of Adult Sexual and Nonsexual Experiences, by Gender and Childhood Sexual Contact Status (percentages)**

	Men		Women	
	Not Touched Sexually	Touched Sexually	Not Touched Sexually	Touched Sexually
Not healthy last year	9.7	11.3[a]	12.2	14.2[a]
Not happy last year	10.8	23.2	12.9	19.6
> 10 sex partners ever	30.5	48.9	7.1	20.8
Homosexual/Bisexual identification	2.0	7.4	.8	3.1
Ever performed oral sex	70.9	79.5	61.8	77.9
Ever received oral sex	73.1	78.8	67.0	82.4
Ever had anal sex with member of opposite gender	22.2	37.1	17.2	31.1
Ever had group sex	13.1	26.2	3.0	9.2
Often think about sex, last year	51.5	72.2	18.2	24.4
Lacked interest in sex, last year	15.1	21.2[a]	32.1	40.1
Unable to experience orgasm, last year	7.6	13.4	22.2	34.4
Experienced orgasm too soon, last year	27.8	34.3[a]	10.5	9.6[a]
Experienced pain during sex, last year	2.7	5.5[a]	12.4	2.5
Sex was not pleasurable, last year	7.8	10.3[a]	19.1	32.3
Was anxious about sexual performance, last year	15.6	27.9	10.7	15.6
Experienced difficulty lubricating, last year	N.A.	N.A.	17.0	28.9
Masturbated in the last year	61.3	78.8	38.9	55.8
Emotional problems interfered with sex, last year	33.4	49.7	40.2	59.2
Ever forced sexually by a man	1.2	10.4	16.0	47.1
Erection difficulties, last year	9.3	18.9	N.A.	N.A.
Ever forced a woman sexually	2.6	6.1	N.A.	N.A.
N	1,166	145	1,361	247

Note: N.A. = not applicable.

[a]These differences between the touched and not touched are not significant at the .05 level.

These findings need to be interpreted carefully. At no point is there any evidence that a majority of those with childhood sexual encounters have problems in their adult sexual lives. The differences, although consistent, are modest.

These childhood sexual contacts are extremely various in character. We attempted to examine whether different constellations of factors characterizing the contacts would produce greater differences in these measures in adulthood. In one preliminary analysis, we created a scale of the "severity" of these contacts, from less to more severe experiences. In doing so, we were not trying to minimize the less severe experiences. We were simply attempting to see whether there were specific factors in the experience that might produce different results. Using one fairly commonsense definition of severity of incident(s), we were unable to detect any effect of more versus less severe childhood experience on subsequent outcomes.[12] Further work is clearly necessary to clarify these results.

These data tend to confirm other research on sexual contacts between children under age twelve or thirteen and adults and older adolescents. These contacts happen to a substantial minority of both boys and girls and are initiated mostly by men who have a preexisting relationship with the child. The experiences of boys are different from those of girls, with more of the former engaging in precocious sexual experiences that are similar to experiences that they will have when older. In addition, men are less likely to define a childhood experience as negative than are women. Although more girls than boys report these events to others, only a minority of these contacts come to light, based on the reports of the children when they were children. More of those respondents who report sexual contacts with adults when they were children are likely to be more sexually active when they are adults than those without such con-

---

12. We scored the various aspects of the experiences in the following way:

1. Those contacts that involved kissing or genital touching were scored as less severe, those involving oral sex, anal sex, or vaginal sex as more severe.

2. A contact with only one person was scored as less severe, while contacts with more than one person were scored as more severe.

3. Contacts with nonrelatives were scored as less severe than those that involved relatives.

4. Contacts that occurred only once or a few times were scored as less severe than those that occurred many times.

5. Contacts that occurred early in life (age 6 and before) were scored as more severe than those that occurred later.

6. Finally, those contacts that had a longer duration were scored as more severe than those that had a shorter duration.

The resulting six-point scale was trichotomized and examined for the same series of adult measures that we examined using the simple contrast between ever being touched and never being touched. Our assumption was that the scale would differentiate among those who had been touched.

tacts. They are also somewhat more likely to report sexual troubles. Given the negative subjective assessments of these experiences (especially by women), it is remarkable that the vast majority do not have more difficulties in adulthood than those without such contacts.

9.4 Conclusion

While the substantive parts of this chapter are somewhat disparate, there are a number of intertwined threads. There has been a steady decline in the age at first intercourse over the past four decades, and more young people experience intercourse in high school with more sex partners. Given the general ignorance of youths about sexuality and the lack of education in responsible sexual relations, it is not surprising that there has been an increase in risky sexual encounters among the young. While the general concern about the problems of sex among young people has been directed toward issues of morality, pregnancy, and disease, it is clear that problems of gender misunderstandings and the potential for violence in young people's sexual lives have been generally unaddressed.

The data on first sexual intercourse demonstrate, at a minimum, that young men come to sex with quite different expectations and desires than do young women. This leaves young women more vulnerable to exploitation, given their greater commitment to love and affection. Young women often go along with intercourse the first time, finding little physical pleasure in it, and a substantial number report being forced to have intercourse. These facts reflect dramatic costs for young women, and they appear to be increasing as young women have intercourse earlier in the life course.

In addition to the one in twenty who reports being forced to have her first intercourse, a far larger proportion report other experiences of forced sex, most often from those who are emotionally close to them. In this case, affectional ties are a cloak for experiences of adult sexual coercion. The contamination of intimacy with violence seems a danger to many women in this society, regardless of their social position.

Finally, a substantial proportion of the women and men in our sample report preadolescent sexual contacts with adults. Many of the men and most of the women who have had such contacts report that they have had negative consequences for their adult lives. Again, the majority of these experiences are with people who were known to the respondent when they were children, often relatives and friends of the family.

These are troubling findings and suggest important difficulties in the social arrangements that organize sexual life in our society. Further analysis of these survey data, as well as the collection of more specifically targeted, high-quality studies, should shed further light on this problem.

PART III

In part II, we described many of the features of the sex lives of adults in the United States. We characterized the sexual repertoire of adults as well as their expressed preferences for one or another sexual practice. We discussed the selection of sex partners and presented data on both the number of partners in various time periods and the characteristics of those partners. We discussed several ways to assess the sexual orientation of adults and measured the heterosexual and homosexual preferences and behaviors of respondents. Finally, we presented evidence on the age at which partnered sexual behavior commences and on the prevalence in our society of sexual victimization defined in several ways.

In this part, we shift the focus from sexual activities themselves to associated behaviors. In some of the cases to which we now turn, we can say with confidence that these associated behaviors and opinions are the direct consequence of sexual activity. In other cases, we cannot determine whether the sexual activity caused the observed behavior and attitudes or whether the behavior and attitudes led to the sexual activity; in these cases we simply note the correlation.

A good example of the former is our investigation of sexually transmitted diseases in chapter 11. For them, sexual activity is clearly the cause of disease, the means by which it is contracted, although even here the fact that the disease has been contracted may subsequently influence sexual behavior and attitudes. When we discuss fertility behavior in chapter 12, again we know that childbearing follows from sexual activity, at least in a simple biological sense. This direction of effect is less clear, however, when we look at the relation between sexual activity and the formation and stability of marital and cohabitational relationships in chapter 13. In that chapter, we do not claim to know more than we do about the direction of causation. In chapter 10, we assume our most agnostic stance, as we investigate the relation between sexual activity and measures of general health and happiness.

CHAPTER 10

Sex, Health, and Happiness

Like most of the other activities on which we expend energy, time, and sometimes money, sex is undertaken as a means of achieving many ends. These include the three "Rs" of sex: *relational sex,* entered into as an expression of love and affection for one's partner and as a sharing of intimacy and vulnerability with that person; *recreational sex,* experienced physically as the joyful and exhilarating feeling of sexual excitement and release; and *reproductive sex,* in which a couple engages with the hope that it might result in a child whom they are eager to nurture and care for.[1] These three only begin to suggest the many extraordinary consequences of our sexual activities. Earlier chapters have sketched the theoretical structure on which we rely to understand why people engage in one or another sex act or engage in sex with one or another sex partner. Here, we want to note that sexual activity has consequences and to emphasize that many of these consequences are positive and satisfying.

Sadly, our survey and book focus on the darker side of sex more than on its brighter side. We are not alone in that focus, and it is unfortunate that concerns about the many unpleasant consequences seem to take precedence over an equally thorough exploration of the joys of sex. We include in this chapter a brief and incomplete discussion of the relation of sex, health, and happiness as a modest effort to redress that balance and as part of our effort to persuade other social scientists to join us in exploring the many aspects of sexuality.

10.1   Health and Happiness

To treat topics as sweeping and complex as health and happiness in a few pages or a single chapter may be foolhardy, but the alternative of ignoring them entirely seems even less satisfying (cf. Bloom 1993). We focus initially on two broad questions that we asked respondents in our survey. Regarding happiness, we asked, "Generally, how happy have you been with your personal life during the past 12 months? Have you been extremely happy; very happy most of the time; generally satisfied, pleased; sometimes fairly unhappy; or unhappy most of the time?" (see appendix C, section 9, question 4). Our basic question about

William Dale Schempp conducted the empirical work in this chapter. Robert T. Michael directed the work and wrote the chapter.
1. For an extended discussion of these normative orientations toward sexuality, see chapter 14.

physical health is similarly subjective, although this particular wording is regularly used in survey research: "In general, would you say your health is excellent, good, fair, or poor?" (see appendix C, section 9, question 1). (See Manning et al. 1982.)

Even shifting the wording of the first question's responses from happiness to satisfaction to unhappiness makes interpretation difficult. Bradburn (1969) provides a more complete discussion of the concept of happiness in survey research and of the sensitivity of responses to question nuances. It turns out that questions of this nature, subjective and global as they are, are particularly sensitive to the precise wording, to the number of categories allowed as to the responses, to the general framing of the question, and to its context in terms of the other questions that have preceded it. We therefore have less confidence about our measures of health and happiness than we have about our questions regarding sexual behavior itself, and this is just another complexity to the analysis on which we embark in this chapter.

Just as we argued in chapter 5 that no single measure of sexual behavior can adequately capture its complicated and variegated manifestations, it is equally true that no single question with four or five response categories can adequately characterize a person's happiness or health. Even with these crude measures, however, we can document systematic patterns that are related to sexual activity. Sexual activity is never undertaken in a social vacuum and is inevitably implicated in one's sense of self (see Rosenzweig and Dailey 1991). The feelings of attractiveness, appeal, and satisfaction derived from sex, whether practiced for recreational, relational, or reproductive purposes, often contribute to our overall sense of well-being, both positively and negatively.

Table 10.1 compares the responses to the two questions about health and happiness from the whole NHSLS sample and similar, but not identical, questions from prior versions of the General Social Survey. The NHSLS asked about happiness in five-part response categories, while the GSS used only three categories, so the questions asked are substantially different (see table 10.1A). Notice that 17.0 percent of the NHSLS respondents said that they were extremely happy, and an additional 40.7 percent were very happy. Thus, well over half of our sample expressed a positive overall assessment of their state of happiness, while less than 15 percent indicated any overall unhappiness. One sees roughly similar responses in the comparisons to the GSS three-category responses, with about 10 percent expressing a negative sentiment. These rough proportions are not atypical of questions of this nature in broadly gauged national surveys.

Table 10.1B shows the distributions of responses to the health question. We see there that the respondents in our NHSLS sample report themselves to be somewhat healthier than do those in the GSS samples of adults aged eighteen to fifty-nine.

Table 10.2 shows these two indicators of happiness and health in more detail, reported by the several master status variables used in previous chapters.

Table 10.1A   **Self-Assessed Happiness and Health—Comparisons of the NHSLS and the GSS: Well-Being Measure (percentages)**

			GSS			
Happiness	NHSLS	Happiness	1988	1989	1990	1991
Extremely happy	17.0					
		Very happy	32.6	30.9	32.6	28.8
Very happy	40.7					
		Pretty happy	57.7	60.1	57.9	59.4
Generally satisfied	29.2					
Fairly unhappy	10.1					
		Not too happy	9.7	9.0	9.6	11.7
Unhappy most times	3.0					

Note: For the NHSLS, N = 3,152. For the GSS, 1988 N = 712, 1989 N = 747, 1990 N = 660, and 1991 N = 732.

Table 10.1B   **Self-Assessed Happiness and Health—Comparisons of the NHSLS and the GSS: Health Measure (percentages)**

		GSS			
Health	NHSLS	1988	1989	1990	1991
Excellent	43.4	35.0	38.1	35.8	35.4
Good	45.3	48.0	46.5	47.4	46.7
Fair	9.4	13.9	13.0	14.2	16.0
Poor	1.9	3.1	2.4	2.6	1.9

Note: See the note to table 10.1A.

Table 10.2A presents the distributions of responses to the question about happiness, table 10.2B the pattern of responses to the health question. The two most salient points to be drawn from this table are, first, that the distributions among these demographic and social characteristics are not dramatically different and, second, that the same few factors surface as affecting both happiness and health. Let us elaborate.

If we look at the few categories in which as many as, say (arbitrarily), 4 percent report being unhappy most of the time, we see that those categories are the older, the less educated, the poor, and the alone, specifically those age forty to forty-four, age fifty-five to fifty-nine, those divorced, widowed, or separated, those who did not complete high school, Native Americans, and those who are poor.[2] Looking instead at table 10.2B, the categories with at least, say,

2. We have information about the income of the household in the past calendar year, 1991. With this and information about the household composition, we can determine whether the household is in poverty. That calculation involves looking up the threshold level of income for a household of that size and structure and simply comparing that threshold level to the household's actual

4 percent reporting themselves to be in poor health are quite similar—those over age fifty, those widowed, those with less than a high school education, Native Americans, and those who are poor. These two sets of categories overlap a great deal.

A confirming (but not an independent) pattern is seen if, instead, we ask which of these many demographic or social categories have an exceptionally high rate of reporting themselves "extremely happy" or, alternatively, in "excellent" health. The groups with more than, say, 20 percent who are extremely happy include those age twenty-five to twenty-nine, those married, Asians, those who are Jewish, and those who are "rich." Similarly, the categories with, say, over 50 percent who are in excellent health are those with a college education or more, the Asians, the Jews and those of other religions (mostly Eastern religions like Buddhism and Hinduism), and those who are "rich." From both ends of the spectrum, then, there is substantial overlap in the social categories that stand out as either exceptionally positive or exceptionally negative in happiness and health.

In general, however, the patterns are not dramatically different across these characteristics. They do not differ much by gender, for example, although, here as elsewhere (Verbrugge 1982; Gove 1984; and Anson et al. 1993), women report themselves to be in somewhat poorer health than do men (despite their lower mortality rate). One sees a clear, but not dramatic, difference by marital status, with married people reporting a somewhat happier and healthier condition and widowed people showing the least favorable conditions. Similar patterns of health when examined in terms of education are also commonly found, and there is much less difference among the various levels of education on the happiness scale. Race/ethnicity does not show a major difference, especially among the three larger groups of whites, blacks, and Hispanics.[3] By religion, the Jewish respondents seem to be both happier and healthier, but the Protestants and Catholics have quite similar distributions, and fewer of those with no religion appear to be extremely happy. Income does show a systematic pattern

income level. Our dummy variable "poor" is defined as 1 if the household's income level is less than that poverty threshold and 0 otherwise; similarly, our dummy variable "rich" is defined as 1 if the household's income level was six or more times its poverty threshold level and 0 otherwise. The category "middle" is 1 if the household is neither "poor" nor "rich" and 0 if it is either rich or poor. The threshold, incidentally, for a family of four in 1991 was $13,812.

3. In other studies, blacks have been found to be less happy than whites, even holding socioeconomic status and education level constant (Bradburn 1969, 47). The 1991 GSS data also show this pattern with the percentage unhappy about twice as high for blacks as for whites at each education level. Our NHSLS data do not show this pattern. Here, the percentages who report themselves unhappy sometimes or most of the time are practically equal for blacks and whites at each education level (less than high school: 18 percent of whites, 21 percent of blacks; high school graduate: 12 percent of whites, 13 percent of blacks; some or more college: 13 percent of whites, 10 percent of blacks) and among those who are "poor" or "rich," relative to the poverty line (poor: 19 percent of whites, 20 percent of blacks; middle income: 13 percent of whites, 8 percent of blacks; rich: 13 percent of whites, too few blacks to calculate). The decline in unhappiness as socioeconomic status rises is in evidence here, but the higher rate for blacks is not.

Table 10.2A   **Happiness, by Master Status (percentages)**

Master Status	Extremely Happy	Very Happy	Generally Satisfied	Fairly Unhappy	Unhappy Most Times
Gender (*N* = 3,153):					
Men	17.8	40.6	29.4	9.4	2.8
Women	16.4	40.7	29.0	10.7	3.2
Age (*N* = 3,148):					
18–24	16.2	43.3	28.9	9.2	2.4
25–29	21.0	42.8	25.8	8.7	1.8
30–34	17.4	41.3	30.0	8.5	2.7
35–39	17.3	40.6	28.8	10.0	3.2
40–44	15.9	34.9	31.3	13.0	4.8
45–49	13.4	43.0	29.6	11.4	2.6
50–54	16.7	41.7	27.4	11.5	2.8
55–59	16.9	35.5	32.5	10.4	4.8
Marital status (*N* = 3,134):					
Married	21.1	46.4	23.8	6.7	2.0
Never married	13.0	38.9	33.0	11.9	3.3
Divorced	12.2	27.4	39.1	15.9	5.5
Widowed	8.3	29.2	43.1	13.9	5.6
Separated	9.7	27.8	31.9	25.0	5.6
Education (*N* = 3,133):					
Less than HS	17.0	35.6	29.4	13.3	4.6
HS graduate	17.0	41.7	29.3	9.0	3.0
Some college	16.7	42.8	28.2	9.9	2.4
Finished college	18.3	38.1	30.8	10.2	2.5
Master's/adv. deg.	15.7	43.7	28.4	9.2	3.1
Race/ethnicity (*N* = 3,153):					
White	17.4	40.9	28.3	10.4	2.9
Black	14.2	39.0	33.6	9.7	3.5
Hispanic	18.7	39.1	31.5	8.1	2.6
Asian	20.3	43.8	28.1	4.7	3.1
Native American	7.3	43.9	26.8	17.1	4.9
Religion (*N* = 3,147):[a]					
None	11.3	35.9	36.2	13.0	3.5
Type I Protestant	18.2	39.0	29.6	9.9	3.2
Type II Protestant	16.2	43.3	27.6	9.4	3.5
Catholic	18.8	40.9	27.9	10.2	2.2
Jewish	24.1	37.0	25.9	9.3	3.7
Other	16.7	32.0	38.5	11.5	1.3
Other Protestant	16.4	54.8	20.5	5.5	2.7
Income (*N* = 2,520):[b]					
Poor	15.8	35.4	29.5	14.9	4.5
Middle	16.3	42.5	29.2	9.4	2.6
Rich	21.1	38.4	27.4	10.5	2.6

[a]For an explanation of the classification of Protestant respondents, see chapter appendix 3.1A. *Other* includes primarily Eastern religions (e.g., Buddhism, Hinduism).

[b]Income was divided in the following way: *poor:* family income is below or at the poverty line for 1991; *middle:* family income is between the official poverty line for 1991 and a figure six times that amount; *rich:* family income is six times or more than the official poverty line for 1991.

Table 10.2B   **Health, by Master Status (percentages)**

Master Status	Health			
	Excellent	Good	Fair	Poor
Gender (N = 3,156):				
Men	45.5	44.7	8.3	1.6
Women	41.7	45.8	10.3	2.1
Age (N = 3,151):				
18–24	45.8	46.8	7.0	.4
25–29	48.9	41.9	8.3	.9
30–34	46.2	46.2	6.4	1.2
35–39	43.7	48.2	7.2	.9
40–44	39.8	47.2	10.4	2.7
45–49	42.4	45.6	10.1	1.9
50–54	34.1	45.6	16.3	4.0
55–59	38.5	36.4	18.2	6.9
Marital status (N = 3,137):				
Married	43.4	45.9	9.3	1.4
Never married	47.7	42.6	7.6	2.2
Divorced	37.4	46.8	13.1	2.8
Widowed	30.6	51.4	13.9	4.2
Separated	43.1	44.4	11.1	1.4
Education (N = 3,136):				
Less than HS	27.6	45.8	20.5	6.2
HS graduate	37.6	50.7	10.3	1.4
Some college	44.7	46.9	6.9	1.4
Finished college	58.1	35.8	5.6	.6
Master's/adv. deg.	57.2	38.4	3.9	.4
Race/ethnicity (N = 3,156):				
White	44.7	45.2	8.4	1.7
Black	38.8	44.8	13.7	2.7
Hispanic	40.4	46.0	11.9	1.7
Asian	50.0	42.2	6.3	1.6
Native American	17.1	58.5	19.5	4.9
Religion (N = 3,150):[a]				
None	40.5	47.7	10.7	1.2
Type I Protestant	47.1	43.3	8.2	1.5
Type II Protestant	37.7	48.5	11.5	2.4
Catholic	46.2	43.7	8.4	1.8
Jewish	61.8	29.1	5.4	3.6
Other	50.6	39.0	9.1	1.3
Other Protestant	44.6	47.3	5.4	2.7
Income (N = 2,523):[b]				
Poor	34.2	46.4	14.0	5.4
Middle	43.6	46.9	8.5	1.0
Rich	54.8	38.6	6.3	.2

[a]For an explanation of the classification of Protestant respondents, see chapter appendix 3.1A. *Other* includes primarily Eastern religions (e.g., Buddhism, Hinduism).

[b]Income was divided in the following way: *poor:* family income is below or at the poverty line for 1991; *middle:* family income is between the official poverty line for 1991 and a figure six times that amount; *rich:* family income is six times or more than the official poverty line for 1991.

here, with those who are poor being both less happy and less healthy than the middle class and those who are rich tending to be both happier and healthier. These patterns are hardly startling, being much as we might have anticipated. They help, in fact, reassure us about the validity of our crude indicators of happiness and health.

Previous studies have also found that unmarried men tend to report themselves more unhappy than unmarried women (Bradburn 1969, 149). But this may have changed over time (Glenn and Weaver 1988). This pattern is not found in the NHSLS data. For example, looking at those aged eighteen to twenty-nine, we find that 9 percent of the men and 15 percent of the women who have never been married report themselves somewhat unhappy or unhappy most of the time, while, among those who are married in that age range, 2 percent of the men and 9 percent of the women do so. At the age range thirty to forty-four, 21 percent of the men and 17 percent of the women who have never been married and 8 percent of the men and 11 percent of the women who are married are unhappy. Therefore, we, like others, find that the level of unhappiness is higher among the never married (and among the divorced as well, see Gove and Shin 1989) than among those who are married, but we do not find the gender difference reported elsewhere.

Noteworthy also is the rather high correlation between the two measures of well-being. Table 10.3 shows that nearly 30 percent of the sample characterize themselves as both quite happy and in excellent health, while another 48.7 percent (24.2 + 9.7 + 14.8) say that they are in at least "good" health and are at least generally happy. About 10 percent are in good or excellent health but are unhappy, and another 10 percent are in fair or poor health but are at least generally happy. Finally, a small proportion, 2.7 percent, are both in fair or poor health and unhappy. The overall Pearson correlation of health and happiness is .249; for subgroups defined by age and gender, that correlation ranges from about .22 to about .33.

10.2 Sexual Correlates of Happiness and Health

In table 10.4, the sample is partitioned by several measures of sexual behavior, and the distribution of reported happiness is shown, collapsing the five-

Table 10.3   **Percentage of Sample in Cells Defined by Health and Happiness**

Health	Happiness			
	Extremely or Very Happy	Generally Satisfied	Sometimes or Most Times Unhappy	Total
Excellent	29.6	9.7	4.1	43.4
Good	24.2	14.8	6.3	45.3
Fair	3.5	4.2	1.8	9.4
Poor	.4	.5	.9	1.9
Total	57.7	29.2	13.1	100.0

Table 10.4　　　**Levels of Happiness, by Sexual Behaviors (percentages)**

	Extremely or Very Happy	Generally Satisfied	Unhappy	% of All
Overall	57.7	29.2	13.1	100.0
Number of sex partners in past 12 months				
0	40.7	35.4	23.9	12.7
1	63.4	27.2	9.4	71.8
2–4	44.9	32.7	22.4	12.8
5+	47.2	37.1	15.7	2.3
Frequency of sex in past 12 months				
Not at all	39.5	36.7	23.8	12.0
1–12 times/year	45.6	32.8	21.6	16.7
2–3 times/month or once/week	59.2	29.3	11.5	36.4
2–3 times/week	69.0	25.1	5.9	27.7
4+ times/week	64.5	22.0	13.6	7.2
Oral or anal sex in last sexual event?				
Yes	57.3	30.0	12.6	32.0
No	62.2	27.0	10.8	68.0
Length of last sexual event				
< 30 minutes	60.7	28.4	10.8	48.8
> 30 minutes	59.7	28.1	12.2	51.2
Frequency of orgasm, past 12 months				
Men:				
Always	61.6	27.6	10.9	72.0
Usually	59.6	30.0	10.4	21.8
Sometimes	65.2	30.4	4.4	3.7
Rarely or never	59.4	37.5	3.1	2.6
Women:				
Always	65.5	26.0	8.5	27.1
Usually	62.6	26.8	10.7	41.3
Sometimes	50.9	34.0	15.1	21.6
Rarely	39.0	31.2	29.9	5.2
Never	51.4	28.6	20.0	4.8
How often do you think about sex?				
< once/month	48.8	32.8	18.5	9.1
Once/month, few times/week	60.2	28.1	11.7	56.2
Every day or more	55.8	30.1	14.1	34.7
Masturbation frequency				
Not at all	62.1	26.8	11.1	48.8
Once/month or less	59.0	29.0	12.0	25.5
> once/month	48.4	33.2	18.5	25.7
Sexual orientation				
Men:				
Heterosexual	62.5	27.0	10.5	94.0
Homosexual	47.1	35.7	17.2	6.0
Women:				
Heterosexual	59.2	28.3	12.5	95.9
Homosexual	45.6	31.6	22.8	4.1

Table 10.4 (continued)

	Extremely or Very Happy	Generally Satisfied	Unhappy	% of All
Sensuous activities—nude beaches and nude photos				
Yes	51.5	35.3	13.2	2.2
No	57.8	29.1	13.1	97.8
Purchases of autoerotic sex aids— movies, magazines, phones, and dancing				
Yes	52.3	33.6	14.1	26.7
No	59.6	27.7	12.7	73.3
Purchases of sex toys—vibrators and other toys				
Yes	51.0	33.7	15.3	3.1
No	57.9	29.1	13.0	96.9

category scale into three. For each partitioning, the row percentages are shown, reflecting the extent to which those in that row mirror the distribution of happiness of the sample as a whole. The top row of the table shows that overall distribution, with nearly 60 percent responding that they are extremely or very happy, another nearly 30 percent saying that they are generally satisfied or pleased, and only a little over 10 percent reporting that they are unhappy (i.e., sometimes fairly unhappy or unhappy most of the time).[4]

When we consider the first partitioning, by the number of sex partners within the past twelve months, we find that the category with the lowest proportion unhappy are those with one sex partner—9.4 percent, compared to the average of 13.1 percent. Those with no sex partners and those with two to four partners have the highest proportions who are unhappy, 23.9 and 22.4 percent, respectively. Looking at the upper end of the spectrum, the same pattern is reflected there, with a somewhat higher rate of those with one sex partner responding that they are extremely or very happy compared to the average of 57.7, while as low a proportion as 40.7 and 44.9 percent of those with no

4. We have not partitioned this table by gender because, in most instances, the differences are quite small. For two of the variables reported on here—orgasm and sexual orientation—we have partitioned by gender. There are only four other variables reported on in this table in which men or women differ from the percentage reported by as much as 8 percentage points: (i) in number of sex partners in the past twelve months, women with five or more partners report that they are less happy—37.0 state that they are extremely or very happy and 25.9 state that they are unhappy; (ii) in frequency of sex in the past 12 months, men who reported that they had no sex at all were less happy—30.0 percent stated that they were extremely happy; (iii) in frequency of thinking about sex, women who thought about it seldom reported that they were more happy—47.2 percent stated that they were extremely or very happy; (iv) of those who went to nude beaches or posed for nude photos, the men reported being much happier (61.8 percent stated that they were extremely or very happy and 23.5 percent said that they were generally satisfied) and the women were less happy (41.2 percent stated that they were extremely or very happy and 47.1 percent were generally satisfied).

sex partners or with two to four sex partners, respectively, are extremely or very happy.

We have also looked in much greater detail at the patterns seen in this panel of happiness by number of sex partners, looking, in particular, within groups defined by the combination of age, gender, and marital status as well as number of sex partners. For those with no partners, the subgroups who are most unhappy are the never-married men aged thirty to forty-four (26.5 percent are unhappy) and the divorced women aged forty-five to fifty-nine (30.2 percent are unhappy). Of those with two to four partners, it is primarily never-married or divorced men aged thirty to forty-four and young single women who are most unhappy. We find in this more detailed tabulation that there are two groups of men and women with one partner who also have quite high rates of unhappiness (i.e., rates of 15.1–19.3 percent), the divorced men and women in the age groups thirty to forty-four and forty-five to fifty-nine.

We have reported here the percentages by row, and this leads to thinking of the relation as one in which the number of sex partners somehow affects the level of happiness. We could have reported, instead, the column percentages, which would have encouraged the notion that a person's level of happiness has somehow led to the number of sex partners that he or she had in the past twelve months. Neither direction of causation is established simply by reporting the percentages one way or the other, of course. Indeed, we stress that we do not know here which is cause and which effect or whether either causes the other. We note simply that there is a relation between the number of sex partners and the reported level of happiness, with those who have one sex partner systematically reporting higher levels of happiness than those who have either more partners in the past year or no partners. This is an intriguing finding worthy of subsequent investigation with more formal modeling that might help sort out the causal ordering and perhaps even help identify the mechanism through which the correlational pattern emerges.

The next portion of Table 10.4 shows the distributions of happiness by the frequency of sex in the past twelve months. Looking first at the proportion who are unhappy, those who have sex two or three times a week have a much lower incidence of reporting themselves unhappy than those who had no sex in the past year or those who had sex less frequently than once a month. This pattern at one end of the spectrum is again reflected in the rates at the other end as well, where we see that 69 percent of those who have had sex two or three times a week report themselves extremely or very happy, while only 39.5 percent of those who have had no sex within the past twelve months did so. We repeat the caveat that we do not know and do not suggest that the frequency of sex itself is causing these respondents to report themselves to be happy or unhappy. Quite plausibly, there is some other factor—health, for example— that is affecting both their sense of happiness and their frequency of sex. We simply have not looked into the issue with enough detail and control to draw an inference about cause and effect. Further investigation is needed.

Regarding the next two categories of sexual behavior shown in the table, neither seems to be related to our measure of happiness. We partitioned the sample into those who did and did not engage in any oral and anal sex during their last sex event, and table 10.4 tells us that the two-thirds of those who did not do so and the one-third of those who did do not differ in their assessment of their own happiness. Similarly, the half of the sample who reported that their last sex event lasted longer than thirty minutes did not differ in their reported happiness from the half who said that their last sex event lasted less than thirty minutes.

The next panel in the table partitions by the frequency of orgasm; here, the patterns differ by gender, so we report the men and women separately. For the men, we first note that, since fewer than thirty men report achieving orgasm rarely and, similarly, fewer than thirty report never achieving orgasm, we combined the two categories (to comply with our general rule of not reporting percentages based on fewer than thirty cases). Among the men, the only pattern of note is the low rates of unhappiness among those who report having orgasms sometimes or rarely or never, as compared to those who report having orgasms more frequently. But that rather large difference in the *unhappy* column is not reflected at the other end of the spectrum, suggesting that the association is not very strong. For the women, on the other hand, there is a strong pattern. While 8.5 percent of those who report always experiencing orgasm say that they are unhappy, a very large proportion (29.9 percent) of those who rarely experience orgasm consider themselves unhappy, and 20.0 percent of those who never do also consider themselves unhappy. This pattern is reflected, as well, at the other end of the spectrum, with as many as 65.5 percent of those women who always experience orgasm but only 39.0 percent of those who only rarely do reporting themselves extremely or very happy. Incidentally, more of those who never experience orgasm do say that they are extremely or very happy, so this pattern is not perfectly consistent.

Partitioning the sample by the frequency with which the respondent reported thinking about sex, we see a slight tendency for those at both extremes—those who report that they think about sex every day or more and those who say that they do so never or less than once a month—to have somewhat higher rates of reporting themselves unhappy and correspondingly lower rates of reporting themselves extremely or very happy. (For related results, see the discussion in chapter 3 on the autoeroticism scale.)

The table also shows that nearly one in five (18.5 percent) of the quarter of the sample who masturbate frequently report themselves to be unhappy, while a much smaller proportion (11.1 percent) of those who say that they do not masturbate at all say that they are unhappy. This is a good example of an observed relation that raises more questions than it answers since this correlation can be interpreted in many ways. Further investigation is certainly indicated.

The next panel of table 10.4 shows the reports by sexual orientation, further partitioned by gender. Homosexual preference here is measured as any one of the following: any same-gender sex partner within the past twelve months, or self-identification as homosexual or bisexual, or answering the question about being attracted to only men, mostly men, both men and women, mostly women, or only women by any of the four categories involving a same-gender partner. (For a thorough discussion of the measures of homosexuality, see chapter 8.) Using this expansive definition of homosexuality, a somewhat higher proportion of the homosexual men and women report themselves to be unhappy, and, correspondingly, a somewhat lower proportion, especially of the men, report themselves to be extremely or very happy. Conjecturing about the reasons for this pattern, we suggest that the disjuncture between a person's own preferences regarding sexual orientation and the overwhelming disapproval of this orientation so often expressed in opinion polls, and the social pressures against this orientation that flow from this disapproval, is likely to have something to do with these findings.

Finally, we constructed three dummy variables indicating whether the respondent said that he or she purchased erotic materials or participated in social events or activities that may be considered erotic. We are interested in whether those who do are particularly happy or not so happy. The first of these three measures attempts to capture behavior that is perhaps erotic but not socially disapproved. The variable is defined by whether in the past twelve months the respondent had his or her picture taken in the nude or attended a public gathering in which the respondent was nude (e.g., a "clothes optional" beach). Only 2.2 percent of the respondents had done either of these things in that time interval (the same percentage of men and women said that they had done so, incidentally). From the table, we see that there is no difference in the distributions partitioned by this variable. However, there is a difference by gender (not shown in the table): 62 percent of the men and 41 percent of the women in the *yes* row are extremely or very happy, and, correspondingly, 24 percent of the men and 47 percent of the women are generally satisfied.

The second of these three measures, also discussed in chapter 3, reflects whether in the past twelve months the respondent bought or rented any X-rated movies or videos, or bought any sexually explicit magazines or books, or called any "pay-by-the-minute" phone sex numbers, or went to night clubs with nude or seminude dancers. Overall, 26.7 percent of respondents said that they had done at least one of these things (by gender, the proportions were 40.6 percent of the men and 15.5 percent of the women). There is no discernible difference in the level of happiness between those who did and did not do any of these things.

The last of these three measures is based on whether in the past twelve months the respondent bought any vibrators or dildos or any other sex toys (see also chapter 3). We separate these from the items in the former measure of purchases of X-rated movies since these items are more frequently used in conjunction with a sex partner, as a complement to partnered sex, while the sex movies, magazines, and telephone sex numbers are more likely used as stimulants to masturbatory, nonpartnered sex. In any case, we see that 3.1 percent of the respondents report buying one of these toys (by gender, 2.9 percent of men and 3.3 percent of women did so). People who buy these items do not appear to be more or less happy than those who do not.

Summarizing the patterns shown in table 10.4, most of the indicators of sexual behavior are not particularly strongly or notably associated with the global measure of happiness. The exceptions to this characterization are that those with one sex partner over the year do stand out as happier while those with no partners or those with two to four partners are less happy. Those who have sex two or three times a week are notably happier as well. For women, those who experience orgasm less frequently in their partnered sex are substantially less happy than those who always or usually do so.

We do not present a detailed table of the distributions by self-reported health status analogous to table 10.4 because only two of the many comparisons are noteworthy. While, overall, 1.9 percent of the sample reported itself to be in poor health, of those with no sex partners in the past twelve months, 6.0 percent are in poor health and a slightly higher proportion than average in fair health. The only other category with as many as 6 percent in poor health are those who report masturbating at least every day—6.3 percent.

10.3 Sexual Satisfaction

The previous section briefly explored the relation between several aspects of sexual behavior and general levels of health and happiness. We also asked three more specifically targeted questions about the emotional and physical pleasure assessment of the sexual experience itself. As described in chapter 3 and elsewhere, we asked an extensive set of questions about the respondent's sexual behavior with his or her primary sex partner in the past twelve months and, separately, about that behavior with a secondary sex partner in that same twelve months if there were two or more partners. The primary partner was considered to be the spouse or cohabitational partner if there was one; otherwise, we simply asked the respondent whom he or she considered to have been the most important or primary sex partner in the past twelve months. The secondary partner was, arbitrarily, the person with whom the respondent had most recently had sex other than the primary partner.

We first asked how sex with the primary (or secondary) partner "made you feel"; in particular, we asked for a yes or no response to whether it made the respondent feel "satisfied," "sad," "loved," "anxious or worried," "thrilled or excited," "guilty," or one of a few other descriptors. We followed that question with, "How physically pleasurable did you find your relationship with (PARTNER) to be: extremely pleasurable, very pleasurable, moderately pleasurable, slightly pleasurable, or not at all pleasurable?" and "How emotionally satisfying did you find your relationship with (PARTNER) to be," extremely, very, moderately, slightly, or not at all satisfying? (For the primary partner and the secondary partner, see appendix C, section 4, questions 49–51 and 77–79, respectively.)

Table 10.5 reports the percentages who, in answer to the latter two questions about physical pleasure and emotional satisfaction, replied that they found their relationships extremely or very pleasurable or satisfying. The table has an intriguing pattern. For both the physical and the emotional measures, the ranking (from the most pleasurable or satisfying) of partners is identical: the spouse exclusively; the cohabitational partner exclusively; the exclusive non–spouse/cohabitational partner; the non–spouse/cohabitational partner with one or more partners in addition; the cohabitational partner, with one or more partners in addition; the spouse, with one or more partners in addition; and the secondary partner, with one or more partners in addition. Evidently, having one sex partner is more rewarding in terms of physical pleasure and emotional satisfaction than having more than one partner, and it is particularly rewarding if that single partner is a marriage partner, next most if that partner is a cohabitational partner, and so forth.

A monogamous sexual partnership embedded in a formal marriage evidently produces the greatest satisfaction and pleasure, judging by the responses to these two questions. Notice how much more pleasurable or satisfying the spouse (or cohabitational partner) is reported to be, for example, when there is no more than one sex partner within the past twelve months. Comparing respondents with and without additional sex partners in the past twelve months, those without other partners are 30 percentage points more likely to rate their sexual relationship with their spouse as extremely or very satisfying. Now, we know that association is not causation, and we cannot say whether

Table 10.5 **Percentage "Extremely" or "Very" Physically Pleased or Emotionally Satisfied by the Sexual Relationship, by Type of Partnership and Number of Partners**

Type of Partner	Physical Pleasure	Emotional Satisfaction
Only one:		
Spouse ($N = 1,587$)	87.4	84.8
Cohabitant ($N = 270$)	84.4	75.6
Neither ($N = 380$)	78.2	71.0
More than one:		
Primary:		
Spouse ($N = 67$)	61.2	56.7
Cohabitant ($N = 94$)	74.5	57.9
Neither ($N = 290$)	77.9	61.7
Secondary:		
Spouse ($N = 3$)	. . .	. . .
Cohabitant ($N = 16$)	. . .	. . .
Neither ($N = 455$)	54.3	33.0

the satisfaction influenced the fidelity or the fidelity helped create the satisfaction, but the strong, systematic pattern exhibited in table 10.5 is striking and demands further exploration.

One explanation, neither ethically nor religiously based, relies on the economic perspective of choice sketched in chapter 1. The greater the commitment to the sex partner—in terms of the long-term nature of the partnership and its sexual exclusivity—the greater is the incentive to invest in skills that are "partner specific," including skills that enhance the enjoyment of sex with that particular partner. It is no more far-fetched to think that sexual partnerships differ in their capacity to please their members than to think of there being differences in the capacity of two people to function successfully as bridge partners, business partners, or dancing partners. The longer the partnership is likely to last, and the more commitment one has to that partnership, the greater is the incentive to learn what pleases that partner, what excites, what frustrates, what angers—in short, what works sexually and what does not. We should thus expect to see that partnerships characterized by commitment and long-term prospects would be relatively successful in achieving sexual satisfaction.

From this economic investment perspective alone, the ranking of expressed satisfaction and pleasure in table 10.5 is quite sensible and confirms the suggestion in chapter 1 that, as individuals live their sexual lives, they make choices, confront scarcity, and engage in strategic behavior. While it might be nice if one could experience the breadth of sexual pleasures that might be out there with many partners and at the same time enjoy the satisfaction and pleasure that come from a long-term, carefully nurtured sexual partnership, it looks like one cannot have it both ways. A choice must be made. The reality seems to be that the quality of the sex is higher and the skill in achieving satisfaction and pleasure is greater when one's limited capacity to please is focused on one partner in the context of a monogamous, long-term partnership.

(Remember that this interpretation assumes what we have not actually investigated: that the causal direction of this observed pattern goes from choice of sex partnership—the marriage or cohabitational relationship and its exclusivity, e.g.—to sexual satisfaction. It is also quite likely that some of the causation runs in the reverse direction, with those who are more successful in satisfying their partner being thereby encouraged to be sexually exclusive and to form a longer-term and more formal partnership such as marriage.)

Next, consider some of the responses to the questions about specific feelings prompted by sex with that particular partner. We asked specifically about five positive feelings (interspersed with the four negative ones): "satisfied," "loved," "thrilled or excited," "wanted or needed," and "taken care of." The four negative feelings were "sad," "anxious or worried," "scared or afraid," and "guilty." Table 10.6 shows the simple correlation of responses to these nine descriptors of the sexual partnership, by gender and for the primary partner when that partner was the only partner (table 10.6A) and when that partner was

Table 10.6A   Zero-Order Correlations between Descriptors of "Feelings" about
                     One's Lover—Primary Partner, with One Partner Only, by Gender

	Satisfied	Loved	Wanted	Cared for	Thrilled	Sad	Anxious	Scared
Men[a]								
Satisfied								
Loved	.41							
Wanted	.26	.36						
Cared for	.20	.40	.39					
Thrilled	.27	.23	.26	.15				
Sad	−.34	−.21	−.17	−.14	−.18			
Anxious	−.22	−.20	−.04	−.07	−.02	.23		
Scared	−.19	−.16	−.03	−.10	−.12	.25	.36	
Guilty	−.16	−.10	−.03	−.08	−.06	.27	.28	.38
Women[b]								
Satisfied								
Loved	.45							
Wanted	.34	.45						
Cared for	.39	.48	.42					
Thrilled	.42	.38	.31	.38				
Sad	−.34	−.30	−.16	−.24	−.19			
Anxious	−.22	−.22	−.11	−.16	−.08	.23		
Scared	−.23	−.15	−.08	−.17	−.07	.42	.42	
Guilty	−.23	−.28	−.13	−.22	−.12	.30	.33	.43

[a]$N = 931$.
[b]$N = 1,288$.

not the only partner (table 10.6B). From table 10.6A, we see that the positive correlations among the several positive descriptors tend to be somewhat higher for the women than for the men; similarly, the positive correlations among the four negative descriptors are also higher for the women than for the men. The negative correlations between pairs of positive and negative descriptors are relatively weak for both men and women. In table 10.6B, a similar pattern is seen for the descriptions of the primary partner in the case of respondents who had more than one partner. None of these many pairwise correlations is overwhelmingly high.

Table 10.7 shows the percentages who responded affirmatively to each of these several descriptors, by the same breakdown as explored in table 10.5, with the positive feelings shown in the top panel and the negative feelings in the bottom. Here again, a remarkably consistent pattern is seen. An exclusive, primary sex partner is associated with the highest rates of positive feelings of love, satisfaction, desire, and excitement. The nonexclusive primary sex partners are the next most positive. The secondary partner is a distant third in these five measures, and that secondary partner is particularly inferior in prompting feeling loved, wanted, or taken care of. That secondary partner is less inade-

Table 10.6B **Primary Partner, with More than One Partner, by Gender**

	Satisfied	Loved	Wanted	Cared for	Thrilled	Sad	Anxious	Scared
Men[a]								
Satisfied								
Loved	.22							
Wanted	.17	.42						
Cared for	.12	.36	.31					
Thrilled	.29	.35	.49	.19				
Sad	−.03	−.06	−.03	−.07	−.12			
Anxious	−.14	−.04	.01	−.05	−.09	.17		
Scared	−.10	−.07	.02	−.01	−.03	.14	.40	
Guilty	−.13	.02	.07	.05	−.14	.22	.31	.30
Women[b]								
Satisfied								
Loved	.50							
Wanted	.47	.53						
Cared for	.34	.31	.29					
Thrilled	.50	.52	.40	.34				
Sad	−.33	−.37	−.36	−.21	−.29			
Anxious	−.27	−.24	−.15	−.08	−.20	.39		
Scared	−.22	−.20	−.18	−.07	−.16	.38	.53	
Guilty	−.11	−.22	−.16	−.01	−.18	.31	.41	.47

[a]$N = 294$.
[b]$N = 176$.

quate in terms of feeling thrill and satisfaction. In all these measures except thrill, the spouse in a monogamous relationship is far more effective than any other type of partner in producing these positive feelings.

Regarding the four negative feelings, again a strong pattern emerges: a spouse or cohabitational partner in a sexually exclusive partnership is much less often associated with these negative feelings. By contrast, in the context of nonmonogamous relationships, a spouse especially is associated with feelings of sadness. But, judging by the bottom row of the table, the feelings of worry and guilt as well as sadness and fear are most often associated with the secondary sex partner: compared to the spouse in a monogamous relationship, the secondary sex partner prompts sadness and worry more than three times as frequently, fear nearly six times as frequently, and feelings of guilt about ten times as frequently.

Most Americans form relatively long-term, sexually exclusive partnerships, and this brief inquiry into the feelings associated with their sex lives with one or another partner surely reinforces the view that, in our culture, having a spouse or a cohabitational partner and no other sex partners is far more likely to be associated with positive feelings about one's sex life and, correspondingly, the fewest negative feelings.

Table 10.7   **How Sex Made Respondent Feel, by Partner Type and Number
                    (percentages)**

	Positive Feelings					
	Satisfied	Loved	Thrilled	Wanted	Taken Care Of	N
One partner only						
Spouse	97.1	97.5	90.9	92.2	89.8	1,584
Cohabitant	95.5	95.2	89.6	88.2	84.0	270
Other	92.9	87.6	90.8	87.1	76.0	380
At least two partners						
Primary:						
Spouse	88.1	86.4	77.6	77.6	68.7	67
Cohabitant	90.5	86.2	91.6	85.1	78.7	95
Other	92.8	83.9	86.6	84.8	72.8	290
Secondary	81.6	48.4	75.6	66.7	53.1	475

	Negative Feelings				
	Sad	Anxious, Worried	Scared, Afraid	Guilty	N
One partner only					
Spouse	3.5	8.2	2.6	2.8	1,584
Cohabitant	5.6	14.8	5.6	4.8	270
Other	5.5	19.3	9.2	12.6	380
At least two partners					
Primary:					
Spouse	16.4	16.4	9.0	10.5	67
Cohabitant	11.6	15.8	12.6	9.5	95
Other	7.2	20.7	11.0	13.8	290
Secondary	16.8	27.9	15.4	27.6	474

10.4   Sexual Dysfunction

In the previous section, we observed that a very large majority of men and women feel loved, satisfied, and even thrilled by their sex partners and that comparatively few are made to feel sad or afraid or guilty by their sex lives. Nevertheless, there are many specific problems that can arise in connection with sexual activity, and we asked about a few of these. Specifically, we asked for a yes or no response to the question, "During the last 12 months has there ever been a period of several months or more when you lacked interest in having sex; were unable to come to a climax; came to a climax too quickly; experienced physical pain during intercourse; did not find sex pleasurable; felt anxious about your ability to perform sexually; or (for men) had trouble achieving or maintaining an erection or (for women) had trouble lubricating?" (see appendix C, section 10, questions 10–11).

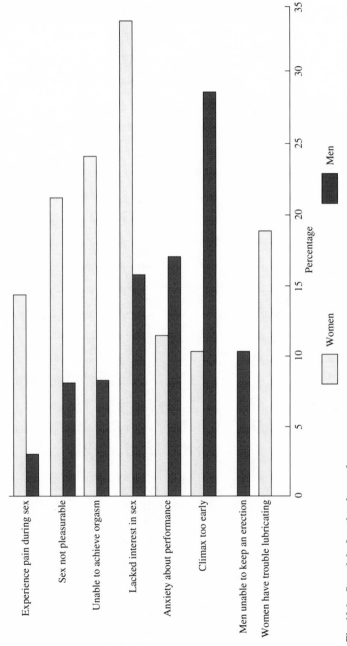

Fig. 10.1 Sexual dysfunction, by gender.

Table 10.8A **Sexual Dysfunction by Master Status, Men (percentage of master status category with dysfunction)**

Master Status	Pain during Sex	Sex Not Pleasurable	Unable to Orgasm	Lacked Interest in Sex	Anxiety about Performance	Climax too Early	Unable to Keep an Erection
Age (N = 1,346):							
18–24	5.7	8.4	4.6	13.6	21.3	26.6	5.6
25–29	1.9	9.7	9.1	15.2	14.8	29.5	9.1
30–34	1.9	9.2	9.1	16.1	13.8	29.2	10.0
35–39	2.0	5.6	6.0	11.9	18.2	30.6	7.5
40–44	3.3	8.9	11.0	19.0	19.3	26.1	9.9
45–49	3.0	6.9	5.9	11.7	15.8	27.3	10.4
50–54	1.9	7.5	14.2	20.4	19.4	25.2	21.5
55–59	4.6	7.0	9.0	24.2	11.4	35.2	20.2
Overall	3.0	8.1	8.3	15.8	17.0	28.5	10.4
Marital status (N = 1,341):							
Married	2.8	6.0	7.7	11.8	13.9	30.2	9.6
Never married	2.8	9.7	8.7	20.0	18.5	25.7	9.9
Divorced	3.8	11.4	9.1	18.2	27.4	32.5	14.6
Widowed	. . .	. . .	. . .	. . .	. . .	. . .	. . .
Separated	. . .	. . .	. . .	. . .	. . .	. . .	. . .
Overall	2.9	8.0	8.1	15.5	17.0	28.5	10.4
Education (N = 1,342):							
Less than HS	4.6	14.7	12.7	22.3	23.2	36.0	15.4
HS graduate	4.1	5.7	8.2	13.2	17.3	32.5	9.5
Some college	2.1	8.9	7.9	15.7	17.8	24.4	10.2
Finished college	2.2	6.6	6.5	15.7	10.9	25.8	9.1
Master's/adv. deg.	1.7	5.2	6.8	13.3	14.5	24.1	9.3
Overall	3.0	8.0	8.3	15.7	16.9	28.5	10.4
Race/ethnicity (N = 1,342):							
White	3.0	7.0	7.4	14.7	16.8	27.7	9.9
Black	3.3	15.2	9.9	20.0	23.7	33.8	14.5
Hispanic	2.0	8.2	10.9	16.7	7.1	25.0	8.9
Asian/Pacific Islander	0.0	6.3	18.8	14.7	15.6	31.3	9.4
Native American	. . .	. . .	. . .	. . .	. . .	. . .	. . .
Overall	3.0	8.1	8.2	15.7	17.0	28.5	10.4
Religion (N = 1,389):[a]							
None	1.6	7.0	8.5	18.3	11.8	26.2	9.6
Type I Protestant	2.9	7.4	7.6	12.7	17.8	25.7	11.7
Type II Protestant	3.1	9.7	8.6	16.5	20.1	32.0	11.2
Catholic	3.3	7.8	7.6	15.3	15.2	29.1	9.0
Jewish	. . .	. . .	. . .	. . .	. . .	. . .	. . .
Other	2.6	7.7	12.8	14.6	10.3	25.6	7.7
Other Protestant	9.1	6.1	14.3	22.9	28.6	15.2	14.3
Overall	3.0	8.0	8.3	15.6	16.9	28.4	10.4
Income (N = 1,098):[b]							
Poor	5.5	15.3	15.9	25.4	20.5	29.7	14.0
Middle	2.8	6.0	7.2	13.0	15.3	28.0	9.1
Rich	1.9	9.1	6.1	15.0	14.2	30.3	11.3
Overall	2.9	7.5	7.9	14.6	15.6	28.6	10.0

Note: ". . ." indicates fewer than thirty cases.

[a]For an explanation of the classification of Protestant respondents, see chapter appendix 3.1A. *Other* includes primarily Eastern religions (e.g., Buddhism, Hinduism).

[b]Income was divided in the following way: *poor:* family income is below or at the poverty line for 1991; *middle:* family income is between the official poverty line for 1991 and a figure six times that amount; *rich:* family income is six times or more the official poverty line for 1991.

Table 10.8B **Sexual Dysfunction by Master Status, Women (percentage of master status category with dysfunction)**

Master Status	Sexual Dysfunction						
	Pain during Sex	Sex Not Pleasurable	Unable to Orgasm	Lacked Interest in Sex	Anxiety about Performance	Climax too Early	Had Trouble Lubricating
Age ($N = 1,622$):							
18–24	21.5	26.6	26.0	32.0	18.4	14.0	19.3
25–29	18.8	26.2	24.4	32.3	13.0	12.8	18.2
30–34	14.2	26.5	27.7	29.5	12.0	10.3	16.2
35–39	13.0	18.3	26.9	37.6	9.5	10.7	18.1
40–44	12.5	15.7	20.8	36.0	10.9	6.9	15.9
45–49	10.3	15.4	18.8	33.7	8.8	7.1	22.6
50–54	7.4	15.3	20.2	30.2	7.8	9.6	21.4
55–59	8.7	16.4	21.8	37.0	4.4	7.6	24.8
Overall	14.4	21.2	24.1	33.4	11.5	10.3	18.8
Marital status ($N = 1,613$):							
Married	14.4	20.5	21.9	29.4	9.7	9.2	21.6
Never married	14.9	23.0	26.6	37.3	15.3	13.4	15.0
Divorced	13.9	22.2	28.6	39.4	13.1	10.8	16.6
Widowed	11.4	11.4	16.7	31.4	4.1	4.6	10.4
Separated	13.3	24.4	25.5	43.8	10.6	13.3	13.0
Overall	14.3	21.2	24.0	33.2	11.4	10.4	18.8
Education ($N = 1,614$):							
Less than HS	16.1	25.8	30.0	43.2	16.2	17.4	14.0
HS graduate	16.8	22.2	28.0	35.4	11.8	11.7	19.5
Some college	14.5	20.5	22.4	32.0	10.4	9.3	19.2
Finished college	9.6	18.4	19.1	27.9	8.3	6.2	19.3
Master's/adv. deg.	9.3	16.5	13.3	23.4	13.3	4.1	23.7
Overall	14.3	21.2	24.0	33.4	11.5	10.3	18.8
Race/Ethnicity ($N = 1,623$):							
White	14.7	19.7	23.2	30.9	10.5	7.5	20.7
Black	12.5	30.0	29.2	44.5	14.5	20.4	13.0
Hispanic	13.6	19.8	20.3	34.6	11.7	18.4	12.0
Asian/Pacific Islander	. . .	. . .	. . .	. . .	. . .	. . .	. . .
Native American	. . .	. . .	. . .	. . .	. . .	. . .	. . .
Overall	14.4	21.2	24.1	33.4	11.5	10.3	18.8
Religion ($N = 1,621$):[a]							
None	20.1	28.5	27.9	29.8	17.7	13.7	19.9
Type I Protestant	11.6	17.0	20.1	30.9	9.6	7.7	19.4
Type II Protestant	16.3	25.2	27.7	38.2	13.4	10.9	19.6
Catholic	14.2	19.1	23.4	32.5	9.6	11.1	17.7
Jewish	. . .	. . .	. . .	. . .	. . .	. . .	. . .
Other	8.6	22.9	20.6	35.1	8.3	2.9	13.9
Other Protestant	10.8	10.5	15.4	25.6	5.3	13.2	15.8
Overall	14.4	21.2	24.0	33.4	11.5	10.3	18.8
Income ($N = 1,297$):[b]							
Poor	16.2	23.3	27.4	39.7	20.0	18.2	13.9
Middle	14.5	21.5	23.6	32.0	10.2	10.6	19.0
Rich	11.4	17.3	20.8	27.5	11.7	4.4	23.7
Overall	14.3	21.1	23.8	32.5	12.0	10.8	18.9

Note: ". . ." indicates fewer than thirty cases.

[a]For an explanation of the classification of Protestant respondents, see chapter appendix 3.1A. *Other* includes primarily Eastern religions (e.g., Buddhism, Hinduism).

[b]Income was divided in the following way: *poor:* family income is below or at the poverty line for 1991; *middle:* family income is between the official poverty line for 1991 and a figure six times that amount; *rich:* family income is six times or more the official poverty line for 1991.

Figure 10.1 shows the overall percentages of men and of women who responded yes. The proportions reporting having one or another of these problems varied from roughly 5 to roughly 25 percent, with the exception that about one-third of the women reported lacking interest in sex for a period of several months or more. Notice also that several of these problems are more common for women while others are more common for men. For men, the more frequent problems are climaxing too early, anxiety about performance, and lack of interest in sex. For women, on the other hand, lack of interest in sex, inability to achieve orgasm, finding sex not pleasurable, having difficulty lubricating for sex, experiencing pain during intercourse, and anxiety about performance all were reported by more than one in ten women.

Table 10.8 shows the percentages with each of these several measures of sexual dysfunction by gender and the master status variables. For the men (table 10.8A), age is associated with several of these sexual problems, as are education level, race/ethnicity, and particularly income. For the women (table 10.8B), several of the problems appear to decline with age, and, here again, there are clear patterns of association with education, race/ethnicity, and income.

Table 10.9 relates these responses to the levels of physical health. The numbers in the table are the percentages of men or women of a given health status who responded yes to experiencing that particular sexual problem. (Only twenty-two men reported their health as poor and we do not report a percentage for them. Thirty-six women reported poor health and we report a percentage when we have at least thirty cases. We decided not to combine those in poor health with those in fair health.) There are two points to be made about this table. First, those who report fair or poor health are much more likely also to report having one or another of these specific sexual problems—the rates of occurrence of the problem rise rather consistently and dramatically as the reported health status declines from excellent to fair. Second, the gradation in the change in the proportion with the problem is much greater for the men than for the women. That is, seldom is the proportion for women in poor health much more than twice the proportion for women in excellent health, but, even excluding the men in poor health, the proportions for men are four or five times as great among those in fair health as among those in excellent health for several of these problems. Perhaps health has a bigger influence on the ability of men to perform and enjoy sex than is the case for women, or perhaps men base their perception of their health status somewhat more directly on their sexual health than do women, or perhaps we happen to have asked about a few sexual problems for which this pattern holds and overlooked others for which it does not.

Table 10.10 is similar in design to table 10.9 but focuses on happiness instead of health. The table reports these proportions for the whole sample and by gender. Here again, we see a steeper gradation across the columns for the men than for the women, and again we see that those who report themselves

Table 10.9   **Sexual Problems by Health Status, by Gender**

		Health Status			
	Total	Excellent	Good	Fair	Poor
Lack interest in having sex					
Men	15.7	11.4	17.0	25.0	. . .
Women	33.4	29.2	34.1	42.0	58.3
Unable to come to a climax (experience an orgasm)					
Men	8.2	4.5	9.3	18.4	. . .
Women	24.1	20.2	25.1	32.6	36.7
Climax (experience an orgasm) too quickly					
Men	28.5	24.8	30.3	40.5	. . .
Women	10.3	9.0	10.3	15.1	. . .
Physical pain during intercourse					
Men	3.0	1.5	3.3	6.4	. . .
Women	14.4	8.6	17.4	22.8	. . .
Did not find sex pleasurable					
Men	8.1	4.9	8.9	18.4	. . .
Women	21.2	18.3	21.9	28.1	. . .
Felt anxious about ability to perform sexually					
Men	17.0	13.1	18.2	28.3	. . .
Women	11.5	8.3	11.9	22.2	10.0
Had trouble achieving or maintaining an erection					
Men	10.4	6.1	11.4	22.6	. . .
Had trouble lubricating					
Women	18.8	16.9	18.7	26.0	23.3

Note: ". . ." indicates fewer than thirty cases.

unhappy are much more likely to report each of these sexual problems than are those who report themselves to be extremely or very happy. This internal consistency is noteworthy itself; it suggests that sexual well-being and overall well-being are intricately connected.

Here, as elsewhere in this chapter, we have barely begun to provide an understanding of the complexity of sexual and general well-being, happiness, or health. We have seen here that, despite the reports of general satisfaction with their sex life, many men and women also report periods in the past year when they experienced one or another sexual problem. These problems vary in their severity from lacking interest or not finding sex pleasurable to physical pain

Table 10.10   **Happiness, by Sexual Dysfunction, Percentage with Dysfunction in Happiness Category**

	Happiness				
Dysfunction	Extremely Happy	Very Happy	Generally Satisfied	Fairly Unhappy	Unhappy Most Times
Lacked interest in sex					
All (25.4%, N = 3,097)	14.5	20.6	29.3	42.1	59.3
Men (15.7%, N = 1,392)	9.6	12.5	18.7	26.0	36.8
Women (33.3%, N = 1,705)	18.9	27.3	38.1	53.3	75.5
Sex not pleasurable					
All (15.2%, N = 2,983)	6.9	11.8	18.9	27.0	41.2
Men (8.1%, N = 1,349)	3.3	5.9	9.4	16.0	35.3
Women (21.1%, N = 1,627)	10.1	16.6	26.9	34.9	45.7
Anxiety about performance					
All (13.9%, N = 3,015)	8.8	10.5	18.6	18.9	28.6
Men (17.0%, N = 1,361)	11.4	14.0	21.5	19.4	42.9
Women (11.4%, N = 1,654)	6.5	7.7	16.2	18.6	18.4
Unable to achieve orgasm					
All (16.9%, N = 3,025)	10.1	13.7	21.3	24.4	32.5
Men (8.3%, N = 1,370)	4.4	6.6	10.6	11.4	22.9
Women (24.0%, N = 1,655)	15.2	19.7	30.3	33.5	39.6
Climax too early					
All (18.6%, N = 2,983)	15.2	17.6	21.2	19.0	25.3
Men (28.5%, N = 1,355)	24.6	26.8	31.9	30.8	35.3
Women (10.3%, N = 1,628)	6.9	9.9	12.1	10.6	17.8
Experienced pain during sex					
All (9.2%, N = 2,968)	5.2	7.7	10.9	15.1	18.5
Men (3.0%, N = 1,348)	1.6	2.2	4.8	2.5	5.7
Women (14.4%, N = 1,620)	8.3	12.3	16.1	24.2	28.3
Unable to keep an erection					
Men (10.4%, N = 1,368)	5.7	10.2	11.7	11.3	27.8
Have trouble lubricating					
Women (18.9%, N = 1,650)	13.3	17.1	20.4	28.3	26.5

and the inability to perform sexually to the satisfaction of the respondent. Much more study is warranted and is feasible, fortunately, with these data as well as with other recent data. Linking the problems to marital and living-arrangement patterns and to other stresses in the lives of the respondents as well as investigating how the sexual experiences affect health and are affected by it should be a high priority for subsequent research.

10.5 Conclusion

This chapter covers a topic of enormous scope and complexity and does so only suggestively. We have found here that, overall, the respondents in our sample report themselves both happy and healthy: nearly 60 percent say that they are very or extremely happy, and almost 90 percent are in good or excellent health. While the correlation between the two is positive, it is far from perfect. About one-quarter of the respondents are healthy but unhappy (about 10 percent), or happy but unhealthy (another 10 percent), or both unhappy and unhealthy (another 3 percent).

When compared by several of the measures of sexual behavior in earlier chapters, we find that those who have one sex partner, those who have sex two or three times a week, and, for women, those who frequently experience orgasm in their partnered sexual activity are substantially happier than are those with either no sex partners or with two or four partners, or those who seldom have sex, or women who seldom experience orgasm. What the causal mechanism is has not been established in any of these cases, but the correlations between many of these sexual behaviors and reported levels of happiness and health suggest that they are closely related and deserve much more research.

Strong relations exist between the type and the number of sex partners and the sexual satisfaction derived from sex with that specific partner. In particular, sex with a spouse in a monogamous relationship seems more consistently associated with emotional satisfaction and physical pleasure than sex with a primary partner while also having a sexual relation with one or more other partners within the past twelve months. Moreover, feelings of being loved or satisfied, or "taken care of," are closely linked to monogamous sex with a spouse or cohabitational partner. Similarly, feelings of sadness, fear, worry, or guilt are strikingly lower in characterizing sex with a spouse or cohabitational partner in a monogamous relationship than in describing sex with a primary or secondary partner for respondents who have had two or more partners within the past twelve months. In every category we asked about except one—the thrill of sex—sex with the secondary sex partner was inferior and generally substantially so. While we had no particular prior conceptions about the likely outcome of our questions about this matter, the respondents offer a remarkably strong case for the efficacy of sexual exclusivity in the context of a formal marriage as most closely associated with a satisfying and pleasurable sex life.

We turn next to a more finely grained investigation of the relation of sexual behavior to one of its many potential consequences, the contraction of a sexually transmitted disease.

CHAPTER 11

Sexually Transmitted Infections

As if the complexities of sexual relationships and practices were not sufficiently challenging in terms of social interaction, psychological meaning, and procreation, disease has always been yet another possible outcome from partnered sex. The consequences of sexual intimacy include the risk of sharing bacterial and viral infections, and the perpetuation and spread of several diseases are an important public repercussion of this very private behavior. No presentation of the patterns of adult sexual behavior in the nation would be complete without a discussion of the incidence and patterns of sexually transmitted infections and diseases (STIs and STDs). They have been part of real-world sex throughout time (for an excellent overview, see Brandt 1987). Moreover, a recent review of the actual causes of death in the United States estimated 30,000 deaths related to sexual behavior, contending that "unprotected intercourse now represents one of the most rapidly increasing causes of death in the country" (McGinnis and Foege 1993, 2210). As the concern about disease, particularly AIDS, was one of the primary motivations prompting this survey project, it is particularly fitting that we devote attention to this issue.

Most of what we know about the distribution of STIs comes from two sources, neither of which is well suited to informing us about infections in the general public. Clinical studies tell us much about those who have an infection, but only by inference can we identify differences between those who have it and those who do not. Official counts reported to the Centers for Disease Control and Prevention (CDC) in Atlanta tell us the number of new reported cases of infection in any given time period, but they cannot tell us how many people are infected or how frequently individuals contract an infection or get another one as well. There are few general population surveys that ask in any detail about STIs or obtain laboratory evidence of infection (except the National Survey of Family Growth; see Johnson, Nahmins, and Madger 1989) and none that have asked these questions and additionally asked detailed questions about sexual behavior of the same men and women (see also Billy et al. 1993; and Catania et al. 1992b). The NHSLS has done so, and this information about both sexual behavior and infection/disease in the general population is one of

Joel A. Feinleib crafted this chapter and generated most of its tables. William Dale Schempp ably assisted in the empirical effort. Robert T. Michael directed their work and wrote the chapter.

the more important contributions that our new data offer; its presentation is the purpose of this chapter.

In particular, we address four main questions in this chapter. (1) What are the lifetime and annual rates of STIs in the U.S. adult population? What are the basic demographic and social correlates of these STIs in this population? (2) What patterns of sexual behavior (i.e., choice of partners and specific sex practices) increase or decrease the risk of contracting an STI, and, most important, what are the observed links between those risky behaviors and the incidence of STIs? (3) What are the sexual behaviors (e.g., acquiring new partners) and practices (e.g., condom use) of those currently or recently infected with STIs, and how do these patterns of behavior contribute to the continuing spread of STIs? (4) What is the extent of knowledge and understanding among the population at large about methods of avoiding STIs, and what changes in behavior are reported in response to the risk of AIDS?

We note at the outset that ours is not an epidemiological study of the populations at highest risk of contracting HIV/AIDS and other STI/STDs. Rather, it is a general survey of the whole range of sexual behaviors engaged in by the U.S. adult population that for the first time permits us to estimate the rates of "risky" sexual behaviors for the whole population and to link that behavior to the contraction of STIs in the population at large. That is, we believe that we have the first general population sample that permits estimation of both the incidence of risky behavior and the incidence of STIs among those same individuals, thus allowing us to identify correlations between the behavior and the outcome.

The reader might have expected a greater emphasis on HIV/AIDS in this chapter because many would agree with the statement by the surgeon general of the United States in an extraordinary booklet mailed to every household in the country in 1988: "AIDS is one of the most serious health problems that has ever faced the American public" (Koop 1988). Indeed, this frightening new virus has changed the social landscape of the nation, forcing discussion of sexual activity into the open in order to provide information to adults and adolescents that might save their lives. This concern about AIDS has been an important motivation for this study, and it is probably one of the more important reasons that the American public has been cooperative in participating in our survey. Yet most of the issues that arise in relating sexual behavior to AIDS pertain as well to the many other sexually transmitted diseases, whether called *venereal diseases* as they once were or *sexually transmitted infections* (STIs) as they are now. (We use the terms *STI* and *STD* in this chapter; the distinction is that the infection causes the disease and that, if an individual remains asymptomatic, the infection may not have been detected.) While AIDS has made "unsafe" sexual behavior a matter of life and death, other more traditional STDs such as gonorrhea, syphilis, and genital herpes vary in the severity of their consequences; if left untreated, however, these diseases as well can have severe effects on health and can become life threatening (see Cotran, Kumar, and Robbins 1989, 343–49 [gonorrhea], 370–71 [syphilis], and 319–20; Holmes et al. 1990).

The CDC estimates that there were over 12 million new cases of STIs in 1991 (CDC 1992). Despite its prominence in the public eye, AIDS represents only a tiny proportion of STIs, with about 50,000 new cases in that year. So, while it has an extraordinarily high fatality rate, the number of cases of HIV/ AIDS in the CDC reports is less than half of 1 percent of all the new STI cases. Consequently, in our data as well, one should expect the HIV/AIDS cases to constitute a very tiny proportion of reported STIs.

Another way to think about this point is that the CDC reports that there are about 114,000 adults (aged eighteen to fifty-nine) in the United States who have AIDS and are alive, and general estimates of those in the nation who are infected with HIV are around 1 million (see Roper, Peterson, and Curran 1993). Now, there were about 146 million adults aged eighteen to fifty-nine in the United States in 1992, so the percentage of living adults with AIDS is about 0.08 percent and the percentage infected with HIV about 0.4 percent. Thus, if in our survey of 3,432 adults we have the same proportion with AIDS as is the case in the United States as a whole, we should expect to find 2.7, or two or three, cases. If we base our expectation on the estimate that 1 million people in this country are infected with HIV, we should expect to find 24 cases. Obviously, there are far too few cases in a small data set such as ours to sustain an analysis of the behavior of those who do and those who do not have HIV/ AIDS. This is another compelling reason why we have not focused on HIV/ AIDS in this chapter.

Understanding how STIs are spread is a major public health objective. Adding urgency, the presence of many of the other STIs is known to increase the likelihood of infection by HIV through sexual contact because of the increased likelihood of lesions or open sores on or around the genitalia (Padian 1990). It is therefore a reasonable strategy to address what we know about these STIs in a consolidated manner since many of the same behaviors affect the risks of contracting and transmitting many different diseases and the presence of some affects the likelihood of contracting others. In this chapter, we look into the observed relations between risks of contracting STIs/STDs and the dynamics of partner choice and sexual practices.

11.1 Lifetime and Annual Rates of STIs

Previous estimates of the number of cases of STIs have generally been based on either studies of at-risk populations, such as people visiting STD clinics, or the official government counts of reported new cases of an infection, which are supposed to be reported to the CDC on diagnosis by a health professional. Both are useful but flawed sources of information about infections because neither permits assessment of the full range of exposure to STIs or estimation of the incidence of ever having had one of these infections in the population at large. Using the clinic counts of an infection, we have no way of knowing what the relevant population group is from which cases come; thus, we cannot estimate the risk of contracting infection in the population as a whole or in a subgroup. Notifications to the CDC from health professionals are subject to different levels of compliance and complex and changing rules, and it is known that compliance differs across states and among various types of health practitioners, say, public health clinics compared to private practices (see Laumann et al. 1993). Moreover, these reported new cases cannot tell us whether they are repeat cases involving the same people or new cases in people who have never before had the infection. In addition, many infections may remain silent or asymptomatic and never be reported; consequently, even if numbers are reported with complete accuracy, we cannot tell how many people in the population have ever had or currently have the infection, that is, the *prevalence* of a specific infection in the population.

The NHSLS survey data permit us to estimate the number of yearly and lifetime cases of STIs in the noninstitutionalized U.S. population aged eighteen to fifty-nine. These estimates are based on self-reports by respondents, regardless of the treatment or diagnosis setting. Consequently, they are obtained in a manner that permits us to estimate a rate of infection, using an appropriate population denominator—the sexually active adult population eighteen to fifty-nine. Additionally, the information can be correlated with the sexual behavior of these respondents, and we can therefore determine whether the "risky behavior," as we tend to characterize it, is in fact linked to the incidence of the infection and thus should be thought of as a formal risk factor. We can do so by looking carefully at sexual behavior, including partner selection and sexual practices. Our sample size is not large, so we have little to say about rare population events and cannot ferret out specialized at-risk populations such as intravenous drug users. The major limitation of these data is that we must depend on respondents' recall and knowledge of medical diagnoses, which is certain to be less than complete. For instance, we asked about pelvic inflammatory disease (PID), which often results from an undiagnosed STD, but respondents may not know the underlying cause of their PID diagnosis. We may therefore undercount the occurrence of, say, chlamydia that leads to PID.[1] In addition, sensitivity about these diseases may lead to a reluctance on the part of respondents to report them, even if they know that they have had them, and this, as well, will result in an undercount of unknown magnitude.

1. In the tables below, when infections are listed separately, we included all cases of diagnosed PID except where the respondent indicated that it was not sexually transmitted. When infections are summarized as "all bacterial STIs," we eliminate the cases of PID where the respondent also had a diagnosis of gonorrhea or chlamydia. Thus, our combined measure presumes a tendency to double count, say, if the respondent was told that her PID resulted from chlamydia.

Survey Questions Asked

Our survey questions about STIs and STDs were designed in consultation with staff of the CDC (see appendix C, section 9, beginning with question 13). We asked specifically and separately about ten infections: gonorrhea, syphilis, genital herpes, chlamydia, genital warts (human papilloma virus [HPV]), hepatitis, HIV/AIDS, and vaginitis and pelvic inflammatory disease (PID) for women, and nongonococcal urethritis (NGU) for men. We asked whether the respondent had ever been told by a doctor that he or she had any of the infections, how many times he or she had been told so, and whether he or she had been told so in the past twelve months. Five of these infections are bacterial and can generally be cured at the early stages (gonorrhea, syphilis, chlamydia, NGU, PID); four are viral and generally recurring and incurable (genital warts, genital herpes, hepatitis B, and HIV). (Hepatitis B is not recurring but may lead to a chronic carrier state in 5–10 percent of infected individuals. For a more extensive discussion, see Cotran, Kumar, and Robbins 1989 or Holmes et al. 1990.) The tenth infection is vaginitis of nonspecific etiology, a category that includes various infections such as trichomoniasis, which the CDC reports as the second most common STD, and various yeast and bacterial infections that are not sexually transmitted. Because we could not distinguish with any precision the sexually transmitted infections from yeast infections and bacterial infections not transmitted sexually, we omitted vaginitis from our analysis in this chapter. We note that there were several cases of other infections that the respondent indicated had not been sexually transmitted, and these, as well, were excluded.[2]

Because bacterial and viral infections differ in level of infectivity and rate of recurrence, we have distinguished between them in most of our analyses here. The bacterial infections can be treated with antibiotics and therefore cured. The viruses, in contrast, cannot be killed by known medication, and many remain latent in the body (i.e., herpes viruses) and can recur from time to time (see Holmes et al. 1990; Donovan 1993). Therefore, the two types of STIs pose different risks. Carriers of such recurring viral infections as herpes, genital warts, and chronic hepatitis B pose a continuing risk of further spread,

---

2. We asked respondents which partner they thought had given them the STI, which provided an opportunity for a response indicating that the infection was not in fact sexually transmitted. We carefully reviewed every reported STI for this and other inconsistencies. Overall, we dropped five cases of HIV/AIDS (discussed in more detail in n. 5 below), seven cases of genital warts, one case of gonorrhea, two cases of syphilis, thirty-one cases of hepatitis, four cases of NGU, fifteen cases of PID, and two cases of genital herpes. We let stand those cases where the respondent did not know who transmitted the infection. Of course, some of these cases, especially of PID, NGU, and hepatitis, may also be nonsexually transmitted. There was some confusion about reported cases of hepatitis since hepatitis A is not sexually transmitted but hepatitis B is. We have eliminated the cases that were evidently type A from the counts of the sexually transmitted hepatitis B. Overall, we cannot count all STIs with complete precision and have had to rely on imperfect methods for adjudicating a few cases in our data set.

whereas bacterial STIs can generally be transmitted only until appropriate antibiotic treatment renders the individual no longer infectious.

Estimates of STIs

Table 11.1 gives the lifetime and annual rates per 1,000 people for the five bacterial and four viral STIs.[3] The combined reported lifetime number of cases for any STI is 169 per 1,000 people, or 16.9 percent. Roughly 11 percent of U.S. adults aged eighteen to fifty-nine report that they have at one time or another had a bacterial STI, and 7.4 percent have had a viral STI. Interestingly, few respondents report having had more than one kind of infection. Of those ever diagnosed with any STI, only 16 percent report having had two or more different types of STI, and only 4 percent of those with an STI report three or more types. Of those ever having any bacterial STI, 33 percent report having two or more separate infections, and less than 13 percent report having three or more cases.

The proportion of respondents who report having been told that they had an STI within the past twelve months is 1.6 percent, with 1.0 percent of the respondents having a bacterial STI within the past twelve months and just over half of 1 percent having been diagnosed as having a viral STI.[4]

Six respondents of the total number of 3,432 in our survey reported being infected with HIV, five in the cross-sectional sample of 3,159 observations and one in the oversample. As discussed above, on the basis of the two national estimates of (*a*) the number of living adults with AIDS and (*b*) the number of people infected with HIV, we expected to find between two and twenty-four cases of HIV/AIDS; six is well within these bounds. Note that the questions

---

3. Throughout this volume, we have reported results based on unweighted data, using the "cross-sectional" sample of 3,159 observations, which is tolerably close to a self-weighting sample. There are a few instances, however, where the use of the weighted data may be important, and these are instances where we estimate national figures as in the first several tables of this chapter on sexually transmitted infections. As in all others, the tables in this chapter report the unweighted results. We have replicated all the tables from 11.1 through 11.8 and have spot-checked many others. If the reader would like a copy of these tables based on weighted data, write or call the NORC Sheatsley Library, 1155 E. 60th St., Chicago IL 60637 (phone, 312-753-7679).

Substantively, there are few differences between the weighted and the unweighted results. We list here all the figures in tables 11.1–11.8 in which the calculated number is different by a magnitude as great as 4 percentage points: *table 11.5:* five or more partners: gonorrhea, 82; PID, 88; any bacterial, 110; any STI, 153; *table 11.6:* females with twenty-one or more partners: bacterial, 292; viral, 320; total, 454; *table 11.8:* black men: any bacterial, 296; any STI, 307; Hispanic men: any bacterial, 64; any STI, 94; black women: gonorrhea, 141; any bacterial, 207; any STI, 220. These are the only numbers in these eight tables that differ by as much as 4 percentage points. Of these, we note that the ratios for men to women in table 11.6 and for blacks to whites in table 11.8 remain essentially unchanged.

4. Note that our survey did not measure the incidence of STIs over a specific twelve-month period, as the CDC does over calendar years. Instead, we asked each respondent whether he or she had been diagnosed by a doctor as having an STI in the twelve months prior to the interview. Since the interviews took place between the months of February 1992 and September 1992, the reported STIs "within the past twelve months" could have occurred anytime during the interval from January 1991 through September 1992.

Table 11.1   **Incidence of Lifetime and Annual STIs (cases per 1,000)**

	Lifetime	Annual		Lifetime	Annual
Gonorrhea	66	2	Genital warts	47	4
Syphilis	8	0	Herpes	21	2
Chlamydia	32	5	Hepatitis	11	0
NGU	19	2	HIV/AIDS	1	0
PID	22	2	Any viral	74	6
Any bacterial	113	10	Any STI	169	16

Note: Comparable values in subsequent tables may differ very slightly because of missing values in the selected correlates.

that we asked respondents were, "Tell me whether you have ever been told by a doctor that you had . . . AIDS, HIV," and, in the self-administered portion of the survey, "Have you been tested for the AIDS virus?" (yes/no and, if yes), then "Did you test positive?" (See appendix C, SAQ 4F, questions 16 and 16A for females, and SAQ 4M, questions 18 and 18A for males.) Thus, these questions should identify more cases than those with symptomatic AIDS but will underestimate the number infected with HIV since not all infected individuals would have been tested. On these grounds, our survey finding of six cases appears to be quite reasonable.[5]

Table 11.2 shows the reported numbers of the bacterial and viral STIs and their total in both the lifetime and the past twelve months, by the *age* of the respondent. Occurrences for any events that occur uniformly over the lifetime

5. Naturally, there is not complete agreement between the answers to the two questions about HIV/AIDS. In total, ten respondents said that a doctor told them that they had HIV/AIDS, while in total twelve said that they had tested positive for HIV. The overlap was five respondents who said that both the doctor and the test revealed the disease, and these are unequivocally recorded in our study as having HIV/AIDS. Of the remaining seven who said that they tested positive but did not say that a doctor told them that they had HIV/AIDS, from their other answers we concluded on a case-by-case basis that they had misunderstood the self-administered question about a "positive" test outcome, thinking of a "positive" test as an indication of no disease rather than the medical connotation of a positive test implying the presence of the disease. (This wording should not be used in a self-administered questionnaire, we conclude.) These seven individuals have not been considered as having HIV/AIDS.

There were five individuals who said that a doctor had told them that they had HIV/AIDS but who did not answer the questions about an HIV/AIDS test yielding a positive result. One of these five provided enough information so that we believe that she had HIV/AIDS. Four others did not— they had not received any treatment for the disease, they did not name a sex partner who they thought gave them the disease, they did not have any other indication of the disease, and they did not engage in any high-risk sexual behavior. Thus, we concluded that these four did not actually have HIV/AIDS.

So the NHSLS data set has six cases of HIV/AIDS reported, as we have identified them. Of the six, three are men and three women. Their ages range from thirty to forty-nine. One of the women injected using shared needles; she and another of the women and one man each had in excess of 100 lifetime male sex partners; all three men were bisexual. Incidentally, there were 1,077 respondents who said that they had had an HIV/AIDS test with a negative result, none of whom said that a doctor had told them that they had HIV/AIDS; ten of that total did not answer the question about the doctor; none of these, of course, was considered as having HIV/AIDS in our study.

will increase with age, of course, as the opportunity for exposure increases. The left-hand panel of table 11.2 shows a different pattern for these STIs, however. For the bacterial infections, we see a notable increase in the reported number of infections from the earliest age interval (eighteen to twenty-four) through the late twenties, no further increase in the reporting through age forty-four, a big jump for the one age group forty-five to forty-nine, and then a precipitous decline through the fifties. (The age group forty-five to forty-nine would have been aged twenty to twenty-five in the period from 1963 through 1972, a time of considerable sexual experimentation and of the Vietnam War, so this group may have had a higher incidence of STIs than those older or younger.) For the viral STIs, the same general pattern is seen—a rise in the twenties, only a mild increase over the interval from thirty to forty-four, and then a dramatic decline to the highest ages we interviewed (age fifty-nine).

Several explanations may account for this pattern. First, it is possible that the older respondents have forgotten infections that they had years before or have chosen not to tell us about them. We have no reason to think this logical possibility is, in fact, a big part of the story since these older respondents did not have difficulty recalling or reluctance reporting any other events that had occurred at a relatively young age. Second, a closely related explanation is a misdiagnosis in the past. Diagnostic tests for many of these infections have only recently been available, so older people may have had these infections at some time in the past but may not have been so diagnosed. (This is a very important difference between self-reported data and serologic data.)

Third, it may be that the younger cohorts are acquiring these infections at a much faster rate than their older counterparts. This could result in the pattern that we see in the table, and it would suggest that, as the younger groups age, the lifetime occurrences at older ages will in the future be higher than they are currently. This is what one would call a *cohort effect*—the younger birth cohorts are now behaving and may well throughout their lifetime behave differ-

Table 11.2   Lifetime and Annual STIs, by Type of Infection and Age (cases per 1,000)

	Lifetime			Annual		
	Bacterial	Viral	Any	Bacterial	Viral	Any
All ages	112	73	166	9	6	15
18–24	102	53	141	31	14	45
25–29	122	71	174	11	7	18
30–34	121	92	191	4	8	10
35–39	123	92	187	4	4	9
40–44	117	97	192	5	2	7
45–49	140	60	183	10	0	10
50–54	74	41	107	0	4	4
55–59	66	53	106	0	0	0

ently than the older birth cohorts. A fourth possibility is that the infections are, and over the past half century have been, mainly contracted at younger ages and that, by the time people reach their mid-thirties, rates of further accumulation of STIs are very low. That too would yield the pattern that we observed here. This is called an *age effect* since it suggests that, although each birth cohort may behave similarly, as it passes through a particular age interval its behavior is systematically different than it is at another age.

We know from chapter 5 that most adults acquire the greatest number of sex partners in their early adulthood and that the rate of acquiring partners falls dramatically as they age and form formal marriages, so this behavior is surely reflected in the rates of accumulation of STIs seen in table 11.2. One further corroboration of the pattern that we see here, but again not useful in distinguishing between the third and the fourth explanations of that pattern, is the evidence in the right-hand panel of the table. There the annual reported occurrence of STDs is clearly seen to be highest among the younger respondents (except for that exceptionally high level of bacterial infection reported by those aged forty-five to forty-nine).

STIs by Number of Partners and Master Statuses

Table 11.3 provides more detail about the reported lifetime infections, showing specific infecting agents and distinguishing men and women while condensing the age groups into three groups instead of the narrow six in table 11.2. Table 11.3 tells us that the lifetime reported cases of these infections are not dramatically different for men and for women—overall, 15.9 percent of

Table 11.3 Lifetime STIs, by Age and Gender (people with at least one sex partner in their lifetime, cases per 1,000)

| | Age | | | | | | Total Population | | |
| | 18–29 | | 30–44 | | 45–59 | | | | |
	M	F	M	F	M	F	M	F	Total
Gonorrhea	47	51	112	54	106	31	90	47	66
Syphilis	9	6	11	8	6	7	9	7	8
Chlamydia	33	81	15	34	6	18	19	44	32
NGU	7	N.A.	25	N.A.	27	N.A.	19	N.A.	19
PID	N.A.	26	N.A.	25	N.A.	14	N.A.	22	22
Any bacterial	83	139	140	107	136	68	121	106	113
Genital warts	31	63	41	74	21	29	33	59	47
Herpes	4	24	19	38	9	18	12	29	21
Hepatitis	7	2	15	10	18	16	13	9	11
HIV/AIDS	0	0	3	1	3	0	2	1	1
Any viral	40	82	70	114	45	59	54	90	74
Any STI	120	194	186	199	160	122	159	178	169

Note: N.A. = not applicable.

the men and 17.8 percent of the women who have ever had a sex partner report having had an STI. The bacterial infection rate is slightly higher for men and the viral infection rate higher for women. For both men and women, the rate of occurrence of chlamydia is much higher for the youngest age group than for any of the older age groups, while the other diseases reflect the general pattern over the lifetime that we saw in table 11.2. The reason for the higher rates of chlamydia in younger groups is probably recent improvements in the reliability, standardization, and expense of clinical testing methods. Thus, higher rates of chlamydia in younger cohorts need not reflect a real increase in number of infections (see Lossick 1985).

Table 11.4 again combines gender and age groups and shows lifetime occurrences of STIs by another important personal characteristic, the number of sex partners reported since age eighteen. Notice how the occurrence of specific infections—both bacterial and viral—rises monotonically and dramatically as the number of sex partners rises from none, to one, to a few, to many over the lifetime. The lifetime occurrence of bacterial STIs, for example, rises from 2.8 percent for those with only one partner since age eighteen, to 15.0 percent for those with five to ten partners, to 30.0 percent for those with more than twenty partners. This is compelling evidence that the number of sex partners is in fact an important risk factor when it comes to contracting these infections.

Table 11.5 shows the corresponding information for the past twelve months. It offers independent corroboration of this strong and striking relation between number of partners and the incidence of infection. Clearly, the number of sex partners that an individual has is a crucial determinant of his or her risk of contracting an STI. Anticipating the discussion later in this chapter, the number of sex partners is the most succinct measure of the extent of exposure to infec-

Table 11.4	Lifetime STIs, by Number of Sex Partners since Age Eighteen (cases per 1,000)					
	Partners since Age 18					
	0	1	2–4	5–10	11–20	21+
Gonorrhea	0	11	30	83	148	206
Syphilis	0	1	4	13	9	21
Chlamydia	0	14	20	44	64	70
NGU	0	0	4	16	31	62
PID	0	9	12	40	77	54
Any bacterial	0	28	58	150	241	300
Genital warts	0	11	37	70	91	98
Herpes	0	5	10	19	51	80
Hepatitis	11	5	5	12	24	25
HIV/AIDS	0	0	0	2	3	7
Any viral	11	17	50	98	159	177
Any STI	11	43	104	234	338	404

Table 11.5   **Annual STIs, by Number of Sex Partners in Past Twelve Months
                    (cases per 1,000)**

	Partners in Past 12 Months			
	0	1	2–4	5+
Gonorrhea	0	2	2	20
Syphilis	0	0	2	0
Chlamydia	0	4	15	20
NGU	0	1	8	0
PID	0	1	12	34
Any bacterial	0	6	28	39
Genital warts	3	3	14	10
Herpes	0	1	5	10
Hepatitis	0	0	0	0
HIV/AIDS	0	0	0	0
Any viral	3	4	19	20
Any STI	3	10	45	59

tion. As the number of exposures rises, the probability of infection consistently rises, and does so dramatically over part of the range.

Table 11.6 reworks the information in table 11.4, discarding the details about specific infections and adding gender. The consistency of patterns in this table is quite striking, as are the high rates among those who report having many sex partners.

There is one very intriguing point that table 11.6 supports. Since we know from human biology that women have a greater susceptibility to a sexually transmitted infection from a given exposure to the infecting agent, we should expect to see that women report having more STIs than men (see Aral and Guinau 1984). But that is not what we see consistently in the bottom row of table 11.6. Now, recall that in chapter 5 we noted that men report having sex with more women than women report having sex with men, and this conclusion from our data is similar to findings by all other researchers using scientifically sound surveys. In chapter 5, we suggested several possibilities as explanations for that finding, but we admitted there that it is not a finding that we (or others) understand very well. Our result here in table 11.6 can be interpreted as confirming the fact that men do have more sex partners than women. Since the rate of infection is higher for women biologically, yet the rate of occurrence of these diseases is about the same for the men and the women, these two facts can be reconciled if men have more exposure than women—that is, if they have more partners.

Of course, there are other explanations that can also reconcile these two facts. One is that men may systematically select as sex partners those who are more likely to have an infection. That can, logically, be the reason that men become infected as readily as women with the same number of partners even

Table 11.6   Lifetime STIs, by Number of Partners, Type of Infection, and Gender
                  (cases per 1,000)

	STI					
	Bacterial		Viral		Any	
Partners since Age 18	M	F	M	F	M	F
1	15	34	18	17	33	48
2–4	35	69	21	64	56	126
5–10	111	187	31	160	136	326
11–20	210	308	108	269	272	481
21+	285	364	131	377	371	547
Total	117	105	54	90	156	175

though, because of anatomy, the male is less efficient than the female in contracting these infections. But this explanation is not borne out by table 11.6.
Look in that table, row by row, at the reported cases of infection for men and
for women. If men's sex partners were themselves more infected with STIs
than women's sex partners, we would see higher rates of infection for men than
for women for each number of partners, or at least for *some* specific numbers
of partners, say, more than ten or more than twenty. But we see just the opposite: for every number of partners, and for both viral and bacterial infections,
the women have much higher rates of infection than the men. Yet, overall (look
at the *total* row in that table), the men and the women show similar rates of
infection. The explanation is that men have more partners—more men are distributed in the lower rows of that table, more women in the upper rows, so the
overall averages happen to come out about the same.

Table 11.7 shows in a little more detail the patterns seen in the left-hand
panel of table 11.2, the reported occurrence of bacterial and viral infection by
detailed age categories, this time separately by gender. We see that, at the
younger ages, when both men and women are having relatively many partners,
the reporting of both types of infections is much higher for the women. As age
increases, the men report having more bacterial infection, while the women
report higher rates than men for the viral infections.[6]

Table 11.8 introduces a final master status variable, race/ethnicity. The occurrence of STIs is greater among blacks than among whites or Hispanics—

6. A note of caution is in order in interpreting tables that combine the several bacterial infections
or the several viral infections, as in table 11.7. As noted above, testing for chlamydia has become
more common in recent years, so the increases in that infection may not reflect any behavioral
change, and that infection is among the bacterial infections included in the table. Also, bacterial
infections in women are more likely to be asymptomatic and thus less often reported by women
than by men, a..d this reporting difference may explain much of the difference that we see here
in the gender comparisons for the bacterial infections. On the other hand, women are also more
likely than men to have medical examinations including tests that reveal sexually transmitted infection.

Table 11.7   **Lifetime STIs, by Detailed Age Group, Type of Infection, and Gender (cases per 1,000)**

| | STI | | | | | |
| | Bacterial | | Viral | | Any | |
Age Group	M	F	M	F	M	F
18–24	54	114	45	68	98	165
25–29	90	117	37	94	125	178
30–34	136	75	50	112	170	178
35–39	133	121	66	100	183	196
40–44	142	63	88	97	194	154
45–49	146	60	39	52	173	111
50–54	85	35	29	50	106	84
55–59	97	54	23	51	108	96
All	109	85	50	82	146	154

Table 11.8   **Lifetime STIs, by Gender and Race/Ethnicity (cases per 1,000)**

| | Men | | | Women | | |
	White	Black	Hispanic	White	Black	Hispanic
Gonorrhea	58	323	87	24	184	15
Syphilis	8	13	19	5	21	0
Chlamydia	19	19	10	43	45	45
NGU	18	19	40	N.A.	N.A.	N.A.
PID	N.A.	N.A.	N.A.	18	42	16
Any bacterial	93	338	109	82	256	71
Genital warts	35	32	30	69	25	30
Herpes	15	6	0	34	16	0
Hepatitis	13	25	0	10	8	8
HIV/AIDS	2	0	10	1	0	0
Any viral	57	64	40	104	45	39
Any STI	135	357	149	169	270	104

Note: N.A. = not applicable.

nearly three times as great for the men and about 60 percent greater for the women—but the discrepancy is due nearly exclusively to gonorrhea. In fact, black women have significantly lower rates of some viral STIs than do white women. Two explanations may account for this pattern. First, as has been argued earlier in this book, salient social characteristics such as race can structure the sexual partnerships that individuals form. If blacks tend to choose only other blacks for partners, and if an easily transmitted infection like gonorrhea is introduced into this community, the smaller pool of potential partners can rapidly develop high infection rates. The same infection rate would take longer to develop in the larger majority population. The second explanation suggests that, because of the structure of Medicaid payments, physicians in public health/STD clinics are induced to diagnose STIs as gonorrhea.[7] Therefore, if blacks tend to be diagnosed in clinics more than other groups, then the reports of gonorrhea may be exaggerated relative to others.

STIs in Multivariate Analysis

Before we investigate other aspects of sexual behavior and how they are related to these infections, we report a multivariate logistic regression analysis, looking at the likelihood that the respondent ever had an STI or ever had either a bacterial or a viral STI (for a brief explanation of this technique, see chapter appendix 11.1A). We include as explanatory variables the respondent's gender, age, race, marital history, and parent's education level, number of lifetime sex partners, and whether the respondent ever participated in group sex, ever had anal sex, ever paid for sex, or was ever paid for sex. We report the results in figure 11.1 to capture the broad outlines of the findings. The variables are listed and the point estimate of the coefficient shown by a circle, a solid circle indicating statistical significance, an open circle nonsignificance. The band surrounding the point estimate is a 95 percent confidence band. We see at once that age, parent's education level, and the information about group sex and anal sex have no apparent relation with whether the respondent ever reported having an STI (anal sex is slightly, positively related to viral STIs).

A coefficient that is less than 1 in the figure indicates that the variable is negatively related to having an STI. So we see that men report having fewer STIs than women, holding constant the number of sex partners and the other variables in the equation. We see that this gender difference is in evidence for all STIs (fig. 11.1A) and also for the bacterial STIs (fig. 11.1B) and the viral STIs (fig. 11.1C). The capacity to hold fixed one variable and look at the relation of another is where this technique is useful. We see the separate or partial effect of each variable, whereas, in most of the tables we show, we see the gross or whole effect of each variable one by one or two by two.

Figure 11.1 tells us that blacks have higher rates of STIs, but we see that this pertains only to bacterial infections and that blacks actually have lower rates of viral STIs. (The National Health and Nutrition Examination Survey data indicate that blacks have substantially higher rates of hepatitis B, suggesting that much of the difference here may be attributable to reporting bias.) The most imposing and persistent effect shown in the figure is that those who report having eleven to twenty or twenty-one or more lifetime sex partners have dramatically higher rates of STIs—two to three times as high, in fact, as those who have only one partner. We also see that those who report ever paying for sex have higher rates of bacterial infections and that those who report having had one type of STI, bacterial or viral, are also somewhat more likely to

---

7. Edward Hook, M.D., suggested this explanation to us, for which we express our thanks.

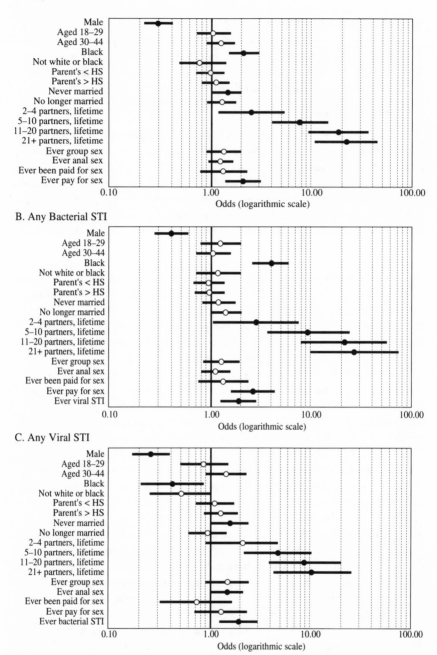

Fig. 11.1 Logistic regressions on ever having an STI, reported by odds ratio point estimates and 95 percent confidence intervals. (Dark circles indicate significance at *a* = .05.) A, Any STIs. B, Bacterial STIs. C, Viral STIs.

have had the other type as well. Clearly, there is much more analysis that can be undertaken here. We next turn to the second question posed near the outset of this chapter, the evidence of a link between specific sexual practices and the incidence of STIs.

11.2   Risky Partners and Risky Practices

In the previous section, we presented data on the reported lifetime and annual cases of various sexually transmitted infections among the adult population. In this section, we examine behavioral and physiological factors that affect the risk of contracting STIs. Although our data set, the NHSLS, was not designed to test complex epidemiological theories, the information that we have on patterns of sexual partnering, choices of sexual practices, and detailed characteristics of up to two sex partners can provide new understanding about the health risks posed by sexual activity.

We distinguish three main components of the risk of contracting an STI and take each up in turn. First, each STI has a rate of *infectivity,* a measure of the likelihood that the infection is spread during a given exposure to an infected person. The infections themselves vary substantially in their intrinsic infectivity, and individuals also vary in their susceptibility to infection. Likewise, different sexual practices affect the likelihood of transmission, and, in the course of an infection within an individual, there are times when the infection is particularly easy to transmit and times when it is less so. These various factors can be pooled, thus yielding a level of infectivity characteristic of each infection. Second, the *partner risk* reflects the critical choice that one makes in selecting a sex partner. Having sex with a person who does *not* have an infection involves no risk of contracting infection, naturally. If one could know with perfect certainty whether a potential sex partner were infectious (i.e., infected and capable of transmitting the infection at that time), choices about whether to have sex with that person and how to protect against disease would be much simpler, but that is not typically or always the case. Uncertainty about whether a potential partner is infectious can be reduced and can be compensated for, as we discuss below. The third component is the *practice risk,* the fact that not all sexual activities are equally likely to result in transmission of an infection and that behavior can be altered in ways that can shift the probability of getting infection from an infectious partner. The second and third of these components are primarily behavioral and subject to the choices that individuals make. The first is more physiological in nature, and we begin with it.

Infectivity

The probability that a sexually transmitted infection is passed from an infected to an uninfected person in a single act of sexual exposure is known as the rate of infectivity or transmissibility of that infection. The rate of infectivity varies from one infection to another, sometimes dramatically. The rate also differs when calculated for a man giving the infection to a woman compared to a woman giving the infection to a man from a single act of vaginal intercourse (see Hearst and Hulley 1988; Lande 1993, 4). Many factors influence this rate of infectivity, including the character of the infection itself, the specific strain of the organism in question, the infectious person's stage of infection, the existence of symptoms such as lesions or open sores, and so forth. Similarly, the health of the uninfected person, his or her genetic makeup, the strength of the immune system, and many other attributes can also affect the likelihood of transmission. Also, the sexual practices in which people engage, the length of time of sexual exposure, the roughness of sexual activity, and so forth can all affect the likelihood of infection. Biologically, women are more vulnerable to certain infections (see Holmes et al. 1990). No single generalization can capture the complexity of the different levels of risk that one might encounter, however, the following discussion is intended to emphasize a few important points, not to elaborate these complexities fully.

Infectivity is a crucial concept in determining what types of partner choices are most relevant to understanding the spread of different infections. An organism with a high rate of infectivity can be contracted after a very few exposures to an infectious person. The infectivity rate of gonorrhea from a man to a woman, for example, is estimated to be 0.50 from a single act of sex with an infectious partner (Lande 1993, 4). Thus, only a single sexual encounter with a man infected with gonorrhea has a fifty-fifty likelihood of transmitting that infection to a woman. In the case of an infection with a high infectivity, such as gonorrhea, limiting the number of sex partners can dramatically lower the risk of getting the infection. By contrast, the infectivity rate for HIV is thought to be on the order of 0.002 from a single act of sex between an infectious man and an uninfected woman (Hearst and Hulley 1988). While the infection can be passed in a single act of sex, the probability is only one in 500 that it will be. Thus, the probability of contracting HIV from sex with an infectious man is not high unless the number of sex acts with that partner is quite high. Table 11.9 shows estimated rates of infectivity for several STIs from one gender to the other during a single act of vaginal intercourse. (We caution that we have

Table 11.9   Estimated Rates of Infectivity for Specific STIs, by Gender

	Male to Female	Female to Male
Gonorrhea	.50	.20
Syphilis	.30	.30
Chlamydia	.40	.20
Herpes	.002	.0004
HIV	.002	.001

Sources: Holmes et al. 1990, 150 (gonorrhea), 214 (syphilis), 182 (chlamydia), 346 (HIV, which is reported as low as 0.00); Peterman et al. 1988 (HIV); Padian et al. 1987 (HIV); Mertz et al. 1992 (herpes).

Table 11.10   **Calculated Probability of Contracting an STI, by Type of Disease, Condom Use, Partner Risk, and Number of Sexual Encounters (male to female transmission, vaginal intercourse)**

STI	Prob. Partner Infected	Est. Rate of Infectivity (%)	Sexual Encounters with Partner			
			1	10	100	1,000
Assuming an infectious partner						
Gonorrhea:						
Always use condom	1.000	50	.05000	.40126	.99408	1.00000
Never use condom	1.000	50	.50000	.99902	1.00000	1.00000
HIV/AIDS:						
Always use condom	1.000	.2	.00020	.00200	.01980	.18129
Never use condom	1.000	.2	.00200	.01982	.18143	.86494
Calculated probability of an infectious partner[a]						
Gonorrhea:						
Always use condom	.001	50	.00005	.00040	.00099	.00100
Never use condom	.001	50	.00050	.00100	.00100	.00100
HIV/AIDS:						
Always use condom	.0001	.2	.00000	.00000	.00000	.00002
Never use condom	.0001	.2	.00000	.00000	.00002	.00009

[a]Assumptions: Condom failure = 10 percent per exposure. Probability that partner is infected: for HIV, see Hearst and Hulley (1988); for gonorrhea, annual incidence for males, NHSLS.

used the best indicators we know to compute these single-event rates of infectivity, but they may be inaccurate, and we use them here primarily to illustrate several points.)

This rate of infectivity applies to the circumstance when one of the partners is infectious. Of course, if the partner is not infected, the risk of contracting the infection falls to zero. Thus, the uncertainty that one faces about getting an infection when choosing a sex partner depends not only on the infectivity rate of that organism but also on the probability that the person has the infection. If we think of the rate of infectivity for organism 1 (say, gonorrhea) as I_1 and the incidence of that infection in the population as P_1, then the product of the two, $I_1 \times P_1$, is an estimate of the risk of getting the infection from a single act of unprotected sex with a person selected at random from the population. Of course, this risk can be reduced by using a condom, and, if we illustrate that reduction in risk by supposing that the condom has a failure rate of C, then we can say that the risk of one act of protected sex with a randomly selected person is calculated as $I_1 \times P_1 \times C$. While this simple formula tells us the risk for a single act of sex, the formula for estimating the risk from having protected sex n times with the same partner is $P_1(1 - (1 - I_1C)^n)$, while the risk from having protected sex n times with a different partner each time is $1 - (1 - P_1I_1C)^n$.

Using these formulas, table 11.10 shows the probability of contracting an infection under different conditions. The top panel assumes that the partner is in fact infectious, and we see that, if the infection is gonorrhea, the risk of infection is one half from a single sex encounter, is practically a certainty after ten sexual encounters if a condom is not used, and is as high as 40 percent even using a condom. For an infection like HIV/AIDS with a low infectivity (.002), on the other hand, the likelihood of contracting the infection is about one in five after 100 sexual encounters with an infectious partner and is dramatically lowered by using a condom.

The bottom portion of table 11.10 assumes not that the sex partner is infectious but instead that the partner has the same likelihood of being infectious as does the average adult in the population, as measured in Hearst and Hulley (1988) for HIV/AIDS and as measured in the NHSLS data for gonorrhea in males. The risks of contracting infection are dramatically lower in this case. While this case reflects averages, we suggest that this is an average that may not apply to many people and may therefore be misleading. The majority of adults who have one or two sex partners are, in fact, at *very* low risk of infection from HIV; on the other hand, the risks faced by others who have relatively many partners are more accurately reflected in the upper panel of table 11.10 than in the lower panel.

Figure 11.2 depicts several scenarios showing the risk of infection at different levels of sexual encounters and for low and high rates of both infectivity and prevalence. The dashed lines show the risk from having sex a specified number of times always with the same partner, the solid lines the risk from having sex the same number of times but with a partner selected independently each encounter. For the low-infectivity case (fig. 11.2A–C), the prevalence of the infection in the population from which the partner is selected determines the level of the risk after a relatively small number of encounters. The risk after, say, twenty-five encounters or contacts is ten times higher in figure 11.2B than in figure 11.2A and another ten times higher in figure 11.2C, where one in four people is infectious. Look at the risk depicted in figure 11.2D–F, where the infectivity is a much higher 0.30. There, the risk of infection is high even when the partner is selected from a low-prevalence population (fig. 11.2D) and approaches certainty when as many as 1.5 percent of the population is infectious. The dotted and solid lines diverge quite dramatically only in figure 11.2D–F, emphasizing that, when considering an infection like gonorrhea, the number of partners as well as the number of sexual contacts with those partners matter considerably. After twenty-five encounters, the risk is about ten times higher if a different partner is involved each time than if one has the same partner every time.

One sees the high risk of contracting gonorrhea from even a single act of unprotected sex, and, with a failure rate for condoms of 10 percent, the risk becomes very high with a large number of exposures despite condom use. For

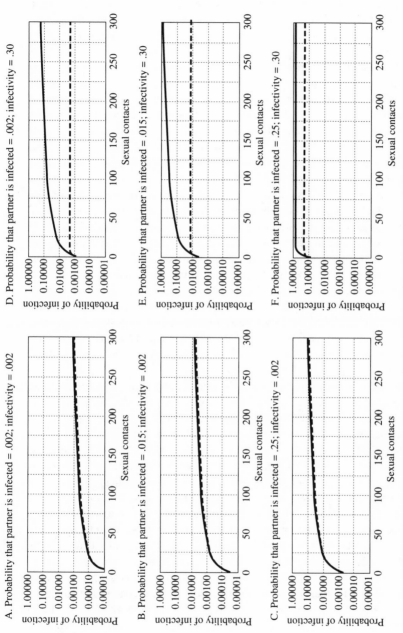

Fig. 11.2 Effect of partnering patterns on the calculated probability of contracting an STI, by the proba-bility the partner is infected, and on the number of sexual contacts. (Solid line indicates new partner with each contact. Dashed line indicates the same partner with every contact.)

HIV, unprotected sex over six months or so (e.g., a hundred times) with an infectious partner also implies a risk of about one in five; it is in the vicinity of these levels of risk that condom use can dramatically lower the probability of transmission.

There is an important relation between the infectivity of the organism and the nature of the sex partner's network. If we imagine a dense social network of people who tend to have sex only within that network and with only a few people who have sex with those in another social network, then the infectivity of an infection can greatly influence how and how rapidly that infection spreads (cf. Potterat 1992). A high-infectivity infection such as gonorrhea that is spread easily by only a few sexual encounters is likely not to remain contained in a given sexual partnership network if there is any bridging from one network to another. An infection like HIV, by contrast, that is not highly infectious is much less likely to be transmitted from one network to another, especially if contacts outside the group are few and sporadic. Hence, HIV/AIDS has been contained in certain pockets of the population, not distributed more evenly across the population (see Jonsen and Stryker 1992). That is a signature characteristic of a low-infectivity infection combined with a highly structured network of sexual partnerships. If either the networks were not so highly structured, with relatively few people moving between network groups, or the infection were more highly infectious, the spread of HIV/AIDS would have been much different than what we have observed in our nation over the past decade. We would have seen, in fact, a pattern observed in Africa, where HIV/AIDS apparently has spread widely throughout heterosexual networks. It is believed that the rate of infectivity of HIV may be significantly higher in Africa because of the prevalence of genital sores and lesions (see Kreiss, Koech, and Plummer 1986; and Greenblatt, Lukehart, and Plummer 1987).

Our discussion of infectivity and prevalence suggests a useful distinction in the choices about sexual behavior as related to sexually transmitted disease. Choices made regarding partners affect the relevant prevalence of infection—selecting partners from a low-risk group, for example, implies a lower prevalence, and selecting fewer partners overall additionally lowers the risk of becoming infected from high-infectivity infections like gonorrhea. Similarly, choices regarding sexual practices affect the relevant rate of infectivity. For example, the use of condoms lowers the infectivity from a sexual contact, and selecting sexual activities that are known to have lower associated infectivity rates can do the same (i.e., anal intercourse is known to have a higher rate of infectivity of HIV than oral or vaginal intercourse, and rough sex that causes breakage of the skin is known to involve higher infectivity of HIV). Interactions among diseases can also be important, as sores associated with one infection can raise the relevant infectivity of another like HIV. We turn next to the evidence in the NHSLS data regarding the risk associated with selecting a partner and then to the risk associated with sexual practices.

Partner Risk

The reasons for selecting one person or another as a sex partner are many and complex, as we discussed in chapter 1. The issue of exposure to the risk of infection is typically not an uppermost concern. There are many attributes of importance in the person one selects as a friend, a companion, or a lover. For the present context, however, let us set aside all the other aspects of the choice and of the search and focus exclusively on the implication for the risk of contracting infection from the choice of a sex partner.

A vast proportion of the total sexual activity in any given interval of time involves a stable sexual relationship that has continued over a long time and does not involve sex with a new partner. So, when we think about the choice of a sex partner, we should remember that, for most individuals, for most of the time, the sex partner was chosen long ago and for reasons that only partially involved sex per se. Yet for a sizable portion of the population—about 20 percent, as we see below—a new sex partner is acquired within the year, and a substantial subset of these select several partners over the course of the year. It is these people for whom the risk of infection is most pertinent. In this selection of a new sex partner, uncertainty abounds. We look at two aspects of partner risk, the *familiarity* with a new partner and the *exclusivity* of partnerships.

We suggest that uncertainty about the sex partner's infection status is reduced by *familiarity* with that partner. There is probably a close correlation between how well and how long one has known the person before having sex and how likely it is that one knows whether that person is currently infectious with an STI. (Of course, it is not the case that infectiousness would necessarily rule out having sex with that person. It probably would not, for example, in the case of a spouse who contracts an STI. Knowing the infection status, however, can lead to sexual practices that compensate for the higher risk. Here, we focus only on the knowledge about the partner; below we consider some forms of compensatory behavior.) Familiarity implies that partners may be more comfortable discussing the issue of infection, more informed about each other's lifestyle and medical history, more caring and concerned about each other, and so more motivated to reveal the risk of infection.

We have in our data set several indicators of familiarity with one's sex partners. We feature six such measures here; all are constructed as dichotomous variables, valued as 1 if the respondent's answer to a question is yes, 0 if no. The six measures are whether the respondent acquired a *new* sex partner during the past twelve months, whether the respondent had sex with any new partner *only one time* during the past year, whether the respondent had sex with a partner over a span of time *shorter than two months* during the past year, whether the respondent had sex with someone whom he or she described as a *casual date or pickup* within the past year, whether any new sex partner acquired within the past year was someone the respondent *knew for only one or two days* before having sex, and whether any new sex partner acquired within the past year was someone whom the respondent *knew for less than one month* before having sex.[8] Obviously, love at first sight or sex on a first date does not imply irrational abandon, but these several measures do let us look at the extent to which adults are familiar with their new sex partners before they are exposed to risks of sexually transmitted infection and disease.[9]

   Table 11.11 shows the percentages of yes answers to these six questions, based on all respondents who were sexually active. We see from the top row of that table that 19.7 percent of those who are sexually active report having a new sex partner within the past twelve months, 8.5 percent a one-time sex partner within the past twelve months, 12.1 percent a partner with whom the sexual relationship lasted less than two months, and 4.7 percent sex with someone they picked up. *Among the subset with a new partner,* 15.1 percent had sex

8. These six questions were not all asked directly in this form in the survey; some have been calculated from answers provided to a series of questions. The first three are taken from section 4 and are based on the calendar dates provided by the respondent about the beginning or ending date of each sexual partnership. The fourth question (about a pickup) was asked directly on the SAQ. The final two questions were asked directly for two partners designated as primary and secondary. The primary sex partner was either the current spouse or cohabitant or the partner the respondent considered to be "most important" during the past twelve months. The secondary partner was the most recent partner not including the primary partner.

   We have dates of the beginning and end of sex partnerships for up to fourteen partners within the past year, and only twelve respondents in our data set report having had more than fourteen partners in the past year, so we have only a little missing information here. A yes answer about any new partners in the past year is restricted to the fourteen partners reported. A yes answer about any one-time sex partner implies that the respondent gave the same date for the first and last sexual events, that the date was at least one month prior to the interview date, and that the respondent reported having sex with this partner only once, so this is a quite conservative and carefully crafted variable. All partners are included here, incidentally; those of the same and the opposite gender are treated indistinguishably in this chapter.

   9. The set of sex partners over which these several measures are calculated differs from measure to measure, as constrained by our questionnaire. Some pertain to any partner, up to a total of fourteen; others pertain only to the primary or the secondary partner; a few others pertain to all the partners within the past year who are reported on the SAQ. In particular, the roster information on all partners up to fourteen is used in defining new partners, one-time partners, and those with whom respondents were involved for less than two months since we have first and last dates of sex with all these partners. The SAQ information on all partners in the past twelve months is used in defining the pickups. The information on the primary and secondary partners only was used in identifying the respondents who had sex with someone they knew for only one or two days or for less than a month before having sex.

   This point raises the question of just how many partners in the past twelve months were not captured by our questioning of only the primary and secondary partners. The answer is that we captured 79 percent of all partners by this scheme. That is, of the 2,262 respondents who had one partner and the 246 respondents who had exactly two partners, we have full details on all these partners (2,262 + [2 × 246] = 2,754 partners). For the 245 respondents who had three or more partners, we have information on only two each, or (2 × 245 =) 490 of the total of 1,374 partners. So, overall, we have information on 3,244 of the total of 4,128 partners within the past twelve months.

Table 11.11   Percentage of Respondents with Various Measures of Unfamiliarity
with Sex Partners (primary [P] or secondary [S]), by Master Status
Variables (cell percentages)

	Any New	Any One Time	Any < 2 Months	Any Casual	Either P or S Known:	
					< 2 Days[a]	< 1 Month[a]
All	19.7	8.5	12.1	4.7	15.1	49.1
Men	25.3	12.2	17.3	8.1	20.7	54.6
Women	15.1	5.4	7.8	2.0	7.2	41.2
18–24	41.5	21.3	30.1	10.7	9.7	41.6
25–29	24.8	12.4	16.4	7.8	23.4	53.8
30–34	19.6	7.2	12.1	4.6	13.9	57.3
35–39	13.8	5.5	7.1	3.4	21.6	57.4
40–44	14.3	4.1	6.0	3.2	23.1	52.3
45–49	10.6	4.6	5.8	1.4	b	b
50–54	8.3	1.4	2.9	.4	b	b
55–59	3.3	.6	.6	.5	b	b
White	18.5	7.8	11.5	5.0	14.7	50.6
Black	26.8	12.9	16.4	3.5	17.6	42.7
Hispanic	21.0	10.6	13.0	4.9	18.8	57.5
Asian	25.0	5.7	9.4	0.0	b	b
Native American	11.4	0.0	8.3	5.1	b	b
Less than HS	18.6	8.6	11.1	4.4	12.5	49.1
HS grad.	17.2	7.0	10.2	4.0	16.5	47.3
Some college	22.1	9.5	13.9	5.8	13.0	47.8
College grad.	22.4	9.2	13.6	4.3	17.1	52.9
Postgrad.	14.3	7.0	10.0	3.2	b	b
Never married	46.3	24.2	33.8	11.5	15.5	46.2
Married	3.6	.9	1.3	.8	14.7	40.5
Div./Wid./Sep.	38.4	11.7	18.4	5.9	12.4	56.4
Not cohabiting	48.8	22.7	32.8	9.7	14.8	48.3
Cohabiting	21.9	7.1	9.3	7.2	12.8	56.6
Married	3.6	.9	1.3	.8	14.7	40.5

[a]Among new partners only.
[b]Fewer than thirty cases.

with someone whom they had previously known for only a day or two, while, broadening the time interval, 49.1 percent had sex with someone whom they had previously known for less than one month. These figures offer compelling evidence that, for adults who are involved in acquiring new sex partners, many of those new partners are relatively unknown before sex and do not become long-term partners; the extent of uncertainty about their infection status is therefore likely to be rather high.

The other sets of rows in table 11.11 show these six measures by the master status variables. We see there that men are more likely to report having sex with less familiar partners, as are younger respondents and most noticeably those who are not currently married or cohabiting. As seen in chapter 5, young unmarried and noncohabiting men tend to have the greatest number of sex partners in a given year. Table 11.11 shows that they are far more likely to have unfamiliar partners than older people involved in more stable relationships. Neither race/ethnicity nor education level shows a consistent pattern across these several measures of familiarity. It is the behavior of the young, unattached males that suggests a dramatically lower level of familiarity by these several indicators.

Exclusivity of sexual partnerships can be explored in our data only as reported by the respondent since we did not interview the respondent's sex partners. After obtaining a roster of all the respondent's sex partners over the past year, we asked specifically about his or her spouse, cohabitational partner, or primary partner and about one other partner, if there was a second one. This is the information that we use here. Exclusivity of sexual partnerships clearly influences the likelihood of contracting infection (Holmes et al. 1990, 29). The more partners either the respondent or the respondent's partners have, the greater the likelihood that the respondent will be exposed to infection.

Uninfected people in long-term sexual relationships that are monogamous for both partners have, by definition, no risk of contracting sexually transmitted diseases (except, of course, for STIs that are acquired in some other manner, such as those that are blood borne, like HIV/AIDS and hepatitis B, or are acquired in other ways, such as medical professionals or researchers exposed on the job or children contracting the infection from their mother at birth). However, if one's partner has had other sex partners, either recently or concurrently, then the potential exposure to infectious people is increased. The more partners that one's partner has had, the greater the risk. A distinction worth note here is between a partner who is serially monogamous—that is, whose other sex partnerships have ended before the current partnership began—and one who has several partners concurrently. An individual who has a partner with multiple partners all in the past must be concerned only with that partner's infection status on entering the relationship. (Recurring outbreaks of previously contracted viral STIs could occur during the relationship, but an individual could theoretically know about the likelihood of such recurrences prospectively.) If that partner is not infected at the start of the relationship, no infection will be introduced later. In contrast, an individual who has a partner with ongoing multiple partnerships must be concerned with the partner's infection status throughout the relationship since each encounter with the concurrent partners may result in infection.

We have explored five questions that reflect the degree of sexual exclusivity between the respondent and his or her primary and secondary partners over the past year. The five measures are as follows. The first is the number of other partners the respondent's sex partner had within the past year (as reported by our respondent). The other four measures are dichotomous variables given the value 1 if the answer is yes and 0 if no to the following four questions: Was this partner sexually involved with another person when the respondent began having sexual relations with him or her? (Incidentally, we calculate this variable only for partnerships that began in the past twelve months since it is the risk faced during the past twelve months that is being examined here.) Did this partner have any other partners during the time the respondent was having sex with that person? (This question tells us about serial monogamy, as reported by the respondent. We note that a positive response by the respondent to this issue may indicate greater knowledge than another respondent actually has.) Does the respondent currently expect that partner to be sexually exclusive? (This goes to the issue of the expectation or understanding between the two, as distinct from the respondent's judgment about whether the partner actually had any other sex partners.) Has the respondent paid or been paid for sex? Those who have sex for money typically have many partners and are potentially exposed to many possible sources of infection.[10]

Table 11.12 shows the results for these indicators of sexual nonexclusivity. The top row reports for the sample as a whole. We see that 83.7 percent of the respondents report that, over the past year, neither their primary nor their secondary sex partner (if they had one) had any other sex partners. This is consistent with the dominant pattern of relatively stable long-term monogamous partnering for the respondents themselves, shown in chapter 5. Another 7 percent of the respondents reported that their partner (or their two partners, if there were two or more) had a total of one other sex partner, 3.6 percent that their partner (or their two partners) had a total of two other partners, and 5.7 percent that their partner(s) had three or more other sex partners.

Looking at the second set of rows in this table, it is interesting to notice that men are more inclined to report that their partners have several other sex partners than are women; that is not consistent with the own-gender reporting of sexual behavior. Looking down the remaining sets of rows in table 11.12, we see that, for the young adults and for the never married and noncohabiting respondents, the report about partners is consistent with self-reported behavior as seen in chapter 5. Similarly, education and race/ethnicity seem to show no strong pattern, either here or in the self-reports.

Regarding the other four measures shown in the right-hand side of table 11.12, one sees rather high rates of nonexclusivity at the beginning of the sexual partnership, but dramatically lower rates of nonexclusivity during the partnership, and quite low rates in terms of the respondent's expectations instead

---

10. As described in n. 9, because of the format of our questions, we can say nothing about the status of the 21 percent of partnerships that are third- or higher-order partnerships, so the first four of these issues pertain to the primary and secondary partners only. The final issue, paid sex, pertains to all partners in the past twelve months, taken from the SAQ.

Table 11.12   Percentage of Respondents with Various Measures of Sexual
               Exclusivity of Sex Partners (primary [P] and secondary [S]), by Master
               Status Variables (first five columns sum to 100 percent; final four columns
               are cell percentages)

| | P and S Partners' Partners Combined | | | | | Either P or S Nonexclusive | | Either P or S Partner's Exclusivity | |
	0 Others	1 Other	2 Others	3 Others	4+ Others	Beginning[a]	During	Not Expected	Any Paid Sex
All	83.7	7.0	3.6	2.4	3.3	21.7	7.6	3.9	.3
Men	79.8	8.3	4.6	2.9	4.4	23.5	8.2	4.6	.4
Women	87.0	5.9	2.7	2.0	2.4	19.4	7.2	3.3	.2
18–24	67.4	11.7	7.6	4.8	8.5	13.4	11.5	4.9	.2
25–29	80.5	8.4	4.3	4.1	2.6	24.0	8.8	3.1	.5
30–34	83.4	8.5	2.2	3.1	2.8	26.9	8.4	2.8	.2
35–39	86.2	5.8	3.2	1.2	3.6	22.0	6.9	4.7	.4
40–44	87.2	5.6	3.3	.8	3.1	30.0	7.9	6.3	0.0
45–49	90.2	6.3	1.6	1.2	.8	b	5.2	2.3	.7
50–54	96.1	1.0	2.4	.5	0.0	b	2.4	3.5	0.0
55–59	96.8	1.3	1.3	.6	0.0	b	3.9	.8	.5
White	85.1	6.4	3.1	2.3	3.1	18.4	6.6	3.4	.2
Black	73.4	11.2	6.6	4.8	3.9	32.9	14.1	7.7	.3
Hispanic	82.9	6.5	4.0	1.0	5.5	32.3	10.7	3.0	1.3
Asian	90.4	7.7	1.9	0.0	0.0	b	1.9	2.1	0.0
Native American	88.6	8.6	2.9	0.0	0.0	b	2.9	b	0.0
Less than HS	85.3	6.8	2.6	1.7	3.7	25.0	9.1	5.2	.2
HS grad.	85.5	5.9	3.3	2.5	2.8	22.0	6.9	3.1	.2
Some college	81.7	7.7	4.6	2.5	3.5	22.0	8.0	3.9	.5
College grad.	82.6	7.8	3.1	2.7	3.8	17.3	7.9	3.1	.2
Postgrad.	85.3	6.6	3.0	2.5	2.5	b	5.7	6.4	0.0
Never married	61.0	16.3	8.2	6.6	7.8	17.0	15.0	9.4	.4
Married	96.8	1.7	.6	.2	.7	35.0	2.2	1.3	.1
Div./Wid./Sep.	68.5	13.0	8.0	4.2	6.2	28.4	18.1	8.0	.7
Not cohabiting	57.9	18.0	9.6	6.7	7.9	21.4	19.0	10.2	.6
Cohabiting	86.2	4.0	2.7	2.2	4.9	11.9	5.8	5.4	0.0
Married	96.8	1.7	.6	.2	.7	35.0	2.2	1.3	.1

[a]Among new partners only.
[b]Fewer than thirty cases.

of his or her estimate of the partner's actual behavior. That is, only 3.9 percent
of all respondents said that they did not expect their partner to be sexually
exclusive with them. The pattern of expectations shown in that column rather
closely mirrors the pattern in the other columns that report actual behavior.
The final column in table 11.12 indicates how infrequent paid sex is reported
to be.

   From these two tables, we see that the sexual partnering of sexually active,
young, unmarried men and women involves more casual and less familiar part-

ners coupled with a greater likelihood of nonexclusivity by either partner. Hence, these young unmarried adults have a much more substantial likelihood of being exposed to infection. This exposure, we have seen above, is reflected in the rates of contraction of STIs.

THE INTERACTION OF RISKY PARTNERS AND MANY PARTNERS

We have identified two aspects of sex partners, familiarity and exclusivity. We have not to this point connected these measures of risk to the more conventional measure, number of sex partners. It is a reasonable presumption that, the fewer the number of partners one has, the more familiar one will be at the outset with that partner, and probably the more sexually exclusive the partnership will be. In fact, a theme that we develop through this chapter is that one of the key reasons that it is risky to have many partners is precisely because they are likely to be less well known, less likely to come from the same social network, and less exclusive, all of which implies that potential exposure to infection rises with the number of partners for several separately identifiable reasons. In the next few tables, we document the close relation between number of partners and the familiarity and exclusivity of these partners.

The next two tables describe the interaction between number of partners and the familiarity and exclusivity of these partners. Two consistent patterns emerge. First, as the number of partners increases, the likelihood increases substantially that at least one partner will have a measure of unfamiliarity or nonexclusivity. In short, as the number of partners rises, the likelihood of having a risky partner increases. Second, the more partners one has, the more likely each of those partners is to be unfamiliar and nonexclusive. Not only is it more likely that there is one risky partner among the total, but it also becomes more likely that many of the partners have risky attributes.

Table 11.13A shows the five measures of familiarity discussed above, this time arrayed by the number of sex partners within the past twelve months. Recall that a higher percentage for any of these five variables implies greater uncertainty about the partner's infection status. One sees dramatic increases in the percentages across each row: those with more partners are much more likely to have a new partner during the year, to have a one-time partner, to have a short-term (lasting less than two months) partner, and to have taken a new sex partner knowing the person less than two days or less than a month. By all five measures, the amount of risk rises with the number of partners. Table 11.13A also shows these results for the primary and secondary partners separately since the questions were asked in the context of the specific partner. In general, but not in every instance, one sees the same pattern of increase for the primary and secondary partner separately as for both together. It is particularly interesting to note that, as the total number of sex partners rises, it is not only the additional (i.e., secondary) partners but also the primary partner who are less well known to the respondent at the outset of the relationship.

Table 11.13A   **Familiarity of Partners, by Number of Partners and Primary and Secondary Partner Status (cell percentages)**

	No. of Partners in Past 12 Months			
	1	2	3+	Total
Any partner new in past 12 months	9.0	63.7	73.8	19.7
Primary partner	9.0	38.2	48.3	15.0
Secondary partner	N.A.	59.3	73.1	66.1
Any one-time partnership	1.1	25.2	60.8	8.5
Primary partner	1.1	3.4	2.1	1.4
Secondary partner		24.8	25.5	25.2
Any partnership < 2 months	2.0	38.6	78.8	12.1
Primary partner	2.1	5.9	10.2	3.2
Secondary partner	N.A.	37.4	35.0	36.2
Either partner known 2 days or less before first sex[a]	4.0	17.2	30.8	15.1
Primary partner	4.0	4.4	9.6	5.6
Secondary partner	N.A.	9.1	19.0	14.3
Either partner known < 1 month before first sex[a]	22.8	66.4	69.7	49.1
Primary partner	22.8	44.6	42.1	33.1
Secondary partner	N.A.	34.4	50.0	42.7

Note: N.A. = not applicable.

[a]Number of new partners used as denominator in calculating these rows.

Table 11.13B shows the analogous information for the exclusivity measures. Here one sees that, whereas 95.6 percent of the partners of respondents with one partner were reported to be sexually exclusive, only 25.1 percent of respondents who had three or more partners had partners who were sexually exclusive. At the other end of the spectrum, practically none of the respondents with one partner reported that their partner had three or more partners, whereas almost 30 percent of those who had three or more partners reported that their partners also had three or more partners. Here is one of the most important conclusions that we reach in this chapter, and it is made more vividly below. But, to anticipate, the risk of infection from having more sex partners rises, not arithmetically as the number of partners rises, but multiplicatively. Generally speaking, table 11.13 suggests that partners are reported to behave like the respondents. As the number of sex partners rises from one, to two, to three, and so forth, the total number of people in the sexual network from whom an infection can be acquired rises, not just from one to two to three, but from one to four (i.e., two squared), to nine (three squared), to sixteen (four squared), and so forth, since each of the two has two partners, each of the three has three partners, etc. This characterization is put too strongly here for clarity of the point, but the pattern is almost that dramatic. The more partners one has, the

Table 11.13B   **Exclusivity of Partners, by Number of Partners and Primary and Secondary Partner Status (column percentages sum to 100 for the first three measures; cell percentages for the bottom four measures)**

	No. of Partners in Past 12 Months			
	1	2	3+	Total
Sum of primary and secondary partner's other partners:				
No other partners	95.6	32.6	25.1	83.7
1 other partner	2.7	26.4	27.2	7.0
2 other partners	.8	14.5	18.4	3.6
3 other partners	.4	12.0	10.9	2.4
4 or more other partners	.4	14.5	18.4	3.3
Primary partner:				
No other partners	95.6	61.1	52.3	89.1
1 other partner	2.7	26.1	26.4	6.6
2 other partners	.8	7.1	9.7	2.1
3 or more other partners	.9	5.8	11.6	2.2
Secondary partner:				
No other partners	N.A.	38.4	31.8	35.2
1 other partner	N.A.	31.1	34.3	32.7
2 other partners	N.A.	9.7	14.6	12.1
3 or more other partners	N.A.	20.9	19.2	20.0
Either partner nonmonogamous, during:	2.2	32.3	36.8	7.6
Primary partner	2.2	18.0	21.8	5.1
Secondary partner	N.A.	24.4	26.2	25.3
Either partner nonmonogamous, beginning:	10.2	28.7	33.3	21.7
Primary partner (new only)	10.2	9.0	9.8	9.8
Secondary partner (new only)	N.A.	16.2	20.5	18.5
Either partner not expected to be monogamous:	1.7	13.9	20.2	3.9
Primary partner	1.7	12.6	12.7	3.2
Secondary partner	N.A.	9.8	34.7	22.0
Any partner paid for sex	.1	.0	3.0	.3

Note: N.A. = not applicable.

more partners one's partners have, so the pool of those to whom one is exposed rises not linearly but multiplicatively.

Table 11.13C simply shows the number of attributes of unfamiliarity or non-exclusivity or both by the number of partners in the past twelve months. Here, too, one sees that respondents with one partner exhibit far greater familiarity and exclusivity with that partner compared to the respondents who have two partners or who have three or more partners.

Table 11.14 shows the same information on familiarity and exclusivity, this

Table 11.13C   **Number of Unfamiliar and Nonexclusive Attributes (column percentages sum to 100 in each panel)**

	No. of Partners in Past 12 Months			
	1	2	3+	Total
Number of unfamiliar partner attributes:				
0	90.6	24.8	7.3	77.3
1	5.8	24.0	8.6	7.7
2	1.9	18.7	15.1	4.5
3	1.3	19.5	31.4	5.6
4+	.4	13.0	37.6	4.9
Number of nonexclusive partner attributes:				
0	93.9	29.3	23.7	81.9
1	2.9	19.9	15.5	5.5
2	1.6	10.2	17.6	3.8
3	.9	15.0	12.6	3.2
4	.2	11.4	11.0	2.2
5+	.4	14.2	19.6	3.4
Number of total risky partner attributes:				
0	86.7	7.7	2.9	72.2
1	6.5	13.4	3.3	6.8
2	3.3	11.0	5.7	4.2
3	1.7	16.7	11.4	3.9
4	.8	11.0	13.9	2.8
5	.4	14.6	16.7	3.1
6+	.6	25.6	46.1	6.9

time partitioning by the relationship between the respondent and the two partners. The first column shows the information for the respondent's formal marriage partner, the second column for cohabitational partners, and the third column for partners who are neither married nor living together. For each attribute, separate rows identify whether the relevant partner was primary or secondary. In the top panel, we see the pattern of much less familiarity with the noncohabitational partner, with the secondary partner even less familiar than the primary partner. A similar qualitative pattern is seen in the bottom panel. Notice in particular how much less sexual exclusivity is both expected and reported for cohabitational partners compared to formally married partners and how different the secondary noncohabitational partners are from the noncohabitational primary partners in this regard as well.

Finally, it is useful to look at the relation between these various measures of riskiness and the incidence of contraction of a sexually transmitted disease. Tables 11.15–11.17 below do so. We saw in table 11.5 that 1.0 percent of the

Table 11.14 **Familiarity and Exclusivity of Partners, by Types of Partnerships and Primary/Secondary Partner Status (cell percentages)**

	Type of Partner			
	Marriage	Cohabitational	Noncohabitational	All Types
Familiarity				
New Partner:				
Primary partner	1.4	16.3	48.0	15.1
Secondary partner	a	a	68.8	66.1
One-time partner:				
Primary partner	0.0	0.0	5.6	1.4
Secondary partner	a	a	26.4	25.2
Less than 2 months partners:				
Primary partner	0.0	.5	12.6	3.2
Secondary partner	a	a	37.8	36.2
Knew partner 2 days or less before first sex				
Primary partner	a	3.2	6.5	5.6
Secondary partner	a	a	14.1	14.3
Knew partner 1 month or less before first sex:				
Primary partner	a	45.2	31.9	33.1
Secondary partner	a	a	42.3	42.7
Exclusivity				
Number of partner's other partners:				
Primary partner:				
No other partners	97.6	83.2	70.3	89.1
1 other partner	1.7	10.1	17.6	6.6
2 other partners	.4	2.9	5.9	2.0
3+ other partners	.3	3.7	6.2	2.2
Secondary partner:				
No other partners	a	a	35.2	35.2
1 other partner	a	a	32.6	32.7
2 other partners	a	a	11.9	12.1
3+ other partners	a	a	20.2	20.0
Partner nonmonogamous, during:				
Primary partner	1.8	9.5	11.4	5.1
Secondary partner	a	a	24.8	25.3
Partner nonmonogamous, beginning:				
Primary partner (new only)	a	8.3	10.5	9.8
Secondary partner (new only)	a	a	18.6	18.5
Do not expect partner's monogamy:				
Primary partner	1.2	5.8	8.4	3.2
Secondary partner	a	a	23.7	22.0

[a]Fewer than thirty cases.

Table 11.15 **Incidence of Diagnosed STIs in the Past Twelve Months, by Familiarity and Exclusivity Measures and Primary/Secondary Partner Status (cell percentages)**

	Any STI without Attribute		Any STI with Attribute	
	%	N	%	N
Familiarity				
Any new partners in past 12 months	1.1	2,135	4.0	530
Primary partner	1.1	2,249	4.5	404
Secondary partner	5.1	157	4.8	312
Any one-time partners	1.3	2,458	5.6	231
Primary partner	1.6	2,582	0.0	37
Secondary partner	5.2	345	3.4	117
Any 2-month or less partners	1.3	2,361	4.6	328
Primary partner	1.6	2,534	2.4	84
Secondary partner	4.4	294	4.8	167
Any casual/pickup partner	1.5	2,803	4.2	142
Knew partner 2 days or less before first sex[a]	4.7	363	3.1	64
Primary partner	4.7	381	[b]	23
Secondary partner	4.0	275	4.4	46
Knew partner 1 month or less before first sex[a]	1.7	241	7.7	234
Primary partner	1.9	269	9.6	135
Secondary partner	2.8	182	5.8	139
Exclusivity				
Number of partner's other partners (column percentage):				
Primary partner:				
No other partners	[a]		1.4	2,313
1 other partner	[a]		2.3	173
2 other partners	[a]		3.8	53
3 or more other partners	[a]		7.1	56
Secondary partner:				
No other partners	[a]		3.6	138
1 other partner	[a]		5.4	129
2 other partners	[a]		0.0	49
3 or more other partners	[a]		7.5	80
Either partner nonmonogamous, during	1.4	2,396	4.6	198
Primary partner	1.4	2,454	5.1	132
Secondary partner	4.4	247	3.5	85

Table 11.15   (continued)

	Any STI without Attribute		Any STI with Attribute	
	%	N	%	N
Either partner nonmonogamous, beginning[a]	3.8	338	6.3	95
Primary partner	3.9	355	7.7	39
Secondary partner	4.0	250	5.2	58
Do not expect partner's monogamy	1.6	2,137	3.5	86
Primary partner	1.6	2,150	4.2	72
Secondary partner	5.3	76	[b]	21

[a]Among those respondents with new partners in the past twelve months.
[b]Fewer than thirty cases.

respondents who had one sex partner within the past year, 4.5 percent of those who had two to four partners, and 5.9 percent of those with five or more partners last year contracted an STI. So there is a clear link between the number of partners and the rate of getting an STI.

The top panel of table 11.15 shows the rate of contracting an STI for those who did or did not respond affirmatively to the several issues measuring familiarity with the partner. The left-hand columns show those who did *not* have a new partner, did *not* have a one-time sex partner, or did *not* have any partnership that lasted less than two months, and so forth, while the right-hand columns show the incidence of STIs for those who *did* have each of these attributes. Clearly, the top panel of this table tells us that those who did have a new partner within the past year were much more likely to have gotten an STI: only 1.1 percent of those with no new partners but 4.0 percent of those who did have a new partner got an infection. All those who had a secondary partner had relatively high rates of STIs, whether the partner was new or not. Those with a one-time sex partner tended to have much higher rates of STIs (except for the small group of thirty-seven cases with a one-time primary partner and no infection). Notice that those who said that they had a "casual" or pickup sex partner were much more likely to report having had an STI—4.2 percent compared to 1.5 percent. While not in evidence for new partners known less than two days, those who had sex with partners whom they knew less than a month had dramatically higher rates of STIs.

The bottom panel of table 11.15 shows the rates of STIs by the sexual exclusivity of the partners; here again, the patterns are quite pronounced. Among primary partners, those whose partner had more partners had higher rates of infection. The same general pattern is seen for the secondary partners. Those who had nonmonogamous partners were much more likely to contract infection, as were those who did not expect sexual exclusivity from their partners.

In short, unfamiliarity with the partner, especially knowing the person less than a month before first having sex, and having nonexclusive partners are both quite strongly associated with a higher incidence of being infected.

Table 11.16 goes more deeply still into the relation between number of partners and STIs. Table 11.16A shows the incidence of STIs by the respondent's and the partner's number of sex partners in the past twelve months. As one moves across or down either panel of this table, the potential exposure to infected partners rises, and, as one would expect, the incidence of infection also rises. For respondents with only one partner who had no other partner, the incidence of infection is 0.9 percent, while an increase in the respondent's own number of partners or in the partner's number of partners or both increases the incidence of infection up to 6.7 percent for those who had three partners and whose primary partner also had two or more. (The rate happens to be even higher—8.2 percent—for those with three or more partners whose primary partner had no other partners.) A similar pattern is in evidence here for the secondary partner.

Table 11.16B again indicates that, as exposure to nonexclusive partners rises, so too does the incidence of STIs. The same is seen in table 11.16C, where respondents who had three or more partners within the past year and who had a primary partner who was known for less than a month before beginning to have sex exhibited an infection rate over 10 percent.

Table 11.17 collapses the several measures of risky partner attributes into a simple sum of risky attributes. The top and middle panels show the incidence of risk by a count of unfamiliarity and nonexclusivity attributes, respectively. In the bottom panel, which combines the two, we see that, as the number of

Table 11.16A   **Incidence of STIs in the Past Twelve Months, by Number of Partners and Primary/Secondary Partners' Number of Partners (cell percentages represent rate of infection)**

	Primary Partner's Other Partners in Past 12 Months				Secondary Partner's Other Partners in Past 12 Months			
	0	1	2+	Total	0	1	2+	Total
Respondents' partners past 12 months:								
1	.9	0.0	5.6	1.0	N.A.	N.A.	N.A.	N.A.
2	3.0	3.5	a	3.2	1.3	4.8	1.6	2.5
3+	8.2	3.6	6.7	6.6	6.6	6.0	7.5	6.7
Total	1.4	2.3	5.5	1.6	3.6	5.4	4.6	4.5

Note: N.A. = not applicable.
[a]Fewer than thirty cases.

Table 11.16B   **Incidence of STIs in the Past Twelve Months, by Number of Partners and Primary/Secondary Partners' Exclusivity Status during Partnership (cell percentages represent rate of infection)**

	Primary Partner Nonexclusive during Relationship with Respondent			Secondary Partner Nonexclusive during Relationship with Respondent		
	No	Yes	Total	No	Yes	Total
Respondents' partners past 12 months:						
1	.9	4.2	1.0	N.A.	N.A.	N.A.
2	2.8	5.3	3.3	3.2	0.0	2.4
3+	6.1	8.7	6.6	5.8	6.8	6.1
Total	1.4	6.1	1.6	4.4	3.5	4.2

Table 11.16C   **Incidence of STIs in the Past Twelve Months, by Number of Partners and Length of Time Respondent Knew Primary/Secondary Partner before First Sex (cell percentages represent rate of infection)**

	Primary Partner Known 1 Month or Less before First Sex			Secondary Partner Known 1 Month or Less before First Sex		
	No	Yes	Total	No	Yes	Total
Respondents' partners past 12 months:						
1	1.3	8.7	3.0	N.A.	N.A.	N.A.
2	0.0	9.8	4.4	1.0	1.9	1.3
3+	4.7	10.4	7.1	4.8	8.0	6.4
Total	1.9	9.6	4.4	2.8	5.8	4.0

risky attributes rises from none, to one, to more, the incidence of infection also rises, up to 9.2 percent for four attributes.

Tables 11.15–11.17 tell us that what we have characterized as *risky* partner attributes do, in fact, raise the likelihood of contracting an STI in the past year. Next, we consider the sexual practices that are typically characterized as risky.

Practice Risk

The nature of sexual activity itself can affect the likelihood of contracting infection since the various ways in which infections are spread can be facili-

Table 11.17   **Incidence of STIs in Past Twelve Months, by Summary Measures of Partner Attributes (row percentages represent rate of infection)**

Sum of Partner Attributes	% Any STD	N
Familiarity:		
0	.9	2,437
1	2.4	209
2	4.8	124
3	4.6	152
4+	6.8	132
Exclusivity:		
0	1.2	2,567
1	1.3	149
2	5.9	102
3	0.0	85
4	5.1	59
5+	7.6	92
Familiarity and exclusivity combined:		
0	.8	2,304
1	2.2	185
2	2.6	116
3	2.9	102
4	9.2	76
5	3.6	84
6+	4.8	188

tated or inhibited by one practice or another. In this section, we look at practices as they are related to the contraction of infection. We distinguish among three types of practices that affect the rate of transmission of infection. First, the sexual activity itself can have some influence. Touching the genitals with one's hand, or with one's mouth, or with one's genitals, can involve different rates of transmission, as can contact that involves the exchange of bodily fluids through kissing, or through vaginal intercourse, or through anal intercourse, for example. Since infections differ in the way in which they are spread, practices carry differing degrees of risk for each different infection. Second, some practices are undertaken expressly to reduce the risk of infection. Condom use during sex is such a practice—indeed, practically the only such practice of note other than avoidance of sexual contact. Third, some practices have an indirect effect on the risk of transmission of infection. These practices include the use of drugs or alcohol in connection with sex since the result is often a reduction in caution, and they sometimes involve rougher sexual activity that can break the skin and increase the risk of transmission of blood-borne infections, and so forth.

We begin with the preventive practice of condom use. Table 11.18 shows the rate of condom use during vaginal intercourse, by the number of partners within the past year. In the data on the most recent sexual event, which is

Table 11.18A **Condom Use during Vaginal Intercourse: During Last Sexual Event, by Number of Partners**

Partners in Past 12 Months	% Used Condom	Total N
1	13.7	1,941
2	25.8	198
3	36.1	72
4	40.5	37
5+	31.2	64
Total	16.3	2,313

Table 11.18B **Condom Use during Vaginal Intercourse: Frequency of Use in the Past Twelve Months with Primary/Secondary Partner, by Number of Partners in the Past Twelve Months (row percentages)**

	Used Condom			
	Never	Some[a]	Always	N
Respondent has 1 partner:				
Primary	69.1	20.1	10.8	2,158
Secondary	N.A.	N.A.	N.A.	N.A.
Respondent has 2 partners:				
Primary	54.2	30.5	15.2	236
Secondary	51.8	17.0	31.2	224
Respondent has 3 or more partners:				
Primary	46.3	33.3	20.4	216
Secondary	42.4	17.6	40.0	205
Total, primary partner	65.9	22.2	12.0	2,610
Total, secondary partner	47.3	17.2	35.4	429

Note: N.A. = not applicable.
[a]Rarely to usually.

reasonably representative of the average sex act, table 11.18A tells us that 16.3 percent of respondents used a condom. But we see that the use of condoms rose substantially with the number of partners the respondent had within the past twelve months. Those who had one partner were least likely to use a condom—only 13.7 percent did so—while, of those who had three partners, one-third used a condom in the last sexual event.

Table 11.18B shows the use of condoms by primary and secondary partner as well as by total number of sex partners within the past twelve months (also see chapter 3, where the practice of condom use is reported). There, we see that the large majority of respondents who have one partner within the year are far less likely to use a condom than are others. They are also exposed to a much decreased risk of infection with their one partner, so this pattern of behavior is quite understandable and reasonable. Also, condoms are more than twice as likely to be used with a secondary partner than with a primary partner. For

Table 11.18C   **Condom Use during Vaginal Intercourse: Frequency of Use in the Past Twelve Months with Primary/Secondary Partner, by Marital/Cohabitational Status (row percentages)**

	Never	Some[a]	Always	N
Primary partner:				
Married	74.7	17.7	7.6	1,622
Cohabitational	63.6	25.2	11.2	357
Noncohabitational	44.4	31.8	23.8	631
Secondary partner:				
Married	[b]	[b]	[b]	3
Cohabitational	[b]	[b]	[b]	15
Noncohabitational	46.7	17.3	36.0	411
Total, primary partner	65.9	22.2	12.0	2,610
Total, secondary partner	47.3	17.2	35.4	429

The header spanning Never, Some[a], Always is "Used Condom".

[a]Rarely to usually.
[b]Fewer than thirty cases.

those with two partners, over half do not ever use a condom, according to table 11.18B, but about one-third always do so with their secondary partner. As the total number of partners rises to three or more, the use of a condom with the secondary partner rises appreciably to 40 percent, but to only 20 percent with the primary partner. In table 11.18C, we see that, for married couples with one partner (by far the most common category in this table), the use of a condom is particularly rare.

Next, we look at drug and alcohol use during sex (for some related results, see section 3.3 of chapter 3). Table 11.19A tells us about the last sexual event. The top number in that table tells us that 1.8 percent of respondents said that alcohol was used the last time they had sex; the subsequent rows tell us the percentage of those who used alcohol or drugs in the past year with their primary or secondary partner. The measure of alcohol use that we employ here is fairly narrowly construed: the respondent or his or her partner is said to use alcohol before or during sex "sometimes" or "usually" or "always," *and* at least one of the two of them is affected "very strongly" by the alcohol, as reported by the respondent. Looking at the left-hand column of table 11.19A, we see that respondents are far more likely to use alcohol with their secondary partner than with their primary partner and that those who have more partners are also more likely to use alcohol. The second column tells us about drug use (drug use is analogously measured). Its use in connection with sex (as in general) is far less widespread than is alcohol use, but the same patterns are seen here: more use as the number of partners rises and generally more use with secondary partners. The third column combines the use of alcohol and drugs and shows the resulting pattern. This does not necessarily mean that the two are

Table 11.19A   **Use of Drugs or Alcohol during the Last Sexual Event and during the Past Twelve Months, by Number and Status of Partners**

Number of Partners	Strongly Affected by:[a]		
	Alcohol	Drugs	Either/Both
Last event	1.8	.3	2.0
During the past 12 months:			
Respondent has 1 partner:			
Primary	2.4	.4	2.6
Secondary	N.A.	N.A.	N.A.
Respondent has 2 partners:			
Primary	3.4	1.3	4.3
Secondary	11.6	2.5	13.3
Respondent has 3 or more partners:			
Primary	4.0	1.3	4.9
Secondary	15.9	.9	16.7
Total, primary partner	2.6	.5	3.0
Total, secondary partner	13.8	1.7	15.0

Note: N.A. = not applicable.

[a]Respondent or partner uses alcohol and/or drugs during sex sometimes, usually, or always, and either respondent or partner or both are affected very strongly.

Table 11.19B   **Condom Use during Last Sexual Event, by Use of Alcohol or Drugs**

Either Partner Strongly Affected[a]	% Using Condoms	N
No	16.2	2,262
Yes	20.9	43

[a]Respondent or partner uses alcohol and/or drugs during sex sometimes, usually, or always, and either respondent or partner or both are affected very strongly.

Table 11.19C   **Condom Use during Past Twelve Months, by Use of Alcohol or Drugs (row percentages)**

Respondent and/or Partner Strongly Affected[a]	Frequency of Condom Use			
	Never	Sometimes	Always	N
Primary partner:				
No	65.5	22.3	12.2	2,426
Yes	73.0	20.3	6.8	74
Secondary partner:				
No	45.4	17.8	36.8	348
Yes	59.3	13.6	27.1	59

[a]Respondent or partner uses alcohol and/or drugs during sex sometimes, usually, or always, and either respondent or partner or both are affected very strongly.

used at the same time, only that the respondent answered the questions about alcohol or drugs or both affirmatively.

The greater use of these substances with secondary partners is an important finding. It may be that alcohol or drugs help "break the ice" with the new or secondary partner, but it surely implies that, if one is "under the influence," it is likely that any up-front resolve to be particularly careful with a secondary partner, or a less well-known partner, may become difficult to carry out. Table 11.19B and table 11.19C make this point vividly. Table 11.19B just shows that, of those who said that they were affected by alcohol or drugs, a somewhat higher proportion did indicate that they used condoms in their most recent sexual event than those who said that they were not using drugs or alcohol. Notice, however, that there were only forty-three respondents in this group. Table 11.19C shows the information in a more relevant manner, by primary and secondary partnership status. We see that, with the secondary partner, those who were affected by alcohol or drugs were notably less likely always to use a condom—27.1 percent compared to 36.8 percent of those who were not using drugs or alcohol. Nearly 60 percent of those who said that they did use drugs or alcohol indicated that they never used condoms with their secondary partners. Here, the risks of contracting infection would appear to be relatively high.

Notice the very different character of primary and secondary partnerships that respondents have described to us here. Compared to the primary partner, the secondary partner is far less familiar to the respondent and is much less sexually exclusive with the respondent. However, the respondents take more precautions in the form of condom use with secondary partners, but then they also engage in more alcohol use than they do with primary partners.

Table 11.20 consolidates much of the information depicted in the last few tables and shows it by the master status variables so that we can see how the risk posed by sexual behavior differs by gender, age, race/ethnicity, education, marital status, and income level. Added to the variables shown in the columns of this table is one discussed in chapter 3 but not previously discussed here, anal intercourse. For HIV/AIDS in particular, anal intercourse is known to be especially dangerous because it is an efficient way of transmitting HIV; accordingly, we include it in table 11.20.[11] For the column showing condom use in the last event and the *always* column under condom use during vaginal intercourse, higher percentages imply lower risk, while, for the *never* column under condom use during vaginal intercourse and the two final columns, a higher percentage reflects a higher risk that infection will be transmitted. Let us consider the patterns in table 11.20 one demographic variable at a time.

Men and women say that they used a condom in about the same proportions in their last sex act (col. 1), but women report slightly less condom use gener-

---

11. Note, however, that anal intercourse is relatively rare. That is why, given our sample size, we are not able to analyze it more fully.

| Table 11.20 | Risky Sex Practices, by Master Status Variables (last event variables array as column percentages; condom frequencies with primary and secondary partners array as percentages; anal sex and alcohol array as column percentages) |

Respondent Characteristic	Last Event Condom Use during Vaginal Intercourse	Frequency of Condom Use during Vaginal Intercourse						Either Primary or Secondary Partner	
		With Primary Partner			With Secondary Partner			Ever Anal Sex	Strong Drug/ Alcohol Effect
		Never	Some	Always	Never	Some	Always		
Total	16.3	65.9	22.1	12.0	47.3	17.2	35.4	9.7	5.1
Men	18.0	60.5	25.4	14.0	45.7	20.0	34.3	10.9	5.5
Women	15.0	70.3	19.4	10.3	50.0	12.8	37.2	8.8	4.8
18–24	28.4	44.9	33.9	21.2	35.0	18.2	46.7	9.1	7.9
25–29	21.8	53.1	32.4	14.5	42.5	18.8	38.8	12.6	7.8
30–34	19.2	61.0	26.4	12.6	44.9	23.2	31.9	10.5	5.4
35–39	15.2	69.5	18.4	12.2	53.7	9.3	37.0	11.0	4.3
40–44	12.3	76.6	14.7	8.7	64.0	18.0	18.0	11.4	4.6
45–49	6.5	81.4	12.8	5.8	b	b	b	10.3	2.9
50–54	5.2	85.0	8.5	6.5	b	b	b	2.4	1.9
55–59	2.4	89.1	8.8	2.0	b	b	b	3.3	1.3
White	15.2	66.8	21.7	11.5	49.5	15.8	34.7	8.9	4.8
Black	23.0	60.1	27.0	12.9	38.5	20.9	40.7	9.6	5.1
Hispanic	15.1	68.8	17.7	13.5	59.4	15.6	25.0	16.1	8.3
Other	19.5	60.0	22.4	17.6	b	b	b	13.3	4.7
Less than HS	12.1	72.7	17.2	10.2	60.0	14.6	25.4	8.8	6.8
HS grad.	13.0	70.8	19.3	9.9	51.4	15.6	33.0	8.2	4.5
Some college	18.5	62.8	23.9	13.2	45.5	19.5	35.1	10.6	5.5
College grad.	18.9	59.2	28.1	12.7	43.2	16.0	40.7	10.4	4.8
Postgrad.	23.6	61.3	22.0	16.7	b	b	b	11.4	2.6
Never married	32.9	40.9	34.9	24.1	37.4	21.0	41.6	11.8	10.1
Currently married	10.6	74.6	17.7	7.7	50.0	16.7	33.3	8.5	2.5
No longer married	16.2	68.9	21.2	9.8	63.9	11.3	24.8	11.4	6.6
Poor[a]	20.4	63.5	23.7	12.8	46.2	16.9	36.9	10.6	9.1
Middle	15.1	66.3	22.7	11.1	48.4	18.4	33.2	10.0	4.6
Rich[a]	16.6	71.1	16.7	12.2	55.8	11.5	32.7	8.8	4.0

[a]For definitions of poor, middle, and rich, see the note to table 10.8.

[b]Fewer than thirty observations.

ally with their primary partner than do men. On the whole, there are not gender differences here of any note.

Age, by contrast, shows a very dramatic relation to condom use. The younger the person is, the higher is the likelihood that a condom was used in the last sex act, and, similarly, the young report much more consistent condom use with both the primary and the secondary partner. The pattern of increased usage among the younger people is very systematic and quite large in magnitude: in the last sexual event, 28.4 percent of those aged eighteen to twenty-four used a condom, as compared to 15.2 percent of those aged thirty-five to thirty-nine or only 2.4 percent of those aged fifty-five to fifty-nine. On the other hand, both anal intercourse and drug or alcohol use is notably lower among those over age fifty. Blacks report higher condom use than do whites, at least in the last sexual event and with the riskier secondary partners. The Hispanic and "other" categories appear to have somewhat higher rates of anal intercourse, and Hispanics also have somewhat elevated rates of drug or alcohol use.

The pattern with education indicates greater use of condoms among the more educated and lower rates of drug or alcohol use, so the pattern by education is the most consistent in suggesting that fewer risks and more precautions are taken with higher levels of schooling. As so often in these tables, marital status has a very large influence on the measure of interest. Here, the currently married are less likely to use a condom in the last event and with the primary partner, but they do have a greater tendency to use condoms during sex with secondary partners: one-third of the married people who had secondary partners said that they always used condoms with that partner. (Note that this number is quite small, with only around fifty respondents.) The bottom segment of table 11.20 tells us that income shows little relation to either condom use or anal sex but that drug or alcohol use is noticeably higher among the poor than among those whose income is greater than the official poverty level.

INTERACTION BETWEEN PARTNER CHOICE AND SEXUAL PRACTICES

In tables 11.11–11.14, we focused on the choice of sex partners, and we saw how familiarity and sexual exclusivity differed by the master status variables and by the number of sex partners. Here, we look at the relation between familiarity and exclusivity and condom use. Table 11.21 reports on condom use during the last sexual event, characterizing the respondent in terms of the several measures of familiarity with and the exclusivity of his or her partners. This table is only suggestive since it does not directly link condom use with the particular partner in the description. Table 11.21 does show, nevertheless, a rather clear pattern of greater use of condoms by those who had less familiar or less sexually exclusive partners. The top panel shows that condom use rates are twice as great by several measures of familiarity of partners, reflecting greater use of condoms when the risks are higher. The bottom panel shows use by exclusivity, and here there is a less clear pattern. As the number of partner's

Table 11.21   Condom Use during Vaginal Intercourse in Last Event, by Partner Familiarity and Exclusivity Measures (cell percentages)

Familiarity	% Using	N
No new partners	12.8	1,890
New partners	32.8	401
No one-time partners	15.2	2,185
Any one-time partners	35.4	127
No < 2 month partners	14.4	2,094
Any < 2 month partners	34.9	218
No casual partners	15.8	2,108
Any casual partners	29.2	106
Neither primary nor secondary partner known 2 days or less[a]	35.0	286
Either primary or secondary partner known 2 days or less[a]	39.0	41
Neither primary nor secondary partner known 1 month or less[a]	38.5	187
Either primary or secondary partner known 1 month or less[a]	29.8	178

Exclusivity	% Using	N
Partners' partners (primary and secondary together) (column percentages)		
0 other partners	14.3	1,939
1 other partner	27.2	147
2 other partners	30.8	78
3 other partners	22.2	45
4 or more other partners	27.5	69
No partner nonmonogamous at beginning[a]	35.5	265
At least 1 partner nonmonogamous at beginning[a]	27.1	70
No partner nonmonogamous during	15.7	2,099
At least 1 partner nonmonogamous during	24.1	166
Monogamy expected	13.6	1,928
No monogamy expected (at least 1 partner)	18.3	71
No partner paid	16.3	2,210
At least 1 partner paid for sex	[b]	4

[a]Based only on new partners within last year.
[b]Fewer than thirty cases.

Table 11.22 **Condom Use in the Past Twelve Months with Primary and Secondary Partners, by Partner Familiarity and Exclusivity Measures (*attribute* and *practice* reference the same partner; within each partner type row percentages sum to 100)**

	With Primary				With Secondary			
	Never	Some	Always	*N*	Never	Some	Always	*N*
Familiarity								
New partners:								
No	69.8	20.6	9.6	2,214	50.3	21.3	28.4	155
Yes	42.0	31.3	26.7	374	45.6	14.8	39.6	270
One-time partners:								
No	66.1	22.5	11.3	2,531	48.9	22.6	28.5	319
Yes	36.7	0.0	63.3	30	40.8	0.0	59.2	98
Less than 2 month partners:								
No	66.6	22.4	11.1	2,493	48.9	21.7	29.4	276
Yes	37.3	17.9	44.8	67	43.6	8.6	47.9	140
Knew partner 2 days or less before first sex:[b]								
No	41.0	31.7	27.2	356	46.2	15.3	38.6	249
Yes	[a]	[a]	[a]	19	46.0	10.8	43.2	37
Knew partner 1 month or less before first sex:[b]								
No	38.6	31.5	29.9	251	47.6	15.1	37.4	166
Yes	49.2	30.6	20.2	124	44.2	14.2	41.7	120
Exclusivity								
Partner's other partners, past 12 months:								
No other partners	67.5	21.5	11.0	2,283	49.6	24.8	29.5	129
1 other partner	50.9	25.8	23.4	167	47.8	16.5	39.7	121
2 or more other partners	61.2	29.6	9.2	98	50.9	13.8	37.1	116
Partner nonmonogamous at beginning:[b]								
No	41.1	31.2	43.1	333	47.4	15.6	40.2	224
Yes	56.2	25.0	18.8	32	53.1	11.8	37.2	51
Partner nonmonogamous during:								
No	66.5	22.0	11.5	2,417	49.3	23.3	31.8	236
Yes	58.4	28.8	12.8	125	56.3	20.0	26.7	75
Do not expect partner's monogamy:								
No	68.9	21.9	9.3	2,136	56.8	31.1	12.2	74
Yes	58.6	28.6	12.9	70	[a]	[a]	[a]	19

Note: Some is defined as "rarely" to "usually." Casual partners are not included in this table because they are defined over all the respondents' partners and not separately as attributes of the primary and secondary partner.

[a]Fewer than thirty cases.

[b]Calculated for new partners in past twelve months only.

sex partners rises from none, to one, to more, the incidence of using condoms rises from 14.3, to 27.2, to 30.8 percent, but no higher.

Table 11.22 links familiarity and condom use directly to the same partners, so here one would expect to see a clearer connection between the perceived risk of infection and the use of a condom—which is what the table does in fact show. Take the first two rows of the top panel, for example. If the primary partner is not a new partner this year—and the vast majority of all cases (2,214 respondents) fall into this category—only 9.6 percent always use a condom, and the risk for these couples is probably quite small. The condom may in fact be being used as a fertility control measure in these cases. If the primary partner is, instead, a new partner this year, then the rate that condoms are always used is 26.7 percent, and if the secondary partner is not a new partner this year, the rate that condoms are always used is 28.4 percent. But, if the secondary partner is a new partner this year, the rate that condoms are always used rises all the way to 39.6 percent.

A similar pattern is seen for those with one-time partners compared to those with no one-time partners. A primary partner with whom one has sex often is likely to be a spouse or regular partner, and, of these 2,531 cases, only 11.3 percent use a condom. For partners who are one-time sex partners, the rate of condom use is much higher: 63.3 and 59.2 percent for primary and secondary partners, respectively.[12] A similar pattern is seen for the measure of familiarity pertaining to having sex with the person over a period of time less than two months. The final two measures in this top panel relate only to new partners within the year, and, there, one sees less patterning within the categories but a relatively high rate of condom use for all categories.

We saw in table 11.15 that having sex with a partner known for less than a month previously is associated with a much higher rate of contracting an STI—a rate of 7.7 compared to 1.7, yet this is the one attribute in table 11.22 that is not associated with substantially higher rates of condom use. Perhaps insisting on a condom in the initial stages of a relationship is particularly awkward, although it would not seem to be so with a one-night partner or with a paid/paying partner. This may be an important window for the transmission of infection.

The lower panel of table 11.22 looks at condom use by the indicators of sexual exclusivity, and here one sees very little pattern that makes much sense. The only explanation that we have for this result is that a respondent who

12. One may question how a one-time partner is a primary partner, but such an individual is so defined for a respondent who had only one sex partner, even if he or she had sex with that person one time only. In that case, there is substantial risk of disease, and the high rate of condom use is surely not inappropriate or surprising. Billy et al. (1993) report that their male respondents had high subjective estimates of the risk of HIV transmission in one-time sexual encounters, even though we have shown in table 11.15 that the one-time risk is not high. In fact, of thirty-seven respondents with one-time primary partners in the past year, none contracted an STI within the year.

knows his or her partner well enough to report on that person's sexual exclusivity may think that he or she knows the partner well enough to know whether a condom is needed. Admittedly, this is one of the more puzzling tables that we show here; we include it for completeness, despite not having a good explanation for its pattern.

Table 11.23 combines information about condom use and incidence of STIs, and here we see that the incidence of STIs is dramatically lower when condoms are always used during vaginal intercourse. Perhaps the most succinct and informative comparison from this table is to contrast the two columns labeled *always* and *total*. The latter shows the incidence of STIs for all respondents in that segment of the row, while the former shows the incidence only for the respondents who always used condoms. In practically every comparison for primary partners, those who always used condoms report far lower rates of STIs: for instance, those who had three or more partners in the past twelve months had an overall rate of infection of 7.0 percent, those who always used condoms only 2.3 percent. However, this pattern is not in evidence for condom use with the secondary partner, as shown in the left-hand portion of the table.

A final note about the several tables that have just been briefly discussed. Two aspects of these tables diminish their capacity to reveal clearly the relations on which we are focusing here. First, many of the characteristics that define the rows in these tables pertain not to the partner in question but rather to the entire set of that respondent's partners. This is so, for example, for the one-time partner, for knowing the partner less than a month prior to having sex, and for many others. Respondents who answered one of these questions affirmatively have been exposed to greater risks than respondents who answered negatively; however, the information about condom use pertains specifically to the primary and secondary partner who is not necessarily a one-time partner, for example.[13] The connections here are therefore weaker than one would like them to be. A tighter analytic link awaits another survey study. Second, many of the cells in these tables have few cases in them. We show no figures based on a group smaller than thirty cases, but even that number is small and has a substantial sampling variance. A larger study with many more observations than we have here could be expected to provide much more precise and robust information in the table shells that we present here. This too awaits a further survey project.

11.3 The Sexual Behavior of Those Infected with STIs

Until now, we have treated our respondents solely from the perspective of being at risk of contracting an STI from a sex partner. In this section, we reverse the perspective and ask what patterns of partnering and practice make the

---

13. For those measures pertaining to any partner, this is strictly true. For those measures pertaining to either the primary or the secondary partner, we have not identified which partner actually exhibited the attribute because of our limited number of observations.

Table 11.23   **Incidence of STIs in the Past Twelve Months, by Primary and Secondary Partner Attributes and Frequency of Condom Use during Vaginal Intercourse (condom use specific to primary or secondary partner; cell percentages represent rate of infection)**

| Partner Attribute | Condom Use during Vaginal Intercourse | | | | | | | | | |
| | Primary Partner | | | | | Secondary Partner | | | | |
	Never	Some	Always	Total	N	Never	Some	Always	Total	N
Partners in past 12 months										
1 partner	.5	2.8	.4	1.0	2,118	N.A.	N.A.	N.A.	N.A.	N.A.
2 partners	3.3	4.2	0.0	3.0	230	4.5	2.6	1.4	2.9	217
3 or more partners	7.0	10.1	2.3	7.0	213	5.7	5.9	8.6	7.4	202
Total	1.1	3.9	0.6	1.7	2,561	5.1	4.2	5.3	5.0	419
Familiarity										
Any new partners	3.9	7.7	0.0	4.1	491	5.4	a	4.3	4.5	286
Any one-time partners	5.6	11.5	1.7	6.2	211	5.4	a	6.8	6.8	177
Any 2 month or less partners	4.7	9.2	1.3	5.1	293	4.0	a	7.6	5.9	236
Any casual partners	4.6	5.7	a	4.7	129	2.1	a	9.3	5.7	106
Either primary or secondary partner known 2 days or less[b]	a	a	a	3.6	56	a	a	a	4.5	44
Either primary or secondary partner known 1 month or less[b]	8.4	12.7	2.2	8.4	215	9.3	a	9.4	8.6	163
Exclusivity										
Sum of primary and secondary partners:										
No other partners	.7	3.0	.4	1.1	2,117	7.7	a	2.4	4.3	117
1 other partner	3.6	9.6	0.0	4.6	175	3.9	a	10.9	7.1	112
2+ other partners	4.8	4.3	3.1	4.4	226	4.4	a	3.3	4.4	182
Either primary or secondary partner nonexclusive at beginning[b]	10.6	a	a	7.1	84	5.7	a	a	7.8	64
Either primary or secondary partner nonexclusive during	3.7	7.6	a	4.9	182	3.1	a	5.1	5.5	128
Either primary or secondary partner, no exclusivity expected	2.0	a	a	3.8	80	a	a	a	6.7	45

Note: N.A. = not applicable.
[a]Fewer than thirty cases.
[b]Among new partners only.

transmission of infection more likely, given that one has been infected. There are numerous sophisticated mathematical and epidemiological studies of the dynamics of infection transmission (for studies of gonorrhea transmission, e.g., see Hethcote and Yorke [1984]), and we make no attempt at any such modeling in this section. Indeed, the NHSLS data do not include the kind of very specific data on which these epidemiological models are built, specifically the data on the exact timing of infection and treatment relative to partner acquisition. Instead, in this section, we describe briefly some general patterns of sexual partnering in the population as a whole that are relevant to these more precise models.

The most important piece of information in understanding transmission dynamics is the number of sex partners that an infected person has during the period when he or she is infectious. Typically, the period of infectiousness follows a short incubation period and lasts until treatment renders the infection no longer communicable. This period varies for different infections and for different manifestations of the same infection; however, we can make a few generalizations. People with bacterial infections such as chlamydia and gonorrhea are typically infectious for about a month if they are symptomatic and for about four months if they are asymptomatic, after which time most everyone has sought and received effective treatment (again, note that these are rather broad generalizations that are useful for establishing some empirical parameters and that we do not claim them to be precise or applicable in every case). People infected with viral STIs have few hopes of cure (there are a few effective treatments for hepatitis B) and therefore can be infectious for years rather than months either continuously, as in the case of HIV/AIDS, or intermittently, as in the case of genital herpes and warts (i.e., mostly during periods when symptoms recur).

For the transmission of high-infectivity infections (mostly the bacterial infections), we are interested in the prevalence of having two or more partners in rapid succession or, indeed, concurrently. Chapter 5 reports that 62 percent of those with two or more partners had concurrent partners at some time in the most recent twelve months. Moreover, as the number of partners in the past twelve months rises, the likelihood of having any concurrent partnerships increases substantially (from 51 percent for those with two partners, to 61 percent for those with three, to 85 percent for those with six or more). While it is not necessarily the case, a person who contracts an STI from one of those partners is very likely to transmit it to another concurrent partner before receiving medical treatment (remember that, with high-infectivity infections, very few exposures are needed before the probability of transmission approaches certainty).

An alternative way of describing this aspect of the dynamics of partnering is to look at the number of months during the most recent twelve-month period when an individual had two or more sex partners. Again, such rapid sequencing of partners involves the greatest probability for spreading infection. Referring back to chapter 5, we report that the mean number of months spent with at least two partners is 2.5 for those with two partners in the year and rises dramatically to 7.6 months for those with six or more partners in the year. Individuals with five or more partners have three or more concurrent partners for an average of four months during the year.

The two points outlined above suggest that for a small proportion of individuals—those with several partners in the year—the period of time between exposure to different individuals is very short. This small group of sexually very active adults may correspond to the hypothesized "core" groups responsible for the continued reproduction of several high-infectivity STIs; that is, these individuals spread the infection to at least one other person before their treatment renders them noninfectious (see, e.g., Hethcote and Yorke 1984; Potterat, Dukes, and Rothenberg 1987; Garnett and Anderson 1993).

In the case of viral STIs, which are typically much less infectious, concern focuses less on numbers of short-term partners than on long-term behavior both in the choice of number of partners and in the choice of safer practices, especially condom use. Table 11.24A enumerates the distribution of sex partners and table 11.24B the frequency of condom use during vaginal intercourse for those who have been diagnosed prior to the past twelve months, comparing them to those with no previous STI diagnosis and those who have previously had only a bacterial STI. Furthermore, we control for age since younger individuals are likely to have been infected more recently and, in some cases (such as herpes and genital warts), are perhaps more likely to manifest symptoms and to be infectious. In fact, in the past twelve months, 21 percent of those with a prior diagnosis of herpes and 7 percent of those with a prior diagnosis of genital warts reported experiencing genital sores or lesions, while 12 percent reported chronic itching of the genital area. (Because of our relatively limited sample size, we cannot analyze separately the behavior of those manifesting symptoms in the current year, although that would be most desirable for this discussion.)

In table 11.24A, the two most notable trends are these. First, individuals with viral STIs have no fewer and perhaps more sex partners in the past twelve months than those never before infected. It does not appear that those who could potentially spread viral STIs moderate their contact with other sex partners in any appreciable way. Second, those with prior bacterial infections in all age groups are much more likely to have several sex partners. A small but significant minority of those who have had bacterial STIs appear to remain in partnering patterns that put them at risk of contracting and then retransmitting high-infectivity infections. In data not reported in this volume, the youngest group with a prior viral infection tends to have sex more frequently than the other two groups: 24 percent report having sex four or more times a week compared with 16 percent of those with past bacterial infections and 10 percent of those with no prior infection. Together, these data perhaps again corroborate the existence of a "core" group.

Table 11.24B reinforces the interpretation given above. Those with prior viral infections, especially the youngest cohort, aged eighteen to twenty-nine, use condoms during vaginal intercourse far less often than those with no prior STIs and those with prior bacterial STIs. (We should note, however, the rather small size of this young group, forty-six.) At best, they take no further precautions. Note that we have made no attempt to distinguish respondents by infection. It may well be that those diagnosed with HIV/AIDS may behave quite differently from those with herpes, but, in our sample, the proportion with

Table 11.24A **Distribution of Number of Partners in the Past Twelve Months, by Sexually Transmitted Infection Status, by Age and Disease Type (row percentages)**

Age Category and STIs prior to Past 12 Months	Sex Partners in the Past 12 Months						
	0	1	2	3	4	5+	N
18–29:							
No STI ever	10.3	65.2	10.5	5.4	2.7	5.9	816
Any viral STI[a]	0.0	69.4	16.3	10.2	0.0	4.1	49
Bacterial STI only[b]	2.8	53.5	16.9	5.6	2.8	18.3	71
30–44:							
No STI ever	10.5	78.6	6.9	2.2	.9	.9	1,120
Any viral STI[a]	9.7	64.5	10.5	5.6	7.2	2.4	124
Bacterial STI only[b]	7.0	62.5	13.3	6.2	3.1	7.8	128
45–59:							
No STI ever	20.5	75.2	2.5	.9	.6	.3	668
Any viral STI[a]	27.5	67.5	2.5	0.0	0.0	2.5	40
Bacterial STI only[b]	20.3	62.5	12.5	3.1	1.6	0.0	64

[a]Genital warts (HPV), genital herpes, hepatitis B, HIV/AIDS.
[b]Gonorrhea, syphilis, chlamydia, PID (women only), NGU (men only).

Table 11.24B **Condom Use with Primary Partner in the Last Sexual Event and during Past Twelve Months (last event in cell percentages; primary partner in row percentages sum to 100)**

Age Category and STIs prior to Past 12 Months	Used in Last Event		With Primary Partner			
	%	N	Never	Some	Always	N
18–29:						
No STI ever	26.3	600	48.4	32.7	18.9	697
Any viral STI[a]	14.0	43	56.5	34.8	8.7	46
Bacterial STI only[b]	22.8	57	49.2	36.9	13.8	65
30–44:						
No STI ever	16.1	874	68.9	19.9	11.2	962
Any viral STI[a]	12.2	90	65.7	21.9	12.4	105
Bacterial STI only[b]	17.5	97	65.8	22.5	11.7	111
45–59:						
No STI ever	5.0	442	84.1	10.7	5.2	503
Any viral STI[a]	c	25	c	c	c	28
Bacterial STI only[b]	7.9	38	87.2	8.5	4.2	47

[a]Genital warts (HPV), genital herpes, hepatitis B, HIV/AIDS.
[b]Gonorrhea, syphilis, chlamydia, PID (women only), NGU (men only).
[c]Fewer than thirty cases.

herpes far outweighs the six HIV-infected individuals. On average, then, there appears to be no particular moderation of sexual behavior among those most likely to contribute to the further spread of infection.

11.4 Reactions to the Risk of Infection

In this section, we consider the two remaining questions raised near the outset of this chapter: What is the extent of knowledge and understanding about methods of avoiding STD infection, and how is this knowledge related to behavior? What portion of the sexually active adult population has changed their sexual behavior in response to the risks of HIV infection, and how have they changed? We begin with the knowledge that adults have regarding strategies for avoiding sexually transmitted infection.

Knowledge about Avoiding STIs and Its Influence on Behavior

The surgeon general's mailing to every household in America in 1988 (see Koop 1988) outlined ways for people to avoid HIV/AIDS. There have been many campaigns before and since to raise public awareness about HIV/AIDS and other STIs, but studies suggest that knowledge may not translate effectively into action. Our survey asked several questions to ascertain how knowledgeable respondents were about methods of avoiding HIV/AIDS and other STIs, and these questions form the basis of the inquiry reported here (see appendix C, section 9, question 19). The general form of the question is to ask the respondent to indicate whether an action like using a condom or having a vasectomy is "very effective," "somewhat effective," or "not at all effective" in preventing one from "getting the AIDS virus through sexual activity."

Table 11.25 shows the distributions of answers to this question. One sees that, in general, the responses were quite accurate in identifying condom use and monogamy with an uninfected partner as very or somewhat effective as preventive measures and in identifying such other activities as use of a diaphragm or a spermicidal cream or a vasectomy as ineffective. The educational campaign to combat ignorance about the risks of HIV/AIDS would appear to have been quite successful. The adult population in the United States does have a functional knowledge about how to prevent contracting HIV/AIDS through sexual activity. Furthermore, this finding is consistent with results from other studies, including Billy et al. (1993) and the National Health Interview Survey. We have looked in detail at the distributions of these answers by the master status variables and by several other behaviors and attitudes, including number of sex partners since age eighteen, whether the respondent ever had an STI, had ever paid for or been paid for sex, had sex education in school, and so forth. Most of these variables show little variation of note, so tables are not presented here. For the percentage who answered correctly that condoms are somewhat or very effective, the range across subgroups was from 86 to 96 percent only, indicating that most all categories of respondents had good knowledge (those with less than a high school education were the least well

Table 11.25   **Knowledge of HIV/AIDS Prevention Techniques (row percentages sum to 100)**

	Effectiveness[a]			
Response	Don't Know	Not at All	Somewhat	Very
Using a diaphragm	3.2	74.5	18.5	3.8
Using a condom	0.2	6.7	52.9	40.2
Using a spermicidal jelly, foam, or cream	2.9	68.1	25.2	3.8
Using a condom with a spermicidal jelly, foam, or cream	1.5	10.2	45.7	42.6
Having a vasectomy	2.1	87.3	5.4	5.3
2 people who do not have HIV/ AIDS having sex only with each other	0.4	7.2	12.9	79.6

[a]Perceived effectiveness "in preventing someone from getting the AIDS virus through sexual activity."

informed, with 86.1 percent answering correctly). Similarly, in response to the question about having sex only with one partner who did not have the AIDS virus, the range of percentages who answered correctly that this was "very effective" was from 70 to 86 percent of the group, so, again with this measure, the population is quite well informed about how to avoid the risk of contracting HIV/AIDS through sexual behavior.[14]

Although adults know about the effectiveness of condoms and monogamy in avoiding the risk of HIV/AIDS, the question remains whether they put that knowledge into practice. Table 11.26 and a few other statistics that we discuss next suggest that the answer is that they do, but insufficiently. Consider the patterns seen in table 11.26, which partitions respondents by the number of partners (top panel) and by their marital/cohabitational status (bottom panel). We see there that, in their last sexual event, those who know that condoms are effective were more likely to use them, but the increase is not dramatic, and the level of usage is not high. On the other hand, there are many instances of

14. One quite intriguing pattern is noted by age. The older respondents were systematically *more* likely correctly to identify monogamy as an effective preventative and were systematically *less* likely than younger respondents correctly to answer that condoms were an effective preventative: the percentages correctly identifying monogamy as effective fell from 84 percent of those aged fifty to fifty-nine to 74 percent of those aged eighteen to twenty-nine, but the percentages identifying condom use as somewhat or very effective rose from 89 percent of those aged fifty to fifty-nine to 96 percent of those aged eighteen to twenty-nine. People learn, but people also hear what they want to hear or retain what conforms to their general belief systems.

We note as well that those who are poor (with an income below the poverty line) are noticeably less well informed than are those with middle or high levels of income: 72.3 percent of the poor correctly answered the question about the efficacy of monogamy, compared to 82.4 percent of the middle- and high-income respondents; 89.0 percent of the poor answered the condom question correctly, compared to 94.0 and 95.8 percent, respectively, of the middle-income and rich respondents.

Table 11.26   Condom Use in the Last Sexual Event and in the Past Twelve Months, by
              Knowledge, Primary/Secondary Partner Status, Number of Partners in the
              Past Twelve Months, and Marital/Cohabitational Status (last event
              in cell percentages; primary and secondary partner in row percentages
              sum to 100)

Perceived Effectiveness of Condoms	Last Event		Primary Partner				Secondary Partner			
	%	N	Never	Some	Always	N	Never	Some	Always	N
Number of partners										
1 partner:										
Not at all	8.1	136	80.9	13.2	5.9	152	N.A.	N.A.	N.A.	N.A.
Somewhat	12.1	1,042	71.5	19.2	9.4	1,153	N.A.	N.A.	N.A.	N.A.
Very	17.1	756	63.7	22.6	13.7	853	N.A.	N.A.	N.A.	N.A.
2 partners:										
Not at all	a	4	a	a	a	6	a	a	a	5
Somewhat	27.0	100	53.9	34.8	11.3	115	53.2	16.5	30.3	109
Very	23.7	93	56.0	25.9	18.1	116	49.1	18.2	32.7	110
3+ partners:										
Not at all	a	7	a	a	a	9	a	a	a	6
Somewhat	36.2	80	55.1	29.6	15.3	98	44.6	18.5	37.0	92
Very	37.2	86	39.4	34.9	25.7	109	39.6	17.0	43.4	106
Marital/cohabitational status										
Married:										
Not at all	5.1	98	81.7	13.0	5.2	115	a	a	a	0
Somewhat	10.0	791	76.3	16.8	6.9	898	a	a	a	2
Very	12.6	525	70.9	19.9	9.1	602	a	a	a	1
Cohabiting:										
Not at all	a	14	a	a	a	20	a	a	a	0
Somewhat	13.3	98	64.8	24.0	11.2	179	a	a	a	6
Very	16.5	79	60.8	27.9	11.4	158	a	a	a	9
Noncohabiting:										
Not at all	19.4	31	59.4	28.1	12.5	32	a	a	a	12
Somewhat	27.8	320	47.7	33.6	18.7	283	47.7	17.6	34.7	193
Very	31.9	323	39.9	30.7	29.4	316	44.7	17.5	37.9	206

Note: N.A. = not applicable.
aFewer than thirty cases.

sex when a condom is not called for and where not using one does not imply
risky behavior. The usage is greater for those who know the right answer and
are having sex with a secondary partner, where the risk would be thought to be
higher; likewise, the rates are higher in noncohabitational sexual unions and
with secondary partners in general. It is nonetheless also the case that the rate
of condom use never reaches 50 percent of the cases, even among those who
know of its efficacy and, on the face of it, are having sex with a partner who
represents substantial risk. So the finding here is both hopeful and sobering.
(This conclusion, also, is consistent with that of Billy et al. 1993, Catania et
al. 1992, and Kost and Forrest 1992b).

We have looked at an analogous pattern of behavior compared to knowledge with regard to the efficacy of monogamy as a strategy for avoiding HIV/AIDS. Here, too, the patterns go in the right directions, but are not very strong. As an example, 15.5 percent of those who know that monogamy is a very effective preventative report having had two or more partners within the last twelve months, while 17.0 percent of those who incorrectly said that monogamy is not at all effective had two or more partners. Similarly, when we looked at whether the respondent had concurrent sex partners, at whether the respondent expects his or her partner to be sexually exclusive, and so forth, there were no notable differences in the responses of those who did and those who did not know that monogamy effectively prevents HIV/AIDS.

We took another approach to the question of the relation between beliefs or judgments and behavior by using a question asked in the context of a set of questions about the respondent's ethical judgments and opinions regarding a wide range of sexually related issues such as pornography, the relation between sex and love, and the sexual needs of men as compared to women. In this series of questions, we asked whether the respondent agreed or disagreed with the statement, "You don't need to use a condom if you know your partner well" (appendix C, section 10, question 11). There is not a clear-cut right answer to this question, so it is legitimately a matter of judgment or emphasis, and we suggest that those who disagree can be considered quite cautious in their approach to avoiding STIs (since the question does not give a context, it is possible that respondents are evincing caution regarding pregnancy as well).

Overall, 59 percent of respondents disagreed with this statement and can be considered cautious about sexually transmitted infections. By gender, 54 percent of men and 63 percent of women disagree, and, by age, the younger disagree most often, with 74 percent of those aged eighteen to twenty-four and about 50 percent of those over age forty-five disagreeing and thus revealing a high level of caution. By race/ethnicity, whites and blacks are more cautious than others, Asians least so. The more education one has, the more likely one is to show caution (i.e., to disagree that one does not need a condom with a partner one knows well). The married respondents are less likely to be cautious by this measure (56 percent disagree) than are the never married (67 percent). It is not surprising that we find that those who said that they believed that condoms were somewhat or very effective in preventing HIV/AIDS were much more likely to disagree (about 60 percent) than those who thought condoms not at all effective (51 percent). Similarly, those who thought monogamy not at all effective in preventing HIV/AIDS were more cautious than those who thought it very effective.

Comparing those who are and are not cautious by this definition (again, measured as disagreement with the statement about not needing a condom with a partner one knows well), those who are more cautious have, in fact, had fewer sex partners, both over their adult lifetime and within the past twelve months. The more cautious also include those men who report having had a same-gender sex partner in the past twelve months, those who have had an STI in the past twelve months, those who report having changed their behavior in response to the HIV/AIDS risk, and those who have been tested for HIV/AIDS.

Table 11.27 shows condom use in the last sex event and with primary and secondary sex partners by this measure of cautiousness and by number of sex partners (top panel) and by marital/cohabitational status (bottom panel). The patterns seen in this table are quite strong: those we describe as more cautious—those who "disagree"—do in fact have noticeably higher rates of condom use, even reaching a rate of 50 percent with secondary partners for those having three or more partners in total (arguably, the riskiest group). Overall, the table tells us that about 22 percent of the cautious used condoms in their last sex act while 9 percent of the less cautious did so. The pattern holds when

Table 11.27 **Condom Use, by Cautiousness, Primary/Secondary Partner Status, Number of Partners in the Past Twelve Months, and Marital/Cohabitational Status (last event in cell percentages; primary and secondary partner in row percentages sum to 100)**

| | Used Condom in Last Event | | Frequency of Condom Use in the Past Twelve Months | | | | | | | |
| | | | With Primary Partner | | | | With Secondary Partner | | | |
	%	N	Never	Some	Always	N	Never	Some	Always	N
Number of partners										
One partner:										
Agree (do not need)	7.3	845	76.9	17.9	5.2	938				
Disagree (do need)	19.0	1,071	62.7	22.0	15.3	1,201				
Two partners:										
Agree (do not need)	17.3	75	71.1	21.1	7.8	90	47.1	24.7	28.2	85
Disagree (do need)	30.6	121	44.5	35.6	19.9	146	54.7	12.2	33.1	139
Three or more partners:										
Agree (do not need)	16.1	62	60.6	28.2	11.3	71	65.7	12.9	21.4	70
Disagree (do need)	46.4	110	39.4	35.2	25.4	142	30.1	20.3	49.6	133
Marital/cohabitational status										
Married:										
Agree (do not need)	6.6	604	80.7	14.6	4.7	700	a	a	a	3
Disagree (do need)	13.7	794	69.9	20.2	9.9	897	a	a	a	0
Cohabiting:										
Agree (do not need)	8.3	96	74.7	20.4	4.9	162	a	a	a	7
Disagree (do need)	20.2	94	54.4	29.0	16.6	193	a	a	a	8
Noncohabiting:										
Agree (do not need)	13.8	269	59.7	30.5	9.9	233	55.9	18.6	25.5	145
Disagree (do need)	40.0	403	35.2	32.7	32.2	395	41.7	16.7	41.7	264
Total:										
Agree (do not need)	8.6	983	75.3	18.8	5.8	1,095	55.5	19.4	25.2	155
Disagree (do need)	22.4	1,302	58.6	24.6	16.7	1,485	42.6	16.2	41.2	272

Note: Statement: "You do not need a condom with a partner you know well" (strongly agree/agree = agree; strongly disagree/disagree = disagree).

aFewer than thirty cases.

we control for marriage and cohabitation, when we control for number of partners, and when we control as well for the primary or secondary status of the partnership.

Attitudes or beliefs about the usefulness of condoms in preventing HIV/AIDS appear to be a more important factor in determining usage than does strict knowledge of the efficacy of condoms. If this distinction proves to be robust and a correct interpretation, it has implications for what an effective strategy may be in persuading adults to use condoms. Influencing their opinion or attitude instead of giving them the flat fact about the matter may pay higher dividends.

The final table in this section—table 11.28—explores this issue further yet. Here, we look at condom use by risk status and by this same measure of caution. The table shows again that there is, in fact, a considerable degree of rationality and responsiveness in the use of condoms. There are those for whom the risks are probably quite small and who do not use condoms extensively. There are also those who are having sex with partners who probably do represent a substantial risk, and, in this circumstance, respondents do actually use condoms more extensively, particularly so if they are among those whom we have characterized as cautious on the basis of their perceived need to use condoms. So the perceptions and the behavior seem to fit together in a sensible and functional manner. Now we give a few details in support of these generalizations.

Table 11.28 shows that the cautious respondents are far more likely always to use a condom with a new primary partner than are the incautious: 36 percent versus 10 percent, respectively, as seen in the top panel of the table. Likewise, the cautious are far less likely never to use a condom with a new primary partner: 32 compared to 61 percent of the incautious. These patterns are seen as well at higher levels of condom use for sex with secondary partners and for new sex partners whom the respondent knew for less than one month before the onset of sexual relations. The middle panel suggests the same pattern. The cautious (those who disagree with the statement) are more likely always to use condoms, however familiar they are with their sex partner, but particularly more likely to use them the less familiar they are with their partner.

Changes in Behavior in Response to HIV/AIDS

We look at two quite different indicators that the respondent has done something in response to the risk of contracting HIV/AIDS: the incidence of having a blood test to determine whether one has HIV/AIDS and the answer to the direct question about whether the respondent has changed his or her behavior in response to the risk of HIV/AIDS. Table 11.29 shows the percentage of respondents who have been tested for HIV/AIDS and also the percentage who responded affirmatively to the question about changing their behavior. From table 11.29A, we see that 26.6 percent of all respondents have been tested for HIV/AIDS—somewhat more men than women, substantially more younger than older people, more blacks than whites or Hispanics, and far more blacks

Table 11.28   **Condom Use in the Past Twelve Months, by Partner Attributes, Cautiousness, and Primary/Secondary Partner Status (cell percentages)**

	% Never Use Condoms		% Always Use Condoms	
	Disagree[a]	Agree[b]	Disagree[a]	Agree[b]
New partners				
New partner within past 12 months:				
New, primary	32	61	36	10
Not new, primary	64	77	13	5
New, secondary	40	56	45	28
Not new, secondary	47	55	34	21
Partners known 1 month or less before first sex				
How long known before sex:[c]				
Known 1 month or less, primary	44	59	26	11
Known 1 month or more, primary	27	62	40	10
Known 1 month or less, secondary	48	[d]	38	[d]
Known 1 month or more, secondary	38	53	44	28
Sum of unfamiliarity attributes				
Familiarity attributes, primary:				
0	65	78	12	5
1	41	66	27	9
2+	39	60	30	13
Familiarity attributes, secondary:				
0	56	60	22	14
1	49	46	36	23
2+	39	56	46	30

[a,b]Agree = strongly agree/agree; Disagree = disagree/strongly disagree, with the statement "You do not need a condom with a partner you know well."

[c]Based only on new partners within the past twelve months.

[d]Fewer than thirty cases.

than Asians or Native Americans. The more educated are more likely to have been tested, as are the nonmarried and those in larger cities.[15]

15. Evidence on the testing of women for the HIV antibody has been reported by Wilson (1993) based on the National Survey of Family Growth 1990 phone survey (NSFG-90). Wilson reports that 35 percent of the women surveyed had been tested. She found that rates were somewhat higher for whites (36 percent) and blacks (35 percent) than for Hispanics (30 percent), for women with thirteen or more years of schooling (40 percent) than for those with twelve or fewer years of schooling (31 percent), for formerly married women (43 percent) than for those who had never married (36 percent) or who were currently married, and for women in their twenties (41 percent) than for those in their thirties (about 35 percent) or between forty and forty-four (28 percent). Wilson also found that women were tested at higher rates in MSA-central cities (40 percent) than in MSA-other (36 percent) or in non-MSAs (32 percent). Our results and the results from the NSFG-90 are similar.

Table 11.29A   **Percentage Who Have Ever Been Tested for HIV/AIDS and Percentage Who Have Changed Behavior in Response to Risk of HIV/AIDS, by Master Status Variables (cell percentages)**

	Ever Tested		Changed Behavior	
	%	N	%	N
Total	26.6	2,943	29.7	3,148
Men	29.4	1,297	35.1	1,406
Women	24.3	1,646	25.4	1,742
18–24	28.4	483	42.9	501
25–29	37.0	430	35.9	457
30–34	31.3	486	32.8	515
35–39	26.1	433	32.6	469
40–44	26.3	388	26.4	413
45–49	20.6	282	19.2	307
50–54	13.2	227	14.4	250
55–59	14.6	213	12.6	231
White	26.5	2,266	26.4	2,407
Black	30.4	365	45.8	402
Hispanic	25.1	215	37.4	235
Asian/Pacific Islander	18.6	59	21.9	64
Native American	15.8	38	37.5	40
Less than HS	24.6	399	28.0	432
HS grad.	22.5	843	27.4	911
Some college	27.7	983	33.0	1,038
College grad.	29.9	485	31.2	519
Postgrad.	34.4	215	23.6	229
Never married	31.4	812	52.4	872
Currently married	23.0	1,568	12.0	1,670
No longer married	30.6	527	47.0	568
Noncohabiting	30.2	1,123	52.1	1,213
Cohabiting	35.6	216	40.5	227
Married	23.0	1,568	12.0	1,670
12 largest central cities	32.9	234	39.9	273
100 largest central cities	34.0	403	40.1	419
Suburb of 12 largest	23.7	333	23.3	356
Suburb of 13–100 largest	25.9	513	27.9	548
Other urban	27.1	1,128	29.6	1,201
Other rural	15.1	332	19.1	351
Poor[a]	25.6	328	38.8	335
Middle[a]	27.0	1,704	28.6	1,758
Rich[a]	31.4	414	28.1	427

[a]Poor = income below official poverty line; rich = income six times the poverty level or higher; middle = income level between "poor" and "rich."

Table 11.29B **Percentage Who Have Ever Been Tested for HIV/AIDS and Percentage Who Have Changed Behavior in Response to Risk of HIV/AIDS, by Number of Partners and Other Sexual Behaviors (cell percentages)**

	Ever Tested		Changed Behavior	
	%	N	%	N
Partners since age 18:				
0	9.4	85	12.8	86
1	16.4	752	9.6	816
2–4	24.4	861	24.8	920
5–10	32.3	647	39.5	678
11–20	36.1	310	47.6	330
21 or more	42.0	269	63.3	286
Partners in past 5 years:				
0	17.1	228	21.2	236
1	20.6	1,545	11.9	1,596
2–4	32.9	750	49.1	772
5–10	40.9	252	67.4	255
11–20	52.0	77	77.5	80
21 or more	58.3	48	68.0	50
Partners in past 12 months:				
0	18.8	341	30.7	371
1	24.6	2,102	20.0	2,241
2–4	36.0	402	68.1	430
5 or more	37.2	98	76.5	102
Any same-gender partners in past 5 years (males)	64.7	51	67.3	52
No same-gender partners in past 5 years (males)	29.3	1,150	34.9	1,195
Ever extramarital sexual relationship	29.3	410	39.3	425
No extramarital sexual relationship	24.7	1,764	17.6	1,823
Never married	30.3	634	53.5	652
Ever pay for sex	31.2	247	36.8	253
Never paid for sex	26.7	2,618	29.7	2,816
Ever been paid for sex	35.2	88	46.7	92
Never been paid for sex	26.8	2,777	29.7	2,977

Table 11.29B shows how dramatically different the rates of testing have been for those who have many partners, for males who have same-gender partners, and for those who have paid or been paid for sex. Those at greater risk, not surprisingly, have a much higher likelihood of having been tested for HIV/AIDS. Table 11.29C reveals the same pattern of greater frequency of testing among those most at risk. We do not find (in tables not shown here) much of a

Table 11.29C   **Percentage Who Have Ever Been Tested for HIV/AIDS and Percentage Who Have Changed Behavior in Response to Risk of HIV/AIDS, by Additional Attributes of Partners (cell percentages)**

	Ever Tested		Changed Behavior	
	%	N	%	N
Unfamiliarity attributes of either primary or secondary partner in past 12 months:				
0	24.1	2,349	20.7	2,497
1	28.4	194	55.2	210
2	43.1	116	65.3	124
3	35.4	144	72.9	155
4+	44.3	131	73.1	134
Nonexclusivity attributes of either primary or secondary partner in past 12 months:				
0	24.3	2,469	22.3	2,623
1	32.1	140	61.2	152
2	44.7	94	73.8	103
3	36.0	86	71.9	89
4	48.2	56	72.9	59
5+	40.4	89	66.7	93
Know either primary or secondary partner less than 1 month[a]	41.4	227	68.7	233
Know neither primary nor secondary partner less than 1 month	28.2	223	56.6	244
Respondent does not expect exclusivity	45.4	86	62.1	87
Respondent expects exclusivity	26.6	2,054	23.5	2,188
Summary of primary and secondary partners' partners:				
0	25.1	2,116	21.0	2,256
1	37.9	174	70.2	188
2	39.6	91	74.0	96
3	44.3	61	70.8	65
4+	41.9	86	68.5	89

[a]Among new partners in the past twelve months.

relation between having been tested and condom use or between having been tested and the familiarity or exclusivity of one's partners. That is, having been tested does not change the choice of partners or practices as far as we can tell. One reason may be that many of those who have been tested may not have done so purely out of self-perceived risk. They may have been tested when donating blood, applying for insurance, entering the military, or routinely after some other diagnosis at an STD clinic. Also, note that almost all those tested do not have HIV/AIDS; thus, they may assume that they do not need to alter their behavior.

There is an interesting literature dealing with the issue of how people respond to risks, and one conclusion in that work is the excessive sensitivity to very small-risk, high-consequence events, like anxiety over the location of nu-clear waste dumps or the collision of the planet with asteroids.[16] Recent work has suggested an interesting bimodality to the response to these low-risk events, one mode with people ignoring the risk as trivial, another evincing excessive concern about these low-probability, high-consequence events (for one such study and a review of the area, see McClelland, Schulze, and Coursey [1993]). If a bimodality does exist in the responses to the low-risk, high-consequence outcome of contracting HIV/AIDS, then those at the one mode with a large concern probably respond by behaving in ways that effectively eliminate that risk—for example, having one sex partner who also is commit-ted to sexual exclusivity. The other mode, those who react by ignoring the slight risk as of little relevance, are those whom we find behaving in ways that reflect disquietingly high risk and that appear to most of us to be irrational.

Table 11.29A tells us that nearly 30 percent of respondents say that they have changed their own sexual behavior as a result of the risk of contracting HIV/AIDS, and more so the men, the younger people, the blacks, the unmar-ried, and those in larger cities.[17] There are dramatically different responses to this question by the number of sex partners one has had since age eighteen, with correspondingly big differences by numbers of partners within the past five years and within the past year. Clearly, those respondents with several part-ners in the past year have not lowered the number of partners so dramatically that they all have but one partner, yet we cannot tell here if they have in fact reduced the total number of recent partners or have changed their sexual prac-tices, selected partners with greater care, and used condoms. The patterns seen across the parts of this table all confirm the same tendency: those who engage in more risky behavior are those who say that they have changed their behavior. This is reassuring, but it may be misleading if the change in behavior is slight, as these men and women are at substantial risk of contracting HIV/AIDS or STIs more generally. Nonetheless, there is an attractive link here between those who appear to be at high risk and those who report some change in their sex-ual behavior.

Multivariate Overview

While the several tables above show relations between important personal background variables and sexual behavior related to risks of infection, most of

16. Kahnemann and Tversky (1979) is an important statement of this phenomenon. The adjec-tives *excessive* or *inadequate* are used in this context when the response is more or less than the response called for from a calculation of the product of the probability of the event happening times the cost if it does occur.

17. Mosher and Pratt (1993) report on the percentage of women between the ages of fourteen and forty-four who, in the 1990 National Survey of Family Growth, said that they had changed their sexual behavior to avoid AIDS. Mosher and Pratt found that, overall, 16 percent of the women surveyed reported a change in behavior, which is somewhat lower than our rate of 25 percent of women respondents. Mosher and Pratt found, as we did, higher rates for younger respondents, for blacks than for Hispanics or whites, and for unmarried respondents.

them do so one or two variables at a time. Here, in a most abbreviated and only suggestive multivariate analysis, we show three statistical, logistic models that estimate the partial influence of some of these key variables, controlling for others (for a discussion of the logistic, see appendix 11.1A). Figure 11.3A reports a logistic model run across all observations on the dummy variable indicating condom use during vaginal intercourse in the last sexual event. We saw in table 11.20 that 16.3 percent of all respondents did use a condom, and that table tells us that men, young adults, blacks, more educated, and unmarried respondents were those more likely to use condoms. This statistical model reported in figure 11.3A shows us that, holding several other characteristics constant, it remains the case that blacks, younger adults (aged eighteen to twenty-four and twenty-five to twenty-nine), and the more educated were systematically among those relatively likely to use a condom in the last sex event, as were those who knew that condoms were effective against HIV/AIDS. Those currently married or cohabiting and those who had had an STI in prior years were relatively unlikely to use a condom in the last sexual event, as were those who thought it unnecessary to use a condom with a partner who is well known to them.

A similar logistic model was estimated on the likelihood of having been tested for HIV/AIDS (fig. 11.3B). Here, we see that the young (those aged twenty-five to twenty-nine), the more educated, those with more sex partners, those who had had an STI in the prior year, those who had recently had a blood transfusion, or those who were intravenous drug users or the sex partner of an intravenous drug user were more likely to have been tested for HIV/AIDS.

Finally, we have estimated the logistic model on the answer to the question about having changed sexual behavior in response to the HIV/AIDS risk (fig. 11.3C). There, we see that males, blacks, those aged twenty-five to twenty-nine, those with relatively many lifetime sex partners, those who have ever had an STI, those who used a condom in the last sexual event, and those who have ever been tested for HIV/AIDS reported changing their sexual behavior because of HIV/AIDS. Those who are currently cohabiting and particularly those currently married were substantially less likely to have changed their behavior.

These logistic models suggest confirmation of the patterns seen in the several tables presented above. Those most at risk of infection are those who have taken steps to reduce that risk, by using condoms, by getting tested for HIV/AIDS, and by indicating, in general, that they have in fact altered their sexual behavior. To this extent, the story told in this chapter is an optimistic one. There is both functional knowledge about and resolve to respond to the risks of sexually transmitted infections. Throughout this chapter, we have seen a fair to moderate degree of sensible behavior among those most at risk of infection. The bottom line on the evidence here is, we suggest, that there is a sizable response to the risks faced, but, nonetheless, a response that is inadequate in magnitude to prevent the transmission of infections, especially the infections with high rates of infectivity. There are signs of success in the fight against

A. Condom Use in Last Sexual Event

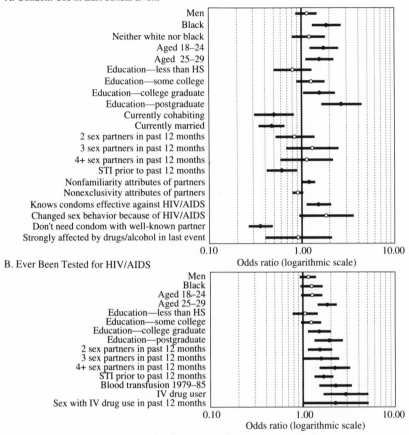

B. Ever Been Tested for HIV/AIDS

C. Reported Change in Sexual Behavior Because of AIDS

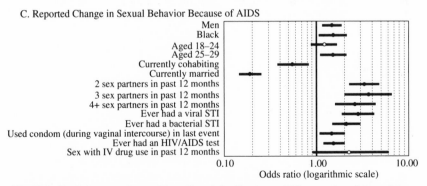

Fig. 11.3 Logistic regressions, odds ratio point estimates and 95 percent confidence intervals. (Solid circles statistically significant at $a = .05$.) A, Condom use in last sexual event. B, Ever been tested for HIV/AIDS. C, Reported change in sexual behavior because of HIV/AIDS.

these infections, but there is much left to be done before they are adequately contained.

APPENDIX 11.1A:
THE LOGISTIC

When we consider a relation between a variable (or many variables) and a proportion of people who have done something, it is often the case that we characterize that relation in a particular form called a *logistic*. A typical shape of a logistic relation is seen in figure 11A.1, where P is the proportion (e.g., the proportion having had a child, or ever been married, or had a sexually transmitted disease, or ever had sexual intercourse), and X might be age, or income, or education level, or race/ethnicity, or some combination of several master status variables or other descriptive variables. A computer program can estimate the relation between P and one or several X's, and our interest here is in the interpretation of the coefficients that are calculated. The mathematical statement of a logistic relation between P and X is of the form

$$P = 1/(1 + e^{-XC}),$$

where each observation or respondent has a value of P and of X and the computer program calculates the value of the coefficient C. There are, unfortunately, three different ways in which one can report these coefficients, and sometimes one or another is more useful, so we describe all three here.

To be explicit, let us consider P to be the proportion of respondents who have ever been married and X to be age in years. For a particular data set (the GSS for the years 1988–91), we estimate that the logistic on these 6,000 observations and the calculated value of C, including an intercept, is $XC = -2.15 + 0.09(\text{age})$. (The standard errors on the intercept and on the age coefficient are 0.12 and 0.003, respectively, with an overall $\chi^2[1]$ of 1,243.4. In these data, the mean age is 45.6 years and the mean proportion 0.80.) Now we move to the interpretation of that coefficient of $+0.09$.

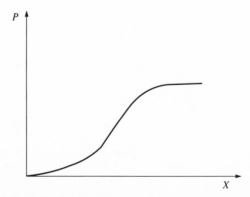

Fig. 11A.1   A logistic relation between the proportion P and the variable X.

The Probability of the Event

For some purposes, it is convenient to think of the proportion as a probability of the event occurring, in this case, the probability of having married by some age. One can show that the change in P for a unit change in X is equal to $C[P(1 - P)]$, evaluated at some level of P such as the mean. Thus, at around the average probability of 0.8, that value is 0.0144 ($= 0.09 \times 0.8 \times 0.2$). Using this value of 0.0144, we would report that the probability of having ever married rises 1.4 percentage points with each year of age around that level. To check this, we compute the probability from the equation at ages thirty-eight, thirty-nine, forty, forty-one, and forty-two, respectively. Those probabilities are .793, .807, .821, .834, and .847, respectively, so the probability does go up by about 1.4 percentage points with each year of age. (Of course, the amount will be different at much younger and much older ages since the shape of the logistic is not a straight line.)

The Odds Ratio

If we calculate the ratio $P/1 - P$, we obtain the odds of the event happening. We can calculate this odds ratio, 0.80/0.20, and can say that, for the whole data set, the odds are four to one that a person has married. Then it would be reasonable to ask how age affects this odds ratio, and one can show that the change in the odds $P/1 - P$ associated with a one-unit change in X is equal to e^C. Using that formula, we calculate its value, which in this case is 1.094 ($= e^{0.09}$). Here, then, we would report that the odds rise by a factor of 1.09 for each additional year of age. If we compute the odds at ages thirty-eight through forty-two, using the values of P listed above, they are 3.83, 4.18, 4.59, 5.02, and 5.54, respectively, or around four to one or five to one at these ages, and we can see that each additional year raises the odds by about 9 percent, or by a factor of 1.09, as the equation suggests. In this case, the increase holds at all ages, which is one reason that this is a convenient way to report the result.

The Log-Odds Ratio

For reasons having more to do with convenience of the computer program than practical application, often one sees results reported as the effect of X on the log-odds ratio, that is, as the effect on the log of the odds. The effect of a unit change in X on the log of the odds is simply the coefficient C, which explains why it is often reported. There is the usefulness here that its sign shows the direction of effect of the variable X on the event, so a negative sign indicates that the event is less likely as the value of X rises, and, for some purposes, that is all that we are interested in. In the case illustrated here, we would report that the effect of age on the log-odds is 0.09, indicating that the proportion rises with age.

CHAPTER 12

Sex and Fertility

One of the things that distinguishes humans from other animals is the absence of a close association between sex and fertility. We have endeavored, with varying degrees of success, to weaken that association from one generation to the next. The evidence in this chapter is that, by now, we have done so quite thoroughly. We have seen in chapter 5 that only 2.8 percent of adults report never having had sex with a partner and in chapter 3 that, of those who have experienced heterosexual sex, over 97 percent have had vaginal intercourse, so we know that the vast majority of adults have engaged in sexual behavior that potentially results in conception. We also note that, in our data set, there are no observations of people who report that they have never had sex with a partner and yet report having borne or fathered a child. The two activities are still related, albeit only weakly.

It will prove useful in the discussion below to catalog the various links in the chain between having sex and having a child (see Davis and Blake 1956). Figure 12.1 identifies several of these. Breaking any one of these links can disconnect the act of sex from having a child. The three steps depicted here—sex, conception, and birth—have between them key decisions and stochastic events that can break one or the other of the links from one of these steps to another.

The link between having sex and conceiving a child involves at least three factors, as suggested in the figure. Some of these three factors—fecundity, sexual practice, and fertility control—are volitional and subject to choice by the person or the partner, while others are not subject to choice but are either personal endowments or stochastic events, as is conception itself. The capacity to produce a fertilized egg is reflected by the fecundity of the man and the woman, and this capacity varies by age, by general health, and by genetic endowment as well as by specific health impairment. Second, sexual practice affects the likelihood of conception, with many sexual activities—oral sex, anal sex, and manual manipulation of the genitals, for example—not at all likely to produce that outcome. Because the definition of a sex partner that we use in our survey did not require vaginal intercourse, it is quite possible for a

Rita C. Butzer and Lucy A. Mackey conducted the empirical work for this chapter. Robert T. Michael directed their work and wrote the chapter.

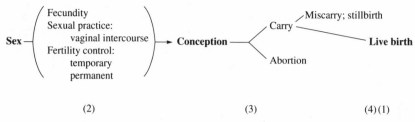

Fig. 12.1 Linkages in the chain of events and decisions that occur between sex and live birth.

respondent to have had a sex partner without having engaged in the one sexual activity that can result in conception.

Third, couples engage in much activity expressly to reduce the likelihood that sex will result in conception, and these several forms of fertility control involve the use of contraception, the timing of sex to avoid the stage of the woman's menstrual cycle in which conception is most likely, and medical procedures that cause sterility in either the man or the woman.

Similarly, we can identify three factors that can break the connection between conception and a live birth, and here again there are some that are subject to choice, such as abortion, and others that are not, such as spontaneous miscarriage and stillbirth. No wonder, then, with all the linkages that must be made to connect the two, that one cannot associate sexual activity and births all that closely.

In this chapter, we discuss several of the links in the chain of association between sexual activity and a live birth. We will discuss the topics as depicted in figure 12.1 by the four numbers at the bottom. (1) We first look at the distributions of live births and compare them to analogous distributions from another data set, the National Survey of Families and Households, and we note the differences in number of children ever born by master status variables. (2) We then look at the incidence of fertility control, noting especially the patterns of incidence of sterility across master status variables. (3) We look in detail at the outcome of conceptions, focusing on the patterns of abortions reported here. (4) We then present some evidence on factors associated with age at first birth, and, in particular, we investigate whether the early onset of vaginal intercourse has a discernible and strong relation to age at first birth.

12.1 The Pattern of Fertility

As the NHSLS is among the first national probability surveys of adult sexual behavior, it is important to establish in as many ways as we can whether respondents accurately informed us about their behavior and views. We do not have a substantial body of high-quality data about sexual practices against which we can compare many of our findings; however, we can compare any results we do have on "sex-related" behaviors. Childbearing is surely one of these, despite the weak link between the two activities. Consequently, in table 12.1,

Table 12.1   **Number of Children Ever Born, by Gender, for Two Data Sets—the NHSLS and the National Survey of Families and Households (NSFH) (row percentages)**

| | Children Ever Born | | | | | | | |
	0	1	2	3	4	5	%	N
Women								
Never married:								
NHSLS	70	13	10	3	2	2	24	
NSFH	68	14	10	5	2	2	19	
Married:								
NHSLS	14	16	32	22	10	6	55	
NSFH	13	18	32	21	8	7	56	
Divorced:								
NHSLS	20	21	25	20	8	5	15	
NSFH	14	20	30	19	9	8	16	
Widowed:								
NHSLS	5	17	25	33	10	10	3	
NSFH	8	11	30	15	14	22	4	
Separated:								
NHSLS	8	19	35	23	10	4	3	
NSFH	9	15	28	21	9	18	5	
All:								
NHSLS	28	16	26	18	8	5		1,737
NSFH	24	17	27	18	8	7		4,137
Men								
Never married:								
NHSLS	91	5	2	0	1	0	34	
NSFH	92	6	1	1	0	0	27	
Married:								
NHSLS	17	21	32	16	8	5	52	
NSFH	18	18	31	17	9	7	58	
Divorced:								
NHSLS	24	19	31	14	7	5	12	
NSFH	24	25	24	15	7	5	11	
Widowed:								
NHSLS	. . .	. . .	. . .	. . .	. . .	. . .	1	
NSFH	16	10	23	23	10	19	1	
Separated:								
NHSLS	. . .	. . .	. . .	. . .	. . .	. . .	2	
NSFH	16	27	24	17	8	7	3	
All:								
NHSLS	43	16	22	10	6	4		1,402
NSFH	38	16	22	12	6	5		3,124

Note: ". . ." indicates fewer than thirty cases.

we show in detail the pattern of number of children ever born as reported by our respondents and by the respondents in another high-quality recent national survey that did not focus on sexual behavior. To enhance the comparison, we look jointly at the pattern by gender and marital status in this table. In other comparisons not shown here, we have made the same comparison by gender and narrow age group or by gender and education level. The conclusions that we reach in all three of these comparisons are reflected in table 12.1: the patterns of children ever born in our sample appear to be very similar indeed to the patterns seen in the comparison survey, the National Survey of Families and Households (NSFH) (for analyses of the NSFH data, see Sweet, Bumpass, and Call 1988).

The right-hand column of table 12.1 tells us the percentage of respondents of that gender who fell into that marital status group, and there we see that the proportions were quite similar among adults aged eighteen to fifty-nine from the two surveys; for example, about 30 percent of the men and 20 percent of the women were never married in each survey, about 55 percent of both men and women were currently married in each, and so forth. Regarding fertility itself, notice how similar the reported behavior is. From the upper panel of the table, we see that, of the women who were never married, for instance, 70 or 68 percent have had no children in both surveys, 13 or 14 percent have had one child, 10 percent have had two children, and 7 or 9 percent have had three or more. For the large group of currently married women, the same pattern is again seen from both surveys: 14 or 13 percent of these women have had no children, 16 or 18 percent have had one child, 32 percent have had two children, and so forth. For the other marital categories for women and for the men as well, one sees here a very close conformity of the patterns of numbers of births reported by the respondents in the two surveys. Table 12.1 also tells us that one-quarter of the women and over 40 percent of the men in our survey have not had a child and that about 13 and 10 percent of the women and men, respectively, have had four or more children.

Table 12.2 reports the distribution of number of children ever born by the several master status variables as well as gender. There one sees the evidence of the high rates of several children for the women and men in the oldest cohorts, who were in their twenties during the peak of the baby boom. Notice that, among those whose fertility is completed (i.e., those over, say, age forty-four), well over 80 percent of both the men and the women have had a child.

Notice the pattern of numbers of children by education level by gender. It has been well established that among women, but not men, those with higher levels of education have fewer children. The explanation for this pattern is that well-educated women's time has a relatively high value as measured by the market earnings that they can receive, and, since raising children is quite time intensive, those whose time has a high value tend to have fewer children. (Since, traditionally, men have not spent so much time raising their children, the higher time value of more educated men has not been associated with lower

Table 12.2A   **Number of Children Ever Born, by Master Status Variable, —Women (row percentages)**

| | \multicolumn{7}{c}{Number of Children Ever Born} | | | | | | |
	0	1	2	3	4	5+	N
All	28	16	26	18	8	5	1,743
Age:							
18–24	64	20	11	4	0	0	274
25–29	37	21	27	11	4	1	232
30–34	26	15	33	18	4	3	290
35–39	18	19	31	18	8	6	265
40–44	21	15	29	23	9	3	229
45–49	11	15	26	30	9	9	168
50–54	15	10	24	21	22	8	143
55–59	6	8	24	26	18	18	140
Marital status:							
Nev. marr., not coh.	72	13	8	3	1	2	335
Nev. marr., coh.	60	14	18	3	4	1	73
Married	14	16	32	22	10	6	947
Div./sep./wid., not coh.	14	21	28	23	9	5	310
Div./sep./wid., coh.	30	16	23	18	5	7	56
Education:							
Less than HS	13	14	22	24	13	14	246
HS grad. or eq.	18	16	29	21	10	5	512
Some coll./voc.	32	17	25	15	7	3	584
Finished coll.	42	16	25	11	4	2	280
Master's/adv. deg.	41	19	23	13	1	3	108
Religion:							
None	45	14	22	13	4	2	151
Type I Prot.	29	16	29	15	7	4	421
Type II Prot.	18	18	25	22	10	8	591
Catholic	32	15	26	16	7	4	473
Jewish	. . .	. . .	. . .	. . .	. . .	. . .	29
Other	40	22	16	8	11	3	37
Race/ethnicity:							
White	30	16	25	17	7	4	1,312
Black	16	17	25	20	9	14	244
Hispanic	22	16	29	20	10	4	133
Asian	. . .	. . .	. . .	. . .	. . .	. . .	28
Native Am.	. . .	. . .	. . .	. . .	. . .	. . .	26

Note: Nev. marr., not coh. = never married, not cohabiting; nev. marr., coh. = never married, cohabiting; div./sep./wid., not coh. = divorced/separated/widowed, not cohabiting; div./sep./wid., coh. = divorced/separated/widowed, cohabiting; less than HS = less than high school; HS grad. or eq. = high school graduate or equivalent; some coll./voc. = some college/vocational school; finished coll. = finished college; master's/adv. deg. = master's/advanced degree; Type I/II Prot. = Type I/II Protestant; Native Am. = Native American. ". . ." indicates fewer than thirty cases.

Table 12.2B   **Number of Children Ever Born, by Master Status Variable—Men (row percentages)**

	Number of Children Ever Born						
	0	1	2	3	4	5+	N
All	43	16	22	10	6	4	1,400
Age:							
18–24	87	8	4	0	0	0	223
25–29	66	21	10	3	1	0	221
30–34	47	23	17	8	3	2	228
35–39	31	17	32	10	8	1	202
40–44	17	22	34	14	8	4	185
45–49	19	13	32	19	9	6	139
50–54	14	7	34	26	15	4	108
55–59	12	8	27	18	11	24	91
Marital status:							
Nev. marr., not coh.	93	4	1	0	1	0	399
Nev. marr., coh.	84	11	3	0	2	0	61
Married	17	21	32	16	8	6	721
Div./sep./wid., not coh.	25	21	28	14	8	4	165
Div./sep./wid., coh.	18	29	26	16	3	8	38
Education:							
Less than HS	40	16	19	10	9	6	189
HS grad. or eq.	39	18	22	10	6	4	402
Some coll./voc.	46	15	21	10	5	2	446
Finished college	49	13	22	10	3	2	237
Master's/adv. deg.	36	18	27	12	5	2	119
Religion:							
None	51	16	16	9	6	2	193
Type I Prot.	41	15	24	12	5	2	322
Type II Prot.	40	16	23	9	7	5	406
Catholic	41	17	20	12	6	4	373
Jewish	. . .	. . .	. . .	. . .	. . .	. . .	26
Other	54	29	12	2	2	0	41
Race/ethnicity:							
White	43	16	23	10	5	3	1,094
Black	43	17	15	10	7	8	155
Hispanic	39	16	14	13	14	5	102
Asian	44	24	20	9	3	0	34
Native Am.	. . .	. . .	. . .	. . .	. . .	. . .	15

Note: See the note to table 12.2A.

fertility.) This pattern is seen in table 12.2 by comparing the differences in numbers of children ever born across education levels for women and for men. For the women, we see quite substantial differences: to suggest the patterns by the extremes, we see that only 17 percent of the women with postgraduate education but 51 percent of those with less than a high school education have three or more children. For men, on the other hand, the comparable percentages are 19 and 25 percent, respectively. The conformity of this well-known, rather subtle pattern of differences for women and not for men is a further indication of the quality of these data.

Table 12.2 shows the differences in fertility by marital status, and these too are as expected. One sees that 72 percent of the women who have never married and are not cohabiting have had no children, but a small percentage of the never-married women have had several. Of the men, 93 percent of those who have never married and are not cohabiting report never having had a child, a proportion that does not seem consistent with the report by the never-married women. In the comparisons by race/ethnicity, black women but not men report relatively high rates of fertility. Among the religious groups, those with no religious affiliation and those of other (mostly Eastern) religions have notably fewer children, and Type II Protestants have substantially more children than Catholics and Type I Protestants, who appear to have quite similar fertility behavior. Clearly, the NHSLS sample reports fertility patterns much like other samples drawn from this population. With that assurance, we turn to the critically important links between sex and conception and between conception and live birth.

12.2   Fertility Control

The mechanisms by which conception is controlled are several, as outlined in figure 12.1 above. There is little known regarding the selection of sexual practice as a means of controlling fertility, and, while our data can support study of this matter, we will not undertake it here. There is growing interest in the patterns of sterilization as a means of controlling fertility, as that practice acquires popularity, and we summarize the information in our data about this practice.

The aspect most frequently studied and thus best understood is the choice of contraceptive technique (see, e.g., Ryder and Westoff 1971; Westoff and Ryder 1977; Kahn, Rindfuss, and Guilkey 1990). Fertility control through contraception is not a major focus of our study, and, faced with the need to keep our survey questionnaire to the tolerable length of ninety minutes on average, we did not inquire about details regarding contraceptives, except for information about condom use as described in chapters 3 and 11. We asked respondents only a few questions about their contraceptive practices, and then only in relation to their primary and secondary partners within the past twelve months or specifically about the last sexual event.[1] Thus, from our data, we cannot characterize the contraceptive strategies (Michael and Willis 1976) that respondents have used over the lifetime, for example, nor can we characterize

1. The question was posed in the context of asking about vaginal intercourse with a specific partner who had been identified as the primary or as a secondary partner. Two questions were asked: "When you had vaginal intercourse with (PARTNER), how often did you use condoms?" and "When you had vaginal intercourse with (PARTNER), how often did you use any other methods of birth control?" The response categories were "always, usually, sometimes, rarely, or never" (see appendix C, section 4, e.g., question 31).

the details of the techniques used. We summarize in this section the frequency of use of contraception (including condom use) and sketch the patterns of its use by several master status variables. Clearly, this is an area deserving much more attention in subsequent research.

There are several reasons why a couple would not use contraception. These include, most obviously, times when the couple wishes to conceive and, additionally, times when the couple may know that conception is not possible (e.g., when one of the two is sterile, when the woman is already pregnant, during the infertile period of the menstrual cycle, and so on). There is also the possibility that the couple is ill informed about the need for or efficacy of contraception, or is unable to acquire contraception (at least at the moment), or does not rationally consider the likelihood of conception when entering into a sexual event that turns out to include vaginal intercourse. Because condoms are the only form of contraception that serves as protection from both disease and conception, the use of that contraceptive will be somewhat different from other contraceptive choices. As our question asked how often the respondent used contraception, we cannot distinguish whether an answer like "sometimes" means that the respondent's sporadic use of contraception was purposive (i.e., there was no risk of conception and therefore no need of contraception) or not (i.e., the couple was thereby risking an unwanted pregnancy). Similarly, a response of "never" does not necessarily mean that the couple faced a high risk of an unwanted conception if they knew one of the two was sterile or if over the past twelve months (the time frame for the question) they had been attempting to conceive. We note these several complexities in order to emphasize that the interpretation of the information in the accompanying tables is not self-evident.

Table 12.3 shows the usage of contraception during the past twelve months separately by gender and by the primary and the secondary sex partner. We see that half of all respondents say that they always use some form of contraception with their primary partner and that a much higher rate always use it with their secondary partner. On the other hand, nearly one-third report that they never use contraception with a primary partner, and about one-quarter never use it with a secondary partner. These patterns for usage with the primary partner are quite similar for the men and the women. These rates are, of course, far higher than the rates of condom use reported in table 11.18B, where about 12 percent used that form of contraceptive and disease prevention with their primary partner and about one-third with their secondary partner. Other patterns can be discerned. For example, usage declines rapidly with age beyond the late forties, as one might expect. It is particularly high for women and men who never married and are living alone, is higher among the more educated men but not the women, is not particularly related to religion, is notably lower for the black women compared to the white or Hispanic women, is lower for the black men than for the white men, and is lower for Catholic men than for Protestant men.

Table 12.3A **Contraception Use in the Past Twelve Months, with Primary Partner, by Gender (row percentages by gender)**

	Contraception Used—Women					Contraception Used—Men				
	Always	Usually	Some/ Rarely	Never	N	Always	Usually	Some/ Rarely	Never	N
All	53	6	9	31	1,436	47	9	13	31	1,186
Age:										
18–24	56	13	18	13	241	62	16	11	12	179
25–29	56	9	11	24	214	56	6	19	19	193
30–34	59	6	9	26	253	39	17	17	26	190
35–39	58	5	5	31	226	49	8	10	33	177
40–44	48	4	6	41	190	47	5	9	39	166
45–49	50	1	9	40	132	35	3	13	49	112
50–54	41	2	6	52	106	45	3	5	47	94
55–59	36	0	3	61	74	34	3	11	52	73
Marital status:										
Nev. marr., not coh.	63	8	15	13	224	63	14	10	12	276
Nev. marr., coh.	61	12	12	15	66	48	9	9	33	54
Married	50	6	8	36	889	41	7	15	37	683
Div./wid./sep., not coh.	54	5	9	31	185	46	7	10	38	121
Div./wid./sep., coh.	58	6	8	28	53	54	3	8	35	37
Education:										
Less than HS	49	4	14	33	192	40	5	14	41	152
HS grad. or eq.	50	4	8	38	437	42	9	14	35	342
Some coll./voc.	58	6	10	26	488	51	9	12	28	374
Finished coll.	54	10	6	30	230	50	9	16	25	205
Master's/adv. deg.	52	11	10	27	81	57	11	7	26	106
Religion:										
None	56	5	12	26	129	51	8	13	29	158
Type I Prot.	52	5	8	34	350	46	8	10	36	278
Type II Prot.	56	6	9	30	479	44	10	14	33	341
Catholic	51	7	10	32	392	48	8	15	29	323
Jewish	. . .	. . .	. . .	. . .	24	. . .	. . .	. . .	. . .	19
Other	44	11	11	33	33	55	18	6	21	33
Race/ethnicity:										
White	54	6	8	32	1,107	49	9	13	30	945
Black	47	6	16	31	268	41	8	17	35	180
Hispanic	52	6	9	33	151	37	9	14	40	108
Asian	. . .	. . .	. . .	. . .	24	. . .	. . .	. . .	. . .	26
Native Am.	. . .	. . .	. . .	. . .	23	. . .	. . .	. . .	. . .	13

Note: See the note to table 12.2A.

Seventy percent of women and 60 percent of men report that they always use contraception with the secondary partner, a higher rate than with the primary partner. There are so few women in the sample with a secondary partner that patterns of contraceptive use cannot be studied here. For the men, the patterns do not look dramatically different between primary and secondary partners.

Table 12.3B   **Contraception Use in the Past Twelve Months, with Secondary Partner, by Gender (row percentages by gender)**

	Contraception Used—Women					Contraception Used—Men				
	Always	Usually	Some/ Rarely	Never	N	Always	Usually	Some/ Rarely	Never	N
All	70	2	4	23	164	60	6	8	26	265
Age:										
18–24	73	4	4	18	67	60	10	9	21	70
25–29	. . .	. . .	. . .	. . .	20	70	3	10	17	60
30–34	. . .	. . .	. . .	. . .	28	66	7	7	20	41
35–39	. . .	. . .	. . .	. . .	21	64	3	6	27	33
40–44	. . .	. . .	. . .	. . .	14	44	3	12	42	36
45–49	. . .	. . .	. . .	. . .	9	. . .	. . .	. . .	. . .	12
50–54	. . .	. . .	. . .	. . .	4	. . .	. . .	. . .	. . .	7
55–59	. . .	. . .	. . .	. . .	1	. . .	. . .	. . .	. . .	5
Marital status:										
Nev. marr., not coh.	69	3	8	21	77	67	8	8	18	145
Nev. marr., coh.	. . .	. . .	. . .	. . .	8	. . .	. . .	. . .	. . .	13
Married	. . .	. . .	. . .	. . .	15	39	3	12	46	33
Div./wid./sep., not coh.	76	0	0	24	53	51	4	10	35	69
Div./wid./sep., coh.	. . .	. . .	. . .	. . .	8	. . .	. . .	. . .	. . .	3
Education:										
Less than HS	. . .	. . .	. . .	. . .	24	32	10	13	45	31
HS grad.	55	2	8	35	40	65	3	9	23	69
Some coll./ voc.	79	3	3	15	67	54	5	11	30	87
Finished coll.	. . .	. . .	. . .	. . .	23	72	7	3	17	58
Master's/adv. deg.	. . .	. . .	. . .	. . .	9	. . .	. . .	. . .	. . .	18
Religion:										
None	. . .	. . .	. . .	. . .	24	67	6	11	17	36
Type I Prot.	71	2	2	24	42	57	4	5	34	56
Type II Prot.	73	0	6	21	52	51	5	10	33	78
Catholic	62	3	3	31	32	67	7	10	16	73
Jewish	. . .	. . .	. . .	. . .	4	. . .	. . .	. . .	. . .	3
Other	. . .	. . .	. . .	. . .	3	. . .	. . .	. . .	. . .	10
Race/ethnicity:										
White	73	3	3	22	114	61	5	8	27	186
Black	63	4	10	24	51	61	8	11	21	66
Hispanic	. . .	. . .	. . .	. . .	20	. . .	. . .	. . .	. . .	27

Note: See the note to table 12.2A.

Table 12.4   **Rates of Sterility, by Cause, Gender, and Master Status (cell percentages)**

	Women			Men		
	All	By Choice	Age 45+	All	By Choice	Age 45+
All	38.3	28.8	74.5	12.8	11.3	27.4
Age:						
18–24	4.7	3.3	N.A.	.9	.9	N.A.
25–29	18.0	16.7	N.A.	.9	.9	N.A.
30–34	24.4	21.6	N.A.	6.6	4.8	N.A.
35–39	36.1	32.3	N.A.	13.3	12.3	N.A.
40–44	48.5	43.2	N.A.	22.0	21.5	N.A.
45–49	63.7	51.8	63.7	22.9	19.3	22.9
50–54	72.0	44.1	72.0	25.7	21.1	25.7
55–59	90.0	40.7	90.0	36.3	33.0	36.3
Marital status:						
Nev. marr., not coh.	13.0	8.0	54.6	.8	.5	. . .
Nev. marr., coh.	15.1	11.0	. . .	4.9	3.3	. . .
Married	45.0	34.2	77.8	18.4	17.1	28.9
Div./wid./sep., not coh.	50.6	38.7	73.0	20.0	14.6	25.4
Div./wid./sep., coh.	37.5	32.1	. . .	15.8	15.8	. . .
Education:						
Less than HS	51.6	38.6	76.8	11.6	8.4	27.3
HS grad.	49.2	37.3	82.9	11.7	11.2	24.0
Some coll./voc.	29.9	23.6	67.0	13.6	12.0	32.3
Finished coll.	27.4	18.9	73.3	11.3	10.5	26.5
Master's/adv. deg.	28.4	17.4	59.0	17.4	14.9	25.0
Religion:						
None	34.9	27.0	. . .	11.9	11.3	32.3
Type I Prot.	42.2	30.8	78.6	16.7	14.5	33.3
Type II Prot.	45.8	36.2	77.4	14.2	12.5	35.0
Catholic	29.4	20.4	67.3	9.8	8.8	14.4
Jewish	. . .	. . .	. . .	. . .	. . .	. . .
Other	27.0	21.6	. . .	4.9	4.9	. . .
Race/ethnicity:						
White	37.8	27.8	75.8	14.2	12.8	30.1
Black	46.3	36.1	72.3	7.0	5.1	20.0
Hispanic	31.6	26.3	. . .	9.7	7.8	. . .
Asian	20.0	. . .	. . .	0.0	0.0	. . .
Native Am.	. . .	. . .	. . .	. . .	. . .	. . .

Note: See the note to table 12.2A. N.A. = not applicable. ". . ." = fewer than thirty cases.

In addition to contraception, sterility also breaks the link between sex and conception. We asked the respondent about his or her own sterility, but we did not seek sufficient information to characterize whether the respondent's sex partner was sterile.[2] Table 12.4 shows the rates of sterility by gender for several master status variables. We give those rates both without identifying the reason for the sterility (the column labeled *all*) and specifying that the sterility is "by choice," meaning that the men have had a vasectomy or the women a tubal ligation. This latter category is not precise because another option in the questioning is "partner sterile" and we do not determine whether that partner is sterile by choice or because of illness, accident, or menopause, for instance. We also show the reported rates of sterility for those over age forty-five.

Overall, 12.8 percent of the men and 38.3 percent of the women in the survey report themselves to be sterile. For the men, particularly, it is of interest to note that a vast majority of those who are sterile report themselves to be so by choice, that is, as a result of a vasectomy, not because of an accident or health problems. Table 12.4 shows that the rate rises with age, particularly so for women, of course. It is interesting to note that most demographic research takes the age range fourteen to forty-four as the fertile interval for women, but, as seen in the third column of table 12.4, a sizable percentage of women over the age of forty-four—even 10 percent of those over age fifty-four—still report themselves to be fertile. As the questions were asked, we clearly sought information about the respondent, not the sexual partnership, so the rates shown in table 12.4 should indicate the rates of sterility of the men or the women, not the partnership.

The table reveals lower rates of sterility among men than among women, as we would expect for a group of adults that includes women who have reached menopause, and low rates at younger ages and among those never married. The patterns by education suggest that sterility declines with education for women but not for men. This probably reflects the fact that the less educated women and men are older, but being older is not so closely associated with sterility for men. Catholics have noticeably lower rates of sterility than non-Catholics. Black women report quite high rates of sterility compared to white women, but black men report far lower rates than white men. Now, as it is only necessary for one partner to be sterile to eliminate the chance of conception, it would be sensible to find that if the member of one gender in a partnership is sterile, the member of the other gender would not be expected to also be sterile. So the pattern seen here for blacks and whites is quite intriguing, but, as we

---

2. Questions 11–16 of section 3 address this issue. There we noted that "some men find it physically impossible to father children" and that "some women find it physically impossible to have (more) children," and we asked, "As far as you know, is it possible or impossible for you to father any (more) children" or "to conceive a(nother) baby, that is, to get pregnant (again)?" If the respondent said that it was not possible, we then inquired about the reason, as can be seen in appendix C. If the respondent said that it was possible for him or her to have a child, we did not inquire about the sterility status of the sex partner.

Table 12.5   **Percentages with Lowered Risk of Conception in the Last Sex Event, by Means of Avoidance, Gender, and Marital Status/Living Arrangement**

Marital Status/ Living Arrangement	% with No Sex Partners in Past 12 Months	Those Sexually Active					
		Had No Vaginal Intercourse	Used Condom	Used Other Contraception	Sterile	Pregnant	At Least One of These Means
Women							
Total	14.5	4.4	15.0	44.7	37.1	3.7	75.9
Never married and not cohabiting	30.3	6.6	31.5	49.2	9.3	5.8	69.5
Never married and cohabiting	1.4	7.7	22.0	47.5	15.3	6.3	72.2
Married	3.7	3.5	11.3	43.6	43.8	3.7	77.5
Div./sep./wid. and not cohabiting	35.8	5.1	17.3	44.3	46.7	.5	80.9
Div./sep./wid. and cohabiting	1.8	4.2	4.2	52.1	36.4	5.6	70.9
Men							
Total	10.9	5.4	18.0	36.9	12.9	3.7	56.1
Never married and not cohabiting	23.2	7.1	40.1	41.2	.6	1.5	58.3
Never married and cohabiting	0.0	1.9	19.2	40.4	1.6	11.8	60.7
Married	2.6	4.8	9.6	32.6	17.9	4.6	53.5
Div./sep./wid. and not cohabiting	23.6	5.5	22.3	48.0	19.8	0.0	61.9
Div./sep./wid. and cohabiting	0.0	8.3	9.1	48.5	15.8	5.7	63.2

do not know the sterility status of the partner in each relationship, we cannot pursue this issue with our data.

Table 12.5 performs the complicated task of identifying the fertility risks on the basis of the sexual practices involved in the last sexual event. The table emphasizes how many complexities there are in assessing this risk, as it adjusts for sexual practice, contraceptive use, sterility, and current pregnancy. The first row of the upper panel, which reports on all women in the sample, shows that 14.5 percent had had no sex partners over the past twelve months and were therefore not at risk of conception. Of the remainder, 4.4 percent of those who did have a sex partner did not engage in vaginal intercourse during their most recent sexual event, so they too are not at risk of conception, but of course they may be at risk of sexually transmitted infection. During that last sexual event, 15 percent of the women reported that their partner used a condom, 44.7 percent used other contraceptives, 37 percent were sterile, and 3.7 percent were pregnant. Combining the several ways of lowering the risk of conception during this one sexual event, but not double counting if more than one were used, we find that 75.9 percent of the sexually active women had some protection from conception in their last sexual event.

The first column of table 12.5 shows that a large proportion (about one-third) of the noncohabiting women had no sex partners in the past year, so they were not at risk of conception. About 23 percent of the noncohabiting men were similarly not at risk. While condom use among the sexually active women varied considerably (from 4 percent of the cohabiting, no longer married women to 32 percent of the noncohabiting, never-married women), the overall risk of conception varied much less—between 70 and 80 percent of all five marital status/living arrangement groups of women are estimated to have had protection against the risk of conception, as seen in the right-hand column of table 12.5. Some groups contained more who were sterile, other groups more who used contraception, but for the women overall the risk of conception does not differ dramatically by marital status.

While the men report lower rates of most of these pregnancy-risk-avoiding behaviors, they too do not differ dramatically from group to group in terms of overall risk, but they do face a higher risk than the women. We caution, again, that, since we did not fully establish the fertility status of both partners, these estimates overstate the risk of conception somewhat.

12.3 The Outcome of Conceptions

In this section, we focus on the outcomes of the conceptions reported by our respondents. As we have recast our data somewhat for this section, we take some time at the outset to clarify their nature. Consider the penultimate row of the top panel of table 12.1, which tells us that 16 percent of the 1,737 women in our study had one child. These 277 women (i.e., 16 percent of 1,737) each contributed one observation on one live birth in this new data file. Similarly, 26 percent of these women had two children, and thus 450 women contributed 900 births to this data file. The 18 percent of these women who had three children constitute 312 women and so 936 births, and so forth. In all, if we count up all the births reported by the women in that row, the total would be a little over 3,100. In the same way, if we calculate all the births reported by the men in the lower panel of table 12.1, the total comes to an additional 1,870 births, so we then have a grand total of over 4,970 births among the men and women in our study. Additionally, these respondents reported on their miscarriages, their abortions, and their stillbirths. Taking all these—the total number of *conceptions* reported by the respondents—we have 6,608 conceptions.

That set of 6,608 conceptions—4,176 reported by women and 2,432 by men—is the data base that we use in this section of the chapter.[3] With these

3. The discrepancy between the men and the women is partially explained by the fact that there are only about 80 percent as many men as women in the survey. Also, as can be seen in table 12.1 for both the NHSLS and the NSFH, a much larger portion of the men report no children.

If we calculate the number of men and of women who reported at least one live birth, that number is 799 men (1402 less the 43 percent who had no children, according to table 12.1), and 1,251 women (1737 less the 28 percent who had no children, according to table 12.1), so 61 percent of the respondents who reported a live birth were women, and from table 12.6 we see that 63 percent of the conceptions were reported by women (4,176 as a percentage of 6,608).

data, we can look at outcomes from these conceptions in terms of live births, stillbirths, miscarriages and abortions; we can see how all 6,608 of these conceptions turned out. (Pregnancies that were in progress at the time of the interview are not included.) Now, some of these conceptions occurred many years ago and are reported by the older respondents in our survey. As we proceed, we sometimes characterize the circumstance as at the time of the conception. We do this, for example, when we describe the marital status and living arrangements of the respondent at the time of that particular conception. At other points in the discussion, we characterize the status of the respondent at the date of the interview in 1992. The difference is important: consider a fifty-four-year-old widower who was responsible for two conceptions years before, one when he was twenty and not yet married, the other when he was thirty and married. Both these conceptions can be characterized in terms of different marital statuses and ages in one or another of the tables below. We make clear how each table is constructed.

Table 12.6 shows the basic outcome of all 6,608 conceptions.[4] The top row of both table 12.6A (women) and table 12.6B (men) shows that about 75 percent of all the conceptions reported have resulted in live births. Averaging over the reports by the women and men, the top row also tells us that miscarriages are the second most frequent outcome of a conception (12.3 percent of the total), that abortions constitute another 10.0 percent of the total conceptions, that a very small percentage are stillbirths, and that the outcome of less than 1 percent of pregnancies was not reported.

It is useful to pause here and note the apparently large difference between the reported rate of abortion here—about 10 percent, overall—and the often cited "abortion ratio" publicized by the Alan Guttmacher Institute. In a recent publication, for instance, that ratio for 1988 was estimated at 28.6 percent overall and as high as 40.6 for women ages eighteen to nineteen and 31.3 for women ages twenty to twenty-four (Henshaw, 1992, 86). Another figure that is often cited is Guttmacher's estimate that 40 percent of pregnancies of women under age twenty ended in abortion by the mid-1980s (Hayes, 1987, 54). These estimates are based not on surveys of individuals but on canvassing abortion service providers to obtain an estimate of the number of abortions performed and then combining these numbers with data on the number of live births from *Vital Statistics,* collected by the National Center for Health Statistics. Knowing the age of the women involved in the live births and the abortions, one can then form the ratio of abortions to live births plus abortions for women of a given age category and for women overall. This is what has been done in several publications. Since our figure includes in the denominator miscarriages and stillbirths as well, that simple difference in the calculation partly explains the

---

4. The reader will notice that the race/ethnicity segments of this table actually report more than 6,608 conceptions. The explanation is that the core 6,608 represent the cross-sectional sample of 3,159 respondents; the black and Hispanic respondents in the oversample are used any time we partition by race/ethnicity, but not when we use the "self-weighting" cross-sectional sample.

differences between the rate we report and the ratio reported by the Gutt-macher Institute.

Far more important, our number includes retrospective information on pregnancies over the whole lifetime and therefore includes pregnancies from the years before abortion was legalized. When we calculate that same ratio of abortions to abortions plus live births for those aged eighteen to twenty-four, we get 29.0 and 34.4 percent from the data in table 12.6 as reported by women and men, respectively. So the Guttmacher estimates and the reports in our data are roughly similar (this is particularly reassuring in light of Jones and For-rest 1992).

From other surveys, it has been concluded that abortions are often under-reported, and probably they are. Perhaps in the present context of reporting on a whole range of sexual behavior under the particular procedures for protecting confidentiality that our survey employed, and knowing that ours would not involve repeated surveying in the future, respondents found the circumstances of our survey as safe and encouraging as any can be. Thus, we may have come quite close to an accurate reporting of the outcomes of all pregnancies.[5]

5. Because of the interest in abortion reporting and the inadequacy of the information in many household surveys, we comment briefly here on the abortion data we have obtained.

The question about abortions was asked twice in our survey, first in the face-to-face interview after about twenty minutes of interviewing in a section of the questionnaire about fertility. It fol-lowed a series of questions about the number of pregnancies, then the number of live births, mis-carriages, stillbirths, and then abortions (see appendix C, section 3, question 10). That variable is called Abort in this footnote. The second time the question was asked was near the end of the ninety-minute interview, in a self-administered portion of the questionnaire in which the answers were not seen by the interviewer (see appendix C, sections 4M and 4F, question 7). That variable is called SAQabort in this note. N.A. indicates no answer.

Comparing the two answers for the men and the women separately, we find the following distri-bution of answers to the two questions:

		Men					Women		
			SAQabort					SAQabort	
		Yes	No	N.A.			Yes	No	N.A.
	Yes	146	1	8		Yes	261	6	13
Abort	No	50	1043	79	Abort	No	32	1231	66
	N.A.	11	63	9		N.A.	9	119	21

So of the cases with two answers, 95.9 percent of men and 97.5 percent of women gave the same answer both times, or if we include the N.A.s (no answers), 84.9 percent of men and 85.9 percent of women gave the same answer both times. The correlation, excluding the N.A.s, is 0.89.

The "no answer" response in the face-to-face interview includes many respondents who were not in fact asked the question about abortions, because if they had listed as many live births as they had reported pregnancies, the questions about miscarriages, stillbirths, and abortions were skipped. (We had urged respondents to include "all your pregnancies, whether they resulted in a live birth, stillbirth, abortion, or miscarriage, even those which ended very early.")

Notice that more respondents—both men and women—said that they (or their partner) had had an abortion in the self-administered questionnaire than in the face to-face interview (52 more men and 22 more women). Clearly, our data are not perfect, but the internal consistency of these data is quite impressive. Incidentally, in section 12.3 of this chapter we have used the variable Abort from the face-to-face interview.

Table 12.6A   **Outcomes of Conceptions, by Master Status—Women**

Social Characteristic	Outcome of Conception (%)					Total N
	Live Birth	Miscarriage	Abortion	Stillbirth	Unknown	
All	75.7	13.4	9.7	.6	.6	4,176
Age:						
18–24	57.5	16.8	23.5	.4	1.9	268
25–29	70.0	14.6	14.6	0.0	.7	424
30–34	73.9	11.2	14.0	.6	.3	679
35–39	76.6	12.4	9.9	.6	.4	684
40–44	76.4	14.0	7.7	1.0	.9	573
45–49	73.5	16.4	9.4	.5	.2	562
50–54	85.0	12.5	1.6	.7	.2	447
55–59	84.3	12.0	2.4	.7	.6	535
Total						4,172
Marital status (current):						
Nev. marr., not coh.	61.2	9.4	27.1	.7	1.7	299
Nev. marr., coh.	49.2	17.5	32.5	0.0	.8	120
Married	78.9	13.5	6.8	.5	.3	2,671
Div./sep./wid., not coh.	75.4	14.2	9.0	.8	.6	878
Div./sep./wid., coh.	68.3	14.8	14.8	.7	1.4	142
Total						4,110
Education:						
Less than HS	80.4	13.4	5.2	.8	.1	841
HS grad. or eq.	78.8	10.4	9.8	.7	.4	1,351
Some coll./voc.	73.3	14.5	11.2	.2	.9	1,255
Finished coll.	70.8	17.1	10.9	.8	.4	496
Master's/adv. deg.	65.3	17.8	14.4	1.0	1.5	202
Total						4,145
Religion (current):						
None	62.4	18.8	17.1	.7	1.0	298
Type I Prot.	74.1	13.5	11.0	.4	1.0	958
Type II Prot.	79.3	12.9	6.7	.7	.4	1,646
Catholic	77.5	12.3	9.5	.5	.2	1,028
Jewish	68.1	15.3	15.3	1.4	0.0	72
Other	58.1	14.0	26.7	1.2	0.0	86
Other Protestant	75.0	14.8	6.8	1.1	2.3	88
Total						4,176
Race/ethnicity:						
White	75.1	14.3	9.5	.5	.6	2,983
Black	78.8	10.7	9.1	1.1	.4	1,041
Hispanic	75.9	12.0	11.4	.8	0.0	493
Asian	66.0	11.3	20.8	0.0	1.9	53
Native Am.	83.1	10.8	4.8	0.0	1.2	83
Total						4,653

Note: See the note to table 12.2A.

Table 12.6B   Outcomes of Conceptions, by Master Status—Men

Social Characteristic	Outcome of Conception (%)					Total N
	Live Birth	Miscarriage	Abortion	Stillbirth	Unknown	
All	76.9	10.5	10.4	.7	1.5	2,432
Age:						
18–24	51.4	14.9	27.0	0.0	6.8	74
25–29	60.0	14.2	23.7	.5	1.6	190
30–34	73.0	11.3	14.1	.6	.9	319
35–39	77.2	9.6	9.6	1.5	2.0	394
40–44	73.1	10.6	13.1	1.3	1.9	480
45–49	81.2	8.3	8.8	.3	1.4	362
50–54	85.0	13.0	1.7	.3	0.0	301
55–59	90.2	7.5	1.6	0.0	.7	307
Total						2,427
Marital status (current):						
Nev. marr., not coh.	33.8	7.4	50.0	.7	8.1	136
Nev. marr., coh.	48.4	22.6	25.8	0.0	3.2	31
Married	82.3	10.6	5.7	.7	.7	1,742
Div./sep./wid., not coh.	73.5	9.3	16.0	0.0	1.3	388
Div./sep./wid., coh.	74.5	7.4	8.5	2.1	7.4	94
Total						2,391
Education:						
Less than HS	81.3	7.4	6.3	1.9	3.0	364
HS grad. or eq.	81.5	10.4	7.2	.1	.7	709
Some coll./voc.	71.1	12.3	13.9	.8	2.0	764
Finished coll.	73.9	11.3	12.9	.8	1.1	371
Master's/adv. deg.	79.2	8.0	11.8	0.0	.9	212
Total						2,420
Religion (current):						
None	72.0	15.3	10.7	1.0	1.0	300
Type I Prot.	78.0	12.2	8.5	.9	.4	551
Type II Prot.	76.5	9.3	12.1	.5	1.7	778
Catholic	79.2	8.6	8.9	.6	2.6	660
Jewish	67.6	11.8	14.7	0.0	5.9	34
Other	63.0	6.5	30.4	0.0	0.0	46
Other Protestant	83.3	11.1	3.7	1.9	0.0	54
Total						2,423
Race/ethnicity:						
White	77.2	11.4	9.8	.8	.9	1,845
Black	74.1	9.2	14.0	0.0	2.8	436
Hispanic	76.7	8.0	11.5	1.0	2.8	288
Asian	63.6	10.9	25.5	0.0	0.0	55
Native Am.	87.1	3.2	6.5	0.0	3.2	31
Total						2,655

Note: See the note to table 12.2A.

Returning to the figures reported in table 12.6, there is no notable difference in the dispositions of the conceptions by the gender of the respondents. The men have a slightly lower rate of reported miscarriages, but the men and women here are reporting essentially the same patterns. There are big differences by other master status variables, however. Age is a major factor, with younger respondents reporting higher rates of miscarriage and dramatically higher rates of abortion and therefore lower rates of live births as a percentage of all conceptions. Here, *age* means age at the time of the interview, not age at the time of the conception, so the older respondents are reporting on the outcomes from their conceptions in earlier years.

Marital status has a profoundly large association with the nature of the outcome of the pregnancy, and here we measure marital status at the time of the interview, not at the time of conception. For the reports by both the women and the men, the differences in rates of abortion by current marital status are on the order of five- to tenfold: the married women (men) report that 6.8 percent (5.7 percent) of conceptions ended in abortion, while the never-married, noncohabiting women (men) report rates of 27.1 percent (50.0 percent). The currently married and previously married women and men report that 70–80 percent of their lifetime conceptions resulted in live births, the never married report much lower rates.

Abortion rates are systematically higher for the more educated men and women, as is the miscarriage rate for women. Recall that the more educated also tend to be younger, so this may partially reflect an age effect. Regarding the pattern by religion, there are differences here, with higher rates of abortion among those of "other religions" and lowest rates for women classified as Type II Protestant and "other Protestant" and for men classified as "other Protestant," Type I Protestant, and Catholic. By race/ethnicity, Asians appear to have higher rates of abortion and lower rates of live births, while the differences between blacks and whites are not very pronounced (we have not yet undertaken multivariate analyses of these data; reports that have studied the decision making and the outcomes in analytically relevant contexts include Leibowitz, Eisen, and Chow 1986 and Cooksey 1990).

In table 12.7A, we partition these data by three variables at once, gender, partnership status (i.e., marriage or cohabitation) *at the time of the outcome of the conception,*[6] and age in 1992, in detailed categories. We can see there the tremendous difference in percentages of live births by partnership status: at each age, those in marriages had much higher rates of live births, those in cohabitational relationships a lower rate, and those living alone by far the lowest rates, at each age interval up to age forty. Notice how high the reported rates of live births are among the men and women who were married at the

---

6. Notice that we have used here the status of the respondent at the time of the outcome from the conception, not at the date of the conception itself. In most cases, these two are identical, but there are a few differences reported in the status over the nine or so months between the conception and its outcome.

time of conception: close to 85 percent or as high as 94.4 percent for the oldest age group of married men. When we look at the incidence or rate of abortion, we see the mirror image (of course these two are not strictly independent of each other): the married men and women have rates of abortion that are 1 to 5 percent of all their conceptions; those who are young and not in a marriage or a cohabitational partnership have rates well in excess of 30 percent in several age groups.

Table 12.7B partitions these same data by four variables, gender, broader age categories, race (white/black), and marital status at the time of the outcome of the conception (married or not married). Look first at the percentages of live births. For whites, both women and men, married young people report a rate of live births dramatically different (nearly double at 80 percent) from that of unmarried young people (40 percent). The difference is smaller, but still in evidence, for the older group. The rates of live births for those who are married are roughly the same for blacks as for whites, but the rates for the unmarried are higher for blacks than for whites—about 70 and 40 percent, respectively. Among older blacks, the rates of live births among the unmarried are, again, higher than among older whites.

Look next at the rates of abortion. In most cases, for both women and men and both whites and blacks, the rates are quite low for those who are married and dramatically higher for young, unmarried whites and black men, but not black women. The rates are much lower for the older groups, of course, as most of their pregnancies occurred before the legalization of abortion, but the rates among the older, unmarried whites are still substantial.

Table 12.8 reorganizes the information about conceptions and abortions, showing them by the respondent's age at the time of the conception or by the year of the conception instead of by the respondent's age at the time of the interview in 1992. In table 12.8A, one sees a U-shaped relation between age and the incidence of abortion. The rate of abortion is higher at younger ages (i.e., under age twenty) and again at older ages (i.e., over age thirty-five for women and age forty for men) and much lower during the principal childbearing ages of twenty through the mid-thirties. The right-hand panel shows a very dramatic increase in the reported rate of abortions beginning in the early 1970s. Clearly, this pattern reflects the legalization of abortion at the time of the *Roe v. Wade* Supreme Court decision in 1973. The consistency of these rates across the genders and with the dramatic increase after 1973 again reinforces the point that we make often throughout this volume, that the respondents have indeed provided accurate information on the behavior we asked about. There was no mention in our interview of *Roe v. Wade,* for example, yet, when we investigate the implied rate of abortion by year, as we do in table 12.8A, we see the clear indication of its effect coming through in the data.

Table 12.8B looks at the outcomes by the number of the conception. That is, the top row of the left-hand panel tells us that 76.5 percent of the first pregnancies or conceptions for which the men were responsible resulted in a live

Table 12.7A **Outcomes of Conceptions, by Gender, Narrow Age Category, and Marital Status/Living Arrangement**

| | Outcome of Conception (%) | | | | | | | | | |
| | Live Birth | | Miscarriage | | Abortion | | Stillbirth | | Total | |
	Men	Women	Men	Women	Men	Women	Men	Women	Men	Women
Age 18–24:										
Within cohab.	[a]	62.3	[a]	18.2	[a]	19.5	[a]	0.0	11	77
Within marr.	83.9	77.4	12.9	17.7	3.2	4.8	0.0	0.0	31	62
Not within										
marr./cohab.	[a]	46.8	[a]	16.1	[a]	36.3	[a]	.8	26	124
N									68	263
Age 25–29:										
Within cohab.	[a]	67.7	[a]	10.8	[a]	21.5	[a]	0.0	23	65
Within marr.	87.0	80.3	12.0	15.9	1.0	3.8	0.0	0.0	100	239
Not within										
marr./cohab.	28.9	50.5	13.5	13.1	55.8	36.5	1.9	0.0	52	107
N									175	411
Age 30–34:										
Within cohab.	62.5	52.4	20.8	14.3	16.7	32.1	0.0	1.2	48	84
Within marr.	89.2	87.0	9.3	10.1	1.6	2.9	0.0	0.0	194	446
Not within										
marr./cohab.	32.1	48.1	7.1	10.1	58.9	39.5	1.8	2.3	56	129
N									298	659
Age 35–39:										
Within cohab.	58.3	66.2	19.4	15.4	22.2	18.5	0.0	0.0	36	65
Within marr.	87.1	85.3	9.4	11.1	1.7	3.0	1.7	.6	287	470
Not within										
marr./cohab.	52.5	56.8	5.1	16.1	40.7	27.1	1.7	0.0	59	118
N									382	653
Age 40–44:										
Within cohab.	56.1	52.8	4.9	8.3	39.0	33.3	0.0	5.6	41	36
Within marr.	85.4	81.9	10.3	13.8	3.7	3.8	.6	.5	329	448
Not within										
marr./cohab.	68.5	69.6	9.3	8.7	22.2	18.8	0.0	2.9	54	69
N									424	553
Age 45–49:										
Within cohab.	[a]	[a]	[a]	[a]	[a]	[a]	[a]	[a]	11	27
Within marr.	87.6	82.9	6.9	13.0	5.5	3.7	0.0	.5	275	409
Not within										
marr./cohab.	63.0	63.2	20.4	6.6	14.8	30.3	1.9	0.0	54	76
N									340	512
Age 50–54:										
Within cohab.	[a]	[a]	[a]	[a]	[a]	[a]	[a]	[a]	12	18
Within marr.	87.0	88.0	10.9	10.9	1.6	.6	.4	.6	247	350
Not within										
marr./cohab.	[a]	85.1	[a]	8.5	[a]	6.4	[a]	0.0	27	47
N									286	415
Age 55–59:										
Within cohab.	[a]	[a]	[a]	[a]	[a]	[a]	[a]	[a]	12	8
Within marr.	94.4	86.2	4.8	11.7	.8	1.5	0.0	.7	251	463

Table 12.7A (continued)

	Outcome of Conception (%)									
	Live Birth		Miscarriage		Abortion		Stillbirth		Total	
	Men	Women	Men	Women	Men	Women	Men	Women	Men	Women
Not within marr./cohab.	[a]	76.6	[a]	10.6	[a]	10.6	[a]	2.1	19	47
N									282	518

[a]Fewer than thirty cases.

Table 12.7B   **Outcomes of Conceptions, by Gender, Broad Age Category, Race, and Marital Status**

	Outcome of Conception (%)									
	Live Birth		Miscarriage		Abortion		Stillbirth		Total	
	Men	Women	Men	Women	Men	Women	Men	Women	Men	Women
18–29										
White:										
Married	85.0	78.3	13.3	19.2	1.8	2.6	0.0	0.0	113	235
Not married	32.0	41.2	20.0	17.0	46.7	41.8	1.3	0.0	75	153
N									188	388
Black:										
Married	[a]	84.8	[a]	6.5	[a]	8.7	[a]	0.0	0	46
Not married	35.4	70.1	12.5	11.3	52.1	18.0	0.0	.5	48	194
N									48	240
30–44										
White:										
Married	86.2	84.2	10.4	12.5	2.4	3.1	.9	0.3	661	1,067
Not married	45.4	37.4	12.1	14.2	41.4	46.8	1.1	1.6	174	254
N									835	1,321
Black:										
Married	91.6	87.5	6.0	8.6	2.4	2.0	0.0	2.0	83	152
Not married	68.8	77.4	12.5	11.1	18.8	9.5	0.0	2.1	96	243
N									179	395
45–59										
White:										
Married	90.5	84.9	7.8	12.5	1.5	2.2	.2	.4	612	1,005
Not married	61.6	66.3	20.5	6.3	16.4	26.3	1.4	1.0	73	95
N									685	1,100
Black:										
Married	90.7	92.8	7.2	5.7	2.1	1.0	0.0	.5	97	194
Not married	97.8	76.7	2.2	11.0	0.0	11.6	0.0	.7	46	146
N									143	340

[a]Fewer than thirty cases.

Table 12.8A   Abortions as a Percentage of Conceptions, by Gender and by Age at
                     Conception or Year of Conception (cell percentages)

	Men	Women		Men	Women
Age at conception			*Year of conception*		
11–14	a	25.6	1950s	2.4	1.9
15–17	27.4	16.4	1960–64	0.0	2.1
18–19	17.3	9.6	1965–69	1.5	3.5
20–24	10.2	8.9	1970–74	10.0	8.5
25–29	7.0	7.1	1975–79	11.4	15.1
30–34	6.8	7.8	1980–84	13.9	11.5
35–39	5.2	13.3	1985–89	13.1	12.5
40–44	18.8	a	1990–92	14.3	17.9
45–49	a	a			
Total	9.5	9.5	Total	9.4	9.5

aFewer than thirty cases.

Table 12.8B   Live Births, Miscarriages, and Abortions as Percentages of
                     Conceptions, by Gender and by the Number of the Conception (row
                     percentages)

	Men			Women		
Number	Live Birth	Miscarriage/ Stillbirth/ Unknown	Abortion	Live Birth	Miscarriage/ Stillbirth/ Unknown	Abortion
1	76.5	11.3	12.2	75.3	11.6	13.1
2	82.9	10.4	6.7	80.4	13.1	6.4
3	82.2	11.7	6.1	77.1	15.8	7.0
4	77.4	14.2	8.5	74.2	17.9	7.9
5	68.8	18.8	12.5	72.2	17.2	10.6
6+	44.6	27.4	28.0	59.5	24.8	15.6

birth and that 12.2 percent were aborted. For the second pregnancy or conception, 82.9 percent resulted in a live birth and 6.7 percent in abortion. By examining the data conception by conception, as we do here, we see that the abortion
rate was higher for first conceptions and for fifth or higher conceptions and
lower for second through fourth conceptions. That is, abortion appears to be
more likely when the pregnancy is the first one or when it follows several
others that have presumably led to live births. This tells us much about the use
of abortion as a means of fertility control in our country. Because many more
adults have a first conception than have, say, a fourth or fifth, the total number
of abortions at first and second parity are much greater. That is, for the women,
for example, we have 1,385 first-conception observations and 1,130 second-
conception observations but only 430 fourth-conception, 227 fifth-conception,

and 262 sixth- and higher-order-conception observations, so the smaller percentage (6.4 percent) of second-order conceptions that were aborted (seventy-two abortions) still constitutes more abortions in total than the higher percentage (15.6 percent) of sixth or higher-order conceptions (forty-one abortions).

This last point suggests yet another way to look at abortion, and that is to ask how many are reported by the women or men who report any. Table 12.9 shows the data in this form. We see that 281 women reported ever having an abortion and that they reported a total of 405 abortions, so the average number of abortions for women who have any is 1.4. Of all those 405 abortions, 71.5 percent were first abortions, 19.2 percent second, 7.2 percent third, and only about 2.1 percent fourth, fifth, sixth, or more abortions. For the men, the pattern is quite similar, with again about three-quarters of the abortions occurring to the partners of men who reported that that was their first experience with ending a pregnancy by abortion. We do see somewhat higher rates of fourth, fifth, and sixth or higher-order abortions for men, and, of course, it is unlikely that all have occurred with the same women.

12.4   Age at Birth of the First Child

In the demographic literature on fertility, one major focus is the person's age at the birth of his or her first child. This is an indicator of considerable social concern when that age is quite young. Having a child while still a child oneself, as an early adolescent, is fraught with risk for both the infant and the young parent, as the capacity of that parent to nurture and provide for the infant is severely tested (see, e.g., Chilman 1980a and 1980b; Baldwin and Cain 1980; Hayes 1987; and Bumpass and McLanahan 1989). As the person ages, different factors have been found to influence age at first birth, and most of the literature addresses age at first birth for women only.

We report here a very limited analysis of the socioeconomic characteristics of the respondents as they are associated with age at birth of first child, another important focus of research (see Michael and Tuma 1985; Rindfuss, Morgan,

Table 12.9   The Distribution of Abortions, by Number of Abortions (percentages)

	Men	Women
Number of abortions		
1	76.3	71.5
2	12.8	19.2
3	5.8	7.2
4	1.9	1.4
5	1.3	0
6+	1.9	.7
Total	100	100
No. of people	156	281
No. of abortions	254	405

and Swicegood 1988; and Chen and Morgan 1991). We look separately at the men and the women. To anticipate our findings, we show three broad patterns. First, we find the same general pattern of entry into parenthood for these men and women as found in other data sets. Second, many of the same variables found in other data sets to be associated with early or late age at first birth appear to be similarly associated in this data set. To this extent, once again, the NHSLS data exhibit much the same patterns as other data sets. This is not surprising, nor particularly noteworthy, except as one might question whether a survey about sexual behavior has respondents of the same general character-istics as more broadly focused surveys, and we again find here that, indeed, they do.

The third finding is only suggestive. It is that sexual behavior as an adoles-cent appears to be systematically related to the likelihood of having a child at a relatively young age. This latter finding is the main point of this section of the chapter, as we wish to suggest by the illustration of the analysis here that information about the sexual behavior of the respondent can be incorporated into analyses of this nature and that doing so can enhance our understanding of entry into parenthood.

Figure 12.2 shows the survival plots of age at first birth by gender, birth cohort, and education level for the NHSLS data. Figure 12.2A shows the plot for women born in the earlier interval, from 1933 through 1952. There we see that, by age eighteen, for example, only about one-third of the women with less than a high school education but nearly 90 percent of the women with more than a high school education had *not* given birth. The midpoint date of birth for this group of women was 1943, so these women turned age eighteen in 1961, soon after the peak of the baby boom, and it is therefore not surprising that these women had a rather early age of entry into parenthood. Notice, also, that, by the time they reached age thirty, only about 10 percent of these less well-educated women, but about one-third of those with a college education, still had not had a child.

For the early cohort of men (fig. 12.2B), we see the slower entry into parent-hood typical of men, with about three-quarters of the less educated and even more of the more educated men not having become a parent by age eighteen. As with other data, we also see a much less pronounced gradation by education level for the men than for the women.

Figures 12.2C and 12.2D show a much slower entry into parenthood in the later cohorts of more educated men and women, but not in the less educated. These cohorts turned age eighteen in 1971–92, when the birth rate was much lower. (For comparison, the total fertility rate per woman in the late 1950s was above 3.4 and had fallen to only about 1.8 by 1982.) These patterns depicted in figure 12.2 are notable primarily for their consistency with other national data.

Next, we turn to a multivariate statistical analysis of the age at which these men and women first have a child. In order to look at the effect, if any, of sexual

Table 12.10   The Pattern of First Births in Age Intervals, by Gender

| | | First Birth Occurred: | | |
Cohort	N^a	Before Age 14	Age 14–17	Age 18–21
Women				
1933–42	298	1	29	127
1943–52	411	0	27	129
1953–62	547	0	37	146
1963–74	483	2	45	119
Men				
1933–42	209	0	4	38
1943–52	335	0	7	59
1953–62	431	1	9	51
1963–74	421	1	3	34

ᵃNumber of observations.

behavior before age eighteen on the age at first birth in the few years after age eighteen, we narrow our focus to the four years of ages eighteen through twenty-one. Before that age, there are few men who have begun their parenting, as seen in the figures just discussed and as can be seen from table 12.10. But, for the women, our decision to begin our analysis at age eighteen implies that we have ignored a modest number of cases of women who began their childbearing before we look at their behavior. This is technically a statistically biasing research strategy, but, as our interest here is to see if sex before age eighteen has an effect, we will proceed with this *left-censored* data, as it is called in the more technical literature.

For the interval from ages eighteen through twenty-one, we have estimated two logistic regression models for each of the four ten-year birth cohorts and for each gender separately. Rather than show all sixteen of these models, we show in table 12.11 the two models for our largest group, the women born in 1953–62. In the statistical model we have included several variables that have often been found to influence the age at which parenthood begins. These include, in addition to the single year age dummy variables, three levels of the respondent's education and of his or her parent's education, race (black or non-black), religion (Catholic, Type II Protestant, or neither), frequency of church attendance, residence in the West region, and having lived in a nonintact family at age fourteen. That regression (model 1) is reported in the left-hand panel of table 12.11. It indicates that the likelihood of the woman having her first child is higher at twenty-one than at eighteen, of course, and also that it is much higher in this four-year interval of her life if she has less than a high school education, somewhat higher if she has a high school education but has not gone to college, higher also if her parents had less than a high school education, and higher if she grew up in a nonintact family. It also shows that she is less likely

A. Women Born 1933–52

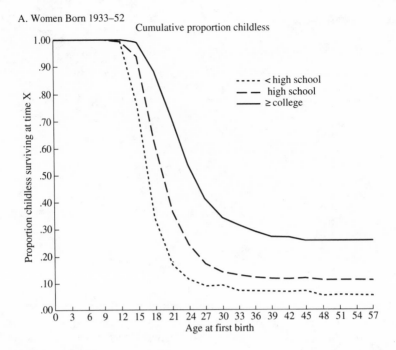

Cumulative proportion childless

.... < high school
— — high school
—— ≥ college

B. Men Born 1933–52

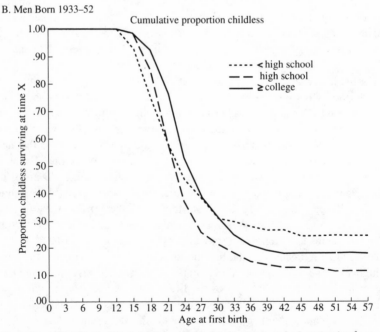

Cumulative proportion childless

.... < high school
— — high school
—— ≥ college

Fig. 12.2   Age at birth of first child, by gender, birth cohort, and education level.

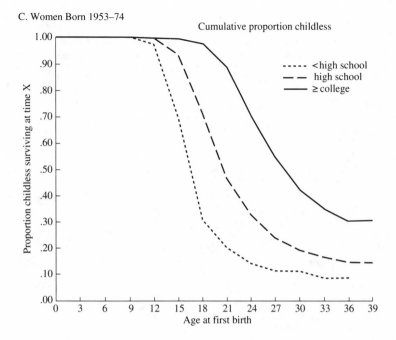

C. Women Born 1953–74

Cumulative proportion childless

Proportion childless surviving at time X

---- <high school
– – high school
—— ≥ college

Age at first birth

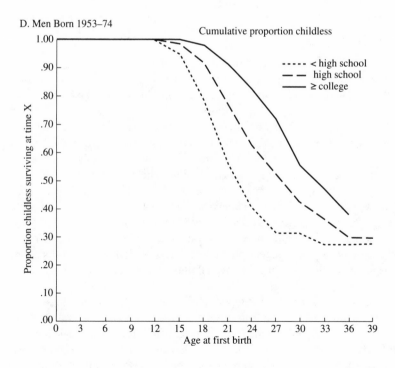

D. Men Born 1953–74

Cumulative proportion childless

Proportion childless surviving at time X

---- < high school
– – high school
—— ≥ college

Age at first birth

Table 12.11   **Logistic Regressions on Age at First Birth, with and without Variables Indicating Sex before Age Eighteen (women born 1953–62)**

	Model 1: Without Information on Sex before Age 18	Model 2: With Information on Sex before Age 18
Age (18)	−.87***	−.98***
Age (19)	−.20	−.26
Age (20)	−.14	−.16
Educ. (< HS)	2.66***	2.33***
Educ. (HS)	1.75***	1.52***
Black	.22	.17
Church	−.11	−.08
West	−.75**	−.70*
Div14	.53**	.46**
Cath.	−.56**	−.50**
Type II Prot.	.16	.16***
ParEduc (< HS)	.68**	.85
ParEduc (HS)	.21	.33
SEX (none)	. . .	−.60
SEX (one)	. . .	.51
SEX (2–4)	. . .	−.05
Constant	−3.96***	−3.69***
χ^{2a}	112.8***	25.9***
−2 ln likelihood	853.4	827.5

Note: *, **, *** imply significance at 90 percent, 95 percent, and 99 percent, respectively.
[a]Degrees of freedom on χ^2 are 13 for Model 1, 3 for Model 2.

to have a child in this four-year age interval if she lives in the West or if she is Catholic. These are not surprising results; to the contrary, most of them are quite typical of analyses of this nature.

What is of greater interest is the comparison of that rather typical left-hand panel (model 1) with model 2, shown in the right-hand panel. In model 2, we have added three additional variables indicating the number of sex partners the women had before age eighteen. The results indicate that, overall, this additional information is in fact related to the likelihood of a woman having a child in the age interval eighteen to twenty-one. The result hints that having no sex partners before age eighteen is associated with a lower probability of having a child in that subsequent four-year interval while having one sex partner tends to be associated with a higher probability, but these individual results are not statistically significant, although, overall, the information about the number of sex partners is.

A statistical model like that reported in table 12.11 is not easy to digest, so we have contrived to present its content in a more accessible way. We have defined five different synthetic cases and estimated from the statistical models the likelihood of each of these five cases having a birth at age eighteen. The five cases are described by a set of characteristics, based on all the variables in the two models shown in table 12.11. For ease of identifying them, we give them letter names. Thus, for example, Mr. or Ms. A is a person with sixteen years of schooling and whose parent also had sixteen years of schooling, is white, is Catholic, and grew up in an intact family not living in the West region. The second case, Mr. or Ms. B, is black, has sixteen years of schooling and a parent with twelve years of schooling, is non-Catholic and non–Type II Protestant but attends church frequently, and grew up in an intact family not living in the West region. Table 12.12 describes Mr. or Ms. C, D, and E as well.

Table 12.13 shows the significance of these eight variables as they are associated with the likelihood of having a birth at age eighteen. Consider first the bottom panel of the table since it shows the pattern for women born in 1953–62, the group for which the statistical model is shown in table 12.11. We see from the top row of that panel that Ms. A has a very low estimated probability of giving birth at age eighteen, .005, or only half of 1 percent. Ms. B has a probability about twice that high, .011, Ms. D a much higher probability, .161, and Ms. E a very high probability, .359. That is, the statistical model implies that a person with the characteristics of Ms. E is dramatically more likely to have a child while she is eighteen than is a person with the characteristics of Ms. A or Ms. B. The purpose of this elaborate description of five types is to reveal how much difference these personal characteristics actually make, as estimated by the statistical model. In the case just described, the difference is very large indeed.

Now consider the effect on the estimated likelihood of having a child at that age of introducing information about the sexual behavior of the respondent prior to age eighteen. That effect is shown in the lower four rows of each panel of table 12.13. For Ms. A, the table says that, if she had had no sex partners before age eighteen, the likelihood of having a child at age eighteen is only .003, whereas, if she had had one and only one sex partner before age eighteen, then the likelihood of having a child at age eighteen is .009, about three times higher but still very low. If she had had two, three, or four partners before age eighteen, the likelihood of having a child at age eighteen is .005; if she had

Table 12.12   **Five Synthetic Cases**

	Designation				
Characteristic	A	B	C	D	E
Education	16	16	12	10	10
Parent's educ.	16	12	12	10	10
Intact at 14?	Yes	Yes	Yes	No	No
Race	White	Black	White	White	Black
West	No	No	Yes	Yes	No
Catholic	Yes	No	Yes	No	No
Type II Protestant	No	No	No	Yes	Yes
Church attend	No	Yes	Yes	Yes	No

Table 12.13   **Estimated Probability of an Eighteen-Year-Old Person Having a Child, Based on Logistic Regressions, by Gender and Cohort**

	Designation[a]				
	A	B	C	D	E
Birth cohort 1933–42					
Men:					
Model 1	.010	.015	.037	.248	.221
Model 2					
No sex partners	.006	.008	.033	.172	.075
One sex partner	.015	.022	.084	.357	.178
2–4 sex partners	.017	.025	.095	.385	.197
5+ sex partners	.018	.027	.100	.400	.207
Women:					
Model 1	.028	.048	.222	.578	.352
Model 2					
No sex partners	.022	.024	.156	.373	.172
One sex partner	.115	.123	.517	.774	.545
2–4 sex partners	.040	.043	.255	.524	.277
5+ sex partners	.118	.126	.523	.779	.551
Birth cohort 1953–62					
Men:					
Model 1	.002	.007	.034	.126	.068
Model 2					
No sex partners	.001	.006	.026	.088	.042
One sex partner	.001	.006	.025	.082	.040
2–4 sex partners	.003	.014	.058	.179	.091
5+ sex partners	.002	.011	.046	.147	.073
Women:					
Model 1	.005	.011	.011	.161	.359
Model 2					
No sex partners	.003	.008	.009	.096	.214
One sex partner	.009	.023	.027	.242	.451
2–4 sex partners	.005	.013	.016	.154	.319
5+ sex partners	.006	.014	.016	.161	.331

[a]See table 12.12 for the definitions of A through E.

five or more sex partners before age eighteen, the likelihood is .006. So, for a person with the characteristics of Ms. A, the probability of having a child at age eighteen is quite low in all cases, although it varies somewhat. But consider next Ms. E. Without including any information about her prior sex behavior (i.e., using model 1), the estimate of the probability that she would have a child at age eighteen was more than one-third. If she had no sex partners prior to age eighteen, however, the estimated probability is .21; if she had one sex partner before age eighteen, the estimate is .45; if she had two or more, it is again about one-third. So, in the case of a woman with the characteristics of Ms. E, prior sexual behavior has a much stronger relation with the likelihood of a birth at age eighteen than in the case of Ms. A or B.

The top two panels of table 12.13 show the estimated probabilities for the men and the women born in 1933–42, who were age eighteen during the period 1951–60, the height of the baby boom. While the probability is low for those with the A and B characteristics, it is quite high for both men and women with D and E characteristics and for women with C characteristics as well. For the men, there is a monotonic increase in the probability as the number of sex partners before age eighteen increases—about a threefold increase as the number of partners rises from none to five or more. For the women, the probability increases severalfold as well, but not monotonically as the number of partners rises. It is lowest for the women who had no sex partners before age eighteen, and highest for those who had five or more, but quite high as well for those who had one partner.

The lower two panels show the estimates for the cohorts born in 1953–62, who were age eighteen in the period 1971–80, the "sexual revolution," but nevertheless a period of far lower fertility rates nationally. We see this lower rate of births for the men and for all the women except those with E characteristics, whose fertility rate remained very high. Again, we see that, while those men in the cohort who had no sex partners or only one before age eighteen had a low probability of becoming a parent at age eighteen, those who had two or more partners had about twice as high a likelihood of becoming a parent. For the women in that cohort, as we discussed above, those who had no sex partners before eighteen had a much lower probability of having a child at age eighteen, but the relation between the number of partners and the probability is not monotonic.

The statistical analysis that we have just described is quite incomplete. One would want to control for marital status, reintroduce those who began their fertility prior to age eighteen, and in several other ways tighten the analysis before having confidence in the results. But this brief foray into multivariate analysis of this important behavior should serve to illustrate that data on sexual behavior itself can enhance our understanding of the factors that influence the important social event of becoming a parent. Obviously, much more work must be done, but data sets that do not have information on detailed sexual behavior are not as adequate in revealing fertility patterns as are those that do. That is the main point that we make in this section.

12.5 Conclusion

In this chapter, we have seen that the respondents in this survey report patterns of fertility behavior that mirror those from other data sets. Given the age range of these respondents, eighteen to fifty-nine in 1992, their fertility spans the period of the baby boom and subsequent low levels of national fertility. The respondents, in fact, report fertility behavior that reflects these well-known national patterns. We have also seen that a majority of men and women report using contraceptives to avoid unwanted fertility but that, overall, about one-third do not use any contraceptives with their primary partners and about one-quarter do not do so with any secondary sex partners.

We have seen that women report much higher rates of sterility than do men, even in the age ranges under forty. There are patterns to sterility by marital status and education level for women, with lower rates for Catholic men and women and relatively high rates for black women but not black men. Overall, about three-quarters of women protect against pregnancy when they have vaginal intercourse, an estimate based on women's responses to our survey questions. But that estimate falls to only about 60 percent, instead of 75 percent, when it is based on men's answers to a similar set of questions.

We have information about the outcomes of conceptions or pregnancies, and we find great similarity in the answers given by men and women, with about three-quarters of the pregnancies resulting in live birth, about 12 percent in miscarriage, and about 10 percent in abortion, overall. When we break that information down by the age of the respondent at conception, we find a U-shaped pattern for the rate of abortions, with rates well over 20 percent for young teenagers, falling to about 7 percent for those in their twenties and early thirties, and rising again to 10–15 percent for women in their late thirties and for men in their early forties. There is clear evidence of the effect of *Roe v. Wade,* as rates of abortion rose abruptly from 1–4 percent to around 12 percent in each time interval since 1973. We also find that most who have an abortion have but one—about three-quarters of all abortions reported in our data are first abortions, and rates of abortion are highest for the first pregnancy and again for the fifth or higher pregnancy, while only about half as frequent for the second, third, and fourth pregnancies.

Finally, we have conducted a brief multivariate analysis of some socioeconomic background factors and their relation to the age at which the respondent first became a parent. We find the typical factors that have been found elsewhere to play a similar role here. For example, for the women in the birth cohort 1953–62, those with less education, with less well-educated parents, who grew up in nonintact families, who were not Catholic, and who did not live in the West region were much more likely to enter parenthood relatively early. We also find that the respondent's sexual behavior prior to age eighteen is related to the probability of becoming a parent in the age interval eighteen to twenty-one. This is the only effect of sex per se on the fertility patterns that we have investigated.

We suggest that the brief inquiry in this chapter illustrates that it can be useful in understanding the traditionally demographic behavior of fertility and contraception use to bring sexual behavior explicitly into the analysis. Much more work on this subject should be and can be done. We turn in the next chapter to another traditional demographic inquiry, the formation and stability of longer-term partnerships.

CHAPTER 13

Sex, Cohabitation, and Marriage

In previous chapters, we have discussed several aspects of sexual partnering, including number of sex partners (in chapter 5) and characteristics of partners relative to the respondent's own characteristics (in chapter 6). This chapter addresses three additional issues about live-in partnerships that last at least one month: at what age are they first formed, how do they begin (with formal marriage or informal cohabitation), and how stable are they? In chapter 1, we discussed the fact that the selection of a longer-term partner is motivated by a number of considerations, only some of which are sexual. There are strong social, economic, and psychological incentives to form a partnership with another person, and, once a partnership is formed, we have seen in several earlier chapters how powerfully the relationship organizes the pattern of sexual behavior. Indeed, no other discretionary characteristic of a person seems to be even close to marital status or living arrangement in its influence on the number of sex partners one has, for example. Only age and gender have a comparably powerful influence on the organization of sexual behavior. So, in the presentation of the patterns of sexual behavior in the adult population, it seems appropriate to devote a chapter to the two primary modes of partnering, formal marriage and informal cohabitation.

Marital behavior has long been a major focus of study by demographers. Two classic and wonderfully informative descriptive volumes that detail marriage and divorce patterns in the United States up to the most recent quarter century are Jacobson (1959) and Carter and Glick (1970). No single volume so dominates the more recent period, but the 1990 Census Monograph by Sweet and Bumpass and the volume by Cherlin (1992) provide and interpret basic background information, while volumes such as Becker (1991), England and Farkas (1986), and Goldscheider and Waite (1991) offer more analytic treatments of the recent changes in family formation and structure, and see Greeley (1991) for a discussion of sexual fidelity in marriage.

Three measures of marital behavior are the usual focus of attention: the age at which the first marriage or first union takes place; the stability of the partnership or the time pattern of dissolution; and, more recently, the choice of form-

Kara Joyner helped craft this chapter and conducted the empirical work. Robert T. Michael directed the work and wrote the chapter.

ing a formal marriage or an informal cohabitational relationship. We look at all three of these measures of partnership behavior. The chapter takes as its objective addressing two sets of questions. First, what is the pattern of marital and cohabitational partnering evinced in the NHSLS data, and do that pattern and its demographic correlates reflect the behavior patterns found in other recent U.S. data sets? Second, how, if at all, does knowledge about prior or contemporaneous sexual behavior add to our understanding of these partnership formation and dissolution patterns? We begin by describing the pattern of entry into a first union.

13.1   Age of Entry into a First Marriage or Cohabitation

The Pattern of Entry by Age

Figure 13.1 depicts the pattern of entry into a first heterosexual union or partnership. Consider figure 13.1A, a survivor plot showing the behavior of men born in the interval 1933–42. The dotted line shows the entry into a formal marriage. We see that, at the young ages of twelve and thirteen, 100 percent of these men were single and had not married and that, as age increases to sixteen, seventeen, and so on, the dotted line declines from 1.00 to .98 and lower. By age eighteen, for example, where the dotted line is at the height of about .94, 6 percent of these men had and 94 percent had not married. By age twenty-two, the height of the dotted line is 54 percent, indicating that, by that age, nearly half these men had in fact married and only half were still never married. By age twenty-seven, only 20 percent were still never married, while 80 percent had married.

The solid line gives us the same information but includes both formal marriage and informal cohabitation in the definition of a union. The vertical distance at any age between the dotted and the solid lines, therefore, tells us the portion who had formed informal cohabitational unions since the solid line is the sum (from the top down) of the marriages and the cohabitations.

Three major behavior patterns are seen in figure 13.1. First, for every cohort, by the late twenties—say, age twenty-seven—more than 70 percent of the men and more than 85 percent of the women had formed a union. Adults overwhelmingly continue to form long-term social and sexual live-in partnerships, as they have for decades. This fact should not be overlooked in all the discussion about the decline of the family: adults overwhelmingly form two-person sociosexual partnerships. Second, it is also true that the rate of formal marriage has fallen dramatically and that the proportion of first unions that are informal cohabitations has risen steadily from one cohort to the next. This tendency is seen most easily by noting the widening vertical gap between the dotted and the solid lines as one goes from the earlier to the later cohorts; that vertical gap reflects the rate of cohabitation. Third, the men are slower to form partnerships than the women, as can be seen by looking at the age at which, say, half the group had formed a union—that is an age of about twenty-two for the men in all four cohorts and an age of twenty or twenty-one for the women. All three of these key patterns seen in figure 13.1 reflect findings common to the social demography of adults in the United States today. Once again, the behavior reported in the NHSLS data set looks like other data, as reported, for instance, by Sweet and Bumpass (1990) regarding marriage and Bumpass, Sweet, and Cherlin (1989) regarding cohabitation offsetting the decline in marriage.

The Socioeconomic Co-factors

There have been many studies by social demographers and economists of socioeconomic factors that are correlated with age of starting a marriage (and, more recently, of starting a cohabitational union). These studies usually find a positive relation of age of entry with schooling level. This can be explained in terms of either strategic decision making by young men and women or the social organization of the circumstances in which the event takes place. There is a clear pattern of delaying entry into marriage until most of one's formal schooling is completed. This may be because of a strategy of selecting a partner who is a good match in terms of interests, capabilities, and potential relative contributions to the partnership or because of the simple constraints of time and attention that searching entails, implying that the natural moment in the life course for obtaining a mate is at about the time one moves from the world of school to the world of work.

This sequence of entering marriage at about the age at which one leaves school implies that those who end their schooling with less than a high school education, for example, are much more likely to marry another who also is leaving school at a relatively early age. This pattern leads to strong positive assortative mating by schooling level. The pattern of positive assortative mating in marriage both mirrors and helps explain the same pattern among sexual partnerships as shown in chapter 6.

Studies have looked at various measures of the age of entry into marriage, including indicators such as the steepness and location of the line depicted in figure 13.1 or the proportion who have married by some specified age. Keeley (1979), for example, studied age at first marriage across states in the United States. He contended that a common statistical model, a log-logistic function as he described it, can capture important uniformities over time and location in the age pattern of first marriage, building on important work by Coale (1971) and Coale and McNeil (1972), who are credited with establishing a similar pattern across nations. By parameterizing the relation between age and entry in this form, Keeley shows that one can understand much of the difference in patterns from state to state by taking account of relative wages of men and women, relative education levels, the ratio of men to women, levels of income, and the density of urban areas, all suggesting that the gains from marriage in one geographic location or another have much to do with the observed pattern of entry into marriage. A related research strategy by Preston and Richards

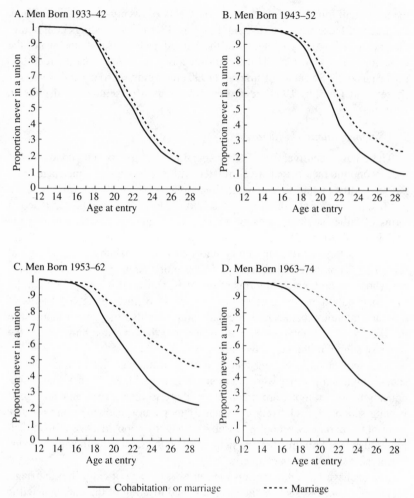

A. Men Born 1933–42

B. Men Born 1943–52

C. Men Born 1953–62

D. Men Born 1963–74

——— Cohabitation or marriage   - - - - Marriage

Fig. 13.1   Pattern of entry into first union, by gender and cohort.

(1975) yields a qualitatively similar conclusion from a study across major metropolitan areas in the United States: factors like female employment opportunities, the sex ratio, the percentage who are Catholic, and the population density go a long way toward explaining the differences in age at entry into marriage (or the proportion who have married by age twenty-two, in these authors' case).

More recently, a number of studies have used individual level longitudinal data to study determinants of early entry into marriage (see, e.g., Michael and Tuma 1985; Axinn and Thornton 1992a; and Goldscheider and Waite 1991). Findings include that marriage occurs at an earlier age if the parents' education

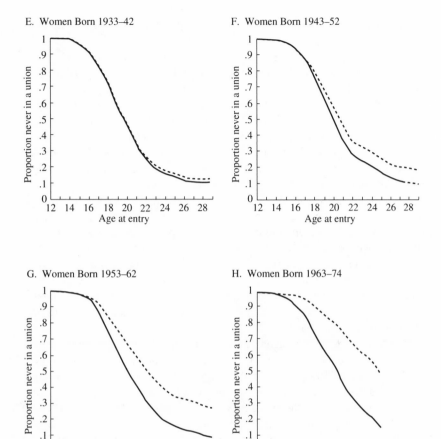

E. Women Born 1933–42

F. Women Born 1943–52

G. Women Born 1953–62

H. Women Born 1963–74

——— Cohabitation or marriage   ----- Marriage

levels are relatively low, if the number of siblings is high, if the person does not live in an intact family at age fourteen, and if the person is neither Catholic nor black and that women marry younger than men.

The Multivariate Analysis

We investigated the relation between age at entry into a partnership and some of these same demographic characteristics, using the NHSLS data. Here, we do not distinguish between a formal marriage and a cohabitation. This behavior is depicted in figure 13.1 as the lower, solid line discussed above. In this section, we do two things. First, we investigate the relation separately for men and for women in each of four ten-year birth cohorts. The characteristics that we feature here are primarily those emphasized in the demographic literature cited above.

In particular, we include in this analysis age (and age squared, in order to capture nonlinearity in the relation), education level, race, religion, parents' education level, whether the respondent lived in the West at age fourteen, and whether the respondent lived with both natural parents at age fourteen. In addition to age, which plays a key role, we have six descriptive characteristics, which are measured in ten specific variables used in this multivariate analysis. To foreshadow the results, we find that our data confirm many of the relations found in other data sets regarding how these several characteristics are associated with the formation of a first partnership.

Second, we introduce into this analysis information about sexual behavior as a teenager and see whether and how that behavior influences the formation of these marital or cohabitational partnerships. There are several restrictions that we must impose on this analysis, but the work serves to illustrate that it is useful to include prior sexual activity in the study of demographic behavior such as age at partnership formation. To anticipate our findings, we show that, indeed, respondents who have sex partners (more precisely, vaginal intercourse partners) prior to turning eighteen are more likely to form a partnership over the following dozen years.

The form of the empirical analysis here is a discrete-time approximation to a continuous-time, event-history logistic regression model, and it is run separately for each of four cohorts and each gender, so we have estimated eight independent relations (regarding the statistical model, see Allison 1982; for a recent application to partnership behavior, see Teachman, Thomas, and Paasch 1991). Each person year is included as an observation, with the dependent variable taking the value 0 if no union was formed in that year and 1 if a marriage or cohabitation was formed in that year. Once a union is formed, that observation is dropped from the analysis for all subsequent ages; the observation is also dropped at the time it is censored by the interview, of course. Age and age squared are included as exogenous variables, and they capture the nonlinear shape of the pattern of the rate of new union formation across the age span from fourteen to thirty. All the other variables in the regression retain a constant value for each year. That is, these other six descriptive variables do not vary over time (or are treated here as if they do not).

Three model specifications are estimated. Model 1 covers the whole time span from childhood (i.e., age fourteen) to age thirty, tracking the event of the formation of a first union; it estimates the partial relations of age and each of the several characteristics on entry into a union. This first model, therefore, covers a wide span of the life course in which a vast majority of first partnerships are formed. Model 2 eliminates those respondents who form their first partnership before age eighteen and then investigates the influence of the same set of characteristics on the formation of the union over the narrower range of ages from eighteen to thirty. Model 3 then adds to model 2 information about the number of sex partners the respondent had had prior to age eighteen so that we can see both what influence that new information has and how it alters the estimated relations with the other demographic variables. (We begin at age eighteen in this analysis in models 2 and 3 in order to have information on sexual behavior that predates the formation of the partnership that we study.)

Table 13.1 shows how many new unions were formed in different age intervals for the men and the women in the four birth cohorts. Notice that, among the men, there are very few unions formed before age eighteen—only four among the 205 men in the oldest cohort, for example, and no more than 6 percent of any of the four cohorts. For the women, there are substantially more unions formed at these early ages. By contrast, over the whole period up to age thirty, nearly 90 percent of men in the birth cohorts up to 1952 and of women in the cohorts up to 1962 have formed a union. Of course, those in the youngest cohort have not yet reached age thirty, so the decline in the proportion who have entered a union in this youngest cohort reflects that truncation of the data at the time of the interview, not a behavioral change necessarily.[1]

Lest the bulk of the analysis of these three models estimated for each of eight gender-cohort groups becomes too great, we show here the estimated statistical models for only one of the eight groups and then characterize the others more qualitatively. We chose the group with the most observations to report here in detail—the women born in 1953–62. The three model estimations for that group are shown in table 13.2.

Consider the left-hand column of table 13.2, model 1. The coefficients reported are the logistic coefficients (for a discussion of their interpretation, see appendix 11.1A). A positive value implies that the characteristic is associated with a greater likelihood of forming a union. Consider the positive coefficient +1.45 for an education level of less than high school (third row, first column) and the positive value of +.75 for an education level of high school (fourth row, first column), where the comparison category is an education level of greater than high school. Women with less than a high school education are more than four times as likely to form a union as (or, put differently, they have a probability of doing so that is 13 percentage points greater than) those with

1. There are several aspects of table 13.1 that can be misleading, and we note a few here. For one thing, in the youngest cohort, the youngest age of any respondent at the time of the survey is eighteen. So, for those young respondents, the data are truncated or censored at their current age, which explains why the proportion who ever marry or cohabit in the young cohort is much lower than in the earlier cohorts—they simply have not lived as many years on which to report. The data analysis that we conduct takes that truncation into account, but table 13.1 reports only the number of cases.

Also, in some instances in the table, one can subtract those no longer eligible as potential partners and get the number of observations in the next higher group, but this cannot be done in every instance. For example, there are 200 men aged eighteen to twenty-one in the oldest cohort, seventy-nine of whom got married or formed a cohabitational relationship in that age interval, so the remaining 121 are then in the next age category, twenty-two to twenty-nine. In that instance, the subtraction yields the number recorded in the next older interval. But this subtraction does not always work because of missing information in the subsequent interval.

Table 13.1   **Number of New Partnerships and Number of Observations, by Gender, Age Interval, and Birth Cohort**

	Men				Women			
	14–17	18–21	22–29	Overall %	14–17	18–21	22–29	Overall %
Cohort born 1933–42:								
Events	4	79	102	90.2	47	144	62	90.4
Observations	205	200	121		280	232	87	
Cohort born 1943–52:								
Events	12	129	143	87.7	45	199	108	88.9
Observations	324	309	180		396	350	150	
Cohort born 1953–62:								
Events	24	144	150	75.7	65	242	161	89.5
Observations	420	394	245		523	454	209	
Cohort born 1963–74:								
Events	23	107	81	51.1[a]	65	182	78	69.0[a]
Observations	413	368	172		471	394	119	

[a]The low percentages for this cohort reflect truncation and not necessarily a change over time.

more than a high school education.[2] Similarly, women with exactly a high school education face odds of forming a union that are about twice as high as (or they have a probability that is about 7 percentage points higher than) women with more than a high school education.

Black women are less likely to form a union according to model 1; the coefficient is −.75, implying that blacks are about half as likely as nonblacks in terms of the odds (or that blacks have a probability about 7 percentage points lower than nonblacks). Catholics are somewhat less likely to form a union than non-Catholics, according to model 1. The other socioeconomic variables in the model do not have statistically significant relations.

Model 2 uses fewer observations, setting aside those respondents who had formed a union before age eighteen. In this model, then, we are addressing a conditional relation, one conditioned by reaching age eighteen without entering a union. Those who did enter a union in those earlier ages (of whom there are sixty-five women in this instance, as one can see in table 13.1) no longer influence the results. We see that the magnitudes of the coefficients are some-

2. For a brief discussion of the logistic equation and the interpretation of its coefficients, see appendix 11.1A. Drawing on that discussion, we note that the change in the odds $P/(1 - P)$ associated with a one-unit change in X is equal to e^c, so we can calculate the effect of the women having less than a high school education compared to having more than a high school education as $e^{1.45} = 4.26$, thus the statement in the text that these women are more than four times as likely to form a union. Alternatively, since the change in P for a unit change in X is equal to $C[P(1 - P)]$, we calculate that women with less than a high school education have a 13 percentage point higher likelihood of forming a union since $P = 470/523 = .899$, and so $C[P(1 - P)] = 1.45$ $[.899(.101)] = .132$.

Table 13.2   **Age at First Union, for Women Born 1953–62—Three Models**

	Model 1		Model 2		Model 3	
Variable	Coef.	Sig.	Coef.	Sig.	Coef.	Sig.
Age	2.19	.00	1.05	.00	1.13	.00
Age^2	−.05	.00	−.02	.00	−.02	.00
Educ (< HS)	1.45	.00	1.17	.00	.86	.00
Educ (HS)	.75	.00	.64	.00	.53	.00
Black	−.75	.00	−.68	.00	−.90	.00
Catholic	−.34	.01	−.20	.15	−.14	.31
Type II Protestant	.20	.17	.22	.18	.31	.07
Attendance	−.16	.17	−.13	.32	−.05	.68
Parent's educ (< HS)	.16	.37	.02	.92	.08	.68
Parent's educ (HS)	.10	.49	.04	.81	.11	.47
West14	.03	.86	−.05	.80	.07	.73
Div14	.18	.22	.07	.68	.05	.79
Sex partner 1					.88	.00
Sex partner 2 or more					.74	.00
Constant	−26.53	.00	−13.53	.00	−15.04	.00
No. of observations	523		454		454	
% with event	89.9		88.8		88.8	
χ^2 (df = 12 or 2)	394.2	.00	55.38	.00	43.4	.00

Note: Model 1 includes all observations, covering entry between ages fourteen and thirty. Model 2 deletes those forming unions before age eighteen, covering entry between eighteen and thirty. Model 3 is the same as model 2, adding two additional explanatory variables.

what different here as compared to model 1, but qualitatively the same few variables show statistical significance—age, education level, and race.[3]

What is of particular interest here is the comparison of model 2 with model 3 when we have added two new variables to the identical model. Here, we can investigate how the model is affected by information about the number of sex partners the women had had before age eighteen. There are two parts to the question: first, how the estimates of the previously entered variables are affected by this new information about sex and, second, how the sexual behavior itself is related to the formation of unions.

Looking first at the twelve coefficients previously estimated, by comparing

3. For completeness, we note here the interpretations of the three coefficients in model 2 that we derived in the text from model 1. Here, education less than high school has a coefficient of 1.17; it implies a greater than threefold increase in the odds (3.22 times) and an increase in the probability by 11.6 percentage points. The coefficient on education level of exactly high school is .64, which implies an increase in the odds of 1.9 or nearly a doubling and a change in the probability of 6.4 percentage points. The coefficient on the variable for black is −.68, which implies that blacks have the odds of forming a union that are about half those of the nonblacks and a probability lower by about 6.8 percentage points.

the coefficients in models 2 and 3 we see that there are, in fact, substantial changes in magnitude. Including the sexual behavior of the women prior to age eighteen does appear to affect the relations between several of the other demographic variables and the formation of a union. The coefficients on education, for example, are noticeably smaller here, while the differences between blacks and nonblacks are actually larger when sexual behavior is held constant. Only one variable—being a Type II Protestant—becomes statistically significant when sexual behavior is held constant (and only at the 90 percent level of significance), suggesting that those who are Type II Protestants are slightly more likely to form a union when prior sexual behavior is held constant.

Considering the coefficients on the two sex variables, we see that those who had one or more sex partners before age eighteen were more likely to form a partnership in the subsequent interval from age eighteen to age thirty—the coefficient of .88 implies that the odds of forming a union for those who had one sex partner were almost two and a half times ($e^{.88} = 2.41$) the odds of those who had none, or that the probability of forming a union was higher by about 9 percentage points ($.88 \times .888 \times .112 = .09$). Those who had two or more sex partners have about the same likelihood as those who had one.

While these past few paragraphs discuss the estimates of models from one of the eight gender-cohort groups, we are most interested in the overall pattern of these results for all eight gender-cohort groups. Because we think that a figure captures the information in this sort of statistical model effectively, we show model 3 for all eight cohorts in figure 13.2. (This type of figure, which we will use throughout the rest of this chapter instead of reporting all the coefficients themselves, was introduced in chapter 11 as fig. 11.1.) From figure 13.2, one can see at a glance which demographic characteristics are associated with a rise or fall in the odds of forming a partnership and the magnitude of those effects (a log scale is used in the figure, so the distance from 1.00 to 2.00 is the same as that from .5 to 1.00).

The figure shows that the likelihood of entering a partnership (a marriage or cohabitation) is higher at older ages of course, as we also saw from figure 13.1, but here this result controls for many other factors. The less educated show a higher likelihood of entering a partnership, especially the women. Blacks are less likely to enter a partnership, consistently so for women, but only in two of the four cohorts for men. In a few cohorts, Type II Protestants are more likely to form a partnership, but not consistently so, and neither frequency of church attendance, being Catholic, nor several other variables examined here—parent's education level, growing up in the West, or growing up in a nonintact family—have a noticeable effect. In no case is there a coefficient that is statistically significant at the 95 percent level of confidence in one model that has a reversed sign in another of these eight independent models, so these relations are relatively stable across the several groups. In all, these estimated models look much like those based on other data sets and reported in the demographic literature.[4]

To get an intuitive sense of the magnitude of the differences implied by the models shown in figure 13.2, we use here again the device used in chapter 12. We define several synthetic cases labeled Mr. or Ms. A, B, C, D, and E (defined in table 12.12 of chapter 12 and used in table 12.13). Table 13.3 shows these results for the men and women in two of the four cohorts. For the men born in 1933–42, the probability of forming a marriage or cohabitation at age eighteen ranges from .03 to .16 on the basis of model 2 for these five synthetic cases, and the information on prior sexual behavior has a very small effect on that probability in many cases, but it does show a larger influence on the probability in the case of people with Mr. C's or D's characteristics. Table 13.3 shows larger differences for the women from that earlier cohort and for both the men and the women in the later cohort. From the bottom panel, for instance, the estimated probability of forming a partnership at eighteen varies from .05 for Ms. B to .30 for Ms. D. Similarly, the information about sexual activity prior to age eighteen also has a much larger influence on the estimated probabilities for the women, particularly those with the characteristics of Ms. C and D.

In comparisons of model 2 with model 3, for the other seven gender-cohort groups (not shown), only one variable has a consistently different pattern when the sex variables are added: the effect of race is stronger and larger in a negative direction. Without the sex variables, blacks are somewhat less likely to form a union, but the coefficient is stronger in model 3 in seven of the eight gender-cohort groups. That is, blacks are more likely to have vaginal intercourse before age eighteen (see table 13.5 below), which, in turn, is associated with a higher probability of forming a union. So, when this influence of sexual behavior is removed statistically, the negative relation between race and forma-

---

4. Model 2 eliminates those who formed their first union before age eighteen, as discussed in the text. We have also run model 1 over the age interval fourteen through seventeen alone, and there we find essentially that nothing shows statistical significance for the men since there are so few men in each cohort who form a union in that early age interval. For the women, however, there are a few consistently significant coefficients: on the variables measuring education, race, parent's education, and being Catholic. The respondent's own education has a very large effect— education of less than twelve years has a coefficient of 2.15–4.07 for each of the four cohorts of women, and education at exactly twelve years has a coefficient of between 1.11 and 2.01, all quite significant. These are quite problematic results to interpret, however, since none of these women have in fact acquired a level of schooling in excess of twelve years by the age of seventeen. So these results are not noteworthy and contaminate the other results in these regressions on fourteen to seventeen-year-olds as well. We note, for completeness, that blacks have much lower rates of union formation, as do Catholics and those whose parents have higher levels of schooling.

We have also run this model on the age interval eighteen through twenty-one alone and on the age interval twenty-two through twenty-nine alone. There, the education variable is well defined, and we can look at the influence of sex (i.e., vaginal intercourse) before age eighteen in each case. The sex variables are stronger in the age interval eighteen to twenty-one than in the subsequent interval from twenty-two to twenty-nine, particularly for women. None is significant for women in the later interval, and they are so for men in only the 1953–62 birth cohort.

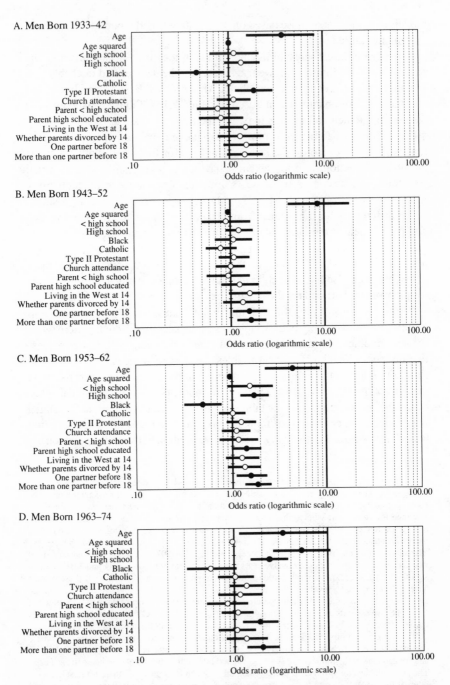

Fig. 13.2 Logistic regression on entry into first union: odds ratio point estimates and 95 percent confidence intervals (solid circles statistically significant at $a = .05$).

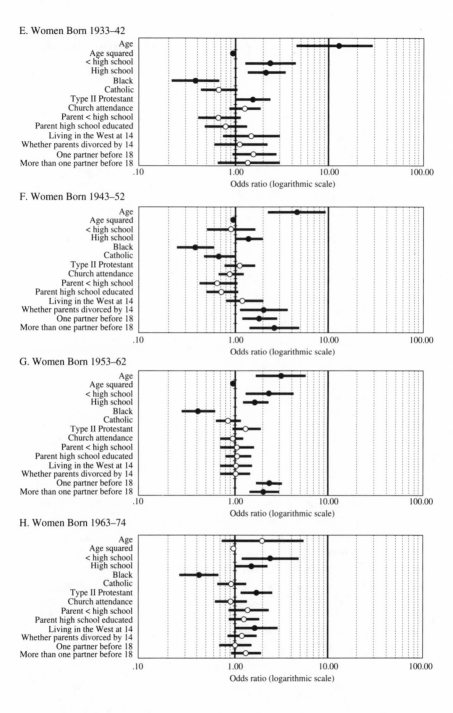

E. Women Born 1933–42

Age	
Age squared	
< high school	
High school	
Black	
Catholic	
Type II Protestant	
Church attendance	
Parent < high school	
Parent high school educated	
Living in the West at 14	
Whether parents divorced by 14	
One partner before 18	
More than one partner before 18	

Odds ratio (logarithmic scale)

F. Women Born 1943–52

Odds ratio (logarithmic scale)

G. Women Born 1953–62

Odds ratio (logarithmic scale)

H. Women Born 1963–74

Odds ratio (logarithmic scale)

Table 13.3   **Estimated Probability of an Eighteen-Year-Old Forming a Marriage or a Cohabitational Partnership (based on logistic regressions, figure 13.2, by gender and cohort)**

| | Demographic Characteristics | | | | |
	A	B	C	D	E
Men, 1933–42					
Model 2	.06	.03	.09	.16	.07
Model 3:					
0 partners	.05	.02	.09	.15	.05
1 partner	.08	.03	.13	.21	.07
2+ partners	.07	.03	.13	.21	.07
Women, 1933–42					
Model 2	.07	.04	.18	.39	.12
Model 3:					
0 partners	.07	.04	.19	.36	.10
1 partner	.10	.06	.27	.48	.15
2+ partners	.09	.05	.24	.44	.13
Men, 1953–62					
Model 2	.04	.03	.11	.14	.07
Model 3:					
0 partners	.03	.02	.09	.11	.04
1 partner	.04	.03	.14	.17	.07
2+ partners	.05	.04	.16	.19	.08
Women, 1953–62					
Model 2	.09	.05	.14	.30	.21
Model 3:					
0 partners	.07	.03	.12	.23	.11
1 partner	.14	.08	.24	.41	.22
2+ partners	.13	.07	.22	.38	.20

tion of a union is made even stronger. None of the other variables exhibits a systematic change when the sex variables are added.

Regarding the relation between sex before age eighteen and the likelihood of forming a union, table 13.4 shows the coefficients on the two sex variables from model 3 for each of the eight gender-cohort groups. (The estimates for the women in the 1953–62 birth cohort are, of course, also shown in table 13.2 and are also depicted in fig. 13.2.)[5] Notice that, in every case, the coefficient is positive: the likelihood of entering a partnership is higher for those who had a sex partner before age eighteen. The differences in the coefficients on the two variables are generally not great—the relation is about the same whether the

5. In each instance in table 13.4, we show as well a χ^2 test on the statistical significance of the set of two variables, and there we see that they are significant for the men in the later three cohorts and for women in the middle two cohorts but that they are not significant overall for the oldest cohort or for the youngest cohort of women.

respondent had one or more than one partner in that interval of time. With the coefficients in the range of .45–.98, this implies that the effect on the odds of forming a partnership is about one and a half to two and a half times higher for those who had a sex partner before age eighteen.

The interpretation of this quite persistent relation between having sex partners before age eighteen and having a higher likelihood of entering a partnership over the next dozen years is certainly not transparent. Let us suggest three different theoretical perspectives through which it is useful to view this relation. Perspective A is that respondents can be classified into two groups, those who want to have a lot of opposite-gender, partnered sex and are thus eager to form a partnership in order to make that sex accessible and easy, and those who are much less concerned about sex and have a disinclination, relatively, toward either having a sex partner early in their teen years or having a partnership later. In this case, the respondents are heterogeneous, and the sex variable simply distinguishes between two groups. Notice that, in this perspective, having sex per se does not influence the likelihood of forming a union; it is only signaling to us in which of the two groups a respondent belongs. We call this the *sex-heterogeneity perspective*. Many examples of this perspective can be found in the family demography literature; one example of a closely related point is the contention that "females who are already more predisposed toward marriage and parenthood may be more interested in and willing to become sexually active at a young age" (Miller and Heaton 1991, 721).

Table 13.4   **Effect of Having Sex Partners before Age Eighteen on the Likelihood of Forming a Partnership (marriage or cohabitation) by Age Thirty**

	Men		Women	
	Coef.	Sig.	Coef.	Sig.
Birth cohort 1933–42				
1 sex partner	.42	.13	.48	.06
2+ sex partners	.38	.07	.34	.37
$\chi^2 (2)$	4.27	.12	3.80	.15
Birth cohort 1943–52				
1 sex partner	.46	.02	.62	.00
2+ sex partners	.50	.00	.98	.00
$\chi^2 (2)$	10.99	.00	16.55	.00
Birth cohort 1953–62				
1 sex partner	.45	.01	.88	.00
2+ sex partners	.62	.00	.74	.00
$\chi^2 (2)$	18.12	.00	43.39	.00
Birth cohort 1963–74				
1 sex partner	.32	.20	.03	.88
2+ sex partners	.71	.00	.29	.10
$\chi^2 (2)$	14.66	.00	2.99	.22

Perspective B is that the respondents are partitioned into two groups that have different behavior, but here, rather than there being a difference in their interest in sex per se, they differ in their beliefs about the appropriateness of having sex outside marriage. Those who hold a traditional view would be less likely to have sex before age eighteen and outside marriage, and they would also be more likely to form a formal marriage than a cohabitational relationship. Thus, it is not clear whether they would be more likely to form a union overall, but, since nearly all the partnerships recorded here for the oldest cohort are formal marriages while over half those formed in the youngest cohort are cohabitational unions, the relation between the sex variables and the likelihood of entry into a partnership should be stronger for the oldest cohorts by this argument. We call this the *attitude-heterogeneity perspective.*

Perspective C is that having one or more sex partners is a form of searching in the effort to find a suitable spouse or partner—a form of intensive searching, one might say. If this is what the sex variable represents, then we would expect to see that those who do search a lot (i.e., those who have one or more sex partners before age eighteen) would be more likely to form a marital or cohabitational partnership: they search more and are consequently more likely to find a partner. We call this the *search perspective.* Marini, among others, argues along these lines, contending that "relationships with members of the opposite sex affect the timing of entry into adult family roles"; in particular, she finds that adolescents who begin to date early, who date frequently, and who "go steady" tend to marry at younger ages (Marini 1985, 314, 339).

While one or another of these perspectives may seem to be a reasonable interpretation of the findings here, there are additional empirical patterns that are not consistent with this positive partial correlation. One example is an inconsistency between this cross-sectional correlation and the trends over time. That is, the proportion of men and women who had no sex partners before age eighteen declined monotonically across the four cohorts, for both whites and blacks in our sample, as seen in table 13.5. Yet we know that the formation of new partnerships (including both marriages and cohabitations) did not increase across these four cohorts. So the cross-sectional evidence in table 13.3—a persistent positive relation between having a sex partner before age eighteen and

Table 13.5   **Percentage of Cohort Having No Sex Partners before Age Eighteen, by Gender and Race**

	Men			Women		
	All	White	Black	All	White	Black
1933–42	58.5	62.4	. . .	81.5	85.0	59.4
1943–52	52.4	55.6	30.8	79.7	82.4	62.5
1953–62	46.7	49.0	28.9	58.8	62.3	35.6
1963–74	39.7	41.0	28.2	47.2	51.6	22.0

having a high likelihood of forming a partnership—is not in evidence across these four cohorts. We need an explanation for this difference in the cross section and the time series, and none of the three perspectives discussed above is adequate. One is tempted to argue that we are simply seeing here an aspect of the sexual revolution—over time there is more sex and a decline in the social commitment to formal marriage bonds—but that is not an explanation, just a description or relabeling of the finding.

A second point also seen from table 13.5 compares blacks and whites. While both groups changed behavior across the four cohorts, with younger cohorts far more likely to have sex before age eighteen, blacks were and are far more likely to do so than whites. Yet we have seen above that blacks are also much less likely to form partnerships. So here too we have an inconsistent pattern: for the whites (and overall in the logistic regressions), those who have sex before eighteen are more likely to form partnerships, but, between whites and blacks, the groups most likely to have sex before age eighteen (the blacks) are less likely to form partnerships. Again, we need an explanation, and none of the three perspectives described above seems to provide it.

13.2   The Choice of a Marriage or a Cohabitational Union

In the preceding section, we disregarded the nature of the union, treating the formal marriages and the informal cohabitations identically and looking at the characteristics that are correlated with entry into either type of first partnership. In this section, we shift that focus and look at the choice between the two types of union, given that a union of one or the other type is formed (for an analogous study, see Clarkberg et al. 1993). Since our early two cohorts have relatively few who first entered a cohabitational relationship, we look here only at the later two cohorts, combining the two into a single statistical model for each gender. Also, we include only those whose partnership began after age eighteen. Here, 56.2 percent of the men and 50.2 percent of the women first entered a cohabitational union, and it is that choice on which we focus.[6]

Figure 13.3 shows the results of a statistical model analogous to model 3 in the section above. For both men and women, we find that the younger cohort is much more likely to form a cohabitational union, as was evident in the descriptive figure 13.1 shown earlier, and as is in evidence as the general time trend in the United States. For the men but not the women, those who formed their partnership at a younger age were more likely to form a cohabitational union. For women, blacks are more likely to form cohabitations than marriages. For both genders, Type II Protestants and those who attend religious services frequently are far less likely to form cohabitational relationships.

6. For an excellent discussion of the pattern and social policy consequences of cohabitation in the United Kingdom, with a review of its pattern throughout Europe, see Kiernan and Estaugh (1993).

Fig. 13.3 **Logistic regression on entry into a cohabitational relationship instead of a marriage: odds ratio point estimates and 95 percent confidence intervals (solid circles statistically significant at** $a = .05$**).**

Those who grew up in nonintact families were also more likely to form cohabitations.

In a broadly analogous statistical model using a large sample of men and women born in about 1954, Willis and Michael (1994) study this same choice of marriage or cohabitation in first unions and report several generally similar results: among whites, those from intact families were much less likely to form a cohabitational relationship than a marriage (as we find here as well), and those whose fathers had higher levels of schooling are more likely to form a cohabitation (as we find here for women but not for men).[7] Using the NSFH data, Bumpass and Sweet (1989, 623) also look at rates of cohabitation before marriage in a multivariate proportional hazard model. They report higher rates of cohabitation among nonblacks, less educated respondents, those whose family of origin was not intact at age eighteen, and those whose parents' education level was higher and, of course, among younger respondents, again reflecting the trend in cohabitation. Most of these tendencies are seen in the NHSLS data reported here as well, except for the effect of race, so the patterns of cohabitation with background demographic factors are relatively well established. Here again, these NHSLS data appear to be similar to other data, given the evident differences in time, statistical model, and context. In all three of these studies, incidentally, Catholics are not found to behave differently than non-Catholics.

Here again, we can use the five synthetic cases of Mr. or Ms. A, B, C, D, and E to see heuristically how much difference these several demographic factors make in the estimate of the probability of forming a cohabitational relationship instead of a formal marriage when a first partnership is formed. Table 13.6 shows that pattern, estimated for a man or woman from the 1953–62 birth cohort, and based on the logistic model depicted in figure 13.3. There we see that these several demographic factors do indeed have a substantial influence on the estimated probability, with Mr. D having a .10 probability of forming a cohabitation, while Mr. E has a .50 probability, Ms. C a .27 probability, and Ms. E a whopping .87 probability. The low rate of cohabiting for Mr. D can be attributed to his having a low level of schooling and attending church frequently, while Mr. E has such a high rate because he grew up in a nonintact family structure at age fourteen and did not attend church frequently. Ms. E has such a high estimated rate because she is black and grew up in a nonintact family. (Remember that these constructed cases are crafted only to illustrate the collective effect of the coefficients in the model; they do not speak to, and surely do not confirm, the causal connections.) When sexual behavior is added in model 3, its effect on the estimated probability is substantial in several cases, as can be seen clearly in table 13.6.

Consider that final variable, sexual behavior before age eighteen, in a little more detail. It indicates that those men and women who had a sex partner before age eighteen were more likely to form an informal cohabitational relationship than a formal marriage. About 60 percent of the men and 50 percent

---

7. In that study, those who first entered their partnership at a later age were more likely to cohabit, a pattern that we do not find here. The reason is probably that that study was based on a single-year birth cohort, so those who formed their partnership at an older age did so at a later date. Our study, however, covers twenty single-year birth cohorts, so those who form a partnership at a later age can have done so at an earlier date than other, younger members of our sample. As suggested by Willis and Michael (1994, 30), their age effects reflect the dramatic trend over time in cohabiting; our age effects do not since our data contain such a wide span of cohorts.

Table 13.6   **Estimated Probability of Entering a Cohabitation Instead of a
                    Marriage, Given That a Partnership is Formed (based on logistic
                    regressions, figure 13.3, by gender and cohort)**

	Demographic Characteristics				
	A	B	C	D	E
Men, 1953–62					
Model 2	.39	.23	.12	.10	.50
Model 3:					
0 partners	.32	.19	.10	.08	.39
1 partner	.43	.27	.15	.13	.50
2+ partners	.44	.28	.15	.13	.52
Women, 1953–62					
Model 2	.64	.68	.27	.39	.87
Model 3:					
0 partners	.60	.62	.25	.33	.79
1 partner	.74	.76	.39	.48	.88
2+ partners	.76	.78	.42	.52	.89

of the women had had a sex partner before age eighteen, and they were systematically more likely to enter into a first, cohabitational partnership. For the women, for example, the odds of forming a cohabitation were nearly twice as high for those who had one sex partner before age eighteen as for those who had not had any, as seen as the magnitude 1.92 in figure 13.3. It is significant that this relation is a partial one, estimated after controlling for cohort, education level, religious behavior, and all other background factors in the model.

It is interesting to interpret this finding using the three perspectives that we discussed above. First, consider the sex-heterogeneity perspective. What form of partnership would those who have a strong inclination toward sex prefer to have, cohabitational or marital? It is not clear. Newcomb (1986) investigates the sexual behavior of people who cohabit and those who do not and provides an extensive literature review of studies that find substantial differences. The definition of *cohabiting* typically includes both married and single people, and the sample sizes are quite small in Newcomb's study and many of those that he cites. Since sex is a relatively important aspect of the decision to form a cohabitational relationship, while a formal marriage involves many more complex decisions integrating families, finances, and so forth, it seems likely, other issues aside, that those for whom sex is a particularly salient issue would be likely to cohabit instead of marry. Thus, from the sex-heterogeneity perspective, we would expect that those who consider sex particularly salient would both have a sex partner before age eighteen and enter a cohabitational partnership. This could explain the positive correlation that we observe here.

Similarly, by the attitude-heterogeneity perspective, those who consider sex outside marriage to be inappropriate would be both less likely to have sex before age eighteen and less likely to form a cohabitational partnership. Thus, here too, we can understand the positive correlation between the two aspects of behavior as simply reflecting consistency of behavior and attitudes in the population.

The interpretation offered by the search perspective depends on what one considers the cohabitational partnership to be. If it were a final form of partnership, then, since those who had sex have done more searching and are therefore better informed than those who have not searched, we might expect them to be more prepared to enter formal marriage. By this argument, those with sex partners before age eighteen would be less likely to form a cohabitation. Alternatively, we might consider cohabitation as another, even more intensive form of searching, as has been argued elsewhere (e.g., Oppenheimer 1988; Willis and Michael 1994). Our empirical evidence and others' show that cohabitation unions tend to endure only briefly, either soon converting to formal marriages or soon dissolving and having a half-life of only about one year. This evidence tends to support the notion of cohabitation as a further component of searching, that is, as tentative partnering. In this interpretation, the two forms of searching would be expected to be positively correlated; thus, those with a sex partner before age eighteen would be more likely to form a cohabitational relationship.

We can check out the attitude-heterogeneity perspective empirically by looking into the answers to two questions that we asked about the respondent's opinion regarding whether it is wrong "if a man and women have sex relations before marriage" and "if they are in their teens, say 14–16 years old." We also asked about agreement with a series of statements, one of which was, "My religious beliefs have shaped and guided my sexual behavior" (see appendix C, section 10, questions 1, 2, and 13; for an extended analysis of differences in attitude regarding sexual issues in the population at large, see chapter 14). We constructed three dummy variables defined as 1 if the answers to these three questions were that premarital sex and teen sex were "always wrong" or "almost always wrong" and if the respondent "strongly agreed" or "agreed" with the statement about religious beliefs guiding his or her sexual behavior. These are attitudes expressed in 1992, so their use in explaining earlier behavior is problematic and intended as suggestive.

Adding these three additional variables to model 3 has an interesting effect. For men, the sex variable loses its statistical power, and the value falls from .53 to only .17, while all three attitude variables are statistically significant—-1.15 for premarital sex, -1.16 for teen sex, and $-.55$ for religion guiding behavior. Moreover, both the cohort variable and the Type II Protestant religion variable lose all significance, and the coefficient on church attendance falls by half, from about -1.51 to $-.78$. For women, while the two sex variables declined in magnitude a little—from .65 to .56 and from .78 to .47—both remain significant at a 95 percent level of confidence. The premarital sex and teen sex opinions are not significant at 95 percent levels for the women, and only the coefficient on religion guiding behavior is significant, with a coefficient of −.88. For the women as well, the Type II Protestant and church attendance variables lose their significance when tested at the 95 percent level.

Clearly, these several variables in model 3—Type II Protestantism, church attendance, birth cohort, and having sex before age eighteen—serve to identify those with traditional moral values, and those values do, in fact, influence whether one enters into a formal marriage or a cohabitational relationship, even among these younger cohorts of men and women born after 1962. To return to the main point, however, for the women but not the men, even holding these opinions constant, we have seen that the sex before age eighteen variables remain significant. This implies that there is also latitude for the search and the sex-heterogeneity perspectives (or, of course, many other perspectives) to play a role here.

13.3   The Stability of Partnerships

The previous two sections considered entry into marital and cohabitational partnerships. In this section, we look at exits. In particular, we focus on the stability of formal marriages and see whether the same factors that appear to influence stability in other data sets do so here as well. In addition, we determine how information about sexual behavior per se influences that stability.

Before we turn to formal marriage, however, we briefly report evidence of the stability of cohabitational partnerships in the NHSLS data. Figure 13.4 shows the pattern of stability of first partnerships that were formed as cohabitations for the men and women separately and for two ten-year birth cohorts separately. Recall that there were very few cohabitations formed as first partnerships among those in the birth cohorts before 1952, so there are not enough cases to analyze from those earlier groups.

Cohabitation can end in any of three ways: by separation, by converting the cohabitational relationship into a formal marriage, or by the death of one of the partners. In this age group, death is not a common way for partnerships to end, so figure 13.4 shows the pattern of exit by the other two routes, formal marriage (the dotted line) and either marriage or dissolution (the solid line). Thus, the vertical distance between the dotted and the solid lines reveals the incidence of dissolution. We caution that the horizontal axis in figure 13.4 depicts months, not years, as in earlier and in later figures. Here, the duration of the cohabitation is short enough that we show the patterns over only a three-year, or thirty-six-month, period. If one does not notice that the axis is defined over months, not years, one might not recognize how short-lived these cohabitational relationships are.

Two findings in figure 13.4 are most noteworthy: (1) about half the cohabitations end within a year; and (2) a large proportion (40 percent or so) end in a formal marriage. Only the younger cohort of men appears to have mostly

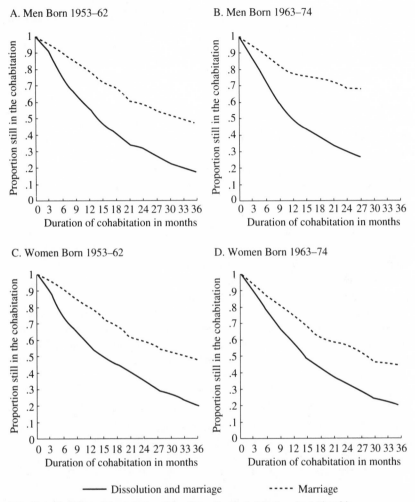

A. Men Born 1953–62

B. Men Born 1963–74

C. Women Born 1953–62

D. Women Born 1963–74

———— Dissolution and marriage ----- Marriage

Fig. 13.4 Stability of first partnerships formed as cohabitational relationships.

dissolutions, not marriages. These two patterns are found in the reports by the men and by the women. They are quite similar to findings elsewhere (see, e.g., Thornton 1988; Bumpass and Sweet 1989; and Willis and Michael 1994).

Turning now to the stability of marriages, figure 13.5 shows the separation pattern for each of the four ten-year birth cohorts for each gender separately. (The horizontal axis is in years, not in months.) Consider what the figure tells us about the rate of separation by the tenth year of marriage, for example. Table 13.7 shows the percentage of divorce by that duration from figure 13.5. The men and women report very similar patterns, as should be the case. Note that, between the first and the second birth cohorts, the rate of dissolution rises

Table 13.7   **Separation by the Tenth Anniversary of Marriage (percentages)**

Cohort	Men	Women
1933–42	18	20
1943–52	33	33
1953–62	39	38
1963–74	. . .	. . .

dramatically, as seen by the much lower lines in the figure for the later cohorts. Nationally, the divorce rate was low and rather constant throughout the 1950s and early 1960s, rose dramatically beginning in about 1966, doubling in magnitude over the next decade, and then leveled off at the higher rate, with a very slight decline more recently (for an investigation of the causes of this pattern over several decades, see Michael 1988). The pattern reported here reflects that national pattern since those in our earliest ten-year birth cohort, born in 1933–42, entered their late teens and early twenties during the late 1940s–mid-1960s, so the first ten years of most of those marriages occurred before the national divorce rate had risen. Accordingly, the rate of dissolution by the tenth anniversary of marriage in that earliest cohort is relatively low, with about 20 percent of marriages ending within ten years. The later birth cohorts experienced the period of higher dissolution rates earlier in their marriage, so we see here much higher rates of dissolution by the tenth year of marriage for those later cohorts—33 percent or higher. This is but one more indication that the NHSLS respondents reported behavior that conforms to well-known demographic trends.

As the following analysis looks at the factors associated with separation, it may be useful to note that these marriages took place at very different ages, as seen in table 13.8. A few of these marriages occurred at a very early age, while others occurred relatively late in life. All are first marriages.

Several demographic attributes have been shown in the literature to influence divorce rates, and we investigate their effect on separations reported in the NHSLS data. They include the respondent's age at marriage, education level, race/ethnicity, birth cohort, whether he or she is Catholic, is a Type II Protestant, attends religious services frequently, lived in the West region at age fourteen, and lived in an intact family at age fourteen, and the higher level of schooling of either parent. In the NHSLS data, we can also include information about the demographic characteristics of the marriage partner and compare these characteristics to those of the respondent. In particular, following up on our discussion of homogamy in chapter 6, we include whether the respondent and partner are of the same religion and the same race/ethnicity, have the same education level, and are of equal ages (within three years of each other).

The analysis here, like the analysis of the entry into a partnership in section 13.1 of this chapter, is a discrete-time (annual), event-history analysis of marital separation estimated as a logistic regression model over the first twelve

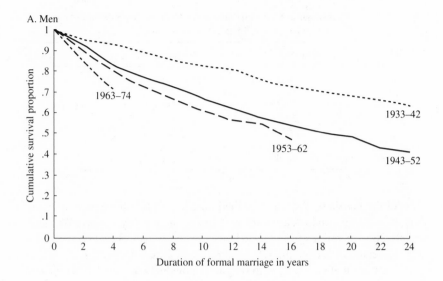

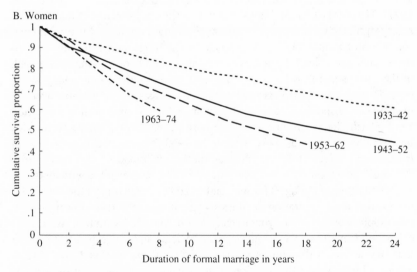

Fig. 13.5 Divorce patterns.

Table 13.8   **Number of First Marriages in the NHSLS, by Age at Marriage and by Gender (all four birth cohorts combined)**

Age	Men	Women
< 16	5	32
16–19	141	441
20–24	424	517
25–29	150	112
30–39	40	31
40–49	4	1
Total	764	1,134

years of the marriage. We combine the four birth cohorts for presentation, although we have conducted extensive logistic analyses by cohort. We have, overall, 266 separations from the 764 observed marriages of male respondents and 415 separations from the 1,134 marriages of female respondents.[8]

We first estimate a model with only the individual characteristics included since, in many data sets, that is all an analyst has to work with if information about former spouses was not collected (see, e.g., Becker, Landes, and Michael 1977). These logistic regressions will not be shown, but we note that they are highly significant statistically. The four cohorts have dramatically different dissolution probabilities. Using the logistic model by gender, with only respondents' characteristics included, we calculate the odds of dissolution for each of the cohorts as follows, expressed in table 13.9 relative to the youngest cohort. That is, men in the earliest cohort had odds of a dissolution over the twelve-year period that are only 21 percent as high as men born in the period 1963–74 (the index group), and those born in the second cohort faced odds that were half as high as those born in the 1963–74 period. Similarly, we can calculate the effect of age at marriage on the likelihood of dissolution from the coefficients on age and age squared. The estimated coefficients are $-.1999(\text{age}) + .0036(\text{age}^2)$ for men and $-.2695 + .0051(\text{age}^2)$ for women, so the likelihood of separation declines as age at marriage rises, but it does so more rapidly at extremely young ages. The minimum dissolution risk can be calculated from these age-at-marriage coefficients and suggests that the age at marriage at which dissolution is least is 27.6 for the men and 26.4 for the women.[9] Interestingly, the duration of the marriage itself does not show a significant relation with the likelihood of dissolution, nor does it in plots of the

8. Incidentally, these rates (34.8 percent of the men and 36.6 percent of the women whose first marriage has ended in separation) are not useful for any purpose since they are averages over very different lengths of marriage (up to twelve years), some of which began before 1950 and others in the early 1990s.

9. The minimum age is that age at which the derivative of the equation $b_1(\text{age}) + b_2(\text{age}^2)$ is equal to 0, and this implies that age is equal to $-b_1/2b_2$; this is the formula from which the minimum ages reported in the text are calculated.

Table 13.9　　　The Odds of Dissolution for Each of the Cohorts, Relative to the
　　　　　　　　Youngest Cohort

Cohort	Men	Women
1933–42	.21	.48
1943–52	.50	.86
1953–62	.53	.91
1963–74	1.00	1.00

Table 13.10　　　Effects of Personal Characteristics on the Dissolution Rate[a]

Coefficient	Men	Women
Cohab	1.86	1.49
Blacks		1.58
Attendance	.55	.51
West14		1.50
Div14		1.63

[a]From multivariate logistic model—statistically significant coefficients only.

annual incidence of dissolution. The cohort matters tremendously, but the duration of the marriage does not.

In this simple model, several characteristics in addition to these several timing variables of cohort, age at marriage, and duration are found to be correlated with the separation rate.[10] In particular, factors that have statistically significant effects, shown in terms of their effect on the odds (e.g., calculated as e^c for each coefficient that is significant at the 95 percent level of confidence), are as given in table 13.10. Those who began their partnership as a cohabitation and then converted it to a formal marriage had a much higher likelihood of separation—higher by a factor of 1.86 for men and about 1.5 for women—than those who did not begin their partnership with a cohabitation. (Incidentally, we defined the start of the marriage as the time of the formal marriage for these previously cohabiting couples, so the cohabitational relationship does not enter into the measure of the duration of the marriage.) This finding replicates the conclusions in several other studies of marriages of those who previously lived together (see, e.g., Bennett, Blanc, and Bloom 1988, who use Swedish data, Schoen 1992, who uses 1986 NSFH data for the United States, and Axinn and Thornton 1992a). Those who frequently attend religious services are only about half as likely to separate. Among the women (but not the men), blacks,

10. Another important variable often included as a determinant of divorce is children (see, e.g., Becker, Landes, and Michael 1977; Waite and Lillard 1991). We have not introduced any time-varying variables here, so we have not introduced children. Subsequent analyses should do so.

those who grew up in the West region, and those who grew up in nonintact families also experienced separation at a rate that was higher by a factor of about 50 percent, for each of these variables.

Next, we added information about the spouse—whether the respondent and spouse differed by race/ethnicity, religion, education level, and age. These several additional factors were highly significant overall for both the men and the women. For the men, these added variables actually strengthened the effect of age at marriage, but they weakened it for the women. They had no other substantial influence on the statistically significant variables for either the men or the women. The differences themselves were quite significant for both genders, and the coefficients that were statistically significant at a 95 percent level are shown in table 13.11. If the couple differed by religious preference, they were more than twice as likely to separate (124 percent more likely for men and 137 percent more likely for women). If they differed by race/ethnicity, the men were 69 percent more likely to separate. The differences by education levels are puzzling: for the male respondents, separation is more likely in cases where the man has a higher education level than his wife, but, for the female respondents, separation is more likely where the woman has a higher education level than her husband. Regarding age difference, no effect is seen for the women, and, for the men, dissolution rates are lowest when the two are of about equal age.

Finally, we added one piece of information about sex before marriage: a variable indicating whether the respondent had ever had vaginal intercourse with any opposite-gender partner before the marriage.[11] For the two genders, 16.5 percent of men and 30.0 percent of women report being virgins at their wedding, and by cohort these proportions are shown in table 13.12. Figure 13.6 shows the full model, which includes the timing variables, the respondent's own characteristics, the similarity of respondent and spouse's characteristics, and the sex variable that indicates whether the respondent was a virgin at the time of the marriage.[12]

---

11. This information is obtained by a series of three queries about the first time the respondent had vaginal intercourse with an opposite-gender partner. The variable is coded as 1.0 if the first intercourse was with a spouse and on the wedding night (see appendix C, section 8, questions 21A, 21C, 21D, and 22).

12. It would have been preferable to have information about extramarital sex partners during this first marriage also, in order to study their effect on the stability of the marriage. Unfortunately, and surprisingly, we cannot conduct that analysis with our data. We asked only about *new* sex partnerships that were started during the marriage, and we did not ask the series of questions that would have allowed us to know whether and how many other earlier sex partners had continued to be sex partners after the marriage began. So this is a weakness in our data.

We do know from questions in the SAQ whether the respondent ever had an extramarital affair, but we cannot link that information back to the first or a specific marriage if the respondent had more than one marriage. There is, in fact, more precision that can be achieved on this point with further data-refinement effort, such as linking the information for those who had only one marriage, but we have not done this as it can introduce a statistical bias. Thus, in this chapter, we have used only information about sexual behavior prior to the start of the marriage.

Table 13.11   **Effects of Differences in Characteristics between Respondent and Spouse on the Dissolution Rate[a]**

Differed by:	Men	Women
Religion	2.24	2.37
Race/ethnicity	1.69	
Educ(1)	.58	.46
Educ(2)	.54	.69
Age(1)	.68	

Note: Educ(1) is defined as 1 if the respondent has more years of schooling than the spouse and as 0 otherwise. Educ(2) is defined as 1 if the respondent and spouse have the same level of schooling and as 0 otherwise. The omitted category, then, is that of the respondent having fewer years of schooling than the spouse.

[a]From multivariate logistic model—statistically significant coefficients only.

Table 13.12   **Proportions of Men and Women Who Were Virgins at Marriage, by Cohort**

Cohort	Men	Women
1933–42	21.9	54.4
1943–52	15.4	28.9
1953–62	13.5	20.0
1963–74	16.3	20.1

Once again, in order to get an intuitive sense of the magnitude of the effects implied by these coefficients, we use the device of Mr. or Ms. A and D. Here we show the calculations for only those two sets of characteristics (defined in table 12.12) and add information about prior sexual behavior and previous cohabitational history. Those calculations are reported in table 13.13. There we see that the differences in ethnicity, religion, education, or age have only a 1 or 3 percentage point effect on the probability of dissolution for the men in the earlier cohort, but a much greater effect on the men in the later cohort. The differences between the men with the characteristics of Mr. A and Mr. D do not have as much effect on dissolution as on the probability of forming a cohabitation or entering a partnership, shown in earlier tables. For the women, the influence is somewhat greater overall, with a similar pattern of effects. For both the men and the women, the influence of differences in all four of the variables—race, religion, education, and age—is quite substantial.

For both genders, we find that the virgins have dramatically more stable first marriages—the odds of separation for those who are virgins at marriage are only .63 as great for men and .76 as great for women as compared to nonvirgins (these are shown in figure 13.6, bottom row). The finding confirms the result reported by Kahn and London (1991) using National Survey of Family

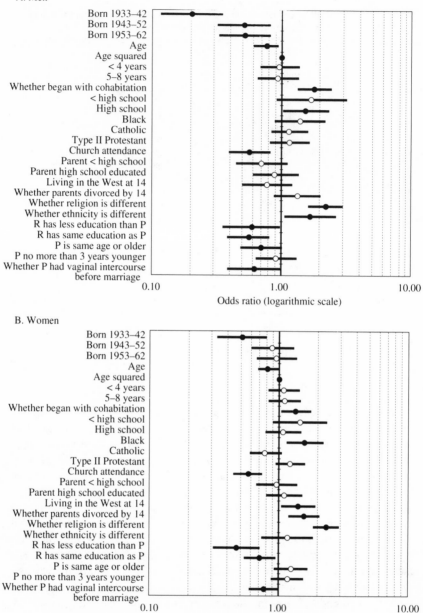

Fig. 13.6 Logistic regression on marital dissolution: odds ratio point estimates and 95 percent confidence intervals (solid circles statistically significant at $a = .05$).

Growth data from 1988—in multivariate analyses, those who are virgins at marriage have much lower rates of separation and divorce.

How might we interpret the finding that virgins exhibit substantially more stability in their marriages, holding constant all the personal characteristics and partnership differences that we control in this analysis? The perspectives that we describe above as sex heterogeneity and attitude heterogeneity offer rather straightforward interpretations. Consider the sex-heterogeneity perspective: those for whom sex is a particularly salient aspect of life are unlikely to be virgins at marriage (particularly so controlling for age at marriage, as we do here), and they are also less likely, all things equal, to be sexually exclusive over the remainder of their life, with the result that divorce is a more likely outcome for them. This will yield the partial correlation that we see—those who are not virgins are more prone to divorce. The attitude-heterogeneity perspective offers just as straightforward an explanation: those who value virginity and think nonmarital sex inappropriate also value the commitment to marriage and are disinclined, relatively, to divorce. So, again in this case, those who are virgins at marriage are those who go to greater lengths to avoid divorce.

What these two explanations provide is the insight that the patterns that we have seen in this chapter reflect continuity of behavior: the sexual behavior that we observe before entering a partnership seems to be consistent with the behavior that we observe regarding that partnership—the age at entry, the form of partnership, and the stability of the marriage. Those who have vaginal intercourse relatively early or have sex before a marriage are those who enter a partnership at an early age, are more likely to enter an informal cohabitational partnership, and are more likely to separate or divorce. This is a not particularly surprising consistency in behavior.

The search perspective is more difficult to employ here since it is not altogether clear how search per se relates to this matter. If we simply think of search as having sex (i.e., vaginal intercourse), then the logic of the argument suggests that the virgin has not conducted as extensive a search of the prospective spouses, or of anyone else for that matter, and so enters the marriage less well informed about an important aspect of the partnership, sexual compatibility. Hence, by this argument, we would expect the better-informed nonvirgin to select the more compatible spouse and thus his or her marriage to be more stable. But this is too simplistic a view of the search process. It seems more likely that the information content has changed substantially over time. It used to be the case that one learned as much about the character of the person as about his or her sexual prowess from his or her willingness to have intercourse premaritally because there was general concurrence that nonmarital sex was inappropriate. In recent times, in contrast, the willingness to have premarital intercourse does not have the same connotation since the practice is far less stigmatized. The information that once was conveyed about the character of the individual by the fact of virginity may have far outweighed the value of

Table 13.13   **Estimated Probability of Dissolution (based on logistic regressions, figure 13.6, by gender)**

| | Demographic Characteristics | | | | | |
| | A | | | D | | |
	No Sex, No Cohab.	Sex, No Cohab.	Sex, Cohab.	No Sex, No Cohab.	Sex, No Cohab.	Sex, Cohab.
Men, 1933–42						
Homogamous	.01	.01	.02	.01	.01	.02
Race/ethnic diff	.01	.02	.04	.01	.02	.03
Religion diff	.02	.03	.05	.01	.02	.03
Educ diff	.01	.02	.04	.01	.02	.03
Age diff	.01	.02	.03	.01	.01	.02
All 4 diff	.07	.11	.18	.05	.08	.14
Men, 1953–62						
Homogamous	.02	.03	.06	.01	.02	.04
Race/ethnic diff	.03	.05	.09	.02	.04	.07
Religion diff	.04	.07	.12	.03	.05	.08
Educ diff	.04	.06	.10	.03	.04	.07
Age diff	.03	.05	.08	.02	.03	.06
All 4 diff	.16	.24	.36	.12	.18	.29
Women, 1933–42						
Homogamous	.01	.02	.02	.03	.04	.05
Race/ethnic diff	.01	.02	.02	.04	.05	.06
Religion diff	.03	.03	.05	.07	.09	.12
Educ diff	.02	.02	.03	.04	.06	.08
Age diff	.01	.02	.02	.04	.05	.05
All 4 diff	.05	.07	.09	.13	.17	.22
Women, 1953–62						
Homogamous	.02	.03	.04	.06	.07	.10
Race/ethnic diff	.02	.03	.04	.07	.08	.11
Religion diff	.05	.06	.08	.12	.16	.20
Educ diff	.03	.04	.05	.08	.10	.13
Age diff	.03	.03	.03	.07	.09	.08
All 4 diff	.09	.12	.16	.22	.27	.34

Note: A is defined as 16 years of schooling for respondent and respondent's parent, white, Catholic, lived in an intact family at age 14; D is defined as 10 years of schooling for respondent and respondent's parent, white, conservative (type II) Protestant who attends church frequently, lived in a non-intact family at age 14, and lived (in 1992) in the West region. These two are shown in table 12.12.

any information about the sex partner obtained from "searching." In fact, the traditional view was that one sought someone as a partner who had not had a sex partner previously. More recently, that consensus has apparently dissolved, as seen in table 13.14, which reports the percentage of respondents in this analysis who believe that premarital sex is always or almost always wrong.

Table 13.14   **Percentage of Respondents Who in 1992 Believe That Premarital Sex Is Always or Almost Always Wrong**

Cohort	Men	Women
1933–42	36	53
1943–52	26	31
1953–62	21	31
1963–74	16	22

Table 13.15   **Coefficient on the Variable Denoting Virginity at Wedding**

Coefficient	Men	Women
Sole variable	−.91*	−.71*
With demographics	−.36	−.24
With attitudes	−.54*	−.50*
With attitudes and demographics	−.22	−.14

*Significant at the 95 percent level.

Thus, the information obtained from having sex with the prospective spouse may now be more oriented toward the sexual nature of the person than toward his or her general character.

We can add the three attitude variables used in section 13.2 above, attitudes about whether premarital sex is wrong, whether teen sex is wrong, and whether religion guides sexual behavior. Kahn and London (1991), for example, suggest that attitudes such as these may lie behind the observed negative relationship between virginity at marriage and marital stability. When entered into our logistic model on dissolution, these three together have a statistically significant additional influence on the stability of the marriage in the direction one would expect—those who consider these nonmarital sexual activities to be wrong have more stable marriages, as do those who report that religion guides their sexual behavior (for a related discussion, see chapter 14). We note that the inclusion of these three attitude variables also knocks the statistical significance from the variable indicating virginity at the wedding. This is also the finding of Kahn and London (1991), but they had no direct measures of attitudes and obtained results inferentially from unobservables.

Virginity at the wedding has been entered into the analysis, in fact, in four different contexts, and we summarize them in table 13.15. When we estimate the logistic with only the one variable that indicates virginity at the wedding, the difference in the odds of divorce is dramatic: the virgin has a likelihood of divorce that is only .40 (for the men) and .49 (for the women) that of the nonvirgin (i.e., $e^{-.9114}$ for men and $e^{-.7135}$ for women). When we add the several demographic variables shown in figure 13.6, the coefficient on virginity declines by about two-thirds for both the men and the women, as table 13.15 shows. Similarly, when we instead add only the three attitude variables to the single-variable logistic, again the coefficient on virginity declines, especially for the men. When both the demographics and the attitudes are included, the coefficient on the virginity variable becomes insignificant, statistically, as seen in the bottom row of table 13.15. In other words, virginity before marriage is not independently related to the probability of dissolution.

13.4   Conclusion

This chapter has focused on the formation and dissolution of long-term partnerships, both as informal cohabitational and as formal marital unions. The choices about marital status and living arrangements have been shown in earlier chapters to be important determinants of many aspects of sexual behavior, and here we have seen evidence of the rapid trend toward cohabitational partnerships, their short duration, and their effect on subsequent formal marriages. The statistical analysis here is only suggestive of the multivariate analyses that can be undertaken to better understand the relation between sexual behavior early in the life course and the character and quality of subsequent partnerships.

CHAPTER 14

Normative Orientations toward Sexuality

Thus far, we have focused primarily on the behavioral component of sex—
what people do and with whom and how often they do it. Yet much of the prior
sociological research on sexuality has focused on people's *attitudes* toward
specific sexual behaviors, such as premarital intercourse, sex between same-
gender partners, masturbation, etc. (e.g., Reiss 1967; Reiss, Anderson, and
Sponaugle 1980; Klassen, Williams, and Levitt 1989). There are two main
reasons for this. One is that many of our cultural understandings about sexuality are tightly bound to moral and religious proscriptions condemning certain
behaviors as wrong, unnatural, or perverse while at the same time permitting
others only in their "proper" context. Consequently, these normative labels
frame much of the public and even academic discourse on sexuality, and attempts to shift the discussion to a different (e.g., scientific) frame are met with
strong resistance. The political history of this very study provides an excellent
case in point.

Another reason for this focus on sexual attitudes is that they serve as a rough
indicator of how people *think about* a particular issue or activity. And many of
the processes that we as social scientists are interested in studying involve these
thoughts. For example, consider the difference between a biological theory of
adolescent sexual behavior and a social scientific theory. The biological theory
might involve hormonal and other physical changes that result in both the capacity for and perhaps an increased interest in sexual activity. Although the
individual may have some awareness of and control over the effects of this
process, the process itself is a physiological one that is not dependent on conscious thought. In contrast, the social scientific theory would likely focus on
such factors as the amount and type of sexual information provided by parents,
the changing sexual activities and expectations of peers, and opportunities for
particular types of sexual relationships. These factors operate not through a
physiological process but rather through their effect on the conscious thoughts
of the individual. Measuring people's attitudes allows us to characterize their

L. Philip Schumm drafted this chapter and generated the tabular and graphic materials, ably
assisted by Christopher Browning. The chapter was prepared under the direction of Edward O.
Laumann.

509

thoughts with respect to a specific set of issues, thereby allowing us to make inferences about the effects of various social processes on these thoughts.

In studying people's attitudes, it is important to keep in mind that the link between attitudes and behavior is rarely straightforward. Not only is it often unclear which causes which, but in certain cases it is also possible for people to behave in a manner inconsistent with their expressed attitudes. For this reason, we resist the temptation to correlate an attitude toward a single behavior with the occurrence of that behavior, claiming that we have in some sense "explained" the behavior. Rather, we examine the association between an individual's overall profile of sexual attitudes and a wide range of different sexual behaviors. This, of course, does not eliminate the indeterminacy regarding causal direction, yet it can be argued that an individual's profile of sexual attitudes is both more informative in characterizing his or her views on sexuality and more stable over time than his or her response to a specific item. This issue of the link between attitudes and behavior will be discussed further in section 14.3.

Our data on sexual attitudes consist of responses to sixteen questions selected to represent a broad range of sexual topics (for the specific wording of these questions, see appendix C, section 10, questions 1–16). We would have liked to include a more comprehensive battery of questions; however, the length and complexity of other sections of the questionnaire prevented us from doing so. Instead, we selected a subset of questions that either have proved to be significant in previous studies of sexual attitudes or were considered by us to be fundamental to understanding an individual's sexual outlook. (Readers interested in seeing a larger set of sexual attitude items should consult Klassen, Williams, and Levitt [1989] or the literature review in Sprecher and McKinney [1993, chap. 1].)

14.1 Different Normative Orientations

In 1964, Ira Reiss used several "wrong/not wrong" questions about the occurrence of premarital sex in different types of relationships to construct a scale of premarital sexual permissiveness (Reiss 1960, 1967). He was able to show that people's responses to the questions depended upon the degree of affection in the relationship—the more affection there was, the more likely people were to approve of premarital sex. This represented the first serious attempt to measure people's attitudes toward a particular sexual behavior.

Reiss's scale of premarital sexual permissiveness, and a subsequent scale he developed for measuring extramarital sexual permissiveness (Reiss, Anderson, and Sponaugle 1980), each focused on people's attitudes about a single activity as it might occur in different relational contexts. Yet many who have studied sexual attitudes have not been as careful to define what exactly they were attempting to measure. Several researchers have loosely applied the concept of permissiveness to interpret people's attitudes about a wide variety of sexual activities, and in the worst cases have simply combined questions about many different behaviors into a general permissiveness scale without checking to see whether or not the data were consistent with this assumption. In fact, the evidence indicates that a single unidimensional concept such as permissiveness cannot alone account for all types of sexual and related behavior. For example, in their study of sexual attitudes, Klassen, Williams, and Levitt (1989) found that many of their attitude questions failed to conform to a unidimensional model. Similarly, Hendrick and Hendrick (1987) identified four different dimensions underlying the set of items that they studied, one of which corresponded to permissiveness. This same finding—that a single dimension cannot alone explain the full range of sexual attitudes—is echoed in the results that we present below.

Although the concept of permissiveness has been used to interpret much of the empirical research on sexual attitudes, an alternative approach has been present within the theoretical literature on sexuality. Briefly, this approach suggests that various social institutions such as religion and the family affect sexual attitudes, not by dictating a specific level of permissiveness, but rather by creating and maintaining several different "orientations" toward sexuality (DeLamater 1987). These orientations are based on certain assumptions about the purpose of sexual activity and consist of both a set of specific attitudes and a logic that sustains them. (Note that this use of the term *sexual orientation* is different from the way in which it is commonly used—to refer to being homosexual or heterosexual.)

Three major normative orientations toward sexuality have been identified in the literature.[1] The first is generally referred to as *procreational* because it is based on the assumption that the primary purpose of sexual activity is to reproduce. The Roman Catholic church has been a strong proponent of this idea and has used it to justify restrictions against those behaviors that do not lead (or are not intended to lead) to conception: masturbation, oral sex, homosexuality, sex outside marriage, even the use of birth control. The second orientation is a *relational* one and is based on the idea that sexual activity is a natural component of an intimate, loving relationship. Unlike the procreational orientation, a relational orientation allows for premarital sex within the context of a loving relationship; it is inconsistent, however, with extramarital sex (to the extent that it represents "cheating on" one's spouse) and with activities such as group sex and casual sex without love. Finally, the third orientation is called *recreational* and is based on the premise that pleasure is the primary purpose of sexual activity. Although it may be accompanied by a proscription against forcing others to comply, this orientation essentially allows for any type of sexual activity among consenting adults.

This is the way in which these orientations are usually described—each is

---

1. These three are not the only sexual orientations that have been identified; others include an ascetic orientation and a therapeutic orientation (DeLamater 1987). We decided that the number of people who might subscribe to these orientations is too small to warrant attention here.

based on a fundamental assumption about the purpose of sexual activity from which a set of appropriate sexual behaviors may be logically derived. However, although these basic assumptions are occasionally used by people to justify their own actions or beliefs, there are also additional factors that significantly affect people's sexual orientations. Acceptance of homosexuality provides a good example. The relational orientation, as originally defined, does not preclude sexual activity within committed, same-gender couples, and the recreational orientation does not preclude any type of sexual activity as long as those involved give their consent. However, our data (as well as previous studies) indicate that a significant number of people who subscribe to an otherwise relational or recreational perspective do not approve of any type of same-gender sexual activity. This fact implies the existence of at least one additional factor determining people's sexual attitudes, and it is reasonable to assume that there may be others. The important point, however, is that there is considerably more empirical variation within these orientations than is conveyed by their basic descriptions.

In addition, although the assumption that the sole purpose of sex is reproduction is still the explicit foundation of the Catholic church's formal position on sexual issues, the fact that Catholic parishioners in the United States (and even some priests) disagree with the church's position on the use of birth control (Greeley 1990) indicates that many Catholics are no longer willing to accept this assumption. Moreover, most Protestant denominations view sex not solely in terms of procreation but also as a sacred expression of love within marriage. These facts suggest that, for the purpose of describing current sexual attitudes, the procreational orientation might be referred to more accurately as a *traditional* orientation, characterized by many of the same attitudes about specific behaviors (especially those occurring outside marriage), but justified instead by an appeal to traditional moral values.

It is important to recognize that, while these orientations may be ordered roughly in terms of their level of permissiveness (procreational being the least permissive, recreational the most), this is not the fundamental distinction among them. Instead, it is the nature of the relationship within which the sexual activity should occur. And it is this distinction, we argue, that is most important for understanding why people approve of certain behaviors while disapproving of others.

Although these three orientations toward sexuality are essentially defined in terms of attitudes regarding the type of relationship within which sex should or should not occur (e.g., premarital, extramarital, homosexual), it is reasonable to assume that an individual's orientation toward sexuality will be reflected in his or her attitudes toward the entire domain of sexually related issues. Thus, in an attempt to identify empirically these and other possible orientations, we performed a cluster analysis in order to identify sets of respondents who exhibited the same or similar profiles of responses across nine different attitude items (for another application of cluster analysis to the study of sexual attitudes, see Lottes 1985).[2] Briefly, cluster analysis is a data-reduction technique in which respondents are classified into distinct sets so that those within each set have the same (or similar) responses to the items in question (for an introduction to cluster analysis, see Everitt 1993 or Anderberg 1973). We carefully examined solutions with between five and twelve clusters and found the solution with seven to strike a good balance between within-cluster homogeneity and parsimony. The results of this analysis are presented in table 14.1.

The actual items are listed in left-most column of the table. Although each question included several possible responses, we chose to dichotomize each item for the purposes of this analysis. One reason for this was to simplify the clustering process—dichotomizing provided a convenient way of combining items with different response categories. More important, however, dichotomizing certain items allowed us to concentrate on that portion of the response variation that was most important to us substantively. For example, consider the response categories for the first four items: "always wrong," "almost always wrong," "sometimes wrong," and "not wrong at all." In this case, our primary interest was in identifying the existence of certain normative rules, rules that, by definition, do not allow exceptions. The willingness of an individual to use situational as opposed to absolute morality—revealed by answering something other than "always wrong"—indicates a qualitatively different way of thinking about a rule than those who accept the rule without exception. And it is this distinction, rather than the distinction between answering "almost always wrong" and "sometimes wrong," for example, that we wanted to emphasize.

The numbers in the table indicate the percentage of individuals in each cluster who answered a particular item in the manner indicated. For example, a full 100 percent of those in the first cluster reported that premarital sex is always wrong, making it the only cluster in which a majority of members held this position. Continuing down the same column, we see that nearly all of those in this first cluster also believe teenage, extramarital, and same-gender sex to be always wrong. Most said that they would not have sex unless they were in love and that their religious beliefs guide their sexual behavior. There appears to be slightly less consensus regarding laws against pornography (70.6 percent said that such laws should exist), although this cluster is in general more favorable toward such laws than are the other six clusters. With respect to abortion, only 56 percent agreed that a woman should be able to obtain one if she has been raped (lower than all other clusters by 30 percentage points or more), and nearly everyone (except for two respondents out of 439) disagreed that abortion should be legal in all cases. Since each of these positions is consistent with what we have described as a traditional orientation toward sexuality, and since

---

2. The remaining seven items were excluded, either because their response categories were not easily comparable to those for the first nine items, or because the nature of their association with other items suggested that they were interpreted by respondents in an ambiguous manner.

Table 14.1   Results of Cluster Analysis Based on Responses to Nine Sexual Attitude Items (column percentages; N = 2,843)

	Traditional			Relational		Recreational	
	Conservative	Pro-Choice	Religious	Conventional	Contemporary Religious	Pro-Life	Libertarian
1. Premarital sex is always wrong	100.0[a]	23.6	0.0	.4	.8	6.5	0.0
2. Premarital sex among teenagers is always wrong	99.5	90.3	78.6	29.1	33.6	65.7	19.7
3. Extramarital sex is always wrong	98.2	91.0	92.1	94.2	52.1	59.3	32.0
4. Same-gender sex is always wrong	96.4	94.4	81.9	65.4	6.4	85.9	9.0
5. There should be laws against the sale of pornography to adults	70.6	47.2	53.1	12.2	11.7	14.9	6.4
6. I would not have sex with someone unless I was in love with them	87.5	66.0	98.0	83.8	65.3	10.1	19.5
7. My religious beliefs have guided my sexual behavior	91.3	72.9	74.7	8.7	100.0	25.0	0.0
8. A woman should be able to obtain a legal abortion if she was raped	56.3	98.6	82.3	99.1	99.3	84.3	99.8
9. A woman should be able to obtain a legal abortion if she wants it for any reason	.5	100.0	0.0	87.4	84.9	9.3	88.6
Total	15.4	15.2	19.1	15.9	9.3	8.7	16.4

Note: The oversample was excluded from the analysis, as were respondents who had missing values for one or more items. Clusters were derived by minimizing the squared Euclidean distance between members within each cluster. All items were dichotomized before clustering.

[a]The percentage of people in the conservative traditional cluster who believe that premarital sex is always wrong.

this cluster is by far the most uniformly conservative, we refer to it as *conservative*. Note that this cluster comprises approximately 15 percent of the total population.

The next cluster differs from the first in that only one-quarter of its members believe that premarital sex is always wrong. Yet, with regard to most other items, this cluster is still generally conservative. This makes it surprising that every respondent in this cluster reported that women should be able to obtain legal abortions in all cases. For this reason, we refer to this cluster as *pro-choice*. The fact that this cluster combines relatively conservative positions on most items with the single most liberal position on abortion is our first indication that the underlying structure of these data may be more than unidimensional. Moreover, note the different image that this gives of how opinions on abortion are distributed in the population. A common way to think about this is that opposition toward abortion is associated with conservative attitudes on other sexual issues, and, for the data as a whole, it is. However, this cluster reveals that 15 percent of the population—a number equal to the size of the conservative cluster—report conservative positions on most items while at the same time unanimously reporting themselves as being pro-choice.

The primary distinction between the traditional clusters (especially the conservative cluster) and those that we have labeled *relational* is that respondents in the latter almost uniformly believe that there are certain situations in which premarital sex is not wrong (most believe that it is wrong only sometimes or not at all).[3] However, with respect to other items, there is considerable variation among the relational clusters. For example, cluster 3 is in many respects similar to the conservative cluster, although somewhat more tolerant with respect to items 2–5. We have labeled this cluster *religious* because roughly three-quarters of its members reported that religious beliefs shape their sexual behavior and because its attitudes against such activities as same-gender sex and abortion are consistent with the formal positions of many religious groups. In contrast, those in the following cluster are more tolerant than those in the religious cluster with regard to teenage sex, homosexuality, pornography, and abortion and are much less likely to report that religious beliefs influence their sexual conduct (only 8.7 percent did so). We refer to this cluster as *conventional* since most still report that both extramarital and same-gender sex— behaviors that many would view as being unconventional—are always wrong.

The remaining relational cluster is much more tolerant of homosexuality, with only 6.4 percent believing that it is always wrong. Surprisingly, however, all respondents in this cluster reported that religious beliefs guide their sexual behavior—more than in any other cluster. We therefore refer to this cluster as *contemporary religious* since its opinions regarding items 1–5 and 9 reflect not

---

3. Only 20 percent of the entire sample claimed that premarital sex is always wrong; 8 percent said that it is almost always wrong, 24 percent wrong only sometimes, and the remaining 48 percent not wrong at all.

traditional religious doctrine but rather the newly adopted positions of more liberal denominations (Roof 1993). Although the fact that half of those in this cluster do not believe that extramarital sex is always wrong may seem inconsistent with what we have described as a relational orientation, this is not necessarily the case. Instead, it may be that many of those in this cluster are what we might call *hyperrelational,* that is, willing to condone extramarital sex in situations where an individual has become emotionally committed to a partner.

Just as the primary distinction between the traditional and the relational clusters is disapproval of premarital sex, the primary distinction between the relational clusters and those that we have labeled *recreational* is that most of those in the latter do not consider love to be a necessary prerequisite for engaging in sex. The first of these clusters is interesting since it combines relatively liberal positions on extramarital sex and pornography with relatively conservative positions on homosexuality and abortion. For this reason, we call this cluster *pro-life.* In contrast, the second recreational cluster reflects consistently liberal views on each of the nine items; we therefore refer to it as *libertarian.* Note that the pro-life cluster provides further evidence of the multidimensional structure of these data. Specifically, it appears that this group's negative position toward both homosexuality and abortion is the result not simply of a lack of permissiveness but also of specific beliefs about the importance of gender in determining appropriate sex partners and about how the consequences of sexual conduct, such as pregnancy, should be handled.

Our examination of table 14.1 confirms the utility of the cluster analysis. First, we see that, for several of the items, the clusters are quite homogeneous, indicating that much of the variation in these data can be described in terms of a few discrete sets of individuals who share a particular profile of responses. This reflects in part the relatively high level of association among many of the items, for, if the items had been generated randomly with respect to each other, a larger number of clusters would have resulted.[4] Of course, the relative homogeneity of the clusters does not alone prove that they are socially significant. However, the fact that most of them can be interpreted on the basis of our theoretical expectations does suggest that they are capturing recognizable ways of thinking about sexuality.

In addition, the cluster analysis emphasizes two important features of the data that would be obscured by automatically attempting to reduce them to one or more underlying scales. The substantive rationale for combining several items into a scale is that the items are measuring roughly the same attributes among all individuals being studied. Indeed, it is this assumption that allows one meaningfully to compare the scores of two different people on an intelli-

---

4. For example, five binary variables, each with a mean of .5 and each generated randomly with respect to the other, would yield thirty-two different response profiles, were the number of observations sufficient. In this case, the fact that the means differ from .5 may limit the total number of randomly generated response profiles.

gence test, for example. However, in this case, we have good reason to believe that some people perceive certain sexual behaviors quite differently than other people do and that these perceptions are likely to affect their attitudes toward these behaviors. For example, it is likely that people's attitudes toward homosexuality depend in part on whether they perceive it to be the result of personal choice or a biologically determined attribute of the individual. The same is also likely to be true of people's attitudes toward abortion, with some interpreting it as killing and others not. As a consequence of these differences, the logic by which these attitudes are related to other sexual attitudes may differ across people. The advantage of the clustering approach is that it does not place any restrictions on this possibility while the scaling approach does.

A second, related feature of the data that is emphasized by focusing on clusters of individuals is the discreteness of the attitude space. By this, we mean that we may think of the population as composed of distinct groups, each with a particular set of attitudes about sexual activities, rather than as a single set of individuals who all vary according to one or more sexual dimensions. Although a formal comparison of these two alternatives is beyond the scope of this chapter, one should recognize that the former is more consistent with the social mechanisms by which these attitudes are adopted and maintained. In contrast to intelligence or depression, which are intrapsychic in nature, sexual attitudes are largely social phenomena; that is, for many people, a particular position on abortion is the result of membership in a particular religious or political group, and voicing that position serves to reaffirm that affiliation. In fact, the same may be argued of attitudes with regard to premarital sex, same-gender sex, and other sexual activities. The effect is that people are motivated to comply exactly with a particular group's position—coming close to it is unlikely to be sufficient. And it is membership in these groups that is likely to have significant effects on people's sexual preferences and behaviors.

Although cluster analysis seems in general to be well suited to the social phenomena that we are attempting to capture, we are still left with the question of whether the clusters that we have identified are the "correct" ones. The fact that these clusters are related to both master status attributes and sexual behavior in predictable ways, as we see below, provides some confirmation of this. However, addressing this question also requires that we pay attention to certain aspects of the way in which these particular clusters were generated.

For example, we generated these clusters using the responses to nine questions and, having no specific alternative available, weighted each of these nine items equally. However, this procedure ignores the fact that these items vary, both with respect to their social and political salience and in the extent to which they are socially recognizable. For example, attitudes concerning abortion are often polarized into two quite visible positions—"pro-choice" and "pro-life"—and the same is often true of attitudes concerning premarital and same-gender sex. In contrast, belief in love as a prerequisite for sex is more latent, meaning that it is less organized politically and less likely to be talked about and recognized by others. A similar dynamic may also operate with regard to extramarital sex since, because it is so overwhelmingly disapproved of, those who do approve of and/or engage in it have strong incentives not to talk about it with others. Consequently, it is possible that these latter attitudes are less important in distinguishing socially relevant clusters than the former. Although these examples suggest that further work be done with weighted versions and/ or subsets of these data, we choose to present the full, unweighted analysis because of its descriptive utility. In addition, although we are primarily interested here in socially relevant differences, we were also open to the possibility that the more latent features of an individual's normative orientation might be associated with his or her sexual behavior.

A second yet related issue involves the specific form of the responses that we used. As we said before, although the original responses to questions 1–7 consisted of four possible categories, we dichotomized them before performing the cluster analysis. This was because, owing to the clustering technique used, including all four categories in the analysis would have meant treating them as though they were interval scale measurements, as though, for example, the distance between "always wrong" and "wrong only sometimes" is exactly twice as large as the distance between "always wrong" and "almost always wrong." And, as we have argued, the social logic of these attitudes strongly suggests that this is not the case. Nevertheless, by using only dichotomous versions of the items, we are ignoring potential subtleties reflected by responses across all four categories. Future work is needed to determine what these shaded responses reveal about how people evaluate particular sexual activities.

Despite these unanswered questions regarding the appropriate weights for different items and the way in which the different response categories should be handled, we argue that the cluster solution presented here is an important first step in identifying different normative orientations toward sexuality and in estimating the distribution of these different orientations in the population. Next, we turn to an examination of the distribution of these orientations within master status groups and different regions of the country.

14.2 The Distribution of Orientations within Master Status Groups

Table 14.2 shows the incidence of each orientation within different master status groups. It is important to recognize that this manner of examining the association between status attributes and sexual attitudes provides a more detailed picture than what has generally been done in the past—studying the association either between attributes and individual attitudes or between attributes and an individual's score on a scale of sexual permissiveness. This is because, as we shall see, it is possible for different combinations of orientations to be over- or underrepresented within particular status groups. Focusing on a single attitude or scale is likely to miss such effects.

Looking first at the overall distributions for men and women (first column),

we see that women are more likely to report either of the traditional orientations and that men are more likely to report either of the recreational orientations. This latter difference is particularly sharp for the pro-life cluster; 13.9
percent of men but only 4.5 per cent of women are in this cluster. This is not
surprising since restricting abortion limits women's options more directly than
it does men's. Among the relational orientations, the gender differences vary.
Specifically, women are more likely than men to subscribe to the religious or
contemporary religious orientations, while there is little difference with respect to the conventional orientation. These first-order gender differences are
consistent with previous research demonstrating greater permissiveness toward
both premarital and extramarital sexuality among men and greater religious
involvement among women. What is less obvious, and what should be noted
carefully as we examine the remainder of the table, are the second-order gender effects, that is, gender differences in the *differences* across other status
categories.

   With regard to race, we see that blacks have the highest percentage of traditionally oriented people and the lowest percentage of libertarians (except for
Hispanic men). Leaving aside for the moment the question of why this is the
case, we note that this finding gives a very different impression than previous
research claiming that blacks are more sexually permissive than whites (e.g.,
Smith 1994; Klassen, Williams, and Levitt 1989).[5] This difference is due
largely to the fact that other studies have focused primarily on the partial effects of race after other variables have been controlled. Indeed, our own multivariate analyses (reported below) indicate that blacks have somewhat lower
odds of being in the conservative cluster after taking into account the effects
of gender. age, marital status, and religion. However, great care must be taken
in interpreting such multivariate models when they are applied to survey data
(for an excellent discussion of the issues involved, see Lieberson 1985).

   Both the pro-choice and the pro-life clusters also exhibit interesting racial
differences. Specifically, there are proportionally fewer whites in the pro-
choice cluster than either blacks or Hispanics, while at the same time there are
proportionally fewer white men in the pro-life cluster than other men. Making
sense of this apparent contradiction requires thinking about the reasons why
people have either a traditional or a recreational approach to sexuality. In the
former case, people are recruited to and maintain a traditional orientation
largely through religious participation. Yet among this group, those who live
in poor areas and are thus disproportionately composed of minority groups

   5. Because some studies have emphasized a positive association between being black and ap-
proving premarital sexuality, one might wonder whether refining the traditional clusters to include
only those who believe that premarital sexuality is always wrong would decrease the percentage
of blacks in these clusters relative to the percentage of whites. However, a simple cross-tabulation
between race and one's attitude toward premarital sexuality indicates not: 21.6 percent of black
men but only 16.6 percent of white men reported that premarital sex is always wrong. The corresponding percentages for women are 27.8 and 20.0, respectively.

Table 14.2   Cluster Membership, by Master Status Groups (column percentages)

Cluster	All	Race			Age			Marital Status[a]			
		White	Black	Hispanic	18–29	30–44	45–59	Never Married	Cohabiting	Married	Div./Sep./Wid.
Men											
Traditional:											
Conservative	13.2	13.3	14.8	7.7	8.7	13.3	19.5	8.6	0.0	19.3	5.3
Pro-choice	13.7	12.7	17.6	17.6	10.4	14.2	17.5	8.4	10.7	17.1	13.3
Relational:											
Religious	15.8	15.8	11.3	20.9	17.3	14.4	16.2	11.6	12.5	18.4	16.5
Conventional	16.3	17.6	8.5	16.5	25.3	12.5	10.6	21.3	28.6	12.7	14.9
Contemporary religious	8.1	8.2	5.6	7.7	4.0	11.5	7.6	8.4	5.4	8.0	7.4
Recreational:											
Pro-life	13.9	12.0	23.9	19.8	13.5	13.8	14.5	13.7	16.1	11.9	20.7
Libertarian	19.1	20.3	18.3	9.9	20.8	20.4	14.2	28.0	26.8	12.7	21.8
N	1,279	1,004	142	91	423	550	303	371	56	648	188
Women											
Traditional:											
Conservative	17.3	16.7	18.7	20.3	12.8	16.1	24.6	11.4	1.5	20.4	17.0
Pro-choice	16.4	13.8	26.6	20.3	12.2	17.7	19.0	15.4	19.7	15.8	18.8
Relational:											
Religious	21.7	22.0	21.0	16.9	20.2	21.3	24.4	15.8	22.7	24.5	20.3
Conventional	15.5	15.1	16.4	16.9	23.2	14.4	8.4	23.2	19.7	13.9	12.4
Contemporary religious	10.4	11.1	8.4	9.3	9.7	11.7	8.9	10.4	7.6	9.7	12.4
Recreational:											
Pro-life	4.5	4.6	3.3	5.9	5.5	4.8	2.8	5.0	0.0	4.5	4.5
Libertarian	14.2	16.6	5.6	10.2	16.4	14.0	11.9	18.8	28.8	11.3	14.5
N	1,564	1,184	214	118	475	694	394	298	66	849	330

Cluster	Education					Religion[b]			
	< HS	HS Grad.	1–3 Yrs. Coll.	4 Yrs. Coll.	Grad. Deg.	None	Prot. I	Prot. II	Catholic
Men									
Traditional:									
Conservative	14.1	14.4	11.4	14.4	12.0	4.5	8.1	28.5	5.9
Pro-choice	17.5	13.9	13.3	13.9	7.4	7.3	16.2	16.0	11.9
Relational:									
Religious	20.9	18.0	17.0	7.2	13.0	7.8	14.8	16.8	21.4
Conventional	14.7	18.8	16.0	13.9	14.8	22.9	17.2	10.1	19.9
Contemporary religious	4.0	4.1	6.3	14.4	22.2	8.4	11.8	3.2	8.3
Recreational:									
Pro-life	20.3	17.4	12.4	8.7	7.4	8.9	13.1	15.5	16.9
Libertarian	8.5	13.4	23.5	27.4	23.1	40.2	18.9	9.9	15.7
N	177	367	412	208	108	179	297	375	337
Women									
Traditional:									
Conservative	23.3	20.0	14.4	14.5	12.5	3.0	11.7	31.8	9.1
Pro-choice	13.2	18.3	18.3	14.9	8.3	7.4	19.2	18.6	13.1
Relational:									
Religious	29.5	21.6	21.6	14.9	21.9	8.9	20.0	22.5	28.6
Conventional	14.1	17.4	15.9	14.0	12.5	25.9	16.1	11.2	16.7
Contemporary religious	4.0	7.0	10.8	18.2	20.8	9.6	15.3	4.7	12.6
Recreational:									
Pro-life	8.4	5.7	3.4	1.7	3.1	5.2	2.9	5.0	5.5
Libertarian	7.5	10.0	15.7	21.9	20.8	40.0	14.8	6.1	14.3
N	227	459	529	242	96	135	385	537	419

[a]Includes only those who have never been married. Those who have been married but are now divorced, widowed, or separated are included in the right-most column.
[b]Type I Protestants are those belonging to most mainline denominations; Type II Protestants consist of Baptists, those belonging to nondenominational churches, and those who have been "born again" (see chapter appendix 3.1A).

are also likely to find themselves (or someone they know) confronted with an unwanted pregnancy—a practical issue that may alter their opinion with regard to abortion. (Note that this interpretation is consistent with the fact that a higher proportion of those with less education are in the pro-choice cluster.) This narrow change in opinion also may be facilitated by the public health groups that work in these areas, many of which are ardent supporters of pro-choice legislation (Laumann and Knoke 1987, chapter 4). In contrast, there is no particular institutional basis supporting a recreational orientation to sexuality and, as a result, there are fewer pressures toward attitudinal consistency. Thus, people with a recreational approach to sex who are intolerant of homosexuality and abortion—such intolerance is more likely among blacks and Hispanics—are able to retain these opinions while at the same time maintaining a recreational orientation.

Among both men and women, the likelihood of being in either traditional cluster increases with increasing age. As we have discussed elsewhere, this likely reflects both a cohort effect and the fact that increasing age is accompanied by a higher probability of being married and having children, events that tend to be associated with a higher degree of sexual conservatism. At the same time, it is also interesting to note that, while the percentage of people in the two recreational clusters generally declines with age, this change is too small to offset fully the increase in the proportion traditional. Consequently, much of the increase in the proportion traditional comes from the sharp decrease in the conventional cluster. In fact, from the youngest to the oldest age category, the conventional cluster is reduced to between half and one-third of its original size. It may be that, for some, the conventional orientation represents a modern, nonreligious alternative to a traditional orientation. Regardless, the fact that this cluster contains one-quarter of all adults under age thirty suggests that it deserves special attention.

As expected, being married both increases one's chances of being in the conservative cluster and decreases one's chances of being in the libertarian cluster. Cohabiting has the opposite effect, consistent with our interpretation throughout the book of the decision to cohabit as reflecting a more liberal orientation toward sexuality. However, it should also be noted that both men and women involved in cohabitational relationships are well represented in the pro-choice cluster and that roughly 40 percent of them are in either the religious or the conventional cluster. These figures document the wide variation in the types of people who cohabit, a point that is often overlooked when focusing on a single measure of the association between cohabiting behavior and attitudes. Such variation may reflect different motivations for cohabiting, such as cohabiting as a prelude to marriage versus cohabiting as an alternative to marriage.

The differences in the prevalence of the different orientations across educational groups are both marked and uniform. For example, with each increase in educational category, the percentages of both men and women in the traditional clusters either decline or remain constant, with only two exceptions. In contrast, the percentages of men and women in the libertarian cluster generally increase with each increase in education level. Both these observations are consistent with prior work demonstrating positive associations between education and approval of premarital sexuality, extramarital sexuality, and same-gender sex. Interestingly, unlike the profile for the libertarian cluster, the percentages of both men and women in the other recreational cluster generally decrease with increasing education. This finding confirms that our cluster analysis was indeed successful in distinguishing between two distinct types of recreational orientations and that the social factors affecting adoption of these two orientations are quite different in nature.

The percentages of those in the contemporary religious cluster increase steadily with increasing education. This result largely reflects the positive association between education and approval of homosexuality since one of the major differences between this cluster and the other two relational clusters is that those in the former are considerably more tolerant of same-gender sex. However, it is also significant that this is the only cluster to combine religious influence on sexual behavior with a relatively tolerant position on several items. Together with the educational composition of this cluster, we interpret this as reflecting either membership in a liberal parish or a willingness to rethink and perhaps reject particular elements of church doctrine.

Like the other status groups, the differences across religious groups are greatest for the traditional and libertarian orientations. Specifically, the conservative orientation occurs most frequently among Type II Protestants, where the percentage is at least triple that for any of the other religious groups. In contrast, the libertarian orientation is most common among those with no religious affiliation, where the percentage is more than double that for the other groups. Type II Protestants, on the other hand, are particularly unlikely to subscribe to this orientation.

Three additional observations confirm our earlier interpretations of the different relational clusters. As expected, the highest proportion of people in the conventional cluster are those with no religious affiliation, consistent with the fact that only 8.7 percent of this cluster reported that religious beliefs influenced their sexual behavior. Second, the contemporary religious orientation is most frequent among Type I Protestants and only somewhat less frequent among Catholics. Unlike Type II Protestants, these two groups contain specific denominations, parishes, or individual members who have accepted more tolerant attitudes toward sexual issues. Similarly, the fact that roughly 9 percent of those with no religious affiliation report having a contemporary religious orientation suggests that such people pursue a less doctrine-oriented form of religious experience. Finally, Catholics are most likely to subscribe to the religious orientation, a finding that is consistent with this cluster's strong disapproval of abortion and homosexuality.

As table 14.2 clearly demonstrates, there are significant differences across master status groups in the probabilities of having specific normative orientations toward sexuality. An important consequence of this is that in many cases it increases the probability that partnerships will form between those with the same or similar orientations, owing to the strong tendency toward equal status contact among sexual relationships documented in chapter 6. This is important, not only because it increases the likelihood that two partners will "get along with" each other, but also, as we show below, because it can increase the likelihood that they will find the same sexual activities to be appealing.

An important limitation of the data in table 14.2 is that they contain only information about the zero-order associations between master statuses and normative orientations. As we have repeatedly argued, such information provides a useful description of reality. Thus, the fact that one-third of black men subscribe to one of the two traditional orientations, as compared to only one-quarter of white or Hispanic men, is itself a social fact with important implications. However, the fact that many of the master statuses are empirically correlated with each other leads us to ask how each one is *partially* associated with membership in the different normative clusters or, in other words, what the effects are of one status variable "controlling for" the effects of the others.

Table 14.3 presents two models: one predicting the odds of being in the conservative cluster, the other predicting the odds of being in the libertarian cluster. Both models may be interpreted as follows. The baseline odds, given at the top of each column, describe the odds of being in each cluster for the baseline group, which is in this case unmarried white men between the ages of eighteen and twenty-nine who have twelve years of education or less and no religious affiliation. The coefficients of the model describe the percentage change in these odds associated with a particular status category relative to the baseline category, holding the other variables constant. Thus, among unmarried people, being female increases one's odds of being in the conservative cluster by 69 percent relative to the odds for men. The effect of being female is somewhat smaller among married people, with the odds increasing by only 11 percent. That the effect of being female is different for married and unmarried respondents is due to the presence of an interaction term in the model between gender and marital status.

Continuing on, we see that blacks are somewhat less likely to be in the conservative cluster, Hispanics more likely. Note that the estimated effect of being black on the odds of being in the conservative cluster is negative, even though blacks as a group have a higher percentage of people in the conservative cluster than do whites. This discrepancy is due to the fact that the model is measuring racial differences while holding the effects of gender, age, marital status, and religion constant.

Being older is associated with an increase in the odds of being in the conservative cluster, an increase of 38 percent for those aged thirty to forty-four and 111 percent for those aged forty-five to fifty-nine. Being married also increases one's odds of being in this cluster, although more for men than for women.

Table 14.3   Two Models Showing Changes in the Odds of Being in a Particular Normative Cluster Associated with Different Master Status Groups

	Traditional Conservative		Recreational Libertarian		
Baseline odds	1 to 58.8		1 to 1.6		
	Unmarried	Married	Whites	Blacks	Hispanics
Gender:					
Men	...	...	...	...	...
Women	+69%[a]	+11%	−11%	−62%	−11%
	All		Men	Women	
Race:					
White	...		...	...	
Black	−39%		+18	−49%	
Hispanic	+77%		−46%	−46%	
Age:			No significant differences		
18–29	...				
30–44	+38%				
45–59	+111%				
	Men	Women	All		
Marital status:					
Not married	...	...	...		
Married	+142%	+59%	−48%		
Education:	No significant differences				
12 years or less			...		
13–15 years			+83%		
16 years or more			+122%		
	All				
Religion:					
None	...		...		
Type I Protestant	+118%		−70%		
Type II Protestant	+886%		−83%		
Catholic	+66%		−68%		

[a]Indicates that the odds of being in the "traditional conservative" cluster are 69 percent higher for unmarried women than for unmarried men; the odds are only 11 percent higher for married women than for married men.

Thus, marriage may be thought of as narrowing the gap between men and women in the odds of being conservative. Surprisingly, education was found to have no statistically significant effects on the odds of being in this cluster once the other variables were taken into account. As expected, each of the three religious categories was associated with increased odds of being in the conservative cluster, with Catholics exhibiting the smallest increase (66 percent), Type I Protestants the next largest (118 percent), and Type II Protestants by far the largest (886 percent). In fact, this increase in odds for Type II Protestants is by far the largest effect recorded in either model.

Looking now at the second model, we see that, in contrast to the first, being female decreases one's odds of being in the libertarian cluster. Yet, in this model, rather than an interaction between gender and marital status, we observe an interaction between gender and race. Thus, the decrease in odds associated with being female is greater for blacks than for the other two racial groups. This interaction may also be described in terms of the estimated effects of race. For men, being black increases one's odds of being in the libertarian cluster, while, for women, it decreases one's odds. Being Hispanic decreases the odds of being in this cluster for both men and women.

Unlike the first model, the model predicting the odds of being in the libertarian cluster shows no statistically significant effects of age. It does, however, show effects for education. Specifically, the odds of being in this cluster increase with each increase in education: 83 percent for those having one to three years of college and 122 percent for those having four years of college or more. In contrast, each category of religious affiliation is associated with a decrease in odds, as is being married.

Together, these two models are helpful in assessing the partial association between master statuses and particular normative orientations toward sexuality. However, we must exercise caution in interpreting these models since they are heavily dependent on the manner in which we have identified the two normative clusters whose membership we are predicting. Further work might be aimed at modeling the odds of being in each of the seven clusters simultaneously, thereby providing a more complete picture of the association between master statuses and normative orientations.

These differences in the incidence of specific normative orientations across master status groups also imply the existence of regional variation in the occurrence of these orientations since the master status groups are not distributed evenly across the country. In addition, some researchers have claimed to find independent effects of region, even after controlling for the differential distribution of master status groups (Klassen, Williams, and Levitt 1989). In order to address this issue of regional variation, table 14.4 presents the proportion of respondents with each of the different orientations, calculated separately for each of the nine census regions of the country. (Readers who are unfamiliar with how these regions are defined may refer to the map in fig. 14.1.) From this table, we see that the incidence of every cluster varies somewhat across the different regions. For example, roughly one-quarter of those in the East South Central and Mountain states report a conservative orientation, whereas the proportions of conservatives in New England and the Pacific states are only 7.5 and 9.9 percent, respectively. Conversely, approximately one-quarter of those in New England and the Pacific states reported a libertarian orientation,

Table 14.4 **Cluster Membership, by Region (column percentages)**

Cluster	New England	Middle Atlantic	East North Central	West North Central	South Atlantic	East South Central	West South Central	Mountain	Pacific
					Region				
Traditional:									
Conservative	7.5	11.7	13.0	11.9	16.8	25.5	22.8	27.6	9.9
Pro-choice	11.8	13.0	14.7	17.4	16.1	16.5	18.0	9.9	16.5
Relational:									
Religious	19.3	18.6	21.0	27.7	16.8	22.5	21.3	18.8	12.1
Conventional	21.1	16.4	17.4	14.5	15.2	10.5	13.5	14.4	18.0
Contemporary religious	6.2	11.7	11.8	8.5	7.9	5.5	3.0	8.8	14.1
Recreational:									
Pro-life	8.7	9.5	7.4	8.1	8.9	10.5	12.4	7.2	7.2
Libertarian	25.5	19.1	14.7	11.9	18.3	9.0	9.0	13.3	22.2

while only 9 percent of those in the South Central states reported this orientation. These differences result primarily from differences in the educational and religious composition of these regions—for instance, the fact that the East South Central states have an especially high concentration of Type II Protestants, the Pacific states a high proportion of people with no religious affiliation.

One way of summarizing the information in this table is to quantify, for any two regions, the extent to which the distribution of orientations within those two regions differs. The index of dissimilarity provides a convenient way of measuring this difference. This index is equivalent to the sum of all positive percentage differences between the 2 percent distributions and, as such, may be interpreted as the proportion of people in either region that would have to be redistributed to make the 2 percent distributions equivalent (see Duncan and Duncan 1955). Calculating this index for all pairs of regions yields a symmetrical matrix of dissimilarity scores. This information can then be represented spatially, as has been done in figure 14.2. In this figure, a larger distance between one pair of regions than between another indicates that the index of dissimilarity calculated for the first pair is greater than that for the second. Thus, we can see that the Pacific states and New England have very similar percentage distributions of the different normative orientations, while those for New England and the Mountain states, for example, are quite different.[6]

The most significant conclusion to be drawn from this figure is the extent to which it fails to reproduce the geographic distances between the regions. Instead, it identifies both the Pacific states and New England as similar, the West South Central and East South Central states as similar, and the two pairs as most different from each other.

6. We used ALSCAL to perform nonmetric multidimensional scaling on the matrix of dissimilarities. For the unidimensional solution, Kruskal's measure of stress was 0.168, indicating an acceptable fit of the model to the data.

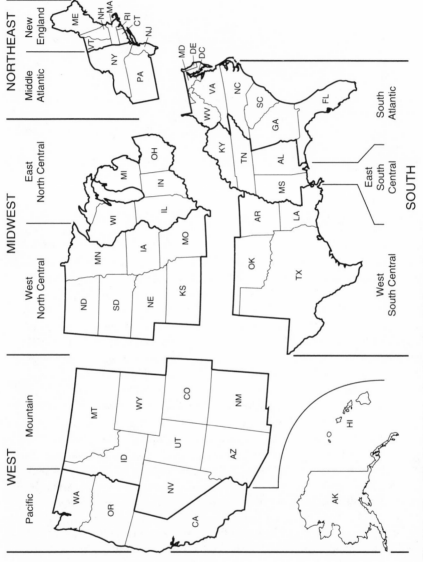

Fig. 14.1 Map of the United States showing census divisions and regions.

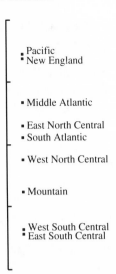

Fig. 14.2 Scale showing the relative similarity of the distribution of sexual orientations within regions.

14.3   Normative Orientations and Sexual Behavior

The fact that membership in the different normative clusters is socially organized—that is, occurs with different frequency across status groups—lends empirical support to our argument that the clusters are capturing distinctive ways of thinking about sexuality and to our larger argument throughout the book that people's understandings of sexuality are strongly conditioned by social factors. In this section, we address the link between the normative orientations, on the one hand, and concrete sexual behavior, on the other. A significant association between these two would both validate our particular cluster solution and would provide a sense of how important these normative orientations are in understanding sexual activity.

It is common to focus on the link *from* attitudes *to* behavior. We often find ourselves searching for the reasons why a person behaved a certain way, and our efforts to modify people's behaviors are often aimed at trying to change their basic attitudes, assuming that such a change will necessarily bring about changes in behavior. Public campaigns promoting the importance of "safe sex" are an excellent example. Yet, as we stated at the outset, past research has shown that the link between attitudes and behavior is complex. Specifically, this link is likely to involve reciprocal causation; that is, while changes in attitudes may bring about changes in behavior, the opposite is also possible. Thus, at a given point in time, the association between people's attitudes and their behaviors is likely to be the joint product of both processes, and to interpret it in terms of only one would be inaccurate.

Unfortunately, the only way to address this problem directly is to collect longitudinal data, an option not available to us here. Instead, we pursue a different strategy in which we use the association between cluster membership and behavior to explore the possibility that people with different normative orientations *perceive* specific sexual activities differently. Although this strategy is based on the assumption that people will try to establish some correspondence, at a cognitive level, between their beliefs and their actions, it does not depend on exactly how this occurs (i.e., whether people change their actions to fit their beliefs, or vice versa).

Table 14.5 presents the percentages of people in each of the seven clusters who reported engaging in several specific behaviors. The figures are calculated separately for men and women, and the overall percentages for men and women are given at the bottom of their respective panels so that the deviation of a particular cluster from the overall mean can be easily determined.

We may think of the different behaviors represented in this table as belonging to two sets. The first set contains those behaviors that correspond exactly to one or more of the attitude items used to derive the clusters. Thus, for example, married people who report having more than one partner during the past year are engaging in extramarital sexual activity (item 3 in table 14.1)—assuming that they were not married *after* having the additional partners. Similarly, those who are unmarried and report having either one or more partners or a positive frequency of sex are engaging in premarital sex—also assuming that they were not divorced, widowed, or separated within the past year. Same-gender sex since age eighteen would also belong to this set. The significance of this correspondence between the behavior and the attitude item is that it generates an automatic hypothesis about how the behavior will be distributed within the different clusters. Specifically, we would expect the frequency of the behavior to be low in those clusters whose members believe that the activity is always wrong and somewhat higher in clusters whose members do not. To the extent that this hypothesis is violated, we must search for an explanation for why people are behaving in a manner seemingly inconsistent with their expressed attitudes.

In contrast, the behaviors in the second set (i.e., thinking about sex, masturbation, and oral and anal sex) have no direct correspondence to the items used to derive the clusters. Therefore, we must rely on a theory about the substantive difference(s) between the clusters in order to construct a hypothesis about whether and how these behaviors will be differentially distributed among them. As a starting point, it will be useful to rely on the concept of permissiveness discussed above. According to this idea, the fundamental distinction among the clusters is their level of permissiveness. And, since permissiveness is a unidimensional concept, it implies that, the more permissive a cluster is, the more likely its members will be to engage in each of the different sexual activities.

Looking now at table 14.5, we see that, among unmarried men, those in the libertarian cluster have the highest probability of having four or more partners during the past year. The same is true for unmarried women, although the difference between the libertarian cluster and all other clusters is much greater. In fact, libertarian women have the same probability of having four or more partners in the past year as libertarian men, an interesting point of comparison. In contrast, those in the conservative cluster have the highest probability of having no partners in the past year, consistent with this cluster's unanimous disapproval of premarital sex. Nevertheless, we still see that 40 percent of unmarried conservative men and 30 percent of unmarried conservative women appear to be behaving in a manner inconsistent with their reported beliefs.[7]

Among married respondents, we may use the number of partners in the past year to look for evidence of extramarital activity. The percentages of those with two or more partners during the past year are highest for those in the two recreational clusters while, as expected, much lower for the other clusters. This point suggests that, indeed, the clusters that we have identified as recreational are distinct from all others in terms of their sexual expression. In particular, recall the fact that the proportion of respondents in the contemporary religious cluster who did not report that extramarital sex is always wrong (47.9 percent) was even somewhat less than the comparable proportion for the pro-life cluster (40.7 percent). However, the actual behavior of the contemporary religious cluster appears closer to that of the other relational and traditional clusters than it does to that of the pro-life cluster. This is an interesting finding—one that is consistent with several different explanations. For example, it may be that those classified as contemporary religious are simply less likely to be judgmental of those who engage in extramarital sex, even though they are unlikely to do so themselves. Alternatively, it may be that they would approve of extramarital sex only in situations where the marriage had already disintegrated and the two partners were in love with each other, a situation that is presumably relatively infrequent.

The data on the frequency of sex provide evidence that sexual behavior is not associated with the normative orientations in a unidimensional fashion, as the concept of permissiveness might predict. For example, among those who are unmarried, the highest frequencies of sex are reported not by the libertarian cluster but rather by the conventional and pro-life clusters for the men and by the pro-choice and conventional clusters for the women. Part of this effect may be due to differences in the number of partners that people have—if, for instance, having a single steady partner affords more opportunities for consistent sexual contact than having several partners. However, it is also possible that frequency alone is an aspect of sexual activity that is less valued by those in the libertarian cluster than by those in certain other clusters.

Thinking about sex occurs most frequently within the libertarian cluster and

---

7. These percentages overestimate the true percentages by some degree since it is possible for some respondents to have been divorced, widowed, or separated during the past twelve months. It is unlikely, however, that this explanation would account for the entire difference.

Table 14.5 Frequency of Participation in Selected Sexual Behaviors, by Attitude Cluster (row percentages)

	No Last Year Partners[a]								Frequency of Sex[a]						
	Unmarried				Married				Unmarried			Married			
Cluster	0	1	2–3	4+	0	1	2–3	4+	None	≤3/Month	1/Week+	None	≤3/Month	1/Week+	N[b]
Men															
Traditional:															
Conservative	59.5	26.2	9.5	4.8	3.2	95.2	.8	.8	60.0	25.0	15.0	1.7	25.9	72.4	40
Pro-choice	25.9	33.3	38.9	1.9	4.5	92.8	2.7	0.0	25.0	34.6	40.4	1.9	37.0	61.1	52
Relational:															
Religious	38.8	43.3	16.4	1.5	1.7	96.6	1.7	0.0	35.4	41.5	23.1	.9	33.0	66.1	65
Conventional	13.4	39.2	36.1	11.3	3.7	92.7	3.7	0.0	14.0	35.5	50.5	1.3	35.0	63.8	80
Contemporary religious	20.0	42.5	30.0	7.5	0.0	96.2	3.8	0.0	13.5	40.5	45.9	0.0	28.6	71.4	37
Recreational:															
Pro-life	10.7	31.0	48.8	9.5	3.9	80.5	10.4	5.2	13.9	31.6	54.4	2.7	26.0	71.2	73
Libertarian	14.8	30.4	40.0	14.8	1.2	85.4	12.2	1.2	15.6	50.8	33.6	0.0	32.5	67.5	77
All	22.2	34.7	34.3	8.9	2.8	91.8	4.5	.9	22.1	38.9	38.9	1.3	31.4	67.3	488
Women															
Traditional:															
Conservative	70.1	21.8	6.9	1.1	4.0	94.8	1.2	0.0	68.7	16.9	14.5	4.7	33.7	61.5	83
Pro-choice	26.8	53.6	19.6	0.0	0.0	97.8	1.5	.7	29.7	28.6	41.8	0.0	38.9	61.1	91
Relational:															
Religious	38.7	55.7	5.7	0.0	3.4	96.2	.5	0.0	39.2	31.4	29.4	3.0	33.0	64.0	102
Conventional	16.8	57.4	23.8	2.0	2.5	96.6	0.0	.8	16.7	36.5	46.9	1.7	33.9	64.3	96
Contemporary religious	16.1	48.4	33.9	1.6	4.9	92.7	2.4	0.0	16.7	55.0	28.3	1.3	32.5	66.2	60

	Think about Sex			Masturbate			Give Oral Sex[d]			Receive Oral Sex[d]			Had Anal Sex during Lifetime	N
	≤2/Month	≤2/Week	Daily +	Never	≤3/Month	1/Week+	Never	Occas.	Always	Never	Occas.	Always		
Recreational:														
Pro-life	13.8	33.0	14.9	5.3	86.8	2.6	14.3	54.9	30.8	5.4	67.6	27.0	c	37
Libertarian	c	45.8	3.1	5.2	92.7	0.0	30.6	36.6	32.8	2.1	64.6	33.3	c	91
All	30.2	20.8	2.9	1.6	95.1	0.4	c	36.6	c	2.6	63.5	33.9	c	552
Men														
Traditional:														
Conservative	13.7	43.5	42.9	53.2	30.8	16.0	51.8	38.0	10.2	55.8	35.5	8.7	14.3	137
Pro-choice	13.1	38.3	48.6	47.4	33.3	19.3	41.9	45.9	12.2	40.9	46.3	12.8	22.8	148
Relational:														
Religious	21.9	39.8	38.3	45.0	41.9	13.1	36.5	47.3	16.2	35.9	50.9	13.2	15.9	167
Conventional	10.1	31.9	58.0	34.8	37.4	27.8	23.0	55.1	21.9	18.7	59.9	21.4	24.4	187
Contemporary religious	6.9	33.3	59.8	18.2	34.3	47.5	10.6	62.8	26.6	14.9	63.8	21.3	34.3	94
Recreational:														
Pro-life	11.8	28.1	60.1	37.6	43.0	19.4	33.5	54.3	12.2	36.6	49.4	14.0	25.6	164
Libertarian	3.7	26.2	70.1	16.8	36.7	46.5	14.9	46.2	38.9	15.8	49.3	34.8	37.2	221
All	11.6	34.0	54.4	36.2	37.1	26.7	30.0	49.4	20.7	30.5	50.4	19.0	24.9	1,118
Women														
Traditional:														
Conservative	47.6	39.7	12.7	77.8	20.2	1.9	56.1	37.4	6.6	55.6	38.4	6.1	11.2	198
Pro-choice	42.4	41.6	16.0	59.7	32.1	8.2	43.2	45.9	10.9	42.8	44.1	13.1	15.4	229
Relational:														
Religious	42.4	43.8	13.8	68.8	26.5	4.6	44.8	46.9	8.4	38.5	51.0	10.5	14.0	286
Conventional	35.8	43.2	21.0	52.2	38.7	9.1	22.7	64.4	13.0	22.6	57.6	19.8	23.0	216
Contemporary religious	26.5	45.7	27.8	37.3	49.0	13.7	18.2	66.4	15.4	15.4	66.4	18.2	26.0	143

(continued)

Table 14.5   (continued)

Men

	Think about Sex			Masturbate				Give Oral Sex[d]			Receive Oral Sex[d]			Had Anal Sex during Lifetime	
	≤2/Month	≤2/Week	Daily +	Never	≤3/Month	1/Week+	N	Never	Occas.	Always	Never	Occas.	Always	Lifetime	N
Recreational:															
Pro-life	37.1	41.4	21.4	58.2	35.8	6.0	169	30.6	56.5	12.9	27.4	56.5	16.1	23.9	62
Libertarian	27.9	38.3	33.8	31.2	54.6	14.2	175	19.0	62.4	18.5	19.0	59.0	22.0	41.7	205
All	38.3	42.0	19.7	57.1	35.1	7.8	1,279	35.2	53.0	11.8	33.2	52.2	14.6	20.8	1,339

Men

	Any Same-Gender Sex since Age 18	N
Traditional:		
Conservative	3.6	169
Pro-choice	1.7	175
Relational:		
Religious	1.5	202
Conventional	4.8	208
Contemporary religious	9.7	103
Recreational:		
Pro-life	2.8	178
Libertarian	11.5	244
All	5.1	1,279

Women

	Any Same-Gender Sex since Age 18	N
Traditional:		
Conservative	1.5	270
Pro-choice	0.0	257
Relational:		
Religious	1.2	340
Conventional	2.5	243
Contemporary religious	7.4	162
Recreational:		
Pro-life	1.4	70
Libertarian	10.8	222
All	3.3	1,564

[a] Percentages for number of partners and frequency of sex have been computed separately for unmarried and married respondents. Owing to small numbers of cases, cohabiting respondents are not included.

[b] Actual N's vary slightly across behavior items owing to missing values; N's given are the smallest from that row.

[c] Fewer than thirty cases.

[d] Frequencies for giving and receiving oral sex are those for the respondent's primary partnership. The response categories were "never," "rarely or sometimes," and "usually or always."

least frequently within the traditional cluster, and, among the clusters in between, there appears to be a rough ordering from lowest to highest. The largest exceptions to this are the pro-choice cluster for men and the contemporary religious cluster for women, both of which have higher probabilities of thinking about sex daily than do the clusters directly above and below them. Interestingly, this pattern is somewhat different than that for masturbation, in which, for both men and women, the contemporary religious and libertarian clusters have by far the highest probability of masturbating once a week or more. If we think of these two behaviors as reflecting an individual's "level" of sexual interest or desire, then the difference in how they are distributed within the various clusters suggests that certain clusters may interpret masturbation differently than others. Specifically, those in the conventional and pro-life clusters, who think about sex relatively frequently, may believe that masturbation is not an appropriate way of dealing with sexual thoughts.

Among both men and women, there are clear patterns in the occurrence of both oral and anal sex. Those in the libertarian cluster are most likely to report engaging in oral sex often, and this difference is much greater among men than among women. This is followed by the conventional and contemporary religious clusters, both of which exhibit somewhat comparable percentages. The remaining clusters are roughly similar, except for the conservative cluster, which is considerably more likely than any other cluster never to have had oral sex. The pattern is similar for ever having anal sex; among men, both the contemporary religious and the libertarian clusters have relatively high percentages, whereas, among women, only the libertarian cluster does so.

One particularly interesting aspect of these patterns is that the two recreational clusters appear to be quite different, a fact that may reflect a more fundamental distinction between the two clusters in their basic approach to sexual matters. For example, Posner (1992) has suggested that the recreational orientation—the *hedonistic* orientation, as he labels it—can be further subdivided into two typical manifestations. The first views sexuality merely as a drive that must be satiated—tantamount, in his imagery, to scratching an itch. The second sees sexuality as a domain of physical interactions to be cultivated. While neither requires love as a prerequisite for the initiation of sex, those people represented by the latter orientation are less likely to view vaginal intercourse as the definitive sexual technique and are therefore more inclined to elaborate on their repertoire of sexual activities. It may be that these two manifestations of the recreational orientation explain, to some extent, the differences that we observe between pro-life and libertarian respondents.

Finally, we see that the occurrence of same-gender sex is largely confined to both the contemporary religious and the libertarian clusters. This is consistent with the fact that these are the two clusters that expressed the most tolerant attitude toward homosexuality, although, as we have said, it is unclear which is the result of which. Yet the relatively high percentages in these two clusters should not overshadow the fact that, for both men and women, each cluster contains at least some respondents who reported having same-gender sex (except for traditional pro-choice women).

14.4   Normative Orientations and Sexual Preferences

In addition to the behaviors in table 14.5, it is reasonable to assume that an individual's normative orientation will be associated with other facets of his or her sexual expression. For example, consider the data that we presented in chapter 4 on the extent to which people find certain sexual activities to be appealing. We demonstrated that, although these appeal items are associated with concrete sexual behaviors, they are more than merely a direct consequence of such behaviors. Rather, they appear to reflect a distinct level of sexual expression—one that is more latent and has to do with what people would prefer if they could construct an ideal sexual event. Thus, although it seems reasonable to assume that such preferences will be associated with people's normative orientations, there is no a priori reason to assume that these associations will mirror those found in table 14.5.

Table 14.6 presents the percentages of people in each normative cluster who reported certain activities to be "very appealing," "somewhat appealing" or "not appealing" (together labeled *in between*), and "not at all appealing" (for an in-depth description and analysis of these items, see chapter 4). In looking at these data, we are interested in more than simply the percentages of people who find each activity to be "very appealing" or "not at all appealing"; we are also interested in the percentage of people who made an intermediate judgment. Our hypothesis is that these intermediate judgments reflect a specific approach to sexuality, one that may be very different from that which leads to responding in either the positive or the negative extreme. This is because many normative understandings about what is or is not appropriate sexual conduct are absolute rather than a matter of degree. Thus, for example, a person who believes that homosexuality is always wrong has only one option when asked about the extent to which he or she finds same-gender sex appealing—namely, not at all! In contrast, a person who may not have had any experience with same-gender sex but does not consider homosexuality to be always wrong has, in one sense, more freedom to look at that question and perhaps answer only "not appealing" rather than "not at all appealing." This is an important distinction, one that may be expected to have significant consequences for how the two individuals will respond to a particular situation.

Looking now at the percentages in table 14.6, we see that, for nearly all the activities, those in the libertarian cluster have both the highest probability of judging the activity to be very appealing and the lowest probability of judging it to be not at all appealing, followed closely in many cases by the contemporary religious cluster. In addition, for many of the activities (except oral sex), these two clusters also have the highest percentage of people who made an intermediate judgment. This suggests that the people in these two clusters are most likely actively to cultivate their sexual repertoire, trying (or being relatively open to trying) different sexual activities when the opportunities arise. The fact that the pro-life cluster does not fit this pattern further confirms our earlier interpretation of the distinction between it and the libertarian cluster.

In general, the highest percentages of "not at all" responses are exhibited by the conservative and religious clusters, with the pro-choice cluster distinguishing itself by being more likely than the other two to make an intermediate judgment. This points to a possible difference among the two traditional clusters that was not evident in the previous section.

Finally, it is interesting that, in all clusters and for both men and women, the percentage of people who find receiving oral sex to be very appealing is greater than the percentage who find giving it to be very appealing. However, the magnitude of these differences varies according to both gender and cluster. Specifically, the biggest difference for men is in the pro-life cluster (a difference of 20.4 percent), whereas the biggest differences for women are in the conventional (18.7 percent), contemporary religious (19.2 percent), and libertarian (21.2 percent) clusters. Note, however, that the percentages of both men and women in each cluster who reported that receiving oral sex is not at all appealing are more nearly equal to the percentages who reported that performing oral sex is not at all appealing.

14.5 Conclusion

In this chapter, we have demonstrated that people's attitudes about a variety of sexual behaviors and sexually related issues may be summarized in terms of several distinct and nonoverlapping clusters, each composed of individuals with the same (or similar) profiles of responses. Moreover, the clusters that we generated correspond roughly to three different "orientations" toward sexuality that have been previously identified in the literature: traditional, relational, and recreational. Thus, our data begin to lend empirical support to what has become a very useful typology for characterizing, at a general level, people's normative orientations toward sexuality.

Having identified several distinct orientations, we then demonstrated the extent to which they are socially organized—that is, the extent to which their occurrence may be predicted by the presence (or absence) of specific master statuses. This general finding provides an important final link in what has been the main argument of this book—namely, that the ways in which people understand sexuality, and hence the behaviors that they engage in with and expect from their partners, are heavily conditioned by the social groups to which they belong. Chapters 3–13 were devoted to examining the associations between social characteristics and various types of sexual expression, and we often interpreted these associations in terms of differences in people's cultural understandings. In this final chapter, we have begun to identify and distinguish between some of these understandings.

In addition, we showed how the different normative orientations that we identified are associated with two forms of sexual expression: a variety of con-

Table 14.6   Responses to Selected Sexual Appeal Items, by Attitude Cluster (row percentages)[a]

Cluster	Sex with Multiple Partners			Sex with Same-Gender Partner			Watching Others Have Sex			Sex with a Stranger			N[b]
	Very	In Between	Not at All	Very	In Between	Not at All	Very	In Between	Not at All	Very	In Between	Not at All	
Men													
Traditional:													
Conservative	4.7	30.2	65.1	0.0	5.9	94.1	3.0	44.4	52.7	2.4	34.3	63.3	169
Pro-choice	8.6	49.1	42.3	1.1	5.1	93.7	1.1	44.0	54.9	3.4	45.1	51.4	175
Relational:													
Religious	4.0	38.8	57.2	1.0	4.0	95.0	1.0	40.3	58.7	0.5	34.8	64.7	201
Conventional	15.5	53.6	30.9	2.9	7.2	89.9	4.8	54.6	40.6	3.4	54.1	42.5	207
Contemporary religious	16.7	62.7	20.6	7.8	11.8	80.4	6.9	69.6	23.5	4.9	66.7	28.4	102
Recreational:													
Pro-life	15.9	54.5	29.5	2.3	3.4	94.4	3.4	53.7	42.9	2.8	59.3	37.9	176
Libertarian	26.2	60.7	13.1	8.6	10.7	80.7	13.5	68.9	17.6	8.6	71.7	19.7	244
All	13.5	49.8	36.7	3.4	6.7	89.9	5.1	53.3	41.6	3.8	52.3	43.8	1,274
Women													
Traditional:													
Conservative	0.0	6.0	94.0	1.1	3.4	95.5	.7	15.4	83.9	0.0	6.4	93.6	267
Pro-choice	1.2	16.0	82.8	2.3	5.4	92.2	.8	26.5	72.8	.4	13.7	85.9	256
Relational:													
Religious	.3	13.2	86.5	1.8	8.5	89.7	1.2	23.5	75.3	.3	11.2	88.5	340
Conventional	.8	19.3	79.8	3.3	11.5	85.2	2.1	35.0	63.0	.8	19.3	79.8	243
Contemporary religious	2.5	29.8	67.7	5.6	19.8	74.7	3.1	46.3	50.6	1.9	25.9	72.2	161
Recreational:													
Pro-life	0.0	20.0	80.0	2.9	11.4	85.7	1.4	24.3	74.3	2.9	22.9	74.3	70
Libertarian	3.6	40.5	55.9	4.5	25.7	69.8	1.8	58.1	40.1	2.7	36.5	60.8	222
All	1.2	19.3	79.5	2.8	11.3	85.8	1.5	31.7	66.8	1.0	17.7	81.3	1,559

Cluster	Receiving Oral Sex			Performing Oral Sex			Passive Anal Intercourse			Active Anal Intercourse			N^{b}
	Very	In Between	Not at All	Very	In Between	Not at All	Very	In Between	Not at All	Very	In Between	Not at All	
Men													
Traditional:													
Conservative	27.1	43.4	29.5	24.0	43.1	32.9	3.0	13.3	83.6	4.4	11.3	84.3	159
Pro-choice	37.4	43.7	19.0	24.7	51.1	24.1	0.0	18.1	81.9	1.2	14.5	84.3	166
Relational:													
Religious	28.6	45.7	25.6	23.7	47.0	29.3	1.5	15.2	83.2	1.5	16.8	81.6	196
Conventional	49.0	41.7	9.2	37.9	50.5	11.7	1.0	12.9	86.1	1.5	14.7	83.8	197
Contemporary religious	58.8	36.3	4.9	45.1	51.0	3.9	6.0	29.0	65.0	6.0	33.0	61.0	100
Recreational:													
Pro-life	46.0	39.2	14.8	25.6	53.4	21.0	2.9	19.5	77.6	6.3	17.1	76.6	174
Libertarian	67.2	28.3	4.5	52.5	43.0	4.5	5.8	30.2	64.0	8.4	31.9	59.7	238
All	45.2	39.5	15.3	33.7	48.1	18.2	2.8	19.6	77.6	4.2	19.7	76.0	1,231
Women													
Traditional:													
Conservative	9.8	45.5	44.7	7.1	39.8	53.0	1.5	6.4	92.1				265
Pro-choice	26.2	39.8	34.0	11.7	49.2	39.1	.4	10.2	89.4				254
Relational:													
Religious	18.1	45.1	36.8	10.4	45.1	44.5	.6	8.3	91.1				336
Conventional	40.8	42.1	17.1	22.1	55.8	22.1	1.2	12.8	86.0				240
Contemporary religious	42.2	49.1	8.7	23.0	62.7	14.3	1.9	16.8	81.4				161
Recreational:													
Pro-life	28.6	45.7	25.7	23.2	40.6	36.2	0.0	10.0	90.0				69
Libertarian	53.2	39.6	7.2	32.0	53.6	14.4	1.8	22.1	76.1				222
All	29.5	43.5	27.0	16.8	49.4	33.8	1.1	11.9	87.0				1,550

[a]Actual response categories were "very appealing," "somewhat appealing," "not appealing," and "not at all appealing." The middle two categories have been combined here.

[b]Actual N's vary slightly across appeal items owing to missing values; N's given are the smallest from that row.

crete sexual behaviors and the extent to which people find certain sexual activities appealing. The strength of these associations goes part of the way toward validating the clusters as capturing real differences among respondents. More important, these data provide an important starting point from which we may speculate about how people's interpretations of different sexual behaviors are associated with their likelihood of engaging in them.

It is important to recognize that this chapter represents only a first cut at analyzing these data. Future work should be directed at examining more closely the psychometric structure of the various attitude items, for it may be that even more parsimonious and theoretically informed descriptions are possible. Once this has been accomplished, it will provide a sound basis for building formal models to relate these normative judgments to both social characteristics and different modes of sexual expression.

EPILOGUE

Measuring social phenomena is a complex endeavor. The instruments and resources that social scientists have at their disposal for collecting data about social behavior are, for some purposes, less than ideal. Although the NHSLS has generated valid and important information, we nevertheless recognize that we have charted only a small portion of the sexual landscape of American society. Future research initiatives—our own included—will ideally base their analyses on more expansive, multifaceted, and contextualized inquiries into the sexual lives of Americans. Part of this enterprise will certainly be the introduction of longitudinal studies of sexual phenomena so that we can better assess the dynamics of change in sexual behavior and attitude over the life course and the historic shifts in cultural and social understandings of sexuality. Yet, while we acknowledge that yawning gaps in our knowledge of sexuality remain, our study has covered a broad base of subjects with reference to a considerable fund of empirical support. In this respect, we hope that we have not overburdened the reader with what might appear an endless litany of tabulated facts. Two of our highest priorities were to make as much of the information that we obtained—in some cases of considerable policy relevance—as possible available to the public in a timely fashion and to do so comprehensively, rather than let our theoretical agenda alone dictate the scope of the book.

In this final section of the book, however, we attempt to highlight those aspects of the material that are especially relevant to our theoretical and policy concerns. Consolidating the framework presented in chapter 1 with insights of subsequent topic-specific chapters, we address the recent history of sexual change and present a summary of the model of sexual exchange that we have employed. Stepping back from the substance of our analysis, we then consider the relation of our work to the general society-wide debate over sexuality. The genesis and development of this project were, of course, deeply affected by the salience of sexual concerns in our society, and this book will, no doubt, have its own effect on that debate.

Revisiting Our Theoretical Agenda

It is important to recognize that this survey was conceived and administered in a particular historical moment. The substance of our inquiries has been influenced by the contemporary place of sexuality in public discourse. Similarly, those whom we have interviewed, of course, live in a particular historical context. Some were born only eighteen years ago, others nearly sixty years ago. That the information that we have gathered is embedded in individuals' histories and life courses has implications for the interpretation of our data in several respects. First, a variety of social forces have set in motion processes that are not in themselves sexual in character but that have had profound consequences for the organization of sexual lives. Second, these forces or events confront individuals at different ages and circumstances and thus have different effects that play out differently. Respondents to a one-time survey are in the midst of their sexual careers, some in one circumstance, some in another; for instance, some are currently married, others divorced at the time of the survey.

Our data represent only a "snapshot" of each of our respondents as these careers unfold. Although we have sought much retrospective information so that we could piece together how those circumstances affect the individual's behavior and how different behavior is from one person to another independent of his or her circumstance at the time of the survey, we can do only so much with a single cross-sectional sample. It will be important to ask these same questions of another sample at another time so that the influence of age, of dated events, and of shared experience at a given age might be sorted out.

Consider the issue of the declining age at first heterosexual intercourse. The rapid increase in the proportion of young people having their first intercourse before age twenty and the increased numbers of partners were not the product of greater sex drive among the young but the result of larger social changes independent of sexuality itself. Over the past century, a middle-class pattern of association among young people has become predominant, a pattern of association that now includes expressions of affection and sexual intimacy before marriage. Increasingly, the period of youth has become more autonomous (free of adult influence) and experienced within schools rather than the workforce. The mass media have directed their attention to the young in more and more forceful ways, celebrating entertainment figures who cultivate a successful sexual persona (e.g., Madonna) rather than an image based on "good character" (e.g., Jimmy Stewart). In the 1940s, sexually transmitted infections began to be controlled, and, in the 1960s, technological advances offered reliable methods of contraception. Social forces—demographic, economic, technological, and social organizational—produced the long-term social trends that have culminated in what some have perceived to be the "revolutionary" transformation of sexuality among young people. As we have seen, however, the so-called sexual revolution of the 1960s may have been more of a social construct than a label for concomitant changes in sexual practice. Indeed, much of the shift in sexual techniques that we have observed may have occurred prior to the 1960s, beginning as early as the 1920s. In any case, these changes may be more appropriately termed *evolutionary* in character.

This perspective—examining the social factors proximate and distal to the actual sexual encounter—has been the center of our attempt to study sexuality.

Most thinking about sexuality starts with the sexual drive, the sexual act, or the sexual pair and reasons outward, viewing the society and the culture as responses to the imperious sexual drive. We have begun our analysis at some remove from the sexual encounter, beginning with variables that are proxies for the great social divisions in our society—gender, ethnicity, religion, age, education (which is one measure of social class), and marital status. The ways in which these factors are organized in any society shape the sexual lives of individuals. As we have moved closer to the sexual act, we have concerned ourselves with the stakeholders in the sexual lives of individuals. In part, the master status variables are themselves concatenations of social networks of people with shared attributes (e.g., women and men, couples and singles); however, we have also considered the characteristics of sexual partnering as expressions of how current sexual stakeholders influence sexual practice. In future studies, more direct measures need to be used to assess the influence of non–sexual stakeholders (e.g., parents, children, friends, coworkers) on the sexual lives of individuals and couples. At the center of these webs of influence and interaction is the sexual couple, who view their negotiations about sexuality as entirely up to them rather than the result of social forces both near and far, which change over the course of the life cycle.

One thread that we have not fully explored is the fundamental tension between what is said about sex publicly and what is done sexually in private. Clearly, public debate about sexuality is often pure rhetoric. Peoples' actual sexual lives do not necessarily correspond to public grandstanding, as when one argues for fidelity but does not practice it and, in the other direction, when one implies having had sexual experiences that in fact have not occurred. This difference between what is said and what is done is not characteristic only of political figures. We have found, for instance, that 58 percent of people who said that premarital sex was always wrong had themselves had sex before marriage. Of those respondents who said that sex as a teenager (ages fourteen to sixteen) was always wrong, 26 percent had engaged in intercourse before age seventeen. This is not necessarily hypocrisy. It can represent the difference between statements of normative standards and the situations in which sexual conduct occurs. While we are convinced of the honesty with which respondents answered our questions, we have not adequately studied the circumstances and patterns surrounding discrepancies between their behavior and their opinions.

Chapter 14 demonstrated the extent to which normative orientations toward sexuality are both variable and patterned across the social structure. Yet, like its behavioral dimension, the subjective component of sexuality should not be seen as operating solely, or even primarily, at the level of the individual. The effect of attitudes on sexuality is mediated by ongoing social and sexual interaction. The initiation of any given sexual event involves a recognition by both parties of a more or less shared set of expectations about the content and character of the ensuing activities. Sexual interaction brings normative orientations into play as cultural resources—subjective categories by which participants negotiate which sexual scripts will be enacted. In addition to the effect of individual level factors, this negotiation process is influenced by a variety of other salient social dimensions of a relationship. These factors include the type of relationship in which the participants are engaged (be it a one-night stand, a long-term relationship, or a marriage), differences in social status between the parties (including the effects of gender, age, race, and education), and the social embeddedness of the relationship (a concept that we have employed to describe the structure of social interest surrounding the sexual relationship). Knowledge of these three factors—the type of relationship, the social distance between the participants, and the embeddedness of the relationship—can give us a great deal of purchase on the sexual scripts and activities that are likely to be negotiated and enacted.

In figure E.1, we display schematically the social organization of sexuality that has animated our analyses throughout the book, and we note the chapters in which each aspect is featured. Each individual—the respondent or focal person and the partner—is embedded in a network of family and friends who become stakeholders in the social and sexual behavior of that person and have influence on choices about the sex partner and sexual practices. Each individual brings his or her own personal characteristics and perspectives on sex and its practice and meaning, and each individual has a history of experience (or inexperience) that influences those preferences and judgments. Potential sex partners meet, interact, negotiate, form expectations, and make decisions about their sexual behavior in the context of other decisions about their partnerships and their nonsexual behavior. The partnerships themselves have attributes that affect sexual behavior, as we have seen in the dramatically different patterns of sexual behavior among married couples and unmarried individuals. The resulting sexual behavior reported by the respondents in our survey is specific to the sexual partnership and affected by it. That behavior is interpreted by the partners and their social network. It also has consequences, some anticipated, others not so, some desired, others not so, some quite private, others quite public. The figure is not a model; we do not think that we have yet melded the many important factors adequately to suggest a formal model. Yet the figure suggests the importance of the social organization of sexuality, and throughout the volume we have found that social context most illuminating in understanding adult sexual behavior.

Commenting on the Public's Concerns

There will be a temptation to simplify the findings from this research into a single message of either *good news* or *bad news* about the status of sexuality in the United States on the basis of one's prior expectations and one's views of what is proper sexual behavior. Many of our findings are surprising and contradict popular perceptions about sexual behavior that, until recently, have not been based on scientific study. We stress that, where it is feasible to compare,

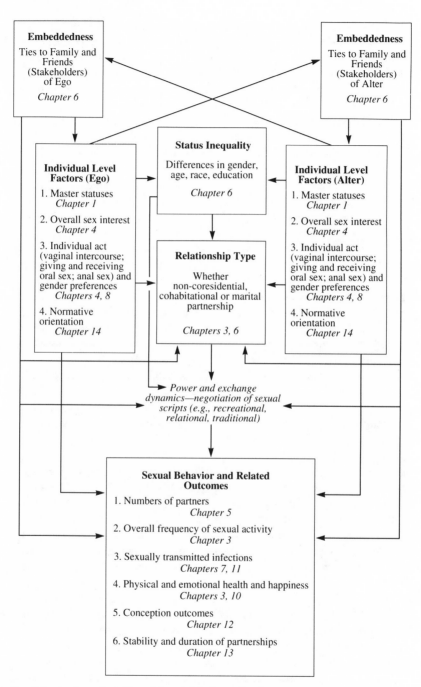

Fig. E.1 A schematic outline of the model of sexual exchange.

our findings are remarkably similar to other recent, high-quality surveys of aspects of sexual behavior. This is the case, for example, as regards the number of sex partners in the past year, the frequency of sex, or the incidence of homosexuality. In other areas where we have looked more extensively than others, we find, for example, that married people are the most likely to find their sexual lives very satisfying, both emotionally and physically.

We suggest that there can be controversy and fruitful debate at four distinct points in considering our findings: One might debate whether the findings are in fact correct and accurate. One can question whether they can be generalized to a larger population, even if they are accurate reflections of the behavior of the 3,432 respondents. One can debate the explanations and meanings that we suggest for the behavior that we observe. Finally, one can debate whether this behavior is proper or improper, good or bad, by some standard. We have addressed accuracy and generalizability at considerable length in this book, and, from the checking and rechecking that we have done, we believe that our facts are both basically correct and quite generalizable to the population of those aged eighteen to fifty-nine living in households in the United States. On these first two issues, we have considerable confidence.

On the matter of interpretation, explanation, and meaning of these facts, we have offered our views and are eager to pursue them and refine them and to learn further about this complex behavior in our own subsequent work and from work by others. Many of our interpretations are suggestions that need further exploration and testing. We have stressed the social context of sexuality, which has been too long ignored but is surely not the only fruitful or important context for viewing sexuality. We welcome the debates, discussions, and progress toward a better understanding that we anticipate will follow the publication of our findings.

We have not addressed the fourth point of controversy, the normative issues. Take, for instance, the fact that married people report themselves to be most satisfied sexually. Someone from the religious Right might contend that this is evidence strongly supporting a "family values" perspective on sex and social relations and will accordingly view this finding as very good news. Alternatively, someone ideologically committed to a recreational view of sex may argue that this is evidence of self-delusion and sexual repressiveness (and will likely dispute the finding as inaccurate) and will consider it rather bad news. We suggest only that the finding implies that couples committed to enduring affectionate relationships dominate the sexual landscape, and we avoid any suggestion as to whether this is a good thing or a bad thing. We are not ethicists or moralists. We do contend that the difficult policy debates in our nation can be more fruitful and the resulting social policy improved by having accurate facts and cohesive interpretation about the sexual behavior of the nation.

One example of information that can improve policy, whatever one's political position, involves education about the risks of HIV/AIDS and other sexually transmitted infections. We have argued that the findings of a low average number of sex partners and of a lack of connectivity between sexual networks imply that there will be only a slow spread of HIV/AIDS in the heterosexual majority population and a continuation of that infection in specific subpopulations. That interpretation of the findings here can be quite useful in the formation of public health policy and educational programs. Having large numbers of sex partners is characteristic of certain phases of the life course and of certain social milieus. Efficient public health and educational interventions to prevent the spread of HIV/AIDS need to take this into account.

There are certainly signs of sexual difficulties. Perhaps one of the most important indicators of difficulties is the pervasive difference in the approach to and understanding of sexuality by women and men. From the earliest heterosexual encounters, the different views of men and women toward sexuality are striking. Men report having their first vaginal intercourse because they are curious or because of peer pressure. Love and affection motivate the initiation of sex for women and are key facets of ongoing sexual relationships. Men report more sex partners, a greater interest in a variety of sexual practices, and more fantasizing about sex, and they are more likely to masturbate. Women report many incidents of sexual coercion, and one in twenty report having been forced to have intercourse the first time it happened. Orgasm is the standard outcome for men in sexual encounters, whereas the rates of orgasm for women are much lower. Older women are particularly disadvantaged in the competition for sex partners and hence in access to sexual expression.

The problem of coerced sex and sexual abuse is particularly troubling since it seems so often to happen under the auspices of affectionate or friendly relations. Adult sexual contacts with children and the sexual coercion of women occur most frequently within the close personal networks of the child or the woman. In the case of coercion, it is clear that men's normal socialization and roles in the sexual encounter undermine their ability to recognize limits set by their female partners. Men and women interpret these violations quite differently, as this survey indicates.

Certain consequences of private sexual behavior are clearly of public importance and both serious and negative in nature. These include HIV/AIDS, other sexually transmitted infections, and sexual coercion. Other aspects or consequences of sexual behavior such as sex before marriage, abortion, and homosexuality are among the social issues about which we as a nation seem to have no clear consensus at this time.

Anticipating controversy about the implications of some of our findings, we note a cautionary tale. One of the great ironies of this research is that it was vehemently opposed by right-wing members of Congress and their supporters out of a fear that the scientific study of sexuality would somehow promote the further breakdown of morals.[1] While the exact content of their fears was never

1. The consequences of this opposition are quite real. It delayed the study by several years and prevented the use of federal grant money in data collection. (For a more detailed political history of the national sex survey, see Laumann et al. 1994a.)

completely clear to us, those fears appear to have been based on the idea that, if research found high rates of sexual licentiousness, this would somehow legitimate and help increase it. On one issue in particular the opponents of this study were quite clear: they were certain that this research would report high rates of homosexual activity and was motivated to promote its acceptance. The fact that this survey found low rates of homosexuality and that these rates are generally similar to every other probability sample survey that has been conducted may be seen as good news by the Right. These findings are likely to be disputed by gay/lesbian rights advocates, who have placed tremendous emphasis on a "10 percent" prevalence estimate of homosexuality. Finding a smaller number of homosexuals than that hotly defended but inaccurate 10 percent does not diminish the civil rights of homosexuals and may not have any implication for the attitudes of voters in support of those rights.

Like many of our readers, we suspect, we have been surprised by many of our empirical findings. We consider the pattern of adult sexual behavior reported here to be generally cohesive, purposive, and amenable to understanding in the social scientific context that we have proposed. We believe that this understanding can contribute to improvements in individual decision making and social policy regarding social issues. Despite methodological doubters and political opponents, we have demonstrated that modern survey research can be used to collect valuable data on sexual behavior and attitudes from representative samples of the American population. Nearly four out of five adults whom we asked to participate in the survey did so, and these 3,432 respondents who provided us with generally honest and accurate information about their sexual lives are grounds for considerable optimism about the sexual health of the nation. With efforts to know and interpret the facts about our sexual lives, we as a nation can become more effective in respecting diversity in our sexuality and in formulating coherent and effective policies that enhance the sexual aspects of our private and public lives.

Sampling Procedures and Data Quality

> Thirty-four percent of Americans are Democrats.
> Three percent of American women aged eighteen to fifty-nine
> are currently pregnant.
> Eighty percent of Americans had an orgasm the last time they had sex.

Anyone who reads a newspaper or watches the evening news is familiar with statements like those presented above. No doubt many people accept them without pausing to consider how researchers discovered how many Americans are members of the Democratic party or are currently expecting a child. However, a skeptical reader might balk at the statement regarding the rate of orgasm, asking, "How could they find out something like that?" When such statements are derived from survey research, they are assertions about the distribution of characteristics in a population that are generated by measuring that characteristic in a carefully selected sample of that population. This process, called *statistical inference,* allows the researcher to make a best estimate for the true value in the population—for example, the actual number of U.S. citizens who identify with the Democratic party or the number of American women who are currently pregnant. Although such estimates frequently inform the public debate about important issues, the actual processes that generated them are often ignored or misunderstood. As a result, people are often either too willing to accept such statements as fact or too willing to dismiss them entirely.

The purpose of this appendix is to identify and discuss the issues involved in using our data to make statements about the distribution of sexual attitudes and practices in the population. In doing do, we hope to eliminate many of the potential sources of skepticism about our results. We first discuss in general terms the process of generating such estimates as well as possible sources of error in order to lay the groundwork for an assessment of the quality of our data.

How do survey researchers generate statements about the distribution of a particular characteristic in the population? How might the techniques used by

This appendix was drafted by Kristen Olson with help from Fang Li and Christopher Browning. It was prepared under the direction of Stuart Michaels and Edward O. Laumann.

survey researchers go astray and produce misleading results? To understand statistical inference, or the procedure by which information from a sample of individuals is used to make inferences about a larger population, consider the following example. Suppose that we are interested in determining the proportion of adults in the United States who had two or more sex partners during the past year. Now suppose that we are able to draw a sample of adults in which every adult in the population had exactly the same nonzero probability of being chosen. Intuitively, this type of sampling (called *simple random sampling*) can be thought of as making a list of every person in the population and then randomly selecting some of these names. We could then ask the respondents whom we have chosen randomly how many partners they had during the past year, and the proportion who answer that they have had two or more would be our estimate of the proportion of American adults with multiple partners.

What factors might contribute to the possible inaccuracy of our estimate of the proportion of American adults with multiple partners? In survey research, two broad categories of error together constitute total error; we refer to these two types of error as *sampling variability* and *nonsampling error.* Sampling variability results from the fact that only part of the population of interest is selected to participate in the survey (Kish 1965, 9–10). In our estimate of the proportion of American adults with multiple partners, for example, the sample drawn will consist of a set of individuals whose characteristics will almost certainly not be exactly the same as the characteristics of the population; that is, our random sample contains a slightly smaller or slightly larger proportion of people with multiple partners than the general population. However, the relation between sample size and sampling variability is well understood and can be easily evaluated; sampling variability is reduced by increasing the size of the sample, and a remarkably high level of precision can be achieved with only 2,000 or 3,000 interviews.[1] Although sampling variability is well understood and can be estimated precisely, estimates of error in survey data based on sampling variability alone do not reflect any of the nonsampling error that may be present in the data. The possibility of nonsampling error is much more difficult to evaluate. A discussion of possible sources of nonsampling error, or an evaluation of the quality of our data, is the main task of this appendix.[2]

Nonsampling error is a result of imperfect procedures of observation that may arise from a flawed sample design or the poor implementation of an ade-

1. Because we know the probabilities of selection for each member of the sample, it is possible to compute the amount of sampling error present in the estimate. This variability is usually reported as an interval around the estimated proportion such as, "We are 95 percent certain that the population proportion (i.e., the proportion that would result if we interviewed every adult) is within 3 percentage points of our estimate." For an excellent introduction to the procedures for computing sampling variability, see Freedman, Pisani, and Purves (1978). An application of the approach estimating sampling error is found in chapter 2, where table 2.2 gives the sampling error for various proportions estimated for several different sample sizes.

2. For a comprehensive discussion of sampling variability and nonsampling error, see Groves (1989). For a more concise discussion of the major issues in survey data quality, see Groves (1987).

quate design. The ideal sample design includes the following: a clearly defined set of individuals about whom the analyst seeks to make generalizations, or a *population of inference;* a method for selecting a representative sample of those individuals, or a *sample frame;* the cooperation of *every member of the sample;* and an *accurate way of measuring* each selected individual's characteristics. If any one of these requirements is compromised, some variety of nonsampling error may occur. If the researcher does not clearly define the population that he or she seeks to describe, or if all individuals belonging to that population are not covered by the sample frame, the sample will not be representative. In this case, *coverage error* may arise because the inference of the distribution of a particular characteristic in an entire population from measurements made on a small sample is reliable only if the individuals included *represent the entire population.* Given a clearly defined population that the researcher seeks to describe (or a population of inference), the researcher must devise some method for choosing a representative sample from that population.

To this end, survey researchers have developed techniques that enable them to draw what is called a *probability sample.* The term *probability sample* refers to the fact that we know (or can estimate with a high degree of precision) the probability that each person had of being chosen to be in the sample. A probability sample allows the researcher to assess the precision of his or her estimates of the distribution of characteristics in the population. By using a probability sample, the researcher can be confident that the distribution of individual characteristics in the sample can be generalized to the population from which the sample is drawn, either directly or after the relative probabilities of each respondent being sampled have been taken into account.[3] We discuss issues related to covering a defined population in the next section of this appendix.

Once the problem of selecting an appropriate sample has been overcome, some thorny issues remain. The researcher must try to secure the cooperation of as many selected individuals as possible in order to avoid the possibility of *nonresponse bias.* If some members of the sample cannot be located or simply refuse to participate, *and* if these individuals are systematically different from those members of the sample who do respond, the survey findings will be biased, or systematically different from the actual population value. For example, suppose that a researcher managed to secure the cooperation of 63 percent of the individuals selected to be in the sample. Also suppose that the

---

3. Probability samples may require the use of weights. That is, if the analyst knows the nonzero probability that each individual had of being included in the sample, he or she can give more "weight" to those respondents who were less likely to be included. For example, in our survey, which is based on a stratified random sample of households, an individual who lives in a household with five other people has a much smaller probability of being included in the sample than an individual who lives alone. To compensate for this bias against individuals in large households, the data can be weighted so that the responses of individuals in large households count more when aggregate statistics are calculated.

remaining 37 percent of selected individuals were systematically different from the others with respect to a particular characteristic of interest, for instance, whether the respondent had ever had an abortion. If women who have ever had an abortion were systematically more likely to be part of the 37 percent who did not answer the questionnaire, then the researcher's estimate of abortions performed would be biased (i.e., lower than the actual number of abortions performed.) If, however, nonparticipants were not systematically different from participants, the researcher's estimate of the number of abortions performed would not suffer from nonresponse bias. Of course, it is usually very difficult, if not impossible, to determine the characteristics of individuals who were unavailable to participate in the survey, and the existence of bias due to nonresponse is therefore difficult to assess. We discuss this topic in more detail later in this appendix.

Selecting a sample that adequately represents a population of interest and assessing any bias that might arise from the nonresponse of individuals in that sample are problems of nonobservation. That is, any estimates based on the sample may be biased because representatives of particular groups (in our example above, women who have ever had an abortion) in the population are left out. However, we must also take into consideration problems that might arise because of errors in the process of gathering the data that the researcher does collect. Errors of this kind are generally referred to as errors of observation or *measurement errors.* Measurement errors may result from failure on the part of the interviewer, the respondent, or the questionnaire. We will be primarily concerned with the possibility of measurement errors on the part of the respondent as well as how the conditions under which the interview took place might have biased responses. These issues will also be considered later in this appendix. Possible errors arising from the survey instrument and failure on the part of the interviewers as well as the measures that we took to avoid them are addressed in chapter 2.

To Whom Do Our Findings Apply?

In the earlier part of this century, the survey sample was developed as a more effective and efficient alternative to the census.[4] Researchers discovered that they could obtain comparable quality information from measuring a carefully selected sample of a population as they can obtain from taking a census, or measuring every unit in that population. Taking measurements on a sample of a population clearly requires less time and money than conducting a census, and, paradoxically, because measures can be taken more carefully, samples can be more accurate than censuses. However, certain issues become problematic when a sample is substituted for a census. In a census, for example, the group

4. For concise histories of the development of survey research, see Rossi, Wright, and Anderson (1983, 2–9) or Babbie (1973, 41–45). For an extended and personal account of the development of survey research methods, see Hyman (1991).

to whom the findings apply is unambiguous; it is the group on whom measurements were made. In a sample, the group to whom the findings apply, or the *population of inference,* is not always obvious. So, when researchers are designing a survey research project, they must define the population from which the sample is drawn very carefully. Furthermore, researchers must ensure that every member of that population has a chance of being selected as part of the sample so that the sample will be representative of the population.

How do researchers gather a *representative* sample? In practice, there are many ways in which researchers may gather samples, but it is generally recognized that the only samples from which valid statistical inference can be drawn are probability samples (Kish 1965, 19). Probability samples are superior because they do not rely on broad assumptions about the distribution of characteristics in the population. In probability sampling, the need for these assumptions of randomization in the population are bypassed by randomization in the selection process (Kish 1965, 19). In probability samples, every individual in the population has a known nonzero probability of being selected. The known nonzero probability allows us to obtain a valid estimate of the magnitude of sampling error. Otherwise, the precision of the estimate cannot be assessed. The most direct way of drawing a probability sample is simple random sampling. To draw a simple random sample of a population, the researcher must list every member of that population and select a sample randomly. In order to draw a simple random sample of the population of the United States, one would have to compile a list of every individual in the United States! Fortunately, there are other, more feasible methods of generating probability samples.

The NHSLS used the most highly regarded of these methods, area probability sampling, to draw our sample. Area probability sampling is highly respected because of the relative dependability of identifying individuals with one and only one place of residence.[5] Residences can be identified, in turn, with one and only one geographic location (Kish 1965, 25). The NHSLS sample frame (based on the 1980 SRC/NORC sample frame)[6] is a multistage area probability design. In such a design, a geographic area, such as the United States, is divided into geographic strata that each contain about the same number of people. From these geographic strata, eighty-four smaller geographic units are drawn. Within these smaller units, clusters of households are drawn. Each geographic area is selected with probability proportional to the total number of people living within it. Finally, one randomly selected individual in each selected household is asked to complete the interview. At all but this last stage, sampling with probability proportional to size is utilized (Davis and

5. Vacation homes and other secondary residences are excluded as a matter of course.

6. Details regarding the design of the 1980 SRC/NORC sample frame are available in the cumulative codebook for the General Social Surveys (Davis and Smith 1991, 700–706) or Herringa and Connor (1984).

Smith 1991). All households have an equal probability of selection, but because only one individual is selected, persons residing in large households are
less likely to be interviewed. Similarly, our full sample was designed to select
more blacks and Hispanics than would otherwise have been the case given their
proportions in the population so that we could make more accurate statistical
inferences about these groups.

The issues of defining a population of inference, sample design, and
avoiding coverage error cannot be considered independently of one another;
the goal is to use a sample frame that will cover the population of inference (in
our case, the adult population in the United States) at a reasonable cost. An
excellent choice for such a large population is area probability sampling, but
it requires that we narrow the scope of our research to those individuals who
reside in households and exclude those who do not.

The U.S. residents who were excluded from the NHSLS population of inference may be quite different from those individuals we surveyed in any number
of ways; therefore, the population of inference should always be kept in mind
when interpreting the statistics reported in this book. The primary goal of the
NHSLS was to produce the most accurate statistics about sexual practices possible. To this end, we decided to concentrate on the most sexually active part
of the population; adults under age fifty-nine. We decided not to interview
non-English-speaking respondents because we could not afford a high-quality
translation of our English questionnaire, nor could we afford the hiring or
travel cost of bilingual interviewers. We also decided to interview only people
over age seventeen since we felt that to do otherwise would require a separate
operation to secure parents' permission to interview minors, a procedure that
might jeopardize the rest of the enterprise. Individuals in group quarters were
excluded because we used an area probability sample design based on household residences.[7] In sum, our population of inference was defined as all people
aged eighteen to fifty-nine with adequate English proficiency living in households located in the fifty states and the District of Columbia between February
and September 1992. Therefore, the NHSLS statistics do not apply to individuals younger than eighteen or older than fifty-nine, or individuals who do not
speak enough English to complete the survey, or individuals living in correctional institutions, college dormitories, military barracks, nursing homes, or
homeless shelters, or homeless individuals.

As of 1 April 1991, 57 percent of the total U.S. population (145 million
individuals) was estimated to be between the ages of eighteen and fifty-nine.
Approximately 65 million individuals (26 percent of the total population) were
younger than eighteen years of age, and 42 million people (17 percent of the

---

7. In no way should these decisions about the allocation of scarce resources be interpreted as a
statement denigrating the importance of understanding sexuality within the groups excluded from
the population of inference; in fact, we very much hope that, in the future, resources will be
available to address precisely such subpopulations' sexual behavior.

total population) were sixty years old or older (Statistical Abstract of the United States 1992, 19). We also limited the population to those individuals who live in households and speak English. The 1990 census allows us to estimate what proportion of the total U.S. population was excluded from our sample because they do not live in households or do not have adequate English proficiency to complete the questionnaire. According to the 1990 census, 2.7 percent of the total population lived in group quarters (correctional institutions, nursing homes, college dormitories, military barracks, homeless shelters, or some other institution or group residence); half of 1 percent (0.5 percent) of the total population was homeless and living on the street. However, these statistics do not necessarily represent the fraction of the U.S. population that was excluded from the population from which our sample was drawn because this distribution is not exactly the same for people aged eighteen to fifty-nine. Unfortunately these data are not directly available at this time, but we can estimate the distribution for individuals aged eighteen to fifty-nine on the basis of the available data and some reasonable assumptions. The results of this analysis are shown in figure A.1. We estimate that about 2.9 percent of the total population aged eighteen to fifty-nine did not reside in households in 1991. These individuals are not represented in our sample. The largest groups of individuals who are most likely to be sexually active are in college, the military, or prison. Because each of these institutions also has a substantial influence on the attitudes and experiences of their members, it would be wise to design and execute specialized research projects to study these groups separately.

Finally, we must estimate how many people were excluded owing to lack of English proficiency. According to the General Social Survey (GSS), 98 percent of the adult household population is English speaking (General Social Surveys, 1972–1991 Cumulative Codebook 1992, 560). The GSS uses the same sampling frame and general procedures as the NHSLS. Assuming that non-English speakers are evenly distributed with respect to age and residence in households or institutions, 2 percent of the people aged eighteen to fifty-nine living in households must be excluded from the population of inference. Some of these may overlap with the population living in group quarters and homeless individuals. At this point, we may conservatively conclude that our population of inference consists of about 138 million people, or 95 percent of the total U.S. population between ages eighteen and fifty-nine.

Response Rate and Nonresponse Error

After a probability sample has been drawn from a defined population, the survey researcher must begin the task of contacting each unit in the population for the purpose of data collection. However, resource and other limitations almost always inhibit the capacity of researchers to contact the residents of every enumerated household. Even for those who are contacted, some proportion will, for whatever reason, fail to produce completed questionnaires. Both situations are classified as instances of *nonresponse*. The proportion of the eligible (and

A. U.S. Population, Ages 18–59

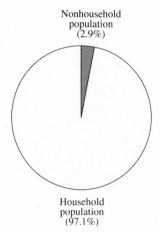

Nonhousehold
population
(2.9%)

Household
population
(97.1%)

B. Nonhousehold Population, Ages 18–59

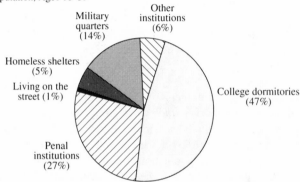

Other
institutions
(6%)

Military
quarters
(14%)

Homeless shelters
(5%)

Living on the
street (1%)

College dormitories
(47%)

Penal
institutions
(27%)

Fig. A.1 Population of inference. A, U.S. population, aged eighteen to fifty-nine. B, Non-household population, aged eighteen to fifty-nine.

not clearly ineligible) sample frame for which no questionnaire is completed is the *nonresponse rate.* Nonresponse rates are relatively easy to calculate and are often used as a proxy for *nonresponse bias,* which is more difficult to measure. *Nonresponse bias* refers to the level of systematic difference between those households that did respond and those that did not. In this section, we consider the extent to which our data may be biased by nonresponse error.

Nonresponse may occur when the interviewer is unable to contact a household selected by the sampling procedures or when the randomly selected household resident is unable or unwilling to provide responses to the questionnaire. The first type of nonresponse occurs when the residents of some proportion of sample households prove difficult if not impossible to contact (a situation that is inevitable in survey research). In some of these cases, the household consists of an individual or individuals who for some reason—possibly related to the nature of their employment or lifestyle—cannot be reached despite the repeated efforts of interviewers. The NHSLS interviewers failed to contact eighty-three of the selected households, or 2 percent of the potentially eligible addresses. When an interviewer successfully contacts the residents of a household, he or she must determine the number of eligible individuals residing there and randomly select a potential respondent among them. This randomly selected member of the household is the only member of the household who is eligible to participate in the survey; otherwise, the problem of self-selection bias is very likely to occur because those individuals who are more willing or more able to respond to a survey are likely to be systematically different from those individuals who are not. Because no substitution is allowed, the second type of nonresponse occurs when a selected eligible respondent cannot or will not provide answers to the questionnaire. Relatively few individuals are unable to complete the questionnaire.[8]

A much more worrisome issue is nonresponse from unwilling potential respondents. Some individuals see social surveys as inconvenient, invasive, or both and simply refuse to participate in them. When a potential respondent refuses to provide answers to the questionnaire, interviewers may attempt to persuade the individual to cooperate. Many methods for gaining the cooperation of potential respondents were available to our interviewers. Interviewers used letters, telephone calls, and videotapes as well as offers of monetary compensation to encourage unwilling individuals to participate. Interviewers found that assuring respondents of the confidentiality of their answers and stressing the importance of the research were very useful techniques for gaining cooperation. Aside from convincing respondents that their answers would contribute to efforts to contain the spread of HIV/AIDS, another effective incentive to participate is the payment of a respondent fee. The respondent fee may compensate for the inconvenience or loss of time that participation would involve. At the beginning of the interviewing process, $10.00 was offered to selected households. In the later stages of the project, when more funds became available, all NHSLS respondents received at least $25.00. Larger respondent fees were offered to more reluctant respondents. Some individuals, however, remained unwilling to participate. In our sample, 736 of the selected individuals, or 17 percent of the eligible potential respondents, refused to participate. An additional 3 percent of eligible potential respondents (115 individuals) did not refuse to participate but were otherwise unwilling or unable to complete the interview.

8. Lack of English proficiency is the main cause of inability to answer the questionnaire. Non-English speakers resided in about 2 percent of the addresses that we selected (204 non-English-speaking potential respondents per 9,004 potentially eligible addresses). One hundred eighty-six households contained only non-English-speaking residents. Of the households where at least one eligible English-speaking individual lived, eighteen of the selected respondents spoke no English. Because such individuals are not included in the population of inference, they are considered out of the scope of the research rather than instances of nonresponse.

Intuitively, we might expect a survey of sexual matters to be particularly vulnerable to refusals owing to the sensitive nature of the subject matter. In fact, concern about levels of respondent cooperation has been a frequently asserted pretext used to justify not undertaking large-scale surveys of sexual behavior in the past. However, the experience of many major surveys of sexual matters in the United States and Europe indicates that individuals are as willing to respond to surveys about sexual matters as they are to surveys of other aspects of their personal lives. In an assessment of the causes and effects of nonresponse to sexual behavior items included in the General Social Survey, Michael and Veldman (1992) found little evidence that the adult population in the United States is not cooperative in providing answers to questions about sexual matters. Furthermore they found no evidence that nonresponse contributed to nonresponse bias. These authors analyzed patterns of nonresponse to a set of self-administered questions pertaining to sexual behavior and found that a comparable proportion of GSS respondents refused to answer the family income question (10 percent) as refused to answer the set of sexuality-related questions (11 percent) (Michael and Veldman 1992, 3). They also found that nonresponse was more strongly related to the structure of the questionnaire (i.e., whether the set of questions was near the end of the ninety-minute interview or not) than to the demographic or social characteristics of those not responding. Michael and Veldman also considered the possibility of bias introduced by nonresponse. Using the Heckman technique for addressing potential bias in model estimation caused by censored data (Heckman 1979), they estimated the effects of nonresponse and found no evidence that nonresponse might bias substantive conclusions (Michael and Veldman 1992, 17). Finally, they noted that, of respondents who were later contacted for the purposes of an unrelated methodological study, only a handful (five respondents out of 696) mentioned the sex questions as a salient part of the interviewing process, and, although they all expressed the sentiment that the questions were too personal, three of the five did in fact answer the questions (Michael and Veldman 1992, 17). Although this methodological analysis of the sexuality-related questions on the General Social Survey indicates that survey data regarding sexuality can be collected in an unbiased manner, it does not directly address the issue of potential nonresponse bias in the NHSLS data. We now turn to this issue.

To what extent were the different types of nonresponse outlined above confronted in our survey, and what are the implications for the findings presented in this book? In order to address these questions, we must first consider the overall rate of nonresponse. A response rate is relatively easy to calculate but more difficult to interpret. As depicted in figure A.2, the method that we used to calculate our rate of response involves taking the number of completed interviews and dividing that figure by the sum of (1) the number of completed interviews, (2) the number of refused eligible units, (3) the number of noncontacted units, and (4) the number of other instances of nonresponse. This figure

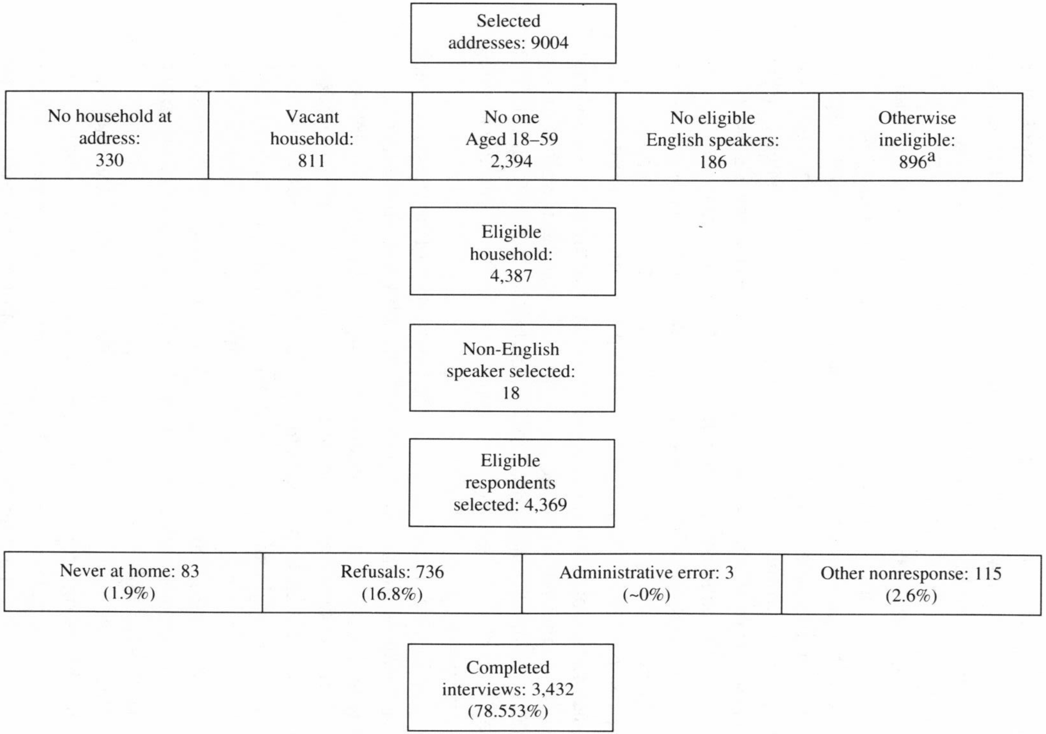

Fig. A.2 Response rate.

Note: The response rate is calculated as follows: (i) *eligible respondents* = (selected addresses) − [(ineligible addresses) + (selected non-English speakers)], or 4,369 = 9,004 − (4,617 + 18); (ii) *response rate* = (completed interviews)/(eligible respondents), or 78.553 = 3,433/4,369).

[a]Because we oversampled blacks and Hispanics relative to their true proportions in the population, in some areas all nonblack and non-Hispanic respondents were considered ineligible.

will be equal to the total number of addresses specified in our original sample frame minus the number of those that were considered out of scope.[9]

How does our response rate compare with response rates obtained in other social surveys? Despite the fact that more than 20 percent of the sample were not interviewed, a 79 percent rate compares very favorably with standard response rates for social surveys. For instance, the equivalent figure for the General Social Survey, a highly respected annual survey administered by the National Opinion Research Center over the past twenty years, has fallen between 74 and 79 percent. The 79 percent rate can be said on a comparative basis to be quite successful. Yet while a *relatively* high response rate is certainly reassuring, it cannot completely allay our concerns. A higher response rate reduces the likelihood that the completed sample will be subject to nonresponse error, but by no means eliminates it. In order to guarantee that the sample is representative of the population of inference, we must ensure that the 21 percent of the sample population whom we did not reach are not systematically different from those whom we did reach. We need to consider the extent to which the pool of nonrespondents differs systematically from those that did participate. Survey researchers have developed reinterview methods to assess the characteristics of nonrespondents; unfortunately, these methods tend to be expensive and unreliable, so we chose not to invest the time and money in assessing the extent of nonresponse bias directly. However, because this is such an important issue, we decided to attempt to assess the possibility of nonresponse bias indirectly.

We began our indirect examination of the possibility of nonresponse bias by making the assumption that those respondents who were most difficult to contact or persuade to participate are most like those whom we did not reach or persuade at all. We can then compare more and less reluctant respondents in order to infer the extent to which nonrespondents differ significantly from respondents. This method cannot prove conclusively that our data are free of nonresponse bias. However, if it is revealed that reluctant respondents are significantly different from nonreluctant respondents with respect to practices, experiences, and attitudes of interest, it would suggest a stronger possibility of the existence of this type of bias.

Three variables were used to measure respondent reluctance: the interviewer's assessment of how difficult the interview, or "case," was to obtain (9 percent of the cases were judged "very difficult"); the number of visits made to the household address by the interviewer (16 percent of the cases required five

9. Addresses that were considered "out of scope" include addresses at which no household existed, addresses at which the household was vacant, households in which no person from age eighteen to age fifty-nine resided, households in which no English speakers resided, and households considered out of scope because of our sampling design. Our sampling design included an oversample of blacks and Hispanics, so in a few areas all nonblack or non-Hispanic households were considered out of scope.

or more visits); and whether the respondent was paid a fee in excess of $25.00 (12 percent of the respondents). We then performed a series of analyses to reveal the relation between these measures of reluctance and key variables related to sexual practices, experiences and attitudes. We identified this subset of diagnostic questions to represent key aspects of the respondents' sexual lives by examining how these items were intercorrelated so that we could identify a subset of these items that seemed to tap independent dimensions of the respondents' sexuality. The diagnostic behavioral and attitude items selected for detailed presentation here include "the number of sex partners in the last twelve months," "performing oral sex in the last event," "believing that homosexuality is always wrong," "having been 'touched' sexually before puberty," and "if respondent masturbated in the last year." Since responses to attitude items on homosexuality, extramarital sex, and abortion displayed strong positive covariation, we included only the item on homosexuality for this analysis.

In order to demonstrate whether reluctant respondents are more or less likely to report particular sexual practices, experiences, or attitudes, we used logistic regression techniques. Logistic regression is an analysis technique that enables the researcher to take into account how *multiple* characteristics of a respondent *influence the likelihood* that the respondent would engage in a particular behavior. (For additional discussion of this statistical procedure, see chapter appendix 11.1A.) In this case, we are interested in how a characteristic of a respondent (the respondent's reluctance) influences the likelihood of reporting particular types of sexual attitudes, practices, and experiences. However, if we considered *only* how the reluctance level of the respondents influenced the likelihood of reporting these attitudes, practices, and experiences *without* taking into account any other variables, we might easily be misled. A classic illustration of how this could happen involves the relation between the birth rate and the number of storks in a given area. In many parts of Europe earlier in this century, one could observe that, the greater the number of storks in a given area, the greater the likelihood that the people there would have a child at any given time, supporting the hypothesis that storks are responsible for bringing babies. Of course, the relation between storks and babies is spurious—if the researcher also considers whether the given area is urban or rural, the relation disappears because the birth rate and the stork population are *both* higher in rural areas and *both* lower in urban areas. Similarly, we might find that more reluctant respondents were less likely to disapprove of homosexuality, for example, which might lead us to believe that people who answered our survey were more likely to disapprove of homosexuality than those who did not. However, people who live in large cities are both more reluctant respondents and more tolerant of homosexual lifestyles than people who do not live in large cities, so, if we simultaneously took into account our respondents' other characteristics that might be related to both attitudes about homosexuality and reluctance, the relation between them is likely to disappear. Thus, logistic regression analysis allows us to separate the effects of multiple variables that might influence the likelihood of a particular outcome.[10]

Table A.1 reports the result of our analyses of whether respondent reluctance contributes to the likelihood of reporting particular sexual practices, experiences, and attitudes. In these analyses, difficulty of the case, the number of household visits required, and receipt of a fee in excess of $25.00 were chosen as the main explanatory variables.[11] That is, these are the characteristics of the respondents that might contribute to the likelihood of reporting particular behaviors. We also included another set of explanatory variables as controls; these consist of such demographic and social characteristics as age, race, education, marital status, and size of place of residence as well as residence in the Eastern, Southern, Midwestern, or Western region of the United States.

We are interested in testing the notion that reluctance affects likelihood of particular responses, but we also want to avoid the spurious associations that might result from neglecting basic demographic and social characteristics that might be related to both reluctance and sexual behavior. Logistic regression allows the researcher to estimate how much these explanatory variables increase or decrease a particular outcome. These outcomes are called *response variables*. In this case, the response variables are the key measures of sexual behavior that we identified above. The estimates listed in table A.1 indicate whether the characteristics represented by explanatory variables are positively or negatively related to a particular outcome represented by the response variable; these estimates also indicate the magnitude of the effect. A relatively small negative estimate indicates that a characteristic (i.e., whether the respondent's case was difficult to get) slightly decreases the likelihood of a respondent reporting a particular sexual practice (i.e., performing oral sex in the last sexual encounter). However, all estimates have a particular margin of error. The probabilities reported in the second column of the table indicate whether the estimate is statistically significant, that is, how often the estimate would be generated if no effect actually existed. Therefore, if the probability associated with an estimate is equal to .86, then this estimate would be generated by random chance in more than eight out of ten samples drawn when no effect actually exists.

The probabilities are important because they allow us to judge whether or not the effect reported should be interpreted substantively or considered essentially equivalent to zero. A common rule of thumb is that an estimate is considered statistically significant if the estimate would only occur by random chance in one trial out of twenty if no effect actually existed, that is, if the probability was equal to or less than .05. Researchers usually want to demonstrate that

10. Detailed explanation of logistic regression may be found in standard texts on categorical data analysis, including Fienberg (1980, 102–5) and Agresti (1990, chap. 4).
11. Because the measures of reluctance are not highly correlated (all less than .35), we included all three in the same model.

Table A.1 Regressions of Measures of Reluctance on Sexual Experiences and Attitudes

Response Variables	Men[a]		Women[b]	
	Estimate	Probability	Estimate	Probability
	Explanatory Variable: Respondent's Case Rated Very Difficult to Get			
Respondent had more than one partner in the past year	.395	.131	−.569	.075
R performed oral sex in the last event	−.047	.862	−.207	.438
R thinks homosexuality is always wrong	.264	.272	.227	.292
R was touched sexually before puberty	−.251	.396	.014	.958
R masturbated in the past year[c]	−.322	.182	−.101	.641
	Explanatory Variable: Respondent's Case Required Five or More In-Person Visits			
Respondent had more than one partner in the past year	−.006	.975	.178	.445
R performed oral sex in the last event	−.014	.945	.388	.049
R thinks homosexuality is always wrong	.082	.655	.004	.978
R was touched sexually before puberty	.095	.661	−.041	.839
R masturbated in the past year[c]	−.593	.001	−.197	.222
	Explanatory Variable: Fee in Excess of $25 Paid to Respondent			
Respondent had more than one partner in the past year	.034	.888	−.176	.514
R performed oral sex in the last event	−.368	.122	−.116	.595
R thinks homosexuality is always wrong	.064	.763	.244	.177
R was touched sexually before puberty	.078	.759	−.361	.126
R masturbated in the past year[c]	.229	.289	−.222	.214

Note: Estimates are based on a series of logistic regressions. The response variable of each regression is listed down the stub column (e.g., respondent had more than one partner in the past year, etc.); in each regression, these response variables were regressed against explanatory variables for the difficulty of the case, the number of visits required, and payment of a large fee as well as control variables for race, education, age, marital status, urban, suburban, or rural residence, and residence in the Eastern, Southern, Midwestern, or Western part of the United States.

[a]$N \approx 1,200$ for regressions on multiple partners and performing oral sex in the last sexual event (only those men who had at least one sex partner in the past year were included in these regressions). $N \approx 1,300$ for all other regressions.

(*continued*)

Table A.1   (continued)

---

[b]$N \approx 1,400$ for regressions on multiple partners and performing oral sex in the last sexual event (only those women who had at least one sex partner in the past year were included in these regressions). $N \approx 1,600$ for all other regressions.

[c]The question regarding masturbation in the past year was asked in a written format; i.e., respondents were given a questionnaire to read and complete privately. All other response and explanatory variables are based on questions administered by the interviewer, which the respondent answered verbally.

effects do exist; in that case, the .05 criterion is conservative. However, because we would like to show that no effect exists (i.e., we want to show that reluctance is unrelated to reports of sexual activity), a criterion of .1 is more appropriate. All estimates with probabilities equal to or less than .1 are highlighted in italic. These logistic regressions support the conclusion that nonreluctant and reluctant respondents are not systematically different with respect to sexual attitudes, experiences, and practices. However, there is marginal support to indicate that women whose cases were rated "very difficult to get" were less likely to report multiple partners. Also, women whose case required five or more visits were somewhat more likely to report performing oral sex. There is also a statistically significant indication that male respondents who required five or more visits are less likely to report masturbating in the past year. However, in the absence of stronger and more general patterns relating masturbation, multiple partners, oral sex, and nonreluctance, these are not particularly worrisome findings. Reluctant and nonreluctant respondents are not very different along important dimensions of sexual life. If we assume that reluctant respondents are more like nonrespondents, these findings suggest that the extent of nonresponse bias is rather small. Of course, this finding is suggestive rather than conclusive. However, in light of the high response rate achieved, the evidence from other research that, when conducted with care and diligence, surveys related to sexuality do not suffer from particularly high rates of nonresponse, and some suggestive findings based on statistical analyses, our data appear to be largely free of significant nonresponse bias.

Measurement Error

Measurement error is simply the failure of the researcher to make accurate measurements of certain characteristics of interest; the failure may be due to the interviewer, the questionnaire, or the respondent. The best way to avoid measurement error on the part of the interviewer and the survey instrument is to take all possible precautions before administering the questionnaire to respondents. However, failures on the part of the respondent (lack of comprehension or candor, for example) often cannot be avoided completely. Here, we attempt to assess the effect of lack of comprehension and candor on the reported characteristics of respondents. In addition, we consider the indirect effect of lack of privacy during the interview on respondents' reported characteristics.

Good comprehension of the questions being asked is crucial in minimizing reporting errors and biases. If the respondent does not understand what he or she is being asked, he or she is likely to under- or overreport certain practices or attitudes. Only 8 percent of the respondents were regarded by the interviewers as having a limited understanding of the interview questions; these people tended to report less frequent sexual activities and more conservative attitudes. For example, 63 percent of those people with limited comprehension reported never engaging in masturbatory behavior, 15 percentage points higher than those who understood the questionnaire well. Similarly, we observe that, while 84 percent of such respondents said that homosexuality was always wrong, 63 percent of those who understood the questionnaire well held such an opinion. In general, studies have consistently found less educated parts of the population express more conservative attitudes on sexual issues and report more conventional sexual behaviors. Here again, we have an ambiguity in interpreting these results. Are the lower reported rates for those who did not understand the survey very well due to failure to understand what they were being asked? Or is there a real difference in their behavioral inclinations when compared to better-educated parts of the population? In any event, the distortions arising from incomprehension of the interview seem to be very modest under the most stringent assumptions because so relatively few are adjudged to be deficient in their comprehension.

Finally, we observe similar patterns for respondents differing in their frankness, as evaluated by the interviewers. Overall, only 5 percent of the total sample were not regarded as being frank by the interviewers. And these respondents apparently underreport certain activities and are more conservative on sex-related issues. For example, 69 percent of the less than frank reported that they never masturbated, fully 21 percentage points higher than those who were considered frank. Table A.2 does not report the more detailed analyses that we conducted to examine how measurement errors might vary across gender, race, education, and other demographic categories. We were able to determine that there was considerable association of selected demographic categories with particular interview conditions. Women, in general, reported fewer masturbatory activities and fewer sex partners; they were also more likely to have other people present during the interview. Asians were assessed as having lower levels of cooperation with the interviewers as well as lower rates of masturbatory and other sexual activities. We conducted more precise statistical assessments of the associations of demographic and social attributes and interview conditions on the main dependent variables describing sexual activities and attitudes.

None of the logistic regression models that we examined supported the notion that comprehensibility and candor substantially affected the results, once

Table A.2 **Regressions of Respondent Error on Sexual Experiences and Attitudes**

Response Variables	Men[a]		Women[b]	
	Estimate	Probability	Estimate	Probability
	Explanatory Variable: Interviewer Judged Respondent to Be Frank			
Respondent had more than one partner in the past year	−.081	.827	.959	.135
R performed oral sex in the last event	.429	.274	.807	.194
R thinks homosexuality is always wrong	.292	.307	.209	.511
R was touched sexually before puberty	*.943*	*.035*	.436	.327
R masturbated in the past year[c]	*.759*	*.008*	*.893*	*.024*
	Explanatory Variable: Respondent's Comprehension of the Questionnaire Was Good or Excellent			
Respondent had more than one partner in the past year	.364	.227	1.212	*.028*
R performed oral sex in the last event	−.039	.884	−.081	.827
R thinks homosexuality is always wrong	*−.491*	*.062*	*−.839*	*.007*
R was touched sexually before puberty	.095	.739	.278	.398
R masturbated in the past year[c]	.319	.151	.137	.586

Note: Estimates are based on a series of logistic regressions. The response variable of each regression is listed down the stub column (e.g., respondent had more than one partner in the past year, etc.); in each regression, these response variables were regressed against explanatory variables for interviewer's judgment of respondent's frankness and comprehension, controlling for presence of onlookers, race, education, age, and marital status, urban, suburban, or rural residence, and residence in the Eastern, Southern, Midwestern or Western part of the United States.

[a]$N \approx 1,200$ for regressions on multiple partners and performing oral sex in the last sexual event (only those men who had at least one sex partner in the past year were included in these regressions). $N \approx 1,300$ for all other regressions.

[b]$N \approx 1,400$ for regressions on multiple partners and performing oral sex in the last sexual event (only those women who had at least one sex partner in the past year were included in these regressions). $N \approx 1,600$ for all other regressions.

[c]The question regarding masturbation in the past year was asked in a written format; i.e., respondents were given a questionnaire to read and complete privately. All other response and explanatory variables are based on questions administered by the interviewer, which the respondent answered verbally.

the basic demographic and social characteristics were taken into account as well. Table A.2 summarizes our analysis of the question of whether those respondents who had acceptable levels of candor and comprehension were systematically different from those who did not. In order to assess the effect of the possibility of measurement errors as a result of lack of candor or comprehension on the respondents' answers, we ran a series of logistic regressions using key response variables relating to sexual practices, experiences, and attitudes. Because bivariate analyses revealed substantive differences in the patterns of relations between these variables for men and women, the logistic regressions were run separately for men and women. The explanatory variables were selected from interviewer's detailed reports about various aspects of the interview itself, including its duration, the presence of other people, and the respondent's comprehension of the questions asked and his or her overall candor and frankness. Comprehension and frankness are the variables most likely to contribute to respondent errors. Interviewers overwhelmingly reported, however, that respondents were both frank and had a good or excellent understanding of the questionnaire. The analyses in table A.2 take the same form as those in table A.1, and the estimates and probabilities reported in table A.2 can be interpreted in exactly the same way. The analyses reported in table A.2 indicate that men who were considered frank were more likely to report being touched sexually before puberty. Perhaps the interviewer may have judged those who admitted this more frank than those who did not. Nevertheless, the interviewer's assessment of frankness is given a measure of independent validation by the finding that both men and women who were judged frank were more likely to report that they masturbated in the past year in the self-administered questionnaire, which the interviewer never saw. Because of the lack of social desirability associated with this practice, we might expect that the response biases would be in the direction of underreporting and that frank respondents would be expected to report a higher incidence of masturbation. Given this argument, table A.2 supports the interviewers' assessments.

Women who were judged to have good comprehension were more likely to report having more than one partner in the last year, although this finding is not highly significant. Both men and women who had good comprehension were less likely to agree with the statement, "Homosexuality is always wrong." However, the direction of the causality is difficult to assess. Were respondents with inadequate comprehension more likely to agree with the statement because they did not understand it? Or are respondents who are less able to understand a questionnaire treating sexual matters simply less tolerant of homosexuality?

As the table shows, however, many key sexuality-related variables are not significantly related to measures of respondent error. Frankness does not contribute to the odds of reporting multiple partners, performing oral sex, or disapproving of homosexuality. Frankness is also unrelated to reports of being touched sexually before puberty for women. Among men, respondents' adjudged comprehension does not contribute to the odds of reporting having multiple partners, performing oral sex, being touched sexually before puberty, or having masturbated in the past year. Among women, comprehension is unrelated to reports of performing oral sex, being touched sexually before puberty, or masturbating in the past year. The conclusion that we draw is that, while a small amount of measurement error can be detected in the data, it plays a negligible role in explaining the substantive results.

We also examined the effect of interview conditions on respondents' answers. Note, first, that we were broadly successful in achieving private interviewing situations where no one other than the respondent and the interviewer was present. In fact, 79 percent of the interviews took place under these conditions. Only 6 percent of the interviews took place with the spouse or other type of sex partner present, and an additional 15 percent had other people present (*other people* defined as anyone other than the spouse or sex partner). These "others" were overwhelmingly likely to be the children or stepchildren of the respondent. Since our strongest priority was to have as complete a participation in the survey as possible, we were prepared to trade the exclusion of others during the interview for an agreement to participate. Based on bivariate analyses, the presence of a "third person" during the interview did seem to induce some differences in reporting certain sexual practices and attitudes. When interviewed alone, 17 percent of the respondents reported having two or more sex partners in the past year, while only 5 percent said so when their partners were present during the interview.

The presence of others also seemed to be associated with a different pattern of reported attitudes. On the basis of these bivariate analyses, we cannot conclude that the presence of others caused the reporting differences in the sense of suppressing the truth. It might well be that respondents were "selected" for the presence of others in a systematic fashion that resulted in their being much less likely to have "two or more" partners to report. It is likely, for example, that mothers of young children had their children present at the interview because they lacked access to childcare. Such a constraint would surely also influence the likelihood of their being able to report sex partners in addition to their husbands. In short, these respondents might well be reporting the truth instead of distorting it to avoid awkwardness with their partners or children (most of whom were too young to understand the questions in any event).

The multivariate analyses indicate that these effects tend to disappear when basic demographic and social characteristics (age, race, education, and marital status) are controlled. Table A.3 presents the results of a series of logistic regression analyses with sexuality-related attributes as the response variables and interviewing conditions and social and demographic controls as the explanatory variables. This table may be interpreted in the same way as tables A.1 and A.2. Table A.3 indicates that men who were interviewed with their spouse or sex partner present were less likely to report having multiple partners, although this is not strongly significant (probability = .051); there is no

Table A.3 **Regressions of Presence of Onlookers on Sexual Experiences and Attitudes**

Response Variables	Men[a]		Women[b]	
	Estimate	Probability	Estimate	Probability
	Explanatory Variable: Respondent's Spouse or Sex Partner Present during Interview			
Respondent had more than one partner in the past year	−.874	*.051*	−.648	.311
R performed oral sex in the last event	.251	.334	.008	.977
R thinks homosexuality is always wrong	.155	.555	.103	.677
R was touched sexually before puberty	.256	.393	−.045	.881
R masturbated in the past year[c]	−.063	.789	.042	.862
	Explanatory Variable: Others Present during Interview			
Respondent had more than one partner in the past year	.263	.314	−.387	.127
R performed oral sex in the last event	−.026	.913	−.334	.113
R thinks homosexuality is always wrong	.248	.254	.025	.864
R was touched sexually before puberty	−.053	.842	*.341*	*.043*
R masturbated in the past year[c]	−.131	.531	−.101	.485

Note: Estimates are based on a series of logistic regressions. The response variable of each regression is listed down the stub column (e.g., respondent had more than one partner in the past year, etc.); in each regression, these response variables were regressed against explanatory variables for presence of onlookers as well as controlling for frankness, comprehension, race, education, age, and marital status.

[a] $N \approx 1,200$ for regressions on multiple partners and performing oral sex in the last sexual event (only those men who had at least one sex partner in the past year were included in these regressions). $N \approx 1,300$ for all other regressions.

[b] $N \approx 1,400$ for regressions on multiple partners and performing oral sex in the last sexual event (only those women who had at least one sex partner in the past year were included in these regressions). $N \approx 1,600$ for all other regressions.

[c] The question regarding masturbation in the past year was asked in a written format; i.e., respondents were given a questionnaire to read and complete privately. All other response and explanatory variables are based on questions administered by the interviewer, which the respondent answered verbally.

similar effect for women. Women who were interviewed with others (anyone other than their spouse or sex partner) were somewhat more likely to report being touched sexually before puberty. None of the other key sexuality-related variables were significantly related to the presence of onlookers. Because only two of the twenty coefficients are significant at the .1 level, it is highly likely that these levels of significance are due to random sampling variability, and it is therefore safe to conclude that the extent of the bias produced by lack of privacy is small.

Conclusions

In this appendix, we have discussed the process of statistical inference and reviewed the procedures for drawing a high-quality sample of survey respondents. We have also considered the errors that might arise in this process. We have described our population of inference (adults aged eighteen to fifty-nine with adequate English proficiency residing in households located in the fifty states and the District of Columbia between February and September 1992) and explained our procedures for drawing a representative sample of these individuals (using a multistage area probability design based on the 1980 SRC/ NORC sample frame). We discussed our relatively high response rate (79 percent) and concluded that the allegedly sensitive nature of the questions asked did not contribute to a high nonresponse rate or a significant amount of nonresponse bias. We also performed a series of multivariate analyses that did not reveal any indication that respondent reluctance was systematically associated with nonresponse bias. Finally, we discussed the possibility of measurement error, noting that the overwhelming majority of respondents were assessed as being frank and as having understood the questionnaire. The majority of interviews also took place privately. Our multivariate analyses of the effects of comprehension, candor, and interviewing conditions revealed that, by and large, these indicators of measurement error were not systematically related to particular sexual practices and attitudes. To conclude, we judge that the data that we gathered and the inferences derived from them are relatively free of significant biases and accurately represent the sexual practices and attitudes of adults in the United States.

Comparisons of the NHSLS with Other Data Sets

In this appendix, we address the issue of whether the sample of respondents in the NHSLS data set appears to be one drawn from the appropriate population of U.S. adults. The sample is designed to represent the adult, noninstitutionalized U.S. population aged eighteen to fifty-nine, inclusively, with oversampling of blacks and English-speaking Hispanics as described in appendix A. It is designed as a stratified, clustered random sample. The sampling strategy employed in collecting our data was designed by NORC and utilizes NORC's national sample frame, which routinely produces excellent samples that quite accurately reflect the targeted U.S. population. In the study of sexual behavior, however, the issue of the representativeness of the sample, like other aspects of the project, deserves particular scrutiny because of concerns about obtaining the needed cooperation of the targeted population in conducting the survey.

There are two basic components to the issue addressed in this appendix. First, is there evidence that the sample of respondents itself is correct in the sense of being a sample that has the same demographic characteristics as other samples drawn for other purposes? Second, to the extent that it is possible to tell from other samples, does it appear that the NHSLS sample of respondents reports the same overall sexual behavior found in other surveys? Our data may have more detail than other surveys about specific sexual events and practices, but there are a few general descriptors of sexual behavior in other data sets—such as information about the number of partners within the past twelve months. Compared to these other samples on the few sexual facts that are available, does it appear that our sample reports the same or different sexual behavior?

The strategy adopted in this appendix is to compare the sample information obtained here against comparable information from other data sources whose quality is known to be high, in order to see whether our sample is drawn from the same population as that from which those other samples have been drawn. We proceed in two steps. We first look at comparisons of general demographic characteristics of three samples—the distributions by gender, age, educational attainment, current marital status, race, Hispanic ethnicity, number of children,

The calculations for this appendix were made by Joel Feinleib and Kara Joyner, under the direction of Robert T. Michael.

religion, and health. The three independent data sources chosen for this comparison include (1) the very large and high-quality national benchmark Current Population Survey from 1991 (CPS91) (collected by the U.S. Bureau of the Census), (2) the far smaller but highly respected General Social Survey from 1991 (GSS91) (collected by NORC), and (3) the 1986–87 survey on subject matter closely related to ours, a sample known as the National Survey of Families and Households (NSFH) (collected by researchers at the University of Wisconsin and Temple University).

From these comparisons, we ascertain whether the NHSLS sample appears to be drawn from the same population demographically as that from which these other samples were drawn. If it is, we can then have greater confidence that our findings from the NHSLS data set can indeed be generalized to the adult (aged eighteen to fifty-nine) U.S. population. If it is not, we must do what we can to "fix" our sample, as is feasible by weighting the sample in ways that statistically overcome certain identified over- or underrepresentation of one demographic group compared to another.

We then look at the second issue, the similarity in sexual behavior itself, comparing what we know from another recent national survey of specific sexual behavior, the annual GSS from 1988 through 1991, to the answers to the same questions asked in the NHSLS. In this comparison, we determine whether our sample reflects the same sexual behavior as the GSS in the few particulars for which the latter provides known population estimates. We note that the two surveys are different in that, whereas the NHSLS is designed specifically and pointedly to obtain information about sexual behavior, the GSS has only a few questions about sexual behavior and was appropriately presented to prospective respondents as something other than a sexual behavior survey. In that survey, the sexual behavior questions constituted only about two minutes of the entire ninety-minute survey. By contrast, in the NHSLS, the entire objective of the ninety-minute interview was to find out about sexual behavior, although, even in our survey, there were many questions about background demographic factors and correlates of sexual behavior. It may be that the initial characterization of ours as a sexual behavior survey caused respondents to be more or less willing to cooperate with us. Or it may be that the focus on sexual behavior within our survey caused respondents to give different responses, either because the extended focus caused them to recall facts differently, or because the focus created a different expectation and thus yielded different social responses. Or it may be that these differences had no apparent effect on the responses obtained. We attempt to reach conclusions about these matters later in the appendix.

Finally, we compare the sexual attitudes of our respondents to those reported in the GSS. Again, the fact of a "sex survey" may or may not affect who willingly cooperates with the survey or the attitudes expressed to the interviewer. It will be useful to know how similar or different the reported attitudes are in our study as compared to the GSS. The final section summarizes conclusions drawn about the demographic characteristics, the sexual practices, and the sexual attitudes of our sample members compared to other samples. As emphasized there, the results reported here support several important conclusions about the NHSLS data and about the feasibility of collecting accurate and useful information about adult sexual behavior from surveys of this nature.

We begin with a discussion of the weights available on our data set and the purposes to which these weights can be put.

Weighting the Sample Data

In the simplest concept of a sample drawn to represent some population, each person in the population has an equal chance of being selected for interview, and all who are selected are in fact interviewed. In that simple world, each sampled person represents the same number of people in the population. If, for example, we took a town of 50,000 people, randomly drew a sample of 1,000 names from a complete list of those 50,000, and completed interviews with the entire 1,000, then each observation in the sample would be said to represent fifty people in the town, and, on the basis of the information obtained from that thousand-person sample, we could make statements about the town's population of 50,000.

In reality, however, two circumstances can cause a sample to diverge from this simple notion. First, the strategy for selecting the respondents can be more complex than in a simple random sample, and our strategy in the NHSLS is more complex, as it is in practically all other large national samples. We use a stratified, clustered sample, meaning that we randomly sample geographic areas and then randomly sample households within those selected areas, which lowers the costs of data collection considerably compared to sampling households without clustering them. We also decided to sample more blacks and Hispanics than others, in order to get enough of these two groups to make group comparisons. We also chose to sample one person from each of the households in our sample, which means that we will have interviewed a disproportionately large number of people who live in one-person households and a disproportionately small number of people who live in three-, four-, or more-person households. These are all sampling decisions that we made that cause our sample to deviate from a simple random sample.

Second, aside from our sampling strategy, we secured a 78.6 percent response rate, so about four out of every five people completed our survey questionnaire, but one in every five did not. Although we are very pleased with this response rate because it is quite high compared to most any other survey, the fact still remains that those who did not cooperate were not necessarily distributed evenly in terms of attributes or behavior compared to all those in the sample. For example, men are known to be more difficult to get as respondents than are women, and, in our sample, like practically every other, we ended up with a few more women than men, even though the proportions of men and women in the population of people aged eighteen to fifty-nine are about fifty-

fifty. This disproportionate nonresponse by one group compared to another also prevents our sample from being a simple "self-weighting" random sample.

Both these reasons for divergence from a simple random sample—our sampling strategy designed to cut costs and add efficiency and the differential nonresponse by those targeted for interviewing—make our actual data set not fully accurate as a representation of the population of adults aged eighteen to fifty-nine. They imply that we may need to adjust for these divergences in order to be able to generalize about the behavior of the population. If, for instance, men average six sex partners over their lifetime and women four partners, then, in a population of an equal number of men and women, we know that, across all people in that population, the average is five sex partners. But, if we have a lot more women than men in our sample, we would calculate an average for the whole population that was closer to the women's average than in fact was true—we might calculate that the overall average was 4.7, for example, when the truth was that the average was 5.0. If, however, we give more weight or emphasis to the observations that are underrepresented, we can adjust for this and get the right answer.

This is exactly what the sample weights in our data set are designed to do. In effect, some observations have a higher likelihood of being in our sample than others—blacks are more likely, for example, since we purposively oversampled them, whereas adults who live in households with many adult members are undersampled because we interviewed only one person from each household. By using the reciprocal of the probability of being in the sample for each observation, we can derive weights that quite precisely adjust our sample so that it can yield accurate generalizations about the population aged eighteen to fifty-nine.

The way the weights are constructed, the average weight is 1.0. An observation from an oversampled category like a black in a household with few adults receives a weight much below 1.0, while an observation from a relatively rare category—a man in a many-adult household, for example—receives a weight far above 1.0.[1]

Table B.1 shows the mean and median sample weights for specific subgroups in our data set. The top panel shows that the average weight for the entire sample is 1.0, as it is by construction. The cross-sectional sample has an

---

1. The weight in the NHSLS data set was calculated by NORC's chief statistician, Martin Frankel. The weight first adjusts for the oversampling, and then a "multidimensional raking or balancing procedure" is applied, which adjusts for any differences by Census region (Northeast, Midwest, South, West), gender (male, female), household size (one, two, three, four, five or more), age (in four intervals: eighteen to twenty-four, twenty-five to thirty-four, thirty-five to forty-four, forty-five to fifty-nine), and race/ethnicity (in four categories: white non-Hispanic, black non-Hispanic, Hispanic, other), based on the 1990 census. About 120 observations in the data set required imputations, mostly of their household size. The weight, therefore, combines a sampling weight (for the oversampling of certain groups), an eligibility weight (for the household size), and a poststratification weight (primarily for differential nonresponse). The weights are scaled to sum to the actual sample size, so the average weight is 1.0.

Table B.1   **Sample Weights, by Key Components**

Group	Mean	Median	N
Entire sample	1.00	.97	3,432
Cross section	1.01	.98	3,159
Oversample	.86	.77	273
Gender:			
Men	1.13	1.09	1,511
Women	.90	.95	1,921
Age:			
18–24	1.09	.92	558
25–34	.93	.97	1,070
35–44	.98	.96	947
45–59	1.05	1.09	850
Marital status:			
Never married	.97	.82	973
Married	1.10	1.05	1,809
Divorced	.67	.45	474
Widowed	.67	.44	74
Separated	1.21	.83	82
Race/ethnicity:			
White	1.05	1.00	2,452
Black	.73	.69	550
Hispanic	.98	.89	321
Other	1.21	1.09	109
Household size:			
1	.41	.41	1,062
2	1.05	1.01	1,844
3 or more	2.02	1.86	526
Region:			
Northeast	1.06	1.00	667
Midwest	.98	.98	834
South	.96	.96	1,234
West	1.03	.97	697

average weight slightly over 1.0, and the oversample, of course, has an average weight substantially below 1.0. Look at the differences by gender. The average man has a weight of 1.13, the average women 0.90. That reflects the fact that the men were more likely to refuse to be interviewed, so the men we did interview get a little more weight, as each man represents more men in the population than each woman does other women. The big differences in the table show up in household size, marital status, and race/ethnicity.

Those who live in one-adult households, those who are divorced or widowed, and blacks and Hispanics are greatly overrepresented in our data set, so these groups have quite low average weights. Those who live in households of three or more adults are particularly underrepresented in our data set, so they have a particularly large average weight. In the data set, the range of weights is from a lowest value of 0.25 to a highest value of 3.71, and, in the entire data set, the twenty-fifth to seventy-fifth quartile range is from 0.46 to 1.21.

In the following sections, we compare the weighted and the unweighted data to other data sets.

Comparison of Demographic Characteristics

The Samples Compared

In the tables shown subsequently in this appendix, the NHSLS data are shown in two columns: one includes all 3,432 observations and is weighted by the sample weights discussed above, and the other represents the cross-sectional sample of 3,159 observations presented in unweighted form. These two summaries of our data are compared to the three other data sets listed above, the 1991 Current Population Survey, the 1991 General Social Survey, and the 1986–87 National Survey of Families and Households. As the data summary at the end of this appendix makes clear, we used only those observations in the age range eighteen to fifty-nine from each of these data sets since our interest here is to determine whether our data appear to be a sample drawn from the same population as the other samples. Not every one of our variables is available in all three of the other data sets, so our comparisons are limited in certain instances.

Each panel of table B.2 shows the percentage distribution for each data set, its total number of observations, and the χ^2 statistic on the null hypothesis that the two samples are drawn from the same population.[2] Where the χ^2 statistic is larger than the critical value, the null hypothesis is rejected, and, where the

2. The χ^2 test statistic is calculated for each pair of distributions, using the NHSLS and the comparison data set. The statistic is calculated as follows: $2 \times (\Sigma\{fo \times [\ln(fe/fo)]\})$, where fo is the observed number of cases in the cell of a contingency table, and fe is the expected number of observations in that cell. The expected number of observations, fe, is equal to (the number of cases observed in the row total $\times$ the number of cases observed in the column total)/(the total number of observations, N). The χ^2 critical value has degrees of freedom equal to (number of rows $-$ 1) $\times$ (number of columns $-$ 1); these critical values for various degrees of freedom at the 95 percent confidence level are shown below. (For more information about the χ^2 test, see any of several good statistics texts, including, e.g., Blalock [1979, chap. 15].) For convenience, we note here the critical value of the χ^2 statistic at the 95 percent confidence level, for each relevant number of degrees of freedom:

df	χ^2	df	χ^2
1	3.84	6	12.59
2	5.99	7	14.08
3	7.82	8	15.51
4	9.49	9	16.92
5	11.07	10	18.31

Table B.2   **Comparison of Demographic Characteristics: Percentage Distribution within Selected Data Sets; χ^2 Tests of Differences**

A. Gender

Category	CPS	GSS	NSFH	Wtd. NHSLS	Unwtd. NHSLS
Men	49.7	43.8	43.0	49.8	44.6
Women	50.3	56.2	57.0	50.2	55.4
Total N	144,697	1,132	7,262	3,432	3,159

	χ^2 Tests of Independence	
	NHSLS-W	NHSLS-U
CPS	.01	31.38*
GSS	12.1*	.23
NSFH	42.76*	2.34
NHSLS-W		17.39*
Critical value @ alpha = .05	3.84	

*Null hypothesis rejected.

B. Age

Category	CPS	GSS	NSFH	Wtd. NHSLS	Unwtd. NHSLS
18–24	18.2	13.7	15.2	17.8	15.9
25–29	14.3	13.3	15.8	13.9	14.5
30–34	15.3	16.5	18.3	15.0	16.5
35–39	14.2	17.2	15.6	13.8	14.9
40–44	13.0	14.8	11.5	13.4	13.2
45–49	9.7	10.0	8.8	10.9	9.8
50–54	8.0	7.7	7.5	8.4	8.0
55–59	7.2	6.9	7.3	6.7	7.3
Total N	144,696	1,132	7,262	3,427	3,154

	χ^2 Tests of Independence	
	NHSLS-W	NHSLS-U
CPS		13.3
GSS		8.31
NSFH		15.76*
NHSLS-W		10.91
Critical value @ alpha = .05	14.08	

*Null hypothesis rejected.

Table B.2   (continued)

C. Education

Category	CPS	GSS	NSFH	Wtd. NHSLS	Unwtd. NHSLS
< HS	15.8	13.5	15.7	14.5	13.9
HS or eq.	64.0	63.5	63.6	63.0	62.2
College	13.9	17.1	16.4	15.6	16.6
Advanced	6.3	5.9	4.2	6.9	7.3
Total N	142,101	1,126	7,239	3,408	3,139

	χ^2 Tests of Independence	
	NHSLS-W	NHSLS-U
CPS	13.31*	29.04*
GSS	3.21	3.13
NSFH	34.21*	43.9*
NHSLS-W		1.87
Critical value @ alpha = .05	7.82	

*Null hypothesis rejected.

D. Marital Status

Category	CPS	GSS	NSFH	Wtd. NHSLS	Unwtd. NHSLS
Never married	27.7	26.9	22.5	27.8	28.2
Married	58.3	54.5	56.9	58.6	53.3
Divorced	9.5	12.5	13.7	9.3	13.9
Separated	3.0	3.5	4.3	2.9	2.3
Widowed	1.6	2.6	2.6	1.4	2.3
Total N	144,095	1,132	7,261	3,411	3,140

	χ^2 Tests of Independence	
	NHSLS-W	NHSLS-U
CPS	.88	82.65*
GSS	17.91*	6.8
NSFH	92.74*	60.49*
NHSLS-W		47.78*
Critical value @ alpha = .05	9.49	

*Null hypothesis rejected.

Table B.2   (continued)

E. Race/Ethnicity

Category	CPS	GSS	NSFH	Wtd. NHSLS	Unwtd. NHSLS
White	75.9			75.2	76.5
Black	11.7			11.8	12.7
Hispanic	9.0			9.2	7.5
Other	3.3			3.8	3.3
Total N	143,388			3,430	3,159

	χ^2 Tests of Independence	
	NHSLS-W	NHSLS-U
CPS	2.42	11.68*
GSS		
NHSLS-W		8.54*
Critical value @ alpha = .05	7.82	

*Null hypothesis rejected.

F. Religious Affiliation

Category	CPS	GSS	NSFH	Wtd. NHSLS	Unwtd. NHSLS
None		7.9	9.1	10.7	11.0
Protestant		61.7	52.3	56.0	57.8
Catholic		26.0	25.8	28.8	27.0
Jewish		2.3	2.0	1.8	1.7
Other		2.2	10.8	2.6	2.5
Total N		1,132	7,191	3,427	3,153

	χ^2 Tests of Independence	
	NHSLS-W	NHSLS-U
CPS		
GSS	15.75*	12.43*
NSFH	230.99*	260.86*
NHSLS-W		2.79
Critical value @ alpha = .05	9.49	

*Null hypothesis rejected.

Table B.2   (continued)

G. Religious Attendance

Category	CPS	GSS	NSFH	Wtd. NHSLS	Unwtd. NHSLS
Never		13.1		15.0	14.8
< 1/year		9.5		8.6	8.3
1 or 2/year		15.2		16.7	16.3
Sev./year		12.9		14.1	14.5
1/month		8.4		6.9	6.9
2–3/month		11.2		9.7	9.6
Nearly weekly		4.8		4.1	3.9
Weekly		18.9		16.8	17.6
Sev./week		5.9		8.1	8.0
Total N		1,113		3,423	3,152

	χ^2 Tests of Independence	
	NHSLS-W	NHSLS-U
CPS		
GSS		11.16
NSFH		
NHSLS-W		.74
Critical value @ alpha = .05	16.92	

*Null hypothesis rejected.

H. Health

Category	CPS	GSS	NSFH	Wtd. NHSLS	Unwtd. NHSLS
Excellent		35.1		43.3	43.4
Good		46.9		45.6	45.3
Fair		16.1		9.2	9.4
Poor		1.9		1.9	1.9
Total N		738		3,429	3,156

	χ^2 Tests of Independence	
	NHSLS-W	NHSLS-U
CPS		
GSS	34.82*	32.98*
NHSLS-W		.11
Critical value @ alpha = .05	7.82	

*Null hypothesis rejected.

statistic is less than the critical value, the null hypothesis is accepted. Let us take table B.2A—by gender—and go through the information shown there.

The CPS distribution tells us that 49.7 percent of that sample of adults aged eighteen to fifty-nine were men, on the basis of the 144,697 observations in the 1991 CPS sample. Because of its very large size and its high quality, the CPS is the best sample against which one might compare a new sample, so this is the comparison that we emphasize here. The unweighted NHSLS has only 44.6 percent men, and the χ^2 statistic comparing these two distributions— the unweighted cross-sectional NHSLS and the CPS—is a whopping 31.4, so we reject the null hypothesis: these two samples are not likely to have come from the same population.

That would be a big concern, and would suggest a problem with our data, but for two other facts also shown in table B.2A. First, when we use the weighted data for this comparison, we see that 49.8 percent of our weighted sample are men, and the χ^2 statistic on that weighted sample compared to the CPS is 0.01, comfortably accepting the null hypothesis of no difference. So, when we weight our data, our sample is practically identical to the CPS in terms of the gender mix. That is precisely why we weight our data for making population projections. Weighting can, and here it does, correct for the under-representation of men in the data set. Of course, if we adjust for any sampling problem by creating a weight, we then cannot argue that the fact that our weighted data conform to the benchmark is evidence that the data are of good quality. We need to look further.

The second piece of information that is reassuring here is in the comparison of our unweighted data and the unweighted data from the other good surveys such as the GSS and the NSFH. Notice that the GSS has 43.8 percent men and the NSFH 43.0 percent men. These are pretty similar to our unweighted 44.6 percent, and ours is in fact closer to the "truth' of 49.7 percent than either of these. When we make the χ^2 comparison of our unweighted data and the GSS, the statistic is 0.23 and not significant; likewise, when we compare our un-weighted data to the NSFH, the χ^2 statistic is 2.34 and not significant. So our unweighted data look like other good-quality unweighted data, and our ad-justed or weighted data look like the population as reflected in the CPS. That statement is reassuring and impressive. To anticipate the discussion below, it implies that the people who willingly answered our long questionnaire about sexual behavior are not different from the population at large in terms of this first characteristic, gender.

One other point before we turn to the substantive findings in table B.2; it pertains to the pattern of tests that we performed. We looked first at the com-parisons of the CPS and our unweighted data. In any instance in which these two did not differ, we did not perform all the other pairwise tests since, if our unweighted data appeared to match the population as reflected in the CPS, there was not much point in making the other comparisons. So, in the compari-sons by age category, for instance, our unweighted NHSLS data and the CPS appear to come from the same population and we therefore conclude that our data are not biased in their age distribution.

The Variables Compared

There are eight variables of concern here: gender, age, education, marital status, race/ethnicity, religious affiliation, religious attendance, and health status. We consider each in turn. We have selected a 95 percent level of confidence for our χ^2 tests and indicate with an asterisk each test in which the null hypothesis of no difference is rejected. Thus, one can tell at a glance from the presence or the absence of an asterisk whether the NHSLS data appear to be drawn from the same population as the alternative data set. Those instances with an asterisk are those for which concern and attention are warranted.

Gender. As discussed above in describing how to read table B.2, our sample has somewhat too few men to be self-weighting, but the weighted data match the CPS quite well, and our unweighted data look very much like other samples such as the GSS and the NSFH. Thus, there is no indication here that men or women are relatively inclined or reluctant to participate in our sexual behavior survey. We should use the weights in our analysis, however, when we combine our sample by gender.

Age. The distribution of our sample by age matches the CPS sample in unweighted form, and the weighting itself does not alter the age distribution of our sample. Moreover, our NHSLS sample matches the GSS age distribution as well. Only the NSFH appears to differ somewhat, and it appears to have fewer in the thirty-five to forty-four age category. There is no need to weight our data when we combine age groups.

Education. The comparison of our sample and the CPS by education level raises a different issue. The χ^2 tests do in fact pass, suggesting that the distributions are not similar. Neither the unweighted nor the weighted data set matches the CPS, although both appear to match the GSS data. Moreover, the actual differences are surely not great—a couple of percentage points fewer high school equivalents and correspondingly more with some college is the essence of the difference. We conclude that these statistically significant but substantively small differences do not merit concern and that it is not necessary (or useful, for that matter) to weight our data when we combine education levels. We note that education was not used in the construction of the weights.

Marital status. The results for marital status are like those for gender—there does appear to be a substantial difference between the unweighted data and the CPS, but the weighting eliminates that difference. Our unweighted data match the unweighted GSS data. Our NHSLS data set appears to have relatively more divorced and relatively fewer married adults than the CPS, and this is likely to be a result of our oversampling people in one-adult households compared to those in multiple-adult households. This is also the case with the GSS sample. Weighting is called for here, but we note again that the reason for the discrepancy appears to have nothing to do with the subject matter of our study and everything to do with the sampling decision regarding interviewing only one adult per household. Because of its sampling decisions, the NSFH differs substantially from all these other data sets in its unweighted form. This difference, too, has a purpose in the context of the subject matter under investigation in that study, and nothing here implies any behavioral response to the content of these surveys that might introduce a substantive bias into the findings.

Race/ethnicity. We purposely oversampled blacks and English-speaking Hispanics in order to have enough observations from each of these two groups to look at behavior within each; these oversampled cases are not included in the unweighted, cross-sectional NHSLS sample shown in the right-hand column of table B.2E. We also followed the current custom of defining those who identified themselves as Hispanic as of that ethnicity and locating only the non-Hispanics in the racial categories. This identifies the black Hispanics in the Hispanic category and thus maximizes its magnitude relative to all other groups. This procedure may or may not be reasonable, but it permits us to compare our data to other surveys. The result of that comparison suggests that it is necessary to weight our data to conform to the U.S. population—the χ^2 statistics on the unweighted cross-sectional sample are significant. In a practical vein, the various distributions all yield about three-quarters of the samples as white, about 12 percent black, and 7–9 percent Hispanic, with a residual category of about 3 percent.

Religion. Regarding religion, we cannot use the CPS data for our comparisons and focus instead on the GSS. In religious affiliation, there is a significant difference between the NHSLS and the GSS, but there is not a difference in terms of attendance at religious services. The differences in affiliation are not great in substance, with a 3 or 4 percentage point difference between those who report themselves to be Protestants and those who report themselves to have no religious affiliation. The NSFH has a much larger percentage who report an other religion. Weighting the data here does not improve the similarity between the NHSLS and the GSS, but the GSS data are also not weighted, and we did not use religion in the construction of the weights.

Health. Health status, as reported in the self-assessed categories of excellent, good, fair, and poor, are compared here against the GSS data as we have no CPS figures to use. Here, as in the case of religious affiliation, there is a statistically significant difference, and, in the case of health status, there is a very substantial difference observed. The respondents in the NHSLS report themselves to be in better health than those in the GSS survey. We have no explanation for this difference. Given the relationship between health and sexual behavior reported in chapter 10, this factor could influence some of our observed patterns.

Conclusions

To summarize the results of this section, we find that, in comparisons of the NHSLS unweighted data and the CPS data, there are statistically significant differences in the compositions of the samples by gender, race/ethnicity, marital status, and education. Regarding the distribution by age, there is no difference between the unweighted NHSLS data and the CPS. In the case of gender, race/ethnicity, and marital status, the *weighted* data do not differ from the CPS. This suggests that, in making projections from our data to the U.S. population, weighting is necessary. Where we partition our data by these master status variables, however, that partitioning itself should suffice to give accurate estimates for subpopulations. Moreover, when we compare our NHSLS data to the GSS, we find that our unweighted cross-sectional sample conforms to the GSS in gender, age, education, and marital status (we did not compare race/ethnicity to the GSS).

Regarding religious affiliation, religious attendance, and health status, we cannot compare our data to the CPS, but we match the GSS in religious attendance, although not in affiliation or health status. Of these discrepancies, the difference in religion appears to be trivial in magnitude, but the NHSLS sample is a noticeably healthier sample than the GSS or the NSFH.

Thus, overall, while there are some differences in the demographic characteristics of the NHSLS and the CPS, there do not appear to be differences that can be attributed to the substantive content of our survey—the differences are no greater than those between the CPS and the GSS or the NSFH and are not, evidently, related to the sexual content of our survey. There is no indication in this series of variable-by-variable comparisons that the NHSLS data have systematically undersampled one group or another because we were asking about sex. We have fewer married and more divorced people, for instance, but that is because we sampled one person from a household and married people, of course, live in households with two adults, not one. The comparisons that we have undertaken here, then, do not suggest to us any particular problem or bias that can be attributed to the topic on which we focus.

Comparison of Reported Sexual Behavior

The previous section compares the NHSLS data to other data sets in terms of demographic characteristics. In this section, we exploit the fact that the 1991 GSS asked the identical set of eleven sexual behavior questions that the NHSLS asked in a self-administered (SAQ) portion of the survey, and we investigate much more directly whether there is any indication that our NHSLS data set reflects different sexual behavior patterns than the GSS. It is possible that a survey that is unabashedly sexual in content might capture a different group of respondents or might yield a different kind of response than a more conventional survey. The NHSLS-GSS comparisons here provide a nearly perfect test of this issue since the GSS was not identified as a sex survey and only a few minutes of that ninety-minute interview were devoted to these eleven sex questions, whereas in the NHSLS we told respondents initially that the content of the whole survey was basically sexual.

The eleven-question SAQ was, in both surveys, handed to the respondent to be filled out, with help from the interviewer only if the respondent requested it. In the 1991 GSS, this sexual behavior SAQ was the final component of the survey, coming at the end of the roughly ninety-minute interview about a wide range of attitudes and behaviors with little or no focus on sexual matters. By contrast, in the NHSLS, the SAQ was administered relatively early in the interview, following the first few minutes of questions about the respondents' demographic characteristics and a few family background questions. We wanted to ask these dozen questions in the sex SAQ before we got into the more detailed sexual behavior topics in order to make this comparison to the GSS SAQ as appropriate as possible.

Only the GSS respondents aged eighteen to fifty-nine are included in this comparison since that is the age range of the NHSLS; only the 1991 GSS data are utilized here, as the earlier waves of GSS data ask only a subset of the sexual behavior questions and in some instances asked them in a somewhat modified form. Here, the NHSLS is reported in four columns of table B.3, and each gender is reported separately. The table shows the unweighted cross-sectional data, the weighted full sample, and the two separate survey waves 1 and 2 of the cross-sectional data. The χ^2 statistic is reported for several pairwise comparisons for each question and for each gender separately.

The finding reported in table B.3 is remarkably strong: there is a practically identical pattern of response to each of these eleven questions in the GSS and the NHSLS for the men and for the women. The two samples were administered in consecutive years, 1991 and 1992, and in rather different contexts, as described above. Yet table B.3 reveals very similar distributions of responses in the two surveys.

Only one of the twenty-two comparisons failed to accept the null hypothesis of no statistical difference between the NHSLS and the GSS data. For the men, there is a slightly lower percentage of sex partners in the past twelve months who are characterized as a spouse or regular partner of the respondent (about 86 percent compared to about 90 percent in the GSS). In all other comparisons performed here, the distributions are not statistically different. They are similar in each of the following ten respects for men and for women: in terms of the number of partners within the past twelve months and in the past five years; the relationship of the partners in the past twelve months to the respondent; the distribution of the partners by gender in the past twelve months and in the past five years; the frequency of sex during the past twelve months; the total

Table B.3   **Comparison of Sexual Behavior, SAQ in GSS and NHSLS by Gender: Percentage Distributions and χ^2 Tests of Independence**

A. Males: How Many Sex Partners Have You Had in the Past 12 Months?

Response	GSS	Wtd. NHSLS	Unwtd. NHSLS	NHSLS Wave 1	NHSLS Wave 2
0	11.6	10.9	11.1	10.0	11.9
1	69.4	67.7	67.6	68.2	67.2
2	9.2	9.6	9.6	9.1	10.0
3	2.4	5.0	4.8	5.6	4.2
4	2.4	2.9	2.8	3.0	2.7
5–10	3.9	3.0	3.1	2.6	3.4
11+	1.2	0.9	1.0	1.6	.5
Total	415	1,435	1,341	573	768

χ^2 Tests of Independence

	NHSLS Wtd.	NHSLS Unwtd.	NHSLS Wave 1	NHSLS Wave 2
GSS	7.07	6.00	8.68	7.82
NHSLS Wtd.		.14		
NHSLS wave 2			7.56	
Critical value @ alpha = .05		12.59		

B. Males: Was One of Your Partners Your Spouse or Regular Sex Partner?

Response	GSS	Wtd. NHSLS	Unwtd. NHSLS	NHSLS Wave 1	NHSLS Wave 2
Yes	89.7	85.5	85.6	85.7	85.5
No	10.3	14.5	14.4	14.3	14.5
Total	358	1,293	1,206	525	681

χ^2 Tests of Independence

	NHSLS Wtd.	NHSLS Unwtd.	NHSLS Wave 1	NHSLS Wave 2
GSS	4.30*	4.17*	3.03	3.90*
NHSLS Wtd.		.00		
NHSLS wave 2			.02	
Critical value @ alpha = .05		3.84		

*Null hypothesis rejected.

Table B.3   (continued)

C. Males: If You Had Other Partners, Please Indicate All Categories That Apply to Them

Response	GSS	Wtd. NHSLS	Unwtd. NHSLS	NHSLS Wave 1	NHSLS Wave 2
Close friend	37.2	44.6	43.9	43.4	44.2
Acquaintance	25.7	22.0	22.5	23.0	22.1
Casual date	29.2	30.4	31.1	30.3	31.7
Paid person	6.2	1.9	1.7	2.6	1.0
Other	1.8	1.1	.9	.7	1.0
Total	113	368	351	152	199

χ^2 Tests of Independence

	NHSLS Wtd.	NHSLS Unwtd.	NHSLS Wave 1	NHSLS Wave 2
GSS	6.59	7.17	3.50	8.35
NHSLS Wtd.		.20		
NHSLS wave 2			1.55	
Critical value @ alpha = .05		9.49		

D. Males: Have Your Sex Partners in the Past 12 Months Been . . .

Response	GSS	Wtd. NHSLS	Unwtd. NHSLS	NHSLS Wave 1	NHSLS Wave 2
Exclusively male	2.8	2.6	2.6	1.8	3.3
Both male and female	.6	0.8	0.8	1.0	.8
Exclusively female	96.6	96.6	96.5	97.3	95.9
Total	355	1,263	1,177	512	666

χ^2 Tests of Independence

	NHSLS Wtd.	NHSLS Unwtd.	NHSLS Wave 1	NHSLS Wave 2
GSS	.57	.73	1.95	1.52
NHSLS Wtd.		.03		
NHSLS wave 2			3.00	
Critical value @ alpha = .05		5.99		

588

Table B.3 (continued)

E. Males: About How Often Did You Have Sex during the Past 12 Months?

Response	GSS	Wtd. NHSLS	Unwtd. NHSLS	NHSLS Wave 1	NHSLS Wave 2
Not at all	9.8	9.6	9.8	8.4	10.8
Once or twice	7.1	6.4	6.6	6.8	6.4
About once/ month	7.8	10.8	11.0	9.7	12.0
2–3 times/ month	16.6	16.7	16.3	17.9	15.1
About once/ week	21.8	19.0	19.2	20.0	18.5
2–3 times/week	28.6	29.4	29.5	29.7	29.3
4 or more/week	8.3	8.1	7.7	7.4	7.9
Total	409	1,423	1,330	569	761

	χ^2 Tests of Independence			
	NHSLS Wtd.	NHSLS Unwtd.	NHSLS Wave 1	NHSLS Wave 2
GSS	4.49	4.63	2.41	8.00
NHSLS Wtd.		.33		
NHSLS wave 2			5.78	
Critical value @ alpha = .05		12.59		

F. Males: How Many Sex Partners Have You Had in the Past 5 Years?

Response	GSS	Wtd. NHSLS	Unwtd. NHSLS	NHSLS Wave 1	NHSLS Wave 2
0	5.4	7.2	7.1	6.9	7.3
1	49.6	45.2	45.7	45.5	45.9
2	9.1	13.0	12.9	12.9	12.9
3	9.6	8.5	8.5	10.1	7.3
4	4.9	6.3	6.2	6.9	5.8
5–10	12.3	12.4	12.0	10.1	13.3
11–20	5.4	4.1	4.2	3.7	4.6
21+	3.5	3.3	3.3	3.9	2.9
Total	405	1,423	1,330	565	765

	χ^2 Tests of Independence			
	NHSLS Wtd.	NHSLS Unwtd.	NHSLS Wave 1	NHSLS Wave 2
GSS	9.59	8.79	8.98	11.28
NHSLS Wtd.		.16		
NHSLS wave 2			8.16	
Critical value @ alpha = .05		14.08		

Table B.3 (continued)

G. Males: Have Your Sex Partners in the Past 5 Years Been . . .

Response	GSS	Wtd. NHSLS	Unwtd. NHSLS	NHSLS Wave 1	NHSLS Wave 2
Exclusively male	3.1	2.3	2.4	1.9	2.8
Both male and					
female	2.1	1.8	1.8	2.2	1.4
Exclusively female	94.8	95.9	95.8	95.9	95.8
Total	385	1,337	1,251	537	714

	χ^2 Tests of Independence			
	NHSLS Wtd.	NHSLS Unwtd.	NHSLS Wave 1	NHSLS Wave 2
GSS	.89	.76	1.52	1.52
NHSLS Wtd.		.02		
NHSLS wave 2			2.34	
Critical value @ alpha = .05		5.99		

H. Males: How Many Female Partners Have You Had Sex with Since Your 18th Birthday?

Response	GSS	Wtd. NHSLS	Unwtd. NHSLS	NHSLS Wave 1	NHSLS Wave 2
0	6.0	5.4	5.5	5.6	5.4
1	16.3	16.9	17.2	17.4	17.1
2	9.6	9.0	8.9	9.0	8.7
3	5.4	7.3	7.2	8.5	6.2
4	7.5	6.5	6.6	6.7	6.5
5–10	26.4	27.6	27.6	26.4	28.6
11–20	15.5	12.7	12.5	12.1	12.8
21–100	11.4	13.0	12.9	12.3	13.4
Over 100	1.8	1.6	1.6	2.0	1.3
Total	386	1,400	1,309	553	756

	χ^2 Tests of Independence			
	NHSLS Wtd.	NHSLS Unwtd.	NHSLS Wave 1	NHSLS Wave 2
GSS	4.92	4.97	5.62	5.81
NHSLS Wtd.		.11		
NHSLS wave 2			4.26	
Critical value @ alpha = .05		15.51		

Table B.3 (continued)

I. Males: How Many Male Partners Have You Had Sex with Since Your 18th Birthday?

Response	GSS	Wtd. NHSLS	Unwtd. NHSLS	NHSLS Wave 1	NHSLS Wave 2
0	94.7	95.9	96.0	97.0	95.3
1	.8	.7	.7	.9	.5
2–4	.8	1.3	1.2	.9	1.4
5–10	1.6	.5	.5	.2	.7
11+	2.1	1.5	1.6	.9	2.2
Total	380	1,362	1,272	532	740

χ^2 Tests of Independence

	NHSLS Wtd.	NHSLS Unwtd.	NHSLS Wave 1	NHSLS Wave 2
GSS	5.13	4.98	8.35	4.37
NHSLS Wtd.		.19		
NHSLS wave 2			4.64	
Critical value @ alpha = .05		9.49		

J. Males: Since Your 18th Birthday, Have You Ever Had Sex with a Person You Paid or Who Paid You for Sex?

Response	GSS	Wtd. NHSLS	Unwtd. NHSLS	NHSLS Wave 1	NHSLS Wave 2
Yes	15.3	16.8	16.4	15.7	17.0
No	84.7	83.2	83.6	84.3	83.0
Total	411	1,426	1,333	567	766

χ^2 Tests of Independence

	NHSLS Wtd.	NHSLS Unwtd.	NHSLS Wave 1	NHSLS Wave 2
GSS	.53	.28	.02	.58
NHSLS Wtd.		.08		
NHSLS wave 2			.40	
Critical value @ alpha = .05		3.84		

K. Males: Have You Ever Had Sex with Someone Other Than Your Wife While You Were Married?

Response	GSS	Wtd. NHSLS	Unwtd. NHSLS	NHSLS Wave 1	NHSLS Wave 2
Yes	21.7	25.2	24.5	22.1	26.4
No	78.3	74.8	75.5	77.9	73.6
Total	281	997	929	392	537

Table B.3 (continued)

	χ^2 Tests of Independence			
	NHSLS Wtd.	NHSLS Unwtd.	NHSLS Wave 1	NHSLS Wave 2
GSS	1.46	.97	.02	2.59
NHSLS Wtd.		.10		
NHSLS wave 2			2.28	
Critical value @ alpha = .05		3.84		

L. Females: How Many Sex Partners Have You Had in the Past 12 Months?

Response	GSS	Wtd. NHSLS	Unwtd. NHSLS	NHSLS Wave 1	NHSLS Wave 2
0	13.4	13.7	13.7	14.2	13.4
1	76.4	74.9	75.5	74.7	76.1
2	6.7	6.6	6.3	6.5	6.1
3+	3.6	4.8	4.5	4.6	4.4
Total	554	1,843	1,675	719	956

	χ^2 Tests of Independence			
	NHSLS Wtd.	NHSLS Unwtd.	NHSLS Wave 1	NHSLS Wave 2
GSS	1.50	.95	1.04	.59
NHSLS Wtd.		.38		
NHSLS wave 2			.46	
Critical value @ alpha = .05		7.82		

M. Females: Was One of Your Partners Your Spouse or Regular Sex Partner?

Response	GSS	Wtd. NHSLS	Unwtd. NHSLS	NHSLS Wave 1	NHSLS Wave 2
Yes	92.1	91.9	92.1	90.9	93.1
No	7.9	8.1	7.9	9.1	6.9
Total	478	1,609	1,461	626	835

	χ^2 Tests of Independence			
	NHSLS Wtd.	NHSLS Unwtd.	NHSLS Wave 1	NHSLS Wave 2
GSS	.01	.00	.47	.45
NHSLS Wtd.		.05		
NHSLS wave 2			2.31	
Critical value @ alpha = .05		5.99		

*Null hypothesis rejected.

Table B.3   (continued)

N. Females: If You Had Other Partners, Please Indicate All Categories That Apply to Them

Response	GSS	Wtd. NHSLS	Unwtd. NHSLS	NHSLS Wave 1	NHSLS Wave 2
Close friend	59.5	56.5	56.8	52.4	60.5
Acquaintance	24.1	21.6	22.0	24.3	20.2
Casual date	15.2	15.3	15.0	17.5	12.9
Other	1.3	6.7	6.2	5.8	6.4
Total	79	255	227	103	124

	χ^2 Tests of Independence			
	NHSLS Wtd.	NHSLS Unwtd.	NHSLS Wave 1	NHSLS Wave 2
GSS	4.60	3.90	3.30	4.03
NHSLS Wtd.		.07		
NHSLS wave 2			2.02	
Critical value @ alpha = .05		7.82		

O. Females: Have Your Sex Partners in the Past 12 Months Been. . .

Response	GSS	Wtd. NHSLS	Unwtd. NHSLS	NHSLS Wave 1	NHSLS Wave 2
Exclusively male	99.4	98.3	98.3	99.0	97.8
Both male and female	.2	.4	.5	.3	.6
Exclusively female	.4	1.3	1.2	.7	1.6
Total	465	1,568	1,424	609	815

	χ^2 Tests of Independence			
	NHSLS Wtd.	NHSLS Unwtd.	NHSLS Wave 1	NHSLS Wave 2
GSS	3.49	3.20	.15	5.21
NHSLS Wtd.		.07		
NHSLS wave 2			4.82	
Critical value @ alpha = .05		5.99		

Table B.3   (continued)

P. Females: About How Often Did You Have Sex during the Past 12 Months?

Response	GSS	Wtd. NHSLS	Unwtd. NHSLS	NHSLS Wave 1	NHSLS Wave 2
Not at all	14.1	13.5	13.6	14.5	13.0
Once or twice	8.0	7.1	7.2	7.1	7.2
About once/ month	8.2	9.1	9.0	10.1	8.1
2–3 times/ month	17.1	17.7	17.7	18.2	17.3
About once/ week	20.6	19.2	19.5	18.4	20.4
2–3 times/week	25.1	26.5	26.3	24.0	28.1
4 or more/week	6.9	6.9	6.7	7.7	6.0
Total	538	1,829	1,664	716	948

	χ^2 Tests of Independence			
	NHSLS Wtd.	NHSLS Unwtd.	NHSLS Wave 1	NHSLS Wave 2
GSS	1.72	1.31	2.85	2.20
NHSLS wtd.		.13		
NHSLS wave 2			7.52	
Critical value @ alpha = .05		12.59		

Q. Females: How Many Sex Partners Have you Had in the Past 5 Years?

Response	GSS	Wtd. NHSLS	Unwtd. NHSLS	NHSLS Wave 1	NHSLS Wave 2
0	6.9	9.0	8.7	9.0	8.5
1	61.9	59.3	59.4	57.7	60.6
2	12.6	12.1	12.3	13.1	11.7
3	8.2	7.2	7.4	7.9	7.0
4	3.5	4.6	4.6	4.6	4.6
5+	6.9	7.8	7.7	7.7	7.6
Total	548	1,837	1,669	711	958

	χ^2 Tests of Independence			
	NHSLS Wtd.	NHSLS Unwtd.	NHSLS Wave 1	NHSLS Wave 2
GSS	.57	.73	1.95	1.52
NHSLS wtd.		.03		
NHSLS wave 2			3.00	
Critical value @ alpha = .05		5.99		

Table B.3   (continued)

R. Females: Have Your Sex Partners in the Past 5 Years Been . . .

Response	GSS	Wtd. NHSLS	Unwtd. NHSLS	NHSLS Wave 1	NHSLS Wave 2
Exclusively male	98.6	97.8	97.9	98.9	97.2
Both male and female	1.0	.8	.8	.3	1.1
Exclusively female	.4	1.4	1.3	.8	1.7
Total	507	1,688	1,537	654	883

	χ^2 Tests of Independence			
	NHSLS Wtd.	NHSLS Unwtd.	NHSLS Wave 1	NHSLS Wave 2
GSS	4.61	3.78	2.47	5.47
NHSLS wtd.		.09		
NHSLS wave 2			7.71*	
Critical value @ alpha = .05		5.99		

*Null hypothesis rejected.

S. Females: How Many Female Partners Have you Had Sex with since Your 18th Birthday?

Response	GSS	Wtd. NHSLS	Unwtd. NHSLS	NHSLS Wave 1	NHSLS Wave 2
0	96.7	97.0	96.9	97.2	96.8
1	1.0	1.0	1.0	.7	1.2
2	1.0	.7	.8	1.2	.4
3+	1.4	1.3	1.3	.9	1.6
Total	509	1,755	1,599	677	922

	χ^2 Tests of Independence			
	NHSLS Wtd.	NHSLS Unwtd.	NHSLS Wave 1	NHSLS Wave 2
GSS	.46	.25	.84	1.78
NHSLS wtd.		.09		
NHSLS wave 2			4.56	
Critical value @ alpha = .05		7.82		

Table B.3   (continued)

T. Females: How Many Male Partners Have you Had Sex with since Your 18th Birthday?

Response	GSS	Wtd. NHSLS	Unwtd. NHSLS	NHSLS Wave 1	NHSLS Wave 2
0	3.8	4.8	4.8	4.4	5.0
1	33.3	30.4	30.1	28.2	31.5
2	15.1	15.8	16.0	16.6	15.4
3	13.2	11.8	11.8	12.3	11.3
4	6.8	8.7	8.6	9.5	8.0
5–10	21.2	20.8	21.1	20.3	21.7
11–20	4.9	4.9	4.9	6.2	4.0
21+	1.7	2.8	2.5	2.3	3.0
Total	529	1,806	1,643	698	945

	χ^2 Tests of Independence			
	NHSLS Wtd.	NHSLS Unwtd.	NHSLS Wave 1	NHSLS Wave 2
GSS	6.54	6.61	7.50	5.76
NHSLS wtd.		.11		
NHSLS wave 2			7.43	
Critical value @ alpha = .05		14.08		

U. Females: Since Your 18th Birthday, Have You Ever Had Sex with a Person You Paid or Who Paid You for Sex?

Response	GSS	Wtd. NHSLS	Unwtd. NHSLS	NHSLS Wave 1	NHSLS Wave 2
Yes	1.4	1.6	1.4	1.5	1.4
No	98.6	98.4	98.6	98.5	98.6
Total	556	1,833	1,667	713	954

	χ^2 Tests of Independence			
	NHSLS Wtd.	NHSLS Unwtd.	NHSLS Wave 1	NHSLS Wave 2
GSS	.11	.00	.02	.01
NHSLS Wtd.		.22		
NHSLS wave 2			.09	
Critical value @ alpha = .05		3.84		

Table B.3   (continued)

V. Females: Have You Ever Had Sex with Someone Other Than Your Husband While You Were Married?

Response	GSS	Wtd. NHSLS	Unwtd. NHSLS	NHSLS Wave 1	NHSLS Wave 2
Yes	13.4	14.5	15.0	14.3	15.4
No	86.6	85.5	85.0	85.7	84.6
Total	424	1,450	1,324	552	772

	χ^2 Tests of Independence			
	NHSLS Wtd.	NHSLS Unwtd.	NHSLS Wave 1	NHSLS Wave 2
GSS	.29	.60	.10	.86
NHSLS wtd.		.12		
NHSLS wave 2			.40	
Critical value @ alpha = .05		3.84		

number of female and of male sex partners since the respondent's eighteenth birthday; whether the respondent ever paid or was paid for sex; and, finally, whether the respondent ever had sex with someone other than his or her spouse while married. This is a very strong indication that these two samples reflect the same sexual behavioral patterns.

There are also two other reassuring findings in table B.3. First, for each of the eleven questions asked, a comparison between the respondents in the first wave of data and those in the second, administered over a consecutive few months, yielded no differences whatsoever. (There is one exception to this statement from the entire set of twenty-two comparisons—regarding the question about whether their sex partners in the past five years have been exclusively males, exclusively females, or both, the two waves of data for the women pass the statistical test at a 95 percent level of confidence.) Overall, therefore, there is very powerful information here that these two waves of data can in fact be pooled and can be used as a single sample, as had been our intention in designing the survey and analysis strategy.

Second, a parallel test was performed on the unweighted cross-sectional data and the weighted full sample, and none of these comparisons showed a significant difference. So, in terms of the sexual behavior reported in these SAQs, the weighted and unweighted data yield the same distributions of responses. This is quite important because it reaffirms that the differences in response rates to our survey and the differences imposed by our sampling strategy (e.g., sampling one person per household or oversampling blacks and Hispanics) are not statistically related to the sexual behavior reported in these SAQs.

In conclusion, there is strong evidence here that those who willingly sit for a survey interview about sexual behavior (the NHSLS) report the same sexual behavior patterns as those who sit for a more conventional general survey (the GSS). Moreover, there is evidence here that asking these questions near the end of a ninety-minute (as in the GSS) or near the beginning of the interview (as in the NHSLS) has no discernible or systematic effect on the nature of the answers given. The comparisons here are quite reassuring that the sample we drew and the answers they offered are not affected by the substantive focus of this survey.

Comparison of Sex-Related Attitudes

There are a few questions in the 1991 GSS that were replicated in the NHSLS pertaining to attitudes about sexual conduct and sex-related issues. A comparison of four of these attitudes and two additional issues is reported in this section. The attitudes pertain to abortion, extramarital sex, and homosexuality. The specific wording of the questions is discussed at the end of this appendix, and the distributions for the GSS and the unweighted and weighted NHSLS are shown in table B.4. The additional issues are whether the respondent knows anyone personally who has HIV/AIDS and whether the respondent, if married, had cohabited prior to his or her formal marriage. These two final items provide yet another indication of whether the NHSLS data set reflects the same general behavior pattern as the GSS sample. We consider these several items one by one since the findings here do not reflect a consistent pattern.

Abortion. There are two questions about abortion asked of the GSS and NHSLS samples. The first asks whether the respondent thinks it should be possible for a pregnant woman to obtain a legal abortion if the woman wants it "for any reason." The GSS has asked this question over many years, and the 1991 yes-no response does not differ very much from earlier years. The NHSLS response, by contrast, shows a notably more liberal stance, with about 52 percent answering yes, compared to 44 percent in the GSS. That difference is statistically significant. The second question we compared asks the same question about abortion but stipulates that the circumstance is that the woman became pregnant as a result of rape. There, the GSS sample had about 87 percent answering yes and the NHSLS 88 percent, which is not a significant difference statistically or substantively.

Extramarital sex. Regarding the attitude toward the acceptability of extramarital sex, the NHSLS respondents have a more conservative attitude than those in the GSS survey, as seen from table B.4D–E. There, 1.2 percent of the whole, unweighted NHSLS sample, but 3.6 percent of the GSS sample, think having sexual relations with someone other than the marriage partner is "not wrong at all"; correspondingly, 77 percent of the NHSLS sample and 74 percent of the GSS sample think that it is "always wrong." The χ^2 test indicates that these two distributions are statistically different.

Table B.4   **Comparison of Sex-Related Attitudes: Percentage Distribution for the GSS and NHSLS; χ^2 Tests of Differences**

A. Abortion—under Any Circumstance

Category	GSS	Wtd. NHSLS	Unwtd. NHSLS
Yes	44.3	50.1	51.7
No	55.7	49.9	48.3
Total N	715	3,255	3,010

	χ^2 Tests of Independence
	NHSLS-U
GSS	12.42*
NHSLS-W	1.57
Critical value @ alpha = .05	3.84

*Null hypothesis rejected.

B. Abortion—under Any Circumstance (males 18–34)

Category	GSS	Wtd. NHSLS	Unwtd. NHSLS
Yes	50.0		52.8
No	50.0		47.2
Total N	148		651

	χ^2 Tests of Independence
	NHSLS-U
GSS	.39
NHSLS-W	
Critical value @ alpha = .05	3.84

C. Abortion—If Rape

Category	GSS	Wtd. NHSLS	Unwtd. NHSLS
Yes	86.8	87.4	88.4
No	13.2	12.6	11.6
Total N	714	3,303	3,045

	χ^2 Tests of Independence
	NHSLS-U
GSS	1.28
NHSLS-W	1.48
Critical value @ alpha = .05	3.84

Table B.4   (continued)

D. Extramarital Sex

Category	GSS	Wtd. NHSLS	Unwtd. NHSLS
Always wrong	74.3	77.5	77.2
Almost always wrong	15.0	13.6	13.9
Sometimes wrong	7.1	7.6	7.7
Not wrong	3.6	1.3	1.2
Total N	719	3,416	3,144

	χ^2 Tests of Independence
	NHSLS-U
GSS	17.39*
NHSLS-W	.16
Critical value @ alpha = .05	7.82

*Null hypothesis rejected.

E. Extramarital Sex (males 18–34)

Category	GSS	Wtd. NHSLS	Unwtd. NHSLS
Always wrong	71.9		70.3
Almost always wrong	16.3		20.5
Sometimes wrong	9.2		7.6
Not wrong	2.6		1.6
Total N	153		707

	χ^2 Tests of Independence
	NHSLS-U
GSS	2.28
NHSLS-W	
Critical value @ alpha = .05	7.82

F. Homosexuality

Category	GSS	Wtd. NHSLS	Unwtd. NHSLS
Always wrong	71.4	66.7	65.0
Almost always wrong	4.3	5.6	5.4
Sometimes wrong	5.2	7.7	8.2
Not wrong	19.1	19.9	21.4
Total N	691	3,367	3,098

	χ^2 Tests of Independence
	NHSLS-U
GSS	13.15*
NHSLS-W	3.04
Critical value @ alpha = .05	7.82

*Null hypothesis rejected.

G. Homosexuality (males 18–34)

Category	GSS	Wtd. NHSLS	Unwtd. NHSLS
Always wrong	73.8		71.1
Almost always wrong	2.0		4.2
Sometimes wrong	4.7		8.6
Not wrong	19.5		16.1
Total N	149		615

	χ^2 Tests of Independence
	NHSLS-U
GSS	5.36
NHSLS-W	
Critical value @ alpha = .05	7.82

H. Knowing Someone with HIV/AIDS

Category	GSS	Wtd. NHSLS	Unwtd. NHSLS
Yes	18.9	27.4	28.9
No	81.1	72.6	71.1
Total N	1,132	3,426	3,157

	χ^2 Tests of Independence
	NHSLS-U
GSS	44.68*
NHSLS-W	1.78
Critical value @ alpha = .05	3.84

*Null hypothesis rejected.

Table B.4   (continued)

I. Knowing Someone with HIV/AIDS (males 18–34)

Category	GSS	Wtd. NHSLS	Unwtd. NHSLS
Yes	13.0		25.6
No	87.0		74.4
Total N	216		676

	χ^2 Tests of Independence
	NHSLS-U
GSS	16.35*
NHSLS-W	
Critical value @ alpha = .05	3.84

*Null hypothesis rejected.

Homosexuality. On attitudes toward homosexuality, the NHSLS respondents appear to be more liberal than are the respondents in the GSS, as seen from table B.4F–G.

Knowing someone with HIV/AIDS. A question tracked in the GSS over several years and asked again in the NHSLS was whether the respondent knew someone personally who had contracted HIV/AIDS. A remarkable inconsistency is revealed in table B.4H–I, where the portion of respondents who reported knowing someone with HIV/AIDS increased from about 19 percent in the 1991 GSS to about 29 percent in the 1992 NHSLS. However, the 1993 GSS reports that 27.8 percent knew someone with HIV/AIDS, a figure that is quite comparable to the NHSLS.

Cohabiting before marriage. As a final comparison, we look at the reported incidence of cohabiting prior to formal marriage in the NSFH and NHSLS samples. Table B.5 shows the proportions of those who have married who indicated that their first union was a formal marriage. One sees here in both surveys the decline over time in the proportion whose first union was a formal marriage or, conversely, the proportion whose first union was a cohabitation. One also sees a somewhat higher rate of formal marriage reported by the women in both samples. The similarity of results from the two surveys is of interest. The reader may notice that the youngest cohort does show a somewhat different experience in the two samples, but that is due to the difference in the dates of these two surveys: the NSFH was conducted in 1986–87, while the NHSLS was conducted in 1992, so those born in the years 1963–74 were only thirteen to twenty-four in 1986 but were eighteen to twenty-nine by 1992, a difference

Table B.5   **Percentage Whose First Union Was a Marriage, NSFH and NHSLS**

| | Men | | Women | |
	NSFH	NHSLS	NSFH	NHSLS
Cohort				
1933–42	89.8	83.6	94.2	93.1
1943–52	75.2	69.7	84.9	78.2
1953–62	52.7	46.9	60.0	57.6
1963–74	29.6	34.3	43.2	36.0

that probably explains the discrepancy between the two samples in the bottom row of table B.5.

Conclusion

We draw several conclusions from the tables in this appendix, and a few are of critical importance to our inquiry. We acknowledge a strong intellectual bias toward these conclusions, but we believe that they are warranted by the evidence adduced here and are not particularly affected by our personal perspectives.

1. Adults in the United States (between ages eighteen and fifty-nine) are willing to be interviewed about their sexual behavior when that interview is conducted in a respectful, confidential, and professional manner. We have seen above that there is no indication that the NHSLS sample differs from other high-quality samples in its demographic characteristics. Our respondents were told before the survey was begun that it was a survey about their own sexual behavior in recent years and that it would go into some detail about that behavior. Appendix A shows that approximately 80 percent of the adults targeted for the survey did in fact agree to sit for about ninety minutes and tell us about their sexual behavior, and this appendix shows that there is no discernible demographic difference between the men and women in this sample and those in other recent household samples such as the GSS with which we compared them. There are differences between our sample and the U.S. population as reflected in the Current Population Survey in terms of gender, marital status, race/ethnicity, and education, but these differences seem to be related to sampling decisions that we made for reasons of cost and efficiency, not to basic differences that can be attributed to sexual behavior. Moreover, the weighted data conform with the CPS data in all respects but education, where a quite small substantive difference persists. There does not appear to be a difference in the willingness to respond to a sexual behavior survey. This is a very optimistic finding, as it suggests that the population at large respects the importance of, and is willing to contribute to, a better understanding about sexual behavior.

2. The adults in the NHSLS sexual behavior survey of 1992 report the same general sexual behavior as do adults in other recent U.S. surveys about sex; thus, the sample appears to be similar to the population at large in terms of its sexual behavior, as best as this can be determined. There is strong suggestive evidence here that the sexual behavior of the NHSLS sample—as well as the demographic characteristics of this sample—is similar to the sexual behavior reported in other national samples. It does not appear to be the case that those who chose to be interviewed in the NHSLS differ in any discernible way in terms of their sexual behavior. They appear to be representative of the population at large.

3. It appears that the sexual behavior reported in the NHSLS is reported without systemic bias or, put more cautiously, that whatever bias is contained in the description of sexual behavior reported here is the same as that reported in other quite recent national surveys that ask these same questions; sexual behavior is also invariant across the two waves of the NHSLS data collection itself. We have no precise way in which we can check the accuracy of the sexual data because we do not have external, reliable, factual bases for the comparison—as we do, for example, in the case of asking about the number of live births or current marital status, where we do have independent accurate information about the population. But the consistency in the answers to a few questions about sexual behavior between the NHSLS and the GSS data, surveys that differ in character, administration, and timing, provide considerable indirect evidence that the answers are honestly given. It would be quite a feat for some untruth to survive this several year, several mode, several team difference in data collection effort. The consistency is reassuring that the information is honestly provided and as accurate as respondents can be.

4. Regarding sexual attitudes, as distinct from behavior, we find that the NHSLS sample differs from the comparison, GSS, sample; the NHSLS respondents hold a more liberal attitude toward homosexuality and abortion for any reason than those in the GSS but a more conservative attitude toward extramarital sex, and they also report a much higher incidence of knowing someone personally with HIV/AIDS. Perhaps the fact of responding to the sexual behavior questions affects the reported attitudes, but the direction of effect is not consistently liberal or conservative, so we are puzzled by this result.

5. The sexual behavior reported in the NHSLS is, in fact, reflective of the sexual behavior of the adult population in the United States, and findings about this behavior can legitimately be generalized to that population. This conclusion motivates the analysis in this book. Were we doubtful about the veracity of the information or about the representativeness of the respondents who provided that information, there would be less incentive to engage in the analysis of these data. We have concluded, to the contrary, that the respondents are a random sample of the adults in the target population and that the sexual behavior that they report is as accurate as the communication between researcher and respondent can sustain at this time.

Data Used for Comparisons in Tables B.2–B.4

SOURCES

> CPS1 (gender, age, and ethnicity, 1991, for ages eighteen to fifty-nine): U.S. Bureau of the Census 1993.
>
> CPS2 (education, 1990, for ages eighteen to fifty-nine): U.S. Bureau of the Census 1992a.
>
> CPS3 (marital status, 1992): U.S. Bureau of the Census 1992b.
>
> GSS (1991, for ages eighteen to fifty-nine): Davis and Smith 1991.
>
> NSFH (1986–87, for ages eighteen to fifty-nine, main sample): Sweet, Bumpass, and Call 1988.

DEFINITIONS OF VARIABLES

> GENDER
>
>> NHSLS-GENDER (gender of respondent from household screener)
>> CPS1
>> GSS-SEX (interviewer coded)
>> NSFH (gender of respondent based on full-time household roster)
>
> AGE
>
>> NHSLS-AGE (date of birth recoded into actual age)
>> CPS1
>> GSS-AGE (date of birth recoded into actual age)
>> NSFH-M2BP01 (age of respondent based on full-time household roster)
>
> MARITAL STATUS
>
>> NHSLS-MARST (constructed variable)
>> CPS3
>> GSS-MARITAL: "Are you currently married, divorced, or separated, or have you ever been married?"
>> NSFH-MARCOHAB (constructed variable)
>
> EDUCATION
>
>> NHSLS-DEGREE (constructed from): "What was the highest grade or year of schooling you completed? 8th grade or less; some high school; finished high school or equivalent, vocational/trade/business school; some college or 2-year degree; finished college, 4 to 5 year degree; master's degree or equivalent; other advanced degree."
>> CPS2
>> GSS-DEGREE (constructed variable)
>> NSFH-EDUCAT (constructed variable)

ETHNICITY

    CPS1

    NHSLS-RACE/HISPANIC: "What is your race?"/"Do you consider yourself Hispanic?"

    GSS-RACE: "What race do you consider yourself?"

    NSFH-M484: "Which of the groups on this card best describes you?"

RELIGION

    NHSLS-RELIG14/RELIG: "In what religion were you raised? (probe if necessary)/(if switched) "What is your current religious preference?" (probe if necessary)

    GSS-RELIG: "What is your religious preference? Is it Protestant, Catholic, Jewish, some other religion, or no religion?"

    NSFH-M486: "What is your religious preference?"

ATTENDANCE

    NHSLS/GSS-ATTEND: "How often do you attend religious services?"

HEALTH

    NHSLS-HEALTH: "Would you say your health is, in general, excellent, good, fair, or poor?"

    GSS-HEALTH: "In general, would you say your health is excellent, good, fair, or poor?"

    NSFH-E207 "Compared with other people your age, how would you describe your health? Very poor, poor, fair, good, excellent?"

ABORTION—UNDER ANY CIRCUMSTANCES

    NHSLS/GSS-ABANY: "Please tell me whether or not you think it should be possible for a pregnant woman to obtain a legal abortion if the woman wants it for any reason?"

ABORTION–IF RAPE

    NHSLS/GSS-ABRAPE: "Please tell me whether or not you think it should be possible for a pregnant woman to obtain a legal abortion if she became pregnant as a result of rape?"

EXTRAMARITAL SEX

    NHSLS/GSS-XMARSEX: "What is your opinion about a married person having sexual relations with someone other than the marriage partner—Is it always wrong, almost always wrong, wrong only sometimes, or not wrong at all?"

HOMOSEXUALITY

    NHSLS/GSS-HOMOSEX: "What about sexual relations between two adults of the same sex? Do you think it is always wrong, almost always wrong, wrong only sometimes, or not wrong at all?"

KNOWING SOMEONE WITH AIDS

    NHSLS/GSS-AIDSKNOW: "How many people have you known personally, either living or dead, who came down with the disease called AIDS?"

The NHSLS Questionnaire

This appendix contains the complete text of the questionnaire used to collect the primary data discussed in this book. Because responses to questions in surveys can vary according to their wording and context, readers and researchers may want to see the exact wording and ordering of the questions. There are a few typographical conventions used in translating this written text into a face-to-face interview and a few terms that need further explanation.

Capitalization. Capital letters are used to distinguish text that is intended only for the interviewer from text that is meant for the respondent. Most of the uppercase text consists of instructions for the interviewer, but it is also used for answer categories that are not to be read to the respondent. When the response categories for a question are in lowercase text, even if they are not part of the question itself, the interviewer is allowed to use these categories to probe the respondent's answer to make sure of the correct category. (See, e.g., section 1, question 3, highest grade or year of schooling.) When the categories are in uppercase text, the interviewer is not allowed to provide the category or categories to the respondent, because we are interested in the respondent's own terminology and understanding of the question. If the respondent provides an unusual answer or one that is not listed, the interviewer records that answer as a verbatim response. (See section 1, questions 4 and 5 about race and ethnicity for examples of this usage.)

Uppercase text is also used to indicate that the interviewer should insert the first name (or initials or another mnemonic) of a specific sex partner (this use of uppercase text is found primarily in sections 2, 4, and 5 of the questionnaire). Because a series of questions are asked about specific partners (spouses, cohabitational partners, and sex partners from the last year), a device was needed to ensure that the interviewer and the respondent were talking about the same person. Rosters at the beginning of these sections collect first names for partners; in subsequent questions, the interviewer substitutes the appropriate name or mnemonic for the uppercase indicator in the question text. Section 2 collects basic information on all spouses and cohabitational partners and detailed information on the first and the most recent such partner where appropriate. The interviewer substitutes the appropriate name when (S/C) or

(S/C's) appears in the question. In sections 4 and 5, the interviewer replaces (PARTNER) or (PARTNER'S) in the text of questions with the actual first name or mnemonic the respondent gave.

Skip patterns. There are several conventions that modify the flow of the questionnaire based on specific responses by indicating to the interviewer which question to ask next. The general rule is that questions are read in the order in which they appear in the questionnaire unless a different order is indicated. There are several ways to indicate that the interviewer should skip questions. Skip patterns that depend on specific responses to a question are usually indicated by placing the question number that should be asked beside the response category code (e.g., section 1, question 2). Braces are sometimes used to indicate a set of responses that all skip to the same question. We tried to provide a clear indication of what question to ask next whenever there was a chance of ambiguity. Other methods of controlling the flow of the questionnaire are indicated by uppercased instructions below a question or before a set of questions and by interviewer boxes, which include special instructions, actions, or questions that determine the flow of the interview. Interviewer boxes, which are numbered like questions, also allow the interviewer to skip from a question to a box rather than to another question.

Hand cards. Throughout the questionnaire, there are references to hand cards (e.g., section 1, question 7; section 2, questions 18, 19, 23, and 24). A spiral-bound booklet of hand cards is given to the respondent at the beginning of the interview. At the beginning of certain questions, the respondent is asked to turn to a specific card that has, in large type, the answer categories for that question and their number codes. There are several reasons for using hand cards. They help break up the monotony of the interview. They help respondents remember all of the answer categories when there are many, when they are especially complicated, or when a small set of categories is used repeatedly over a whole set of questions (for examples of the latter, see section 4, questions 27–34 and 69–76). Hand cards also provide a sense of comfort and privacy when answering certain questions about specific sexual practices that occurred in certain events, such as early sexual experiences. In answer to these questions (section 8, questions 3, 25, 32, 34, 44, and 45D) the respondent is asked only for the number on the card. The full response categories are not printed in the questionnaire. This way respondents do not have to verbalize names of specific sexual acts and they do not necessarily feel they are revealing them to the interviewer.

SAQs. There are two basic parts to the NHSLS questionnaire. The first part is the face-to-face interview. The second part is the four separate self-administered questionnaires (SAQs) that are used during the course of the face-to-face interview. All of the SAQs appear at the end of the main questionnaire reprinted here. In the actual instrument, they are bound separately and are given to the respondent as a set the first time they are needed (see box 1.1 after section 1, question 34). At various times during the interview the respondent is asked to fill out the next SAQ. After the final SAQ is filled out (at the very end of the interview, section 10, after question 16), the respondent is asked to put the set into the envelope provided and seal it before returning it to the interviewer. The main purpose of the SAQs is to increase the respondents' sense of privacy and to improve the honest reporting of some of the most sensitive information in the questionnaire (about, e.g., income, masturbation, lifetime experience of sexual practices, abortion, drug use). The second SAQ, while hardly especially sensitive in the context of this survey, is a replication of a set of self-administered questions used in the General Social Survey (GSS). The questions in the fourth SAQ are asked differently for men and women so there are two forms, SAQ 4F (females only) and SAQ 4M (males only).

Contents

INTERVIEWER: RECORD TIME |___|___|:|___|___| AM...1
                                                 PM...2

SECTION 1: DEMOGRAPHY

☞

1. What is your date of birth?

|___|___| |___|___| |___|___|
  MONTH   DAY   YEAR

CALCULATE YEAR THAT R WAS
18 YEARS OLD ——————>

YEAR OF BIRTH   19|___|___|

AGE 18   +   1   8

YEAR AT AGE 18   ——————

We will be using this Life History Calendar later on to help to recall the dates of specific events in your life from the time you were 18 through this year. The calendar divides each year into quarters representing the 4 seasons: W (January-March); SP (April-June); SU (July-September); F (October-December). At this time I need to enter the years in the space indicated for each year from the time you were 18 until now.

RECORD YEAR AT 18 IN FIRST COLUMN OF THE LHC. ENTER SUCCEEDING YEARS IN APPROPRIATE BOXES UP THROUGH CURRENT YEAR.

2. Were you born in the United States? (PROBE: That is, in one of the 50 states or in the District of Columbia.)

Yes 1 (Q.3)
No . . . . 2 (ASK A)
DON'T KNOW 3 (Q.3)

A.   In what year did you first move to the United States to
live?   19 |___|___|

3. What was the highest grade or year of schooling you completed?

8th grade or less 01
Some high school 02
Finished high school or equivalent . . 03
Vocational/trade/business school . . . 04
Some college or 2-year degree 05
Finished college, 4 to 5-year degree . 06
Master's degree or equivalent 07
Other advanced degree 08

4. What is your race? (PROBE: Which would you say best describes your racial
background?)

WHITE 1
BLACK 2
ALASKAN NATIVE/NATIVE AMERICAN 3
ASIAN/PACIFIC ISLANDER 4
OTHER (SPECIFY)_____ 5

THIS PAGE LEFT INTENTIONALLY BLANK

1.1

5. Do you consider yourself Hispanic?

Yes . . . . 1 (ASK A)
No 2 (Q.6)
DON'T KNOW 3 (Q.6)

A. Would you say you are Mexican, Puerto Rican, Cuban or something else?

Mexican, Mexican-American, Chicano . . 1
Puerto Rican, Puertorriqueno, or Boricua . . 2
Cuban, Cubano . . 3
OTHER LATIN AMERICAN, LATINO, HISPANIC, OR SPANISH DESCENT (SPECIFY) ___ 4

6. Now I'd like you to think about when you were fourteen years old, and what your household was like then. Where were you living when you were 14 years old? (PROBE FOR CITY, STATE; ALSO PROBE FOR COUNTRY, IF NOT USA.)

_____ CITY

_____ STATE

_____ COUNTRY IF NOT USA

7. HAND CARD #1 Which of the categories on this card comes closest to the type of place you were living in when you were 14 years old . . .

In open country but not on a farm . . . 1
On a farm . . . 2
In a small city or town (under 50,000) . . . 3
In a medium-size city (50,000-250,000) . . . 4
In a suburb near a large city . . . 5
In a large city (over 250,000) . . . 6
DON'T KNOW . . . 7

1.2

8. Were you living with both your own mother and father when you were 14? (IF NO: With whom were you living around that time?) IF RESPONDENT MARRIED OR LEFT HOME BY AGE 14, PROBE FOR BEFORE THAT.

BOTH OWN MOTHER AND FATHER 01 (Q.9)
FATHER AND STEPMOTHER . . . . 02 (ASK A)
MOTHER AND STEP FATHER . . . . 03 (ASK A)
FATHER - NO MOTHER OR STEPMOTHER . . . 04 (ASK A)
MOTHER - NO FATHER OR STEPFATHER . . . 05 (ASK A)
OTHER MALE RELATIVE (SPECIFY)___ 06 (ASK A)
OTHER FEMALE RELATIVE (SPECIFY)___ 07 (ASK A)
OTHER ARRANGEMENT WITH BOTH FEMALE AND MALE RELATIVES - E.G., GRANDPARENTS (SPECIFY)___ 08 (ASK A)
OTHER(SPECIFY)___ 00 (ASK A)

A. IF NOT LIVING WITH BOTH OWN MOTHER AND FATHER: Why were you not living with your own mother and father?

ONE OR BOTH PARENTS DIED 01
PARENTS DIVORCED OR SEPARATED 02
FATHER ABSENT IN ARMED FORCES 03
ONE OR BOTH PARENTS IN INSTITUTION . . 04
OTHER (SPECIFY)___ 05
DON'T KNOW . . . 06

IF NO FATHER/FATHER SUBSTITUTE IN Q. 8, GO TO INSTRUCTION ABOVE Q. 12, PG. 1.4

9. What was the highest grade or year of schooling your (father/FATHER SUBSTITUTE) completed?

8th grade or less 01
Some high school 02
Finished high school or equivalent . . 03
Vocational/trade/business school . . . 04
Some college or 2-year degree 05
Finished college, 4 to 5-year degree . 06
Master's or equivalent 07
Other advanced degree 08

1.3

10. Did your (father/FATHER SUBSTITUTE) work for pay when you were 14 years old?

Yes 1 (Q.11)
No 2 (Q.12)
DON'T KNOW 3 (Q.12)

11. What kind of work did your (father/FATHER SUBSTITUTE) do when you were 14 years old? That is, what was his job called? (RECORD VERBATIM).

OCCUPATION: _____ . |__|__|__|

A. IF NOT ALREADY ANSWERED, ASK: What did your (father/FATHER SUBSTITUTE) actually do in that job? Tell me what were some of his main duties?

_____
_____

B. What kind of place did your (father/FATHER SUBSTITUTE) work for?

INDUSTRY _____ . |__|__|__|

IF NO MOTHER/MOTHER SUBSTITUTE IN Q. 8 GO TO Q. 14, PG. 1.5.

12. What was the highest grade or year of schooling your (mother/MOTHER SUBSTITUTE) completed?

8th grade or less 01
Some high school 02
Finished high school or equivalent 03
Vocational/trade/business school 04
Some college or 2-year degree 05
Finished college, 4 to 5-year degree . . . 06
Master's or equivalent 07
Other advanced degree 08

1.4

13. Did your (mother/MOTHER SUBSTITUTE) work for pay when you were 14 years old?

Yes 1
No 2
DON'T KNOW 3

14. How many brothers did you have? (Count those born alive, but no longer living, as well as those alive now. Also include stepbrothers, and sons adopted by your parents.)

|__|__|

A. How many sisters did you have? (Count those born alive, but no longer living, as well as those alive now. Also include stepsisters, and daughters adopted by your parents.)

|__|__|

IF ANY BROTHERS OR SISTERS ASK B. IF NO BROTHERS AND NO SISTERS (Q. 14 AND Q. 14A BOTH EQUAL "00"), GO TO Q. 15.

B. Were you the oldest, youngest, (or in the middle)?

Oldest 1
Youngest 2
Middle 3

15. In what religion were you raised? (PROBE IF NECESSARY: Was it Protestant, Roman Catholic, Jewish, Orthodox--such as Greek or Russian, Hindu, Muslim, some other religion or no religion at all)? (PROBE: IF MORE THAN ONE ANSWER, ASK FOR THE ONE RELIGION THEY FELT CLOSEST TO AT AGE 14.)

Protestant (CHRISTIAN) . . . . 01 (ASK A)
Roman Catholic 02 (Q.16)
Jewish 03 (Q.16)
Orthodox (such as Greek or Russian) 04 (Q.16)
Hindu, Muslim, or other Eastern Religion 05 (Q.16)
Other religion (SPECIFY) _____ 06 (Q.16)
None 07 (Q.16)

A. What specific denomination is that, if any?

Baptist 01
Methodist 02
Lutheran 03
Presbyterian 04
Episcopalian 05
Other (SPECIFY) _____ 06

1.5

16. Is your current religious preference the same, that is (RELIGION CIRCLED AT Q.15 OR Q.15A?)

Yes 1 (Q.17)
No . . . . 2 (ASK A)

A. What is your current religious preference? (PROBE IF NECESSARY: Is it Protestant, Roman Catholic, Jewish, Orthodox -- such as Greek or Russian, Hindu, Muslim or some other religion or no religion at all)?

Protestant (CHRISTIAN) . . . . 01 (ASK B)
Roman Catholic 02 (Q.17)
Jewish 03 (Q.18)
Orthodox (such as Greek or Russian) 04 (Q.18)
Hindu, Muslim, or other Eastern Religion 05 (Q.18)
Other religion (SPECIFY) 06 (Q.18)
None 07 (Q.18)

B. What specific denomination is that, if any?

Baptist 01
Methodist 02
Lutheran 03   (Q.17)
Presbyterian 04
Episcopalian 05
Other (SPECIFY) 06

17. ASK OF PROTESTANTS AND CATHOLICS ONLY. ALL OTHER SKIP TO Q. 18: Would you say you have been "born again" or have had a "born again" experience -- that is, a turning point in your life when you committed yourself to Christ?

YES . . . . 01 (ASK A)
NO . . . . 02 (ASK Q.18)

A. At what age did you have this experience? |__|__|

18. How often do you attend religious services? (USE CATEGORIES AS PROBES, IF NECESSARY.)

Never 0
Less than once a year 1
About once or twice a year 2
Several times a year 3
About once a month 4
2-3 times a month 5
Nearly every week 6
Every week 7
Several times a week 8

1.6

19. At what age did you first leave home? For example, going away to school, going into the military, or establishing your own residence (by yourself or with others).

AGE IN YEARS . . . . |__|__|
STILL LIVING AT HOME 00

Now I'd like to ask some questions about military service.

20. Not counting the reserves, are you currently serving full time in any branch of the armed services, have you served in the past, or have you never served?

Currently serving . . . . 1 (ASK A)
Served in the past . . . . 2 (ASK A AND B)
Never served . . . . 3 (Q. 21)

A. At what age did you begin serving in the armed forces?
AGE IN YEARS |__|__|

B. [IF SERVED IN PAST] At what age were you discharged from the armed forces?
AGE IN YEARS |__|__|

21. Next, I'd like to ask you some questions about any time you may have spent in (a military jail), jail, prison, reform school or detention center. Did you ever spend one night or more in any of these places?

Yes . . . . 1 (ASK A)
No . . . . 2 (Q. 22)

A. Altogether, how much time have you spent in a reform school, detention center, jail or prison? (RECORD NUMBER OF YEARS/MONTHS/NIGHTS).

|__|__| YEARS
OR
|__|__| MONTHS
OR
|__|__| NIGHTS

B. At what age were you first confined to one of these places for one night or more?
AGE IN YEARS |__|__|

1.7

22. At what age did you get your first full-time job, for which you were paid, not counting seasonal or summer work?

AGE IN YEARS . . . . |__|__|
NEVER . . . . 00 (ASK Q.23)

23. Now I'd like some information about what you were doing last week. Last week, were you going to school?

Yes, in school 1
Yes, in school but temporarily
      not in classes 2
No 3

24. Last week, did you spend any time doing household chores? By household chores we mean any work you did around the house that you were not paid for, including yard work and auto maintenance.

Yes . . . . 1 (ASK A)
No . . . . 2 (Q. 25)

A. IF DOING HOUSEHOLD CHORES: How many hours did you spend doing household chores last week?

HOURS |__|__|

25. Were you working for pay last week?

Yes . . . . 1 (ASK A)
No . . . . 2 (Q. 26)

A. IF WORKING FOR PAY: How many hours did you work for pay last week, at all jobs?

HOURS |__|__| (Q. 28)

26. Last week, did you have a job, but did not go to work because of temporary illness, vacation, layoff, or strike?

Yes . . . . 1 (ASK A)
No . . . . 2 (Q. 27)

A. IF HAD A JOB, BUT NOT AT WORK: How many hours per week do you usually work for pay, at all jobs?

HOURS |__|__| (Q. 28)

1.8

27. IF NOT WORKING OR NOT AT WORK: Are you retired?

Yes 1
No 2
NEVER WORKED FOR PAY . . 3 (SKIP TO BOX 1.1, PG. 1.11)

28. What kind of work (do/did) you normally do? That is, what (is/was) your job called? (RECORD VERBATIM).

OCCUPATION: _____

A. IF NOT ALREADY ANSWERED, ASK: What (do/did) you actually do in that job? Tell me what (are/were) some of your main duties?

_____
_____

|__|__|__|

B. What kind of place (do/did) you work for?

INDUSTRY _____
_____

|__|__|__|

29. What (is/was) your usual wage rate, before taxes, at this job? ENTER AMOUNT, AND CIRCLE ONE BELOW. IF NECESSARY, ASK: Is that per hour, day, week or what?

$ |__|__|__|.|__|__|

Per hour 01
Per day 02
Per week 03
Bi-weekly 04
Per month 05
Per year 06
Other (SPECIFY) _____ 07

1.9

30. How many hours (do/did) you work at this job in a usual week?

|___|___|
OF HOURS

31. How often (do/did) you work evenings and weekends?

More than twice a week 01
Every week 02
About once a month 03
A few times a year 04
Almost never 05
Never 06

Close contact between a worker and a client, customer or co-worker is a necessary part of some jobs.

32. At your job, is it frequently the case that you are alone with one of your clients, customers or co-workers? (For example, a home repair man, a nurse).

Yes 01
No 02

33. Does your job require that you touch your clients, customers or co-workers? (For example, a dentist, a shoe salesperson.)

Yes 01
No 02

34. Does your job require that you discuss the personal concerns of your clients, customers or co-workers? (For example, a teacher, a lawyer.)

Yes 01
No 02

BOX 1.1

ADMINISTER SAQ #1. IF THE R CANNOT READ AND ASKS FOR YOUR HELP, YOU MAY ASSIST HIM/HER IN FILLING OUT THIS FORM.

READ THE FOLLOWING TO R:
Now I have a form for you to fill out yourself. Please read the question and put an answer down for each part. When you are finished please put it in the "privacy" envelope. (PROBE: By household income, we mean the total income of everyone living in the house.)

R filled out SAQ 1
Interviewer assisted with SAQ . . . 2
R refused SAQ 7

35. Compare your total household income from all sources in 1991 with your total household income four years ago (in 1988). Has it...

Risen a lot (e.g. by 20% or more) 1
Risen somewhat 2
Remained about the same 3
Fallen somewhat 4
Fallen a lot (e.g. by 20% or more) 5

36. Generally speaking, do you usually think of yourself as a Republican, Democrat, Independent, or what?

Republican . . . . 1 (BOX 1.2)
Democrat . . . . 2 (BOX 1.2)
Independent . . . . 3 (ASK A)
Other (SPECIFY)_____ . . . . . . 4 (ASK A)
No Preference . . . . 8 (ASK A)

A. IF INDEPENDENT OR "NO PREFERENCE" OR "OTHER": Do you think of yourself as closer to the Republican or Democratic Party?

Republican 1
Democrat 2
Neither 8

BOX 1.2

ADMINISTER SAQ #2 AT THIS TIME. IF R CANNOT READ AND ASKS FOR YOUR HELP, YOU MAY ASSIST HIM/HER IN FILLING OUT THIS FORM.

READ THE FOLLOWING TO R:
Now I have another form for you to fill out yourself. Please read the questions and circle the appropriate code. When you are finished please put it in the "privacy" envelope.

R filled out SAQ 1
Interviewer assisted with SAQ . . . 2
R refused SAQ 7

SECTION 2: MARRIAGE AND COHAB
(USE LIFE HISTORY CALENDAR--"LHC")

 Now I'd like to ask you some questions about the times you've lived with someone in a sexual relationship. Please include all relationships, with men or women, where you lived together for a month or more. Also include anyone you currently live with.

1. Have you ever been married or lived with someone in a sexual relationship for a month or more? We will refer to this as a Spouse/Cohab (S/C) relationship.

Yes 1

No . . . . 2 (Q. 14, Page 2.4)

THIS PAGE LEFT INTENTIONALLY BLANK

2.1

2. How many different people have you been married to or lived in a sexual relationship with for a month or more? Please do not include any living arrangements which lasted less than one month, unless it's someone you are currently living with.

|_|_|

A. Please start with the first time that you got married or lived in a sexual relationship. What is that person's first name? RECORD ON LINE "1" BELOW AND ON LINE "1" OF LHC. CIRCLE "S/C" NEXT TO NAME. IF MORE S/Cs REMAIN, ASK 2B UNTIL ALL S/Cs ARE ACCOUNTED FOR.

B. What is the name of your next Spouse or Cohab? RECORD "S/C NAME" ON LINE "2" ON "3" ETC. OF BOTH S/C ROSTER AND THE LHC UNTIL ALL S/Cs ARE ACCOUNTED FOR. CIRCLE "S/C" NEXT TO ALL NAMES RECORDED ON LHC. THEN, ASK Q.3-12 FOR ALL SPOUSE/COHABS ENTERED BELOW:

S/C ROSTER: [BE SURE TO RECORD ALL ANSWERS IN THE BOXES BELOW]

2A. S/C NAME	3. What is (S/C)s sex? M....1 F....2	4. What is (S/C)s ethnic/racial background? White....1 Black....2 Hispanic..3 Asian.....4 Other.....5	5. What is (is/was) the highest level of education that (S/C) completed? Less than 12th...1 H.S. graduate..2 Some college/Vocational school..3 College grad...4 More than college grad........5 DON'T KNOW.......8	6. How many years older or younger than you is (S/C)? (IF SAME AGE – MEANING LESS THAN "1" YEAR OLDER OR YOUNGER, RECORD "0" YRS. IN OLDER BOX) IF DK, PROBE OLDER OR YOUNGER AN PUT DK IN APPROPRIATE BOX. YEARS YOUNGER / YEARS OLDER	7. When did you begin living with (S/C)? RECORD BELOW AND ENTER IN LHC. IF YOUNGER, RECORD SEASON ON LHC. MONTH YEAR
	M F	W B H A O		YEARS YOUNGER — YEARS OLDER	MONTH YEAR
1.	1 2	1 2 3 4 5	1 2 3 4 5 8		
2.	1 2	1 2 3 4 5	1 2 3 4 5 8		
3.	1 2	1 2 3 4 5	1 2 3 4 5 8		
4.	1 2	1 2 3 4 5	1 2 3 4 5 8		
5.	1 2	1 2 3 4 5	1 2 3 4 5 8		
6.	1 2	1 2 3 4 5	1 2 3 4 5 8		
7.	1 2	1 2 3 4 5	1 2 3 4 5 8		
8.	1 2	1 2 3 4 5	1 2 3 4 5 8		
9.	1 2	1 2 3 4 5	1 2 3 4 5 8		

IF MORE THAN 9 S/Cs, USE A SECOND QUESTIONNAIRE.

2.2

[BE SURE TO RECORD ALL ANSWERS IN THE BOXES BELOW]

8. IF M/M OR F/F COUPLE, SKIP TO Q.12. ASK ALL M/F: Were you married/to (S/C) when you started living together? Yes..1 (Q.10) No...2 (Q.9) (YES/NO)	9. Did you and (S/C) ever marry? Yes...1 (ASK A) No....2 (GO TO Q.12) A. When did you and (S/C) get married? RECORD "M" IN SEASON ON LHC & RECORD DATE BELOW (Y N — MO YEAR)	10. Did this marriage end? Yes...1 (ASK B) No....2 (ASK A) A. Do you still live with (S/C)? Yes..1 (Q.13 DRAW A LINE TO CURRENT DATE ON LHC) No...2 (ASK B) B. When did you stop living with (S/C)? RECORD "X" IN SEASON ON LHC & RECORD DATE BELOW & DRAW LINE FROM 1ST "X" TO LAST "X" (Y N Y N — MO YEAR)	11. How did this marriage end? Were you... divorced..1 (ASK A) widowed?..2 (Q.13) separated.3 (Q.13) A. When was your divorce finalized? RECORD MONTH AND YEAR BELOW AND GO TO Q.13. (D W S — MO YEAR)	12. Did you stop living together? Yes...1 (ASK A) No....2 (DRAW LINE ON LHC TO CURRENT DATE) A. When did you stop living together? RECORD "X" IN SEASON ON LHC. DRAW LINE FROM 1ST "X" TO LAST "X". SKIP TO Q.13 BELOW. (Y N — MO YEAR)
YES NO	Y N — MO YEAR	Y N Y N — MO YEAR	D W S — MO YEAR	Y N — MO YEAR
1 2	1 2 — 19	1 2 1 2 — 19	1 2 3 — 19	1 2 — 19
1 2	1 2 — 19	1 2 1 2 — 19	1 2 3 — 19	1 2 — 19
1 2	1 2 — 19	1 2 1 2 — 19	1 2 3 — 19	1 2 — 19
1 2	1 2 — 19	1 2 1 2 — 19	1 2 3 — 19	1 2 — 19
1 2	1 2 — 19	1 2 1 2 — 19	1 2 3 — 19	1 2 — 19
1 2	1 2 — 19	1 2 1 2 — 19	1 2 3 — 19	1 2 — 19
1 2	1 2 — 19	1 2 1 2 — 19	1 2 3 — 19	1 2 — 19
1 2	1 2 — 19	1 2 1 2 — 19	1 2 3 — 19	1 2 — 19
1 2	1 2 — 19	1 2 1 2 — 19	1 2 3 — 19	1 2 — 19

13. ASK QUESTIONS 3-12 FOR ALL S/Cs RECORDED ON THE S/C ROSTER. THEN ASK Q. 14.

2.3

14. Again, it is very important that we get complete information about all of the times that you have been married or lived in a sexual relationship with someone. Sometimes people don't mention live-in relationships that lasted a short time or ended badly. Have we missed any times where you lived in a sexual relationship with someone for a month or longer?

YES 1   (CORRECT NUMBER AT Q.2.
ADD NAME TO S/C ROSTER & LHC.
ADJUST S/C NUMBERS ON ROSTER & LHC,
THEN ASK Q. 3-13.)

NO 2

IF ANY S/Cs RECORDED ON ROSTER ON PG. 2.2, GO ON TO Q. 15.
IF NO S/Cs RECORDED ON ROSTER ON PG. 2.2, SKIP TO SECTION 3, PG. 3.1.

FIRST (OR ONLY) SPOUSE/COHAB (S/C)

ASK Q'S 15-19 BELOW ABOUT "S/C" RECORDED ON LINE 1 ON LHC.

RECORD (S/C) **NAME:** _____

15. What (has/did) (S/C) (done/do) most of the period you lived together?
(Is/was) that . . .

Work full time, ...	1 (Q.16)
Work part-time, ...	2 (Q.16)
Unemployed, laid off, looking for work, . .	3 (Q.16)
Retired, ...	4 (Q.16)
In School, ...	5 (Q.17)
or keeping house?	6 (Q.17)
DON'T KNOW	8 (Q.17)

16. (When you were living together,) what kind of work (does/did) (S/C) do?
That is, what (is/was) (his/her) job called? (RECORD VERBATIM).

OCCUPATION: _____

|_____|___|___|

A. IF NOT ALREADY ANSWERED, ASK: What (does/did) (S/C) actually do in that job?
Tell me what (are/were) some of (his/her) main duties?

_____
_____
_____

B. What kind of place (does/did) (S/C) work for?

INDUSTRY _____
_____

|_____|___|___|

17. What (is/was) (S/C's) religious preference?
PROBE IF NECESSARY: (Is/was) (S/C) Protestant, Roman Catholic, Jewish, Orthodox --
such as Greek or Russian, Hindu, Muslim, some other religion or no religion at all?

Protestant (CHRISTIAN)	01 (ASK A)
Roman Catholic	02 (ASK B)
Jewish	03 (ASK B)
Orthodox (such as Greek or Russian) . . .	04 (ASK B)
Hindu, Muslim, or other Eastern Religion . .	05 (ASK B)
Other religion (SPECIFY) _____	07 (ASK B)
None	08 (ASK B)
DON'T KNOW	98 (ASK B)

A. What specific denomination is that, if any?

Baptist 01
Methodist 02
Lutheran 03
Presbyterian 04
Episcopalian 05
Other (SPECIFY) _____ 06

B. How often (does/did) (S/C) attend religious services; (is/was) it...

Never 00
Less than once a year 01
About once or twice a year 02
Several times a year 03
About once a month 04
2-3 times a month 05
Nearly every week 06
Every week 07
Several times a week 08

18. **HAND CARD #2** On a scale of 1 to 4, with 1 being a lot and 4 being not at all, tell me how much you (enjoy/enjoyed) spending time with (S/C)'s...

	A LOT	SOME	A LITTLE	NOT AT ALL	DOES NOT APPLY
family?	1	2	3	4	7
friends?	1	2	3	4	7

19. **HAND CARD #2** On a scale of 1 to 4, with 1 being a lot and 4 being not at all, tell me how much (S/C) (enjoys/enjoyed) spending time with your...

	A LOT	SOME	A LITTLE	NOT AT ALL	DOES NOT APPLY
family?	1	2	3	4	7
friends?	1	2	3	4	7

IF **2 OR MORE** S/Cs RECORDED ON ROSTER ON PG. 2.2, GO ON TO Q.20
IF **ONLY 1** S/C RECORDED ON ROSTER ON PG. 2.2, GO ON TO SECTION 3, PG. 3.1

CURRENT (MOST RECENT) "S/C"

ASK Q's 20-24 ABOUT MOST RECENT "S/C" RECORDED ON LHC

RECORD (S/C) NAME: _____

20. What (has/did) (S/C) (done/do) most of the period you lived together (Is/Was) that ...

work full time, ... 1 (Q.21)
work part-time, ... 2 (Q.21)
unemployed, laid off, looking for work, . 3 (Q.21)
retired, ... 4 (Q.21)
in School, ... 5 (Q.22)
or keeping house? 6 (Q.22)
DON'T KNOW 8 (Q.22)

21. (When you were living together,) what kind of work (does/did) (S/C) do? That is, what (is/was) (his/her) job called? (RECORD VERBATIM).

OCCUPATION: _____

. |__|__|__|

A. IF NOT ALREADY ANSWERED, ASK: What (does/did) (S/C) actually do in that job? Tell me what (are/were) some of (his/her) main duties?

B. What kind of place (does/did) (S/C) work for?

INDUSTRY _____

. |__|__|__|

22. What (is/was) (S/C's) religious preference?
PROBE IF NECESSARY: (Is/was) (S/C) Protestant, Roman Catholic, Jewish, Orthodox -- such as Greek or Russian, Hindu, Muslim, some other religion or no religion at all?

Protestant (CHRISTIAN) . . . . 01 (ASK A)
Roman Catholic . . . . 02 (ASK B)
Jewish . . . . 03 (ASK B)
Orthodox (such as Greek or Russian) . . . 04 (ASK B)
Hindu, Muslim, or other Eastern Religion . 05 (ASK B)
CHRISTIAN . . . . 06 (ASK B)
Other religion (SPECIFY) _____ 07 (ASK B)
None . . . . 08 (ASK B)
DON'T KNOW . . . . 98 (ASK B)

FOR WOMEN:

1. Now I would like to ask you about any pregnancies you might have had. I'm interested in all your pregnancies, whether they resulted in a live birth, stillbirth, abortion, or miscarriage, even those which ended very early. How many pregnancies have you ever had, NOT including a current pregnancy?

|___|___|

ONE OR MORE PREGNANCIES, GO TO Q.3.
ZERO PREGNANCIES, GO TO Q.14.

FOR MEN:

2. Now I would like to ask you about any pregnancies that any of your sexual partners might have had by you. I'm interested in all pregnancies, whether they resulted in a live birth, stillbirth, abortion, or miscarriage, even those which ended very early. How many pregnancies have your sexual partners ever had by you, NOT including any current pregnancies?

|___|___|

ONE OR MORE PREGNANCIES, GO TO Q.3.
ZERO PREGNANCIES, GO TO Q. 11.

ASK OF BOTH MEN AND WOMEN:

3. How many children have you ever had, counting only live births?

|___|___|

GO TO BOX 3-B

IF THERE ARE MORE THAN 5 CHILDREN, PULL OUT EXTRA CHILD PAGES

BOX 3-A

MEN ONLY IF ANSWER TO Q.2 IS GREATER THAN ANSWER TO Q.3, CHECK HERE ____
WOMEN ONLY IF ANSWER TO Q.1 IS GREATER THAN ANSWER TO Q.3, CHECK HERE ____

BOX 3-B

HAS RESPONDENT HAD ANY LIVE BIRTHS?

YES . . . . 1 (ASK Q.4-7 FOR EACH LIVE BIRTH)
NO . . . . 2 (IF BOX 3A CHECKED, ASK Q.8.
IF BOX 3A NOT CHECKED, GO TO BOX 3-D, PAGE 3.5)

3.1

A. What specific denomination is that, if any?

Baptist 01
Methodist 02
Lutheran 03
Presbyterian 04
Episcopalian 05
Other (SPECIFY) _____ 06

B. How often (does/did) (S/C) attend religious services: (is/was) it...

Never 00
Less than once a year 01
About once or twice a year . . . 02
Several times a year 03
About once a month 04
2-3 times a month 05
Nearly every week 06
Every week 07
Or several times a week? 08

23. HAND CARD# 2 On a scale of 1 to 4, with 1 being a lot and 4 being not at all, tell me how much you (enjoy/enjoyed) spending time with (S/C)'s...

	A LOT	SOME	A LITTLE	NOT AT ALL	DOES NOT APPLY
family?	1	2	3	4	7
friends?	1	2	3	4	7

24. HAND CARD #2 On a scale of 1 to 4, with 1 being a lot and 4 being not at all, tell me how much (S/C) (enjoys/enjoyed) spending time with your...

	A LOT	SOME	A LITTLE	NOT AT ALL	DOES NOT APPLY
family?	1	2	3	4	7
friends?	1	2	3	4	7

GO ON TO NEXT SECTION

2.8

	CHILD 1	CHILD 2	CHILD 3	CHILD 4	CHILD 5
ASK Q. 4-7 FOR 1ST CHILD					
4. When was your (1st, 2nd, etc) child born?	mo/ day/ year |__|/|__|/|__|__|	mo/ day/ year |__|/|__|/|__|__|	mo/ day/ year |__|/|__|/|__|__|	mo/ day/ year |__|/|__|/|__|__|	mo/ day/ year |__|/|__|/|__|__|
5. Was the baby a boy or a girl?	boy . . . . . . .1 girl 2	boy . . . . . . .1 girl 2	boy . . . . . . .1 girl 2	boy . . . . . . .1 girl 2	boy . . . . . . .1 girl 2
6. What is this child's natural (mother's/father's) first name?					
7. HAND CARD #3 Where does (CHILD) usually live?					
In this household. .	01	01	01	01	01
with (his/her) (mother/father). .	02	02	02	02	02
with other surrogate parents . . .	03	03	03	03	03
away at school . . .	04	04	04	04	04
living on (his/her) own.	05	05	05	05	05
other (SPECIFY). . .	06	06	06	06	06
deceased	07 (ASK A)	07 (ASK A)	07 (ASK A)	07 (ASK A)	07 (ASK A)
DON'T KNOW	08	08	08	08	08
A. IF DECEASED ASK: When did (CHILD NAME) die?	|__|__| MONTH |__|__| YEAR	|__|__| MONTH |__|__| YEAR	|__|__| MONTH |__|__| YEAR	|__|__| MONTH |__|__| YEAR	|__|__| MONTH |__|__| YEAR
	IF THERE IS ANOTHER LIVE BIRTH, GO TO Q.4. IF THERE ARE NO MORE LIVE BIRTHS, GO TO BOX 3-C, PG. 3.4	IF THERE IS ANOTHER LIVE BIRTH, GO TO Q.4. IF THERE ARE NO MORE LIVE BIRTHS, GO TO BOX 3-C, PG. 3.4	IF THERE IS ANOTHER LIVE BIRTH, GO TO Q.4. IF THERE ARE NO MORE LIVE BIRTHS, GO TO BOX 3-C, PG. 3.4	IF THERE IS ANOTHER LIVE BIRTH, GO TO Q.4. IF THERE ARE NO MORE LIVE BIRTHS, GO TO BOX 3-C, PG. 3.4	IF THERE IS ANOTHER LIVE BIRTH, USE CONTINUATION PAGES. IF THERE ARE NO MORE LIVE BIRTHS, GO TO BOX 3-C, PG. 3.4

BOX 3-D	IS RESPONDENT MALE OR FEMALE?
	MALE. 1 (Q.11)
	FEMALE. 2 (Q.14)

ALL MALE RESPONDENTS:

11. Is anyone currently pregnant by you?

    Yes . . . . 1 (ASK A, B)
    No 2 (Q.12)

    A. What is the mother's first name?

    _____

    B. When is the baby due?

    |__|__| |__|__|
    MONTH   YEAR

12. Some men find it physically impossible to father children. As far as you know, is it possible or impossible for you to father any (more) children?

    Possible . . . . 1 (SECTION 4)
    Impossible 2 (Q.13)
    DON'T KNOW, NOT SURE . . 8 (SECTION 4)

13. What is the reason that it is physically impossible for you to father a(nother) baby?
    RECORD VERBATIM AND CODE ALL THAT APPLY.

    _____

    _____

    IMPOSSIBLE DUE TO VASECTOMY OR OTHER
       STERILIZATION OPERATION . . . . 1 | (GO TO
    IMPOSSIBLE DUE TO ACCIDENT OR ILLNESS . . 2 | SECTION 4)
    RESPONDENT STERILE FOR OTHER REASONS . . 3
    PARTNER STERILE 4
    COUPLE UNABLE TO CONCEIVE 5

BOX 3-C	IS BOX 3-A CHECKED? THAT IS, MORE PREGNANCIES THAN CHILDREN
	YES . . . . 1 (GO TO Q.8)
	NO. . . . . 2 (GO TO BOX 3-D, PG. 3.5)

	A.	B.

8. Did any of these pregnancies end in miscarriage?

    YES . . . . . .1 (ASK A, B)
    NO 2 (Q.9)

    A. How many? |__|__|

    B. When did this happen?
    |__|__| |__|__| MONTH YEAR
    |__|__| |__|__| MONTH YEAR
    |__|__| |__|__| MONTH YEAR

9. Did any of these pregnancies end in stillbirth?

    YES . . . . . . 1 (ASK A, B)
    NO 2 (Q.10)

    A. How many? |__|__|

    B. When did this happen?
    |__|__| |__|__| MONTH YEAR
    |__|__| |__|__| MONTH YEAR
    |__|__| |__|__| MONTH YEAR

10. Did any of these pregnancies end in abortion?

    YES . . . . . . 1 (ASK A, B)
    NO . . . . . . 2 (BOX 3-D, PG. 3.5)

    A. How many? |__|__|

    B. When did this happen?
    |__|__| |__|__| MONTH YEAR
    |__|__| |__|__| MONTH YEAR
    |__|__| |__|__| MONTH YEAR

SECTION 4: **PARTNER IDENTIFICATION AND 1 YEAR SEXUAL ACTIVITY**
(USE LIFE HISTORY CALENDAR "LHC")

☞

Now I am going to be asking some questions about your sexual activity during
the last 12 months. People mean different things by sex or sexual activity,
but in answering these questions, we need everyone to use the same definition.
Here, by "sex" or "sexual activity", we mean any mutually voluntary activity
with another person that involves genital contact and sexual excitement or
arousal, that is, feeling really turned on, even if intercourse or orgasm did
not occur.

In answering these questions, please include all persons or times (in the last
12 months where you had direct physical contact with the genitals (the sex
organs) of someone else and sexual excitement or arousal occurred. Certain
activities such as close dancing or kissing without genital contact should NOT
be included. Also, this set of questions does NOT refer to occasions where
force was used and activity was against someone's will.

4.1

ALL FEMALE RESPONDENTS:

14. Are you pregnant now?

Yes . . . . 1 (ASK A, B)
No 2 (Q.15)

A. What is the father's first name?

_____

B. How many months have you been pregnant?

|____|____|
MONTHS

IF CURRENTLY PREGNANT, GO TO SECTION 4.

15. Some women find it physically impossible to have (more) children. As far
as you know, is it possible or impossible for you to conceive a(nother)
baby, that is, to get pregnant (again)?

Possible . . . . 1 (SECTION 4)
Impossible 2 (Q.16)
DON'T KNOW, NOT SURE . . . . . 8 (SECTION 4)

16. What is the reason that it is physically impossible for you to have
a(nother) baby?
RECORD VERBATIM AND CODE ALL THAT APPLY.

_____

IMPOSSIBLE DUE TO TUBAL LIGATION OR
OTHER STERILIZATION OPERATION 1
IMPOSSIBLE FOR RESPONDENT DUE TO
ACCIDENT OR ILLNESS 2
RESPONDENT STERILE FOR OTHER REASONS . . 3
PARTNER STERILE 4   (GO TO
COUPLE UNABLE TO CONCEIVE 5   SECTION 4)
RESPONDENT NOT YET FERTILE, PERIOD
HAS NOT STARTED 6
RESPONDENT HAS REACHED MENOPAUSE 7

3.6

1. Thinking back over the past 12 months, how many people, including men and women, have you had sexual activity with, even if only one time?

NONE. 0   SKIP TO BOX 6A, SECTION 6, p. 6.1

|_|_|_|

2. Since I will be asking some questions about (this/these) sexual partner(s), please tell me a first name or some other way to refer to (this person/each of these people).

(IF NECESSARY: You may refer to them in any way you want -- first name, initials, nicknames. I just need some way to refer to these partners so that when I ask you some follow-up questions we both know whom we are talking about.)

(IF MORE THAN "9" PARTNERS IN Q. 1: Please begin with the person you consider to have been your most important or primary sexual partner during the last 12 months?)

RECORD NAMES ON PARTNER ROSTER AND RECORD ALL NEW NAMES ON LHC.
CIRCLE "P" NEXT TO EACH NAME ON LHC.
IF THE NAME OF ANY SEX PARTNER IN THE LAST YEAR IS THE SAME AS "CURRENT S/C", CONFIRM RELATIONSHIP AND DATES AND CIRCLE "P" NEXT TO NAME ON LHC.

PARTNER ROSTER:

2 PARTNER NAME	3. IF BOTH "P" AND "S/C" ARE CIRCLED FOR PARTNER ON CALENDAR SKIP TO Q. 7. What is (PARTNER'S) sex? M......1 F......2		4. What is (PARTNER'S) ethnic/racial background? White.....1 Black.....2 Hispanic..3 Asian.....4 Other.....5					5. What (is/was) the highest level of education that (PARTNER) completed? < 12th......1 H.S. grad...2 Some col/Voca-tional......3 College grad..4 More than coll grad......5 DON'T KNOW....8						6. How many years older or younger than you is (PARTNER)? (IF SAME AGE - MEANING LESS THAN "1 YEAR OLDER OR YOUNGER, RECORD "0" YRS. IN OLDER BOX) (IF DK, PROBE OLDER OR YOUNGER, AND PUT DK IN APPROPRIATE BOX)	
	M	F	W	B	H	A	O							YOUNGER	OLDER
1	1	2	1	2	3	4	5	1	2	3	4	5	8		
2	1	2	1	2	3	4	5	1	2	3	4	5	8		
3	1	2	1	2	3	4	5	1	2	3	4	5	8		
4	1	2	1	2	3	4	5	1	2	3	4	5	8		
5	1	2	1	2	3	4	5	1	2	3	4	5	8		
6	1	2	1	2	3	4	5	1	2	3	4	5	8		
7	1	2	1	2	3	4	5	1	2	3	4	5	8		
8	1	2	1	2	3	4	5	1	2	3	4	5	8		
9	1	2	1	2	3	4	5	1	2	3	4	5	8		

IF MORE THAN 9 PARTNERS, ONLY RECORD NAMES & INFORMATION ON 9 PARTNERS. THIS SHOULD INCLUDE ANY PARTNER CONSIDERED "MOST IMPORTANT" OR "PRIMARY" DURING LAST 12 MONTHS.

4.2

7. Was the first time you had sex with (PARTNER) in the last 12 months? Yes.........1 (Q. 8A)		8.A. When did you first have sex with (PARTNER)? RECORD MONTH & YEAR BELOW & ASK Q. 9A.		9.A. How many times did you have sex with (PARTNER) in the last 12 months? Was that... Only once.....1 (Q.11) 2 to 10 times..2 (Q.10) or more than 10 times?...3 (Q.10) RECORD BELOW			10. In the past 12 months, when did you (most recently) have sex with (PARTNER)? RECORD MONTH & YEAR BELOW. GO TO Q. 11.	
No.........2 (Q. 8B)		8.B. When did you first have sex with (PARTNER)? RECORD MONTH & YEAR BELOW & ASK Q. 9B.		9.B. How many times did you have sex with (PARTNER) in the last 12 months? Was that... Only once.....1 (Q.10) 2 to 10 times..2 (Q.10) or more than 10 times?...3 (Q.10) RECORD BELOW			
Yes	No	Month	Year	1	2	3	Month	Year
1	2			1	2	3		
1	2			1	2	3		
1	2			1	2	3		
1	2			1	2	3		
1	2			1	2	3		
1	2			1	2	3		
1	2			1	2	3		
1	2			1	2	3		

11. ARE THERE ANY MORE PARTNERS ON ROSTER?

YES. . . . . . (ASK Qs. 3-10 FOR NEXT PARTNER)

NO . . . . . . (GO TO Q. 12)

4.3

12. **IF ONLY ONE PARTNER ON ROSTER:** RECORD NAME: _____.

   A. IS THIS PERSON AN S/C?

        YES 1 (Q.17)
        NO 2 (Q.14)

13. **IF MORE THAN ONE PARTNER ON ROSTER:**

   A. IS ANY SEX PARTNER FOR THE PAST YEAR A S/C (THAT IS, BOTH "S/C" AND "P" AND CIRCLED NEXT TO A NAME ON LHC)?

        YES . . . . . 1 (CONFIRM RELATIONSHIP AND SKIP TO Q. 17 ON PAGE 4.5.)
        NO . . . . . 2 (ASK B)

   B. Which of the people that you mentioned do you consider to have been your most important or primary sexual partner during the last 12 months?

      RECORD NAME: _____
      IF NO PRIMARY PARTNER, ASK C.   . GO TO Q. 14.

   C. Of the people that you mentioned, who did you have sex with most recently?

      RECORD NAME: _____   . GO TO Q. 14.

14. What (is/was) (PARTNER's) (PARTNER's) religious preference? (PROBE IF NECESSARY: (Is/Was) (s/he) Protestant, Roman Catholic, Jewish, Orthodox -- such as Greek or Russian, Hindu, Muslim, some other religion, or no religion at all?)

    Protestant . . . . . 01 (ASK A)
    Roman Catholic 02 (Q.15)
    Jewish 03 (Q.15)
    Orthodox (such as Greek or Russian) . 04 (Q.15)
    Hindu, Muslim, or other Eastern religion . 05 (Q.15)
    Other religion (SPECIFY) _____ 06 (Q.15)
    None 00 (Q.15)
    DON'T KNOW 98 (Q.15)

   A. What specific denomination is that, if any?

    Baptist 01
    Methodist 02
    Lutheran 03
    Presbyterian 04
    Episcopalian 05
    Other (SPECIFY) _____ 06

15. How often (does/did) (PARTNER) attend religious services; (is/was) it...

    Never 00
    Less than once a year 01
    About once or twice a year . . . 02
    Several times a year 03
    About once a month 04
    2-3 times a month 05
    Nearly every week 06
    Every week 07
    Several times a week 08

16. What (does/did) (PARTNER) do most of the time (while you were involved)? (Is/Was) that ...

    Work full time, ... 1 (ASK A)
    Work part-time, ... 2 (ASK A)
    Unemployed, laid off, looking for work, . 3 (ASK A)
    Retired, ... 4 (ASK A)
    In school, or 5 (Q.18)
    Keeping house? 6 (Q.18)
    DON'T KNOW 8 (Q.18)

   A. (When you were involved,) what kind of work (does/did) (PARTNER) do? That is, what (is/was) (his/her) job called? (RECORD VERBATIM).

      OCCUPATION:_____   . |__|__|__|

   B. IF NOT ALREADY ANSWERED, ASK: What (does/did) (PARTNER) actually do in that job? Tell me what (are/were) some of (his/her) main duties?

      _____

   C. What kind of place (does/did) (PARTNER) work for?

      INDUSTRY_____   . |__|__|__|

      (SKIP TO Q. 18)

17. RECORD S/C NAME _____   AND ASK Q.18

18. Where did you meet (PARTNER)?

    CODE ALL THAT APPLY.

    Work 01
    School 02
    Church/church activity 03
    Personal ads/ Dating service . . . 04
    Vacation/business trip 05
    Bar/night club/dance club 06
    Social organization/health club/ gym/volunteer-service activity . . 07
    Private party 08
    Other (SPECIFY) _____ 09

19. **HAND CARD #4** Who introduced you to (PARTNER)? CODE ALL THAT APPLY.

    family 01
    friends or acquaintances 02
    co-workers 03
    classmates 04
    neighbors 05
    introduced self or partner introduced self . 06
    Other (SPECIFY) _____ 07

20. (Is/Was) (PARTNER) married, living with someone else in a sexual relationship, separated, divorced, or in a steady relationship with someone else when you first became sexually involved?

    Married 1
    Living with someone else 2
    Separated 3
    In a steady relationship 4
    Divorced 5
    None of these 6
    DON'T KNOW 8

21. How long did you know (PARTNER) prior to having sexual activity for the first time? Was that...

    less than one day, ... 1
    one or two days, ... 2
    more than two days but less than a month, ... 3
    more than one month but less than a year, ... 4
    or more than one year? 5

BOX 4.1

    DURING THE LAST TWELVE MONTHS, HOW MANY TIMES DID RESPONDENT
    HAVE SEXUAL ACTIVITY WITH (PARTNER)?
    (Q. 9.A./9.B. ON PG. 4.3)

    ONLY ONCE . . . . 1 (GO TO 1 TIME SEX, Q. 41, PG. 4.12)
    2-10 TIMES . . . . . . 2 (Q. 23)
    MORE THAN 10 TIMES . . 4 (Q. 22)

22. During the last 12 months, (while you were sexually involved,) about how often did you have sex with (PARTNER)? Was it...

    Once a day or more 1
    3 to 6 times a week 2
    Once or twice a week 3
    2 to 3 times a month 4
    Once a month or less 5

A. (Did/Do) you expect (PARTNER) to have sexual activity only with you during the time you (were/are) sexually involved?

    Yes 1
    No 2
    NOT AT FIRST, BUT LATER I DID 3
    I DID AT FIRST, BUT NOT LATER 4

B. (Did/Does) (PARTNER) expect you to have sex only with (him/her) during the time you (were/are) sexually involved?

    Yes 1
    No 2
    NOT AT FIRST, BUT LATER (SHE/HE) DID 3
    (SHE/HE) DID AT FIRST, BUT NOT LATER 4

4.6

23. **(IF CURRENT SPOUSE/COHAB: SKIP TO Q. 27.)** Do you expect to have sex with (PARTNER) again?

    Yes 1
    No . . . . 2 (Q. 25)
    DON'T KNOW 8

24. How much longer do you expect the relationship with (PARTNER) to last?

    A few more days 1
    A few more weeks 2
    More than 1 month but less than 1 year 3
    Several years 4
    Lifetime 5

25. Did (PARTNER) get to know your family, that is your parents or brothers and sisters, during the relationship?

    Yes 1
    No 2

26. Did (PARTNER) get to know your close friends during the relationship?

    Yes 1
    No 2

FOR QS. 27 - 34, USE HAND CARD #5 (where applicable)

27. Now I would like to ask you some questions about alcohol use. How often (did/do) you or your partner drink alcohol before or during sex?

    Always 1
    Usually 2
    Sometimes 3
    Rarely 4
    Never 5 (Q.28)

A. Was that usually you, your partner, or both?

    RESPONDENT ONLY . . . . 1 (ASK B ONLY)
    PARTNER ONLY . . . . 2 (ASK C ONLY)
    RESPONDENT AND PARTNER . . . . 3 (ASK B AND C)

B. On average, how strongly were you affected by the alcohol, very strongly, somewhat, not at all?

    Very Strongly 1
    Somewhat 2
    Not At All 3
    DON'T KNOW 8

C. On average, how strongly was PARTNER affected by the alcohol, very strongly, somewhat, not at all?

    Very Strongly 1
    Somewhat 2
    Not At All 3
    DON'T KNOW 8

4.7

28. How often (do/did) either you or (PARTNER) use any drugs to get high or intoxicated before or during sex?

```
Always  . . . . . . . . . . . . . . . 1
Usually . . . . . . . . . . . . . . . 2
Sometimes . . . . . . . . . . . . . . 3
Rarely  . . . . . . . . . . . . . . . 4
Never   . . . . . . . . . . . . . . . 5   (Q.29)
```

A. Was that usually you, your partner, or both?

```
RESPONDENT ONLY . . . . . . . . . . 1   (ASK B ONLY)
PARTNER ONLY  . . . . . . . . . . . 2   (ASK C ONLY)
RESPONDENT AND PARTNER  . . . . . . 3   (ASK B AND C)
```

B. On average, how strongly were you affected by the drugs, very strongly, somewhat, not at all?

```
Very Strongly . . . . . . . . . . . 1
Somewhat  . . . . . . . . . . . . . 2
Not At All  . . . . . . . . . . . . 3
DON'T KNOW  . . . . . . . . . . . . 8
```

C. On average, how strongly was PARTNER affected by the drugs, very strongly, somewhat, not at all?

```
Very Strongly . . . . . . . . . . . 1
Somewhat  . . . . . . . . . . . . . 2
Not At All  . . . . . . . . . . . . 3
DON'T KNOW  . . . . . . . . . . . . 8
```

29. Now I'd like you to think about the times you had sex with (PARTNER) during the past 12 months. If you were not sexually involved the whole time, please think only about the period of time when you were involved.

First, I will ask you some questions about oral sex. By oral sex we mean stimulating the genitals with the mouth, that is licking or kissing your partner's genitals or when your partner does this to you.

When you had sex with (PARTNER), how often did (he/she) perform oral sex on you? Was it...

```
always  . . . . . . . . . . . . . . . 1
usually . . . . . . . . . . . . . . . 2
sometimes . . . . . . . . . . . . . . 3
rarely, or  . . . . . . . . . . . . . 4
never?  . . . . . . . . . . . . . . . 5
```

30. When you had sex with (PARTNER), how often did you perform oral sex on (him/her)? Was it...

```
always  . . . . . . . . . . . . . . . 1
usually . . . . . . . . . . . . . . . 2
sometimes . . . . . . . . . . . . . . 3
rarely, or  . . . . . . . . . . . . . 4
never?  . . . . . . . . . . . . . . . 5
```

MALE/FEMALE -- Q.31
MALE/MALE COUPLE -- Q.32
FEMALE/FEMALE COUPLE -- Q.33

MALE/FEMALE COUPLES ONLY:

31. Now I will ask you some questions about vaginal intercourse. By **vaginal intercourse**, we mean when a man's penis is inside a woman's vagina. Was it...

When you had sex with (PARTNER), how often did you have vaginal intercourse? Was it...

```
always  . . . . . . . . . . . . . . . 1
usually . . . . . . . . . . . . . . . 2
sometimes . . . . . . . . . . . . . . 3
rarely, or  . . . . . . . . . . . . . 4
never?  . . . . . . . . . . . . . . . 5   (Q.32)
```

A. When you had vaginal intercourse with (PARTNER), how often did you use condoms?

```
always  . . . . . . . . . . . . . . . 1
usually . . . . . . . . . . . . . . . 2
sometimes . . . . . . . . . . . . . . 3
rarely, or  . . . . . . . . . . . . . 4
never?  . . . . . . . . . . . . . . . 5
```

B. When you had vaginal intercourse with (PARTNER), how often did you use any other methods of birth control?

```
always  . . . . . . . . . . . . . . . 1
usually . . . . . . . . . . . . . . . 2
sometimes . . . . . . . . . . . . . . 3
rarely, or  . . . . . . . . . . . . . 4
never?  . . . . . . . . . . . . . . . 5
```

MALE/FEMALE AND MALE/MALE ONLY:

32. Now I'm going to ask you some questions about anal intercourse. By **Anal intercourse**, we mean when a man's penis is inside his partner's anus or rectum.

When you had sex with (PARTNER), how often did you have anal intercourse with (PARTNER)? Was it...

```
always  . . . . . . . . . . . . . . . 1
usually . . . . . . . . . . . . . . . 2
sometimes . . . . . . . . . . . . . . 3
rarely, or  . . . . . . . . . . . . . 4
never?  . . . . . . . . . . . . . . . 5   (Q.33)
```

A. When you had anal intercourse with (PARTNER), how often did you use condoms?

```
always  . . . . . . . . . . . . . . . 1
usually . . . . . . . . . . . . . . . 2
sometimes . . . . . . . . . . . . . . 3
rarely, or  . . . . . . . . . . . . . 4
never?  . . . . . . . . . . . . . . . 5
```

MALE/MALE COUPLE ONLY:

B. When you had anal intercourse, were you always the active (inserting) partner, the passive (receiving) partner or sometimes both?

```
Active exclusively  . . . . . . . . . 1
Passive exclusively . . . . . . . . . 2
Both  . . . . . . . . . . . . . . . . 3
```

33. When you and (PARTNER) had sex during the past 12 months, did you always, usually, sometimes, rarely, or never have an orgasm, that is come or come to climax?

```
always . . . . . . . . . . . . 1
usually . . . . . . . . . . . . 2
sometimes . . . . . . . . . . . 3
rarely, or . . . . . . . . . . 4
never . . . . . . . . . . . . . 5
```

34. When you and (PARTNER) had sex during the past 12 months, did (PARTNER) always, usually, sometimes, rarely, or never have an orgasm, that is come or come to climax?

```
always . . . . . . . . . . . . 1
usually . . . . . . . . . . . . 2
sometimes . . . . . . . . . . . 3
rarely, or . . . . . . . . . . 4
never? . . . . . . . . . . . . 5
```

35. Now I would like to ask you how sex with (PARTNER) made you feel. Please, tell me if sex with (PARTNER) made you feel:

	YES	NO
a. satisfied	1	2
b. sad	1	2
c. loved	1	2
d. anxious or worried	1	2
e. wanted or needed	1	2
f. taken care of	1	2
g. scared or afraid	1	2
h. thrilled or excited	1	2
i. guilty	1	2
j. OTHER (SPECIFY)_____	1	2

36. How physically pleasurable did you find your relationship with (PARTNER) to be, extremely pleasurable, very pleasurable, moderately pleasurable, slightly pleasurable, or not at all pleasurable?

```
Extremely . . . . . . . . . . . 1
Very . . . . . . . . . . . . . 2
Moderately . . . . . . . . . . 3
Slightly . . . . . . . . . . . 4
Not at all . . . . . . . . . . 5
```

37. How emotionally satisfying did you find your relationship with (PARTNER) to be, extremely satisfying, very satisfying, moderately satisfying, slightly satisfying, or not at all satisfying?

```
Extremely . . . . . . . . . . . 1
Very . . . . . . . . . . . . . 2
Moderately . . . . . . . . . . 3
Slightly . . . . . . . . . . . 4
Not at all . . . . . . . . . . 5
```

4.10

---

38. People engage in sexual activities for a variety of reasons. What were your reasons for having sex with (PARTNER) during the past 12 months? Was it...
(CODE 'YES' OR 'NO' FOR EACH)

	Y	N
a. to make-up after a fight or misunderstanding?	1	2
b. to relieve sexual tension (arousal)?	1	2
c. because your partner wanted you to?	1	2
MALE/FEMALE ONLY:		
d. to get pregnant?	1	2
e. to express love or affection?	1	2
f. to express or experience something else?	1	2

(IF YES) What was that? _____

39. As far as you know, during the past 12 months has (PARTNER) had other sexual partners?

```
Yes . . . . . . . . . . . 1 (ASK A)
No . . . . . . . . . . . . 2 (Q. 40)
```

A. About how many partners was that? RECORD NUMBER. IF DON'T KNOW PROBE FOR BEST GUESS. |__|__|

B. Were these partners all men, all women or both?

```
men . . . . . . . . . . . 1
women . . . . . . . . . . 2
both . . . . . . . . . . . 3
DON'T KNOW . . . . . . . . 4
```

C. Did (PARTNER) have sex with any of these people during the time you and (PARTNER) were sexually involved?

```
Yes . . . . . . . . . . . 1
No . . . . . . . . . . . . 2
```

40. HOW MANY CIRCLED "P"s REMAIN ON THE LHC?

```
NONE . . . . . . . . 0  (GO ON TO SECTION 5: MOST RECENT SEX)
ONE . . . . . . . . . 1  (GO TO Q. 55, p.4.17 & RECORD NAME)
TWO OR MORE . . . . . 2  (ASK A)
```

A. Other than the person you just told me about, who did you have sex with most recently?

GO TO Q. 55, PG. 4.17 (PARTNER #2 -- LAST YEAR) & RECORD NAME

4.11

SKIP FROM BOX 4.1, PG. 4.6

41. Do you expect to have sex with (PARTNER) again?

       Yes 1
       No . . . . 2 (Q. 42)
       DON'T KNOW 8

A. How much longer do you expect the relationship with (PARTNER) to last?

       A few more days 1
       A few more weeks 2
       More than 1 month but less than 1 year . . 3
       Several years 4
       Lifetime 5

I'd like you to think about the one time you had sex with (PARTNER) in the last 12 months.

42. First, I would like to ask you some questions about alcohol use. Did you or your partner drink any alcohol before or during sex?

       Yes 1
       No . . . . 2 (Q. 43)

A. Was that you, your partner, or both?

       RESPONDENT ONLY . . . . 1 (ASK B ONLY)
       PARTNER ONLY . . . . 2 (ASK C ONLY)
       RESPONDENT AND PARTNER . . . . . 3 (ASK B AND C)

B. How strongly were you affected by the alcohol, very strongly, somewhat, not at all?

       Very Strongly 1
       Somewhat 2
       Not At All 3

C. How strongly was (PARTNER) affected by the alcohol, very strongly, somewhat, not at all?

       Very Strongly 1
       Somewhat 2
       Not At All 3
       DON'T KNOW 8

43. Did either you or (PARTNER) use any drugs to get high or intoxicated before or during sex?

       Yes 1
       No . . . . 2 (Q. 44)

A. Was that you, your partner, or both?

       RESPONDENT ONLY . . . . 1 (ASK B ONLY)
       PARTNER ONLY . . . . 2 (ASK C ONLY)
       RESPONDENT AND PARTNER . . . . . 3 (ASK B AND C)

B. How strongly were you affected by the drugs, very strongly, somewhat, not at all?

       Very Strongly 1
       Somewhat 2
       Not At All 3
       DON'T KNOW 8

C. How strongly was PARTNER affected by the drugs, very strongly, somewhat, not at all?

       Very Strongly 1
       Somewhat 2
       Not At All 3
       DON'T KNOW 8

44. First, I will ask you some questions about oral sex. By oral sex we mean stimulating the genitals with the mouth, that is licking or kissing your partner's genitals or when your partner does this to you.

When you had sex with (PARTNER), did (he/she) perform oral sex on you?

       Yes 1
       No 2

A. Did you perform oral sex on (him/her)?

       Yes 1
       No 2

MALE/FEMALE COUPLE -- Q.45
MALE/MALE COUPLE -- Q.46
FEMALE/FEMALE COUPLE -- Q.47

MALE/FEMALE COUPLES ONLY:

45. Now I will ask you some questions about vaginal intercourse. By **vaginal intercourse**, we mean when a man's penis is inside a woman's vagina. When you had sex with (PARTNER), did you have vaginal intercourse?

    Yes 1
    No . . . . 2 (Q. 46)

   A. When you had vaginal intercourse with (PARTNER), did you use condoms?

      Yes 1
      No 2

   B. When you had vaginal intercourse with (PARTNER), did you use any other methods of birth control?

      Yes 1
      No 2

MALE/FEMALE AND MALE/MALE ONLY:

46. Now I'm going to ask you some questions about anal intercourse. By **anal intercourse**, we mean when a man's penis is inside his partner's anus or rectum. When you had sex with (PARTNER), did you have anal intercourse with (PARTNER)?

    Yes 1
    No . . . . 2 (Q. 47)

   A. When you had anal intercourse with (PARTNER), did you use condoms?

      Yes 1
      No 2

MALE/MALE COUPLE ONLY:

   B. When you had anal intercourse, were you the active (inserting) partner, the passive (receiving) partner or both?

      Active exclusively 1
      Passive exclusively 2
      Both 3

47. When you and (PARTNER) had sex, did you have an orgasm, that is come or come to climax?

    Yes 1
    No 2

48. Did (PARTNER) have an orgasm, that is come or come to climax?

    Yes 1
    No 2

49. Now I would like to ask you how sex with (PARTNER) made you feel. Please, tell me if sex with (PARTNER) made you feel:

	YES	NO
a. satisfied	1	2
b. sad	1	2
c. loved	1	2
d. anxious or worried	1	2
e. wanted or needed	1	2
f. taken care of	1	2
g. scared or afraid	1	2
h. thrilled or excited	1	2
i. guilty	1	2
j. other (SPECIFY)_____	1	2

50. How physically pleasurable did you find your relationship with (PARTNER) to be: extremely pleasurable, very pleasurable, moderately pleasurable, slightly pleasurable, or not at all pleasurable?

    Extremely 1
    Very 2
    Moderately 3
    Slightly 4
    Not at all 5

51. How emotionally satisfying did you find your relationship with (PARTNER) to be, extremely satisfying, very satisfying, moderately satisfying, slightly satisfying, or not at all satisfying?

    Extremely 1
    Very 2
    Moderately 3
    Slightly 4
    Not at all 5

52. People engage in sexual activities for a variety of reasons. What were your reasons for having sex with (PARTNER)? Was it...

(CODE 'YES' OR 'NO' FOR EACH)

	Y	N
a. to make-up after a fight or misunderstanding?	1	2
b. to relieve sexual tension (arousal)?	1	2
c. because your partner wanted you to?	1	2
MALE/FEMALE ONLY:		
d. to get pregnant?	1	2
e. to express love or affection?	1	2
f. to express or experience something else?	1	2

(IF YES) What was that? _____

53. As far as you know, during the past 12 months has (PARTNER) had other sexual partners?

Yes . . . . 1 (ASK A)
No . . . . 2 (Q. 54)

A. About how many partners was that? RECORD NUMBER. IF DON'T KNOW PROBE FOR BEST GUESS.

|__|__|

B. Were these partners all men, all women or both?

men 1
women 2
both 3
DON'T KNOW 4

54. HOW MANY CIRCLED "P's REMAIN ON THE LHC?

NONE . . . . 0 (GO ON TO SECTION 5: MOST RECENT SEX)
ONE . . . . 1 (GO TO Q. 55, P. 4.17 & RECORD NAME)
TWO OR MORE . . . . 2 (ASK A)

A. Other than the person you just told me about, who did you have sex with most recently?

GO TO Q. 55, PG. 4.17 (PARTNER #2 -- LAST YEAR) & RECORD NAME

RECORD PARTNER NAME: _____   PARTNER #2 -- LAST YEAR

55. IS THIS PARTNER AN S/C?

YES . . . . . 1 (Q.59, PG. 4.18)
NO 2 (Q.56)

56. What (is/was) (PARTNER'S) religious preference? (PROBE IF NECESSARY: (Is/Was) (s/he) Protestant, Roman Catholic, Jewish, Orthodox -- such as Greek or Russian, Hindu, Muslim, some other religion, or no religion at all?)

Protestant . . . . 01 (ASK A)
Roman Catholic 02 (Q.57)
Jewish 03 (Q.57)
Orthodox (such as Greek or Russian) . . . 04 (Q.57)
Hindu, Muslim, or other Eastern religion . 05 (Q.57)
Other religion (SPECIFY) _____ 06 (Q.57)
None 00 (Q.58)
DON'T KNOW 98 (Q.57)

A. What specific denomination is that, if any?

Baptist 01
Methodist 02
Lutheran 03
Presbyterian 04
Episcopalian 05
Other (SPECIFY) _____ 06

57. How often (does/did) (PARTNER) attend religious services; (is/was) it...

Never 00
Less than once a year 01
About once or twice a year 02
Several times a year 03
About once a month 04
2-3 times a month 05
Nearly every week 06
Every week 07
Several times a week 08

58. What (does/did) (PARTNER) do most of the time (while you were involved)? (Is/Was) that . . .

```
Work full time, . . . . . . . . . . . . . . 1 (ASK A)
Work part-time, . . . . . . . . . . . . . . 2 (ASK A)
Unemployed, laid off, looking for work, . . 3 (ASK A)
Retired, . . . . . . . . . . . . . . . . . . 4 (ASK A)
In School, . . . . . . . . . . . . . . . . . 5 (Q.60)
or keeping house? . . . . . . . . . . . . . 6 (Q.60)
DON'T KNOW . . . . . . . . . . . . . . . . . 8 (Q.60)
```

A. (When you were involved,) what kind of work (does/did) (PARTNER) do? That is, what (is/was) (his/her) job called? (RECORD VERBATIM).

OCCUPATION: _____ |__|__|__|

B. IF NOT ALREADY ANSWERED, ASK: What (does/did) (PARTNER) actually do in that job? Tell me what (are/were) some of (his/her) main duties?

C. What kind of place (does/did) (PARTNER) work for?

INDUSTRY _____ |__|__|__|

(SKIP TO Q. 60)

59. RECORD S/C NAME _____ AND ASK Qs. 60 - 69 ABOUT (HIM/HER)

60. Where did you meet (PARTNER)? CODE ALL THAT APPLY.

```
Work . . . . . . . . . . . . . . . . . . . . . . . . 01
School . . . . . . . . . . . . . . . . . . . . . . . 02
Church/church activity . . . . . . . . . . . . . . . 03
Personal ads/ Dating service . . . . . . . . . . . . 04
Vacation/business trip . . . . . . . . . . . . . . . 05
Bar/night club/dance club . . . . . . . . . . . . . . 06
Social organization/health club/
   gym/volunteer-service activity . . . . . . . . . . 07
Private party . . . . . . . . . . . . . . . . . . . . 08
Other (SPECIFY)_____ . . . . . . . . . . . . . . 09
```

61. **HAND CARD #4** Who introduced you to (PARTNER)? CODE ALL THAT APPLY.

```
family . . . . . . . . . . . . . . . . . . . . . . . 01
mutual friends or acquaintances . . . . . . . . . . . 02
co-workers . . . . . . . . . . . . . . . . . . . . . 03
classmates . . . . . . . . . . . . . . . . . . . . . 04
neighbors . . . . . . . . . . . . . . . . . . . . . . 05
introduced self or partner introduced self . . . . . 06
Other (SPECIFY)_____ . . . . . . . . . . . . . . 07
```

4.18

---

52. (Is/Was) (PARTNER) married, living with someone else in a sexual relationship, separated, divorced, or in a steady relationship with someone else when you first became sexually involved?

```
Married . . . . . . . . . . . . . . . . . . 1
Living with someone else . . . . . . . . . 2
Separated . . . . . . . . . . . . . . . . . 3
In a steady relationship . . . . . . . . . 4
Divorced . . . . . . . . . . . . . . . . . . 5
None of these . . . . . . . . . . . . . . . 6
DON'T KNOW . . . . . . . . . . . . . . . . . 8
```

63. How long did you know (PARTNER) prior to having sexual activity for the first time?

```
less than one day . . . . . . . . . . . . . . . . . . . . 1
one or two days . . . . . . . . . . . . . . . . . . . . . 2
more than two days but less than a month . . . . . . . . 3
more than one month but less than a year . . . . . . . . 4
more than one year . . . . . . . . . . . . . . . . . . . 5
```

BOX 4.2

DURING THE LAST TWELVE MONTHS, HOW MANY TIMES DID RESPONDENT HAVE SEXUAL ACTIVITY WITH (PARTNER)? (Q. 9.A./9.B. IN PARTNER ROSTER, PG. 4.3.)

```
ONLY ONCE . . . . . . 1 (GO TO 1 TIME SEX, Q. 82, PG. 4.25)
2-10 TIMES . . . . . 3 (Q. 65)
MORE THAN 10 TIMES . 4 (Q. 64)
```

64. During the last 12 months about how often did you have sex with (PARTNER)? Was it . . .

```
Once a day or more . . . . . . . . . . . . . 1
3 to 6 times a week . . . . . . . . . . . . . 2
Once or twice a week . . . . . . . . . . . . 3
2 to 3 times a month . . . . . . . . . . . . 4
Once a month or less . . . . . . . . . . . . 5
```

A. (Did/Do) you expect (PARTNER) to have sexual activity only with you during the time you (were/are) sexually involved?

```
Yes . . . . . . . . . . . . . . . . . . . . . 1
No . . . . . . . . . . . . . . . . . . . . . . 2
Not at first, but later I did . . . . . . . . 3
I did at first, but not later . . . . . . . . 4
```

B. (Did/Do) (PARTNER) expect you to have sex only with (him/her) during the time you (were/are) sexually involved?

```
Yes . . . . . . . . . . . . . . . . . . . . . . 1
No . . . . . . . . . . . . . . . . . . . . . . . 2
Not at first, but later, (she/he) did . . . . . 3
(She/he) did at first, but not later . . . . . 4
```

65. IF CURRENT SPOUSE/COHAB: SKIP TO Q 69. Do you expect to have sex with (PARTNER) again?

```
Yes . . . . . . . . . . . . . . . . . . . . . 1
No . . . . . . . . . . . . . . . . . . . . . . 2 (Q. 67)
DON'T KNOW . . . . . . . . . . . . . . . . . . 8
```

66. How much longer do you expect the relationship with (PARTNER) to last?

```
A few more days . . . . . . . . . . . . . . . . . . 1
A few more weeks . . . . . . . . . . . . . . . . . . 2
More than 1 month but less than 1 year . . . . . . . 3
Several years . . . . . . . . . . . . . . . . . . . 4
Lifetime . . . . . . . . . . . . . . . . . . . . . . 5
```

4.19

67. Did (PARTNER) get to know your family, that is your parents or brothers and sisters, during the relationship?

```
Yes . . . . . . . . . . . . . . . . . . 1
No . . . . . . . . . . . . . . . . . . . 2
```

68. Did (PARTNER) get to know your close friends during the relationship?

```
Yes . . . . . . . . . . . . . . . . . . 1
No . . . . . . . . . . . . . . . . . . . 2
```

FOR QS. 69 - 76, USE HAND CARD #5 (where applicable)

69. Now I would like to ask you some questions about alcohol use. How often (did/do) you or your partner drink alcohol before or during sex?

```
Always . . . . . . . . . . . . . . . . 1
Usually . . . . . . . . . . . . . . . . 2
Sometimes . . . . . . . . . . . . . . . 3
Rarely . . . . . . . . . . . . . . . . 4
Never . . . . . . . . . . . . . . . . . 5 (Q.70)
```

A. Was that usually you, your partner, or both?

```
RESPONDENT ONLY . . . . . . . . . . . . 1 (ASK B ONLY)
PARTNER ONLY . . . . . . . . . . . . . . 2 (ASK C ONLY)
RESPONDENT AND PARTNER . . . . . . . . . 3 (ASK B AND C)
```

B. On average, how strongly were you affected by the alcohol, very strongly, somewhat, not at all?

```
Very strongly . . . . . . . . . . . . . 1
Somewhat . . . . . . . . . . . . . . . . 2
Not At All . . . . . . . . . . . . . . . 3
DON'T KNOW . . . . . . . . . . . . . . . 8
```

C. On average, how strongly was PARTNER affected by the alcohol, very strongly, somewhat, not at all?

```
Very strongly . . . . . . . . . . . . . 1
Somewhat . . . . . . . . . . . . . . . . 2
Not At All . . . . . . . . . . . . . . . 3
DON'T KNOW . . . . . . . . . . . . . . . 8
```

70. How often (do/did) either you or (PARTNER) use drugs to get high or intoxicated before or during sex?

```
Always . . . . . . . . . . . . . . . . 1
Usually . . . . . . . . . . . . . . . . 2
Sometimes . . . . . . . . . . . . . . . 3
Rarely . . . . . . . . . . . . . . . . 4
Never . . . . . . . . . . . . . . . . . 5 (Q.71)
```

A. Was that usually you, your partner, or both?

```
RESPONDENT ONLY . . . . . . . . . . . . 1 (ASK B ONLY)
PARTNER ONLY . . . . . . . . . . . . . . 2 (ASK C ONLY)
RESPONDENT AND PARTNER . . . . . . . . . 3 (ASK B AND C)
```

B. On average, how strongly were you affected by the drugs, very strongly, somewhat, not at all?

```
Very strongly . . . . . . . . . . . . . 1
Somewhat . . . . . . . . . . . . . . . . 2
Not At All . . . . . . . . . . . . . . . 3
DON'T KNOW . . . . . . . . . . . . . . . 8
```

C. On average, how strongly was PARTNER affected by the drugs, very strongly, somewhat, not at all?

```
Very strongly . . . . . . . . . . . . . 1
Somewhat . . . . . . . . . . . . . . . . 2
Not At All . . . . . . . . . . . . . . . 3
DON'T KNOW . . . . . . . . . . . . . . . 8
```

71. Now I'd like you to think about the times you had sex with (PARTNER) during the past 12 months. If you were not sexually involved the whole year, please think only about the period of time when you were involved. First, I will ask you some questions about oral sex. When you had sex with (PARTNER), how often did (PARTNER) perform oral sex on you? Was it...

```
always . . . . . . . . . . . . . . . . 1
usually . . . . . . . . . . . . . . . . 2
sometimes . . . . . . . . . . . . . . . 3
rarely, or . . . . . . . . . . . . . . 4
never? . . . . . . . . . . . . . . . . 5
```

72. When you had sex with (PARTNER), how often did you perform oral sex on (him/her)? Was it...

```
always . . . . . . . . . . . . . . . . 1
usually . . . . . . . . . . . . . . . . 2
sometimes . . . . . . . . . . . . . . . 3
rarely, or . . . . . . . . . . . . . . 4
never? . . . . . . . . . . . . . . . . 5
```

MALE/FEMALE COUPLES ONLY:

73. Now I will ask you some questions about vaginal intercourse. When you had sex with (PARTNER), how often did you have vaginal intercourse? Was it...

```
always . . . . . . . . . . .  1
usually . . . . . . . . . . . 2
sometimes . . . . . . . . . . 3
rarely, or . . . . . . . . .  4
never? . . . . . . . . . . .  5  (Q.74)
```

A. When you had vaginal intercourse with (PARTNER), how often did you use condoms?

```
always . . . . . . . . . . .  1
usually . . . . . . . . . . . 2
sometimes . . . . . . . . . . 3
rarely, or . . . . . . . . .  4
never? . . . . . . . . . . .  5
```

B. When you had vaginal intercourse with (PARTNER), how often did you use any other methods of birth control?

```
always . . . . . . . . . . .  1
usually . . . . . . . . . . . 2
sometimes . . . . . . . . . . 3
rarely, or . . . . . . . . .  4
never? . . . . . . . . . . .  5
```

MALE/FEMALE AND MALE/MALE ONLY:

74. Now I'm going to ask you some questions about anal intercourse. When you had sex with (PARTNER), how often did you have anal intercourse with (PARTNER)? Was it...

```
always . . . . . . . . . . .  1
usually . . . . . . . . . . . 2
sometimes . . . . . . . . . . 3
rarely, or . . . . . . . . .  4
never? . . . . . . . . . . .  5  (Q. 75)
```

A. When you had anal intercourse with (PARTNER), how often did you use condoms?

```
always . . . . . . . . . . .  1
usually . . . . . . . . . . . 2
sometimes . . . . . . . . . . 3
rarely, or . . . . . . . . .  4
never? . . . . . . . . . . .  5
```

MALE/MALE COUPLE ONLY:

B. When you had anal intercourse, were you always the active (inserting) partner, the passive (receiving) partner or sometimes both?

```
Active exclusively . . . . .  1
Passive exclusively . . . . . 2
Both . . . . . . . . . . . .  3
```

75. When you and (PARTNER) had sex during the past 12 months, did you always, usually, sometimes, rarely, or never have an orgasm, that is come or come to climax?

```
Always . . . . . . . . . . .  1
Usually . . . . . . . . . . . 2
Sometimes . . . . . . . . . . 3
Rarely, or . . . . . . . . .  4
Never . . . . . . . . . . . . 5
```

76. When you and (PARTNER) had sex during the past 12 months, did (PARTNER) always, usually, sometimes, rarely, or never have an orgasm, that is come or come to climax?

```
always . . . . . . . . . . .  1
usually . . . . . . . . . . . 2
sometimes . . . . . . . . . . 3
rarely, or . . . . . . . . .  4
never? . . . . . . . . . . .  5
```

77. Now I would like to ask you how sex with (PARTNER) made you feel. Please, tell me if sex with (PARTNER) made you feel:

	YES	NO
a. satisfied	1	2
b. sad	1	2
c. loved	1	2
d. anxious or worried	1	2
e. wanted or needed	1	2
f. taken care of	1	2
g. scared or afraid	1	2
h. thrilled or excited	1	2
i. guilty	1	2
j. other (SPECIFY)_____	1	2

78. How physically pleasurable did you find your relationship with (PARTNER) to be: extremely pleasurable, very pleasurable, moderately pleasurable, slightly pleasurable, or not at all pleasurable?

```
Extremely . . . . . . . . .  1
Very . . . . . . . . . . . .  2
Moderately . . . . . . . . .  3
Slightly . . . . . . . . . .  4
Not at all . . . . . . . . .  5
```

79. How emotionally satisfying did you find your relationship with (PARTNER) to be extremely satisfying, very satisfying, moderately satisfying, slightly satisfying, or not at all satisfying?

```
Extremely . . . . . . . . .  1
Very . . . . . . . . . . . .  2
Moderately . . . . . . . . .  3
Slightly . . . . . . . . . .  4
Not at all . . . . . . . . .  5
```

ALTERNATIVE QUESTIONS FOR ONE-TIME SEX PARTNER
PARTNER #2 -- LAST YEAR

SKIP FROM BOX 4.2, PG. 4.19

82. Do you expect to have sex with (PARTNER) again?

```
Yes . . . . . . . . . . . . . . . . . . . . 1
NO . . . . . . . . . . . . . . . . . . . . . 2 (Q. 83)
DON'T KNOW . . . . . . . . . . . . . . . . . 8
```

A. How much longer do you expect the relationship with (PARTNER) to last?

```
A few more days . . . . . . . . . . . . . 1
A few more weeks . . . . . . . . . . . . . 2
More than 1 month but less than 1 year . . 3
Several years . . . . . . . . . . . . . . . 4
Lifetime . . . . . . . . . . . . . . . . . 5
```

I'd like you to think about the one time you had sex with (PARTNER) in the last 12 months.

83. First, I would like to ask you some questions about alcohol use. Did you or (PARTNER) drink any alcohol before or during sex?

```
Yes . . . . . . . . . . . . . . . . . . . . 1
No . . . . . . . . . . . . . . . . . . . . . 2 (Q. 84)
```

A. Was that you, your partner, or both?

```
RESPONDENT ONLY . . . . . . . . . . . 1 (ASK B ONLY)
PARTNER ONLY . . . . . . . . . . . . 2 (ASK C ONLY)
RESPONDENT AND PARTNER . . . . . . . 3 (ASK B AND C)
```

B. How strongly were you affected by the alcohol, very strongly, somewhat, not at all?

```
Very strongly . . . . . . . . . . . . . 1
Somewhat . . . . . . . . . . . . . . . . 2
Not At All . . . . . . . . . . . . . . . 3
```

C. How strongly was (PARTNER) affected by the alcohol, very strongly, somewhat, not at all?

```
Very Strongly . . . . . . . . . . . . . 1
Somewhat . . . . . . . . . . . . . . . . 2
Not At All . . . . . . . . . . . . . . . 3
DON'T KNOW . . . . . . . . . . . . . . . 8
```

---

80. People engage in sexual activities for a variety of reasons. What were your reasons for having sex with (PARTNER) during the past 12 months? Was it...

(CODE 'YES' OR 'NO' FOR EACH)

```
                                                        Y   N
                                                       --- ---
a.  to make-up after a fight or misunderstanding? . . . 1   2
b.  to relieve sexual tension (arousal)? . . . . . . . . 1   2
c.  because your partner wanted you to? . . . . . . . .  1   2
MALE/FEMALE ONLY:
d.  to get pregnant? . . . . . . . . . . . . . . . . . . 1   2
e.  to express love or affection? . . . . . . . . . . . 1   2
f.  to express or experience something else? . . . . .  1   2
    (IF YES) What was that? _____
```

81. As far as you know, during the past 12 months has (PARTNER) had other sexual partners?

```
Yes . . . . . . . . . . . . . . . . 1 (ASK A)
No. . . . . . . . . . . . . . . . . 2 (GO TO SECTION 5
```

A. About how many partners was that? RECORD NUMBER. IF DON'T KNOW PROBE FOR BEST GUESS.

|__|__|

B. Were these partners all men, all women or both?

```
men. . . . . . . . . . . . . . . . . . . . . 1
women. . . . . . . . . . . . . . . . . . . . 2
both . . . . . . . . . . . . . . . . . . . . 3
DON'T KNOW . . . . . . . . . . . . . . . . . 4
```

C. Did (PARTNER) have sex with any of these people during the time you and (PARTNER) were sexually involved?

```
Yes . . . . . . . . . . . . . . . . . . . . 1
No. . . . . . . . . . . . . . . . . . . . . 2
```

GO TO SECTION 5

84. Did either you or (PARTNER) use drugs to get high or intoxicated before or during sex?

Yes 1
No . . . . 2 (Q. 85)

A. Was that you, your partner, or both?

RESPONDENT ONLY . . . . 1 (ASK B ONLY)
PARTNER ONLY . . . . 2 (ASK C ONLY)
RESPONDENT AND PARTNER . . . . 3 (ASK B AND C)

B. How strongly were you affected by the drugs, very strongly, somewhat, not at all?

Very Strongly 1
Somewhat 2
Not At All 3
DON'T KNOW 8

C. How strongly was PARTNER affected by the drugs, very strongly, somewhat, not at all?

Very strongly 1
Somewhat 2
Not At All 3
DON'T KNOW 8

85. First, I will ask you some questions about oral sex.

When you had sex with (PARTNER), did (he/she) perform oral sex on you?

Yes 1
No 2

A. Did you perform oral sex on (him/her)?

Yes 1
No 2

MALE/FEMALE COUPLE -- Q.86
MALE/MALE COUPLE -- Q.87
FEMALE/FEMALE COUPLE -- Q.88

MALE/FEMALE COUPLES ONLY:

86. When you had sex with (PARTNER), did you have vaginal intercourse?

Yes 1
No . . . . 2 (Q. 87)

A. When you had vaginal intercourse with (PARTNER), did you use condoms?

Yes 1
No 2

B. When you had vaginal intercourse with (PARTNER), did you use any other methods of birth control?

Yes 1
No 2

MALE/FEMALE AND MALE/MALE ONLY:

Now I'm going to ask you some questions about anal intercourse.

When you had sex with (PARTNER), did you have anal intercourse with (PARTNER)?

Yes 1
No . . . . 2 (Q. 88)

87.

A. When you had anal intercourse with (PARTNER), did you use condoms?

Yes 1
No 2

MALE/MALE COUPLES ONLY:

B. When you had anal intercourse, were you the active (inserting) partner, the passive (receiving) partner or both?

Active exclusively 1
Passive exclusively 2
Both 3

88. When you and (PARTNER) had sex, did you have an orgasm, that is come or come to climax?

Yes 1
No 2

89. Did (PARTNER) have an orgasm, that is come or come to climax?

Yes 1
No 2

90. Now I would like to ask you how sex with (PARTNER) made you feel. Please, tell me if sex with (PARTNER) made you feel:

	YES	NO
a. satisfied	1	2
b. sad	1	2
c. loved	1	2
d. anxious or worried	1	2
e. wanted or needed	1	2
f. taken care of	1	2
g. scared or afraid	1	2
h. thrilled or excited	1	2
i. guilty	1	2
j. other (SPECIFY)_____	1	2

91. How physically pleasurable did you find your relationship with (PARTNER) to be: extremely pleasurable, very pleasurable, moderately pleasurable, slightly pleasurable, or not at all pleasurable?

Extremely 1
Very 2
Moderately 3
Slightly 4
Not at all 5

92. How emotionally satisfying did you find your relationship with (PARTNER) to be, extremely satisfying, very satisfying, moderately satisfying, slightly satisfying, or not at all satisfying?

Extremely 1
Very 2
Moderately 3
Slightly 4
Not at all 5

93. People engage in sexual activities for a variety of reasons. What were your reasons for having sex with (PARTNER)? Was it...

(CODE 'YES' OR 'NO' FOR EACH) Y N

a. to make-up after a fight or misunderstanding? 1   2

b. to relieve sexual tension (arousal)? 1   2

c. because your partner wanted you to? 1   2

d. MALE/FEMALE ONLY:
to get pregnant? 1   2

e. to express love or affection? 1   2

f. to express or experience something else? 1   2
(IF YES) What was that? _____

94. As far as you know, during the past 12 months has (PARTNER) had other sexual partners?

Yes . . . . 1 (ASK A)
No . . . . 2 (GO TO SECTION 5)

A. About how many partners was that? RECORD NUMBER. IF DON'T KNOW PROBE FOR BEST GUESS.
|___|___|

B. Were these partners all men, all women or both?

men 1
women 2
both 3
DON'T KNOW 4

GO TO SECTION 5

4.28

SECTION 5: LAST EVENT

Now I'm going to ask you some questions about the very last time you had sex, that is, the most recent time you had sex in the last 12 months. These questions focus on that one time, not on any other time that you had sex with this partner.

1. Who did you have sex with most recently?
ENTER NAME: _____

2. When did you last have sex?
___/___/___ mo/day/year

3. Where did you last have sex?

Your home 1
Partner's home 2
Someone else's home 3
Hotel or motel 4
Car or van 5
At work 6
A public place like a park . . . 7
Somewhere else (SPECIFY) 8

DON'T KNOW 98
REFUSED 97

4. How long did this sexual activity last -- from the time physical (sexual) contact began to when it ended.

15 minutes or less 1
More than 15 but less than 30 minutes 2
More than 30 but less than 1 hour 3
More than 1 hour but less than 2 hours 4
2 hours or longer 5

IF R HAD SEX WITH THIS PARTNER MORE THAN ONE TIME (Q. 9.A./9.B. ON PG. 4.3), GO TO Q.5, PG. 5.2.
IF R AND PARTNER ONLY EVER HAD SEX ONE TIME, GO TO NEXT SECTION: LIFETIME SEXUAL ACTIVITY, PG. 6.1

5.1

Now I would like to ask you some questions about alcohol use. During the most recent time you had sex, did you or (PARTNER) drink alcohol before or during sex?

YES 1
NO 2 (Q.6)

A. Was that you, (PARTNER), or both of you?

RESPONDENT ONLY . . . . 1 (ASK B ONLY)
PARTNER ONLY . . . . 2 (ASK C ONLY)
RESPONDENT AND PARTNER . . . . . . 3 (ASK B AND C)

B. How strongly were you affected by the alcohol, very strongly, somewhat, not at all?

Very Strongly 1
Somewhat 2
Not At All 3
DON'T KNOW 8

C. How strongly was (PARTNER) affected by the alcohol, very strongly, somewhat, not at all?

Very Strongly 1
Somewhat 2
Not At All 3
DON'T KNOW 8

6. This most recent time you had sex, did either you or (PARTNER) use drugs to get high or intoxicated before or during sex?

YES 1
NO . . . . 2 (Q. 7)

A. Was that you, (PARTNER), or both?

RESPONDENT ONLY . . . . 1 (ASK B ONLY)
PARTNER ONLY . . . . 2 (ASK C ONLY)
RESPONDENT AND PARTNER . . . . . . 3 (ASK B AND C)

B. How strongly were you affected by the drugs, very strongly, somewhat, not at all?

Very Strongly 1
Somewhat 2
Not At All 3
DON'T KNOW 8

C. How strongly was (PARTNER) affected by the drugs, very strongly, somewhat, not at all?

Very Strongly 1
Somewhat 2
Not At All 3
DON'T KNOW 8

7. During the most recent time you had sex, did (PARTNER) perform oral sex on you?

YES 1
NO 2

8. When you had sex this time with (PARTNER), did you perform oral sex on (him/her)?

YES 1
NO 2

MALE/FEMALE COUPLE -- Q.9
MALE/MALE COUPLE -- Q.10
FEMALE/FEMALE COUPLE -- Q.11

MALE/FEMALE COUPLES ONLY:

9. When you had sex with (PARTNER) this most recent time, did you have vaginal intercourse?

YES 1
NO 2 (Q.10)

A. When you had vaginal intercourse this time with (PARTNER), did you use condoms?

YES 1
NO 2

B. When you had vaginal intercourse this time with (PARTNER), did you use any other methods of disease prevention or birth control?

YES 1
NO 2

MALE/FEMALE AND MALE/MALE ONLY:

10. When you had sex with (PARTNER) this most recent time, did you have anal intercourse?

YES . . . . 1 (ASK A)
NO 2 (Q.11)

A. This most recent time, when you had anal intercourse with (PARTNER), did you use condoms?

YES 1
NO 2

MALE/MALE COUPLE ONLY:

B. On this occasion, when you had anal intercourse, were you the active (inserting) partner, the passive (receiving) partner or both?

Active exclusively 1
Passive exclusively 2
Both 3

SECTION 6: LIFETIME SEXUAL ACTIVITY

USE LHC (LIFE HISTORY CALENDAR)

☞

BOX 6A	HOW OLD IS RESPONDENT?
	AGE 18 . . . . 1 (GO TO SECTION 7, PG 7.1)
	AGE 19 TO 59 . . . . . 2 (READ INSTRUCTIONS BELOW)

I have already asked about some of your sexual partners. [IF ANY S/C OR PARTNERS LISTED ON LHC: You have told me about some people you had sex with and they are listed on this calendar. (POINT TO THE S/C &/OR P NAMES ON LHC.) Now, I would like to ask you about any other sexual partners you may have had since your 18th birthday.]

In answering these questions, please count only those people who you had sex with for the first time since your 18th birthday and do not include anybody that you have already told me about. We will use this calendar (SHOW LHC) to make this easier. (POINT TO PERIODS BETWEEN 18th BIRTHDAY AND UP UNTIL 12 MONTHS AGO.)

(Do not include any S/Cs that ended before your 18th birthday)

Again, in this section we are only interested in the partners not already on this calendar who you had sex with for the first time between this period (POINT TO AGE 18 ON LHC) and this period (POINT TO 12 MONTHS AGO).

6.1

---

11. When you and (PARTNER) had sex this most recent time, did you have an orgasm, that is come or come to climax?

YES 1
NO 2 (Q.12)

A. How many times did you have an orgasm?

|_|_|

12. When you and (PARTNER) had sex this most recent time, did (PARTNER) have an orgasm, that is come or come to climax?

YES 1
NO 2

13. People engage in sexual activities for a variety of reasons. What were your reasons for having sex with (PARTNER) on this occasion?

Was it ....

(CODE 'YES' OR 'NO' FOR EACH)

	Y	N
a. to make-up after a fight or misunderstanding?	1	2
b. to relieve sexual tension (arousal)?	1	2
c. because your partner wanted you to?	1	2
MALE/FEMALE ONLY:		
d. to get pregnant?	1	2
e. to express love or affection?	1	2
f. to express or experience something else?	1	2

IF YES: What was that? _____

5.4

(USE LHC)
IF NO S/C BETWEEN AGE 18 & 12 MONTHS AGO, GO TO BOX 6G ON PAGE 6.12.

IF A S/C BEGAN BEFORE AGE 18, GO TO BOX 6C ON PAGE 6.4.

IF ANY S/Cs BETWEEN AGE 18 & 12 MONTHS AGO, ASK. Q.1 BELOW.

[NOTE: DO NOT INCLUDE ANY S/Cs THAT ENDED BEFORE AGE 18]

1. (POINT TO PERIOD ON LHC) Thinking back, since your 18th birthday and during the time before you started living with (1ST S/C), how many people, including men and women, did you begin having sex with, even if only one time? Please remember, I only want you to tell me about those persons that you have not told me about already.

|__|__|

NONE . . . . 0(BOX 6C, PG. 6.4)
ONE . . . . 1(ASK Q.2)
TWO OR MORE . . . . 2(ASK Q.6, PG. 6.3)

2. Was this partner male or female?
male 1
female 2

3. What would you say best describes (his/her) racial background? Is that...
White. 1
Black. 2
Hispanic, ... 3
Asian, ... 4
or other? 5

4. What was the highest level of education this person received?
Less than 12th grade, ... 1
high school graduate, ... 2
some college or
   vocational school, . . . 3
college graduate, . . . 4
or more than college grad? . . 5

5. How many times did you have sex with this partner? Was that...
One time, ... 1 | GO TO
2 to 10 times, ... 2 | BOX 6C
or more than 10 times? . . 3 | PG. 6.4

6.2

6. How many of these partners were...
male? . . . . [__|__|__]
female? . . . . [__|__|__]

7. How many of these partners would you describe as...
White? . . . . [__|__|__]
Black? . . . . [__|__|__]
Hispanic? . . . . [__|__|__]
Asian? . . . . [__|__|__]
Other? . . . . [__|__|__]

8. How many of these people had as their highest level of education...
Less than 12th grade? . . . [__|__|__]
High school graduate? . . . [__|__|__]
Some college or
   vocational school? . . . [__|__|__]
College graduate . . . . . [__|__|__]
or more than college grad? . [__|__|__]
DON'T KNOW

9. How many of these partners did you have sex with...
only one time? . . . . . . [__|__|__]
2 to 10 times? . . . . . . [__|__|__]
More than 10 times? . . . . [__|__|__]

10. You have just told me about |__|__|__| (NUMBER RECORDED IN Q.1, PG. 6.2) partner(s). During this time, did you ever have sex with one partner while still involved in a sexual relationship with another partner?

Yes 1
No 2

6.3

16. How many of these partners were
male? . . . . |__|__|
female? . . . . |__|__|

17. How many of these partners would you describe as
White? . . . . |__|__|
Black? . . . . |__|__|
Hispanic? . . . . |__|__|
Asian? . . . . |__|__|
Or other? . . . . |__|__|

18. How many of these people had as their highest level of education...
Less than 12th grade? . . . |__|__|
High school graduate? . . . |__|__|
Some college or
vocational school? . . . |__|__|
College graduate . . . . . . |__|__|
More than college grad? . . |__|__|
DON'T KNOW . . . . |__|__|

19. How many of these partners did you have sex with...
only one time? . . . . |__|__|
2 to 10 times? . . . . |__|__|
More than 10 times? . . . . |__|__|

20. During this time, did you also continue to have sex with any of the partners you were sexually involved with before the time you started living with (1ST S/C)?

Yes 1
No 2

6.5

BOX 6C	(USE LHC)
DURING	IF 1ST S/C RELATIONSHIP ENDED MORE THAN 12 MONTHS AGO, ASK Q.11 BELOW.
	IF 1ST S/C IS CURRENT S/C OR ENDED LESS THAN 12 MONTHS AGO, GO TO BOX 6H ON PG. 6.14.
	[NOTE: DO NOT INCLUDE ANY S/Cs THAT ENDED BEFORE AGE 18]

11. Now, I am going to ask you some questions about any other sexual partners you may have had during the time you were living with (1ST S/C). While living with (1ST S/C), how many people, including men and women, did you begin having sex with, even if only one time? Again, please count only those persons that you have not told me about already and who you had sex with for the first time after you were age 18.

|__|__|__|
NONE . . . . 0 (BOX 6D, PG. 6.6)
ONE . . . . 1 (ASK Q.12)
TWO OR MORE . . . . 2 (ASK Q.16, PG 6.5)

12. Was this partner male or female?
male 1
female . . . 2

13. What would you say best describes (his/her) racial background? Is that ...
White, ... 1
Black, ... 2
Hispanic, ... 3
Asian, ... 4
or other? 5

14. What was the highest level of education this person received?
Less than 12th grade, . . . 1
high School graduate, . . . 2
some college or
vocational school, . . . 3
college graduate, ... 4
or more than college grad? . . . 5

15. How many times did you have sex with this partner? Was that...
one time, ... 1|
2 to 10 times, ... 2|GO TO Q.20, PG 6.5
or more than 10 times? . . 3|

6.4

BOX 6D BETWEEN	(USE LHC)
	IF 2 OR MORE S/C RELATIONSHIPS RECORDED ON LHC, ASK Q.21 BELOW.
	OTHERWISE SKIP TO BOX 6I ON PG. 6.16.

21. Now, I am going to ask you some questions about any other sexual partners between the time you were living with (1ST S/C) and (2ND S/C). During this period, how many people, including men and women, did you begin having sex with, even if only one time? **Again, please remember, do not include any persons that you have already told me about.**

|__|__|

NONE . . . . 0 (GO TO BOX 6E ON PG. 6.8)
ONE . . . . 1(ASK Q.22)
TWO OR MORE . . . . 2(ASK Q.26, PG. 6.7)

22. Was this partner male or female?

male 1
female 2

23. What would you say best describes (his/her) racial background? Is that...

White, ... 1
Black, ... 2
Hispanic, ... 3
Asian, ... 4
or other? 5

24. What was the highest level of education this person received?

Less than 12th grade, ... 1
high school graduate, ... 2
some college or vocational school, ... 3
college graduate, ... 4
or more than college grad? 5

25. How many times did you have sex with this partner? Was that...

one time 1
2 to 10 times . . . . 2 | GO TO Q.31 PG 6.7 |
or more than 10 times? . . . 3

6.6

26. How many of these partners were...

male? . . . . |__|__|__|
Female? . . . . |__|__|__|

27. How many of these partners would you describe as . . .

White? . . . . |__|__|__|
Black? . . . . |__|__|__|
Hispanic? . . . . |__|__|__|
Asian? . . . . |__|__|__|
Or other? . . . . |__|__|__|

28. How many of these people had as their highest level of education...

Less than 12th grade? . . . . |__|__|__|
High school graduate? . . . . |__|__|__|
Some college or vocational school? . . . |__|__|__|
College graduate? . . . . |__|__|__|
More than college grad? . . . |__|__|__|
DON'T KNOW . . . . |__|__|__|

29. How many of these partners did you have sex with...

only one time? . . . . . . |__|__|__|
2 to 10 times? . . . . . . |__|__|__|
More than 10 times? . . . |__|__|__|

30. You have just told me about |__|__|__| (NUMBER RECORDED IN Q.21 ON PG. 6.6) partner(s). During this time, did you ever have sex with one of these people while still involved in a sexual relationship with another person?

Yes 1
No 2

31. During this time, did you also continue to have sex with any of the partners you told me about earlier (POINT TO EARLIER PERIODS ON LHC)?

Yes 1
No 2

6.7

BOX 6E DURING	(USE LHC)

IF 2ND S/C ENDED **MORE** THAN 12 MONTHS AGO, ASK Q. 32 BELOW.

IF 2ND S/C IS **CURRENT** S/C OR ENDED **LESS** THAN 12 MONTHS AGO, GO TO BOX 6H P.6.14.

32. Now, I am going to ask you some questions about any other sexual partners you may have had during the time you were living with (2ND S/C). While living with (2ND S/C), how many people, including men and women, did you begin having sex with, even if only one time? **Please remember, I only want you to include those persons that you have not told me about before.**

```
|__|__|__|
    NONE . . . . . . . . . . . . .    0  (GO TO BOX 6F
                                            ON PG. 6.10)
    ONE . . . . . . . . . . . . . .   1  (ASK Q.33)
    TWO OR MORE . . . . . . . . . .   2  (ASK Q.37, PG. 6.9)
```

33. Was this partner male or female?

```
    male . . . . . . . . . . . . . .   1
    female . . . . . . . . . . . . .   2
```

34. What would you say best describes (his/her) racial background? Is that...

```
    White, . . . . . . . . . . . . .   1
    Black, . . . . . . . . . . . . .   2
    Hispanic, . . . . . . . . . . . .  3
    Asian, . . . . . . . . . . . . .   4
    or other? . . . . . . . . . . . .  5
```

35. What was the highest level of education this person received?

```
    Less than 12th grade, . . . . . .        1
    high school graduate, . . . . . .        2
    some college or
        vocational school, . . . . .         3
    college graduate, . . . . . . . .        4
    or more than college grad? . . .         5
```

36. How many times did you have sex with this partner? Was that...

```
    One time . . . . . . . . . . .    1|
    2 to 10 times, . . . . . . . .    2|GO TO Q.41 PG. 6.9
    more than 10 times? . . . . . .   3|
```

6.8

37. How many of these partners were...

```
    male? . . . . . . . . . .   |__|__|__|
    Female? . . . . . . . . .   |__|__|__|
```

38. How many of these partners would you describe as . . .

```
    White? . . . . . . . . . .   |__|__|__|
    Black? . . . . . . . . . .   |__|__|__|
    Hispanic? . . . . . . . .    |__|__|__|
    Asian? . . . . . . . . . .   |__|__|__|
    Or other? . . . . . . . .    |__|__|__|
```

39. How many of these people had as their highest level of education...

```
    Less than 12th grade? . . .         |__|__|__|
    High school graduate? . . .         |__|__|__|
    Some college or
        vocational school? . . .        |__|__|__|
    College graduate? . . . . .         |__|__|__|
    Or more than college grad?          |__|__|__|
    DON'T KNOW . . . . . . . . .         |__|__|__|
```

40. How many of these partners did you have sex with...

```
    only one time? . . . . . .   |__|__|__|
    2 to 10 times? . . . . . .    |__|__|__|
    More than 10 times? . . . .   |__|__|__|
```

41. During this time, did you also continue to have sex with any of the partners you told me about earlier (POINT TO EARLIER PERIODS ON LHC)?

```
    Yes . . . . . . . . . . . . . . .   1
    No  . . . . . . . . . . . . . . .   2
```

6.9

BOX 6F
BETWEEN

(USE LHC)
IF 3 OR MORE S/C'S, ASK Q.42 BELOW.
OTHERWISE SKIP TO BOX 6I ON PG. 6.16.

42. Now, I am going to ask you some questions about any **other** sexual partners since the time you stopped living with (2ND S/C) and up until 12 months ago. During this period (POINT TO PERIOD ON LHC), how many people, including men and women, did you begin having sex with, even if only one time? **Please remember, I only want you to tell me about those persons that you have not told me about already.**

|__|__|

NONE . . . . 0 (GO TO SECTION 7 ON PG. 7.1)
ONE . . . . 1 (ASK Q.43)
TWO OR MORE . . . . 2 (ASK Q.47, PG. 6.11)

43. Was this partner male or female?

male 1
female 2

44. What would you say best describes (his/her) racial background? Is that ...

White, ... 1
Black, ... 2
Hispanic, ... 3
Asian, ... 4
or other? 5

45. What was the highest level of education this person received?

Less than 12th grade, . . . 1
high school graduate, . . . 2
some college or
    vocational school, . . . 3
college graduate, ... 4
or more than college grad? . 5

46. How many times did you have sex with this partner? Was that...

One time . . . . 1|
2 to 10 times . . . . 2| GO TO Q.52, P.6.11
more than 10 times? . . . . 3|

6.10

47. How many of these partners were...

male? . . . . . . |__|__|__|
female? . . . . . |__|__|__|

48. How many of these partners would you describe as...

White? . . . . |__|__|__|
Black? . . . . |__|__|__|
Hispanic? . . . . |__|__|__|
Asian? . . . . |__|__|__|
Or other? . . . . |__|__|__|

49. How many of these people had as their highest level of education...

Less than 12th grade? . . . |__|__|__|
High school graduate? . . . |__|__|__|
Some college or
    vocational school? . . . |__|__|__|
College graduate? . . . . . |__|__|__|
More than college grad? . . |__|__|__|
DON'T KNOW . . . . |__|__|__|

50. How many of these partners did you have sex with...

only one time? . . . . . . |__|__|__|
2 to 10 times? . . . . |__|__|__|
More than 10 times? . . . . |__|__|__|

51. You have just told me about |__|__|__| (NUMBER RECORDED IN Q.42 PG. 6.10) partner(s). During this time, did you ever have sex with one of these people while still involved in a sexual relationship with another person?

Yes 1
No 2

52. During this time, did you also continue to have sex with any of the partners you told me about earlier (POINT TO EARLIER PERIODS ON LHC)?

Yes . . . . 1| GO TO SECTION 7
                       PG. 7.1
No . . . . 2| GO TO SECTION 7
                       PG. 7.1

6.11

BOX 6G
NO S/Cs
(USE LHC)
IF NO S/C BETWEEN AGE 18 AND 12 MONTHS AGO, ASK Q. 53 BELOW.

53. Now, I am going to ask you some questions about your sexual partners since you were 18 years old. Thinking back, during the time since you were age 18 and not including the partners you already told me about (listed on this chart), how many people, including men and women, did you engage in sexual activity with, even if only one time? Please remember, I only want you to include those persons that you have not told me about before.

|_|_|_|
NONE . . . . 0 (GO TO SECTION 7, PG. 7.1)
ONE . . . . 1 (ASK Q.54)
TWO OR MORE . . . . 2 (ASK Q.58, PG. 6.13)

54. Was this partner male or female?
male 1
female 2

55. What would you say best describes (his/her) racial background? Is that ...
White, ... 1
Black, ... 2
Hispanic, ... 3
Asian, ... 4
or other? 5

56. What was the highest level of education this person received?
Less than 12th grade, . . . 1
high school graduate, . . . 2
some college or
vocational school, . . . 3
college graduate, . . . 4
or more than college grad? . . . 5

57. How many times did you have sex with this partner? Was that...
One time . . . . 1 | GO ON TO
2 to 10 times . . . . 2 | SECTION 7
or more than 10 times? . . 3 | PG. 7.1

6.12

---

58. How many of these partners were
male? |_|_|_|
female? |_|_|_|

59. How many of these partners would you describe as
White? |_|_|_|
Black? |_|_|_|
Hispanic? |_|_|_|
Asian? |_|_|_|
Or other? |_|_|_|

60. How many of these people had as their highest level of education...
Less than 12th grade? |_|_|_|
High school graduate?
Some college or
vocational school?
College graduate?
More than college grad?
DON'T KNOW

61. How many of these partners did you have sex with
only one time? |_|_|_|
2 to 10 times?
More than 10 times?

62. You have just told me about |_|_|_| (NUMBER RECORDED IN Q.53 ON PG. 6.12) partner(s). During this time, did you ever have sex with one of these people while still involved in a sexual relationship with another person?
Yes . . . . 1 |SECTION 7 PG. 7.1
No . . . . 2 |SECTION 7 PG. 7.1

6.13

BOX 6H CURRENT S/C	(USE LHC) IF R HAS <u>CURRENT</u> S/C OR A S/C THAT ENDED <u>LESS THAN</u> 12 MONTHS AGO, ASK Q. 63 BELOW.

63. Now, I am going to ask you some questions about any <u>other</u> sexual partners you may have had during the time you were living with (CURRENT S/C) but <u>not</u> including the people you had sex with during the last 12 months. How many people, including men and women, did you engage in sexual activity with, even if only one time? Please remember, I <u>only want</u> you to include <u>those persons</u> that you have <u>not</u> told me about before.

[___|___|___]
NONE . . . . 0 (GO TO SECTION 7 PG. 7.1)

ONE . . . . . . 1 (ASK Q. 64)

TWO OR MORE . . . 2 (ASK Q. 68, PG 6.15)

64. Was this partner male or female?

male 1
female 2

65. What would you say best describes (his/her) racial background? Is that ...

White, ... 1
Black, ... 2
Hispanic, ... 3
Asian, ... 4
or other? 5

66. What was the highest level of education this person received?

Less than 12th grade, . . . 1
high school graduate, . . . 2
some college or vocational school, . . . 3
college graduate, . . . 4
more than college grad? . . . 5

67. How many times did you have sex with this partner? Was that...

one time, ... 1|
2 to 10 times, ... 2|GO TO Q. 72 P. 6.15
or more than 10 times? . . 3|

6.14

68. How many of these partners were . . . .

male? . . . . [___|___|___]
female? . . . . [___|___|___]

69. How many of these partners would you describe as . . . .

White? . . . . [___|___|___]
Black? . . . . [___|___|___]
Hispanic? . . . . [___|___|___]
Asian? . . . . [___|___|___]
Or other? . . . . [___|___|___]

70. How many of these people had as their highest level of education. .

Less than 12th grade? . . . [___|___|___]
High school graduate? . . . [___|___|___]
Some college or vocational school? . . . [___|___|___]
College graduate? . . . . . [___|___|___]
More than college grad? . . [___|___|___]
DON'T KNOW . . . . [___|___|___]

71. How many of these partners did you have sex with

only one time? . . . . . . [___|___|___]
2 to 10 times? . . . . . . [___|___|___]
More than 10 times? . . . . [___|___|___]

72. During this time, did you also continue to have sex with any of the partners you told me about earlier (POINT TO EARLIER PERIODS ON LHC)?

Yes . . . . 1 | (GO ON TO
No . . . . 2 | SECTION 7, PG 7.1)

6.15

BOX 6I (USE LHC)
LESS THAN
3 S/Cs
IF LAST S/C ENDED MORE THAN 12 MONTHS AGO, ASK Q. 73 BELOW.

73. Now, I am going to ask you some questions about any other sexual partners you had after the time you stopped living with (LAST S/C). How many people, including men and women, did you engage in sexual activity with, even if only one time? Please remember, I only want you to include those persons that you have not told me about before.

|__|__|
NONE . . . . 0 (GO TO SECTION 7 PG. 7.1)
ONE . . . . 1 (ASK Q.74)
TWO OR MORE . . . . 2 (ASK Q.78, PG. 6.17)

74. Was this partner male or female?

male 1
female 2

75. What would you say best describes (his/her) racial background?

White, ... 1
Black, ... 2
Hispanic, ... 3
Asian, ... 4
or other? 5

76. What was the highest level of education this person received?

Less than 12th grade, . . . 1
high school graduate, . . . 2
some college or
  vocational school, . . . 3
college graduate, . . . 4
more than college grad? . . 5

77. How many times did you have sex with this partner? Was that...

one time, ... 1|
2 to 10 times, ... 2| Q. 83. PG. 6.17
more than 10 times? . . . 3|

6.16

78. How many of these partners were . . . .

male? . . . . . . |__|__|
female? . . . . . |__|__|

79. How many of these partners would you describe as . . .

White? . . . . . . |__|__|
Black? . . . . . . |__|__|
Hispanic? . . . . |__|__|
Asian? . . . . . . |__|__|
Or other? . . . . |__|__|

80. How many of these people had as their highest level of education...

Less than 12th grade? . . . |__|__|
High school graduate? . . . |__|__|
Some college or
  vocational school? . . . |__|__|
College graduate? . . . . . |__|__|
more than college grad? . . |__|__|
DON'T KNOW . . . . |__|__|

81. How many of these partners did you have sex with

only one time? . . . . . |__|__|
2 to 10 times? . . . . . |__|__|
More than 10 times? . . . |__|__|

82. You have just told me about |__|__|__| (NUMBER RECORDED IN Q.73, PG. 6.16) partner(s). During this time, did you ever have sex with one partner while still involved in a sexual relationship with another partner?

Yes 1
No 2

83. During this time, did you also continue to have sex with any of the partners you told me about earlier (POINT TO EARLIER PERIODS ON LHC)?

Yes . . . . 1 | (GO ON TO
No . . . . 2 | SECTION 7, PG 7.1)

6.17

SECTION 7: FANTASY

☞

BOX (7.1)

ADMINISTER SAQ #3. IF THE R CANNOT READ AND ASKS FOR YOUR HELP, YOU MAY ASSIST HIM/HER IN FILLING OUT THIS FORM.

READ THE FOLLOWING TO R:
Now I have another form for you to fill out yourself. Please read the questions and circle the appropriate code. When you are finished place it in the "privacy" envelope

R filled out SAQ	1
Interviewer assisted with SAQ .	2
R refused SAQ	7

People think about sex in different ways and find some activities more appealing than others. In order for us to better understand how people think about sex. I now have some questions concerning your feelings about sex.

1. On the average, how often do you think about sex?

less than once a month	1
one to a few times a month	2
one to a few times a week	3
every day	4
several times a day	5
I NEVER THINK ABOUT SEX	6 (Q.4)

2. How often does thinking about sex make you feel guilty?

never	1
rarely	2
occasionally	3
often	4
nearly always	5

7.1

THIS PAGE LEFT INTENTIONALLY BLANK

3. Do your thoughts or fantasies about sex usually involve a story or are they more like images or pictures?

Story 1
Pictures 2
Both 3
NEITHER/NA 4

4. On a scale of 1 to 4, where 1 is very appealing and 4 is not at all appealing, how would you rate each of these activities:

HAND CARD #6

	very appealing	somewhat appealing	not appealing	not at all appealing
a. having sex with more than one person at the same time	1	2	3	4
b. having sex with someone of the same sex	1	2	3	4
c. forcing someone to do something sexual that he/she doesn't want to do	1	2	3	4
d. being forced into doing something sexual that you don't want to do	1	2	3	4
e. seeing other people doing sexual things	1	2	3	4
f. having sex with someone you don't personally know	1	2	3	4

5. On a scale of 1 to 4, where 1 is very appealing and 4 is not at all appealing, how would you rate each of these activities:

HAND CARD #6

	very appealing	somewhat appealing	not appealing	not at all appealing
a. watching partner undress/strip	1	2	3	4
b. vaginal intercourse	1	2	3	4
c. using a dildo or vibrator	1	2	3	4
d. a partner performing oral sex on you	1	2	3	4
e. performing oral sex on a partner	1	2	3	4
f. partner stimulating your anus with his/her fingers	1	2	3	4
g. stimulating partner's anus with your fingers	1	2	3	4
h. passive anal intercourse	1	2	3	4

ASK MALES ONLY
| i. active anal intercourse | 1 | 2 | 3 | 4 |

Now, I'd like to ask some questions about your early sexual experience. This series of questions is intended to help us understand the importance of various events that occur during sexual development.

1. IF R FEMALE, ASK: How old were you when you reached puberty? By puberty I mean when you had your first menstrual period?

   IF R MALE, ASK: How old were you when you reached puberty? By puberty I mean when your voice changed or when you began to grow pubic hair.

|___|___|
AGE

2. When you were growing up, in which of the following ways did you learn about sexual matters? From: (CIRCLE ALL THAT APPLY)

Mother	01
Father	02
Brother(s)	03
Sister(s)	04
Other relative(s)	05
Lessons at school	06
Friends of about my own age . . .	07
MEN: First girlfriend or sexual partner	08
WOMEN: First boyfriend or sexual partner	08
Doctor, nurse or clinic	09
Television	10
Radio	11
Books	12
Magazines or newspapers	13
OTHER (SPECIFY)	14
CAN'T REMEMBER AT ALL (PROBE BEFORE CODING) . . .	98 (GO TO Q.3)

IF TWO OR MORE ARE CIRCLED IN Q. 2 ABOVE, ASK A.   OTHERWISE GO TO Q.3

8.1

Many materials are sold for the enhancement of sexual enjoyment.

6. In the last 12 months did you...

	Yes	No
buy or rent any x-rated movies or videos?	1	2
buy any sexually explicit magazines or books?	1	2
buy any vibrators or dildos?	1	2
buy any other sex toys?	1	2
call any "pay by the minute" sex phone numbers? . . .	1	2
buy anything else for sex? (Specify)_____	1	2

7. (IF YES TO ANY OF Q.6:) About how much money would you estimate you spent on these kinds of things over the past 12 months?

$ |__|__,|__|__|__|

There are many activities that people participate in to enhance their sexual experiences or to give an outlet to their sexual feelings. I am going to ask you about your participation in some of these activities.

8. In the last 12 months did you...

	Yes	No
go to night clubs with nude or semi-nude dancers?	1	2
get a professional massage?	1	2
hire a prostitute or pay anyone to have sex with you?	1	2
attend a public gathering in which you were nude? . .	1	2
have your picture taken in the nude?	1	2

9. (IF YES TO ANY OF Q.8:) About how many times in the last 12 months did you do (this/these)?

|__|__|__|

GO TO SECTION 8

7.4

A. From which one of those did you learn the most?

Mother	01
Father	02
Brother(s)	03
Sister(s)	04
Other relative(s)	05
Lessons at school	06
Friends of about my own age	07
MEN: First girlfriend or sexual partner	08
WOMEN: First boyfriend or sexual partner	08
Doctor, nurse or clinic	09
Television	10
Radio	11
Books	12
Magazines or newspapers	13
OTHER (SPECIFY)	14
CAN'T CHOSE JUST ONE (STATE MAIN ONES)	96
DON'T KNOW/CAN'T REMEMBER AT ALL	98

3. Before you were (AGE IN Q.1 / IF Q.1 = DK, THEN USE "12 or 13 years old") did anyone touch you sexually?

Yes 1
No . . . . 2(Q.20, Pg. 8.7)

A. HAND CARD #7 Before you were (AGE IN Q.1 / IF Q.1 = DK; 12 or 13 years old) what happened sexually? Just give me the numbers from this card.

01
02
03
04
05
06

Now I'd like to talk about those individuals that touched you sexually.....

4. With how many persons did this happen?

|___|___|
NUMBER
IF ONE ASK Q.5
IF TWO OR MORE ASK Q.12, PAGE 8.5

8.2

5. What was this person's sex?

Male 1
Female 2

A. Had this person reached puberty, that is was this person at least 12 or 13 years old?

Yes . . . . 1 (B)
No . . . . 2 (Q.20, PAGE 8.7)

|___|___|
ENTER AGE

B. How old was this person?

C. What was (his/her) relationship to you? RECORD VERBATIM AND CODE ONE ONLY.

_____

STRANGER	01
TEACHER	02
FAMILY FRIEND/AQUAINTANCE	03
RELATIVE (UNCLE/COUSIN)	04
MOTHER'S BOY FRIEND	05
RESPONDENT'S OLDER FRIEND	06
OLDER BROTHER	07
STEP FATHER	08
FATHER	09
OTHER	10

6. Did this happen only once, a few times, or many times?

once 1
a few times 2
many times 3

7. How old were you when this happened? (IF HAPPENED ONLY ONCE OR R GIVES AGE STARTED, RECORD AGE IN "FROM" BOX AND ENTER 00 IN "TO" BOX. ACCEPT A "FROM-TO" ANSWER IF GIVEN.)

|___|___| TO |___|___|
FROM AGE   AGE

8.3

8. While you were a child, did anyone else know about this?

yes 1 (Q.9)
no 2 (Q.11)

9. Who knew?
RECORD VERBATIM AND CODE ALL THAT APPLY.

MOTHER 01
FATHER 02
STEP PARENT 03
BROTHER/SISTER 04
OTHER RELATIVE 05
OTHER CHILD 06
ADULT FRIEND 07
MINISTER/CLERGY 08
TEACHER 09
OTHER 10
DON'T KNOW 98

10. Did you tell them or did they discover it some other way?

I told them 1
Some other way 2

11. Do you think that this experience has had any effect on your life since then?

Yes . . . . 1(A)
No . . . . 2(Q.20, P. 8.7)

A. In what ways? RECORD VERBATIM. (PROBES: affect sex life, relationships with men or women)

_____

_____

(SKIP TO Q.20, PAGE 8.7)

8.4

12. Thinking about these persons, how many were...

Male? . . . . ___
Female? . . . . . ___

A. How many of these people were...

13 years old or younger . . . . . ___
14 to 17 years old . . . . ___
18 years or older . . . . ___

B. Thinking about these persons, what were their relationships to you? How many were... (RECORD VERBATIM AND ENTER THE NUMBER OF PERSONS THAT FALL INTO EACH CATEGORY.

No. of persons

STRANGER . . . . ___
TEACHER . . . . ___
FAMILY FRIEND/ACQUAINTANCE . . . . ___
RELATIVE (UNCLE/COUSIN) . . . . . ___
MOTHER'S BOY FRIEND . . . . ___
RESPONDENT'S OLDER FRIEND . . . . ___
OLDER BROTHER . . . . ___
STEP FATHER . . . . ___
FATHER . . . . ___
OTHER . . . . ___

13. With how many of these people, did this happen......

just one time? . . . . ___
a few more times? . . . . ___
many more times? . . . . ___

14. How old were you when this started?

___ AGE

15. How old were you when this ended?

___ AGE

16. While you were a child, did anyone else know about these events?

Yes . . . . 1(Q. 17)
No . . . . 2(Q. 19)

8.5

17. Who knew?
RECORD VERBATIM AND CODE ALL THAT APPLY.

MOTHER 01
FATHER 02
STEP PARENT 03
BROTHER/SISTER 04
OTHER RELATIVE 05
OTHER CHILD 06
ADULT FRIEND 07
MINISTER/CLERGY 08
TEACHER 09
OTHER 10
DON'T KNOW 98

18. Did you tell them or did they discover some other way?

I told them 1
Some other way 2

19. Do you think that these experiences have had any effect on your life since then?

Yes . . . . 1(A)
No . . . . 2(Q.20)

A. In what ways? RECORD VERBATIM. (PROBES: affect sex life, relationships with men or women)

8.6

---

20. Now I would like to ask you some questions about what you did sexually after you were (AGE IN Q.1 / IF Q.1 = DK, THEN USE "12 or 13 years old"). How old were you the first time you had vaginal intercourse with a (OPPOSITE SEX OF R; male/female)?

|___|___|
  AGE

NEVER . . . . 00 (SKIP TO Q.27, P. 8.10)

21. Was this first intercourse...

something you wanted to happen at the time? 1(ASK C)
something you went along with, but did not want to happen? . . . . . 2(ASK D)
something that you were forced to do against your will? . . . . . . 3(ASK A)

A. HAND CARD #8 What was your relationship to this person? RECORD ONE ONLY.
1(Q.24, P. 8.9)

Spouse 1
Someone you were in love with but not married to . . . 2
Someone you knew well but were not in love with . . . 3
Someone you knew but not well . . . 4
Someone you just met . . . 5
Someone you paid to have sex . . . 6
Someone who paid you to have sex . . . 7
Someone you didn't know, a stranger . . . 8
Someone else? (SPECIFY) . . . 9

B. In what ways were you forced to have sex? RECORD VERBATIM AND CODE ALL THAT APPLY.

THREATS OF OR USE OF PHYSICAL FORCE 1
THREATS TO USE OR USE OF WEAPON, SUCH AS A KNIFE OR GUN 2
OTHER THREATS OR INTIMIDATION (COERCION, BLACKMAIL, THREATS TO OTHERS) 3
-(Q.23, P. 8.9)

8.7

C. **HAND CARD #9** There are many different reasons why people decide to have vaginal intercourse for the first time. What was the main reason you chose to have vaginal intercourse for the first time? CODE ONE ONLY.

```
affection for partner . . . . . . . .  1
peer pressure . . . . . . . . . . . .  2
curious/ready for sex . . . . . . . .  3
wanted to have a baby . . . . . . . .  4  ⎫
physical pleasure . . . . . . . . . .  5  ⎬ (Q.22)
under the influence of                    ⎭
   drugs or alcohol . . . . . . . . .  6
wedding night . . . . . . . . . . . .  7
other (SPECIFY)_____ . . .  8

DON'T KNOW/DON'T REMEMBER . . . . . . 98
```

D. **HAND CARD #9** There are many different reasons why people go along with having vaginal intercourse for the first time, even when they don't want to. What was the main reason you decided to go along with having sexual intercourse this first time? CODE ONE ONLY

```
affection for partner . . . . . . . .  1
peer pressure . . . . . . . . . . . .  2
curious/ready for sex . . . . . . . .  3
wanted to have a baby . . . . . . . .  4  ⎫
physical pleasure . . . . . . . . . .  5  ⎬ (Q.22)
under the influence of                    ⎭
   drugs or alcohol . . . . . . . . .  6
wedding night . . . . . . . . . . . .  7
other (SPECIFY)_____ . . .  8

DON'T KNOW/DON'T REMEMBER . . . . . . 98
```

22. **HAND CARD #8** The _first_ time you had vaginal intercourse with this person, what was your relationship to (OPPOSITE SEX OF R; him/her)?

```
Spouse . . . . . . . . . . . . . . . . . .  1(Q.24)
Someone you were in love
   with but not married to . . . . . . . .  2
Someone you knew well but
   were not in love with . . . . . . . . .  3
Someone you knew but not well . . . . . .  4
Someone you just met . . . . . . . . . . .  5
Someone you paid to have sex . . . . . . .  6
Someone who paid you to have sex . . . . .  7
Someone you didn't know, a stranger . . .  8
Someone else? (SPECIFY)_____ . . . .  9
```

23. Was this person a relative?

```
Yes . . . . . . . . . . . .  1(A)
No  . . . . . . . . . . . .  2(Q.24)
```

A. What was their relationship to you? RECORD VERBATIM AND CODE
   _____

```
FATHER . . . . . . . . . . . . . . . .  1
MOTHER . . . . . . . . . . . . . . . .  2
BROTHER . . . . . . . . . . . . . . . .  3
SISTER . . . . . . . . . . . . . . . .  4
UNCLE . . . . . . . . . . . . . . . . .  5
AUNT . . . . . . . . . . . . . . . . .  6
COUSIN . . . . . . . . . . . . . . . .  7
OTHER_____ . . . . . . . . .  8
```

24. Did you or your partner use birth control this first time?

```
Yes . . . . . . . . .  1
No  . . . . . . . . .  2
DON'T KNOW . . . . .  8
```

654

25. **HAND CARD #7** What happened sexually? Just give me the numbers from this card. CODE ALL THAT APPLY.

```
01
02
03
04
05
06
```

26. How many times did you have vaginal intercourse with that person? Was it...

```
just one time. . . . . . . . . . . . 1
two to ten times . . . . . . . . . . 2
or more than ten times? . . . . . . 3
STILL HAVING INTERCOURSE . . . . . . 4
```

BOX	WAS FIRST SEX FORCED? (SEE Q.21)
8-A	YES. 1 (Q.28)
	NO 2 (Q.27)

27. After puberty, that is after you were (AGE IN Q.1./12 or 13 years old), did a (OPPOSITE SEX OF R - male/female) force you to do anything sexually that you did not want to do?

```
Yes . . . . . . . . . 1 (Q.29)
No . . . . . . . . . . 2 (BOX 8-B, PAGE 8.12)
```

28. Other than the first time, have you ever been forced by a (OPPOSITE SEX OF R; male/female) to do anything sexually that you did not want to do?

```
Yes . . . . . . . . . 1 (ASK Q.29)
No . . . . . . . . . . 2 (BOX 8-B, PAGE 8.12)
```

29. With how many different persons did this happen?

|___|___| NUMBER

IF ONE, ASK Q.30.

IF TWO OR MORE, SKIP TO Q.33, P. 8.12.

30. **HAND CARD #8** What was your relationship to that person?
CODE ONLY ONE

```
Spouse . . . . . . . . . . . . . . . . . . 1
Someone you were in love
  with but not married to . . . . . . . 2
Someone you knew well but
  were not in love with . . . . . . . . 3
Someone you knew but not well . . . . . 4
Someone you just met . . . . . . . . . . 5
Someone you paid to have sex . . . . . . 6
Someone who paid you to have sex . . . . 7
Someone you didn't know, a stranger . . 8
Someone else? (SPECIFY) . . . . . . . . 9
_____
```

31. How many times did this happen?

|___|___| NUMBER

32. **HAND CARD #7** What happened sexually? Just give me the numbers from this card. CODE ALL THAT APPLY.

```
01
02   -- (SKIP TO BOX
03       8B, PG 8.12)
04
05
06
```

33. **HAND CARD #8** Thinking about these persons, how many were........

Spouse . . . . |___|___|
Someone you were in love
  with but not married to . . . . |___|___|
Someone you knew well but
  were not in love with . . . . . . |___|___|
Someone you knew but not well . . |___|___|
Someone you just met . . . . . . |___|___|
Someone you paid to have sex . . |___|___|
Someone who paid you to have sex . . |___|___|
Someone you didn't know, a stranger . . |___|___|
Someone else? (SPECIFY)_____ |___|___|

34. With how many persons did this happen......

just one time . . . . |___|___|
two to ten times . . . . |___|___|
or more than ten times? . . . . . |___|___|

HAND CARD #7 Which of the following ever happened sexually? Just give
me the numbers on this card. CODE ALL THAT APPLY.

01
02
03
04
05
06

BOX	WAS FIRST VAGINAL INTERCOURSE BEFORE AGE 18? (SEE Q. 20, PG 8.7)	
8-B	YES.	. . .1 (Q.35)
	NO.	. . .2 (Q.40, PG. 8.14)
	NEVER HAD VAGINAL INTERCOURSE.	. . .3 (Q.40, PG. 8.14)

8.12

---

35. Other than this first person (and/or any forced sex you already told me
about), how many different (OPPOSITE SEX OF R; males/females) did you
have vaginal intercourse with before you were 18 [17 if R is 18 at time
of interview]?

|___|___|
NUMBER

IF NONE................................00 (GO TO Q.40, PG. 8.14)
IF ONE.................................01 (GO TO Q.36)
IF MORE THAN ONE.......................02 (GO TO Q.38)

36. How many times did you have vaginal intercourse with that person? Was
it...

just one time. 1
two to ten times? 2
or more than ten times? 3
STILL HAVING INTERCOURSE 4

37. **HAND CARD #8** What was your relationship to that person?

Spouse 1
Someone you were in love
  with but not married to 2
Someone you knew well but
  were not in love with 3
Someone you knew but not well 4
Someone you just met 5
Someone you paid to have sex 6
Someone who paid you to have sex 7
Someone you didn't know, a stranger . . . 8
Someone else? (SPECIFY)_____ . . . 9

(SKIP TO Q.40, PG. 8.14)

38. How many of these persons did you have vaginal intercourse with...

just one time . . . . |___|___|
two to ten times . . . . |___|___|
or more than ten times? . . . . |___|___|

8.13

39. **HAND CARD #8** The first time you had sex with these people, how many of these partners were... (READ EACH CATEGORY BELOW). FOR EACH, RECORD NUMBER OF PARTNERS.

Spouse . . . . |_|_|
Someone you were in love
  with but not married to . . . |_|_|
Someone you knew well but
  were not in love with. . . . . |_|_|
Someone you just met . . . . . . |_|_|
Someone you knew but not well. . |_|_|
Someone you paid to have sex . . |_|_|
Someone who paid you to have sex |_|_|
Someone you didn't know, a stranger |_|_|
Someone else? (SPECIFY)_____

👉 40. Now I would like to ask you some questions about sexual experience with (SAME SEX AS R; males/females) after you were 12 or 13, that is, after puberty. How old were you the first time that you had sex with a (SAME SEX AS R; male/female)?

ENTER AGE |_|_|

NEVER . . . . 00 (Q.47, PG. 8.19)

41. Was this ....

something you wanted to happen
  at the time . . . . 1 (ASK C)
something you went along with,
  but did not strongly desire, or . . 2 (ASK D)
something that you were forced
  to do against your will? . . . . 3 (ASK A)

8.14

A. **HAND CARD #10** What was your relationship to this person? RECORD VERBATIM

Someone you were in love with . . . 1
Someone you knew well but
  were not in love with. . . . 2
Someone you knew but not well . . . 3
Someone you just met 4
Someone you paid to have sex . . . 5
Someone who paid you to have sex . . 6
Someone you didn't know, a stranger . 7
A relative 8
Someone else? (SPECIFY)_____ . 9

B. In what ways were you forced to have sex? RECORD VERBATIM CODE ALL THAT APPLY.

_____

THREATS OF OR USE OF PHYSICAL FORCE . . . 1
THREATS TO USE OR USE OF WEAPON,
  SUCH AS A KNIFE OR GUN . . . 2   -(Q.43, PG. 8.16)
OTHER THREATS OR INTIMIDATION (COERCION) . 3
BLACKMAIL, THREATS TO OTHERS)

C. **HAND CARD #11** There are many reasons why people decide to have sexual activity for the first time with a person of the same sex. What was the main reason you chose to have sexual contact for the first time? CODE ONE ONLY

affection for partner 1
peer pressure 2
curious/ready for sex 3   (Q.42, PG. 8.16)
physical pleasure 4
under the influence of
  drugs or alcohol 5
Other (SPECIFY)_____ . 6

DON'T KNOW/DON'T REMEMBER 98

8.15

D. **HAND CARD #11** There are many reasons why people go along with having sexual activity for the first time with a person of the same sex, even when they don't want to. What was the main reason you decided to go along with having sexual contact this first time?
CODE ONE ONLY

affection for partner 1
peer pressure 2
curious/ready for sex 3
physical pleasure . . . . 4 ⎫ (Q.42)
under the influence of
 drugs or alcohol 5
Other (SPECIFY)_____ . . . 6

DON'T KNOW/DON'T REMEMBER 98

42. **HAND CARD #10** What was your relationship to the person at the time that you had sexual activity with for the first time?

Someone you were in love with 1
Someone you knew well but
 were not in love with 2
Someone you knew but not well 3
Someone you just met 4
Someone you paid to have sex 5
Someone who paid you to have sex 6
Someone you didn't know, a stranger 7
A relative 8
Someone else? (SPECIFY)_____ . . 9

43. Was your first (SAME SEX AS R: male/female) partner older, younger or the same age as you?

Older . . . . 1 (ASK A)
Younger . . . . 2 (ASK A)
Same Age . . . . 3 (Q. 44)

A. How many years (older/younger) than you?

|__|__| YEARS YOUNGER/OLDER

8.16

44. What did this involve? Just give me the number on the card. CODE ALL THAT APPLY.

HAND CARD #12 FOR MALE R.   **HAND CARD #13 FOR FEMALE R.**

01   11
02   12
03   13
04   14
05   15
06   16
07   17

45. How many times did you have sex with that person after the first time? Was it...

never again 1
just one time 2
two to ten times 3
or more than ten times? 4
STILL HAVING SEX 5

BOX 8-C	WAS FIRST SAME SEX FORCED? (SEE Q.41, PG. 8.14)
	YES. 1 (Q.45B)
	NO 2 (Q.45A)

A. Have you ever been forced to do anything sexual that you did not want to do by a person of the same sex?

Yes . . . . 1 (ASK C)
No . . . . 2 (BOX 8-D, PG. 8.18)

B. Other than this first time, have you ever been forced to do anything sexual that you did not want to do by a person of the same sex?

Yes . . . . 1 (ASK C)
No . . . . 2 (BOX 8-D, PG. 8.18)

C. How many times has this happened?

|__|__|

8.17

D. **HAND CARD #7** What kind(s) of sexual activity happened? Just give me numbers from this card. CODE ALL THAT APPLY.

01
02
03
04
05
06

BOX 8-D	WAS FIRST SAME SEX PARTNER BEFORE AGE 18? (SEE Q.40, PG. 8.14)
	YES......1 (Q. 46)
	NO.......2 (Q. 47)

46. Other than this first person, how many different (SAME SEX AS R - males/females) did you have sex with before you were 18 [17 if R is 18 at time of interview]?

|___|___|
NUMBER

IF NONE . . . . 00 (Q.47, PG. 8.19)
IF ONE . . . . 01 (A,B)
IF MORE THAN ONE . . . 02 (C,D)

A. How many times did you have sex with that person? Was it...

just one time 1
two to ten times 2
or more than ten times? . . 3
STILL HAVING SEX 4

B. **HAND CARD #10** What was your relationship to that person?

Someone you were in love with 1
Someone you knew well but were not in love with . . 2
Someone you knew but not well 3
Someone you just met 4
Someone you paid to have sex 5
Someone who paid you to have sex 6
Someone you didn't know, a stranger 7
A relative 8
Someone else? (SPECIFY)_____ 9

-(Q.47, Pg. 8.19)

8.18

C. How many of these persons did you have sex with...

only once? 01
2-10 times? . . . . . |___|
more than 10 times? . . |___|

D. **HAND CARD #10** How many of these partners were ...

Someone you were in love with . . . . 01 |___|___|
Someone you knew well but were not in love with . 02 |___|___|
Someone you knew but not well . . . . 03 |___|___|
Someone you just met . . . . 04 |___|___|
Someone you paid to have sex . . . . 05 |___|___|
Someone who paid you to have sex . . . . 06 |___|___|
Someone you didn't know, a stranger . . . . . . 07 |___|___|
A relative . . . . 08 |___|___|
Someone else? (SPECIFY)_____ 09 |___|___|

FEMALE R ONLY:

47. In general, are you sexually attracted to . .

only men, ... 01
mostly men, ... 02
both men and women, . . 03
mostly women, ... 04
only women? 05

MALE R ONLY:

48. In general are you sexually attracted to .

only women, ... 01
mostly women, ... 02
both women and men, . . 03
mostly men, ... 04
only men? 05

49. Do you think of yourself as...

heterosexual, ... 01
homosexual, ... 02
bisexual, ... 03
or something else? (SPECIFY)_____ 04
NORMAL/STRAIGHT 05
DON'T KNOW 98

CONTINUE TO SECTION 9

8.19

SECTION 9: PHYSICAL HEALTH

Now I would like to ask you a few questions about your health and some health related topics.

1. In general, would you say your health is . . .

   excellent, ... 1
   good, ... 2
   fair, or 3
   poor? 4

2. **MALES ONLY:** Are you circumcised?

   Yes 1
   No 2

3. Have you ever received a blood transfusion?

   Yes . . . . 1 (ASK A)
   No . . . . 2 (Q. 4)

   A. In what month and year did you receive a blood transfusion?

      (Record all occurrences)

      |___|___|
       MO   YR

      |___|___|
       MO   YR

      |___|___|
       MO   YR

      |___|___|
       MO   YR

4. Generally, how happy have you been with your personal life during the past 12 months? Have you been . . .

   Extremely happy, ... 1
   Very happy most of the time, ... 2
   Generally satisfied, pleased, ... 3
   Sometimes fairly unhappy, or 4
   Unhappy most of the time? 5

9.1

THIS PAGE LEFT INTENTIONALLY BLANK

Sometimes people go through periods in which they are not interested in sex or are having trouble achieving sexual gratification. I have just a few questions about whether you have experienced this in the past 12 months.

10. During the last 12 months has there ever been a period of several months or more when you...(READ A-H BELOW) CIRCLE YES OR NO FOR EACH. NOTE: IF NO SEX DURING LAST 12 MONTHS, SKIP C,D & E.

	Yes	No
A. lacked interest in having sex?	1	2
B. were unable to come to a climax (experience an orgasm)?	1	2
C. came to a climax (experienced an orgasm) too quickly?	1	2
D. experienced physical pain during intercourse?	1	2
E. did not find sex pleasurable (even if it was not painful)?	1	2
F. felt anxious just before having sex about your ability to perform sexually?	1	2
MALE R's ONLY:		
G. had trouble achieving or maintaining an erection?	1	2
FEMALE R's ONLY:		
H. had trouble lubricating?	1	2

IF R ANSWERED "NO" TO ALL OF THE ABOVE SKIP TO INTRODUCTION TO Q. 13, P. 9.6. OTHERWISE, ASK Q. 11.

11. During the past 12 months, have you ever avoided sex because of the problem(s) you mentioned?

Yes 1
No 2

9.3

5. During the past 12 months, about how regularly did you drink alcoholic beverages? Would you say that it was . . .

Daily, ... 1
Several times a week, ... 2
Several times a month, ... 3
Once a month or less, or 4
Not at all? 5 (Q.7)

6. On a typical day when you drank, about how many drinks did you usually have?

ENTER NUMBER |__|

7. During the past 12 months, how much of the time has your physical health interfered with your sexual activities? Would you say that it was . . .

all of the time, ... 1
most of the time, ... 2
some of the time, ... 3
a little of the time, or 4
none of the time? 5

8. During the past 12 months, how much of the time have emotional problems interfered with your sexual activities? Would you say that it was . . .

all of the time, ... 1
most of the time, ... 2
some of the time, ... 3
a little of the time, or 4
none of the time? 5

9. During the past 12 months, how much of the time has stress or pressures in your life interfered with your sexual activities? Would you say that it was . . .

all of the time, ... 1
most of the time, ... 2
some of the time, ... 3
a little of the time, or 4
none of the time? 5

9.2

12. Sometimes when people have problems like this, they go to someone for help such as a doctor or a counselor of some sort. In the past 12 months, have you gone to any of the following people for help with the sexual problem(s) you have experienced:

	<u>Yes</u>	<u>No</u>
A private psychiatrist or psychologist?	1	2
A psychiatrist or psychologist in a clinic?	1	2
Another type of private doctor?	1	2
Another type of doctor in a clinic?	1	2
A marriage counselor?	1	2
A clergy person?	1	2
Someone else? (SPECIFY)_____ .	1	2

THIS PAGE LEFT INTENTIONALLY BLANK

There are several diseases or infections that can be transmitted during sex. These are sometimes called venereal diseases or VD. We will be using the term sexually transmitted diseases or STD's to refer to them.

13. Now I would like to ask you a few questions about these diseases.

(ASK ALL RESPONDENTS A. ASK B-E FOR EACH STD CIRCLED YES (1) IN A. IF ALL NO (2), SKIP TO Q. 14, P. 9.8.)

A. HAND CARD #14. As I read each STD, tell me whether you have ever been told by a doctor that you had it. (READ & CIRCLE "YES" OR "NO" FOR EACH.)

B. How many times have you ever been told by a doctor you had (STD)?

C. Have you been told by a doctor you had (STD) in the past 12 months?

	A. YES NO	B.	C. YES NO
a. Gonorrhea (clap, drip)	1 2	|_|_|	1 2
b. Syphilis (bad blood)	1 2	|_|_|	1 2
c. Herpes (genital herpes)	1 2	|_|_|	1 2
d. Chlamydia	1 2	|_|_|	1 2
e. Genital Warts (venereal warts, Human Papilloma Virus or HPV)	1 2	|_|_|	1 2
f. Hepatitis	1 2	|_|_|	1 2
g. AIDS, HIV	1 2	|_|_|	1 2
h. FEMALE R'S ONLY Vaginitis - such as Yeast Infection or Candidiasis, Trich or Trichomonas (Trichomoniasis)	1 2	|_|_|	1 2
i. FEMALE R'S ONLY Pelvic Inflammatory Disease (PID)	1 2	|_|_|	1 2
j. MALE R'S ONLY NGU (Nongonococcal Urethritis)	1 2	|_|_|	1 2
k. OTHER (Specify:) _____	1 2	|_|_|	1 2

IF ALL "NO", SKIP TO Q. 14, PG. 9.8.

9.6

D. Where did you go for treatment? CIRCLE FOR EACH YES IN COLUMN D.

Was it . . .
private or group practice . 1
a hospital emergency room . 2
family planning clinic. . . 3
an STD clinic 4
some other clinic 5
somewhere else? 6

E. Which partner do you think may have given you (STD)? RECORD NAME IN SPACE BELOW

	D.	E.
a.	1 2 3 4 5 6	a. _____
b.	1 2 3 4 5 6	b. _____
c.	1 2 3 4 5 6	c. _____
d.	1 2 3 4 5 6	d. _____
e.	1 2 3 4 5 6	e. _____
f.	1 2 3 4 5 6	f. _____
g.	1 2 3 4 5 6	g. _____
h.	1 2 3 4 5 6	h. Or not partner-related (such as yeast infection)? _____
i.	1 2 3 4 5 6	i. _____
j.	1 2 3 4 5 6	j. _____
k.	1 2 3 4 5 6	k. _____

GO TO BOX 9-A ON NEXT PAGE

9.7

14. Have you ever wondered if you had a sexually-transmitted disease?

Yes 1
No 2

BOX	SEE Q. 13, COL. D. ARE ANY "4'S" CIRCLED (HAS RESPONDENT GONE TO AN STD CLINIC)?
9-A	YES. . . . . 1 (GO TO Q.16) NO. . . . . 2 (Q. 15)

15. Have you ever gone to a sexually-transmitted disease or STD clinic for any reason?

Yes 1
No . . . . 2 (GO TO Q.18)

16. When was the most recent time you visited an STD clinic?

|___|___| |___|
MONTH   YEAR

17. What was your main reason for going to the STD clinic? RECORD VERBATIM.

REFERRED BY A SEXUAL PARTNER? 1

CONTACTED BY THE CLINIC AS A
CONTACT TO AN STD CASE? 2

EXPERIENCING SYMPTOMS? 3

GOING FOR AN STD FOLLOW UP? 4

FOR A CHECK-UP? 5

GOING FOR SOME OTHER REASON? 6

18. During the past 12 months, have you ever experienced any of the following symptoms:

	Yes	No
painful or difficult urination?	1	2
painful intercourse?	1	2
lesions or sores in the genital area? . . .	1	2
intense chronic itching of genital area? . .	1	2
(FEMALE R's ONLY:) vaginal discharge?	1	2

19. Next, I am going to read you some methods that people use to prevent getting the AIDS virus through sexual activity. For each one, please tell me whether you think it is very effective, somewhat effective, or not at all effective in preventing someone from getting the AIDS virus through sexual activity.

	Very Effective	Somewhat Effective	Not at all Effective
A. Using a diaphragm?	3	2	1
B. Using a condom?	3	2	1
C. Using a spermicidal jelly, foam, or cream?	3	2	1
D. Using a condom w/a spermicide jelly, foam or cream?	3	2	1
E. Having a vasectomy?	3	2	1
F. Two people who do not have the AIDS virus having sex only with each other?	3	2	1

20. Have you made any kind of changes in your sexual behavior because of AIDS?

    Yes . . . . 1 (Q. 21)
    No . . . . 2 (Q. 22)

21. What have you changed? RECORD VERBATIM.

    _____

    _____

    _____

22. How many people have you known personally, either living or dead, who came down with the disease called AIDS?

    |__|__|
     NUMBER

    None . . . . 00 (GO TO SECTION 10)

23. HAND CARD #15 Think about the person you have known best, living or dead, who came down with AIDS. Please tell me the letter of the category on the card which best describes your relationship to that person.

    A. Husband or wife 01
    B. Partner or lover 02
    C. Son or daughter 03
    D. Other relative 04
    E. Friend 05
    F. Neighbor 06
    G. Co-worker 07
    H. Acquaintance 08
    I. Patient 09
    J. Other 10

24. We would like to know a few other things about that person.

    A. Is that person currently living, or has that person died?

       Living 1
       Died 2

B. (Is/Was) that person male or female?

   Male 1
   Female 2

C. How old (is/was) that person? (Is/Was) (he/she)...

   10 years or under 1
   11 - 20 2
   21 - 40 3
   Or 41 years or older 4

D. What (is/was) that person's race? (Is/Was) it black, white, Hispanic or other?

   Black 1
   White 2
   Hispanic 3
   Other 4

E. What state does/did this person live in?

   State_____ |__|

BOX
9-B
   IF Q. 22 EQUALS 1 . . . . 1 (GO TO SECTION 10)
   IF Q. 22 EQUALS 2 OR MORE . . . 2 (ASK Q. 25)

25. HAND CARD #15 Think about the person you have known next best, living or dead, who came down with AIDS. Please tell me the letter of the category on the card which best describes your relationship to that person.

   A. Husband or wife 01
   B. Partner or lover 02
   C. Son or daughter 03
   D. Other relative 04
   E. Friend 05
   F. Neighbor 06
   G. Co-worker 07
   H. Acquaintance 08
   I. Patient 09
   J. Other 10

26. We would like to know a few other things about that person.

A. Is that person currently living, or has that person died?

    Living 1
    Died 2

B. (Is/Was) that person male or female?

    Male 1
    Female 2

C. How old (is/was) that person? (Is/Was) (he/she). . . .

    10 years or under 1
    11 - 20 2
    21 - 40 3
    Or 41 years or older 4

D. What (is/was) that person's race? (Is/Was) it black, white, Hispanic or other?

    Black 1
    White 2
    Hispanic 3
    Other 4

E. What state does/did this person live in?

    State _____ |_|_|

BOX	
9-C	IF Q. 22 EQUALS 2 . . . . . 1 (GO TO SECTION 10)
	IF Q. 22 EQUALS 3 OR MORE. . . . 2 (ASK Q. 27)

27. **HAND CARD #15** Think about the person you have known next best, living or dead, who came down with AIDS. Please tell me the letter of the category on the card which best describes your relationship to that person.

    A. Husband or wife 01
    B. Partner or lover 02
    C. Son or daughter 03
    D. Other relative 04
    E. Friend 05
    F. Neighbor 06
    G. Co-worker 07
    H. Acquaintance 08
    I. Patient 09
    J. Other 10

28. We would like to know a few other things about that person.

A. Is that person currently living, or has that person died?

    Living 1
    Died 2

B. (Is/Was) that person male or female?

    Male 1
    Female 2

C. How old (is/was) that person? (Is/Was) (he/she). . .

    10 years or under 1
    11 - 20 2
    21 - 40 3
    Or 41 years or older 4

D. What (is/was) that person's race? (Is/Was) it black, white, Hispanic or other?

    Black 1
    White 2
    Hispanic 3
    Other 4

E. What state does/did this person live in?

    State _____ |_|_|

BOX	
9-D	IF Q. 22 EQUALS 3 OR MORE . . . YOU NEED NOT RECORD MORE THAN 3.

666

1. There's been a lot of discussion about the way morals and attitudes about sex are changing in this country. If a man and a woman have sex relations before marriage, do you think it is always wrong, almost always wrong, wrong only sometimes, or not wrong at all?

   always wrong 1
   almost always wrong 2
   wrong only sometimes 3
   not wrong at all 4

2. What if they are in their teens, say 14-16 years old? In that case, do you think sex relations before marriage are always wrong, almost always wrong, wrong only sometimes, or not wrong at all?

   always wrong 1
   almost always wrong 2
   wrong only sometimes 3
   not wrong at all 4

3. What is your opinion about a married person having sexual relations with someone other than the marriage partner--is it always wrong, almost always wrong, sometimes wrong, or not wrong at all?

   always wrong 1
   almost always wrong 2
   wrong only sometimes 3
   not wrong at all 4

4. What is your opinion about sexual relations between two adults of the same sex -- do you think it is always wrong, almost always wrong, wrong only sometimes, or not wrong at all.

   always wrong 1
   almost always wrong 2
   wrong only sometimes 3
   not wrong at all 4

THIS PAGE LEFT INTENTIONALLY BLANK

10.1

5. When do you think a woman is most likely to become pregnant? Is it . . .

   right before her period 1
   during her period 2
   right after her period 3
   about 2 weeks after
     her period begins 4
   anytime during the
     cycle? 5
   DON'T KNOW 8

<u>HAND CARD #16 FOR Q. 6-14</u>

Please tell me if you strongly agree, agree, disagree, or strongly disagree with the following statements.

6. Men have greater sexual needs than women.

   strongly agree 1
   agree 2
   disagree 3
   strongly disagree 4

7. Any kind of sexual activity between adults is okay as long as both persons freely agree to it.

   strongly agree 1
   agree 2
   disagree 3
   strongly disagree 4

8. There should be laws against the sale of pornography to adults (persons 18 years of age and older).

   strongly agree 1
   agree 2
   disagree 3
   strongly disagree 4

9. I am a better lover after a drink or two.

   strongly agree 1
   agree 2
   disagree 3
   strongly disagree 4
   I DON'T DRINK 5

10. I feel guilty when I think about someone else when I am having sex with my partner.

    strongly agree 1
    agree 2
    disagree 3
    strongly disagree . . . 4
    NA 5

11. You don't need to use a condom if you know your partner well.

    strongly agree 1
    agree 2
    disagree 3
    strongly disagree . . . 4

12. I would not have sex with someone unless I was in love with them.

    strongly agree 1
    agree 2
    disagree 3
    strongly disagree . . . 4

13. My religious beliefs have shaped and guided my sexual behavior.

    strongly agree 1
    agree 2
    disagree 3
    strongly disagree . . . 4

14. I try to make sure that my partner has an orgasm when we have sex.

    strongly agree 1
    agree 2
    disagree 3
    strongly disagree . . . 4
    NA 5

668

SECTION 11: INTERVIEWER COMMENTS

PLEASE COMPLETE THESE QUESTIONS WHILE RESPONDENT IS COMPLETING SELF-ADMINISTERED QUESTIONS OR AS SOON AS YOU LEAVE RESPONDENT.

1. WHAT IS YOUR INTERVIEWER ID? |__|__|__|__|__|

2. WHO IS YOUR FIELD MANAGER? _____

3. DATE CASE COMPLETED: MONTH |__|__| DAY |__|__| YEAR 199 |__|

4. WHAT OTHER PERSONS WERE PRESENT DURING THE INTERVIEW? CIRCLE ALL THAT APPLY.

CHILDREN UNDER 6 1
OLDER CHILDREN 2
SPOUSE/PARTNER 3
OTHER RELATIVES 4
OTHER ADULTS 5
NO ONE AT ALL 6

5. R'S GENERAL UNDERSTANDING OF THE QUESTIONS WAS . . . .

EXCELLENT . . . 1
GOOD 2
FAIR 3
POOR 4

6. HOW COOPERATIVE WAS THE R DURING MOST OF THE INTERVIEW?

VERY COOPERATIVE 1
SOMEWHAT COOPERATIVE 2
NOT VERY COOPERATIVE 3
NOT AT ALL COOPERATIVE . . . 4

7. WHAT SUBJECTS OR PARTICULAR QUESTIONS DID THE R REFUSE TO DISCUSS OR SEEM TO BE SENSITIVE ABOUT?

11.1

---

15. Please tell me whether or not you think it should be possible for a pregnant woman to obtain a legal abortion . . .

a. if she became pregnant as a result of rape?

yes 1
no 2
DK 8
NA 9

b. if the woman wants it for any reason?

yes 1
no 2
DK 8
NA 9

16. Who do you think usually enjoys sex more -- men, women, or do they both enjoy it the same amount?

men 1
women 2
BOTH THE SAME 3
DK 8

BOX
10.1

ADMINISTER SAQ #4 AT THIS TIME. IF R CANNOT READ AND ASKS FOR YOUR HELP, YOU MAY ASSIST HIM/HER IN FILLING OUT THIS FORM.

READ THE FOLLOWING TO R:
Now I have another form for you to fill out yourself. Please read the questions and circle the appropriate code. When you are finished place the sheet in the "privacy" envelope and seal it.

R filled out SAQ 1
Interviewer assisted with SAQ . . . 2
R refused SAQ 7

Thank you very much for participating in this study. We greatly appreciate your time. Your help on this survey will have influence on how we as a nation deal with sexual issues and diseases like AIDS.

INTERVIEWER: RECORD TIME |__|__:|__|__| AM....1 PM....2

10.4

8. WHICH SECTIONS OF THE QUESTIONNAIRE DID THE R SEEM TO BE SENSITIVE ABOUT?

[LIST HERE]

9. HOW FRANK WAS THE R?

ENTIRELY FRANK 1
MOSTLY FRANK 2
SOMEWHAT FRANK 3
PROBABLY NOT FRANK 4

10. HOW DID YOU FEEL ABOUT THE R?

STRONGLY LIKED R 1
LIKED R SOMEWHAT 2
WAS INDIFFERENT TO R 3
DISLIKED R SOMEWHAT 4
STRONGLY DISLIKED R 5

11. WHAT ELSE WOULD YOU LIKE TO ADD THAT WOULD HELP US BETTER UNDERSTAND THE R AS A PERSON OR THE CONDITIONS UNDER WHICH THE INTERVIEW TOOK PLACE?

12. TYPE OF STRUCTURE IN WHICH R LIVES:

TRAILER 01
DETACHED SINGLE FAMILY HOUSE 02
2 FAMILY HOUSE, 2 UNITS SIDE BY SIDE . . 03
2 FAMILY HOUSE, 2 UNITS ONE ABOVE THE OTHER . 04
DETACHED 3-4 UNIT APARTMENT HOUSE . . 05
ROWHOUSE (3 OR MORE UNITS IN AN ATTACHED ROW) . 06
APARTMENT HOUSE (5 OR MORE UNITS,
  3 STORIES OR LESS) 07
APARTMENT HOUSE (5 OR MORE UNITS,
  4 STORIES OR MORE) 08
APARTMENT IN A PARTLY COMMERCIAL STRUCTURE . 09
OTHER (SPECIFY:)

_____ . . 10

11.2

13. COMPARED TO HOUSE/APARTMENTS IN THE NEIGHBORHOOD, WOULD YOU SAY THE HOUSE/APARTMENT WAS...

FAR ABOVE AVERAGE 05
ABOVE AVERAGE 04
AVERAGE 03
BELOW AVERAGE 02
FAR BELOW AVERAGE 01

14. COUNTING THIS CASE, HOW MANY INTERVIEWS HAVE YOU COMPLETED FOR THIS SURVEY SO FAR?

THIS IS MY FIRST CASE . . . 01
SECOND CASE 02
THIRD CASE 03
FOURTH CASE 04
FIFTH CASE 05
SIXTH CASE 06
SEVENTH CASE 07
EIGHTH CASE 08
NINTH CASE 09
TENTH CASE 10
ELEVENTH CASE OR MORE . . . 11

15. HOW MANY SEPARATE ATTEMPTS (PHONE CONTACTS, PERSONAL VISITS) WERE MADE TO COMPLETE THIS CASE? COUNT THE INTERVIEW AS AN ATTEMPT.

|___|___| ATTEMPTS

16. HOW MANY OF THESE ATTEMPTS WERE IN PERSON VISITS?

|___|___| IN-PERSON VISITS

17. HOW DIFFICULT WAS THIS CASE TO GET?

VERY EASY 1
SOMEWHAT EASY 2
SOMEWHAT DIFFICULT 3
VERY DIFFICULT 4

18. ABOUT HOW LONG WAS THE INTERVIEW TIME?

|___| HOUR(S) AND |___|___| MINUTES

19. COUNTING EVERYTHING -- TRAVEL, CONTACTS, PHONE CALLS, IN-PERSON VISITS, THE INTERVIEW, MAILING CASE -- ABOUT HOW LONG DID IT TAKE TO COMPLETE THIS CASE?

|___|___| HOUR(S) AND |___|___| MINUTES

11.3

D

CASE I.D. |__|__|__|__|__|__|

NORC
5408
2/92

Self-Administered Questionnaire

CONFIDENTIAL

Please place this questionnaire in the "privacy" envelope. It will be sealed at the end of the interview.

National Health and Social Life Survey (NHSLS)
University of Chicago
NORC

---

20. WHICH OF THE FOLLOWING WERE DONE ON THIS CASE?   (CIRCLE ALL THAT APPLY)

SPECIAL PERMISSION TO ACCESS LOCKED
BUILDING OR SECURE COMMUNITY 01

NOTE OR LETTER LEFT AT DOOR 02
NOTE OR LETTER MAILED TO R 03
    (ATTACH COPY IF POSSIBLE)

SPECIALIZED LETTER FROM FM 04
SPECIALIZED LETTER FROM CHICAGO OFFICE . 05
SPECIALIZED LETTER FROM CLIENT 06
CERTIFIED LETTER 07
MAILGRAM OR FED EX LETTER 08

RESPONDENT FEE (AMOUNT _____) . . . 09

CASE TRANSFER TO ANOTHER INTERVIEWER . . 10

IN-PERSON CONVERSION ATTEMPT 11
PHONE CONVERSION ATTEMPT 12
CHICAGO OFFICE PHONE CONVERSION ATTEMPT . 13
CLIENT PHONE CONVERSION ATTEMPT 14
NONE 00

OTHER SPECIAL EFFORT (SPECIFY:)

_____
_____
_____ . 15

21. WHAT CAN WE LEARN FROM THIS CASE ABOUT HOW TO RUN THIS SURVEY BETTER?

11.4

Write in below your best estimate of your yearly household income <u>before taxes</u> for all of 1991. Include your spouse's (husband, wife, or live-in partner) income where asked. EVERY LINE SHOULD HAVE DOLLAR AMOUNT ENTRY. IF YOU DID NOT RECEIVE ANY INCOME FROM A SOURCE, ENTER A ZERO, "0."

		AMOUNT RECEIVED 1991
SOURCE		
A.	Your own wage-earnings IF NONE: ENTER "0"	$ |___|.|___|___|___|.|___|___|___|
B.	Your spouse's/partner's wage-earnings IF NONE: ENTER '0'	$ |___|.|___|___|___|.|___|___|___|
C.	Additional household member's wage earnings IF NONE: ENTER "0"	$ |___|.|___|___|___|.|___|___|___|
D.	Child support and alimony. IF NONE: ENTER "0"	$ |___|.|___|___|___|.|___|___|___|
E.	Other income from investments to any household member (eg. interest, dividends, rental, pension) IF NONE: ENTER "0"	$ |___|.|___|___|___|.|___|___|___|
F.	Other income from government programs to any household member (eg. social security, unemployment, AFDC, welfare). IF NONE: ENTER"0"	$ |___|.|___|___|___|.|___|___|___|
G.	Gifts, fellowships, all other sources IF NONE: ENTER "0"	$ |___|.|___|___|___|.|___|___|___|
TOTAL HOUSEHOLD INCOME (ADD TOGETHER PARTS a-g)		$ |___|.|___|___|___|.|___|___|___|

**THANK YOU FOR YOUR COOPERATION.
PLEASE PLACE FORM IN PRIVACY ENVELOPE.**

There is a great deal of concern today about the AIDS epidemic and how to deal with it. Because of the grave nature of this problem, we are going to ask you some personal questions and we need your frank and honest responses. Your answers are confidential and will be used only for statistical reports.

The Past 12 Months

1. How many sex partners have you had in the last 12 months?

   PLEASE CIRCLE <u>ONE</u> ANSWER

No partners. . .(Skip to Question 5)	00
1 partner	01
2 partners	02
3 partners	03
4 partners	04
5 - 10 partners	05
11 - 20 partners	06
21 - 100 partners	07
More than 100 partners	08

2. Was one of the partners your husband or wife or regular sexual partner?

Yes	1
No	2

3. If you had NO other partners beside your husband or wife or regular sexual partner, PLEASE GO TO QUESTION 4.

   If you had other partners, please indicate all categories that apply to them.

   CIRCLE <u>ALL THE ANSWERS</u> THAT APPLY.

Close personal friend	1
Neighbor, co-worker, or long-term acquaintance	2
Casual date or pick-up	3
Person you paid or paid you for sex	4
Other (PLEASE SPECIFY)	
_____	5

4. Have your sex partners in the last 12 months been...

   PLEASE CIRCLE <u>ONE</u> ANSWER.

Exclusively male	1
Both male and female	2
Exclusively female	3

5. About how often did you have sex during the past 12 months?

Not at all	0
Once or twice	1
About once a month	2
Two or three times a month	3
About once a week	4
Two or three times a week	5
Four or more times a week	6

CONTINUE ON TO THE NEXT PAGE ⟶

SAQ NO. 3   CASE ID |__|__|__|__|__|__|

Masturbation is a very common practice. In order to understand the full range of sexual behavior, we need to know the answers to a few questions about your experiences with masturbation. By masturbation, we mean self-sex or self-stimulation, that is, stimulating your genitals (sex organs) to the point of arousal, but not necessarily to orgasm or climax. The following questions are not about activity with a sexual partner, but about times when you were alone or when other people were not aware of what you were doing.

1. On average, in the past 12 months how often did you masturbate? CIRCLE ONE NUMBER ONLY.

More than once a day ... 01
Every day ... 02
Several times a week ... 03
Once a week ... 04
2-3 times a month ... 05
Once a month ... 06
Every other month ... 07
3-5 times a year ... 08
1-2 times a year ... 09
0 times this year ... (Circle 10 and Skip to Q. 5) ... 10

2. When masturbating in the past 12 months, how often did you reach orgasm, that is come or come to climax?

Always ... 1
Usually ... 2
Sometimes ... 3
Rarely ... 4
Never ... 5

CONTINUE ON TO THE NEXT PAGE

The Past 5 Years

6. Now, think about the past five years—the time since February/March/April 1987, and including the past 12 months, how many sex partners have you had in that five year period?

No partners ... (Skip to Question 8) ... 00
1 partner ... 01
2 partners ... 02
3 partners ... 03
4 partners ... 04
5 - 10 partners ... 05
11 - 20 partners ... 06
21 - 100 partners ... 07
More than 100 partners ... 08

7. Have your sex partners in the last five years been...

PLEASE CIRCLE ONE ANSWER.

Exclusively male ... 1
Both male and female ... 2
Exclusively female ... 3

Since Your 18th Birthday

8. Now thinking about the time since your 18th birthday (again, including the recent past that you have already told us about) how many female partners have you ever had sex with?

_____ Female Partners.

9. Again, thinking about the time since your 18th birthday (including the recent past that you have already told us about) how many male partners have you ever had sex with?

_____ Male Partners.

10. Thinking about the time since your 18th birthday, have you ever had sex with a person you paid or who paid you for sex?

Yes ... 1
No ... 2

While Married

11. Have you ever had sex with someone other than your husband or wife while you were married?

Yes ... 1
No ... 2
Never Married ... 3

THANK YOU FOR YOUR COOPERATION.
PLEASE PLACE FORM IN PRIVACY ENVELOPE.

Please answer the following questions on this form by circling the number corresponding to the correct answer. Some questions you may have answered earlier. Sometimes people find it easier to write the answers to some questions on paper instead of saying them to another person. In thinking about these questions, you may also have remembered activities or events you didn't mention.

The first 6 questions relate to what you have done sexually with a man since you reached puberty (that is since you were about 13 years old).

1. Have you ever performed oral sex on a man?

     YES 1
     NO 2

2. Has a man ever performed oral sex on you?

     YES 1
     NO 2

3. Have you ever had anal sex?

     YES 1
     NO 2

4. Have you ever been paid by a man to have sex?

     YES 1
     NO 2

5. Have you ever been forced by a man to do something that you did not want to do?

     YES 1
     NO 2

6. Have you ever forced a man to do something sexual that he did not want to do?

     YES 1
     NO 2

CONTINUE ON TO THE NEXT PAGE ——→

---

3. People masturbate for many reasons. Thinking about the past 12 months, please circle the number beside all the reasons why you usually masturbated. CIRCLE ALL THAT APPLY.

     to relax 1

     to relieve sexual tension 2

     because of unavailability of partners 3

     because you wanted physical pleasure 4

     because you were bored 5

     because your partner did not want to have sex 6

     to get to sleep 7

     because you are afraid of getting AIDS or another disease 8

     Other (Please specify) _____ 9

4. Do you feel guilty after you masturbate?

     Always 1

     Usually 2

     Sometimes 3

     Rarely 4

     Never 5

5. THANK YOU FOR YOUR COOPERATION. PLEASE PLACE FORM IN PRIVACY ENVELOPE.

674

FEMALES ONLY

7. Have you ever had an abortion?

    YES 1
    NO 2

Questions 8-14 are about what you have done sexually with another woman since you reached puberty (that is since you were about 13).

8. Have you ever performed oral sex on another woman?

    YES 1
    NO 2

9. Has another woman ever performed oral sex on you?

    YES 1
    NO 2

10. Have you ever done anything else sexual with another woman?

    YES 1
    NO 2

11. Have you ever paid another woman to have sex?

    YES 1
    NO 2

12. Have you ever been paid by another woman to have sex?

    YES 1
    NO 2

13. Have you ever forced another woman to do something sexual that she did not want to do?

    YES 1
    NO 2

14. Have you ever been forced by a woman to do something sexual that you did not want to do?

    YES 1
    NO 2

CONTINUE ON TO THE NEXT PAGE

2

FEMALES ONLY

15. Have you ever had group sex, that is sex with more than one person at the same time?

    YES 1
    NO 2

16. Have you been tested for the AIDS virus?

    YES 1   (ANSWER PART A BELOW)
    NO 2   (SKIP PART A)

    A. Did you test positive?

        YES 1
        NO 2
        Don't know 8

17. Have you ever injected drugs, that is taken drugs using a needle, that weren't prescribed by a doctor?

    YES 1   (ANSWER PART A BELOW)
    NO 2   (SKIP PART A)

    A. When you injected drugs, did you ever use a needle or syringe (that is "works") after someone else used it, or may have used it?

        YES 1
        NO 2

CONTINUE ON TO THE NEXT PAGE

3

SAQ NO. 4M   CASE ID |_|_|_|_|

Please answer the following questions on this form, by circling the number corresponding to the correct answer. Some questions you may have answered earlier. Sometimes people find it easier to write the answers to some questions on paper instead of saying them to another person. In thinking about these questions, you may also have remembered activities or events you didn't mention.

The first 6 questions are about what you have done sexually with a woman since you reached puberty (that is since you were about 13 years old).

1. Have you ever performed oral sex on a woman?

   YES 1
   NO 2

2. Has a woman ever performed oral sex on you?

   YES 1
   NO 2

3. Have you ever had anal sex with a woman?

   YES 1
   NO 2

4. Have you ever paid a woman to have sex?

   YES 1
   NO 2

5. Have you ever been paid by a woman to have sex?

   YES 1
   NO 2

6. Have you ever forced a woman to do something sexual that she did not want to do?

   YES 1
   NO 2

CONTINUE ON TO THE NEXT PAGE ⟶

1

FEMALES ONLY

18. Have any of your sexual partners ever injected drugs other than those prescribed by a doctor?

    YES 1   (ANSWER PARTS A, B & C BELOW)
    NO 2   (SKIP PARTS A, B & C)

A. How many partners have ever injected drugs? NUMBER |_|_|

B. Did you have sex with any of these partners during the last 12 months?

    YES 1
    NO 2

C. With which partner(s) was this? Just write down a name or initial you used earlier in reporting this/these partner(s).

    _____
    _____
    _____

19. Sometimes at work, women find themselves the object of sexual advances, propositions, or unwanted sexual discussions from co-workers or supervisors. The advances sometimes involve physical contact and sometimes just involve sexual conversations. Has this ever happened to you?

    YES 1
    NO 2

**THANK YOU FOR YOUR COOPERATION.
PLEASE PLACE FORM IN PRIVACY ENVELOPE, SEAL IT AND
GIVE IT TO THE INTERVIEWER.**

STOP

4

676

7. Have you ever had a sexual partner who became pregnant by you and ended that pregnancy by an abortion?

YES 1
NO 2

Questions 8-16 are about what you have done sexually with a man since you reached puberty (that is since you were about 13).

8. Have you ever performed oral sex on a man?

YES 1
NO 2

9. Has a man ever performed oral sex on you?

YES 1
NO 2

10. Have you ever had anal intercourse with a man where you were the inserting partner?

YES 1
NO 2

11. Have you ever had anal intercourse with a man where you were the receiving partner?

YES 1
NO 2

12. Have you ever done anything else sexual with a man?

YES 1
NO 2

13. Have you ever paid a man to have sex?

YES 1
NO 2

CONTINUE ON TO THE NEXT PAGE

2

14. Have you ever been paid by a man to have sex?

YES 1
NO 2

15. Have you ever forced a man to do something sexual that he did not want to do?

YES 1
NO 2

16. Have you ever been forced by a man to do something sexual that you did not want to do?

YES 1
NO 2

17. Have you ever had group sex, that is sex with more than one person at the same time?

YES 1
NO 2

18. Have you been tested for the AIDS virus?

YES .... 1 (ANSWER PART A BELOW)
NO .... 2 (SKIP PART A)

A. Did you test positive?

YES 1
NO 2
Don't know 8

CONTINUE ON TO THE NEXT PAGE

3

19. Have you ever injected drugs, that is taken drugs using a needle, that weren't prescribed by a doctor?

       YES 1   (ANSWER   PART   A
                               BELOW)
       NO 2   (SKIP PART A)

   A. When you injected drugs, did you ever use a needle or syringe (that is "works") after someone else used it, or may have used it?

       YES 1
       NO 2

20. Have any of your sexual partners ever injected drugs other than those prescribed by a doctor?

       YES 1   (ANSWER PARTS A, B &
                               C BELOW)
       NO 2   (SKIP PARTS A, B & C)

   A. How many partners have ever injected drugs? NUMBER |__|__|

   B. Did you have sex with any of these partners during the last 12 months?

       YES 1
       NO 2

   C. With which partner(s) was this? Just write down a name or initial you used earlier in reporting this/these partner(s).

       _____
       _____
       _____

21. Sometimes at work, men find themselves the object of sexual advances, propositions, or unwanted sexual discussions from co-workers or supervisors. The advances sometimes involve physical contact and sometimes just involve sexual conversations. Has this ever happened to you?

       YES 1
       NO 2

**THANK YOU FOR YOUR COOPERATION.
PLEASE PLACE THIS FORM IN PRIVACY ENVELOPE,
SEAL IT AND GIVE IT TO THE INTERVIEWER.**

4

REFERENCES

Agresti, Alan. 1990. *Categorical data analysis.* New York: Wiley.

Ajzen, Icek, and Martin Fishbein. 1977. Attitude-behavior relations: A theoretical analysis and review of empirical research. *Psychological Bulletin* 84:888–918.

Albrecht, Gary L., and Helen Gift. 1975. Adult socialization: Ambiguity and adult life crises. In *Life span developmental psychology: Normative life crises,* ed. Nancy Datan and Leon Ginsberg. New York: Academic.

Allison, P., ed. 1982. *Discrete-time methods for the analysis of event history.* San Francisco: Jossey-Bass.

Alter-Reid, K., M. S. Gibbs, J. R. Lachenmeyer, J. Sigal, and N. A. Massoth. 1986. Sexual abuse of children: A review of the empirical findings. *Clinical Psychological Review* 6:249–66.

Altmann, Michael. 1993. Reinterpreting network measures for models of disease transmission. *Social Networks* 15:1–17.

Anderberg, Michael R. 1973. *Cluster analysis for applications.* New York: Academic.

Andersen, Ronald, et al. 1979. *Total survey error.* San Francisco: Jossey-Bass.

Anderson, Roy M. 1991. The transmission dynamics of sexually transmitted diseases: The behavioral component. In *Research issues in human behavior and sexually transmitted diseases in the AIDS era,* eds. Judith N. Wasserheit, Sevgi O. Aral, and King K. Holmes. Washington, D.C.: American Society for Microbiology.

———, ed. 1982. *Population dynamics of infectious diseases.* London: Chapman & Hall.

Anderson, R. M., S. Gupta, and W. Ng. 1990. The significance of sexual partner contact networks for the transmission dynamics of HIV. *Journal of Acquired Immune Deficiency Syndromes* 3:417–29.

Anderson, Roy M., and Robert M. May. 1988. Epidemiological parameters of HIV transmission. *Nature* 333:514–19.

———. 1991. *Infectious diseases of humans: Dynamics and control.* New York: Oxford University Press.

———. 1992. Understanding the AIDS pandemic. *Scientific American,* May:58–66.

Anderson, Roy M., Robert M. May, G. F. Medley, and A. Johnson. 1986. A preliminary study of the transmission dynamics of the human immunodeficiency virus (HIV), the causative agent of AIDS. *IMA Journal of Mathematics Applied in Medicine and Biology* 3:229–63.

Anson, O., E. Paran, L. Neumann, and D. Chernichovsky. 1993. Gender differences in health perceptives and their predictors. *Social Science and Medicine* 36, no. 4:419–27.

Aral, Sevgi O., and M. E. Guinau. 1984. Women and sexually transmitted diseases. In *Sexually transmitted diseases,* ed. King K. Holmes et al. New York: McGraw-Hill.

Aral, Sevgi O., and King K. Holmes. 1984. Epidemiology of sexually transmitted diseases. In *Sexually transmitted diseases,* ed. King K. Holmes et al. New York: McGraw-Hill.

679

Athanasiou, Robert. 1973. A review of public attitudes on sexual issues. In *Contemporary sexual behavior: Critical issues in the 1970's*, eds. Joseph Zubin and John Money. Baltimore: Johns Hopkins University Press.

Athanasiou, Robert, Philip Shaver, and Carol Tavris. 1970. Report to the readers of *Psychology Today* on the *PT* sex survey. *Psychology Today*, July, 39–52.

Axinn, William, and Arland Thornton. 1992a. The influence of parental resources on the timing of the transition to marriage. *Social Science Research* 21, no. 3 (September): 261–85.

———. 1992b. The relationship between cohabitation and divorce: Selectivity or causal influence. *Demography* 29:357–74.

Babbie, Earl R. 1973. Survey research methods. Belmont, Calif.: Wadsworth.

Bailey, Kenneth D. 1974. Cluster analysis. In *Sociological methodology 1975*, ed. David R. Heise. San Francisco: Jossey-Bass.

Bailey, N. T. J. 1975. *The mathematical theory of infectious diseases and its applications.* 2d ed. New York: Hafner.

———. 1979. Introduction to the modelling of venereal disease. *Journal of Mathematical Biology* 8:301–22.

Baker, Wayne E. 1984. The social structure of a national securities market. *American Journal of Sociology* 89, no. 4:775–811.

———. 1990. Market networks and corporate behavior. *American Journal of Sociology* 96:589–625.

———. 1991. Using network analysis for organizational diagnosis. Paper presented at the eleventh International Sunbelt Social Network Conference. Tampa, Fla.

Baldwin, Wendy, and Virginia Cain. 1980. The children of teenage parents. *Family Planning Perspectives* 12, no. 1:34–43.

Baltes, Paul B., and Orville G. Brim. 1978. *Life span development and behavior.* New York: Academic.

Bancroft, John. 1987. A physiological approach. In *Theories of human sexuality*, ed. James H. Geer and William T. O'Donohue. New York: Plenum.

Barringer, Felicity. Sex survey of American men finds 1% are gay. *New York Times*, April 15, 1993: A1, A9.

Bartell, Gilbert D. 1970. Group sex among the mid-Americans. *Journal of Sex Research* 6 (May): 113–30.

Becker, Gary S. 1991. *A treatise on the family.* Cambridge, Mass.: Harvard University Press.

Becker, Gary S., Elisabeth M. Landes, and Robert T. Michael. 1977. An economic analysis of marital instability. *Journal of Political Economy* 85, no. 6:1141–87.

Becker, Marshall. 1974. Personal health behavior and the health belief model. *Health Education Monographs* 2:326–473.

Becker, Marshall, et al. 1977. Selected psychosocial models and correlates of individual health-related behavior. *Medical Care* 15:27–46.

Beiber, I. 1962. *Homosexuality: A psychoanalytic study.* New York: Basic.

Bell, Alan P., and Martin S. Weinberg. 1978. *Homosexualities.* New York: Simon & Schuster.

Bell, Alan P., Martin S. Weinberg, and Sue Kiefer-Hammersmith. 1980. *Sexual preference.* New York: Simon & Schuster.

Bennett, Neil G., Ann K. Blanc, and David E. Bloom. 1988. Commitment and the modern union: Assessing the link between premarital cohabitation and subsequent union stability. *American Sociological Review* 53:127–38.

Berger, Alan S., John H. Gagnon, and William Simon. 1973. Youth and pornography in social context. *Archives of Sexual Behavior* 1, no. 4:279–308.

Berkowitz, Stephen. 1982. *An introduction to structural analysis: The network approach to social research.* Toronto: Butterworth.

Bernard, H. Russell, Eugene C. Johnsen, Peter D. Killworth, Christopher McCarty, Gene A. Shelley, and Scott Robinson. 1990. Comparing four different methods for measuring personal social networks. *Social Networks* 12:172–215.

Billy, John O. G., Joseph Lee Rodgers, and J. Richard Udry. 1984. Adolescent sexual behavior and friendship choice. *Social Forces* 62:653–78.

Billy, John O. G., Koray Tanfer, William R. Grady, and Daniel H. Klepenger. 1993. The sexual behavior of men in the United States. *Family Planning Perspectives* 25, no. 2:52–60.

Blair, Ellen, Seymour Sudman, Norman M. Bradburn, and Carol Stocking. 1977. How to ask questions about drinking and sex: Response effects in measuring consumer behavior. *Journal of Marketing Research* 14:316–21.

Blalock, Herbert M. 1979. *Social statistics.* 2d ed. New York: McGraw-Hill.

———. 1984. Contextual-effects models: Theoretical and methodological issues. *Annual Review of Sociology* 10:353–72.

Blau, Peter M. 1964. *Exchange and power in social life.* New York: Wiley.

———. 1974. Presidential address: Parameters of social structure. *American Sociological Review* 39:615–35.

———. 1977. A macrosociological theory of social structure. *American Journal of Sociology* 83, no. 1:26–54.

———. 1986. *Exchange and power in social life.* New York: Wiley.

Blau, Peter M., and Otis Dudley Duncan. 1967. *The American occupational structure.* New York: Wiley.

Bloom, Allan D. 1993. *Love and friendship.* New York: Simon & Schuster.

Blumstein, Philip, and Pepper Schwartz. 1983. *American couples.* New York: Morrow.

Blythe, S. P., and C. Castillo-Chavez. 1990. Scaling of sexual activity. *Nature* 344: 202.

Blythe, S. P., C. Castillo-Chavez, and J. S. Palmer. 1991. Toward a unified theory of sexual mixing and pair formation. *Mathematical Biosciences* 107:379–405.

Bogue, Donald J., Robert Bursik, and Judith Mayo. 1979. *Communicating to combat VD.* Community and Family Study Center Monographs. Chicago: University of Chicago.

Bongaarts, John. 1978. A framework for analyzing the proximate determinants of fertility. *Population and Development Review* 4:105–32.

Booth, Alan, and David Johnson. 1988. Premarital cohabitation and marital success. *Journal of Family Issues* 9:255–72.

Boruch, Robert. 1989. Resolving privacy problems in AIDS: A primer. In *Health services research methodology: A focus on AIDS,* ed. L. Sechrest, H. Freeman, and A. Mulley. Washington, D.C.: National Center for Health Services Research and Health Care Technology Assessment.

Bott, Elizabeth. 1971. *Family and social network.* 2d ed. London: Tavistock.

Bradburn, Norman M. 1969. *The structure of psychological wellbeing.* Chicago: Aldine.

Bradburn, Norman M., Lance Rips, and Stephen Shevell. 1987. Answering autobiographical questions: The impact of memory and inference on surveys. *Science* 236 (10 April): 157–61.

Bradburn, Norman M., and Seymour Sudman. 1983. *Asking questions: A practical guide to questionnaire design.* San Francisco: Jossey-Bass.

Bradburn, Norman M., Seymour Sudman, Ed Blair, and Carol Stocking. 1978. Question threat and response bias. *Public Opinion Quarterly* 42:221–34.

Bradburn, Norman M., Seymour Sudman, et al. 1979. *Improving interview method and design.* San Francisco: Jossey-Bass.

Brady, John Paul, and Eugene E. Levitt. 1965. The scalability of sexual experiences. *Psychological Record* 15:275–79.

Brandt, Allan. 1987. *No magic bullet.* Oxford: Oxford University Press.

Breiger, Ronald L. 1988. The duality of persons and groups. In *Social structure: A network approach,* ed. Barry Wellman and Stephen D. Berkowitz, 83–98. Cambridge: Cambridge University Press.

Briere, J., and M. Runtz. 1987. Post sexual abuse trauma: Data and implications for clinical practice. *Journal of Interpersonal Violence* 8:367–79.

———. 1993. Childhood sexual abuse: Long-term sequelae and implications for psychological assessment. *Journal of Interpersonal Violence* 8:312–30.

Brim, Orville G., and Stanton Wheeler. 1966. *Socialization after childhood: Two essays.* New York: Wiley.

Brines, Julie, 1994. Economic dependency, gender, and the division of labor at home. *American Journal of Sociology* 100. Forthcoming.

Brines, Julie, and Kara Joyner. 1993. The ties that bind: Principles of stability in married and cohabiting relationships. Paper presented at the annual meeting of the *Population Association of America,* Cincinnati.

Brookman, Richard R. 1990. Adolescent sexual behavior. In *Sexually transmitted diseases,* eds. King K. Holmes et al. New York: McGraw-Hill.

Browne, A., and D. Finkelhor. 1986. Impact of child sexual abuse: A review of the research. *Psychological Bulletin* 99:66–77.

Brownmiller, Susan. 1975. *Against our will: Men, women, and rape.* New York: Simon & Schuster.

Bumpass, Larry, and Sara McLanahan. 1989. Unmarried motherhood: Recent trends, composition and black-white differences. *Demography* 26, no. 2:279–86.

Bumpass, Larry, and Ronald R. Rindfuss. 1984. The effect of marital dissolution on contraceptive protection. *Family Planning Perspectives* 16 (Nov./Dec.):271–74.

Bumpass, Larry L., and James A. Sweet. 1989. National estimates of cohabitation. *Demography* 26, no. 4:615–25.

Bumpass, Larry, James A. Sweet, and Andrew J. Cherlin. 1989. The role of cohabitation in declining rates of marriage. *Journal of Marriage and the Family* 59:913–27.

Bumpass, Larry L., and Charles F. Westoff. 1970. *The later years of childbearing.* Princeton, N.J.: Princeton University Press.

Bureau of Justice Statistics. 1984. *Criminal victimization in the United States, 1982.* Washington, D.C.: U.S. Department of Justice.

Burt, Ronald S. 1980. Models of network structure. *Annual Review of Sociology* 6:79–141.

———. 1982. *Toward a structural theory of action: Networks of social structure, perception and action.* New York: Academic.

———. 1987. Social contagion and innovation: Cohesion versus structural equivalence. *American Journal of Sociology* 92, no. 6:1287–1335.

———. 1992. *Structural holes: The social structure of competition.* Cambridge, Mass.: Harvard University Press.

Burt, Ronald S., and Miguel G. Guilarte. 1986. A note on scaling the General Social Survey network item response categories. *Social Networks* 8:387–96.

Buss, David M. 1989. Sex differences in human mate preferences: Evolutionary hypotheses tested in 37 cultures. *Behavioral and Brain Sciences* 12:1–49.

Cahill, C., S. Llewelyn, and C. Pearson. 1991. Long-term effects of sexual abuse which occurred in adulthood. A review. *British Journal of Clinical Psychology* 30:117–30.

Caldwell, John C., Pat Caldwell, and Pat Quiggin. 1989. The social context of AIDS in sub-Saharan Africa. *Population and Development Review* 15, no. 2:185–234.

Cannon, Kenneth L., and Richard Long. 1971. Premarital sexual behavior in the sixties. *Journal of Marriage and the Family* 33, no. 1:36–49.

Carns, D. E. 1975. Talking about sex: Notes on first coitus and the double sexual standard. *Journal of Marriage and the Family* 35:677–88.

Carrier, J. M. 1989. Sexual behavior and the spread of AIDS in Mexico. *Medical Anthropology* 10:129–42.

Carroll, Jackson W., and Wade Clark Roof, eds. 1993. *Beyond establishment: Protestant identity in a post-Protestant age.* Louisville: John Knox Press.

Carter, Hugh, and Paul C. Glick. 1970. *Marriage and divorce: A social and economic study.* Cambridge, Mass.: Harvard University Press.

Castillo, C. O., and J. H. Geer. 1993. Ambiguous stimuli: Sex in the eye of the beholder. *Archives of Sexual Behavior* 22: 131–43.

Catania, J. A., et al. 1992a. Condom use in multi-ethnic neighborhoods of San Francisco: The population-based AMEN (AIDS in Multi-Ethnic Neighborhoods) study. *American Journal of Public Health* 82, no. 2:284–87.

———. 1992b. Prevalence of AIDS-related risk factors and condom use in the United States. *Science* 258 (Nov. 13):1101–6.

Catania, J. A., D. Gibson, D. D. Chitwood, and T. Coates. 1990. Methodological problems in AIDS behavioral research: Influences on measurement error and participation bias in studies of sexual behavior. *Psychological Bulletin* 108:339–62.

Catania, J. A., L. McDermott, and L. Pollack. 1986. Questionnaire response bias and face-to-face interview sample bias in sexuality research. *Journal of Sex Research* 22:52–72.

Catania, J. A., H. Turner, R. C. Pierce, E. Golden, C. Stocking, D. Binson, and K. Mast. 1993. Response bias in surveys of AIDS-related sexual behavior. In *Methodological issues in AIDS mental health research,* ed. D. G. Ostrow and R. Kessler, 133–62. New York: Plenum.

Cates, Willard. 1986. Priorities for STDs in the late 1980s and beyond. *Sexually Transmitted Diseases* 13, no. 2:114–17.

Centers for Disease Control (CDC). 1985. Sexually transmitted disease statistics calendar year 1984. In *Sexually Transmitted Disease Statistics Calendar Year 1984.* Atlanta.

———. 1992a. Sexual behavior and high school students—United States, 1990. *Morbidity and Mortality Weekly Report* 40:885–88.

———. 1992b. *STD/HIV prevention 1991 annual report.* Atlanta.

Chauncey, George, Jr. 1983. From sexual inversion to homosexuality: Medicine and the changing conceptualization of female deviance. *Salmagundi* 58–59:114–46.

Chen, Renbao, and S. Philip Morgan. 1991. Recent trends in timing of first birth in the United States. *Demography* 28, no. 4:513–34.

Cherlin, Andrew J. 1978. Remarriage as an incomplete institution. *American Journal of Sociology* 84:634–50.

———. 1992. *Marriage, divorce, remarriage.* Cambridge, Mass.: Harvard University Press.

Chilman, Catherine S. 1978. *Adolescent sexuality in a changing American society.* Washington, D.C.: Department of Health, Education, and Welfare.

———. 1980a. *Adolescent sexuality in a changing American society.* DHEW–NIH Publication no. 80-1426. Washington, D.C.: U.S. Government Printing Office.

———. 1980b. *Adolescent pregnancy and childbearing: Findings from research.* DHEW–NIH Publication no. 81-2077. Washington, D.C.: U.S. Government Printing Office.

Clancy, Kevin, and Walter Gove. 1974. Sex differences in mental illness: An analysis of response bias in self-reports. *American Journal of Sociology* 80 (July 1974): 205–16.

Clarkberg, Marin, Rafe Stolzenberg, and Linda Waite. 1993. Values and cohabitation. Paper presented at the annual meeting of the Population Association of America, Cincinnati.

Clausen, John. 1972. Life course of individuals. In *Aging and society,* ed. M. W. Riley et al. New York: Russell Sage.

Clayton, Richard R., and Janet L. Bokemeier. 1980. Premarital sex in the seventies. *Journal of Marriage and the Family* 42, no. 4:759–75.

Clogg, Clifford C., and Leo A. Goodman. 1984. Simultaneous latent structure analysis in several groups. In *Sociological methodology 1985,* ed. Nancy B. Tuma. San Francisco: Jossey-Bass.

Coale, J. Ansley. 1971. Age patterns in marriage. *Population Studies* 25 (July): 193–214.

Coale, J. Ansley, and D. R. McNeil. 1972. The distribution by age of the frequency of first marriage in a female cohort. *Journal of the American Statistical Association* 67 (Dec.): 743–49.

Coates, Randall A., et al. 1986. The reliability of sexual histories in AIDS-related research: Evaluation of an interview-administered questionnaire. *Canadian Journal of Public Health* 77 (September–October): 343–48.

Cochran, W., F. Mosteller, and J. Tukey, 1953. Statistical problems of the Kinsey Report. *Journal of the American Statistical Association* 48:673–716.

Cohen, Jere M. 1977. Sources of peer group homogeneity. *Sociology of Education* 50:227–41.

———. 1980. Socio-economic status and high-school friendship choice: Elmtown's youth revisited. *Social Networks* 2:65–74.

Coleman, James S. 1958. Relational analysis: The study of social organizations with survey methods. *Human Organization* 17:28–36.

———. 1961. *The adolescent society.* New York: Free Press.

———. 1980. The structure of society and the nature of social research. *Knowledge: Creation, Diffusion, Utilization* 1, no. 3:333–50.

———. 1986a. Micro-foundations and macro–social theory. In *Approaches to social theory,* ed. Singwort Lindberg, James Coleman, and Stephen Nowak. New York: Russell Sage.

———. 1986b. Social theory, social research, and a theory of action. *American Journal of Sociology* 91, no. 6:1309–35.

———. 1988. The family's move from center to periphery, and its implication for schooling. In *Center: Ideas and institutions,* ed. Liah Greenfeld and Michel Martin. Chicago: University of Chicago Press.

———. 1990. *Foundations of social theory.* Cambridge, Mass.: Belknap.

Converse, Philip. 1964. The nature of belief systems in mass politics. In *Ideology and discontent,* ed. David Apter. New York: Free Press.

Cook, Mark, and Kevin Howells, eds. 1980. *Adult sexual interest in children.* New York: Academic.

Cook, S., and C. Selltiz. 1972. A multiple-indicator approach to attitude measurement. In *Racial attitudes in America: Analyses and findings of social psychology,* ed. S. Brigham and T. Weissbach. New York: Harper & Row.

Cooksey, Elizabeth C. 1990. Factors in the resolution of adolescent premarital pregnancies. *Demography* 27, no. 2:207–19.

Cotran, Ramzi S., Vinay Kumar, and Stanley L. Robbins. 1989. *Pathologic basis of disease.* Philadelphia: Saunders.

Cox, Brenda C., and Steven B. Cohen. 1985. *Methodological issues for health care surveys.* New York: Dekker.

Coxon, Anthony P. M. 1986. *Report of a pilot study: Project on sexual lifestyles of non-heterosexual males.* Cardiff: University College.

————. 1993. Networks and nemesis: The use of social networks as method and substance in researching gay men's response to HIV/AIDS. Paper presented at the ARHN Working Group on Sexual Behavior Research Conference on International Perspectives in Sex Research, Rio de Janeiro.

Coyle, Susan L., Robert F. Boruch, and Charles F. Turner. 1991. *Evaluating AIDS prevention programs.* Washington, D.C.: National Academy Press.

Crosbie, Paul V., and Dianne Bitte. 1982. A test of Luker's theory of contraceptive risk-taking. *Studies in Family Planning* 13:67–78.

Cummings, K. Michael, Marshall H. Becker, and Marla C. Maile. 1980. Bringing the models together: An empirical approach to combining variables used to explain health actions. *Journal of Behavioral Medicine* 3:123–45.

Curtis, L. A. 1976. Present and future measures of victimization in forcible rape. In *Sexual Assault,* ed. M. J. Walker and S. L. Brodsky. Lexington, Mass.: Heath.

Cvetkovich, George, Barbara Grote, E. James Lieberman, and Warren Miller. 1978. Sex role development and teenage fertility-related behavior. *Adolescence* 13:231–36.

Daniel, W. W. 1979. *Collecting sensitive data by randomized response: With annotated bibliography.* Atlanta: Georgia State University Business Publications.

Darrow, William W., H. W. Jaffe, P. A. Thomas, et al. 1987. Multicenter study of HIV antibody in U.S. prostitutes. Paper presented at the Third International Conference on AIDS, Washington, D.C.

Darrow, William W., and M. L. Pauli. 1984. Health behavior and sexually transmitted diseases. In *Sexually transmitted diseases,* ed. King K. Holmes et al. New York: McGraw-Hill.

Davidson, Arnold I. 1987. Sex and the emergence of sexuality. *Critical Inquiry* 14 (Autumn): 16–48.

Davis, James Allan, and Tom W. Smith. 1991. *General Social Surveys, 1972–1991: Cumulative codebook.* Chicago: National Opinion Research Center.

Davis, K., and J. Blake. 1956. Social structure and fertility. An analytic framework. *Economic Development and Cultural Change* 4 (April): 211–35.

Davis, Murray S. 1984. *Smut.* Chicago: University of Chicago Press.

DeLamater, John. 1981. The social control of sexuality. *Annual Review of Sociology* 7:263–90.

————. 1987. A sociological approach. In *Theories of human sexuality,* ed. James H. Geer and William T. O'Donohue. New York: Plenum.

DeLamater, John, and Patricia MacCorquodale. 1979a. *Premarital sexuality: Attitudes, relationships, behavior.* Madison: University of Wisconsin.

————. 1979b. Self image and premarital sexuality. *Journal of Marriage and the Family* 41, no. 2:327–39.

Demaris, Alfred, and William MacDonald. 1993. Premarital cohabitation and marital instability: A test of the unconventionality hypothesis. *Journal of Marriage and the Family* 55:399–407.

D'Emilio, John. 1983. *Sexual politics, sexual communities: The making of a homosexual minority in the United States.* Chicago: University of Chicago Press.

D'Emilio, John, and Estelle B. Freedman. 1988. *Intimate matters: A history of sexuality in America.* New York: Harper & Row.

Department of Health and Human Services. 1986. *Contraceptive use, United States, 1982.* Washington, D.C.

DiMaggio, Paul, and John Mohr. 1985. Cultural capital, educational attainment, and marital selection. *American Journal of Sociology* 90:1231–61.

Dolcini, M. Margaret, Joseph A. Catania, Thomas J. Coates, Ron Stall, Ester S. Hudes, John H. Gagnon, and Lance M. Pollack. 1993. Demographic characteristics of heterosexuals with multiple partners: The National AIDS Behavioral Surveys. *Family Planning Perspectives* 25:208–14.

Donovan, P. 1993. *Testing positive: STD and the public health response.* New York: Alan Guttmacher Institute.

Dunbar, John, Marvin Brown, and Donald M. Amoroso. 1973. Some correlates of attitudes toward homosexuality. *Journal of Social Psychology* 89:271–79.

Duncan, Otis Dudley, and Beverly Duncan. 1955. A methodological analysis of segregation indices. *American Sociological Review* 20:210–17.

Dworkin, Andrea. 1987. *Intercourse.* New York: Free Press.

Edwards, Allen L. 1957. *Techniques of attitude scale construction.* New York: Appleton-Century-Crofts.

Eggert, Leona L., and Malcolm R. Parks. 1987. Communication network involvement in adolescents' friendships and romantic relationships. In *Communication yearbook.* Vol. 10, ed. M. L. McLaughlin, 283–322. Newbury Park, Calif.: Sage.

Ehrenreich, Barbara. 1986. *Re-making love: The feminization of sex.* Garden City, N.Y.: Anchor.

Einhorn, D. H., et al., eds. 1981. *Past and present in middle life.* New York: Academic.

Elder, Glen H. 1979. Historical change in life patterns and personality. In *Life span development of behavior,* ed. Paul Baltes and Orville G. Brim. New York: Academic.

———. 1984. Family history and the life course. In *The family,* ed. Ross Parks et al. Chicago: University of Chicago Press.

Emerson, Richard M. 1981. Social exchange theory. In *Social psychology: Sociological perspective,* ed. M. Rosenberg and R. H. Turner. New York: Basic Books.

Emmons, C., et al. 1986. Psychosocial predictors of reported behavior change in homosexual men at risk for AIDS. *Health Education Quarterly* 13, no. 4:331–45.

England, Paula, and George Farkas. 1986. *Households, employment, and gender: A social, economic, and demographic view.* New York: Aldine de Gruyter.

England, Paula, and Barbara Stanek Kilbourne. 1990. Markets, marriages, and other mates: The problem of power. In *Beyond the marketplace: rethinking economy and society,* ed. Roger Friedland and A. F. Robertson, 163–88. New York: Aldine de Gruyter.

Ensminger, Margaret. 1987. Adolescent sexual behavior as it relates to other transition behaviors in youth. In *Risking the future,* ed. Sandra L. Hofferth and Cheryl D. Hayes. Washington, D.C.: National Academy Press.

Erbring, Lutz, and Alice A. Young. 1979. Individuals and social structure: Contextual effects as endogenous feedback. *Sociological Methods and Research* 7, no. 4:396–430.

Evans, Mariah D. 1984. *Modernization, economic conditions and family formation.* Chicago: University of Chicago, Department of Sociology.

Everitt, Brian. 1993. *Cluster analysis.* New York: Halsted Press.

Fararo, Thomas, and John Skvoretz. 1986. E-state structuralism. *American Sociological Review* 51, no. 5:591–602.

Fararo, Thomas J., and Morris H. Sunshine. 1964. *A study of a biased friendship net.* Syracuse, N.Y.: Syracuse University Press.

Fay, R. E., Charles F. Turner, A. D. Klassen, and John H. Gagnon. 1989. Prevalence and patterns of same-gender contact among men. *Science* 243:338–48.

Feingold, Alan. 1988. Matching for attractiveness in romantic partners and same-sex friends. A meta-analysis and theoretical critique. *Psychological Bulletin* 104: 226–35.

Ferrel, Mary Z., William L. Tolone, and Robert H. Walsh. 1977. Maturational and societal changes in the sexual double-standard: A panel analysis (1967–71; 1970–74). *Journal of Marriage and the Family* 39:255–71.

Fichtner, R. R. 1983. Syphilis in the United States: 1967–1979. *Sexually Transmitted Diseases* 10, no. 2:77–80.

Fienberg, Stephen E. 1980. *The analysis of cross-classified categorical data.* Cambridge, Mass.: MIT Press.

Fienberg, Stephen E., and William M. Mason. 1978. Identification and estimation of age-period-cohort models in the analysis of discrete archival data. In *Sociological methodology 1979,* ed. Karl E. Schuessler. San Francisco: Jossey-Bass.

Finkel, Madelon Lubin, and David J. Finkel. 1975. Sexual and contraceptive knowledge, attitudes, and behavior of male adolescents. *Family Planning Perspectives* 7:256–60.

Finkelhor, David. 1979. *Sexually victimized children.* New York: Free Press.

———. 1984. *Sexual abuse: New research and theory.* New York: Free Press.

Fischer, Claude S. 1982. What do we mean by "friend"? An inductive study. *Social Networks* 3:287–306.

Fishbein, Martin. 1972. Toward an understanding of family planning behaviors. *Journal of Applied Social Psychology* 2:214–27.

———. 1973. Theoretical and methodological considerations in the prediction of family planning intentions and behavior. *Representative Research in Social Psychology* 4:37–52.

Fisher, Andrew A. 1977. The health belief model and contraceptive behavior: Limits to the application of a conceptual framework. *Health Education Monographs* 5:244–50.

Forrest, Jacqueline Darroch, and Stanley K. Henshaw. 1983. What U.S. women think and do about contraception. *Family Planning Perspectives* 15:157–66.

Forrest, Jacqueline Darroch, and Susheela Singh. 1990. The sexual and reproductive behavior of American women, 1982–1988. *Family Planning Perspectives* 22:206–14.

Foucault, Michel. 1978. *The history of sexuality.* New York: Pantheon.

Fox, Greer L. 1981. The family's role in adolescent sexual behavior. In *Teenage pregnancy in a family context,* ed. T. Ooms. Philadelphia: Temple University Press.

———. 1982. *The childbearing decision.* Beverly Hills, Calif.: Sage.

Francis, Donald P., and James Chin. 1987. The prevention of acquired immunodeficiency syndrome in the United States. *Journal of the American Medical Association* 257, no. 10:1357–66.

Frank, Kenneth A. 1993. *Identifying cohesive subgroups.* Ph.D. diss., Department of Education, University of Chicago.

Freedman, David, Robert Pisani, and Roger Purves. 1978. *Statistics.* New York: Norton.

Freeman, Linton C. 1978. Segregation in social networks. *Sociological Methods and Research* 6, no. 4:411–29.

———. 1979. Centrality in social networks: Conceptual clarification. *Social Networks* 1:215–39.

Furstenberg, Frank F. 1982. Conjugal succession: Reentering marriage after divorce. *Life Span,* 176–92.

Furstenberg, Frank, R. Lincoln, and Jane Menken. 1982. Parental involvement: Selling family planning clinics short. *Family Planning Perspectives* 14:140–44.

Furstenberg, Frank, S. Phillip Morgan, Kristin A. Moore, and James L. Peterson. 1987. Race differences in the timing of adolescent intercourse. *American Sociological Review* 52 (August): 511–18.

————. 1982. What is not what in theory construction. In *Social structure and behavior: Essays in honor of William Hamilton Sewell,* ed. Robert Hauser et al. New York: Academic.

Haefner, D. P., and J. P. Kirscht. 1970. Motivational and behavioral effects of modifying health beliefs. *Public Health Reports* 85, no. 6 (June): 478–84.

Hallinan, Maureen T., and Richard A. Williams. 1989. Interracial friendship choices in secondary schools. *American Sociological Review* 54:67–78.

————. 1990. Students' characteristics and the peer-influence process. *Sociology of Education* 63:122–32.

Halperin, David M. 1990. *One hundred years of homosexuality and other essays on Greek love.* New York: Routledge.

Haraldsdottir, Sigridur, Sunetra Gupta, and Roy M. Anderson. 1992. Preliminary studies of sexual networks in a male homosexual community in Iceland. *Journal of Acquired Immune Deficiency Syndromes* 5:374–81.

Harary, Frank. 1969. *Graph theory.* Reading, Mass.: Addison-Wesley.

Harary, Frank, Robert Z. Norman, and Dorwin Cartwright. 1965. *Structural models: An introduction to the theory of directed graphs.* New York: Wiley.

Hare, E. H. 1962. Masturbatory insanity: The history of an idea. *Journal of Mental Science* 108:1–25.

Hart, G. 1977. *Sexual maladjustment and disease.* Chicago: Nelson-Hall.

Hayes, Cheryl D., ed. 1987. *Risking the future: Adolescent sexuality, pregnancy and childbearing.* Washington, D.C.: National Academy Press.

Hayes, J., and C. K. Prokop. 1976. Sociopsychiatric characteristics of clinic patrons with repeat gonorrhea infections. *Journal of the American Venereal Disease Association* 3:43.

Hearst, N., and S. Hulley. 1988. Preventing heterosexual spread of AIDS: Are we giving our patients the best advice. *Journal of the American Medical Association* 259, no. 16 (22–29 April): 24–29.

Heckman, James J. 1979. Sample selection bias as a specification error. *Econometrica* 47:153–62.

Heckman, James J., and Robert J. Willis. 1976. Estimation of a stochastic model of reproduction: An econometric approach. In *Household consumption and production,* ed. N. E. Terleckyj. New York: National Bureau of Economic Research.

Heinz, John P., and Edward O. Laumann. 1982. *Chicago lawyers: The social structure of the bar.* Chicago: Russell Sage Foundation and American Bar Foundation.

Hendrick, S. S., and C. Hendrick. 1987. Multidimensionality of sexual attitudes. *Journal of Sex Research* 23:502–26.

Henshaw, Stanley K. 1992. Abortion trends in 1987 and 1988: Age and race. *Family Planning Perspectives* 24, no. 2:85–86, 96.

Herceg-Baron, R., and Frank Furstenberg. 1982. Adolescent contraceptive use: The impact of family support systems. In *The child-bearing decision,* ed. G. L. Fox. Beverly Hills, Calif.: Sage.

Herdt, Gilbert, ed. 1992. *Gay culture in America: Essays from the field.* Boston: Beacon.

Herdt, Gilbert, and Robert J. Stoller. 1990. *Intimate communications: Erotics and the study of culture.* New York: Columbia University Press.

Herringa, Steven G., and Judith H. Connor. 1984. *The 1980 SRC/NORC national sample design and development.* Ann Arbor, Mich.: Institute for Social Research.

Herzberg, Frederick. 1973. *Work and the nature of man.* New York: New American Library.

Hessol, N., et al. 1987. The natural history of human immunodeficiency virus in a cohort of homosexual and bisexual men: A 7-year prospective study. Paper presented at the Third International Conference on AIDS, Washington, D.C.

Hethcote, H. W., and J. A. Yorke. 1984. *Gonorrhea transmission dynamics and control: Lecture notes in biomathematics.* Vol. 56. Berlin: Springer-Verlag.

Hite, Shere. 1979. *The Hite Report on female sexuality.* New York: Knopf.

———. 1981. *The Hite Report on male sexuality.* New York: Knopf.

Hofferth, Sandra L., and Cheryl D. Hayes. 1978. The variable order of events in the life course. *American Sociological Review* 43 (August): 573–86.

Hogan, Dennis. 1981. *Transition and social change: The early lives of American men.* New York: Academic.

Hogan, Dennis, Nan Astone, and Evelyn Kitagawa. 1985. Social and environmental factors influencing contraceptive use among black adolescents. *Family Planning Perspectives* 17, no. 4 (July/August): 165–69.

Holmes, King K., Per-Anders Mardh, P. Frederick Sparling, and Paul J. Wiesner. 1990. *Sexually transmitted diseases.* 2d ed. New York: McGraw-Hill.

Hooker, E. 1966. The homosexual community. In *Perspectives in pathology,* ed. J. C. Palmer and M. J. Goldstein. Oxford: Oxford University Press.

Huckfeldt, Robert, and John Sprague. 1988. Choice, social structure, and political information: The informational coercion of minorities. *American Journal of Political Science* 32:467–82.

Hudson, Walter, Gerald J. Murphy, and Paula S. Nurius. 1983. A short-form scale to measure liberal versus conservative orientations toward human sexual expression. *Journal of Sex Research* 19, no. 3:258–72.

Humphreys, Laud. 1970. *Tearoom trade.* Chicago: Aldine.

Hunt, Morton, et al. 1974. *Sexual behavior in the 1970s.* Chicago: Playboy.

Hyman, Herbert Hiram. 1991. *Taking society's measure: A personal history of survey research.* New York: Russell Sage Foundation.

Insko, Chester A., Robert R. Blake, Robert B. Cialdini, and Stanley A. Mulaik. 1970. Attitude toward birth control and cognitive consistency: Theoretical and practical implications of survey data. *Journal of Personality and Social Psychology* 16, no. 2:228–37.

Institute of Medicine. 1986. *Confronting AIDS: Directions for public health, health care, and research.* Washington, D.C.: National Academy Press.

Jackson, J., K. Calhoun, A. Amick, H. Maddever, and V. Habif. 1990. Young adult women who report childhood sexual abuse: Subsequent adjustment. *Archives of Sexual Behavior* 19:211–21.

Jacobson, Paul H. 1959. *American marriage and divorce.* New York: Holt, Rinehart & Winston.

Janus, Samuel S., and Cynthia L. Janus. 1993. *The Janus Report on sexual behavior.* New York: Wiley.

Jasso, Guillermina. 1985. Marital coital frequency and the passage of time: Estimating the separate effects of spouses' ages and marital duration, birth and marriage cohorts and period influences. *American Sociological Review* 50:224–41.

———. 1986. Is it outlier deletion or is it sample truncation? Notes on science and sexuality (reply to Kahn and Udry). *American Sociological Review* 51, no. 5:738–42.

Jessor, Richard, et al. 1983. Time of first intercourse: A prospective study. *Journal of Personality and Social Psychology* 44, no. 3:608–26.

Jessor, Shirley L., and Richard Jessor. 1975. Transition from virginity to non-virginity among youth: A social-psychological study over time. *Developmental Psychology* 11:473–84.

Johnson, Anne M., Jane Wadsworth, Kaye Wellings, and Julia Field. 1994. *Sexual attitudes and lifestyles.* London: Blackwell Scientific Publications.

Sweet, J. A., L. L. Bumpass, and V. R. A. Call. 1988. The design and content of the National Survey of Families and Households. Working Paper no. NSFH1. Madison: Center for Demography and Ecology, University of Wisconsin.

Symons, Donald. 1979. *The evolution of human sexuality.* Oxford: Oxford University Press.

Tanfer, Koray. 1987. Patterns of premarital cohabitation among never-married women in the U.S. *Journal of Marriage and the Family* 49:483–97.

———. 1992. Coital frequency among single women: Normative constraints and situational opportunities. *Journal of Sex Research* 29:221–50.

Tanfer, Koray, and M. Horn. 1985. Contraceptive use, pregnancy, and fertility patterns among single women in their 20's. *Family Planning Perspectives* 17:10–18.

Tavris, Carol, and Susan Sadd. 1978. *The Redbook Report on female sexuality.* New York: Dell.

Taylor, B. J. 1978. *The psychological and behavioral effects of genital herpes in women.* Seattle: University of Washington, Department of Psychology.

Teachman, Jay, J. Thomas, and K. Paasch. 1991. Legal status and the stability of coresidential unions. *Demography* 28, no. 4:571–86.

Thomson, E., and U. Colella. 1992. Cohabitation and marital stability: Quality or commitment. *Journal of Marriage and the Family* 54:259–67.

Thornton, Arland. 1988. Cohabitation and marriage in the 1980s. *Demography* 25 (November): 497–508.

———. 1991. Influence on the marital history of parents on the marital and cohabitational experiences of children. *American Journal of Sociology* 96, no. 4:868–94.

Tourangeau, Roger, and A. Smith. 1985. Finding subgroups for surveys. *Public Opinion Quarterly* 49:351–65.

Trussell, James, and Charles F. Westoff. 1980. Contraceptive practice and trends in coital frequency. *Family Planning Perspectives* 12:246–49.

Tryon, Robert C., and Daniel E. Bailey. 1970. *Cluster analysis.* New York: McGraw-Hill.

Tsai, M., S. Feldman-Summers, and M. Edgar. 1979. Childhood molestation: Variables related to differential impacts on psychosexual functioning in adult women. *Journal of Abnormal Psychology* 88:407–17.

Turner, Charles F., Heather G. Miller, and Lincoln E. Moses, eds. 1989. *AIDS, sexual behavior and intravenous drug use.* Washington, D.C.: National Academy Press.

Tversky, Amos, and Daniel Kahneman. 1981. The framing of decisions and the psychology of choice. *Science* 185 (27 September): 1124–31.

Udry, J. Richard. 1988. Biological predispositions and social control in adolescent sexual behavior. *American Sociological Review* 53, no. 5:709–22.

Udry, J. Richard, John O. G. Billy, Naomi M. Morris, Terry R. Groff, and Madhwa H. Raj. 1985. Serum androgenic hormones motivate sexual behavior in adolescent boys. *Fertility and Sterility* 43:90–94.

Udry, J. Richard, and Benjamin C. Campbell. 1994. Getting started on sexual behavior. In *Sexuality across the life course,* ed. Alice S. Rossi. Chicago: University of Chicago Press.

U.S. Bureau of Census. 1980. *Current population reports 1980–81.* Series P-20, no. 362. Washington, D.C.: U.S. Government Printing Office.

———. 1992a. What's it worth? Educational background and economic status: Spring 1990. *Current Population Reports.* Series P270, no. 32. Washington, D.C.: U.S. Government Printing Office.

———. 1992b. Marital status and living arrangements: March 1992. *Current Population Reports.* Series P20, no. 468. Washington, D.C.: U.S. Government Printing Office.

———. 1993. U.S. population estimates by age, sex, race, and Hispanic origin: 1980 to 1991. *Current Population Reports.* Series 25, no. 1095. Washington, D.C.: U.S. Government Printing Office.

Vance, Carole S. 1984. *Pleasure and danger.* London: Routledge & Kegan Paul.

Vener, A.,ʿand C. Stewart. 1974. Adolescent sexual behavior in middle America revisited. 1970–1973. *Journal of Marriage and the Family* 36:728–35.

———. 1982. The sexual behavior of adolescents in Middle America: Generational and American-British comparisons. *Journal of Marriage and the Family* 34:696–705.

Verbrugge, Lois M. 1977. The structure of adult friendship choices. *Social Forces* 56:576–97.

———. 1979. Multiplexity in adult friendships. *Social Forces* 57:1286–1309.

———. 1982. Sex differentials in health. *Public Health Reports* 97, no. 5:417–37.

Voeller, Bruce. 1990. Some uses and abuses of the Kinsey scale. In *Homosexuality-Heterosexuality: Concepts of sexual orientation,* ed. David P. McWhirter, Stephanie A. Saunders, and June Machover Reinisch. New York: Oxford University Press.

Waite, Linda, and L. Lillard. 1991. Children and marital disruption. *American Journal of Sociology* 96:930–53.

Waller, Willard, and Reuben Hill. 1951. *The family.* New York: Dryden.

Warner, S. L. 1965. Randomized response: A survey technique for eliminating evasive answer bias. *Journal of the American Statistical Association* 60:63–69.

Wasserheit, Judith N. 1992. Epidemiological synergy: Interrelationships between human immunodeficiency virus infection and other sexually transmitted diseases. *Sexually Transmitted Disease* 19:61–77.

Weinberg, Martin S., and Colin J. Williams. 1974. *Male homosexuals: Their problems and adaptations.* New York: Oxford University Press.

———. 1980. Sexual embourgeoisment? Social class and sexual activity: 1938–1970. *American Sociological Review* 45, no. 1:33–48.

Wellings, Kaye, Julia Field, Anne Johnson, and Jane Wadsworth. 1994. *Sexual behavior in Britain: The National Survey of Sexual Attitudes and Lifestyles.* New York: Penguin.

Wellman, Barry, and Stephen D. Berkowitz, ed. 1988. *Social structures: A network approach.* New York: Cambridge University Press.

Wellman, Barry, and Scot Wortly. 1990. Different strokes from different folks: Community ties and social support. *American Journal of Sociology* 96:558–88.

Wells, James A., and Randall L. Sell. 1990. *Project HOPE's International Survey of AIDS Educational Messages and Behavior Change: France, the United Kingdom and the United States.* Chevy Chase, Md.: Project HOPE.

Westoff, Charles F., and Norman B. Ryder. 1968. Duration of use of oral contraceptives in the U.S.—1960–65. *Public Health Reports* 83, no. 4:277–87.

———. 1974. Coital frequency and contraception. *Family Planning Perspective* 6 (Summer): 136–41.

———. 1977. *The contraceptive revolution.* Princeton, N.J.: Princeton University Press.

White, Edmund. 1980. *States of desire.* New York: Dutton.

Widom, Kathy. 1989a. The cycle of violence. *Science* 244, no. 14, 160–66.

———. 1989b. Does violence beget violence: A critical examination of the literature. *Psychological Bulletin* 106, no. 1:3–28.

Willis, Robert J., and Robert T. Michael. 1994. Innovation in family formation: Evidence on cohabitation in the United States. In *The family, the market and the state in aging societies,* ed. John Eruisch and Kazuo Ogawa. London: Oxford University Press.

Wilson, Jacqueline B. 1993. Human immunodeficiency virus antibody testing in women 15–44 years of age. In *Advance Data.* Centers for Disease Control and Prevention, no. 238. Washington, D.C.: U.S. Department of Health and Human Services.

Winick, Charles. 1985. A content analysis of sexually explicit magazines sold in an adult bookstore. *Journal of Sex Research* 21, no. 2:206–10.

World Health Organization. 1986. *WHO Expert Committee on Venereal Diseases and Treponematoses.* Geneva.

Yaffee, M., and E. Nelson. 1983. *The influence of pornography on behavior.* London: Academic.

Yamaguchi, Kazuo. 1990. Homophily and social distance in the choice of multiple friends: An analysis based on conditionally symmetric log-bilinear association models. *Journal of the American Statistical Association* 85, no. 410:356–66.

Yllo, Kersti, and David Finkelhor. 1985. *License to rape: Sexual abuse of wives.* New York: Holt, Rinehart & Winston.

Zelnik, Melvin, and John F. Kantner. 1972a. The probability of premarital intercourse. *Social Science Research* 1:335–41.

———. 1972b. Sexuality, contraception and pregnancy among young unwed females in the U.S. In *Demographic and social aspects of population growth,* ed. Charles F. Westoff and R. Parke. Washington, D.C.: U.S. Government Printing Office.

———. 1980. Sexual activity, contraceptive use and pregnancy among metropolitan-area teenagers: 1971–1979. *Family Planning Perspectives* 12:230–37.

Zelnik, Melvin, John F. Kantner, and Kathleen Ford. 1981. *Sex and pregnancy in adolescence.* New York: Sage.

Zubin, Joseph, and John Money, eds. 1973. *Contemporary sexual behavior: Critical issues in the 1970s.* Baltimore: Johns Hopkins University Press.

AUTHOR INDEX

SUBJECT INDEX

Abortion: attitudes about, 513–18; comparison of NHSLS and GSS questions about, 597–98; distribution by number, 465; effect of *Roe v. Wade,* 461, 474; as outcome of conception, 455–65

Adolescents: age at first intercourse, 322–27; effect of scripts on behavior, 7; experience of boys before age eighteen, 327–28, 488–91; masturbation concept, 136; number of partners before age eighteen, 327–33; premarital intercourse among girls and boys, 322–24; sex before age eighteen, 200–206; sexual behavior before age eighteen, 466–73, 488–91, 493–94; sexual contacts with children, 339–47

Age: alcohol use, 123; anal sex experience, 99, 107–9; attitudes toward sex, 518–29; autoeroticism, 141–45; comparison of NHSLS data with GSS and CPS data, 582; as component of master status, 32; conception outcomes, 455–65; condom use, 418; contraception, 448–55; duration of sexual event, 93–95; of entry into marriage or cohabitation, 476–91; of first heterosexual intercourse, 322–33, 542; at first intercourse: earlier research, 322–24; at first intercourse: NHSLS research, 324–27; at first union or marriage, 206–7; forced sex, 333–39; happiness and health, 353–57; homophilous compared to heterophilous partnerships, 260–66; homophilous relationships, 254–66; lifetime sexually transmitted infections, 384–91; masturbation, 81–83; number of children ever born, 445–48; number of sex partners over time, 177–86, 188–92, 194–203; number of sex partners related to first union with opposite gender, 203–16; oral sex experience, 98–107; partnered sex, 88–95; same-gender sexuality, 302–9, 313–20; sexual abuse, 339–47; sexual dysfunction, 370–74; sexually

transmitted infections, 382–89; sexual practices with opposite-gender partners, 97–121; sexual preferences, 149–71; sexual satisfaction, 112–21; sterility, 453–54

AIDS (acquired immunodeficiency syndrome): among homosexual men, 283–84; changes in sexual behavior related to risk of, 432–37; comparison of attitudes in NHSLS and GSS surveys, 600–601; prediction of spread, 547; as proportion of sexually transmitted infections, 378, 381–82; response to educational campaign, 427–40; response to epidemic, 38–41, 46, 377; uneven distribution in population, 396

Alcohol use: in context of sexual activity, 116–17t, 121–24, 131–32; related to age, 123; in risky sex practices, 414–18

American Teen Sex Survey, 41

Anal sex: in context of relationship status, 129–30; practiced by opposite-gender partners, 107–9; preference for, 158–59; as route of AIDS transmission, 38, 416; same-gender, 313–20

Assortative mating, 231

Attitude-heterogeneity perspective, 490, 494–96, 505

Attitudes toward sex: association with behavior, 510–12, 529–37; assumptions about sexual activity, 511–12; cluster analysis, 512–29, 537; comparison of NHSLS and GSS, 597–602; link to sexual behavior, 529–36; within master status groups, 518–29; procreational, relational, and recreational, 511–12; sexual preferences, 536–37. *See also* Permissiveness

Autoerotic activity: characteristics and distribution of, 134–45; masturbation, 80–86; social factors in practice of, 83–84. *See also* Masturbation; Pornographic material; Sex toys; Sexual fantasy